# III
## ENCYCLOPEDIA OF
# WORLD

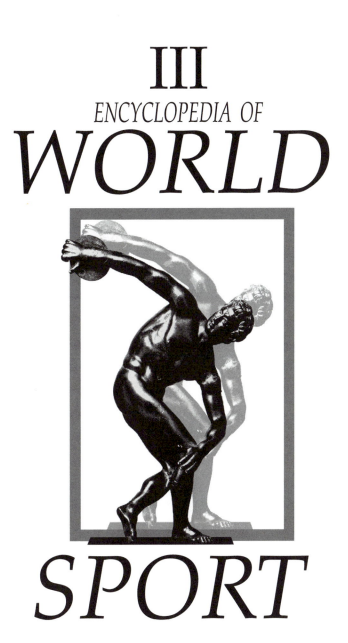

# SPORT

*From Ancient Times to the Present*

# III
## ENCYCLOPEDIA OF
# WORLD

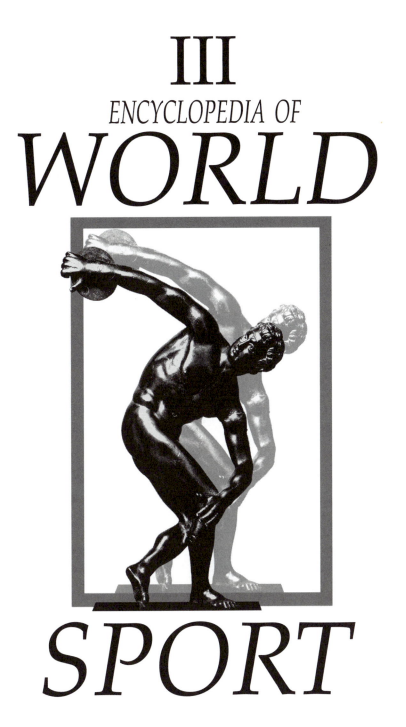

# SPORT

*From Ancient Times to the Present*

*David Levinson and Karen Christensen, Editors*

**ABC-CLIO**

*Santa Barbara, California*
*Denver, Colorado*
*Oxford, England*

## Berkshire Reference Works Project Staff

*Writers*
Bonnie Dyer-Bennet
John Townes
Alan Trevithick

*Technical Support*
Qiang Li

*Editorial Assistants*
Bonnie Dyer-Bennet
Patricia Welsh

Library of Congress Cataloging-in-Publication Data

Encyclopedia of world sport : from ancient times to the present /
      David Levinson and Karen Christenson, editors.
            p.     cm.
         Includes bibliographical references (p.    ) and index.
         1. Sports—Encyclopedias. I. Levinson, David, 1947–    .
      II. Christensen, Karen.
      GV567.E56   1996
      796'.03—DC21                                                 96-45437

ISBN 0-87436-819-7

02 01 00 99 98 97 96 95   10 9 8 7 6 5 4 3 2 1

ABC-CLIO, Inc.
130 Cremona Drive, P.O. Box 1911
Santa Barbara, California 93116-1911


This book is printed on acid-free paper ⊗.
Manufactured in the United States of America

# CONTENTS

ENCYCLOPEDIA OF
# WORLD SPORT
**From Ancient Times to the Present**

# VOLUME II

# Sailboarding

Sailboarding, also called boardsailing and wind-surfing, is a young sport that grew from obscurity to full Olympic status within 20 years. The invention of sailboarding is a most controversial aspect of the sport (see sidebar) having claimants in the United States, England, and Australia. The essential concept is a mix of surfing and sailing. A mast is attached to a board via a universal joint. This makes the rig (mast, sail, and boom) movable in any direction; this free-sail system makes sailboarding different from sailing. Another difference is that the sailor is in a standing position and must support the rig by holding onto a wishbone-shaped boom. A sailor steers by adjusting sail position and shifting weight on the board. In the weight movement, the similarity to surfing becomes apparent. The sport demands more balance and skill than pure strength, and men and women of all ages enjoy the sport in its many variations, which include racing, freestyle, speed, and endurance sailing.

## Origins

Although many people accept that sailboarding began in California, it grew there rather slowly. By contrast, in Europe in the 1970s, the sport grew extremely rapidly, especially in Holland, Germany, and France. Because it was an entirely new sport, designs changed very rapidly as early sailboarders began to test the limits of what could be achieved. Some sailors were happy sailing and racing on the traditional dinghy sailing types of courses, while others explored the freestyle possibilities of the sport. Sailboarding on the big waves of Hawaii led Larry Stanley to develop footstraps in 1977. The original ones were made from surfboard leash holders and were needed for control and stability. Only later did the possibilities footstraps created become clear. They, along with shorter boards, made aerial maneuvers not only possible but, for many, the goal.

## Development

As boards shortened and maneuverability increased, stability and even flotation decreased.

Thus, at the expert end of the market, boards were so small they sank unless they were moving. Beginners' boards were generally longer, and certainly more stable and buoyant. In the 1980s, funboards that tried to combine the best of both approaches appeared. One result was that mass numbers of sailboarders began trying to perfect the techniques that have become what advanced sailboarding is all about: water starting (using the wind to pull the sailor up and out of the water and into the sailing position), footsteering, and various types of turning maneuvers. Fully battened sails (sails with fiberglass strips inserted into pockets stretching from the leech, or back edge of the sail, to the mast) are a feature of high-performance boards. Such a sail has a semi-permanent curve induced in it, making it behave more like an airplane wing, and the airfoil shape increases speed.

As control increased, the time spent on the board increased, and arm strength became the limiting factor. Harnesses, first designed to fit around the chest and later changed to give support to the hips, were the answer. Small lines are attached to each side of the boom and the sailor hooks the harness on to these, thus taking most of the strain off the arms. All these developments led people to claim that sailboarding was the fastest-growing sport of the 1980s.

Attractions of sailboarding are its relative inexpensiveness (compared to many other forms of sailing) and its flexibility and ease of use. Most sailboarders cartop their sailboards to wherever the wind best suits their level of skill, and by changing to a larger or smaller sail can keep the power in the sail manageable over a wide range of wind strengths. It is quite simple and quick (about 30 minutes) to get a board off the roof, rig (assemble) it, and be on the water. For some, another appeal may be the colorful nature of the sport. Sails, wetsuits, and a variety of gear associated with the sport are often very highly colored, and "looking good" both on the water and the beach is important to some, as is the social side of the sport.

## Practice

As is the case in sailing, sailboarding has a vocabulary that can make it seem like an entirely new language. Other than the board and rig (the sail, mast, and boom), the sailor will need a wetsuit in all but the warmest water, for beginners tend to spend more time swimming than sailing. Wet suit bootees (with a good grip) also help maintain warmth. Personal flotation is required in some places, although there are people who feel that the beginner is safer to sink after a fall, and so avoid being hit by the falling mast.

A beginner should first get used to balancing on the board before adding the sail. The idea is to position the board across the wind with the mast pointing away from the wind. This position makes it easiest to get going. The sailor stands on the board and slowly pulls the rig up from the water (called uphauling) until the boom is reached. The hand nearer the front should cross over the other and grasp the boom near the mast and then the back hand grasps the boom about 1 meter (3 feet) back. Pulling in with the back hand traps air in the sail and moves the board forward. Steering is performed by raking the rig. Leaning it back pivots the boat more toward the wind, and leaning it forward turns the boat more away from the wind. If either of these maneuvers is carried on long enough, the board will eventually turn completely around—the former is called coming about, and the latter is called jibing. More advanced sailboarders do not uphaul (in fact they cannot, because their boards are likely to be sinkers) but rather waterstart, and neither do they steer with the sail, but rather by banking the board with their feet.

In addition to the different techniques used by those at different levels of skill, there are also variations in the sport itself. Some types of sailboards are designed for racing in which, like sailing, competitors jockey for position at the starting gun (or start off the beach) and then sail around a series of buoys in a predetermined order and direction. Rules are similar to and based upon sailing, and there are various categories of sailboard according to the design. Division I boards are those that are flat bottomed while division II boards have round bottoms. One-design classes feature identical boards. There are also slalom races and marathon events. A true marathon feat occurred in 1981–1982 when a Frenchman, Christian Marty, sailed across the Atlantic Ocean from Dakar, Senegal, to America Cayenne, French Guiana, eating and sleeping on board. He sailed eight hours a day, often from a sitting position using an extension boom, and support boats brought him his meals. At night, he placed a large

*Only a few decades old, sailboarding caught on rapidly in parts of the United States, northwest Europe, and Australia.*

inflatable collar around the board for stability. The crossing took him 37 days, 16 hours, 14 minutes.

Olympic sailboarding was held for the first time at the Summer Games in Los Angeles in 1984 with 38 countries participating. The board chosen was the Windglider, and events were held for both women and men. Another major sailboarding competition is the Pan Am Cup sailed off the Hawaiian island of Oahu. It has three competitions: races around triangle-shaped courses, a long distance race of 20 miles, and ins-and-outs (sailing back and forth through surf).

Instead of head-to-head competition, another branch of sailboarding is speed sailing. In fact, sailboards have held the world speed record for all forms of sailing craft. In November 1988, Eric

## The Many "Inventors" of Sailboarding

Most books on sailboarding give credit for the invention of windsurfing to two Californians, Jim Drake and Hoyle Schweitzer, although possibly the first written record of the sport is in the August 1965 volume of *Popular Science Monthly*. In this very brief (four-page) article entitled "Sailboarding: Exciting New Water Sport," S. Newman Darby of Pennsylvania wrote that "a sport so new that fewer than 10 people have yet mastered it promises to become inexpensive sailing fun for many." Although the craft illustrated is crude by modern comparisons, it was nonetheless steered by pivoting the mast and sail, giving it the essential difference from regular sailing, and he himself used the term "sailboarding." Major differences with modern sailboards, however, are that Darby's sail resembled a giant kite with wooden cross members, making it a square sail, and the mast was toward the stern, or back, of the board. The article includes a brief section on how to sail the sailboard, complete building instructions, and information on how to buy boards built by the author. Only a few were sold and the sailboard went unpatented.

In 1967, Drake (an aeronautical engineer and sailor, who wanted a simple way to get on the water fast) met Schweitzer (a surfer, who was looking for a less exhausting method of getting to the waves than paddling) and they began to discuss ideas and build prototypes to solve both of their problems. The first prototype was called a "Baja Board." Drake states that his ideas came from discussions with another scientist, Fred Payne, in 1961. In April 1969, Drake presented a paper ("Windsurfing—A New Concept in Sailing") on what was to become known as the Windsurfer—a sailboard with a universal joint and wishbone boom. Drake apparently got the idea for the all-important universal joint "while driving westbound, alone, on the San Bernardino Freeway" (Winner and Jones 1980, 12) in southern California. Schweitzer was soon producing Windsurfers made from what was then a new material, polyethylene, and he took out patents in the United States, Great Britain, West Germany, Australia, Canada, and Japan—places where he thought he would be most successful. He was not able to afford patents in other countries, and in France in particular, where the sport subsequently gained enormous popularity, he had not applied for a patent. Schweitzer bought out Drake (reputedly for $36,000) in 1970 and began to work on marketing Windsurfers full time. In Europe, he sold 100 in 1970, 1,000 in 1971, 3,000 in 1973, and over 5,000 in 1975. The Dutch company Ten Cate was licensed to begin mass-producing them in Europe. From 1973 to 1978, it is estimated that 150,000 sailboards of all types were built in Europe; in North America it was about twenty times fewer. Other companies had begun building similar craft without license, so Schweitzer had to try to enforce his patent rights. In the course of these legal battles, a couple of other people surfaced who also claimed to have invented sailboarding. In England, in 1984, Peter Chilvers stated he had built and sailed such a craft off the south coast in 1958. The judge upheld this claim, making Chilvers the inventor of the craft in Britain. Across the world, in Australia, Richard Eastaugh made a similar claim that he had sailboarded in Sydney Harbor soon after World War II. His claim, too, was upheld.

—Shirley H. M. Reekie

Beale of Great Britain achieved a speed of 40-1/2 knots (approximately 76 kilometers [47 miles] per hour) at Les Saintes Maries de la Mer, France.

Other sailboards are designed for freestyle sailing, in which performers attempt very intricate maneuvers. An example is sailing the board on its edge (or rail), called rail-riding. Robbie Naish and Ken Winner, both Americans, have excelled in freestyle. Another branch of freestyle is sailboard jumping, both competitive and not. People now sail indoors, using jet engines to provide wind, and there is a professional indoor circuit. The sailboard principle is also used for both ice and land versions of the sport. Sailboards are not limited to just one sail or sailor. Tandem sailboards, with two sails and two sailors, as well as three-sailed tridems, do exist. Steering requires great cooperation from the sailors, but the boards are steered in the same general way as a one-sailed board.

In addition to Hawaii (especially Oahu), the Columbia River Gorge in Oregon is a favorite place with U.S. sailboarders. Lake Garda and northeast Sardinia in Italy, Brittany and the Riviera in France, the Canary Islands, the west coast of Cornwall in Great Britain, and Perth, Australia, are all well-known sailboarding locations.

—Shirley H. M. Reekie

**Bibliography:** Darby, S. Newman. (1965) "Sailboarding: Exciting New Water Sport." *Popular Science Monthly* 187, 2 (August): 138–141.

Evans, Jeremy. (1983) *Complete Guide to Windsurfing*. London: Bell & Hyman.

Knox-Johnston, Robin. (1990) *History of Yachting*. Oxford, UK: Phaidon.

Turner, Stephen. (1986) *Windsurfing*. New York: Gallery.

Winner, Ken, and Roger Jones. (1980) *Windsurfing with Ken Winner*. San Francisco: Harper & Row.

# Sailing

Sailing is a mode of transportation across water that uses wind to power sails. It was likely invented in a variety of different forms across the world. Sailing first became a sport of the wealthy in the seventeenth and eighteenth centuries. It developed rapidly in the nineteenth and twentieth centuries, branching out into various forms. Some sailors choose the competitiveness of racing, and some like the freedom to cruise. Today, larger boats can remain at sea for months, but many people sail smaller day boats, or dinghies, on lakes or close to shore. Mass production and use of new materials, such as fiberglass, has brought the price of small boats within the range of many buyers. In the Olympic Games, yachting has been present since 1900, and continuously since 1908. Sailing is a sport where women can compete against men, and where children, adolescents, young, middle-aged, and older adults, and those with disabilities can be co-competitors. On windy days, sailing is a tough physical challenge, but on calmer days the sport is an excellent form of relaxation.

Sailboats come in a variety of sizes, rigs (mast and sail configuration), and costs. To those outside sailing, possibly the best-known aspect of the sport is the America's Cup series of races in which extremely costly, state-of-the-art boats are used. The vast majority of sailors, however, sail smaller, much less expensive dinghies or keelboats. Sailing as a sport, being based on a very old form of transportation, has a complete and rich vocabulary of its own. Although it is not physically difficult to sail, to sail well requires an understanding of the various forces and effects of wind and water. A series of rules is designed to keep boats from colliding with each other. A knowledge of when a boat has right of way, and when she (boats have traditionally been referred to as "she") must yield is crucial to safe sailboat handling. A more detailed set of rules for racing has been developed to cover the closer encounters of competition.

## Origins

Possibly the first type of sailboat was a simple, raftlike structure from which was raised a mast to which a cloth sail was hung. Many cultures developed their own unique designs of sailing craft, including peoples of the Middle East who sailed boats made of reeds circa 3500 B.C.E. and who today still sail the very distinctive *dhows*; Greeks and Romans who sailed galleys circa 1000 B.C.E.; the Chinese who developed the distinctive junk circa 300 C.E.; and the Vikings who sailed longboats from 700 C.E. The rig gives each type of sailing boat unique and recognizable characteristics. Each sailboat was designed to work well in the prevailing conditions of wind direction and strength, number of crew available, and locally available construction materials.

Sailing as a sport, as distinct from a mode of transportation, possibly began in the Netherlands. Many words (including the word "yacht") are derived from Dutch words. In the 1660s, a race took place in London, England, between King Charles II's boat (a gift from Holland) and one owned by the Duke of York. The first regatta was organized in 1720 at the Water Club of Cork, Ireland. Sailing as a sport remained the province of the wealthy, however, until the late nineteenth century when smaller dinghies were built and raced. Certainly the sport had, and continues to have, patronage from the royal families of Europe, and the socially prominent and wealthy families of the United States, so that the sport has always had somewhat of an aura of wealth and exclusivity. An example of this is the oldest club in continuous existence which was founded as simply the Yacht Club (the first to use such terminology) in London in 1815. It received royal patronage and became known as the Royal Yacht Club in 1820 and the Royal Yacht Squadron in 1830.

Before boats were mass-produced, each was completely unique; consequently, various systems of handicapping were developed to obtain some kind of meaningful racing. The first successful system was developed in 1886 by a yacht designer named Dixon Kemp. The boat's waterline length in feet was multiplied by the sail area in square feet and divided by 6,000. For example, a 15-foot (4.5-meter) boat, with a 200-square-foot (18.6-square-meter) sail area, would be visual equivalent of

$$\frac{15 \times 200}{6,000} = \frac{3,000}{6,000} = \frac{1}{2} \quad \text{rating}$$

*Sailing is one of several modes of transportation that have become popular as sports. Wide variations in boat design and cost make it possible for many people to enjoy the sport.*

(a Half-Rater is a type of boat; see below). In 1907, handicapping by rating was replaced by handicapping by meters, in which the handicap was determined by boat length, sail area, and a variety of other measurements. There were 6-, 8-, 12-, and 15-meter yachts. The 12-meter survived to become the prototype for much of the later twentieth century America's Cup racing and various meter classes became early Olympic classes.

## Boats

Today, boats come in a wide variety of sizes, shapes, rigs, and costs, each designed for a different purpose. Boats have been specially designed for children as young as six to sail and race alone; their requirements are clearly different from those of a wealthy business owner taking out clients for a day's sailing. Sailors with disabilities include those who are blind, who often have a very keen sense of wind direction (and who have

a sighted crew member on board), and quadriplegics who sail in a wheelchair on board boats specially designed for their needs.

Regardless of specific differences, however, certain principles apply to all types of sailing boats. One way to understand the principles of sailing is to first examine the earliest boats and then see how modifications over the years have enabled sailboats to increase the range and efficiency of what can be achieved. Early boats were probably only able to sail in the same direction as the wind was blowing. This direction, or point of sailing, relative to the wind is called running. The boat was merely blown along, and the direction of travel was wherever the wind blew. It is still a relatively slow direction to sail because although the sail is pushed along by the wind, the sail also encounters much resistance from the air in front of it. The sail works most efficiently when it is out at 90° to the boat to catch maximum wind.

Over the years, advances in rig design allowed

sailors to sail perpendicularly across the wind. This point of sailing is called reaching. Although the sideways force on the boat is quite large, the boat's hull (or the body of the boat), plus the centerboard or keel (central underwater fin) and rudder (pivoted underwater fin at the back that allows the boat to be steered) all help to redirect the sideways force of the wind into forward motion of the boat. The most efficient sail position is half out; any further out and the sail would luff, or flutter; any further in and the sail would not catch so much wind.

Eventually, boats were designed that were capable of making forward progress in a direction 45° to the wind. This is called beating, or sailing close hauled. This name is used because the most efficient sail position is hauled in close to the boat; any further out, and the sail would luff and lose power. Again, the boat's resistance to going sideways enables the boat to make some forward progress and also to slip slightly sideways (called leeway). No boat can sail directly into the wind, because on that heading the sail would act like a flag, with wind on each side, and harness no power. Boats can, however, make indirect progress directly upwind by zigzagging back and forth.

Bernoulli's principle, which explains how planes are able to get lift, can be used to explain how a sail works. If one imagines the sail to be like a wing, the curved surface makes air travel over it faster than over a flat surface, so that in front (or on top in a plane) of the curved surface is fast-moving air at low pressure, while the other surface has slower moving air and higher pressure. This gives a plane lift and a sail forward motion.

In addition to being able to sail in the various directions of a run, reach, and beat (and all those in between) a sailor should know about turning the boat around in two different ways, which have crucially different components. The choice is to turn the bow (front) into the wind, or to turn the stern (back) into the wind. The end result may be exactly the same, but the process is different. When turning the bow into the wind (called coming, or going, about), there is a time when the sail flutters like a flag, and only momentum allows the boat to complete her turn. In turning away from the wind (called jibing, or gybing), the wind is always filling, thus propelling, the sail, first on one side and then after the sail is forced by the wind to swing across, on the other side. Old sailing ships, such as square riggers, had to turn by

this method (called wearing ship) because they were too heavy and slow to come about. Modern sailing boats can do either type of turn, and skippers usually choose whichever is the quicker or smaller rotation. To make the boat come about, the tiller (steering stick) is moved toward the sail side. The turn happens quite slowly, relying on the boat's momentum. To make the jibe turn, the tiller is moved away from the sail side. The sail can swing across quickly and unless the skipper knows what to do, jibing can put a lot of force on the boat, resulting in either damage or a capsize.

Unlike other vehicles, there is no brake on a sailboat. As long as there is wind, or power, in the sail, the boat will move. To slow down, or stop, the goal is to angle the boat or sail so that wind power is no longer caught by the sail. This can be achieved by either turning the boat into the wind or by letting out the sail. Either way, the sail loses power as a driving force and begins to act like a flag with the wind passing over both sides. Getting started again involves once trapping wind in the sail by angling the sail more across the wind. This can be achieved by either using the tiller and rudder to turn the boat or by pushing the sail out by the boom (the pole along the foot of the sail) at an angle to the wind.

## Sailing Categories

Sailing can be divided into several categories according to the type of vessel and usage. All sizes of boat may be either raced or just sailed from place to place. Dinghies, considered day boats, usually stay close to shore. Larger boats, such as keelboats, cruisers, or ocean racers, may go far offshore.

Cruising is a nonracing branch of sailing in which larger boats, usually with sleeping accommodation, are sailed on voyages ranging from overnight to around the world. Some of the smaller cruisers can be trailered, but usually cruisers are kept moored at anchor or in a marina. Most cruisers have fixed keels, rather than moveable centerboards. Keels are heavy and give the boat much greater stability than a dinghy. After a knockdown, or capsize, a keelboat should right herself. Cruising involves knowledge of not only sailing skills, but also of navigation, anchoring, and meteorology, or indeed any fixing skill needed when out of sight of land, miles from outside assistance. Cruisers are usually equipped with a variety of instruments ranging from a compass and depth sounder to sophisticated Global Positioning System (GPS) navigation aids. Owing to their size and weight of parts, cruisers have a range of devices designed to help the crew gain a mechanical advantage in their work. They include winches for hoisting sails or pulling them in, capstans or windlasses (both types of winch) used to hoist the anchor and chain, and most are fitted with engines.

Cruisers usually carry a variety of sails that are changed to suit the prevailing weather conditions. Generally, as the wind rises in strength, smaller sails are used to keep the boat from being overpowered. Cruising may also include sailing at night, or in fog, and, on the open sea, the crew should know the International Regulations for Preventing Collisions at Sea (often shortened to COLREGS). The first "rules of the road" were probably developed by the Romans, but the current rules were agreed to by international charter in 1972. These regulations include the requirements to display and recognize appropriate lights at night, to make and understand relevant sound signals in fog or in vessels' close proximity to each other, and to keep a good lookout at all times. Boats must know when the onus is on them to take avoidance action for other sailboats or powerboats. Even though there is a general understanding that power gives way to sail, many situations exist where the sailboat must give way. Two examples are when the powerboat/tanker is dredging, or in a narrow channel. In general, the boat with the greater maneuverability keeps out of the way of the one with more restricted ability to maneuver.

Three basic right-of-way rules apply to sailboats meeting other sailboats. They are the opposite tack rule, the overtaking rule, and the windward rule. In order to understand these, one must appreciate that when a sailboat has the wind blowing over her starboard side (and thus her boom is on the port side) she is said to be on starboard tack. A boat with the wind blowing over her port side (with her boom to starboard) is on port tack. When boats on opposite tacks meet, the one on port tack is required to keep clear of the one on starboard tack. When one boat is overtaking another, and they are on the same tack, the overtaking boat must keep clear. When two boats meet, on the same tack, the one to windward

(closer to the wind, that is on the nonsail side of the other) must keep clear of the one to leeward (downwind).

Some of the most popular and well-known designs of keelboats, some designed for racing and some for cruising, are the Catalina 22, Contessa 32, J24, and 12 meter. Many America's Cup races of the mid- to late-twentieth century were raced in the 12 meter class. The America's Cup is probably the most famous of all yacht race trophies.

Ocean, or offshore, racing may be said to have begun in October 1866, as the result of a wager. Three boats raced across the Atlantic, from New York to the Isle of Wight, England. *Henrietta* (32.6 meters [107 feet]) beat *Vesta* (32 meters [105 feet]) and *Fleetwing* (32.3 meters [106 feet]) in a very close race. Crews of early ocean racers were usually professional seamen, and sometimes the owner was not even on board. In the 1920s, amateur sailors took over much of ocean racing and the sport was not without controversy. Some people connected with the sailing world felt that racing in the open sea was too dangerous and, as a result, ocean racing grew up as a sport somewhat removed from dinghy and inshore keelboat racing. The Offshore Racing Council (ORC), headquartered in England, organizes the sport. Ocean racers are divided into classes for racing purposes: Class 1, 70 feet–33 feet (21–10 meters), Class II, 32.9 feet–29 feet (9.9–8.8 meters), Class III, 28.9 feet–25.5 feet (8.7–7.6 meters), Class IV, 25.4 feet–23 feet (7.5–7 meters), and Class V, 22.9 feet–21 feet (6.9–6.4 meters).

A 630-mile (1,014-kilometer) race from Newport, Rhode Island, to Bermuda was first held in 1906 and since 1924 has been held every two years (except during World War II). On the other side of the Atlantic, and subsequently in the intervening year from the Bermuda Race, is the Fastnet Race, held since 1925. This race starts at Cowes, on the Isle of Wight, off England's south coast, goes west past Plymouth, Devon, and up to the southwest coast of Ireland. Boats there round the Fastnet Rock and lighthouse, and return to finish in Plymouth, for a distance of 605 miles (973 kilometers). The Fastnet Race has long had a well-deserved reputation for encountering heavy weather, but in the 1970s there was a series of light wind races. Perhaps designers forgot too soon the potential power of the sea, for in 1979, after a light wind start, hurricane-force winds blew over the largest

# America's Cup

The America's Cup trophy began as the Hundred Guinea Cup, in England, because that is what it cost to make in 1851. It was given for a race around the Isle of Wight off England's south coast held that same year. The British organizers, the Royal Yacht Squadron, wrote to the newly founded New York Yacht Club, inviting American boats to sail over and race against them for the summer. The New York Yacht Club accepted and had a new boat purpose-built. The boat was a 101-foot (30.6-meter) schooner (sails in front and behind the mast, with two or more masts) named *America*. After seeing *America*'s speed, no British boat wanted to race her, but she was invited to race in the Hundred Guinea Cup race. Starting at anchor, as was the custom in those days, 14 British boats and the lone American boat began to race at 10 A.M. on the morning of 22 August. The course was printed in the program as being around the Nab Light, the most easterly point of the course, but the race card called only for the yachts to sail around the island. The distance was about 50 miles (80 kilometers), and no handicaps or time allowances were to be given.

In very light wind, *America* was the last to get underway but soon overtook all but four boats. These four went around the outside of the Nab Light rock, but *America* went inside and into the lead. *America* was never caught and won the race at 8:37 P.M. The first British boat was more than 10 minutes behind. A protest was made about the course sailed by *America* but was later withdrawn. Captain John Cox Stevens (1785–1857) was pre-

sented with the trophy later that evening. A story arose that Queen Victoria (1819–1901), on the Isle of Wight at the time of the race, was told that *America* was leading. When she asked which boat was second, she is supposed to have been told, "Your Majesty, there is no second." Had the then-current system of handicapping in place been used for the race, *America* would have probably won by about two minutes. As it was, *America*'s design influenced British boats for years to come.

Captain Stevens brought the cup home to New York, but sold *America* in Britain. In 1857, the New York Yacht Club offered the cup won by *America* as a trophy for a sailing match open to any country. (Match racing is one boat against one other.) The cup became known as the America's Cup and was one of the earliest international trophies in any sport. The next competition for it occurred in 1870 and it has continued to be contested at intervals ranging from 1 to 21 years ever since. The United States successfully defended the cup against all comers until 1983 when the longest winning stretch in any sport was ended by the Australians. Since then, Dennis Conner (1943– ), sailing for the United States, regained the trophy he lost before, then lost it again, this time to New Zealand. The race is always hosted by the previous winners. The schooner *America* remained in England until the U.S. Civil War when the boat was bought for the South. *America* ended up as a training ship at the U.S. Naval Academy but fell to pieces in 1945.

—Shirley H. M. Reekie

fleet ever assembled for the race—303 boats. The boats were scattered all over the southern Irish Sea and many broke apart or were dismasted in the steep, breaking waves. Fifteen crew members lost their lives; only 85 boats finished. Many lessons were learned about boat design, rescue operations, and life rafts from this notorious race. The Fastnet Race is one of a series of races that make up the Admiral's Cup, one of the premier trophies in offshore racing. The 630-mile Sydney-Hobart, Australia, race, first held in 1945, is the third major offshore race. It always starts on Boxing Day (26 December). Another major ocean race is the Transpac, or Transpacific (held every two years in the odd-numbered years), which starts in Los Angeles and finishes in Hawaii, 2,225 miles (3,580 kilometers) away. An unusual feature of this race is that the wind usually blows in the same direction as the race, making it a run across the ocean.

Sponsorship has become a major feature of offshore racing. The Whitbread Round the World Race, first held in 1973 and 1974, is for fully crewed boats, while the BOC Challenge (begun in 1982 and 1983) is for single-handed racing around the world. Single-handed sailing around the world began in 1895 when Joshua Slocum (1844–1909), an American sea captain born in Nova Scotia, started his voyage aboard *Spray*, a 36-foot (11.2-meter) boat. He went counterclockwise around, making use of prevailing winds and currents, and it took him three years, with many stops. His book, *Sailing Alone around the World*, has become a classic in sailing literature.

In addition to keelboats and ocean racers are dinghies. These are the smallest, but most numerous, types of boats, and are distinguished by having retractable centerboards. They are usually raced by one-design class, which means that all boats in the fleet are of the same type and exactly alike. The oldest one-design centerboard dinghy class boat still raced is the 13-foot (4-meter) clinker-built (overlapping planks) Water Wag from Ireland. They date from 1887 but were re-designed in 1900 by Mamie Doyle, the daughter of the original designer. In 1897, the A Scow was designed and raced on the Great Lakes of North America, and several still race. Designed in 1898 but not raced until 1899, and taking the name from the handicapping system then used, is the Seabird Half Rater. Continuously sailed, raced, and built without major redesign, a fleet of over 30 are raced at Trearddur Bay, Wales, and all bear the names of seabirds.

Some dinghies have a very simple rig—one sail—but others can have a mainsail (a jibsail), a spinnaker (a balloonlike sail used in front of the mast on downwind legs, often brightly colored), and even a trapeze (a device that allows the crew to hook on to a wire, stand on the edge of the boat and lever their weight way over the side to assist in keeping the boat upright in windy conditions). [Some of the more modern and popular dinghies of the hundreds of classes worldwide, are the Optimist, Mirror, Sunfish, 420, 5-0-5, Snipe (all mono-hulls), and the Hobiecat 16 (a catamaran, or twin-hulled boat).] Another branch of dinghy sailing is that made up of restricted or development classes. These boats are definitely not like each other because, although there are certain restrictions on what may be changed, the whole point is to encourage change and development. The International 14 is an example of this type of boat.

## Racing

Sailing races can be of various types. In one design, mentioned previously, identical boats race together in fleet races. In handicap races, boats of different types race each other. Boats may start together, have their finish times recorded, and then work out who won on handicap. A visible handicap may be used in which the slower boats start first and the faster boats start last, at time intervals based on their handicap; the first boat over the finish line wins. Racing may also be subdivided into fleet racing, also mentioned previously, match races (one-on-one races, such as used in America's Cup races), or team racing (in which boats race as members of teams, instead of individually; tactics between and among teams add to the interest).

A sailboat race is run by a race committee that issues instructions about the start procedure, the course to be raced, the finish, and the scoring. A sailing race is unusual compared to races in other sports for two major reasons: the start is with competitors (boats) in motion and there is usually no referee watching all the interactions on the water. The race begins with a countdown (of 10, 5, or 3 minutes) to the start which is signaled to the boats by flags and/or sound. During this time, the boats time and practice starts and jockey for position, each one trying to be in the most advantageous place—exactly on the start line, going fast in the direction of the first buoy, when the starting signal is made. The course is predetermined and is most often triangular. It is a series of buoys which must be rounded in an agreed upon order and direction, for a certain number of laps. The point of sailing that requires the most skill to sail well, and which gives the most opportunity for individually different courses, is a beat. The start line is thus usually set perpendicular to the wind, giving a beat to the first buoy. The next leg may be a reach, or run.

The rules for sailboat racing include the three basic right-of-way rules described earlier, plus many others necessary for sailing at very close quarters. Because the rules may seem complex and intimidating to beginning racers, an attempt is being made to simplify them starting in 1997. Rules are always revised in the year following the Olympic Games by the London-based International Yacht Racing Union (IYRU). The rules cover, for example, the start, what to do at an obstruction (such as a rock) and rounding buoys. Additionally, there are precise definitions, prohibitions on certain forms of propulsion (such as fanning or rocking) and details on penalties. For example, if a boat hits a buoy, she must do a 360-degree turn (come about then jibe—or vice versa—in the same direction) to give herself a time penalty before continuing. If a boat hits another boat and admits she was in the wrong, she may usually put herself right by completing a 720-degree-turn penalty.

An unusual feature of sailing races is that there is usually no referee. It would, in fact, be impossible for a referee to see every situation anywhere on the course. Instead, all competitors are honor-bound to try to sail by the rules to the best of their knowledge and ability, but if one sailor thinks another has wrongly interpreted a rule, the only remedy is to protest. This involves flying a small flag on board and telling the other boat of the intention to protest. Protesting is not unsportsmanlike behavior because it is the only way, after the race, to get a ruling on a situation. At the protest hearing, a committee establishes the facts from the evidence of both parties and decides what action to take. This can range from doing nothing to disqualifying a boat or boats.

Sailing on sand, land, and ice also exists, but their rules for racing are completely different from water sailing. Speeds in these land-based sports are usually much higher than on water because of the lower resistance needed to go over a hard, flat surface than through water. Top speeds for sailing on land approach 70 miles (110 kilometers) per hour, whereas the top speed for sailing on water in time trials are around 45 miles (70 kilometers) per hour. The fastest sailing craft are sailboards and catamarans.

## Outlook

The construction of sailboats has changed greatly in the last 50 years. Until then, most boats were built of wood, and the two major methods of construction were carvel (in which planks were laid edge to edge) and clinker (in which planks were overlapped). Next came the use of marine ply and with that, boat building began to be something people without great woodworking skills could do. Most boats today are fiberglass; some are made of aluminum or cement, and a few from expensive new materials such as Kevlar. Wood continues to be the material many believe looks the best, however. Sails, traditionally made from flax or cotton, both of which had the tendency to rot if left wet, have also become dependent on technology. Today, sails are made from Dacron or sometimes Kevlar; the lighter spinnaker sails use nylon or Mylar.

As a sport, sailing is enjoyed around the world, and 108 countries are affiliated to the IYRU. Until recently, sailing has been a difficult sport to watch, because the boats cover a wide area, and sometimes take very different paths to the next buoy, making it hard even for experts to know which boat is leading. As with so many other sports, television may hold the key to the sport's increased popularity. Use of microcameras mounted high in the rigging or at deck level may be part of the answer. Another solution, long fought by some in sailing but now seemingly here to stay, may be the growth of professional sailing opportunities.

—Shirley H. M. Reekie

**Bibliography:** Bond, Bob. (1980) *The Handbook of Sailing.* New York: Knopf.

Johnson, Peter. (1989) *The Sail Magazine Book of Sailing.* New York: Knopf.

Knox-Johnston, Robin. (1990) *History of Yachting.* Oxford, UK: Phaidon.

Richey, Michael W., ed. (1980) *The Sailing Encyclopedia.* New York: Lippincott & Crowell.

Reekie, Shirley H. M. (1986) *Sailing Made Simple.* Champaign, IL: Leisure Press.

# Sailing, Ice Skate

Ice skate sailing is a Northern European and North American winter recreation exclusively practiced outdoors in the daytime. Participants sail erect, wear ice skates on their feet, and hold sails measuring 3.3 to 8.8 square meters (35 to 95 square feet) with their hands and shoulders. They sail round trips, reaching speeds that more than double the true wind velocity. Sheathed ice picks around the sailors' necks are indispensable for self-rescues; the picks give a secure grip on the ice. Life vests and helmets are advisable. Ice skate sailing requires smooth, thick, snow-free ice occupying at least 10 acres, and steady winds of 15 to 40 kilometers (10 to 25 miles) per hour. Frozen lakes, ponds, and reservoirs lend themselves to the sport, as do icy estuaries and the Baltic Sea.

## Origins

Modern ice skate sailing lacks any certain date or place of origin. It began no earlier than the seventeenth century, when Dutch skaters began to use sharp-edged, iron blades. Iron blades replaced the broad, dull bone blades used for five millennia. Skaters with bone blades propelled themselves only by poling. By contrast, the sharp edges of modern metal blades enable skate sailors to keep a course inclined to the prevailing wind. They reduced downwind drifting and allowed fast braking. An assured grip on the slippery ice made it feasible to sail a round trip, which entails tacking upwind.

In the next century the Swedish botanist and

*In ice skate sailing the sailor assumes the role of the mast. A group of men enjoy ice skate sailing on a lake in Sweden in the early twentieth century.*

explorer Carolus Linnaeus (1707–1778) sighted skaters "with sails like wings." Skate sails in the mid-nineteenth century carried fowlers across the ice separating Denmark from Sweden, bearing the hunters to their prey. Late nineteenth-century Norwegian ice sailors used 100 centimeter (39-inch) skate blades. On the icy Muggelsee near Berlin, a three-person sail propelled German skaters at the turn of the century.

Organized races began near Stockholm on Lilla Värtan Lake in 1887, with sails occupying about 4.2 square meters (45 square feet). For nearly 50 years, Swedish skaters have sailed cross-legged standing only on their leeward blades. In the early 1970s, the Stockholm marine inventor Anders Ansar (1942– ) devised the aerodynamically efficient icewing, which encloses the ice skate sailor and resembles the upturned tip of an airplane wing (Marchaj 1988). Its ratio of sailing speed to true wind speed equals four, while that of traditional skate sails reaches about two and

one-half. In the 1980s, 8.8 square meter (95 square feet) skate sails known as Dragon sails dominated Swedish races (Sahlin 1989). These 3.6-meter (12-foot) tall behemoths cleared the ice only because the competitors wore skates with blades that were 20 centimeters (8 inches) high to elevate their crafts.

Crossing the frozen Whittlesea Mere in England during 1896, a skater named Adams sailed 48 kilometers (30 miles) within 60 minutes, using a parallel trapezium (a four-sided figure with the two longer lines, of equal length, converging without intersecting and the two shorter, unequal in length, parallel to one another) skate sail with its long axis vertical. Sail skaters raced weekly on the salty ice of Cove Pond in Stamford, Connecticut. Their speed "reached forty-five miles [72 kilometers] per hour. And it could [have been] faster except that there is a limit to human endurance," reported the *New York Times* of 14 February 1915. Skate sailors on Lake George, New

## Twentieth-Century Ice Skate Sailing in New Jersey

The winter of 1994 brought an ice storm to the Middle Atlantic States. Thinking it's the wind ill that profits nobody, two New Jerseyans tried overland ice skate sailing. Excerpts from their reports follow.

### Paradise Lost

On Friday, January 7, 1994, rain fell for many hours during the day and night, and it continued to fall into Saturday morning. The air temperature was then 25°F, when snow—not rain—should have descended. The rain landed on top of two inches of old snow. The drops bounced up, froze, and fell back as small pellets of ice. The pellets fused and formed a one-and-one-half-inch-thick layer of ice that followed the contours of the land. They created a textured ice surface that was reasonably easy to walk and drive on, similar to packed snow. The ice sheet provided a smooth, consistent skating surface everywhere but under trees. Although the surface was somewhat slow, you could skate almost anywhere on open land.

The wind was blowing up the small hill in North Branch Park, New Jersey, so I sailed the slopes on ice skates while my companion raced cars. How well I could tack uphill was surprising. To ascend I sailed at an angle varying from slight in a light wind to nearly straight up in a gust. To go downhill I "skied," holding the sail overhead. A long time spent sailing uphill and gliding downhill gave me a taste of what it was like to combine the techniques of skate sailing with those of skiing. I was looking forward to larger and more challenging hills when, alas, the snows came on Wednesday, January 12. They ruined the ice surface on the land.

The next weekend brought fine ice to the Navesink River at Redbank, New Jersey. While sailing over this ice, I concluded that it was too flat: I had seen paradise.

—Richard H. Pace

### Overland Ice Skate Sailing

The highest lawn in the park offered the strongest wind, which blew perpendicularly to the adjoining Milltown Road. The wind direction and road location meant that I was necessarily sailing parallel to moving automobiles. When my bearing opposed that of passing cars, then the passengers' heads turned as I flashed by. Some drivers rose from their seats as they stood on their brakes, stopping short to watch my 65 square-foot *Hopatcong* ice skate sail, which bears eight-inch white polka dots on royal blue sail cloth.

Other drivers steered the same heading as mine, so I chased their cars in an undeclared race. It began beside a tennis court, where I sailed cross-legged on one foot, borne only by what had been the leeward skate. Simultaneously I lay on the sail—and thereby on the wind—to hurtle over the uneven ice sheet at 20 to 30 mph. The racecourse then dropped me onto a rutted, ice-coated lane, entered through a gateway flanked by massive, knee-high railings. Dodging the log railings averted impending amputations with a blunt instrument. Having crossed the lane, I re-entered the lawn. There a shoulder-high, two-rail fence separated the race track from the road. To avoid decapitation, I bypassed a rusty cable, which inclined fifteen feet upward from a protruding iron stake to a roadside utility pole. Next, I slammed over the icy trenches of another driveway and rose sharply onto a rolling, frozen lawn that shone yellow beneath the ice. A safe end to the 1,000-foot run sent me around a grand sign announcing the site of the Park Commissioner's headquarters. My too-short runs were extraordinarily thrilling because they occurred in three dimensions over unfamiliar ground. All told, they made overland ice skate sailing unforgettable.

—Richard Friary

York, hurtled at more than 110 kilometers (70 miles) per hour in the 1930s.

## Practice

An exhilarating sense of harmony rewards a fast, controlled run over smooth, transparent ice. Wind and ice and sail and skates are the notes of this chord, which the sailor links like a musical staff. The wind and ice furnish the aerohydrodynamic forces that produce forward thrust. The sail wrests energy from the wind while the skates resist sideslipping like the keel of a sailboat. A sailor's body acts as an animate mast to transmit force from the wind to the ice. It serves as ballast when he heels the sail; whereas his arms steer the sail as a tiller guides a boat by the rudder. A skate sailor is therefore indispensable to beginning and sustaining his own sailing motion.

The other attractions of this ultimate sailing sport are high speed combined with low cost; the portability of equipment, the opportunity to brake, and the few demands made upon newcomers. An ability to skate without extending one's arms is the only prerequisite skill. The sport appeals to 8-year-old and 80-year-old skaters of both sexes, who must be fit, alert, and properly equipped.

The best sailing skates unite long, flat blades to stiff, high boots. Long blades run 38 to 60 centimeters (15 to 24 inches) and prevent foot and leg vibrations at high speeds. Comparatively flat, they reduce sideslipping. Traditional racing skates, with radii of curvature not less than 19 to 25 meters (62 to 82 feet), make acceptable sailing skates. However, their soft, low boots provide little support on rough ice and little insulation in the coldest weather. Boot warmth is important because a moving skate sailor's feet produce scant heat despite his motion. Racing skate boots provide the greatest ankle maneuverability, which some expert skate sailors prize and others spurn.

Skate blades must be sharp for the sailor to hold a course, and as little as a day's sailing over hard ice will dull them. Thus, a skate sailor must sharpen his blades often, using a skate stand and a long whetstone (Hollum 1984). The blades of sailing skates are usually sharpened manually and ground flat.

Often likened to simple kites, the shapes of many contemporary skate sails derive from parallel trapeziums. Balanced sails, which show no tendency to turn upwind or downwind, add jib and tail sections that are triangles or circle segments. The cloth of a traditional skate sail stretches tautly over a framework of spars, including a horizontal boom and a vertical mast. Such a sail is the popular Hopatcong model.

Devised in 1917 by Wally van B. Claussen (1888–1966), founder of the Skate-Sailing Association of America, the Hopatcong skate sail is named for the largest lake in New Jersey. In two cloth pockets at the jib and tail reside flexible, tapered bows that curve in circle arcs when the sail stretches over its mast and boom. The resulting tension flattens the leading and trailing edges and thereby prevents luffing, especially at the jib. Shared features suggest a common but unidentified ancestor for the Dragon and Hopatcong sails.

A skate sail must fit its sailor. In choosing a sail, sailors heed its area, ratio of sail area to body weight, height, and the distance between the mast-boom crossing and the sail center-of-effort. Experienced sailors use smaller sails in stronger winds, and larger sails in lighter ones. In an all-winds sail that is most useful to a novice, a good

## Nineteenth-Century Ice Skate Sailing in Sweden

W. W. Thomas, Jr., United States Envoy Extraordinary and Minister Plenipotentiary to Sweden and Norway, saw skate sailing in the Stockholm archipelago. An 1893 book, *Sweden and the Swedes* (New York: Rand McNally, 177–178), from which the following passage is taken, records his observations.

One afternoon, as I came in sight of the frozen *vik* [strait], I stopped to gaze upon a lively winter picture. Among the dark masses of the skaters, twenty or thirty white sails were swiftly skimming over the ice; some bearing away before the wind, others tacking to and fro from shore to shore; all gleaming brilliantly white in the level rays of the low December sun.

Here were the sails, to be sure; but where was the boat—and the mast? There were neither; or, rather, a boy in his own proper person was both. Every sail was in the form of a truncated capital A—thus $A$; and a skater taking the cross-bar over his shoulder and leaning against the breeze, shot away with the speed of the wind.

The sail extended upward a foot and a half above the head, and the sailor was always in the lee of his sail. When beating to windward, the sail is not turned around in coming about; only the boy turns, and, taking the cross-bar over his other shoulder, speeds gaily away on the other tack.

The light canvas is stretched flat as a board, and the skater can sail very near the wind, leaning well to windward if the breeze be strong. The greatest speed, however, is gained with the wind over the quarter. In this position a mile has been sailed in Sweden in less than two minutes. Swiftly blown over the ice without exertion, you experience the sensation of flying more nearly, perhaps, than in any other mode of locomotion.

I believe the form of this skating-sail is peculiar to Sweden. It is simple and practical, and so light that at the end of an afternoon's sport the Swedish lad rolls up his canvas on the poles, and carries the roll home as easily as his skates.

—Richard Friary

choice of ratio is a minimum of one square foot of area for every three pounds of body weight. A 68-kilogram (150-pound) sailor, therefore, would carry 4.6 square meters (50 square feet) of sail at least. In the largest sail that a given skater can maneuver, the sail half-height should equal his shoulder height less the distance by which he bends his knees when he sails. A greater half-height would allow the mast to strike the ice, which could topple the sailor. The distance between the crossing and the center must approximate the sailor's reach. If it greatly exceeds his reach, the sail turns uncontrollably upwind.

Many skate sailors make their own sails for economy, self-satisfaction, or design. Sail plans are published, and suitable sailcloth and materials for the windows and spars are identified (Andresen 1974; Claussen 1926; Forsman 1996; Goldberg 1973; Jefferson 1957; Lieghley 1938; Sahlin 1989). Professional sailmakers prepare individual skate sails on request, and cottage industries sporadically arise to make them on relatively large scales.

The techniques of ice skate sailing include a proper stance. A cruising sailor stands to leeward of a *Hopatcong* skate sail, bending his knees to absorb any shocks caused by rough ice. The horizontal boom rests on his windward shoulder and both hands grip the vertical mast below the boom. The sailor's feet run parallel and 10 to 13 centimeters (4 to 5 inches) apart, while the upwind foot precedes the downwind one.

To steer upwind, the sailor slides the boom backward on his shoulder. This motion increases the sail area aft of the skater, who pivots like a weather vane. A 180-degree turn into the wind calls for sliding the boom far aft. The sail turns strongly into the wind, and slows and luffs, when raising it overhead becomes necessary. This task demands both hands, first to lift the mast and afterwards to seize it on either side of the boom. When the sailor has transferred his grip, the sail plane parallels the ice surface and the wind passes ineffectively over the craft. Now he completes the turn using only his skates, lowering the boom to his other shoulder as he begins sailing straight on the new course.

Pushing the boom forward on the sailor's shoulder brings a downwind turn. A 180-degree turn to leeward is feasible if the skater slides the sail over his back, raising the craft as little as possible lest the wind steal it. This maneuver requires practice, so beginners turn upwind only.

A sail skater propelled by the wind can slow by changing his course angle or raising and turning the sail overhead. The sailor can use his skates to brake safely only with the sail plane parallel to the ice sheet. Releasing the sail, reducing its area, or heeling it also reduce speed. Heeling a skate sail decreases sailing speed because it lessens the effective sail area. It also counters the sideforce of the wind, which tends to thrust the sailor downwind. Heeling requires a sailor to stand on his windward blade edges, leaning on his upwind shoulder and hip. Boldly, he commits his body weight to the sail, which inclines as much as 60 degrees from the vertical. Lying on the wind is comfortable and safe when the breeze is steady and the blades sharp. If the wind dies momentarily, a proficient sailor recovers his balance by turning to windward.

—Richard Friary

**See also** Sailing, Icewing and Roller Skate; Sandyachting.

**Bibliography:** Andresen, Jack. (1974) "Skate Sailing." In *Sailing on Ice*. New York: A. S. Barnes.

Catton, Bruce. (1972) *Waiting for the Morning Train: An American Boyhood*. Garden City, NY: Doubleday,

Claudy, C. H. (1910) "Skate-Sailing for Life." *St. Nicholas* 37 (February): 298.

Claussen, Wally van B. (1926) *Practical Suggestions for Making and Using Skate Sails*. Distributed by the Skate-Sailing Association of America.

Forsman, T. (1996) World Wide Web home page for the Skate Sailing section of the Swedish Ice Sailing Association at http://www.ludd.luth.se/users/tomasf/skridske.html.

Friary, Richard. (1990) "Lying on the Wind: Ice Skate Sailing." *Speedskating Times* Part 1, 1, 5 (April): 6; Part 2, 1, 6 (May): 6.

———. (1996) *Skate Sailing*. Indianapolis: Masters Press.

Goldberg, Daniel E. (1973) Skate Sail, U. S. Patent 3,768,823 (30 October).

Hollum, Diane. (1984) "Equipment." In *The Complete Book of Speed Skating*. Hillside, NJ: Enslow Publishers.

*L'Illustration*. (1901) 3026 (February 23): 119.

Jefferson, Rufus C. (1957) *Skate Sailing*. North Minneapolis, MN: Harrison & Smith.

Lieghley, E. O. (1938) "Go like the Wind." *Popular Mechanics* 69 (January): 114.

Marchaj, C. A. (1988) "Land and Hard-water Sailing Craft." In *Aero-Hydrodynamics of Sailing*. Camden, ME: International Marine Publishing.

Mathus, F. K. (1962) "Eisseglen ein wenig bekanntes Vergnügen." *Neues Zürcher Zeitung* (10 February).

Sahlin, Alexander. (1989) *Skridskosegling: Teknik och Prylar*. 2d ed. Distributed by the Skate-Sailing Section of the Swedish Ice Sailing Association. English version, *Skate Sailing: Techniques and Equipment*, distributed by the Skate-Sailing Association of America.

# Sailing, Icewing and Roller Skate

Icewing, roller skate, and ski sailing are closely related to ice skate sailing. They all require hand-held sails, a standing sailor, and special footgear. In each sport, it is possible to sail upwind at an angle to the true-wind direction. Round trips under sail are feasible, so the sailor returns to the starting point with no chase vehicle needed to recover him. The sailing speeds can exceed the wind speeds, except on directly downwind courses. Traveling straight downwind brings the slowest speeds, as in other kinds of sailing. Of the three sports, roller skate and ski sailing enjoy the greatest international popularity, although icewing sailing features the highest ratio of sailing speed to wind speed.

## Icewing Sailing

Because of its aerodynamic shape, an icewing can sail at 90 kilometers (56 miles) per hour in a 24 kilometer (15 mile) per hour breeze. It resembles the detached tip of an airplane wing stood erect, and is a semi-rigid craft. It encloses its sailor completely, so it represents the greatest innovation in ice skate sailing during the twentieth century. Its streamlining abolishes the air turbulence created by its sailor's body. Of all hand-held sails, only the icewing achieves this aerodynamic effect. Its wing-like shape thrusts it forward at nearly four times the wind speed, while Hopatcong ice skate sails reach a value of two to two and one-half.

The icewing was invented by Anders Ansar (1942 – ) in Stockholm, Sweden, in 1973. It consists of two cloth sails, a solid top, and a rigid, curved leading edge. The two sails comprise the port and starboard sides of the craft, joining one another at the aft end and supported by a framework of aluminum tubing. For forward and side visibility, transparent plastic forms the rigid leading edge and each sail has a flexible window. The interior of the wing bears straps supporting it on the sailor's shoulders, freeing his hands for steering. Each wing weighs 9 to 13.5 kilograms (20 to 30 pounds), occupies 4.6 to 7.4 square meters (50 to 80 square feet), and stands only a little higher than its sailor. Ready-to-sail icewings, as well as building plans, are available from Sweden.

To sail an icewing requires suitable ice skates. Flat, sharp, and long blades minimize sideslipping and lend stability over rough ice or at high speeds. Such blades oppose the sideforce of the wind, permitting the sailor to hold a course. Blades about 60 centimeters (24 inches) long avert tiring leg vibrations, while flat ones prevent rocking in a vertical plane. Swedish icewing sailors favor custom skates made from downhill ski boots for support and with quick-release bindings for convenience.

A novice should choose smooth ice and a light breeze for a first voyage in an icewing. Otherwise, cautions Ansar, "bad ice and strong winds [might] put you in a situation you cannot handle. Suddenly you are sailing at 50 mph [130 kilometers per hour], wondering where the brake is and how to make a turn."

Entering an icewing calls for a companion's help because the craft lacks any opening except the bottom. The helper lifts the icewing, placing it over the squatting sailor who faces into the wind. The sailor then rises to his feet, seizing the forward control bar and positioning his shoulders beneath the straps that hold the vessel above the ice. He turns about 90 degrees to bring the wind to bear on one of the sails, adjusting his course angle once his run begins. The sailor steers by maneuvering a horizontal control bar located at waist height.

National icewing races take place annually, often near Stockholm on the Baltic Sea. An informal 1979 contest matched a lone wing sailor against iceboat skippers on Brewster Lake, New York. The DN and Skeeter ice boats that took part can attain ratios of sailing speeds to wind speeds of about four and five, respectively. The icewing inventor Anders Ansar sailed his craft to victory!

## Roller Skate Sailing

Roller-skate sailing dates from the 1930s in the United States, but takes place internationally. It rewards a liking for speed: a roller skate sailor can reach 72 kilometers (45 miles) per hour despite the resistance offered by the surface. The sport is versatile because many kinds of hard surfaces are suitable during much of the year. Paved lots and rural roads are more abundant than frozen lakes, claims one advocate of roller skate sailing. In the United States, diurnal sailors traverse the hard-packed sands of the Mojave Desert, as well as the concrete of abandoned airport runways; nocturnal roller skate sailors haunt the parking lots of eastern shopping malls; and one midwestern sportsman swears by night sailing on the road in front of his home (he says the diffused glow of headlights in the sky above a nearby hill warns of approaching automobiles).

Roller skate sailors in California and Colorado use sails seen only infrequently in the eastern states. Some of these sails are triangular, occupying only 3 to 4 square meters (35 to 40 square feet), but they are commercially available. The shape of other commercial roller skate sails comprises a circle segment forward of an isosceles triangle, and the sailor stands to windward of the sail. The areas of these sails range from 2.0 to 5.7 square meters (21 to 61 square feet). *Hopatcong* skate sails, which are often homemade, can also be employed with roller skates. These sails, more familiar in the eastern states, are usually sailed from leeward but can also be sailed from windward.

The triangular roller skate sails popular in California require special sailing techniques. The sailor stands upwind of the sail, grasping one of the two spars that compose two sides of the triangle. He holds this spar nearly vertical and rests the lower sail edge on one thigh. Sailing in a high wind calls for rotating the sail from this position until one spar parallels the ground. To heel, the sailor places his skates along the same line but facing in opposite directions, and he leans backward. To come about with a triangular roller skate sail requires the sailor to raise the sail overhead, and to lower it to his opposite side when he has completed the turn. Jibing is so awkward compared to coming about that roller skate sailors turn downwind only in light winds. They do so by rotating the sail in front of themselves.

In-line roller skates with plastic wheels, smooth bearings, and rigid boots are the preferred footgear. Sailing with skates having side-by-side wheels is feasible, too. Wise roller skate sailors wear helmets as well as elbow, knee, and wrist guards. As land sailors, they are safe from aqueous debacles but, like ice sailors, must inspect their sailing surface for obstacles. Roller skate sailors who sail heeled must beware sta-

*This roller skate sailor uses a Roller Sail, which can also be employed by ice skaters, skateboarders, surfboarders, and others.*

tionary objects blocking the wind. Parked vehicles, for example, can create a low-pressure area on their leeward sides that fails to support a sail inclined from the vertical. Without support from the sail, the sailor may swoop or fall.

## Ski Sailing

Skiers began to sail as early as 1917, and the sport of ski sailing finds participants in North America and Northern Europe. A variety of sail types are appropriate, including the kite-like American Hopatcong, the dihedral Finnish Skimbat, and the inflatable German parawing. The Hopatcong is sailed from its leeward side, the Skimbat from windward, and the parawing is maneuvered beneath its underside.

Ski sailing requires downhill skis and Alpine boots. The metal edges of these skis prevent side slipping. They are essential to the sport because they permit the sailor to hold a course; without them he would drift haplessly downwind. Rigid boots and bindings translate foot motions into the exacting ski movements that high-speed steering demands. The height, rigidity, and forward lean of modern downhill boots help support a heeling Hopatcong sailor. Cross-country skis lacking metal edges, as well as soft low boots and flexible bindings, find little use in ski sailing.

The resistance of snow to skis exceeds that of ice to skates, so ski sailing requires a faster wind and a larger sail than ice skate sailing. Hopatcong sails ranging from 5 to 6 square meters (55 to 65 square feet) are useful, depending on the true-wind speed and the sailor's weight and skill. With a Hopatcong sail, the techniques of ski sailing resemble those of ice skate sailing, with the exceptions of heeling and turning. To heel, a ski sailor bends his knees more than a skate sailor does, adopting a semi-seated posture for stability. This posture reduces the area of the largest standard Hopatcong sail that a sailor of a given height can handle. Over resistant snow, a ski sailor must turn in increments, first stepping with one foot, then with the other.

Wind-packed snow 5 centimeters (2 inches) thick offers an ideal surface for fast ski sailing. Loose, deep snow reduces speed, while a hard, icy surface affords too little traction, even to metal-edged skis. Ski sailing conditions often improve with time. Wind and other physical processes like recrystallization convert loosely packed snow to dense snow, and this change increases sailing speed. Ski sailing at 80 kilometers (50 miles) per hour over a flat surface is not only feasible but thrilling. Some ski sailors in Minnesota combine high speeds with 6-meter (20-foot) horizontal leaps from platforms made of snow.

Ski sailing offers many advantages over ice skate sailing, regardless of the sail type employed: (1) The use of skis often allows sailing during a greater part of the winter than does the use of skates. The snow needed for ski sailing can obstruct the ice required for skate sailing, effectively shortening the season for ice skate sailing. Ski sailors can gain the passable surface that skate sailors lose in a blizzard. (2) Sailing on skis can extend the sailing season to Spring. Thick ice often remains over lakes when the snow has melted. Sailing over lake ice becomes possible when the surface softens enough to give skis purchase. (3) Ski sailing affords more places to sail: snow-covered fields and even golf courses offer large suitable areas. It does not confine the sailor to lakes or estuaries, and ski sailing over land entails no risk of falling into the water. (4) Snow fallen over rolling terrain adopts the contours of the land and allows out-of-plane sailing, an exciting variation impossible over horizontal ice sheets. (5) Skis and boots are easier to acquire than sailing skates; they can be purchased new or used or they can be rented.

—Richard Friary

**See also** Sailing, Ice Skate; Sailing, Parawing.

**Bibliography:** Forsman, T. (1996) World Wide Web home page for the Skate Sailing section of the Swedish Ice Sailing Association at http://www.ludd.luth.se/users/tomasf/skridske.html.

Friary, R. (1996) *Skate Sailing.* Indianapolis, IN: Masters Press.

# Sailing, Parawing

Parawing sailing was introduced in Europe in the 1980s to provide a new, exciting, and highly maneuverable way for a person to sail—on land—during all seasons of the year on a variety of terrain. The parawing consists of a ram-air inflatable soft-fabric wing measuring from 25 to 120 square feet (0.9 to 4.7 square meters) attached by multiple lines up to 30 feet (9 meters) long to a control bar held by the sailor and sometimes attached to the sailor by means of a quick release snap swivel and body harness. Sailors can use larger or smaller parawings to accommodate wind and other conditions.

While the imagination is the only limit to the kinds of vehicles for which a parawing may provide propulsion power, participants of the sport today primarily use parawings while wearing various sliding or rolling devices on their feet. It appears that sailing on skis is the most popular and practical usage. Parawings are sailed over snow or ice with the sailor wearing skis or skates, over sand beaches or salt flats with the sailor wearing land or sand skis or foot steered "buggies," over paved surfaces with sailor wearing in-line skates, or over turf with the sailor using grass skis, buggies, or various roller devices.

The sailor uses the parawing as a sail for propulsion, converting the pull and "lift" of the wing to forward motion. As a sailboat tacks across and into the wind to change course and direction, so does the parawing sailor also take advantage of the same forces—particularly the phenomenon of "apparent wind," a concept well known by other high speed sailing applications such as ice boats and board sailors.

Parawing sailing is distinctly different from, al-

*There's virtually no limit to the kind of vehicle parawings can propel; parawing sailing on skis—on snow, ice, sand, or turf—is one of the most popular forms of the sport.*

though related to, similar sports that utilize the wind for propulsion. The most closely related sports include power kiting and kite buggy sailing, free-skate winter board sailing, skate sailing, and ice boating.

The sport of parawing sailing was invented in the early 1980s by German sports enthusiast Wolf Beringer. Beringer, "the king of the parawing," conceived of the unique control system that allows changing the angle of attack of a parafoil wing and developed the first parawing designs. He was the inspiration for the founding of the International Parawing Club and has become a European legend with his graceful and athletic stunts, including airborne lifts, jumps, and glides. Along with other early parawing sailors he developed competition events and rules.

In 1990, a successful Antarctic expedition to the South Pole led by explorers Reinhold Messner and Arved Fuchs used parawings to pull men on skis trailing sledges an average of 104 kilometers (65 miles) per day.

In 1992, kite designer and builder Hans Schepker and skier George Theriault, inspired by Wolf Beringer, teamed up to design and produce parawings in America. Theriault became the first person in North America to sail with a parawing using snow and grass skis. He founded the North American Parawing Association, which publishes a newsletter and promotes the sport. In 1995, Charlie Meding, an early member of the association, placed fifth in the fifteenth annual World Ice and Snow Sailing Championships held in Madison, Wisconsin. Meding was the sole parawing sailor competing in the kite and handheld category.

While one would assume that parawing sailing

Flying a parawing on skis, in-line roller skates, grass skis, or land/sand rollers is an awesome experience. The more you resist the pull of the wind against the parawing (especially if you are wearing a harness), the faster you will be propelled by the wing. Also, as you become accustomed to sailing in progressively stronger winds, the more you will be able to trust your body weight to the harness. Eventually, you will find yourself whipping along, supported by the parawing, driving forward, in total control, sailing upwind/across the wind and downwind, fully maneuverable and going like a bat out of hell.

If you don't like the idea of sliding on skis, or rolling devices, then you are probably a buggy person. The lightweight stainless steel tricycle buggy is exceptional fun on fields and the beach. You use the parawing for propulsion, steer with your feet, and achieve exciting levels of speed and control while staying close to the ground with complete stability.

—*Parawing News,* 1994

is a sport that would primarily appeal to younger "risk takers" or those who seek thrills through participation in "extreme" sports, in fact, parawing sailing appeals to many age groups. The person of middle or advanced age, for example, can participate without indulging in great athleticism by utilizing the exceptional maneuverability of the parawing and carefully selecting the appropriate sized parawing to suit the conditions.

—George Theriault

# Sandyachting

Sandyachting is the sailing of certain types of yacht on sand. Landyachting or landsailing involves the sailing of almost identical yachts on land—dry salt lakes, airfields, parking lots, or even school playing fields. Iceyachting is the sailing of similar yachts on ice using skates. Speedsailing is a separate, clearly defined sport involving the use of windsurfer rigs on large skateboards.

Sandyachting is an exhilarating sport that uses the power of the wind to propel a wheeled craft along a sandy surface at speeds of up to 130 kilometers (80 miles) per hour. All that is required to go sandyachting is a large expanse of flat hard sand, a wind, and a sail mounted on a wheeled framework capable of carrying one person or more. Almost every suitable beach will have had a sandyacht of some description sailed on it at some time.

The power of the wind is free. It costs nothing to tie an old bed sheet to a simple pole mast and mount it on a timber framework with a wheel at each corner and enjoy being blown down the beach, even at only a walking pace—such is the simple appeal of sandyachting. The silence, the speed, the ecological soundness of the whole concept, and the sheer beauty of some beaches are added attractions. The outbuildings of most houses near suitable beaches will often contain a basic sandyacht.

## Origins

The competitive sport of sandyachting has evolved naturally from the random sailing by individuals on isolated beaches since the turn of the century, but its origins can be traced back to the Chinese, who in 550 C.E. developed the first wind-driven carriages and sail-powered chariots for battle purposes. By 1600 the Chinese had developed land or sandyachting to such an extent that the Chinese royalty even took part in races. Massive troop-carrying yachts were developed for use on Belgian beaches and a 28-seater built in 1600 was used for 190 years for ferrying dignitaries and tourists between Scheveningen and Petten along the Belgian coast. The yacht inspired numerous engineers to design similar craft, with varying degrees of success.

The French and Americans both tried sailing on the railroads in the 1830s, but insurmountable problems were encountered with the unreliable strength and direction of the wind. The invention of the steam engine finally stopped further development of wind-powered carriages on the railroads.

The discovery of gold in 1849 in California resulted in innovative pioneers mounting sails on their Conestoga wagons to speed up travel to gold country, and a wealth of colorful folklore exists concerning such characters as Windwagon Smith.

# Development

Sandyachting as a competitive sport can be traced back to the Dumont brothers of De Panne, Belgium, in 1898. Their activities attracted the attention of cross-channel aviator Louis Bleriot in 1905 and development began in earnest. By 1912 sandyachts were a common sight on the fashionable beaches on the French and Belgian coasts, with rides being offered and yachts available for hire. A competition in 1913 at Hardelot attracted 43 competitors. The yachts were generally four-wheelers of varying size, using bicycle technology and pneumatic tires, with sails borrowed from sailing boats. World War I abruptly stopped further development of the sport.

By the 1920s yachts were being sighted on British beaches and speeds of 65 kilometers (40 miles) per hour were being achieved. During the 1930s sandyachts became popular once more at French and Belgian beach resorts, and the introduction of spoked motorcycle and car wheels solved a major problem as bicycle wheels had proved incapable of withstanding the considerable side-thrust forces involved.

The Americans were also sailing by the 1930s, but the single momentous event that shaped the future development of the sport occurred in the basement workshops of the *Detroit Evening News* in 1937, where employees built a little iceyacht and christened it "The Detroit News" (DN). Twenty-six years later, the Dutch mounted wheels on The Detroit News and revolutionized the sport by establishing the ideal configuration for a sandyacht, namely with one steerable wheel at the front, and two rear wheels with an axle between them.

In Great Britain the 1950s were the most dramatic and innovative years in the development of the sport. Ingenious designers produced yachts of every shape and size imaginable in the quest to find the optimum configuration. One particularly popular design was the "crabber," with a fixed sail and independent steering to all three wheels to enable the yacht to be positioned correctly to the direction of the wind, so that the yacht appeared to move sideways—in a crablike fashion—along the beach.

The general philosophy was the bigger the yacht, the faster. Some huge yachts were built during the evolutionary heyday of the sport, but

*Any stretch of sand is ideal for sandyachting; yachters can race along at speeds up to 80 miles per hour.*

most needed a strong wind to get them moving at reasonable speeds.

The arrival of the DN on continental beaches in the early 1960s revolutionized the sport because the DN was tiny, simple in design, cheap to build, light, and extremely efficient with a sail of only 5.5 square meters (6.6 square yards). In light winds, the DN's maneuverability and acceleration gave it instant superiority.

The International Federation of Sand and Land Yachts Clubs (FISLY) was formed in 1962 with representatives from France, Germany, Belgium, and Great Britain. The first official European championships were held in 1963, with all yachts racing together in an open class. As the DNs were racing with yachts two or three times their size, the fleet was subdivided in 1965 into three classes according to sail size.

The DN proved that big was not necessarily best and yachts began to come down in size. By 1970 the massive Class 1 dinosaurs were almost extinct, but the DN concept had been quickly refined and developed within the increasingly popular Class 3, with the addition of an aerodynamic body shell and a powerful aerofoil section wing mast.

In 1975 a second revolution occurred with the introduction of the Windskate, a tiny yacht of tubular construction, 1.37 meters (1.5 yards) wide and 1.6 meters (1.75 yards) long, with a sail of 4 square meters (4.8 square yards). It was an instant success and became Class 4, but the lack of a formal specification meant that the yacht was quickly lengthened and widened in the quest for higher speeds. By 1978 a wing mast had been mounted on a stretched Class 4 yacht and for two years chaos prevailed. In 1980 Class 5 evolved to accommodate the simpler smaller tubular yachts with a basic pole mast and 5 square meters (6 square yards) of sail. The more elaborate wing-masted development yachts remained in Class 4, but the class quickly died out as the wing mast concept had been developed already within Class 3. While a few Class 2's remain on the continental beaches and in the United States and Canada, where designers have been able to take advantage of iceyacht technology, only Classes 3 and 5 remain today, though both enjoy equal popularity.

Specification for Class 3 include a maximum wheel base of 3.8 meters (4.15 yard) and a maximum width of 3.5 meters (3.8 yards). The design is free but generally consists of a fiberglass composite cigar-shaped fuselage supported by a flexible wooden axle, with a 7.35-square-meter (8.8 square yards) sail mounted on a rotating wing mast. The minimum weight is 100 kg (220 pounds), and the top speed is around 130 kilometers per hour. In the mid-1990s prices ranged from around $400 second hand to around $6,000 for a new, modern competitive yacht.

Class 5 specifications include a maximum wheel base of 2.5 meters (2.7 yards) and a maximum width of 2.0 meters (2.2 yards). The design is free but is generally of tubular metal construction with an open-topped seat. The front wheel is often from a child's BMX-type bicycle, with cast aluminum motorbike rear wheels. The sail is 5 square meters (6 square yards) with a tubular pole mast. The minimum weight is 50 kilograms (110 pounds), and the top speed is around 105 kilometers (65 miles) per hour. Prices in the mid-1990s ranged from around $400 second hand to around $2,500 plus for a new, competitive modern yacht.

## Practice

The competitive sport of sandyachting exists in most countries where there are suitable beaches for racing, and modern sandyachts are either small or large. Both sizes have the same basic three-wheeled "T" shape configuration with a single steerable front wheel and two rear wheels. The mast and sail are mounted halfway between the back axle and the front wheel, with the pilot lying prone on his back as close to the ground as is physically possible, in a specially made seat located behind the mast, with his feet on a bar connected to the steering mechanism of the front wheel. The small yachts are of basic tubular steel or aluminum construction, with a sail of up to 5 square meters (6 square yards), capable of achieving 97 to 113 kilometers (60 to 70 miles) per hour. The larger yachts have aerodynamic bodies, a wide timber axle and front runner plank, with a composite fiberglass wing mast supported by wire stays with 7.35 square meters (8.8 square yards) or more of sail area, depending on the Class rules of the country, and can achieve speeds of 130 to 137 kilometers (80 to 85 miles) per hour. Carbon fiber composite materials and Kevlar are often incorporated into the design of the body and the wing mast. The speed record for a landyacht is 152.13 kilometers (94.55 miles) per hour, set by Frenchman Bertrand Lambert in May 1991 in a 48 kilometer (31 mile) per hour wind using an asymmetric solid aerofoil sail. The speed of 160 kilometers (100 miles) per hour should be easily achievable and several yachts have been developed to break this barrier, but without success to date.

Sandyachts can sail three or four times the speed of the wind and can sail upwind at an angle of 40 degrees to the eye of the wind. Technically this is achieved by sailing using the "apparent wind," a concept that defies simple explanation but is a delight to discover. A modern racing sandyacht with 5 square meters (6 square yards) of sail can achieve 80 kilometers per hour in a wind of 24 kilometers (15 miles) per hour. Wheels have been refined to minimize rolling resistance and the choice of ultra-smooth round profile tire is critical. The technique is to pull the sail in gently as the yacht accelerates, until the sail is pulled in as tightly as possible once maximum speed has been achieved, to minimize drag. A modern sandyacht can out-accelerate a sports car and can out-perform the best rally driver on corners. The speeds may sound frightening but are only achievable using the latest competitive yachts. Inferior yachts will be restricted by their design to achieving lower speeds and hence it is a very safe sport. Injuries are very rare indeed, even at the international competitive level.

The excitement of racing lies in the cut and thrust of close competition. Yachts start from stationary positions on a two- or three-row grid, with pilots pushing their yachts initially to build up speed and find clean (unobstructed) wind before jumping in. Starts can be spectacularly chaotic and minor collisions are common. A typical course will involve two turning marks 3.2 kilometers (2 miles) apart, sailed in a clockwise direction. A typical race is 30 minutes long with the winner being shown the checkered flag after 30 minutes of sailing. The sailing rules are simple and clearly defined, particularly concerning procedure and priority at turning marks. As sandyachts have no brakes, gybe (with the wind) turns are often taken at full speed and on two wheels. The low center of gravity means the yacht slides sideways easily and cornering is best likened to rally driving in that turning into the skid is required to prevent an involuntary spin. It is utterly exhilarating to be in the center of a group of tightly packed yachts all skidding broadside together around a corner, all on the brink of losing control—and yet accidents are very rare indeed.

The minority sport of sandyachting has approximately 150 active participants within the United Kingdom and owes its lack of popularity to its total dependence on weather conditions. It is alive and well in the United States, but is still a minority sport, with at most 1,000 participants. It is thriving in France, where it seems it is compulsory for school children to try it and yachts have priority on the beach. Germany and Belgium are strong on the sport, followed by the Netherlands.

It is also popular in New Zealand and Australia.

Serious, competitive sandyacht racing occurs during the winter months in Europe, when the beaches are less crowded but invariably wet. A drysuit, goggles, helmet, gloves, and Wellington boots are essential to keep dry and warm, but if a suitable deserted beach can be found in summer, sailing in shorts and a tee-shirt is a delight. Sailing is not permitted on all suitable beaches, and those who attempt to sail before obtaining clearance from the relevant regulatory authority risk inciting an often permanent ban on the sport.

—A. R. Parr

**Bibliography:** Parr, Andrew. (1991) *Sandyachting—A History of the Sport and Its Development in Britain.* Pembrokeshire, UK: Gomer Press.

# Senior Games

The U.S. National Senior Sports Classic is a series of athletic competitions for people who are over the age of 50. It is also known as the Senior Olympics, which was its original name. This national championship is part of a larger network of events that provide venues for older people who want to remain physically active and participate in organized competitive sports throughout their lives. This is sometimes referred to as the Senior Games movement.

The U.S. National Senior Sports Classic and the Senior Olympics have been held once every two years since 1987. The week-long event's basic format is similar to the Olympic Games, with a concentrated schedule of track-and-field events, swimming, tennis, and other sports held in a specific host city. The event is sponsored by the U.S. National Senior Sports Organization, by regional organizations that are affiliated with it, and by residents of the city where the championship is held.

In addition, the U.S. National Senior Sports Organization and associated organizations sponsor numerous Senior Games events that take place on the state and regional levels between the biennial championships. Hundreds of thousands of people compete in these meets. Many of the re-

*A contestant in the triple jump at the 1994 Senior Games. Modeled after the Olympic Games, this week-long competition for people over 50 is held every two years.*

gional Senior Games serve as qualifying events for the national championships.

The National Senior Sports Classic is primarily oriented to the United States, where the majority of competitors live. However, the event is also open to participants from other nations, and residents of Canada, Mexico, and other countries compete in it.

## Origins and Development

The concept of organized athletic competitions for older people became increasingly popular after 1960. Numerous individual events and circuits for older athletes were organized in the subsequent decades. Participants and supporters of Senior Games organized the first multisport National Senior Olympics in 1987 in St. Louis, Missouri. The U.S. National Senior Sports Organization was subsequently formed to coordinate the National Senior Sports Classic and related events on an ongoing basis. The U.S. National Senior Sports Organization, headquartered in St. Louis, is a non-profit, volunteer-based membership organization. It is overseen by a board of directors elected by the members, and it also has a paid office staff. Local activities are organized by the associated regional and state Senior Games organizations.

In 1989, the second National Senior Sports Classic was held in St. Louis. Since then, the event has been held in a different location each time. In 1991 it was moved to Syracuse, New York. In 1993 it took place in Baton Rouge, Louisiana. The 1995 National Senior Sports Classic was in San Antonio, Texas, and the 1997 championship was scheduled to be hosted by Tucson, Arizona. The National Senior Sports Classic network grew rapidly in its first decade, as the number of athletes and events increased. The 1987 Senior Olympics attracted approximately 2,500 athletes. The second national championship in 1989 drew an estimated 3,400 athletes. In 1991, approximately 5,000 people participated in the National Senior Sports Classic, a number that increased to 7,200 in the 1993 event. The 1995 National Senior Sports Classic had a field of almost 8,300 competitors, and approximately 40 percent of those who were invited attended the actual event. The regional events experienced similar growth, with as many as a quarter of a million participants.

The Senior Games movement reflects the increasing number of people who are living longer. It has also been stimulated by society's overall emphasis on health and fitness and by the greater awareness of the physical and psychological benefits of sports for older people. Medical research has indicated that regular exercise and proper nutrition can slow the detrimental effects of aging. Many experts believe that such activities can even improve the physical condition of people who had been sedentary in their earlier lives. The social involvement that organized athletic activity offers is widely believed to have important psychological benefits for older people too.

Participation in senior athletics is expected to continue to grow significantly as the large generation born after 1945 advances in age. The people born in the first year of this "Baby Boom" reached the age of 50 in 1996, and the over-50 population was projected to continue to increase markedly in the latter 1990s and early twenty-first century.

## Events and Athletes

A variety of sports are featured in the National Senior Sports Classics and in the regional Senior Games. They include traditional Olympic events and other challenging sports, as well as less physically demanding activities. The more popular of the sports in the 1995 National Senior Sports Classic included swimming (with 3,516 people competing), track and field (3,418 competitors), softball (1,614 players), cycling (1,450 racers), bowling (1,381 players), tennis (1,311 players) and volleyball (879 players). The 1995 roster also included competitions in archery, badminton, basketball, golf, horseshoes, racquetball, shuffleboard, table tennis, and a triathlon, among other sports. In addition, opening and closing ceremonies and social events are scheduled during the week of the national championships.

Senior Games and National Senior Sports Classic events combine the competitive elements of sports with the goal of encouraging widespread participation in athletic activity for its own sake. Competitors become eligible to participate in the National Senior Sports Classic by placing in the top positions in state and regional meets. Approximately 20,000 people qualified for eligibility in the 1995 National Senior Sports Classic. Medals and ribbons are awarded to the top finishers in each sport and age category. For many of the athletes, advancing to the top levels of the competitions is an important goal.

However, the Senior Games philosophy emphasizes the goal of providing an incentive and opportunity for people of all levels of ability to benefit from athletics. This applies especially at the regional and state levels of the Senior Games. Many of the participating athletes are more focused on the process of training and on accomplishing their own goals and individual "personal best" in a sport rather than on the element of competition with others.

The athletes are very diverse in their back-grounds and situations. At the 1995 National Senior Sports Classic championships, an estimated 66 percent of the competitors were male and 34 percent were female. Some competitors focus on individual sports. Others compete in several events. Many of the participants have been life-long athletes, including former competitors and medalists in the Olympics and other top athletic events and circuits. The National Senior Sports Classic also attracts people who only developed an interest in exercise or a particular sport in their later years. While many competitors are as healthy as their younger counterparts, some of the athletes compete despite specific physical disabilities, such as arthritis. Some have become active in competitive sports as a result of training programs they undertook to deal with heart disease, cancer, and other surgeries or illnesses. Proponents of Senior Games cite the experience of many of the athletes as evidence that age or specific disabilities need not be a barrier to activity. Among the oldest contestants in 1995 was Harley Potter, a 102-year-old golfer who took up that sport in his nineties. Arda Perkins advanced to the national championship as a swimmer in her late seventies, despite being blind. During the 1991 National Senior Sports Classic, Richard Bernabe, 73, competed in the tennis championships, while his 96-year-old father received a bronze medal in the 100-yard dash.

Individual sports are organized into divisions based on age. Originally, the National Senior Sports Classic was limited to people 55 and over. The age requirement for the 1997 National Senior Sports Classic was lowered to 50. (Some regional events, however, retained the minimum age of 55.) Most age classes cover four years. The largest age group has traditionally been people in their sixties. In the 1995 National Senior Sports Classic a total of 2,292 competitors participated in the 60–64 age class, and 1,931 athletes entered events in the division for people 65–69. The next largest category that year was for those who were 55–59, with 1,792 participants. This was followed by people age 70–74, with 1,159 participants, while there were 641 athletes 75–79. A total of 438 competitors were 80–89, 21 athletes were 90–99, and 2 were 100 years old or older.

In addition to overseeing the Senior Sports Classic events, the U.S. National Senior Sports Organization is involved in educational projects related to sports and fitness for older people, and also serves as an advocate on related issues. The U.S. National Senior Sports Organization participates in national policy and educational conferences and boards such as the White House Conference on Aging and the National Recreation and Parks Congress, among others. While it is an independent organization, the U.S. National Senior Sports Organization is designated by the U.S. National Olympic Committee as its representative among seniors. The Senior Sports Classic also receives support and sponsorship from General Mills, Johnson & Johnson, and other corporations that produce products and service for older adults.

—John Townes

**Bibliography:** Pena, Nelson. (1991) "Old Glory." *Bicycling* (December).

Stathoplos, Demmie. (1995) "Silver Threads among the Gold." *Sports Illustrated* (3 July).

U.S. National Senior Sports Organization. (1995) *USNO Newsletter* (Fall/Winter).

Wilson, Lillie. (1991) "At the Senior Olympics." *American Demographics* (May).

# Shinty

Shinty (derived from the Gaelic word *sinteag* for "leap") is first mentioned in the Highlands and Inner and Outer Hebridean Islands of Scotland toward the end of the eighteenth century. As with mob-football, which enjoyed much popular support on the Scottish borders, the game was a highly physical contact and collision sport carried out on a vast playing area with a minimum of rules, regulations, rest, or intermission. The primitive structure of the activity and its amalgam of community festival and unmasked violence are neatly summarized in this description:

Games were contested between whole clans or parishes without limit as to numbers or time until darkness stopped play among the walking wounded. The field of play was undelineated except by the occasional pail of *visge-beatha* (whisky). In an interclan match,

a combatant who had failed to disable at least one opponent within a reasonable time had his curved stick (caman) confiscated as a punishment by the chieftain so that he could only kick the ball (cnaige) or his opponents (McWhirter and McWhirter 1975).

## Origins

Historians are not in agreement on the origins of shinty. R. W. Henderson, an American librarian, distinguished sports historian, and expert on the evolution of ball games, wrote:

It has been claimed that shinty came to Scotland by way of Ireland, but so far evidence is not conclusive. In Irish mythology Cuchulain, Fionn, and Fingall play huge club and ball games over the land of the Gaels, and many are the mythological men who are proficient with ball and club. Allowing for the fact that these legends date back hundreds of years B.C., we must again remember that they were written A.D. The highly imaginative, romantic, legendary accounts should not be taken as historical sources.

Hugh Dan Maclennan, a leading shinty expert, has a differing view as to the origins of shinty. Maclennan played the sport at Lochaber High School in Fort William during the 1970s and then gained a Blue (the equivalent of an athletic "letter" in the United States) at Glasgow University. After playing for Fort William and then Inverness, Maclennan turned to journalism and broadcasting. In 1990, he received the first ever "Shinty Reporter of the Year Award."

Maclennan underscores the fact that shinty (in the Gaelic tongue the word is *camanachd*) has a long history. The U.S. national pastime (baseball) and national passion (football) have histories of between 100 and 150 years. Shinty, by contrast, may have pagan roots and goes back thousands of years: "Introduced to North-West Scotland along with Christianity and the Gaelic language nearly two thousand years ago by Irish missionaries, the game can safely lay claim to being Scotland's national sport."

Maclennan cites the *Inverness Courier* (18 July 1842) as one of the earliest "modern" accounts of a shinty match. Later in the nineteenth century,

# Shinty

*"The Shinty Players," an 1840 painting by D. Cunliffe.*

general agreement on a dress code could not be reached. Some teams played in knickerbockers, others wore the kilt. The Glenforsa team in 1880 achieved an athletic compromise by playing in knickerbockers of the MacKenzie tartan.

## Development

Shinty cannot claim to be a major sport. Scotland's premier sport is soccer, followed by rugby. Many more Scottish children take part in golf, track-and-field athletics, swimming, netball, basketball, and other sports than take part in shinty. Playing members number only in the low thousands, but there are currently 40 shinty clubs, and while the regional base continues to be in the Highlands and Islands, that is not the whole story. There are, for example, university clubs at Aberdeen, St. Andrews, and Edinburgh; there is a Lowland club at Tayforth; and émigré Scots can play for London Camanachd. Maclennan cautions that shinty should not be seen as just a minor sport played regionally in Scotland. Wherever Scots have traveled, they have taken shinty with them as a part of their cultural baggage. For example, soldiers of the Lovat Scouts played shinty during the Boer War in South Africa at the beginning of the twentieth century.

In the period up to 1914 and the onset of World War I, shinty developed rapidly, and the need for a list of playing rules that could be agreed to by all players became clear, and codifying the rules helped in the game's expansion. Following World War I and up to the 1950s, however, a variety of

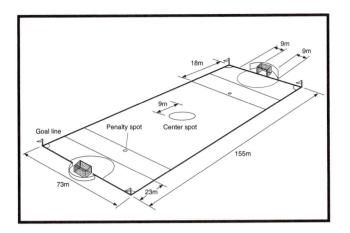

socioeconomic factors resulted in the decline of shinty. Demographic shifts saw significant numbers of Scots move away from the Highlands and Islands and resettle in industrialized Glasgow and the North of England. Maclennan quotes one shinty player, Roger Hutchinson, who says, "The game of shinty ceased to be played during the first four decades of the 20th century. It was an inexorable decline."

Shinty originally bore a close similarity to Ireland's premier sport, hurling. Today, while there are occasional mixed contests (for example, the Shinty/Hurling match between Scotland and Ireland under 21 years teams played at Bught Park, Inverness, Scotland, on 25 July 1992), the games, as played at an elite level, have major differences in technique. In shinty, there are twelve players on each team and seven officials are required. Unlike most field games, the pitch size is not fixed and varies greatly from club to club. The recommended size of a playing field is 170 yards (155 meters) by 80 yards (73 meters). This is considerably larger than the area required for American football, rugby, or soccer (association football). The goal posts may seem much like those used in American football or rugby union football, but they are actually much narrower: the crossbars are only 4 yards (3.6 meters) wide. The crooked, broad-bladed shinty stick bears some resemblance to a field hockey stick.

## Practice

The 12 players on a shinty team include a hailkeeper (goal-keeper), a full-back, three half-backs, a center back, a center-field, a center-forward, three half-forwards, and a full forward. A game lasts 90 minutes, with a half-time interval of 5 minutes. The game is essentially an aerial sport with the ball being tossed and flicked and passed. Only the goal-keeper may handle the ball. This is the major contrast with hurling, in which all players may catch and strike the ball. A goal is scored when the ball passes wholly over the goal line, between the goal posts, and under the crossbar, which is set at a height of ten feet.

The game is tough. Fouls such as kicking, catching, or throwing the ball, obstruction, pushing, charging, hacking, and jumping at an opponent are severely penalized. Shinty, like hurling, is a game where the level of ball flow, spatial movement, and player fluidity create a special type of spectator exhilaration.

The ball has a core of cork and worsted wool and is covered with leather. The stick has a cylindrical shaft. The head must be able to go through a 63-millimeter (2-1/2 inch) diameter ring.

In recent years, vigorous corporate sponsorship and segments of the tourist industry have helped to promote and revitalize the sport. This has resulted in Prince Edward associating himself with the development of a youth shinty league, and Diana, the Princess of Wales, was given a shinty stick at a meeting of the Bute Highland Games in the early 1990s. English cricket star Ian Botham has "had a go" at the game, and, in 1991, two Scottish teams (Skye and Kinguissie) visited Cape Breton and reintroduced the game to Canada's Maritime Region after an absence of 150 years.

What is shinty's future? Is it to be a modern sport or an antiquarian fragment of Celtic culture? Maclennan makes this observation:

For life-force and continuing success, the game must continue to aspire to skill and spectacle at the highest level. If these remain the ideals of the greatest game in the world, and as long as the unique enduring comradeship "after battle" can be maintained, then shinty will maintain the traditions which were founded thousands of years ago and have stood the test of time. It will also remain one of Scotland's truly national assets.

—Scott A. G. M. Crawford

See also Hurling.

**Bibliography:** Arlott, J. A., ed. (1975) *The Oxford Companion to World Sports and Games.* London: Oxford University Press.

Cuddon, J. A. (1979) *International Dictionary of Sports and Games.* New York: Schocken Books.

Henderson, R. W. (1974) *Ball, Bat and Bishop: The Origin of Ball Games.* Detroit: Gale Research Company.

Maclennan, H. D. (1993) *Shinty: 100 Years of the Camanachd Association.* Nairn, UK: Balnain Books.

McWhirter, N., and R. McWhirter. (1975) *Guinness Book of Records.* London: Guinness Superlatives.

*Shinty Yearbook 1994–95.* Inverness, UK: Highland Printers.

Smout, T. C. (1986) *A Century of the Scottish People, 1830–1950.* New Haven, CT: Yale University Press.

# Shooting, Clay Target

There are three disciplines of clay target shooting: (1) trapshooting, (2) skeet shooting, and (3) sporting clays. A shotgun is used in all three. Trapshooting is the precursor to the latter two. It dates from the early nineteenth century when English gentlemen shot at live birds released from traps. In 1880, saucer-shaped clay targets replaced live birds, and spring-operated throwers catapulted them into the air. Currently there are two types of trapshooting: (1) American (also known as Down the Line) and (2) International, which includes Olympic, Universal, Automatic, and Double Trap. All types use one or two clay targets thrown at various angles, heights, and speeds from trap machines. The specifics of scoring, the number of traps, the shooting positions, the distance the targets are thrown, and the release of the clay targets vary between the types of trapshooting and from country to country.

Skeet began in the United States in 1926. There are three types of skeet: (1) American or Amateur Trapshooting Association (ATA), also known as the National Skeet Shooting Association (NSSA), (2) International, and (3) English. The significant differences in types of skeet are the starting position of the gun, the number of shooting positions, the variable-time release system for throwing the targets, and the distance to which targets are thrown.

Sporting clays began in the early 1900s and more clearly resembles field shooting than the other shotgun disciplines because it introduces a variety of target sizes, angles, and speeds to simulate different species of game. There are three popular styles of sporting clays: (1) English, (2) FITASC, which is the abbreviation of the Fédération Internationale de Tir aux Armes Sportives de Chasse (also known as International Sporting Parcours de Chasse), and (3) Five Stand. The major differences are in course design, number of traps, and variety of targets.

## Origin and Development

With the development of the shotgun, shooting at flying birds gained in popularity and developed into the sport of trapshooting. It is difficult to state an exact date for the beginning of trapshooting, but it was fairly well developed in England by 1750 and discussed in an old English publication, the *Sporting Magazine*, in 1793. In the early stage of its history it appears that trapshooting was purely an English sport, as no other European records have been found. Trapshooting clubs began to form shortly after 1800, and the "Old Hats" public house located near London, was the first place mentioned as a favorite resort for pigeon shooters. From England, trapshooting spread to other West European countries, to North America, and to the British colonies and dominions. The year 1831 has often been chosen as the beginning of organized trapshooting in North America.

The term *trapshooting* derives from the fact that the original trapshooters imprisoned live birds in a series of traps and then fired at the birds a few moments after an operator released them. Live pigeon shooting became a very popular sport, and competitions were held throughout Europe and North America. By the late 1860s, trapshooters in England and North America found they were depleting the supply of live birds, and negative public sentiment against the sport began to develop. As a result, trapshooters looked for a suitable inanimate substitute.

The first substitute was the glass ball target and trap, which was developed in England, probably around 1860, and introduced to North America in 1866. Captain Adam H. Bogardus (1833–1913) of Elkhart, Indiana, improved the

*Skeet shooting from the* Canadian Empress *as it sails through the St. Lawrence Seaway.*

trap and target and originated the first simple rules of glass ball competition. He, thus, is considered "the father of glass ball shooting." Glass ball competitions were popular throughout the United States and Canada in the 1870s and 1880s. However, the glass ball did not satisfactorily simulate the bird in flight. The invention of the clay pigeon, or clay target, in 1880 by George Ligowsky (1856–1891) of Cinncinnati, Ohio, began a new era in trapshooting. It was more challenging to the shooters, and its flight more closely resembled a live bird's flight.

To introduce clay pigeons throughout the United States, a series of 25 matches were arranged between Captain Bogardus and Doc Carver (1840–1927), a high-profile trapshooter. Another individual who helped to promote the various forms of trapshooting throughout the United States and Europe was Annie Oakley (1860–1926). Her fame created an interest in trapshooting among the women of her time, and in the 1910s she taught hundreds of women to shoot.

The Interstate Trapshooting Association, organized in 1892, laid the groundwork for trapshooting as it is known today and held what is regarded as the first Grand American Handicap Tournament. In 1918, it changed its name to the American Trapshooting Association to recognize Canadian shooters. A change in structure in 1924 resulted in yet another name change; it became the Amateur Trapshooting Association (ATA), which now has 74,000 registered members.

At the end of the nineteenth century, trapshooting clubs and competitions were common throughout North America and Europe. With the establishment of annual national championships, international competitions seemed to follow naturally. Trapshooting was introduced as a sanctioned international sport at the Second Olympiad in Paris, France, in 1900 and has been included at every subsequent Olympic Games with the exception of 1904, 1932, 1936, and 1948. La Fédération Internationale de Tir aux Armes Sportives de Chasse (FITASC), created in 1921, united international shooting sports bodies in 1929 to establish both the World Shooting Championships and the European Shooting Championships. The Union Internationale de Tir (UIT), in 1947, took over the responsibility for international trapshooting in the Olympics and the World Championships. Women began competing in the European Championships in 1954 and in the World Championships in 1962.

Skeet shooting was devised by three upland game hunters in 1910 as a way to practice hunting techniques. It was originally known as "Round the Clock Shooting," as the shooting arrangement was a complete circle of 25 yards (22.9 meters) with the circle marked off like the face of a clock. Changes were made to make it more appealing: two traps were used to throw targets, double target shooting was added, shooting was done in a half circle, and a new set of rules was established. The sport was officially introduced to the United States in 1926 by William H. Foster, the editor of *National Sportsman* and *Hunting and Fishing* magazines. The first American Skeet Shooting Championship was held in 1935. Skeet was introduced in Britain and Europe in the 1930s, and both the British and the Europeans modified the sport to suit their own needs and developed their own set of rules. The National Skeet Shooting Association (NSSA), with 17,000 current registered shooters, was founded in the early 1930s and hosts the World American Skeet Shooting Championship annually. The UIT has hosted the World International Skeet Championships since 1947 and the European Championships since 1954. Women began competing in the World Championships in 1962. International skeet became an Olympic sport in the 1968 Olympics in Mexico City.

At the turn of the century with the growth of trapshooting and the London shooting schools, some shooters in England changed the location and number of trap machines to better simulate live bird shooting, and sporting clays was developed. Initially sporting clays was the link between game shooting and competitive trap and skeet shooting and was used as practice for both. In the last 20 years, sporting clays in and of itself has become a serious competitive sport internationally. FITASC organized the first Sporting Clays World Championships for men and women in 1979. Although sporting clays was very popular in Europe, it did not become an organized sport in North America until the mid-1980s. Currently the National Sporting Clays Association (NSCA) has 14,000 registered members in North America and hosts the National Sporting Clays Championships annually in September.

## Trapshooting

In the beginning, early clay target shooting followed as nearly as possible the rules and customs of live pigeon shooting; the original form included five traps set in a straight line in front of the shooter. This form was modified in the 1880s by W. G. Sargent of Joplin, Missouri, to include three traps and five shooter positions arranged in a radial formation 16 yards (14.6 meters) from the traps. At the turn of the century this system was superseded in Canada and the United States by a single automatic trap that threw targets at a fixed elevation but at random angles. Shooters, however, still used the same five positions.

The single automatic trap became the basis of American-style (ATA) trapshooting, which is found predominantly in Canada and the United States; a variation of this type of shooting referred to as Down the Line (DTL) is found in the United Kingdom, Australia, and New Zealand. In American trapshooting, one machine in a ground-level traphouse is used to throw the clay target between 48 and 52 yards (44 and 47 meters) at unexpected angles between 0 and 22 degrees right and left of center. Shooters use a 12 gauge shotgun to shoot at the clay targets. In a trap squad (usually five people), shooting is done from five positions in a crescent-shaped formation 16 yards behind the trap, and only one shot is taken at each target. Shooting is done in rotation with the person in position number one firing first and so on until everyone has shot at five targets and then rotates to the next position. Each shooter, using a 12 gauge shotgun, shoots five targets at each position for a total of 25 targets. There are three events: (1) singles, (2) handicap, and (2) doubles. The usual competition consists of 200 singles targets, 100 handicap, and 100 doubles. Singles and doubles are shot from the 16-yard line and shooters are placed in classes according to known ability. In doubles, two targets are released simultaneously from one machine, one angling left at 22 degrees, the other right at 22 degrees. Handicap is shot at increasing distances back from the trap, from 19 yards (17.4 meters) to a maximum of 27 yards (24.7 meters). Handicap events are usually 100 targets and the angles are the same as singles. An individual's assigned handicap is determined by the handicap committee of the ATA and is based on performance in registered shoots. Each August the ATA hosts the Grand American where approximately 5,000 shooters compete along 1.63 miles (2.7 kilometers) of shooting line with 100 trapfields.

Down the Line (DTL) is similar to American trap because one machine is used to throw the clay target, and shooters shoot in squads of five, taking five shots from each position. DTL differs in that two shots are allowed at each target, a hit with the first barrel scoring three points, and one with the second barrrel scoring two points. A perfect score is 100 hits with the first barrel, or 300 points. The usual DTL competition consists of 100 targets. Handicap is to a maximum of 23 yards (21 meters), and there is no doubles event.

While in the 1890s North American clubs were going to fewer traps, in Europe the first-class clubs went to 15 traps. They were fixed on the ground level, and behind there was a trench that hid the traps from the shooters. This type of trapshooting developed into the current International-style trapshooting where 15 traps are arranged in a straight line in a traphouse (bunker/pit). Five shooting positions are in a straight line situated 15 meters (16.5 yards) to the rear and parallel to the traps, one position for each group of three traps. Traps are adjusted to throw all targets away from the shooters within a 45-degree angle right or left of the center trap in each group and at different heights for a distance of 62 to 75 meters (68 to 82 yards). The traps are released by a voice-activated system that guarantees equal distribution of targets to each shooter in a series of 25 targets: 10 targets to the right, 10 targets to the left, and 5 targets to the center. A squad consists of six shooters who move from one position to the next after each shot, eventually shooting five targets from each position. Competitors are allowed two shots at each clay target; one point is given for each clay target broken in the air. International-style trapshooting (also known as Olympic trap) is shot in most countries throughout the world. Since 1993, the World International Trapshooting Championships and Olympics consist of 125 targets plus a

25-target final. (Once all competitors have shot 125 targets, the top 6 shooters shoot a final of 25 targets to determine the winner.) The final score is added to the 125 for a total of 150.

Two variations of International trapshooting are Universal and Automatic trap. In Universal trap, a group of five traps throw targets at various angles and heights, while in Automatic trap one multi-oscillating machine is used to throw targets. Squads of six shooters shoot from five shooting positions. The speed of the targets is not as fast as those in Olympic trap but the angles are more extreme.

In the mid-1980s, the UIT introduced a new international clay target event called Double Trap. In Double Trap two clay targets are thrown simultaneously from two of three traps situated in a traphouse. Three different settings using a combination of two of the three traps are used in competition. The left-hand trap is set at an angle of 5 degrees to the left; the center trap is set at 0 degrees; and the right-hand trap is set at 5 degrees to the right. The traps are set to throw the target a height of 3 or 3.5 meters (3.3 or 3.8 yards) at 10 meters (11 yards) out and a distance between 55 and 65 meters (60.3 and 71.31 yards). The traps are released by a voice-activated system, which guarantees the simultaneous and constant release of two targets from the predetermined traps. The five shooting positions are in a straight line, equidistant apart, 15 meters (16.5 yards) to the rear and parallel to the traphouse. In international Double Trap competitions men shoot at 150 targets plus a 50-target final and women at 120 targets plus a 40-target final. Once all competitors have shot, the top 6 shooters shoot a final of 50 targets for the men and 40 for the women to determine the winner. The final score is added to the 150, for the men for a total of 200 targets, and added to the 120 for the women, for a total of 160 targets. Double Trap became an Olympic sport for both men and women in 1996.

## Skeet Shooting

Skeet shooting uses the same clay targets and traps used in trapshooting, but the field is set up quite differently. Originally intended as a way to help shooters improve their field shooting, it is now an intensely competitive and popular sport. The skeet field consists of a high house and a low house and eight shooting stations arranged on a segment of a half circle. The center of the circle is marked by a stake, which also marks the target crossing point. Station 1 is located at the left end of the half circle beside the high house, and station 7 at the right end beside the low house. Stations 2 through 6 are located on the circle at points equidistant from each other. Station 8 is located at the midpoint of a line between the high and low houses. The houses face each other 40 yards (36.6 meters) apart. Each house contains a trap that throws a target in the direction of the other trap but over the center of the circle and always in the same line and at the same elevation.

In American NSSA skeet, shooters shoot a combination of single and double targets from eight stations. Shooters use four different gauges of shotguns: 12, 20, 28, and .410 and shoot at 100 targets with each gauge. Targets are thrown 60 yards (54.9 meters) in still air conditions. English skeet is different in that shooters shoot from seven positions (there is no station 8), the targets are thrown 55 yards (50.3 meters), and the event is shot with only a 12-gauge shotgun.

In International skeet, shooters shoot singles and doubles from eight stations. The targets must travel between 65 and 67 meters (71.3 and 72.5 yards). The starting position of the gun must be low, with the end of the stock level with the shooter's hip bone and must not be moved until the target is visible. The traps are released by an electric-manual or electric-microphone system with a time device providing for the release of the targets from instant release up to a maximum of three seconds. Since 1993, UIT competitions have consisted of 125 targets and a final of 25.

## Sporting Clays

Sporting clays comes the closest to simulating actual field shooting of any shotgun sport. Rather than using standardized distances and targets, sporting clays provides a variety of target sizes, angles, speeds, and changes in terrain to add an element of surprise. Sporting clays courses are designed so that the flight of the target simulates a species of game, such as ducks, pheasants, or rabbits. There are at least six types of targets: standard, mini, rocket, rabbit, battue, and midi. Each club specifies the number of stations and the number of targets that constitutes a round,

typically 50 to 100 targets, with one or more shots taken from each station.

In English sporting clays there are a number of different "stands" or stations, which can be shot in any order. At each stand the competitor shoots at three to five pairs depending on whether it is a 30-, 50-, or 100-target competition. There are three varieties of pairs: (1) simultaneous pairs—the targets are released together; (2) following pairs—the second target follows the first with very little delay; and (3) report pairs—the second clay is released at the sound of the competitor's shot at the first clay.

In FITASC sporting clays (also known as International Sporting Parcours de Chasse) an event can consist of one parcours, a sequence of 25 targets, up to eight parcours for a 200-target event. The major difference between English sporting clays and FITASC is in the number of trap machines required, which varies considerably, depending on a variety of factors, thus creating greater target variation. In FITASC no two targets on each parcours are the same, differing in distance, speed, and angle. Specialty targets are used on each and every parcours.

There are two ways to shoot FITASC—the traditional and the new. Traditional uses three or four shooting stations set in a horseshoe, line, or oval shape, depending on space and safety zones available. The stations are set according to the terrain and the targets presented, with safety the first consideration at all times. Each station is shot in turn. Forty-five yards (41.2 meters) is generally the maximum distance shot on any parcours. A major drawback is that shooting can be slow. The new way of shooting FITASC differs in two major ways. Each parcours still consists of 25 targets, but four shooting positions are the norm, and each of the four stations has a minimum of three dedicated machines. With the new system each parcours can accommodate a squad on each station and therefore takes less time to complete.

In Five Stand sporting clays, five different shooting stands are in a line. The shooter gets a presentation of five targets, usually a single and two pairs, from each stand. The menu of target presentation at each stand is different so there is a variety of targets. It is common in the United States to set a Five Stand course on a combined American trap and skeet field.

Clay target shooting is practiced in most countries of the world. It is popular with people of both sexes and all ages and abilities, because shooters can choose whether to participate recreationally or competitively at local, regional, national, or international levels. At least one of the clay target shooting disciplines is included in all the major international sporting events, such as the Olympics, Pan American Games, European Championships, and World Championships.

—Susan Nattrass

**Bibliography:** Amateur Trapshooting Association. (1995) *1996 Official Trapshooting Rules.* Vandalia, OH: ATA.

Campbell, Robert. (1967) *Skeet Shooting with D. Lee Braun.* New York: Rutledge Books.

———. (1969) *Trapshooting with D. Lee Braun and the Remington Pros.* New York: Rutledge Books.

Chapel, C. E. (1949) *Field, Skeet and Trapshooting.* New York: Coward-McCann.

Croft, Peter. (1990) *Clayshooting.* London: Ward Lock.

Eaton, D. H. (1920) *Trapshooting: The Patriotic Sport.* Cincinnati, OH: Sportsmen's Review Publishing.

Hinman, Bob. (1971) *The Golden Age of Shotgunning.* New York: Winchester Press.

Lugs, Jaroslav. (1968) *A History of Shooting.* Middlesex: Spring Books.

Menke, Frank G. (1960) *The Encyclopedia of Sports.* 2d rev. ed. New York: A. S. Barnes.

National Sporting Clays Association. (1965) *Sporting Clays.* Houston, TX: NSSA/NSCA.

Nattrass, Susan M. (1974) "The Development of International Clay Pigeon Shooting," M.A. thesis, University of Alberta, Edmonton.

Smith, Lawrence B. (1931) *Better Trapshooting.* New York: E. P. Dutton.

Union Internationale de Tir. (1993) *Special Technical Rules for Clay Target Shooting.* Munich: UIT.

# Shooting, Pistol

A pistol or handgun is, literally, a gun that can be shot with the hand. The sport of pistol shooting involves shooting handguns at targets. Pistol shooting, together with rifle and shotgun shooting, are disciplines within the sport of shooting. The objective of all these disciplines is for the shooter to aim precisely and release a projectile from a gun to strike a distant target as close to its center as possible.

Features that make pistol shooting a sport are pistols that are specifically designed and built for target shooting, that the shooting is done at targets that can be scored and ranked, and that the shooting is carefully controlled with strict safety standards and competition rules. Pistol shooting at targets developed when duelists wanted to be prepared to hit their adversaries. Target pistol shooting became popular toward the end of the nineteenth century and was first organized on an international basis when three pistol events were included in the first modern Olympic Games in Athens in 1896. Modern target pistol shooting features three different men's and two different women's events in the Olympic Games. It offers many additional events at the international and national levels.

## Origins

There is little certainty as to where the term *pistol* originated. Some argue the birthplace of the pistol was in Italy, where they were associated with the city of Pistoia. Czechs argue the name pistol derives from a short Bohemian handgun known as a *pistala* (pipe). Pistols came into common use in the sixteenth and seventeenth centuries, but they were not widely used in target shooting until the eighteenth century.

The first use of pistols in target shooting was associated with the practice of dueling. In the eighteenth century, the pistol gradually replaced the sword as the favorite weapon of duelists. The best way for a potential duelist to survive was to practice shooting at targets. Many elements of dueling are still seen in modern pistol sport. Dueling's strict protocol and the seconds' responsibility to ensure fair play are precursors of today's competition rules. The best gun makers made matched sets of dueling pistols with fast locks, light triggers, and precise sights that are still desired features on modern target pistols.

Nineteenth-century exhibition shooting with pistols encouraged the development of accuracy and skill by public performers. Pistol exhibitions at circuses or large public gatherings occurred in many countries, including Germany and the United States. In the United States, William F. "Buffalo Bill" Cody and Annie Oakley promoted an appreciation of pistol shooting skills through exhibitions.

*Contestants at the 1988 Olympics in Seoul. Target pistol shooting developed out of dueling practice; gradually accurate shooting became an end in itself, and pistol shooting was included in the first modern Olympics in 1896.*

At the end of the nineteenth century, clubs to promote pistol shooting were organized in France, Germany, the United States, and some other countries. A few target pistol shooters became well known throughout the world. A milestone for modern target pistol shooting occurred in 1896 when three pistol events were on the program of the first modern Olympic Games in Athens. A free pistol event similar to an event on that program was introduced to the World Shooting Championship program in 1900. Recognition in the Olympic and world championships made pistol shooting an international sport. This gave impetus to the development of standard rules that now are accepted and practiced by pistol shooters throughout the world.

The 50-meter (54.7-yard) free pistol event has been on every world championship program since 1900 and, with minor changes, on most Olympic programs. A second major pistol event, 25-meter (27.3-yard) rapid fire pistol, now involves shooting five shots at five different targets, but its rules have changed dramatically since an ancestor of that event was on the 1896 program. The event had origins in dueling practice and the more modern police and military training. In 1912, the rapid fire target was a full-sized man with scoring rings. By 1935, the target became a side-facing silhouette of a man where only hits counted. By 1939, the rounded outline of a man changed to straight lines where the target retained a rectangular body and smaller rectangular head. The head and feet did not disappear from the rapid fire target until the 1980s when it took its present form of a square with round scoring rings.

A center-fire pistol event, for large-caliber pistols, was added to the world championship program in 1947. A 25-meter standard pistol event for semi-automatic .22 caliber rimfire pistols and a 10-meter (33-foot) air pistol event were added in 1970. An experimental women's pistol event was on the world championship program in 1962. A woman's sport pistol event was added to the Olympic program in 1984 and air pistol events for men and women were added to the Olympic program in 1988.

## Olympic Pistol Champions

During the 100-year history of the modern Olympic Games, 39 gold medals have been awarded in men's pistol events and 5 in women's. The personal stories of these special champions offer fascinating insights into this sport.

The first modern Olympic Games in Athens in 1896 produced an act of sportsmanship that would be incomprehensible in today's environment of medal counts and winning at all costs. Two brothers, John and Sumner Paine, who were among the finest pistol shots of their time, were selected to represent the United States at the Games. The Paines arrived in Athens not even knowing the conditions of the competition, but they quickly asserted their dominance. In the first pistol event, John won with 442 points, Sumner was second with 380 points, while the third-place shooter had less than 200 points. John decided that since he had already won a gold medal, he would withdraw from the second event. Sumner won that event with an equally wide margin over the second-place shooter. The Paine brothers decided neither should take advantage of the situation and both withdrew from the third pistol event, giving up almost certain chances to win gold and silver medals.

Károly Tackács was a national pistol champion in Hungary in the 1930s. During World War II, Tackács suffered the loss of the right arm he used to shoot his pistol. Nevertheless, after the war, he retrained himself to shoot with his left hand and Tackács won the Olympic rapid fire pistol event in both 1948 and 1952.

When the People's Republic of China team came to Los Angeles in 1984, no athlete from that country had ever won an Olympic medal. The first medal of those Games was awarded to the surprising winner of the men's 50 meter free pistol event, 27-year-old Haifeng Xu, a department store clerk who made sports history in his country and returned home a celebrity.

The 1992 Olympic Games in Barcelona produced dramatic evidence that shooting is a life-long sport. In the free pistol event, 16-year-old Konstantin Lukashik of Belarus and 58-year-old Ragnar Skanaker of Sweden were contesting for the gold medal. Lukashik won the event to became the youngest shooter ever to win an Olympic medal and Skanaker the oldest in the post–World War II period when he finished third.

—Gary Anderson

The most significant changes in pistol shooting were the development of air pistol events and of women's pistol shooting. Air pistol shooting made it possible for the sport to be practiced widely in many countries that did not have large ranges or widespread access to pistols that shoot powder-burning cartridges. Women participated in pistol shooting as early as the late 1800s, but their numbers were small until women's pistol shooting became an Olympic event.

## Practice

Modern target pistol shooting is governed worldwide by the International Shooting Union, also known as the Union Internationale de Tir (UIT). The UIT, founded in 1907, has become one of the world's largest international sports federations with over 135 member nations. Five separate continental shooting confederations are included within its governing structure. Two of the 11 women's shooting events officially recognized by the UIT are pistol events, and both are on the Olympic Games shooting program as well. Five of the 19 men's shooting events recognized by the UIT are pistol events, and 3 of those events are on the current Olympic program.

In pistol shooting governed by the UIT, the shooter must stand erect, holding and aiming the pistol toward the target with one hand only. Some forms of police and combat pistol shooting allow or even stress holding the pistol with both hands to achieve a more stable position. International sports rules, in contrast, specifically require the more difficult one-handed pistol shooting to emphasize and test the skills of participating athletes. Competitive pistol shooters must train several hours daily for 8 to 12 years before they can attain the ability to compete for gold medals at the international level.

Pistols used for target shooting differ from ordinary pistols in several aspects. Target pistols have longer barrels and are heavier to enhance their accuracy and the ability of the shooter to aim them precisely at targets. Target pistols must have larger sights that can be adjusted with a high degree of precision. Target pistols usually have special, orthopedic grips that are carved to fit the hands of the shooter. Pistols used in some events are single-shot pistols, while even those used in multiple-shot events seldom utilize magazines holding more than five shots. Target pistols are made with much greater precision to produce the accuracy required to hit difficult competition targets consistently.

Pistol targets have black, circular aiming areas printed in the center of a rectangular white back-

## Fast Draw

Fast draw is a gun sport in which revolvers are drawn from a holster and used to "shoot" a target. Fast draw requires speed in drawing the revolver and accuracy in hitting the target. The best shooters can draw and hit a target in from .25 to .40 of a second, depending on the nature of the event. The sport is the safest of all gun sports, as bullets are not used. Instead, targets are hit with wax bullets or balloons are broken by the force of a blank cartridge. Fast draw began in Hollywood, California, in the 1950s as a carryover from Western movies and television shows in which the heroes were portrayed as the "fastest guns in the West." The sport was at first popular among actors and stuntmen and the first contest was held in 1954. The sport now has participants all across the United States who compete in local and regional events and the annual World Championships. The governing organization is the World Fast Draw Association which sanctions events, sets the rules, publishes a monthly magazine, maintains records, and presents awards.

The equipment required is a single action revolver with a caliber no smaller than .32 and no larger than .45, a traditional or open-style holster, and wax bullets or blank loads. Targets include a silhouette, impact target disc, a balloon-Disc, and four and nine inch balloons. A signal light on the target indicates that the competitor should draw and shot. A timer is activated with the signal light and is turned off by a sensor on the target when the target is hit. Competitions are of two major types. In elimination events two competitors fire simultaneously at identical targets, with the first one to hit the target the winner. In index events the winner is determined by the lowest total score of a series of draws. Draws can vary by type of ammunition, type of target, size of the target, distance of target, and standing or walking. Competitions are held and records are kept in both men's and women's divisions. While blanks and wax bullets do not cause the same level of injury as real bullets, they can cause serious injury. Thus, safety precautions are stressed and the Association claims that no serious injury to a competitor or spectator has occurred in 25 years of competition.

—David Levinson

be able to hold a relatively heavy pistol steady for long periods of time while carefully aligning the sights of the pistol with the target and releasing the trigger. In some events, the precision of the shooter is tested and shots can be fired quite slowly. In other events, the shooter must start with a loaded pistol at a ready position where the pistol is pointed down from the target at a 45 degree angle. At a ready signal, the shooter must raise the pistol and fire one or more shots in a very short period of time.

In addition to the UIT events, pistol shooting events for police training, for so-called combat or defense shooting, and for shooting at animal-shaped silhouettes were developed in some countries, especially the United States. The pistol events most widely practiced throughout the world, however, are the events recognized and promoted by the UIT.

Today, target pistol shooting is a sport for the young and the old, for women and for men, for people from many different countries all over the world and for many fine sportsmen and sportswomen who are numbered among its millions of worldwide participants.

—Gary Anderson

**See also** Shooting, Rifle.

**Bibliography:** Anderson, Gary L. (1995) "Olympics 1996, Where Shooting Will Be Seen Differently." In *Gun Digest 1996*, edited by Ken Warner. Northbrook, IL: DBI Books.

Antal, Laslo. (1983) *Competitive Pistol Shooting*. East Ardsley, Wakefield, UK: EP Publishing.

Antal, Laslo, and Ragnar Skanaker. (1985) *Pistol Shooting*. Liverpool, UK: Laslo Antal & Ragnar Skanaker.

Blair, Wesley. (1984) *The Complete Book of Target Shooting*. Harrisburg, PA: Stackpole Books.

Crossman, Jim. (1978) *Olympic Shooting*. Washington, DC: National Rifle Association of America.

International Shooting Union. (1995) *General Technical Rules and Special Technical Rules*. Munich: International Shooting Union.

Palmer, A. J. (1977) *The International Shooting Union, Official History 1907–1977*. Wiesbaden, Germany: International Shooting Union.

Peterson, Harold L. (1962) *Treasury of the Gun*. New York: Golden Press.

Standl, Hans. (1976) *Pistol Shooting as a Sport*. Trans. by Anita Pennington. New York: Crown Publishers.

Trench, Charles Chenevix. (1972) *A History of Marksmanship*. Chicago: Follett.

Yur'yev, A. A. (1985) *Competitive Shooting*. Trans. by Gary L. Anderson. Washington, DC: National Rifle Association of America.

ground. Both the black bull's-eye and the area around the central black have scoring rings printed on the target. Their values range from a large outer one ring to a central ten ring. Shots count the value of the scoring ring they hit.

To succeed at pistol shooting, the shooter must

# Shooting, Rifle

Rifles are firearms with shoulder stocks that shoot single projectiles. They are characterized by precise sights that facilitate accurate aiming and long barrels with internal grooves or rifling. Rifles are held to the shoulder with both hands when they are aimed at a target and shot.

Rifle shooting is a discipline within the sport of shooting while shooting is, together with archery, one of two primary marksmanship sports. The objective of all marksmanship sports is to precisely aim and release a projectile from a gun or bow to strike a distant target as close to its center as possible. Shooting, as a sport, tests, measures, and ranks the marksmanship skills of its participants.

Rifle shooting evolved from early forms of marksmanship such as archery, through crossbow and musket shooting, into the extreme tests of human accuracy presented by modern target rifle events. Rifle shooting includes many unique events distinguished by different kinds of rifles, distances, targets, shooting positions, types of shooting, and levels of competition.

## Origins

Records of marksmanship sports were found in ancient Egypt and Assyria as early as 2000 B.C.E. The history extends from ancient longbows through crossbows during the Middle Ages. Rifle shooting's direct ancestry began with matchlock and wheel-lock muskets that were used in target contests as early as the fifteenth and sixteenth centuries. Shooting rituals utilizing matchlock arms developed independently in Japan during this period.

Firearms with more accurate rifled barrels began to appear in competitions in Central Europe by the sixteenth century. The development of rifled barrels with internal, spiral grooves to spin and stabilize projectiles made rifles accurate enough that their impacts could be precisely controlled by shooters. This facilitated their use in formal target training and competitions.

Marksmanship training, first with crossbows and later with muskets and then rifled arms, was organized to help citizens defend their cities and soldiers be more effective in battle. Crossbow-shooting clubs were established in German-speaking cities in the thirteenth, fourteenth, and fifteenth centuries so citizens could practice for their common defense. In the military, manuals of arms evolved from directions to load and fire quickly to instructions to load, aim, and fire with precision.

Traditions celebrating the skills of the best shooters promoted rifle marksmanship as a valued skill and rewarding sport. Earlier, the legendary Swiss crossbowman William Tell became a revered figure because he was skillful enough to shoot an apple from his son's head. German shooting clubs culminated regular shooting practices with shooting festivals that blossomed as an important element of German culture. The shooting skills that Swiss men developed for military purposes were contested in well-organized shooting tournaments for crossbows as early as 1504. Military units like Morgan's Virginia riflemen of the American Revolutionary War were feared and effective because of their soldiers' marksmanship skills. In the American frontier of the 1700s, "rifle frolics" offering prizes of beef, turkey, or other food items for the best shooters became festive community gatherings.

Crossbow and rifle shooting contests were local events for six centuries or more before they were organized at national levels during the nineteenth century. The Swiss Société Suisse des Carabiniers was founded in 1824, the British National Rifle Association in 1859, the German Deutscher Schützenbund in 1861, the American National Rifle Association in 1871, and the French Fédération Française des Sociétés de Tir in 1884. These organizations established common rules to standardize rifle shooting.

Diverse national rifle shooting traditions began to converge in 1896 when two rifle events were on the program of the first modern Olympic Games in Athens and in 1897 when five European nations held the first World Shooting Championship in Lyon, France. Those international contests led to the formation, in 1907, of the International Shooting Union, also known as the Union Internationale de Tir (UIT), the world governing body of shooting. Today, the UIT recognizes six different rifle events for men and three for women that are widely practiced throughout

*Deena Wigger of the United States demonstrates the prone position, one of the five standard positions assumed in contemporary shooting competitions.*

the world. Five of the nine UIT rifle events are on the current program for the Olympic Games.

## Practice

All rifle shooting events now use paper or electronic targets that have scoring rings with values from one to ten points. The size of the target and its scoring rings varies depending upon the shooting distance and type of shooting, but the central ten rings of all modern rifle targets are small and difficult to hit. The ten ring on the 50-meter (55-yard) small-bore rifle target, for example, is 10.4 millimeters (0.41 inches) in diameter. It is smaller than a dime and more than half a football field away.

Three different shooting distances are used in UIT and most national competitions. All rifle events in the first world championship were fired at a distance of 300 meters (328 yards) with center-fire target rifles. Small-bore events for .22 cal-

iber rimfire target rifles shot at targets 50 meters away were added to the Olympic program in 1908 and the world championship program in 1929. Air rifle events for 4.5 millimeter (0.177 inches) caliber target air rifles shot at targets 10 meters (33 feet) away were added to the world championship program in 1970 and the Olympic program in 1984. A major change in modern rifle shooting is a decline in the use of center-fire rifles whose use evolved from military marksmanship training and a dramatic increase in the use of air rifles. Air rifles that use compressed air or $CO_2$ to propel small lead pellets account for the growth of shooting in many countries. They do not require the large ranges or expensive equipment necessary for center-fire rifle shooting.

National shooting programs in British Commonwealth countries and the United States, whose shooting traditions originated from military-oriented programs, still offer shooting events at longer distances of 900 meters (984

## The Evolution of Rifle Targets

The first formal rifle targets were large, circular wooden discs. The discs usually had a central aiming mark painted on them. Wooden shooting-festival targets in German-speaking lands were sometimes painted with motifs commemorating a special occasion that was celebrated through a festival. Target motifs included city or club foundings or anniversaries, holidays, weddings, or birthdays of esteemed club members. Today these older, painted, wooden targets are carefully preserved as extremely valuable artifacts of shooting and cultural history.

Targets for long-range rifle shooting in the United States, England, and British Commonwealth countries in the mid- to late-nineteenth century were large, rectangular iron plates. They were white-washed to show hit locations. Hitting the targets emitted loud clangs that signaled success to shooters and spectators as far away as 914 meters (1,000 yards).

Targets used throughout the twentieth century were printed on paper. They typically have central black areas that offer aiming marks for shooters. Thin white scoring rings are printed on the black bull's-eye. Additional lower-value scoring rings may be printed in the white area around the central black area. A shot is scored according to the value of the scoring ring it hits. When a shot hits two or more scoring rings, it is scored the value of the highest scoring ring it touches. Paper targets are cheap and easily available. Their major disadvantage is that several competition officials are required to score them and official scoring cannot take place until after the shooters finish.

The most modern targets, now used in the Olympics and World Shooting Championships, are electronic targets that instantly display the scores of each shot on computer screens and television monitors. Microphones are mounted in the corners of the targets and computers record sound waves coming off of bullets passing through the target to pinpoint shot locations to an level of accuracy as precise as one one-hundredth of a millimeter.

Electronic targets now make it possible for rifle events to have finals where the top eight shooters conclude a competition event with ten additional shots that are scored in tenths. In this system, a center ten counts as much as 10.9 points, while a shot that just touches the ten ring counts 10.0 points. Finals where every shot is shown on large television monitors and recorded on electronic scoreboards now make shooting in the Olympic Games and other major competitions an extremely exciting spectator sport.

—Gary Anderson

yards) or 1,000 yards (914 meters). Some traditional U.S. small-bore rifle events are still shot at distances of 50 yards (45.7 meters) and 100 yards (91.4 meters), while many indoor events are shot at a distance of 50 feet (15.2 meters).

Target rifles differ from hunting and military rifles through their greater weight, more precise sights, and special triggers that produce the highest degrees of accuracy. There are two basic rifle configurations used in international competition. The traditional target rifle is called a free rifle. It derives from rifles used in the late nineteenth century that featured hook buttplates to assist in uniformly positioning the rifle on the shooter's shoulder and palm rests that extend below the rifle to help the shooter hold the rifle when standing. Free rifles with hook buttplates, palm rests, thumbhole stocks, and additional accessories are used in men's 300-meter and 50-meter events.

The second rifle configuration is called a standard rifle. It has a lighter weight limit and cannot have hook buttplates, thumbhole stocks, or palm rests. Standard rifles represent an attempt to compete with a lighter, simpler, and less costly target rifle. This style of rifle is used by women in their 50-meter events, by men in a 300-meter standard rifle event, and by both men and women in 10-meter air rifle events.

Shooters assume three different positions to hold the rifle and aim at their targets. The most challenging shooting position is standing. The shooter must stand on both feet and hold the rifle on the shoulder with both hands and no other support. UIT rules allow the shooter to rest the arm that supports the forward part of the rifle on the side or hip. The standing position is the most difficult because the center of gravity of the position is higher and the method of supporting the rifle is less stable. The next most difficult position is kneeling. There the shooter kneels on his/her heel and rests the arm that supports the rifle on the forward knee. The shooter is also allowed to use a sling or supporting strap attached between the upper portion of the supporting arm and the rifle to help steady the rifle. The third major shooting position is prone. There the shooter lies on the firing station supporting his/her upper body and the rifle with both arms resting on the elbows. A sling also is permitted in the prone position.

National programs in the United States and a few other countries also require shooting in the sitting position. In this position, the shooter sits on his or her buttocks, supports the rifle with both arms, and rests both elbows on the legs extended in front of the shooter. A sling is permitted here too. A fifth shooting position is used in benchrest shooting, which is practiced in some countries, most notably the United States. In this position the rifle is rested on special supports placed on top of a bench or table. In this form of shooting, marksmanship error is reduced to a minimum in order to test the innate accuracy of the rifle and ammunition.

The type of shooting done in competitions governed by the UIT is called slow-fire or precision shooting. Shooters are given sufficient time to aim carefully and control each shot. Competitions governed by the International Military Sport Council and some national programs include rapid-fire shooting, where shooters are given a short period of time to fire a series of shots. Usually this requires shooting ten shots in one or two minutes. Other forms of rifle shooting include shooting at steel animal silhouettes, popular in the Americas, and field shooting, popular in Scandinavia.

The most important rifle shooting contests today are the rifle events in the Olympic Games and World Shooting Championships. These events are practiced by the more than 135 member federations of the UIT and make rifle shooting one of the world's most popular competitive sports.

—Gary Anderson

**See also** Shooting, Pistol.

**Bibliography:** Anderson, Gary L. (1995) "Olympics 1996, Where Shooting Will Be Seen Differently." In *Gun Digest 1996*, edited by Ken Warner. Northbrook, IL: DBI Books.

———. (1972) *Marksmanship.* New York: Simon and Schuster.

Blair, Wesley. (1984) *The Complete Book of Target Shooting.* Harrisburg, PA: Stackpole Books.

Crossman, Col. Jim. (1978) *Olympic Shooting.* Washington, DC: National Rifle Association of America.

Horneber, Ralf. (1993) *Olympic Target Rifle Shooting.* Trans. by Bill Murray. Munich: F. C. Meyer Verlag.

International Shooting Union. (1995) *General Technical Rules and Special Technical Rules.* Munich: International Shooting Union.

Palmer, A. J. (1977) *The International Shooting Union, Official History 1907–1977.* Wiesbaden, Germany: International Shooting Union.

Parish, David, and John Anthony. (1981) *Target Rifle Shooting.* East Ardsley, Wakefield, UK: EP Publishing.

Peterson, Harold L. (1962) *Treasury of the Gun.* New York: Golden Press.

Pullum, Bill, and Frank T. Hanenkrat. (1995) *The New Position Rifle Shooting.* Peachtree City, GA: Target Sports Education Center.

———. (1973) *Position Rifle Shooting.* New York: Winchester Press.

Trench, Charles Chenevix. (1972) *A History of Marksmanship.* Chicago: Follett Publishing Company.

Yur'yev, A. A. (1985) *Competitive Shooting.* Trans. by Gary L. Anderson. Washington, DC: National Rifle Association of America.

# Shooting, Single-Shot

The sport of shooting at targets with rifles reflects the evolution of rifled shoulder arms, since every age used its most modern and accurate arm. A rifle is a shoulder arm with twisted grooves in the barrel that give the bullet a gyroscopic, stabilizing spin while in flight to the target, thus enhancing accuracy. In the latter half of the nineteenth century, rifles evolved from muzzle loaders to one-shot cartridge breech loaders. The single-shot rifle, as its name indicates, is able to fire only one shot at a time, in contrast to the repeating rifles developed shortly after the U.S. Civil War. This is the era to which contemporary single-shot target shooting belongs. There are four facets of the sport today:

1. German *schuetzen* shooting, from the standing position at 200 meters (219 yards) in Europe and 200 yards (183 meters) in America.
2. British long-range shooting, from the prone position at up to 914 meters (1,000 yards)
3. American benchrest shooting, from a shooting bench at various distances
4. Silhouette shooting at steel targets from any position and at various distances

## Origins

The first contests for accuracy in the United States were usually backwoods affairs, with rifles

*Single-shot shooting employs a type of rifle developed between the Civil War and World War I, an era when marksmanship was first emphasized by the military.*

fired over a log at an "X" inscribed on a distant board. Rifles were loaded with the powder and bullet pushed down from the muzzle. The powder charge was ignited with a flint that scraped against a serrated piece of steel, sending a spray of sparks into a pan that then flashed through a touch hole into the main charge. In the 1830s, the charge was ignited with a percussion cap that had match-head fulminate priming compound seated on a nipple. This was struck and ignited by a hammer. After the Civil War of the 1860s, rifles contained the bullet, powder, and primer all in individual brass cartridge cases that could be loaded from the breech. This allowed soldiers to stay sheltered from enemy fire, since now they did not have to stand up to load their rifles from the muzzle. The military then was not interested in accurate fire, despite the significant achievements of the American colonists using rifled Pennsylvania arms in the Revolutionary War and on the frontier. The dominant tactic of the period was to "fill the air with lead"—soldiers were not even trained in marksmanship until after the Civil War. That thinking was changed by the German-American *schuetzen* tradition and by American victories against the British using long-range rifles.

## Development

Although there were informal shooting competitions on the frontier in the nineteenth century United States, competitive shooting did not begin in earnest until the immigration of many German-

mans who had failed to establish democracy in Germany's revolution of 1848. They brought with them a number of social customs, one of which was shooting at targets from a standing position at 200 meters. They established *Schuetzenvereins*, or gun clubs, that became the basis for many U.S. shooting clubs. These were popular until the anti-German sentiments of World War I brought about their demise.

The victory of the U.S. rifle team over the Irish in the 1874 long-range (1,000-yard) rifle competition on Long Island engendered a new interest in marksmanship in the U.S. military and sparked the popularity of shooting single-shot rifles from the prone position.

## Practice

### The Schuetzen Tradition

After the failure of the 1848 revolution in Germany, many of the rebels fled to the United States to escape persecution and retaliation. These immigrants brought with them their custom of gathering in clubs, some of which centered on target shooting. These clubs introduced accurate target shooting from the standing position, and their rifles were designed specifically for that purpose. Members of the clubs were the core of the U.S. team in the Olympic international free rifle shooting tournaments after the turn of the century. The German-American shooting tournaments were organized in *Bunds*, or unions, of regional target-shooting groups, and sometimes drew hundreds of competitors. There were parades to the *Schuetzenparks* before the shooting, and afterward dances and banquets with the consumption of much beer. The best marksman in the tournament was crowned the *Schuetzenkoenig*, the shooting king, and he presided over the ball at the end of the festival.

When World War I began, many Americans considered anything of German origin to be undesirable, so many of the *Vereins* either ceased to exist or became Americanized. With renewed anti-German sentiment in World War II, most of the rest ceased to exist altogether. However, the specialized *schuetzen* rifles and shooting paraphernalia were still in former members' attics, and in 1948 some members of the National Muzzle Loading Rifle Association decided to establish an organization that would allow competition with these rifles. They formed the American Single Shot Rifle Association (ASSRA) to promote fellowship among those interested in the use, study, and preservation of single-shot rifles developed between the close of the Civil War and the onset of World War I. Since then, the ASSRA has grown to well over 2,000 members. It sanctions single-shot rifle matches for over 50 local and regional clubs, publishes a bimonthly journal of information and news, and maintains an archive of target-shooting history. The rifles used in ASSRA competition fired at 200 yards (183 meters) are limited to those that can load a single cartridge (brass case, powder, and bullet). The empty brass case must be removed before the next cartridge can be inserted and fired.

Target shooting with rifles has taken on many other forms since the turn of the century, mostly dictated by the military emphasis on accurate rapid fire for the training of soldiers for combat. Modern military weapons are both semiautomatic (one shot per trigger pull) and full automatic (many shots per trigger pull) and today's competitive target shooting reflects those developments. Two organizations remain time-bound, however, to the older traditions: the ASSRA and the National Muzzle Loading Rifle Association, which sponsors competition with rifles that use black powder and are loaded from the muzzle.

### The Long-Range Tradition

Shooting with rifles at longer distances (sometimes over 1,000 yards) requires a different technique than that of *schuetzen* shooting, which uses the relatively unstable standing position. In long-range shooting, the bullet can be in flight for several seconds and be affected by wind currents, for which compensation must be made when aiming. Shooters in this sport lie prone, facing the target with the rifle in front of them, or supine, with the rifle cradled between upraised knees. The rifles themselves usually are of larger caliber and have considerably more recoil.

In 1873 the Irish Long Range Rifle Team won the Elcho Shield Trophy of the British Isles and looked for another team to challenge in long-range rifle competition. They challenged "the colonists" in America with an advertisement in the *New York Herald*. The New York Amateur Rifle Club accepted the challenge and received en-

## Colonists Triumph

After 12 years of competition the Irish team won the British long-range Elcho Shield trophy in 1873 and challenged the American "colonists" to a similar match at distances of up to 1,000 yards. The Americans accepted, although they had no previous experience of shooting at such long ranges. Thus, the international match began on 25 September 1874, at the newly constructed Creedmoor range on Long Island.

At 800 yards the Americans were ahead after one and one-half hours of shooting, with a score of 326 to 317. At 900 yards the Irish team closed that 9-point gap by scoring 312 against the American score of 310, even with a shot on the wrong target by J. K. Millner of the Irish team, which was a center shot that did not count. Thus, the 1,000-yard stage was to determine the outcome of this first international match.

The Irish closed the gap further at 1,000 yards, so that they were ahead by a point when it came time for Colonel John Bodine of the American team to fire the last shot of the match. If he missed the target, the Americans would lose by one point. If he made a center shot (bull's-eye), the Americans would win by three points. Clearly the pressure was on, and Bodine opened a ginger ale bottle before hand to refresh himself. The bottle exploded and cut his hand. A cry of dismay rose from the crowd of some 8,000 spectators who were crowding the firing line down toward the targets. Bodine casually wrapped a handkerchief around his cut hand and got into position. A swath in the crowd of spectators was made so that he could have a sight of the target. Then he fired the final shot. All eyes were riveted on the target for the signal of what his score might be, and they saw the white bull's-eye scoring disc slowly rise over the target over a half mile away. A roar of jubilation rose from the spectators as the Americans won the match by 3 points and Colonel Bodine became the savior of America's national honor.

The illustrations of the teams from the account of the match in *Harper's Weekly* show the American team all of erect posture with top hats, turned toward the hero Bodine. The Irish team members, on the other hand, are hatless and slouched around Millner, who is beset with remorse for the crossfire that did not count, and he is given the hand of succor from Arthur Leech, the Irish Team Captain.

This American victory began a long history of U.S. interest in the accurate shooting sports.

—Rudi Prusok

dorsement from the newly formed National Rifle Association. Both organizations established a long-distance range at Long Island's Creedmoor Range and contracted the Sharps and Remington rifle companies to manufacture breech loader rifles for the event. The Irish were still using muzzle loaders, and so the event was a challenge of technology as well as marksmanship.

To everyone's surprise, the Irish team almost tied the American team until the last shot was fired, when Col. John Bodine scored with a center shot to win the match by three points for the Americans. The New Yorkers were jubilant and the development of accurate long-range shooting was underway for American sports shooters and the American military. Today, that tradition continues in the long-range international matches of the ASSRA against European and Canadian teams, which feature the kinds of single-shot rifles used in the original competitions.

## The Benchrest Tradition

While the *schuetzen* and long-range traditions demand that the rifle be held by the shooter without other support, the benchrest tradition allows the rifle to be fired from a shooting table and rested on a sandbag or other support near the muzzle. This stability permits testing of the various components that make a rifle shoot accurately (bullet, lubricant, powder charge) without the factor of human error and has helped to develop superaccurate rifles with heavy barrels. Such rifles were used with great success in the Civil War by the Union's Berdan's Raiders, a company of snipers, and were developed further from muzzle loaders to breech loaders at the Walnut Hill Range of the Massachusetts Rifle Association. However, there was no formal benchrest competition until 1947, with the formation of the National Benchrest Shooters Association in Johnstown, New York, and the subsequent splinter organization of the International Benchrest Shooters (IBS) in 1970. The latter publishes a monthly magazine and allows any kind of rifle to be used. The same benchrest tradition is preserved in the ASSRA, which has held regular benchrest matches since 1948, but unlike with the IBS, only the old single-shot cartridge rifles are used.

## Silhouette Shooting

A recent development of single-shot rifle competition is shooting at steel targets that resemble game animals in silhouette. The sport originated in Mexico in the 1950s as *siluetas metalicas*, but that term applies now only to high-power rifle shooting at metal targets. The French-derived *silhouette* is used as a generic term for shooting with any weapon at animal-shaped targets. The purpose is to knock over the steel targets at longer ranges, so the sport is one that requires not only accuracy, but also the use of larger and heavier bullets to carry enough energy to the target to topple it. In the relatively recent single-shot rifle phase of the sport, the rifles used are large-caliber, black powder cartridge single shots of the kind used in buffalo-hunting days.

—Rudi Prusok

**See also** Shooting, Rifle.

**Bibliography:** Blannin, A. (1877) *Hasty Notes of a Flying Trip with the Victorian Rifle Team to England and America in 1877.* Melbourne, UK: Privately printed.

Gillmore, Russell S. (1974) *Crack Shots and Patriots: The National Rifle Association and America's Military Sporting Tradition, 1871–1929.* Ph.D. dissertation, University of Wisconsin, Madison.

Kelver, Gerald O. (1975) *100 Years of Shooters and Gunmakers of Single Shot Rifles.* Brighton, CO: Gerald Kelver.

Leech, Arthur B. (1875) *Irish Riflemen in America.* London: Edward Stanford.

Lugs, Jaroslav. (1968) *A History of Shooting.* Middlesex, UK: Spring Books.

National Rifle Association Staff. (1978) "Silhouette Shooting Comes of Age." *American Rifleman* (May): 35–40.

*Precision Shooting* (journal of the International Benchrest Shooters).

Roberts, Ned H., and Kenneth L. Waters. (1967) *The Breech-Loading Single-Shot Match Rifle.* New York: D. Van Nostrand.

Trefethen, James B. (1967) *Americans and Their Guns.* Harrisburg, PA: Stackpole.

Trench, Charles C. (1980) *A History of Marksmanship.* New York: Exeter Books.

# Shooting, Trap and Skeet

**See** Shooting, Clay Target

# Shuffleboard

Shuffleboard is played on a long, rectangular court with a flat, smooth surface. Players stand at one end and use a long stick, called a cue, to aim and push a flat, round disk, which then slides toward a scoring area at the opposite end. The scoring area is usually a triangle, marked into the court's surface, that is divided into smaller numbered zones. When the disc stops sliding inside a numbered zone, that number is added to the player's score. The player or team with the most points at the end of the game is the winner.

Shuffleboard is a popular pastime that is frequently played on cruise ships, and at resorts, camps, public parks, and retirement communities. At its most basic level, shuffleboard can be played for light exercise and amusement by people who do not have the strength or endurance for more rigorous sports. With only a moderate push, the discs can be made to slide down the court, and the basic skill of aiming the disc can be easily learned. However, when played at advanced levels, shuffleboard requires a great deal of concentration, strategy, and physical skill. Expert players make shots with great force and accuracy, and the discs can move very fast on the court. Players can also use their shots to accomplish other actions, such as knocking their opponents' discs out of scoring areas.

## Origins

Contemporary shuffleboard was developed in the late nineteenth and early twentieth centuries. It is based on elements of numerous older games. Shuffleboard has similarities to the historic sport of lawn bowling, with discs used instead of balls. It is also closely related to the outdoor winter sport of curling, in which players slide an object called a "stone" down a long course marked on the ice.

The most direct ancestors of shuffleboard were games that originated in Britain during the Middle Ages and the Renaissance. These were all based on the action of pushing a flat disc towards a scoring area. Many had similar names, such as "shovel board," "shove groat," and "shove

ha'penny." There were many variations of these earlier versions of shuffleboard. Some were played on large courts marked out on a floor or the ground and used wooden discs. Other versions were played on tabletops, using coins. In some of the tabletop versions, players used their palms or fingers to shoot the coins to the scoring areas. In others, they used flat sticks to shove the coins. Some of these tabletop games are still popular in Britain and elsewhere.

The forerunners of shuffleboard had mixed reputations. Early games were associated with the aristocracy, and a playing area or game table at home was considered a status symbol. However, the games also became popular among the lower classes, and playing tables were common in taverns. Some of the games were associated with gambling and were officially discouraged.

The basic elements of these old games were revived and given their contemporary identity as shuffleboard in the late nineteenth century. This revival coincided with the growth of the cruise-ship industry. These large ships carried passengers across the oceans and emphasized comfort and luxury. The cruise-line owners needed to develop recreational activities for passengers. These older sliding games were appropriate for ships, so the companies devised new versions of them to be played on large courts on the decks.

In 1913, the Ball family set up a shuffleboard court on land, at their hotel in Daytona Beach, Florida. The land-based game spread to other Florida resorts, and in the following decades became popular in other regions and nations. Shuffleboard courts were often included in the public parks that were being built in the early twentieth century. Children also played makeshift forms of shuffleboard.

In the early stages of this revival, there were many versions of the basic game of shuffleboard, some with different names. Players at individual resorts or localities often invented their own rules. In the 1920s, an effort began in Florida to establish a standard form of shuffleboard, and the National Shuffleboard Association was formed to coordinate the sport's development. The association held its first organized competition in 1931. The development of official rules made it possible for players from different locales to compete on an organized basis, which helped to further popularize the game. Shuffleboard is

*At the tournament level shuffleboard calls for great concentration, strategy, and skill, but the sport remains associated in the popular mind with retirement communities and cruise ships.*

widely played today, and numerous local, regional, and national leagues and tournaments are held in many locations. Florida remains a focal point for the sport, and a national winter tournament is held there annually.

## Practice

Shuffleboard courts can be located inside or outdoors. The playing surface must be smooth enough to allow the disc to slide down it, and is usually a hard surface such as wood, concrete, or terrazo.

The designs of shuffleboard courts and the rules of the games may vary to accommodate space limitations and other conditions. Shuffleboard can also be played informally, on courts marked with chalk on basement floors or driveways. Very simple homemade equipment can be used, such as cues made from worn-out broom handles.

The official version of shuffleboard, however, has specific rules and guidelines. The standard shuffleboard disc is 2.54 centimeters (1 inch) thick and 15.24 centimeters (6 inches) in diameter, and it is made of wood, rubber, plastic, or other hard material. The cue is a straight stick between 1.5 and 1.9 meters (5 feet and 6 feet, 3 inches) long. At its base, the cue has a curved, open section that holds and guides the disc on the floor. Players hold the cue near its top at a semi-upright angle and push it forward to make their shots.

The standard shuffleboard court is 16 meters (52 feet) long and 1.8 meters (6 feet) wide. The two scoring areas are triangles located near the ends of the court that are furthest apart. The tips

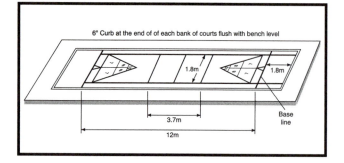

6" Curb at the end of of each bank of courts flush with bench level

1.8m

1.8m

Base line

3.7m

12m

of these triangles point toward each other (and the opposite end of the court). The narrow tip of each triangle is a small triangular scoring area worth 10 points. Behind that, the middle section of the triangle is divided into two equally-sized scoring areas marked for eight points. Behind these (at the triangle's base) are two adjacent seven-point zones. Extending behind the base of the triangle is a 10-off zone, a narrow 46 centimeter (18 inches) wide strip that extends across the court. The player tries to avoid landing his disc in this zone, because it subtracts ten points from his score.

Midway down the court (between the two triangles, three feet from their tips) is a 12-foot (3.7-meter)-long area marked by parallel "dead lines," which extend all across the court. Discs that stop in this area are removed from the game. At the two farthest ends of the court, behind the base of the triangles, are marked blocks that extends about 1.8 meters (6 feet) back from the 10-off zone. Players stand in this area to make their shots. One person stands on the right side, and the other on the left.

Each player has four discs, either red or black. In singles, the two players stand at the same end of the court and take turns making shots. When shuffleboard is played as doubles, one member of each team stands at either end, next to their opponents. Players from each team alternate shots. In singles, the players then move to the other end for another round of eight shots. Games are generally played until a score of 50, 75, or 100 is reached.

The disc must stop completely within the scoring area, without touching its lines, to count. In addition to building up his own score, a player may also make shots that deliberately lower the other player's score by using his disc to knock the

opponent's disc out of a numbered zone or into the 10-off area. This is called *caroming*. Players can also use one disc to protect another disc from being struck by their opponent or to block the other player's access to a scoring area. A player is penalized, with points subtracted from his score, for infractions such as stepping over the line when making a shot. The points are tallied up for a round after all of the discs have been shot from a side.

Shuffleboard uses a combination of skills. The game requires both offensive and defensive strategy. These include the ability to determine and control the speed, distance, and angle that the disc will move, so that it will stop on a specified place on the court. When making carom shots, the skillful player tries to figure how to strike the opponent's disc with her own at an angle that will send both into the desired area of the court.

Players decide on their priorities when making shots. They weigh the relative importance of focusing on their own scores or lowering their opponent's and decide if they can simultaneously accomplish both. A player may, for example, aim the first shots into the scoring areas furthest down the court, to keep the nearer sections clear of discs for their later shots. With all of these considerations, a shuffleboard match can become very intricate and challenging for players.

—John Townes

# Sidesaddle Riding

**See** Horseback Riding, Sidesaddle

# Single-Shot Shooting

**See** Shooting, Single-shot

# Skateboarding

Skateboarding, a sport in which a person rides a four-wheeled board, has spread through much of the West. The origins and traditions of skateboarding, like many other board activities, lie in North America, but particularly California. Like surfing and snowboarding, skateboarding was popularized by members of the new leisure movement of the 1960s. This movement instilled a specific set of values and philosophies in skateboarding that attracted various alternative youth movements, which have largely retained them to the present day. As in surfing and snowboarding, these attitudes continue to generate controversy.

## Origins

The first skateboard was probably an adaptation of the fruit-crate skate-scooters made in the 1930s. Californian surfers popularized skateboarding in the late 1950s as an activity for days when there were no waves. Skateboarders, or "sidewalk surfers," formed part of the same subculture as surfers. Thus, skateboarders adopted the surfers' hedonistic, carefree philosophies and lifestyle, as well as the cooperative, fun, and self-expressive tenets of leisure seekers in the 1960s. The two activities also shared technical similarities, and skateboarders often mimicked surfing maneuvers when riding the curves of swimming pools, sewer pipes, and street curbs.

## Development

Skateboarding is a demanding activity: scrapes, bruises, and even broken limbs are regular occurrences. However, skateboarders take pride in their ability to push their limits. Like many other activities with a high risk of injury, and perhaps because of girls' socialization, skateboarding is overwhelmingly a male pursuit.

The sport has passed through four distinct historical phases: "sidewalk surfing" in the 1960s, the punk and skatepark era in the 1970s, ramp skating in the late 1980s, and "grunge" in the 1990s. Skateboarding evolved in the early 1960s with the surf boom and was quickly popularized

*Called the best skateboarder in the world, 19-year-old Tony Hawk demonstrates his talents flying 15 feet above the ground at an exhibition in Toronto in 1988.*

by the media. Yet the public also condemned the activity for the same reason it opposed surfing—board riders were depicted as selfish, irresponsible itinerants and louts. City authorities banned skateboarding after medical and safety authorities in North America described it as dangerous. By 1967, skateboarding had gone underground.

In 1973 the urethane wheel resurrected skateboarding. It provided skaters with greater control of their boards and so increased their repertoire of tricks and moves. Skateboard parks consisting of specially designed pools, pipes, and obstacle courses became the rage.

In the late 1970s, punk, an antisocial subculture involving extremes of music, fashion, and attitude, adopted skateboarding. It appealed to punks because skateboarders rejected mainstream bourgeois values and because it carried the cachet of being an ideologically "pure" activity, as opposed to being institutionally oriented. However, exacerbated by skateboarding's links with punks, the "skateboard menace" again concerned some sectors of the public. Medical authorities repeated their condemnation of the activity, city councils banned skateboarding or enforced existing ordinances, skateparks had trouble obtaining insurance, and many new parks closed down.

The National Skateboarding Association (NSA) was formed in 1981 with assistance from the Boy Scouts of America. The NSA attempted to give skateboarding a legitimate and positive image through competition and sponsorship from major companies. Many skateboarders, however, resisted the group. They wanted skateboarding to remain an unorganized activity, true to its original ideals. *Sports Illustrated* described the debate at the time as "Anarchists to the left. Little Leaguers to the right."

Skateboarding videos revitalized skateboarding for the third time in the mid-1980s. While surfing-inspired ramp and pool skating was the dominant form of the sport, many stayed on the streets. Downhill slalom-type skateboarding had largely died out. Despite the best efforts of the NSA, skateboarding remained unorganized, individualistic, and rebellious, while competitions were largely ignored. The skateboarding subculture became even more extreme in some ways, its fans' favorite music moving toward "thrash," a combination of heavy metal and punk played at twice the speed of either styles. Fashion also began tending toward the punk-influenced skull-and-cross-bones and snake themes.

Meanwhile, skateboarding began to have an influence on the newly popular activity of snowboarding. Ski resorts started to build skateboard-park-like snowboard courses that included half-pipes and ramps. With the advent of the freestyle snowboard, snowboarders increasingly looked to ramp and street skateboarding for moves and fashions.

The fourth and current phase of popularity is influenced by grunge, an underground youth style that rejects high consumption and yuppie competitiveness. Grunge youth repopularized such cooperative, individualistic activities as skateboarding and has proved to be an important source of new revenue for big business since the turn of the decade. In the 1990s, skateboarders prefer street skating, a form of the sport almost totally divorced from surfing's influence. Hip-hop, an urban style of music and fashion, also has a large influence on skateboarding style and philosophy.

Each phase of skateboarding has been characterized by a paradox. Soon after marketing agencies sell skateboarding as a clean-cut, all-American activity, albeit a little mischievous, city councils take a different view and have banned skateboarding in many areas. Indeed, street skateboarding in the 1990s remains unpopular with city councils and some sectors of the public. Damage caused by street skateboarding tricks does nothing to alter unfavorable opinions. In addition, many pedestrians feel threatened by the fast-moving, weaving skateboarders. Some skateboarders have moved back to skateparks, but the majority continue to practice their sport as "urban guerrillas," running a gauntlet of police and municipal authorities.

—Duncan Humphreys

See also Extreme Sports.

**Bibliography:** Beal, Becky. (1995) "Disqualifying the Official: An Exploration of Social Resistance through the Subculture of Skateboarding." *Sociology of Sport Journal* 12: 252–267.

Davidson, Judith A. (1985) "Sport and Modern Technology: The Rise of Skateboarding, 1963–1978." *Journal of Popular Culture* 18, 4: 145–157.

# Skating, Figure

Skating has evolved from its prehistoric origins as winter transport into an aristocratic pastime and private club recreation and then into a year-round Olympic sport, performing art, and big business. Men and women have been dancing since time began, so it was inevitable that they would find a way to do it on ice and then see who could do it best. While speed skating and ice hockey have scarcely changed since their inception, except for improved equipment and rules changes, figure skating continues to evolve because of its individual creative element.

*European champion and world and Olympic medalist Surya Bonaly of France exemplifies a generation of young, stylish figure skaters.*

Skating is thoroughly woven into Western culture at all levels as one of the stereotypical sights of winter. Santa, animals, and others skate on Christmas cards, stamps, and porcelain plates; as figurines and as mechanical store-window displays. At first limited by geography, the global growth of skating over the past five centuries has been influenced by socioeconomic factors, individual personalities, technology, movies, and especially television. Skating is now online with Web sites and, because of extensive television coverage, even nonskaters are knowledgeable enough to discuss the sport's finer points.

## Origins

Flint-shaped bone blades found all over northern Europe—one still thong-tied to the foot of a Neolithic skeleton found in a bog in Friesland (in what is now the northern Netherlands)—document skating's ancestry. The earliest literary mention of skating appears in the Scandinavian Eddas, tales collected in the tenth century that date back to 156 C.E., in which reference is made to the "beauty, arrows and skates" of Uller, god of winter, who "runs on bones of animals," as well as to runic heroes who count skating among their manly feats.

For the Dutch, who started building canals in the twelfth century, skating was a necessity. By the 1500s it had become such an integral part of the Lowlands landscape that the Flemish artist Pieter Brueghel even painted skaters into his *Census at Bethlehem* (1556). Rembrandt, the Avercamps, Bol, van Goyen and other artists peopled their flat horizons with burghers on blades, scenes little changed when the American children's writer Mary Mapes Dodge described them in *Hans Brinker or the Silver Skates* (1865). During their Golden Age in the seventeenth century, the Dutch put their society on ice, complete with tented shops and food stalls. Because the commercial aspects of covering 48 to 64 kilometers (30 to 40 miles) a day demanded speed, racing as a sport was already well advanced. The Elfstedtentocht (Eleven-City Tour), a 198-kilometer (124-mile) race linking 11 Friesland cities, is still an annual event—if the canals freeze. Although they invented the Dutch roll, a semicircle skated on the outer edge, the Dutch have generally focused on speed, not figure skating.

In England skating was an import, perhaps brought as early as the fifth and sixth centuries by invading Saxons and certainly no later than 1066 with the Norman invasion. In 1180, Londoners were tying on bones and pushing along with "picked staffs," not for travel but as "play on yce," according to Archbishop Thomas à Becket's clerk, William FitzStephen. Seeing them knock each other down, breaking bones, he concluded, "youth desirous of glorie, in this exerciseth it selfe against the time of warre."

In 1660 the deposed Stuarts returned from exile at the Netherlands court, bringing with them the Dutch roll and more elegant iron skates, on Dutch ice since the 1400s. On 15 December 1662, diarist Samuel Pepys noted Charles II's son, the Duke of Monmouth, and his coterie skating in St. James's Park and remarked that "he slides very well."

## Development

During the Great Frost of 1683, vividly featured in Virginia Woolf's *Orlando*, the court, along with Nell Gwynn, much of London, and Pepys himself, were out on the frozen Thames. By 1742, the first skating club was founded in Edinburgh. A skating portrait of a dour, cross-armed Reverend Robert Walker, who joined in 1780, hangs in the Scottish National Gallery. Admission to the club was limited to men (women were not admitted until well over a century later) of eminent lineage who could skate a circle on each foot and jump over three hats. Those circles and the turns on them became the basis of modern figure skating, and triple jumps of a different sort—no hats—the desideratum of elite competitors, male and female alike.

In the mid-1700s, skating spread across Europe and to North America as sophisticated recreation. Unlike the working class, the gentry had the time, energy, and inclination for such leisure sport. The ice was still free. American painter Benjamin West, later president of the Royal Academy, visiting London in 1760, was invited to show off his Philadelphia style in Kensington Gardens. His compatriot Gilbert Stuart, noted for his portrait of George Washington, immortalized the sport in *The Skater* (1782), which hangs in the National Gallery of Art, Washington, D.C. In Germany, the great writer Goethe (1749–1832), skating even by moonlight, wrote, "I owe to these hours . . . the most rapid and successful development of my potential projects." Both Marie Antoinette and Napoleon, related by fate to the guillotine blade, were seen on skating blades.

The sport's first textbook was British Artillery Lieutenant Robert Jones's 1772 *Treatise on Skating*. Today's typical recreational skater probably does little more than the basic plain skating, rolls, and stops Jones described. He dismissed going backward as "unnecessary and unpleasant" and warned that only those "possessed of some genius" should attempt the "more masterly parts." He also lamented the absence of women.

Confined to frozen village ponds with no place to go but around, the Victorians soon began inventing elaborate geometric, filigree, and grapevine figures made possible by the extended heel and shorter radius curve of the blade developed by Henry Boswell in the 1830s. (Mention of the outside loop turn in G. U. A. Vieth's 1790 text, *Über das Schrittschuhfahren*, suggests that the Germans had already invented such a blade.) Abandoning the grace Jones had advocated, Victorians skated these figures with top-hatted, rigid reserve, arms tight by their sides. Perhaps they were influenced by "scientific method" and the machine standardization of the Industrial Revolution. From these early figures were devised "combined figures" for two to eight skaters who traced patterns to and from an orange on the ice marking a center, rather like a minuet or sedate quadrille. The emphasis was on "doing it properly."

Across the Channel, the scene was altogether more expressive of *joie de vivre*. To the Parisians, skating was festive, and aesthetic form was as important as technical proficiency, as Jean Garcin, leader of *Les Gilets Rouges* (elite skaters named for their red vests) prescribed in *Le Vrai Patineur* (1830). These two impulses, precision and appearance, self-control and self-expression, interact to this day and are both present in competitive scoring in the marks for technical merit and presentation.

Skating continued to develop in the nineteenth century. The Philadelphia Skating Club and Humane Society, the latter phrase referring to the club policy of men members carrying ropes to effect rescues of people who had fallen through the ice, was founded in 1849. Winslow Homer documented for *Harper's* magazine some of the 50,000 New Yorkers who turned out to skate when Central Park opened in 1860; 150 of them went on to form the Skating Club of New York in 1863. That same year, the St. Petersburg club was founded in Russia; even the czar came to skate on the Neva River. Tolstoy wrote a skating scene into *Anna Karenina* (1877). Quebec City had the first covered rink—a roof over natural ice—in the late 1850s. Even though an indoor artificially frozen ice rink had been built in London as early as 1876, competitive events continued to be held outside until 1967.

The New York eye for creativity was also focused on the print—the mark the blade leaves on the ice—rather than how the skater looked performing the figures. Blinded by decorum, the Americans and then the English ignored the one man most responsible for inspiring today's "international style." Trained as a ballet master and committed to having skaters dance on ice to live music, Jackson Haines (b. 1845) left his wife and three children in 1865 to teach and exhibit across continental Europe and Russia. His imaginative blend of charismatic physicality, costuming, and theatrical flair made him a star. His portrait still hangs at the Wiener Eislauf Verein (Vienna Skating Club); Prague named a street for him; and Finland incised "The American Skating King" on his tombstone when he died there in 1879, still unsung at home.

Private skating clubs and associations were sufficiently organized by 1892 for Austria, Germany, Great Britain, the Netherlands, Hungary, and Sweden to found the Internationale Eislauf Vereinigung, now the International Skating Union (ISU), which governs speed and figure skating. Canada joined in 1894, under the aegis of Louis Rubenstein, the U.S. Figure Skating Association in 1923. The World Figure Skating Championships have been held annually since 1896, except during the two world wars and in 1961, after a plane crash killed the entire U.S. team. As of 1996, there were 55 member nations, including a number of countries not commonly associated with ice skating, such as Israel, Mexico, and Thailand.

For most of its history, skating's face on the podium has been Caucasian, and Anglo-Saxon. This is changing. The 1932 Olympics were the first in which Japan took part. In 1977 Minoru Sano placed third at the World Figure Skating Championship, an event held annually in March, and Emi Watanabe placed third in 1979. Midori Ito (1990) and Yuka Sato (1994) have also won world championships. Kristi Yamaguchi of the United States was both a World (1991, 1992) and Olympic (1992) champion before she began her lucrative professional career. China's Chen Lu won the world championship in 1995 and the United States' Michelle Kwan in 1996.

South Africa is the only African ISU member, and there are few skaters of African descent. Notable are Debi Thomas (United States, 1986 World Gold), who competed while a premedical student at Stanford, and Surya Bonaly (France), a European champion and world and Olympic medalist.

## Figures

The four edges combined with the three turns—bracket, loop, rocker—and counterturns placed on two- and three-lobed "eights" that the English developed became the ISU 42-figure compulsory syllabus. Nearly 100 years after Haines's death, figures were still 60 percent of the score, with freestyle score making up the remainder. Then, in 1972, after Austria's Beatrix Schuba won an Olympic and three World titles on the strength of her impeccable figures, despite lackluster freestyle performance, they were reduced to 40 percent, and a do-or-die short program with compulsory moves and mandatory deductions for omitted or failed elements was added for 20 percent.

Figures, which had been two-thirds the cost and time of becoming a singles champion, were dropped from international competition in 1990. The U.S. Figure Skating Association kept them as events separate from freestyle and designed a "Moves in the Field" skill ladder, incorporating all the turns and edges in patterns covering the whole ice surface, that call for dynamic footwork linkage rather than meticulously traced, compass-pure circles. Club registrations tripled.

## Singles

The first world championship, for men only, was held in St. Petersburg in 1896. In 1902, because there was no specific rule barring women, the ISU had to let Britain's Mrs. Edgar (Madge) Syers (b. 1882) compete. When this unforeseen interloper placed second to defending champion Ulrich Salchow (b. 1877) of Sweden in a field of four, the ISU was so undone that if inaugurated a separate women's event in 1908, the same year pairs competition was instituted.

Men had invented most of the important ice skating moves—Haines's sitspin, the Axel, Salchow, Lutz, the loop jump—and it was a male-dominated sport until Norway's Sonja Henie (b. 1912) burst on the skating scene in 1924 with ballet-trained vigor, invention, and speed to break all precedents. At the time skating was a sober sport for mature adults. Men wore black tights or knickers and knee hose, women wide-brimmed, top-heavy hats and angle-length skirts. Sonja Henie changed all that. Not since the French ambassador to the Netherlands wrote to Louis XIV about the Princess of Orange skating "in petticoats shorter than are generally worn by ladies so strictly decorous, these tucked up half-way to her waist" had a skating skirt been so short. Because she was only 11, Henie got away with it and then went on to win 10 world and 3 Olympic titles, wearing colored costumes that rippled during spins and beige, then white, boots. Her corkscrew Axel had no lift or carry, and she had none of today's double or triple jumps (no woman did until Britain's Cecilia Colledge landed a double Salchow in the 1936 European championships), but Henie raised skating to a new plane.

Her magnetic spirit, showmanship, and marketing sense, 11 Hollywood movies, and stardom in a traveling ice show made her a millionaire. She created a skating boom and put a feminine stamp on the sport for more than 50 years as the public looked for the next Sonja. Canada's Barbara Ann Scott (b. 1928) and Americans Tenley Albright (b. 1935) (later a surgeon), Carol Heiss (b. 1940), Peggy Fleming (b. 1948), Janet Lynn (b. 1953) ("the best skater never to win"), and Dorothy Hamill (b. 1957) (whose haircut the world copied)—all bore the "skating princess" aura of popular fantasy.

If Henie gave the sport its glamour, its guts came from postwar North American men. Dick Button (b. 1929) of the United States, aided and abetted by Swiss émigré coach Gus Lussi, launched his challenge to conventional style with a whole new concept of aggressive power skating. In 1948, 66 years after Norway's Axel Paulson (b. 1855) debuted his eponymous jump, Button doubled it—a forward take-off, two and a half revolutions, landing backward. The first triple was by Canada's Vern Taylor in 1978; the first by a woman by Midori Ito in 1990. Now men do triple Axels in combination with other double and triple jumps without doing a turn or step in between.

Button invented the flying camel, and his flying sitspin, split, and double jumps soared higher than the barrier at the edge of the rink. He did double loop jumps, three in a row on the same foot—perhaps thinking of those three hats—and the first triple loop (1952). He wore trousers, not tights, and a short white mess jacket, to depart further from tradition.

The idea was to be muscularly athletic; the artistry would be in making it look easy and natural. Button won seven U.S. championships, five world championships and two Olympic golds from 1946 to 1952, the year he graduated from Harvard College. After Harvard Law School, he continued to influence skating as a television producer and commentator.

Hayes Alan Jenkins (b. 1933) (also a Harvard lawyer) and his doctor brother David kept the heat on for the next two Olympics, and the world championships in between. With Jimmy Grogan (b. 1931), Ronny Robertson (b. 1937), and Tim Brown (b. 1938) on the podium with silvers, "American style" dominated the 1950s as wartorn Europe rebuilt. In 1961 the U.S. skating community suffered a devastating loss when the entire post-Olympic team was killed in an air crash.

Canada's Donald Jackson (b. 1940) was the next to break the triples barrier, making up a 45-point figures deficit with the first-ever triple Lutz to win the 1962 world championship. It took twelve years for the feat to be defeated by Jan Hoffman (b. 1955) of East Germany, and not until 1978 did a woman Denise Biellmann (b. 1962) of Switzerland do a triple Lutz.

In the 1970s, several developments revolutionized figure skating. The more challenging elements became essential—in1978 Dorothy Hamill was the last woman to win a major championship without a triple jump. After Elaine Zayak (b. 1965) of the United States unleashed four triple toe loops and two triple Salchows to win the 1982 world championship, a breakthrough for women's athleticism, the ISU ruled that no triple could be repeated except in combination with another jump. Women are now landing triples, while men are throwing quads.

Two men, the aristocratic classicist John Curry (b. 1949) of Great Britain and the baroquely flamboyant Toller Cranston (b. 1949) of Canada, each with a uniquely personal idiom, gave permission for men to be more expressive and creative. Even into the 1970s men had hardly dared raise their arms above shoulder level. Curry, whom many consider the most complete skater the world has seen, who could hold an audience transfixed with a single edge, parlayed his World and Olympic wins (1976) into television specials and a world-touring ice dance company that has performed at the Kennedy Center and the Metropolitan Opera House. Seeing skating as a performing art like ballet, he commissioned works by such choreographers as Twyla Tharp, Norman Maen, Kenneth MacMillan and Peter Martens.

While his intentions would be echoed by subsequent skating stars like the USA's Paul Wylie (second, 1992 Olympics), skating styles cannot be cloned. Indeed, in the 1980s, skating produced more athletic-looking world and Olympic medalists: The humorous American Scott Hamilton (b. 1958). The smooth pop styling of Britain's Robin Cousins. The USA's Brian Boitano (b. 1963) as romantic hero. The rock-star magnetism of France's Philippe Candeloro (b. 1972). From Canada, Kurt Browning (b. 1966), the actor, and motocross rider/martial artist Elvis Stojko (b. 1972). Each put an individualistic stamp on a sport that is ultimately judged on essence, not by time, tape, or ball placement.

## Pairs

Centuries of skating hand in hand led to a first tepid world pairs event in 1908. The development of modern pairs skating depended on improvements in women's skating (including liberation from long skirts) and the advent of Russian skaters.

Until the 1930s, a typical program consisted of shadow-skated footwork (where the two skaters move exactly in tandem in me-and-my-shadow fashion) between highlights such as spirals, one or two half-turn jumps, and tiny lifts, skated to march or ballroom dance music. The look was precise, safe, and genteel.

The top prewar teams were Andrée (b. 1901) and Pierre (b. 1902) Brunet of France, and Maxi Herber (b. 1920) and Ernst Bayer (b. 1905) of Germany, who added speed to perfectly synchronized Axels and change-foot spins to music specially composed to fit their style. Karol (b. 1952) and Peter (b. 1948) Kennedy of the United States were the first North American pair to break the European grip, winning the world gold medal in 1952. They were followed by Canadians Frances Dafoe (b. 1929) and Norris Bowden (b. 1926) (1954–1955), and Barbara Wagner (b. 1938) and Robert Paul (b. 1937), whose athleticism and hint of romance clinched four world championships and the 1960 Olympics. Maria (b. 1942) and Otto (b. 1940) Jelinek, after a perilous escape from communist Czechoslovakia in 1948, returned to triumph for Canada at the Prague world championships in 1962.

No Russian/Soviet had competed since Nicholas Panin won the Olympic special figures in 1908. Because Russian skating development had stopped, the Soviets came to every postwar event, not to skate, but to film and learn.

Shrewdly, drawing on their rich ballet heritage, they concentrated first on pairs and later on dance, neither of which requires costly and time-consuming figures practice. In 1958, when Tatyana (b. 1946) and Stanislav (b. 1935) Zhuk placed eighth and Ludmilla (Belousova) (b. 1935) and Oleg (b. 1932) Protopopov thirteenth in their first world championships, the USSR still had only one indoor rink. The British had fewer than 40. But the United States and Canada had some 600 each, more than twice as many in each country as in all of Europe.

By 1969, the Protopopovs, then aged 32 and 35, considered old at that time—had won four world and two Olympic titles and their fluid refinement was seen as the future for pairs. Instead, the pendulum swung to tiny Irina Rodnina (b. 1949) charging in with Alexei Ulanov (b. 1947) to her first world championship to usurp the throne with a routine of spectacular speed, daring, and difficulty. They were the first of the small-and-tall pairs, in which the size difference made it easy to move the woman around in the air.

When Ulanov quit to marry and compete with a woman from a rival pair, Rodnina returned with Alexander Zaitsev, later her husband, to beat them. Altogether, she won ten world and three Olympic titles, part of the 1964–1994 "Russian gold rush," capped by the passionate intensity of Natalya Mishkuteniok (b. 1970) and Artur Dmitriev (b. 1968) (1992) and the radiant, romantic unison of Ykaterina Gordeeva (b. 1971) and Sergei Grinkov (b. 1967) (1988 and 1994). Grinkov's sudden heart failure at age 28 in 1995 was lead-story news around the world, indicating figure skating's importance in public consciousness.

The Russian pairs' 1965–1996 string of world gold was broken only five times; in the Olympics (1964–1994) never.

Having gone way beyond hand-in-hand, pairs programs now include triple jumps, lifts, twists, and 7.6-meter (25-foot) triple throws, as well as increasingly complex footwork influenced by ice dancers.

## Ice Dancing

Since the advent of Jayne Torvill (b. 1957) and Christopher Dean (b. 1958) of Great Britain in the 1980s, ice dancing, the last discipline to be developed, is often the first ticket to sell out at international meets. In the early years of organized figure skating, ice dancing got off to a feeble start, largely because there were only three dances, and "touch" social dancing was not popular until the second decade of the twentieth century. Although Jones's 1772 book described the 3-turn, it was not until 1885 that it was developed into a waltz. Two other dances, the rousing 14-step (1889) and Kilian (1909), were performed to marches.

In the 1930s, the English, by then a nation of ballroom dance adepts, saw the possibility of adapting other social dances to ice. New-dance contests produced foxtrots, tangos, a quickstep, blues, more waltzes, a paso doble and rumba, creating an enjoyable club activity and a set-pattern test and competition schedule. Still, a world championship, with an added free-dance worth 40 percent, was not held until 1952. Even with an original set-pattern dance event added in 1967, the International Olympic committee (IOC) did not consider dance athletic enough for the games until 1976, after the Soviets started steadily winning world dance in 1970 with their dramatic projection.

The British, having established the standard of upright and static posture, even in free-dance, not surprisingly won the first 11 championships. Former pair skaters Eva Romanova and Pavel Roman of Czechoslovakia took the championships from 1962 to 1965 with added lean and flourish. Britain came back with 1966–1969 champions Diane Towler and Bernard Ford who dared to abandon social dance music and instead used a film score; they inserted a mini-lift and death spiral in their lightning footwork. The Soviets entered world ice dance competition in 1966 and Ludmilla Pakhomova and Victor Ryshkin placed tenth. A year later, Pakhomova returned with Alexander Gorshkov, dropping to thirteenth place. Their compulsories, learned from books, were marked as much as six places lower than their free dance. But they went on to coin five world titles, capped by the first Olympic dance crown awarded in 1976.

Skaters from Western Europe and the United States were then better technicians, but what the Soviets may have lacked in technique, they more than made up for in facial and upper body expression. The "English style" was polite, the Russian, passionate, opening the possibility for ice dance to be a fully realized artistic medium.

Judging ice dance presents considerable difficulty, since the dance itself and the skating technique must be evaluated as a whole, unlike singles and pairs where it is easier to spot errors in individual elements. Dancing demands more sheer skating—blade to blade, never apart—than pairs. It also demands more subtle edge control, flow, complex footwork, holds, and positions. Seeing two compulsory dances that they already know helps judges winnow the field before they look at the original dance (to a preselected rhythm) and the free-dance (to music of the skater's own choosing.).

Judges engaging in political placement swapping was not unheard of from the beginning. Following the Soviet insurgence, bloc-judging occurred on both sides of the Iron Curtain, with some judges being suspended for overt nationalistic bias. Television coverage, press criticism, knowledgeable arena audiences, and rules changes have forced greater objectivity.

There was no judicial disagreement about the incomparable and inimitable Jayne Torvill and Christopher Dean—during their first amateur career, after winning four world titles and the 1984 Olympics, they had garnered 136 perfect marks of 6.0. Like John Curry, they brought a many-leveled quality of mind, an intelligence, to movement that was organic rather than assumed, combined with intense discipline, to create the impression that they weren't really on skates at all. Some parts of their innovative choreography, such as knee slides, lying on the ice, holding the partner's book, blade, or leg, and over the shoulder lifts, would subsequently be ruled illegal by tradition-minded judges. The ISU continues its tinkering with the rules to find a balance between the strictly ballroom tradition and the competitors' urge to explore new forms of contemporary interpretive dance.

## Team Skating

From a 1956 teen-age marching drill team organized as a recreational outlet for club skaters in Ann Arbor, Michigan, there has developed the highly competitive international sport of precision skating. Line, circle, block, wheel, and intersecting formations, edges incorporating intricate footwork and single jumps, but no lifts, are skated in unison to music. Teams have from 12 to 24 skaters, with juvenile through adult divisions. The fastest-growing skating discipline in the world, it received official recognition as an ISU world event in 1994 and has corporate sponsorship and television coverage.

Similarly, carnivals, which spawned the professional ice shows, have been a traditional club activity since the 1930s, but amateur show skating was not put into competition until 1980. From France the sport has spread across Europe. The first U.S. team, established in 1990 in Burlington, Vermont, hosted the 1996 international event.

## The Business of Skating

After complaining for years that government support in communist countries made their skaters "paid professionals," in the early 1980s, it finally occurred to Western associations to seek capitalistic corporate sponsorship to augment existing income from sale of TV rights. The Victorians had resisted testing for merit badges, lest it lead to competition, professionalism, and betting. Such amateur "purity" also limited participation to those with means, forcing parents of some promising skaters to take second jobs and mortgages, while praying for private patronage to support their training. Amateurs are now termed "eligibles," and skaters duly registered to do so with their national association may perform, compete, and teach for pay without penalty. The ISU itself sponsors open and grand prix events with money prizes.

The multimillion-dollar professional contracts offered to Olympic medalists prompted Tonya Harding (b. 1970), to say her competitive motivation was "dollars," and her husband and cohorts attacked rival Nancy Kerrigan (b. 1969) to prevent her from competing in the 1992 U.S. National championships. Harding went on to compete in that year's Olympics, but the U.S. Figure Skating Association divested her of her U.S. title and association membership.

Figure skating is now, unavoidably, big business. U.S. television networks, observing that its ratings were second only to those of football—sometimes even equaling Superbowl figures—greatly increased coverage of skating in the 1990s. Accompanying skating's greater visibility has been a revolution in skating fashion, which formed part of the show-business spectacle of major skating events. Into the 1960s, the form was to carry the free leg—the one not bearing the skater's weight—bent. Today, this looks merely quaint. Flapping trousers and bent free legs were

replaced, in the sixties, by aerodynamic lines of stretch ski cloth. In the 1980s, women's high-necked, minimally decorated dresses gave way to elaborately body-revealing and flashily decorated stretch fabrics. The 1990s, some longer skirts in chiffon appeared; but ironically, tights on men, which the Victorians had found inoffensive, were banned by the ISU in 1992.

—Astrid Hagenguth

**Bibliography:** Brown, Nigel. (1959) *Ice Skating: A History*. New York: A. S. Barnes.

Copley-Graves, Lynn. (1992) *Figure Skating History: The Evolution of Dance on Ice*. Columbus, OH: Platoro Press.

Hennessy, John. (1983) *Torvill & Dean*. New York: St. Martin's Press.

Money, Keith, and Curry, John. (1978) *John Curry*. New York: Alfred A. Knopf.

Ogilvie, Robert S. (1985) *Competitive Figure Skating: A Parent's Guide*. New York: Harper & Row.

*Patinage* (Rouen, France).

*Pirouette* (Stuttgart, Germany).

*Skating* (Colorado Springs, CO).

Smith, Beverly. (1994) *Figure Skating: A Celebration*. Toronto: McClelland & Stewart.

Steere, Michael. (1985) *Scott Hamilton: A Behind-the-Scenes Look at the Life and Competitive Times of America's Favorite Figure Skater*. New York: St. Martin's Press.

Whedon, Julia. (1988) *The Fine Art of Ice Skating*. New York: Harry N. Abrams

# Skating, Ice Speed

Skating has its origins in the pre-Christian era. The sport appears as early as the Scandinavian literature of the second century B.C.E.

The first known illustration of skating is a Dutch wood engraving from 1498, depicting St. Lydwina of Schiedam, the patron saint of skaters, who in 1396, fell and broke a rib while skating at the age of 16. Samuel Pepys, the English diarist, gives an account of skating with Nell Gwynn (mistress of King Charles II) during London's interminable winter of 1683. Nearly a century later French sources described Marie Antoinette as helping to popularize skating in 1776. Napoleon Bonaparte nearly drowned in 1791 when he fell through the ice while skating at Auxerre.

## Origins

By the middle of the nineteenth century, according to Brown, the national sport of Holland was speed skating. The most successful speed skaters were workers whose occupation led them to skate quickly on a daily basis. Thus, canal workers enjoyed great success in various competitions, some of which offered sizable purses.

A key in the development and growth of speed skating was the advent of artificial "ice palaces," or rinks. While early attempts to produce real ice by artificial means were not commercially successful, by the 1890s real progress had been made. As of 1900, New York, Paris, and London each had two rinks. Brighton, Brussels, Munich, Philadelphia, Brooklyn, and Baltimore had one each. In 1909, the world's first open-air artificial ice rink was opened in Vienna, Austria. It was designed by Edward Engelmann, an engineer and former European skating champion.

Ice speed skating eventually spread to Holland's neighbors, including Austria, Germany, and France. The Frieslanders of North Holland, helped by their close geographical proximity, introduced the sport to the Fens district of England. The first record of this "Fenland skating" dates to 1814.

## Development

The first international speed skating competition took place at Hamburg, Germany, in 1889. This was followed by the inaugural men's world championships in 1893. (Although men's speed skating was included on the program of the Chamonix Olympics in 1924, it was not until the Squaw Valley Olympics in 1960 that women's speed skating appeared.)

In the twentieth century, the sport of speed skating has been closely bound up with the Olympics. While the Olympics provide the sport with tremendous publicity, speed skating should be understood in its proper setting—as a major event in the winter sports calendar. As with skiing, the speed skating World Cup has created an annual circuit of events, and today the star speed skater travels the world from Cortina d' Ampezzo, Italy, to Sapporo, Japan.

Men's speed skating first appeared at the 1924 Chamonix Olympics. At these inaugural games

*Speed skaters on a 200-kilometer track on a picturesque canal in the Netherlands, where the sport of speed skating originated.*

men competed in the 500, 1,500, 5,000, and 10,000-meter (546.81-, 1,640.42-, 5,468.07-, and 10,936.13-yard) races. There was also a four-race combined event, but it was never included again in the Olympics. Nordic countries did exceptionally well, winning four of five gold medals. Speed skating had mushroomed in Scandinavia because of its ideal climate and a plethora of iced surfaces suited for speed skating.

While no country has dominated men's speed skating, certain countries such as Norway, Finland, and Holland have always been highly successful. At the final of the 5,000-meter race at the 1952 Oslo Olympics, a packed house of 24,000 people stamped and cheered as 28-year-old Norwegian truck driver Hjalmar Anderson achieved the largest winning margin in the history of the event. This margin (over 10 seconds) can be likened to a distance track runner breasting the tape as the runner-up comes off the final turn.

In North America speed skating for many years was administered by an overall skating body. However, in 1960 the Canadian Amateur Speed Skating Association was founded. Four years later the United States followed suit by setting up the International Speed Skating Association.

Speed skating came of age in the United States at the 1980 Lake Placid Olympics when 22-year-old Eric Heiden, a native of Madison, Wisconsin, took five gold medals and inspired a generation of young American skaters. At the 1994 Olympics in Lillehammer, Norway, two other American speed skaters, Bonnie Blair (1964– ) and David Jansen (1965– ), won medals. Nevertheless, the vast Norwegian audiences were energized and excited by the exploits of their native son, Johann Olav Koss (1968– ). He was a triple gold medal winner and lived up to a favorite crowd slogan which touted his athletic supremacy—"Koss er Boss."

Until Heiden's sweep at the 1980 Olympics, the greatest Olympic speed skaters were either Norwegian or Dutch. Ivar Ballangrud (Norway), Anderson (Norway), and Ard Schenk (Netherlands) all won at least three gold medals at a single Olympics. Indeed, Schenk won four gold medals at the 1972 Sapporo Olympics. Speed skating is not just confined to North America and Europe, however. There are national skating associations on every continent. There is even one in a country—Australia—where surf, sand, sea, and outback dominate the lifestyle and the terrain.

Women's speed skating events were introduced to the Olympics in 1960. At the 1960 Squaw Valley Olympics, women competed in the 500-, 1,000-, 1,500-, and 3,000-meter (3,280.84-yard) events. Three of the four gold medals went to the Soviet Union—a factor that has been attributed to a greater number of training facilities. In 1980, there were 1,202 Olympic-sized speed skating rinks in the Soviet Union versus only 2 in the United States.

At the 1984 Innsbruck Olympic Games, the great Soviet skater Lydia Skoblikova (1939– ) became the first person to win four gold medals at one winter Olympics. This feat took her to a career total of six Olympic golds. Speed skating has produced a number of athletes who keep making comebacks. While Skoblikova is remembered for winning six gold medals, her greatest achievement may be one of longevity—she took part in the 3,000-meter race at the Grenoble Olympics in 1968.

## Practice

International championship meets are normally two days long. Usually, the 500- and 5,000-meter events are staged on the first day and the 1,500- and 10,000-meter events occur on the following day. The best all-around performer over these four distances, as calculated on a points basis, becomes the overall individual champion.

Success at speed skating requires a true all-around athlete who has the quickness of a dash sprinter and the staying power of a long-distance performer. This is comparable to a track runner training to perform well in both the 100-meter dash and the 10,000-meter race. In the world of speed skating, the champion performer is genuinely versatile, possessing a blend of speed and stamina, explosive power and controlled energy, pace and endurance. It is a sport that has both technically superb skaters who fly and glide over the ice and powerful skaters who use explosive strength to muscle their way to the finish line.

In the 1950s and 1960s, thousands of excited Norwegian spectators would gather outdoors in temperatures well below freezing to cheer on their local, regional, and national champions. One of these skating heroes was Knut Johansen. In 1960 Johansen set what many at the time believed was an unbeatable time of 15 minutes, 46.6 seconds over 10,000 meters. In many respects, this was the equivalent for ice skating of the elusive four-minute mile in track and field. Today, great skaters complete 10,000 meters in less than 14 minutes.

Modern speed skating is immediately recognizable by its competition format: two skaters going against one another and the clock. During the race the competitors alternate at preset intervals between the inside and outside lanes to prevent one skater from having an unfair advantage. This is known as "crossing over," and is difficult considering the skaters are moving at speeds sometimes in excess of 48 kilometers (30 miles) per hour. At that velocity, the margin between keeping the honed steel skating blade in contact with the surface of the ice and letting it slip is infinitesimal.

A new type of speed skating, called "pack start" or short-track racing, was introduced at Calgary in 1988. Today, short-track racing is an integral part of Olympic and world speed skating. The primary events are the 500-, 1,000-, and 3,000-meter relays for women and the 500-, 1,000-, and 5,000-meter relays for men. The tremendous attraction of short-track racing is that it revolves around groups of competitors in close contact. It is very similar to the "bunching up" of track runners in the final lap of the 800 or 1,500 meters. The problem with traditional speed skating is that there are only two skaters and they have to stay in their own lanes. Short-track racing is much more exciting for spectators than traditional speed skating since there can be contact collisions, shadowing, drafting, and a cut-and-thrust atmosphere that makes it a civilized version of roller derby.

—Scott A. G. M. Crawford

**Bibliography:** Blair, B. (1995) Public lecture at Illinois Wesleyan University, Bloomington, 6 December.

Brokaw, I. (1925) *The Art of Skating*. New York: American Sports Publishing.

Brown, N. (1959) *Ice Skating—A History*. New York: A. S Barnes.

Hickok, R. (1992) *The Encyclopedia of North American Sports*. New York: Facts on File.

Holum, D. (1984) *The Complete Handbook of Speed Skating*. Hillside, NJ: Enslow Publishing.

McCallum, J., and C. Stone (1995) "Scorecard." *Sports Illustrated* (4 December).

Muskat, C. (1995) "Fleet Flame Is Lingering." *Chicago Tribune* (19 November).

Rushin, S. (1995) "The Last Lap." *Sports Illustrated* (27 February).

Thomas, R. McG. (1994) "Jansen Now Skating in Corporate Arena." *New York Times* (2 March).

Vamplew, W., and K. Moore, J. O'Hara, R. Cashman, I. Jobling. (1992) *Oxford Companion to Australian Sport*. Melbourne: Oxford University Press.

Wallechinsky, D. (1984) *The Complete Book of the Olympics*. New York: Viking Press.

Wolff, A. (1994) "Fourth Down." *Sports Illustrated* (21 February).

# Skating, In-line

In-line skating is a variant of roller skating employing a series of wheels, generally four or five, set in a straight line mimicking the ice skate. Freed from the necessity of a frozen surface, the modern in-line skate sacrifices the precise control of the dual-axle roller skate for greater speed, superior adaptability to a variety of surfaces, and easier mastery. Recreational outdoor skating is undoubtedly the most popular in-line activity. Speed skating, roller hockey, and stunt or "aggressive" skating are other variants of in-line skating. As in other skating sports, participants receive the benefits of low-impact cardiovascular exercise and toning to all major muscle groups. In-line skating is an activity open to all ages; industry figures claim an even split between male and female skaters, with an average age of 27. The current popularity of in-line skating began in the United States and has spread to Europe and parts of Asia.

## Origins

Although in-line skating did not enjoy widespread popularity before the 1980s, in-lines are actually the oldest type of roller skate. In the earliest recorded attempt to move skating from the winter ice, Joseph Merlin (1735–?), a member of the Dutch Royal Academy of Sciences and maker of musical instruments, introduced roller skating to the public at a London reception in 1760. While playing the violin and rolling about for the crowd's entertainment, Merlin, his violin, and a large mirror discovered that it was not possible to turn or brake on the new invention. Merlin survived the discovery. The violin and mirror did not.

In-line skates were used in theatrical productions in the late eighteenth and early nineteenth centuries as a substitute for ice skates. Experimentation with different configurations eventually resulted in the superior maneuverability of the cushioned dual-axle roller skate. The in-line concept survived into the 1970s largely as an off-season training tool for skiers and ice skaters, benefiting from the introduction of plastic components and Polyurethane wheels. In 1979 Scott Olson, a 19-year-old American semiprofessional

*In-line skating is popular with adults as a form of cardio-vascular conditioning and with young people as another vehicle for stunts similar to stunt skateboarding.*

skates use leather or leather and nylon boots that sacrifice some of those qualities for increased flexibility and decreased weight. Beneath the boot lies the frame, or plate. This component mounts the wheels and can be constructed of plastic, nylon, or metal. Frames can incorporate a number of features depending upon their intended purpose, including "rocker" features to enhance maneuverability, brake pads, and even active braking systems. Wheels are chosen to suit the surface and activity of the skater, with variations in size and hardness.

In-line skating enjoyed explosive growth in the later 1980s and early 1990s. In the United States alone an estimated 12 million people tried the sport at least once in 1993. In-line skates may now be found around the world, for both recreational and practical purposes. One reflection of this is their adoption by the American Amish community, renowned for its rejection of modern technology and recreational pursuits, as a means of transportation. While the Amish continue to shun the use of electricity, automobiles, and most modern conveniences, they have accepted in-line skating because of its simplicity and practicality. Use of the skates for pure entertainment is still frowned upon, however.

hockey player, discovered the in-line skate as an off-season training aide. Olson modified the design for hockey use and sold the patent rights to a private investor in 1984. The resultant company, Rollerblade, launched a major marketing campaign that popularized in-line skating and made the company's name synonymous with in-line skates.

## Development

The modern in-line skate bears only a geometric resemblance to its predecessor of the nineteenth century. Early in-lines were wooden platforms mounting wooden wheels, attached to the foot with straps of leather or fabric. Modern skates employ space-age materials. The boot, or shell, encases the foot. Recreational in-lines and their heavier stunt versions generally have an outer plastic shell and a removable lining for comfort, offering support and stability. Hockey and racing

## Practice

Skaters are not limited to tamely rolling along sidewalks and in skating rinks. That use, although undoubtedly the most popular in-line activity, serves as the introduction to a number of organized sports. The least regulated of these is "aggressive" skating—the performance of various acrobatic stunts, similar to stunt skateboarding in nature and its largely adolescent demographics. Aggressive skating also inherited some of skateboarding's bad reputation due to their close relationship and the damage each inflicted upon public property through both skating stunts and the often rebellious behavior of youthful subcultures. The in-line industry's formation in 1992 of the Skatesmart program, which promotes skating safety, attempted to adjust this image.

Organized competitive roller skating is governed internationally by the Fédération Internationale de Roller-Skating (FIRS), which accepts in-line skates in all categories and has established speed and hockey divisions reserved for in-line

## Skatesmart

In-line skating is, for most participants, an outdoor activity. Skaters are commonly found on sidewalks, in parks, on quiet streets, and deserted parking lots. As with skateboarding and other skating activities, many enthusiasts are children. Recreational skaters generally learn by trial and error, frequently without even the knowledgeable advice of a more experienced skater. The combination of a hazardous environment, poor training, and a growing body of participants, many of them young or unskilled, has had predictable results. In 1993, the United States alone recorded some 83,000 injuries requiring emergency room treatment due to in-line skating. In-line skating can be one of the most hazardous recreational activities for children under the age of 12.

Part of this is inherent in the nature of the in-line skate. They are deceptively easy to use and the uninitiated frequently fail to appreciate the speeds even the novice can easily reach. Handling skates effectively, in particular maneuvering suddenly, stopping, or falling so as to minimize injury, is a skill that requires time and instruction and is often overlooked. In-line skating without proper safety equipment and skills can result in serious injury. Among the most common are broken wrists and arms, twisted ankles, and damaged knees. As with any high-speed sport, participants are exposed to the risk of head and neck injury.

In response to the number of skating injuries, a coalition of skaters and manufacturers launched the Skatesmart program in 1992. That program and others like it stress the importance of proper equipment, training, and behavior to make in-line skating a safe and enjoyable activity. This voluntary action of the industry has increasingly popularized the use of safety gear and reduced the risks associated with the sport for those who follow its guidelines and has reduced some of the early opposition to in-line skating from the medical community.

At a minimum, outdoor skaters should always wear knee and wrist protection and approved bicycle-style safety helmets. Skating should be done only upon smooth surfaces well away from vehicle traffic. New skaters should always seek competent instruction; proper training is a requirement before any advanced activities should be undertaken.

—Jeffery Charlston

One discipline of competitive skating, roller hockey, enjoyed a particularly substantial boost in popularity with the introduction of in-line skates. The 1992 Olympic Games in Barcelona featured an exhibition of roller hockey, the first roller sport in the Olympics. The game itself is based upon ice hockey with a few modifications relating to the different surfaces involved. In keeping with its early link to the ice hockey community, in-line roller hockey has formed professional leagues and includes professional ice hockey players in its ranks.

In-lines quickly replaced traditional roller skates in speed competitions, both those sanctioned by FIRS and recognized national governing organizations and the less formal events, which increased in number as the popularity of in-line skating grew. The in-line configuration allows for larger wheels and a reduced area in contact with the skating surface, resulting in greater efficiency and decreased drag in comparison with traditional roller skates. Additionally, the larger wheels are more tolerant of rough surfaces, improving the appeal of outdoor and long-distance competitions.

Only one discipline of internationally organized skating remains untouched by in-line skates. Artistic roller skating is still dominated by dual-axle skates due to their superior maneuverability and control. But artistic events are open to in-lines and inventors continue to improve in-line designs. One European innovation exhibited at the 1994 American national championships featured a modified four-wheel in-line configuration intended for artistic skating. In time even the conservative world of figure skating may welcome in-line skaters.

The rapid spread of in-line skating may be attributed both to its close relationship to the existing international ice and roller skating communities and to in-line skates' excellent outdoor adaptability. Beyond the ready appeal of rapid and exhilarating motion to young skaters, in-lines offer a mode of transportation almost as efficient as the bicycle in a much more compact form. That factor may weigh heavily in in-line skating's urban popularity, as it reduces the logistical and security concerns associated with bicycling. To date in-line skating has not spread far into cultures lacking an existing familiarity with ice or roller skating and/or the bicycle. The sport

skaters. The codified and regimented nature of these activities stands in stark contrast to the more informal world of stunt skating, as does organized skating's appeal to a broader range of age groups.

continues to grow in popularity however, with participants and manufacturers in the Americas, Europe, Asia, and Australia.

—Jeffery Charlston

**Bibliography:** Himmelberg, Michele. (1995) "Skating Fast and Safe." *Parenting* 9 (August): 142.

Italia, Bob. (1991) *In-line Skating.* Minneapolis: Rockbottom.

Joyner, Stephen. (1993) *Complete Guide and Resource to In-line Skating.* Cincinnati, OH: Betterway.

National Museum of Roller Skating. (1983) *First Fifty Years: American Roller Skates 1860–1910.* Lincoln, NE: National Museum of Roller Skating.

Nesbitt, Lloyd. (1993) " The In-line Skating Experience." *Physician and Sportsmedicine* 21 (August): 81–82.

Rappelfeld, Joel. (1992) *The Complete Blader.* New York: St. Martin's.

Wickelgren, Ingrid. (1994) "In-line Injuries Soar." *Current Science* 80 (23 September): 8–9.

# Skating, Roller

The roller skating sports developed as competitive activities from the use of roller skates for transportation and recreation and are modeled on ice sports.

## Origins

No one is absolutely sure when the first roller skates were used. It is likely that the first roller skates were an adaptation of ice skates and used for transportation rather than sport.

The first recognized inventor of roller skates was a Belgian manufacturer named Joseph Merlin, who produced the first roller skates with metal wheels in 1760. He presented his invention in London at a fancy ball by rolling across the floor while playing an expensive violin. The story follows that because Merlin's skates were unable to be turned or stopped, he glided gracefully into a huge mirror and suffered serious injuries.

The first time roller skates were successfully seen in public was in 1849 when a Frenchman named Louis Legrange used them to simulate ice skating in the play *Le Prophete.* He created his skates by mounting tiny rollers down the center of ice skates.

In the mid-1800s, a number of other inventors took up the call and many different types of skates were produced. All, however, suffered from the same problems that Merlin's skates had—the inability to be effectively controlled or stopped.

A New Yorker by the name of James Plimpton solved the problem of controlling roller skates in 1863. Plimpton's skates used a rubber cushion to anchor the axles. This cushion would compress when the body was leaned, enabling the wheels of the skate to turn slightly when the skater shifted his or her weight. Plimpton's design is considered the basis for the modern roller skate.

Plimpton opened a number of rinks across America and in Europe. He had envisioned roller skating to be a pastime of the rich only. But soon after his patents expired, cheaper imitations flooded the market and skating became popular with all classes.

## Development

Organized roller skating sports developed as the popularity of roller skates increased in the late nineteenth and early twentieth centuries. Roller hockey teams were playing throughout Europe as early as 1901.

Although the sport was disrupted somewhat during World War I, it quickly regained its momentum and the first world championship of roller hockey was held in Stuttgart, Germany, in 1936. The first world speed roller skating championships occurred just a year later in Monza, Italy. Competitive artistic roller skating existed at the same time, although the first artistic roller skating world championships were not held until 1947 in Washington, D.C.

World championships in all three recognized disciplines of competitive roller skating—artistic, speed, and hockey—have been held annually (for the most part) ever since. The first U.S. roller skating speed championships were held in 1937 in Detroit, and the first world dance and figures championships in 1947.

## Practice

All three types of roller skating are governed in the United States by the United States Amateur

Confederation of Roller Skating (USAC/RS), which is recognized by the United States Olympic Committee as the national governing body for all roller sports. The sport is governed internationally by the Fédération Internationale de Roller Skating (FIRS).

Artistic skating is further broken down into dance, singles and pairs freestyle, and figures. Dance skating requires athletes to perform preannounced skating dance programs, a detailed series of steps at various points around the floor. Each dance has its own set of steps, tempo, rhythm, and progression. Athletes are judged based on their performance of the steps and adherence to the music. Artistic skating—both singles and pairs—is very similar to ice figure skating, where athletes perform difficult routines set to music. The skaters are judged on the maneuvers—such as jumps and spins—as well as use of music, appearance, flow of the program as a whole, and artistic impression of the program. Figures is the grandfather of all artistic roller skating disciplines, stressing skating fundamentals. This sport requires competitors to trace painted circles on the floor. The skaters are judged on their carriage, their ability to stay on the lines, and the degree to which they make the entire program look effortless.

Speed skating is one of the fastest sports in the world where speed is generated by human energy. It is a noncontact sport, requiring skaters to maneuver cleanly through the pack and into winning position. Skaters are disqualified for unsportsmanlike conduct, such as blocking, forcing another skater out of position, or using their arms, legs, or hands in any way that impedes the progress of other competitors.

Speed skating is divided into indoor and outdoor varieties, with indoor racing being an almost exclusively American pastime. Indoors, speed skaters take on a flat, 100-meter (110-yard) track in individual and relay events. Indoor speed skating is broken down even further by equipment (conventional four-wheeled skates or in-line skates), gender, and age divisions. In individual competition, skaters compete in three different distances, receiving 30, 20, or 10 points for first through third places in each distance, respectively, the champion being the one with the highest point total at the end of the competition. Relays are staged in combinations of same-sex or

*Artistic roller skating competitions include many of the same events as their ice-based counterparts.*

mixed. In order to perform a legal tag in a relay, the incoming skater gives the relay partner a push from behind to help accelerate the new skater into the flow of traffic.

Outdoor speed skating is the internationally accepted version of the sport. This form of speed skating is competed on both banked tracks and road courses. The banked track is usually about 200 meters (219 yards) and has parabolic curves. The U.S. home track is inside the 7-Eleven Velodrome in Colorado Springs, Colorado. A road competition is held on a flat course, which may be a closed course or an open stretch of road. Distances of 300, 500, 1,500, 3,000, 5,000, 10,000, and 20,000 meters (328, 547, 1,646, 3,281, 5,468, 10,936, and 21,872 yards) are competed on the track, which also includes a relay. On the road, the same distances are run, with the relay being replaced by a marathon. Competitors may wear either four-wheeled "quads" or in-line skates in outdoor speed skating competition, with in-lines being the skate of choice for nearly all competitors.

Not only are in-line skates popular among recreational skaters, the design's dominance over traditional quad skates in speed skating competitions prompted USAC/RS to create separate divisions in sanctioned indoor meets. Recognizing in-line skates' impact on the sport, USAC/RS also successfully lobbied FIRS to permit in-lines in international competition. In-line skates made their debut at the 1992 world speed skating championships.

For the past few years, popularity of in-line roller hockey has been booming in the United States and the rest of the world. But roller hockey on conventional skates has been popular throughout the world for many years. The conventional roller hockey game has been popular in many countries, most notably Spain, Italy, Portugal, and throughout South America. In fact, in many of those countries it is second in popularity only to soccer.

The conventional roller hockey game is played with a hard, black rubber ball, quad skates, and a short, curved, wooden stick. Four players and a goalkeeper on each team work together to try to put the ball in the net of their opponent while attempting to stop the opposition from doing the same. Although the game is played with an essentially noncontact principle, players do have to take steps to protect themselves from injury through the use of padding, helmets, and reinforced skates. A well-hit shot can send the ball shooting off the stick at more than 128 kilometers (80 miles) per hour.

The in-line version of roller hockey is much more closely related to its ice hockey cousin in the equipment used—including the rubber puck, the amount of physical contact, and the high speeds, but still with four players and a goalie per side. In-line roller hockey players also need to protect themselves as a puck can travel at speeds approaching 160 kilometers (100 miles) per hour off a strong slapshot. Roller hockey accommodates both male and female players in coed and separate divisions, which allow for play by both young and old alike.

The conventional version of roller hockey was a demonstration sport at the 1992 Olympic Games in Barcelona. But the international popularity of in-line hockey can be recognized by the fact that 1995 saw the first-ever world championship for that sport in Chicago.

—Andy Seeley

**Bibliography:** Bass, Howard. (1958) *The Skating Age.*
Phillips, Ann-Victoria (1979). *The Complete Book of Roller Skating.* New York: Womman.

# Ski Jumping

Ski jumping is one of the two main techniques of Nordic skiing, the other being cross country. The two were originally staged in combination. Jumping on skis began as part of the Nordic (Norwegian, Swedish, and Finnish) skiing culture, from which it has spread over most of the world (wherever climate or technology allows). Ski jumping has gone through the same processes of modernization and diffusion throughout the world as most other modern sports, broadening the ideological context of what was once a "national" Norwegian sport. Ski jumping competitions more and more resemble other international sports.

## Origins

Ski jumping as an activity first appeared in the Nordic region. Ski jumping as a sport seems to be a more specific Norwegian invention. International ski historians disagree, however, about where exactly in Norway ski jumping got its start. Traditionally, Telemark has been identified as "the cradle of skiing." The local term for skiing down hills with or without jumps was *laam.* Olav Bø (1993) attributes to Telemark two forms of ski competitions: downhill/slalom (laam) and jumping. Jumping followed from the skills developed in mastering the terrain of the mountain slopes. Recent research questions the assumption of a specific local origin and concludes that early skiing had several local strongholds in Norway: from the southeastern inland (including Telemark), stretching north and east through Trøndelag all the way to the Lappish Finnmark. Around the turn of the eighteenth century sources give evidence of ski jumping among the military ski companies. The early sagas and legends of the Norse Viking era suggest similar challenges.

The first formal jumping competitions were most often combined events, either downhill with a terminating jump, or cross-country with one or more jumps included. From the 1860s, local competitions were sometimes staged as pure jumping contests, with a race in Trysil in 1862 being the first known pure jumping competition. During this decade, also, attempts to formalize the activity into a sport got their start with races in the capital at Kristiania (present-day Oslo). The first contests in 1867 and 1868 introduced the activity to the urban middle classes. The townspeople were undoubtedly impressed with what they saw—and wanted to control it: they made themselves referees and evaluators of how the sport was to develop into *ski-idræt,* the concept of sport as a path to both physical and moral development. From 1879 the annual Huseby races in Kristiania strengthened the urban hegemony. These races were central arenas for both experimentation and development, as well as for ideological discussions and consolidations. In 1892 the organizers (*Foreningen til Ski-idrættens Fremme*) moved the race to the larger Holmenkollen hill, which ever since has housed one of the major events in the sport of skiing. Ski jumping also started to appear in other countries and in other parts of the world.

*Initially practiced only in hilly landscapes like those of Norway, where the sport originated, ski jumping has increasingly relied on constructed arenas.*

## Practice

Ski jumping means jumping, with skis on, for the purpose of achieving length and landing upright on skis. Referees evaluate the style of the jumper in the air and while landing and award points accordingly. Length is measured in meters from the edge of the jump. Style points from 1 to 20 are assigned by the five referees, of which the lowest and highest number does not count. It is the flight through the air—only a few seconds—and the landing that determine whether the jump is successful or not. Norms and rules of evaluation have undergone dramatic changes. The overall tendency has been to diminish the importance of style, while the length of the jump has been given more weight. In 1996 landing style still counts as much as before.

A ski-jumping hill consists of four parts: (1) the inrun, today most often a constructed scaffold to give sufficient speed before the jump; (2) the jump itself—in modern hills it is not constructed to give upward jumps but rather to follow the shape of the hill in a downward angle; (3) the

landing (*unnarenn*), which is also the steepest part of the hill; and (4) the end of the run, or the halt. "Telemark landing" is still required to get top score (20 points) from the referees. In the old days, the halt was to be done with a "Telemark turn," a turn in which, in contrast to traditional turns, the skis are not parallel.

Ski jumping as a sport and leisure activity was, like other outdoor winter sports, originally dependent on cold temperatures and snow. Hilly landscapes, however, do not seem to be a necessary condition for ski jumping; after the turn of the nineteenth century constructed arenas became ever more prevalent. Since the 1970s ski jumping has also been practiced in the summertime on artificial surfaces such as porcelain and plastic.

## Cultural Variation

Ski jumping initially spread from Norway to neighboring countries and to the countries to which Norwegians emigrated. Ski jumping came to Sweden through Norwegian soldiers posted in Stockholm as part of the union military system. Here the alleged first "international ski jumping contest" took place in 1886. The international contingent was made up of troops from the Norwegian Jægerkorps posted in Stockholm from 1856 to 1888. The spread continued to Finland, where skiers rather hesitantly took up the "Norwegian habit" around the turn of the century. The original Finnish form of skiing at that time definitely was cross-country. If one considers the Finnish topography, this preference is not surprising. The Alps regions also seems to have been introduced to ski jumping through Norwegian students and ski instructors, either directly or indirectly. In Germany three Norwegians were among the founders of the Schneeschuhverein München (Ski Association of Munich), which organized a jumping contest in 1894. At about the same time, jumping was introduced to Austria. In Switzerland, France, and Italy the first real contests did not occur until after the turn of the century. Czechoslovakia, Poland, and Yugoslavia also embraced the sport after 1900. As early as the middle of the nineteenth century, however, jumping had been brought to North America by Norwegian immigrants. By the beginning of the twentieth century ski jumps had been performed in such remote areas as Australia and South Africa as well.

The history of ski jumping in Norway made it, according to some historians, the part of skiing that was most specifically Norwegian. In the final decades of the nineteenth century ski jumping was embraced by spokesmen of a "national stand" and eventually regarded as the unrivaled national sport. Ski jumping's national connotation came out of a growing tension in the union with Sweden and the need of the emerging nation to define itself and its national culture. In this situation skiing in general and ski jumping in particular stood out as characteristically Norwegian. Accordingly, one of the first official appearances by Norway's newly imported king and queen after they had arrived late in the autumn of 1905 was at the Holmenkollen ski-jumping festival. In his youth, the young Prince Olav (who later became king) actually jumped the hill.

As skiing and ski jumping were transplanted from their Norwegian origins to new, more modern and materialistic settings, the sport experienced important cultural and ideological changes. In North America, for example, the height of the jump was considered important and worth measuring. When Torjus Hemmestveit (1861–1930) of Telemark set a "world record" in Red Wing, Minnesota, in 1893, it was measured at 31 meters (103 feet). It was also noted that he rose 11 meters (36 feet) in the air at the highest point—although it's unclear how that number could be substantiated.

Even if ski jumping acquired a royal mark only in Norway, the development of the sport and the fact that other nations experienced success in ski jumping have given it a central role in the sports life of nations such as Finland and Austria. After 16-year-old Toni Nieminen won the Olympic large-hill competition at Albertville in 1992, he was met by vast crowds of Finns and was so celebrated that the authorities granted him a driver's license almost two years before ordinary citizens.

## Technique and Equipment

Until the 1880s the skis used for jumping were not very specialized. Skiers used whatever skis they possessed, since the major skiing event was a combined race in which ingredients from jumping, downhill, and cross-country were integrated. The combined cross-country and jumping event had a particularly strong position in Norway. To be allowed to jump the Holmenkollen hill, adult jumpers (20–32 years) had to take part in the preceding cross-country. This rule stood until 1933 as a means of ensuring versatility. As early as the 1880s, however, the combination event was held as two separate races, enabling the skiers to change from jumping to cross-country skis or the other way around. Jumping skis became heavier, thicker, and longer than previous ones. The materials also became more specialized: imported hickory replaced homegrown wood and indeed kept its position as the most-used material until fiberglass materials took over in the 1970s. Bindings, boots, jumping-suits, and wax underwent similar changes, ever more so as the emphasis on length and winning has increased. The development of equipment should therefore be seen in connection with the ideological discussion about specialization versus many-sidedness—a debate that became heated after "foreigners," especially jumpers from the United States who were not particularly interested in ideological questions of correct skiing equipment and style, entered the sport. The fiberglass revolution was accompanied by a centralizing of the ski-manufacturing industry in the hands of a few Central European firms; the skis are no longer produced in their country of origin.

## Rules and Style

Changes in style have been very much connected to the changes in equipment. Modern equipment makes for longer, more aerodynamic jumps and larger hills. Still, the ideal jump should always seek to cover an optimal distance, but it should also harmonize the take-off, the flight, and the landing. The regulations for judging the style have varied, but until the 1990s these criteria prevailed. The development from the original Telemark "drawn-up" style performed by legendary jumper Sondre Nordheim (1825–1897)—in which the jumper drew his skis up under himself (as in today's freestyle skiing) presumably in an attempt to increase the length of the jump (or to impress the spectators)—to the current style had many phases. First, in the "upright style," the skiers stood up straight during the jump, arms along the side. As the hills grew larger, more aerodynamic styles forced their way in. Jacob Tullin Thams (1898–1954), Olympic victor in 1924, pioneered the transition to a more aerodynamic style of jumping. In a further development, the "Kongsberg bend," named after the famous Ruud brothers from Kongsberg, Norway, and their townsman Reidar Andersen (1911–1993), was notable for a marked bend in the hip, arms out, and controlled arm rotations.

After World War II the "Finn style" introduced a new marked step and increased emphasis on aerodynamics. The "Recknagel" style, named after Helmut Recknagel (1937– ), 1960 Olympic gold medalist from the German Democratic Republic, introduced a new version of the Finn style that featured arms pointing forward, over the head. However, not all jumpers adopted this style, and into the 1960s the dominant way of jumping was arms along the side, parallel skis, and an ever more aerodynamic posture in the air. Bjørn Wirkola (1943– ), 1966 world champion in both "normal hill" and "large hill" was especially noted for his graceful and elegant Telemark landing. The next new invention came with a change

of the sitting position in the in-run, promoted by the East Germans in the early 1970s, changing arms position from front to back. The last big innovation was the "V-style," introduced by the Swede Jan Bokløv (1966– ) in 1986. His revolutionary idea was, instead of jumping with parallel skis, to jump with the skis spread in a V-shape (seen from behind). This style did not dominate the jumps immediately, but today it is the rule in competition. The advent of this style is interesting because it is both a consequence of one of ski jumping's original ideals—to adjust both the jumper's body and his skis as closely as possible to the laws of physics—and a violation of those ideals. The immediate result of V-style jumps was longer jumps and fewer style points, since it broke the ideal of even parallel skis. Just before the 1992 season, the approved rules for judging style were changed to allow the maximum score for V-style jumps as well. The Telemark landing, however, with bent knees, one foot ahead of the other, has remained obligatory.

## Controversies

The development of style illustrates some of the ideological discussions that have characterized the sport. Conservative officials—represented by the Fédération Internationale de Ski (FIS) and the judges—and innovative jumpers disagree over new styles, new equipment, new dress. According to traditional Norwegian *idretts* (sport) ideology, ski jumping should not be artificially constructed acrobatics but a test of the skier's ability to meet and conquer natural obstructions in the terrain. To build scaffolds for increasing the length and speed in the in-runs was viewed as artificial and not praiseworthy, not in the correct way of thinking ski-*idrett*. Even though this ideology has been steadily eroded, some of its elements have survived, if just barely, in the fact that ski jumping remains an aesthetic sport: the skier who has the longest jumps does not necessarily win the competition. The style referees will have their say, even if the norms for evaluating what is considered a "correct jump" have changed tremendously over the years.

The conservative ideology can also be seen in the official attitude toward ski flying (jumping hills of over 145 meters [476 feet]) and the registration of records of jumping length. Initially an interest of jumpers and race organizers from the

United States, record keeping was long seen as undesirable in the sport of ski jumping. "World records" have always been unofficial, meaning not approved by ski sport's governing body, the FIS. Official world championships in ski flying did not take place before 1972.

One episode from a recent championship shows that the desire to restrain the striving for records in the sport of ski jumping is still alive. In Planica, Slovenia, in 1994, officials decided that jumps over a certain measure (191 meters [209 feet]) would be counted as equal in length. The official reason for this was partly to ensure the skiers' safety (after some bad falls in Kulm in 1987) and partly to prevent the private hill owners from building larger and larger hills to ensure themselves a "world record." The decision created a heated discussion, with officials being accused of trying to turn back the clock. As it happened, the debate was short-lived, and soon the technological development both in the V-style and in reshaping the profile of the hills made it possible for 1994 Olympic champion Espen Bredesen (1968– ) of Norway to jump 209 meters (686 yards) in 1994 just as safely—some would argue more safely—as the longest traditional-style jumps. The philosophy of ski jumping—and the goals of the sport—have, however, remained clear. A ski jump is more than getting as far down a hill as possible. Bredesen's jump is therefore not registered as an official world record. Records like these do not exist in the official sport of ski jumping.

## Modern Competitive Jumping

Ski jumping has grown significantly as a modern competitive sport. Around the turn of the century, the Holmenkollen races were the main event. Finland began its Finnish "Ski-games" in Lahti in 1922. After World War II, Sweden initiated "Ski-games" in Falun in 1947, while the big event in Central Europe became the German-Austrian "Springer-Turnee," first staged in 1952–1953. Meanwhile, the Olympic Winter Games had grown from their inception in 1924 to rival the prestige of Holmenkollen, and in 1926 the FIS inaugurated a world championship in Nordic skiing (jumping, cross-country, and combination). Since the 1979–1980 competition the annual World Cup has distributed competitive events more evenly throughout the jumping

world, including Eastern and Central Europe, Japan, and North America.

In the early years Norway dominated the international scene. From 1924 until 1952 Norwegian jumpers won all Olympic races as well as a substantial number of world championships. Thereafter, the geographical distribution of medals has been more even. Jumpers from Finland, Austria, Germany—especially the former East Germany, and Czechoslovakia outjumped the Norwegians for quite some time. The last decades have seen a true international diffusion of the sport; world-class jumpers have come from nations as varied as Japan, Italy, Sweden, France, Slovenia, Switzerland, Poland, and Russia, as well as from ski-jumping strongholds in Canada and the United States.

Sondre Nordheim lives on in ski mythology as the early Telemark great. Matti Nykänen (1963– ) of Finland is a modern great, the jumper who has won the most championships after World War II. He collected 19 medals from Olympic Games and world championships. In the 1988 Calgary Winter Games he won both individual contests by a clear margin, as well as the team competition for Finland. The same year he also won the World Cup and the Springer-Turnee. In Sarajevo four years earlier, the then-18-year-old Nykänen had taken home Olympic gold and silver medals.

Earlier jumpers had fewer chances of gaining gold medals. However, the performances of Birger Ruud (1911–) of Norway are difficult to match. He emerged on the jumping scene as one of the three Ruud brothers, all highly successful with gold medals from either world championships or Olympic games. Every Olympic jumping contest between 1928 and 1948 had a Ruud on the winners' podium; the brothers won 7 out of 10 available international titles between 1928 and 1938. Of the three, Birger stood out. He won the last two Olympic gold medals before World War II (1932 and 1936) and came back 16 years after his first win to capture a silver medal in the 1948 Games at St. Moritz. His versatility is illustrated by the fact that he also won the downhill race—which only counted as a part of the alpine combination—in Garmisch-Partenkirchen in 1936.

Another modern jumper who made a remarkable comeback was the German Jens Weissflog (1964– ) who won a gold and a silver medal in the 1984 Games (representing the German Democratic

Republic) and came back after a ten-year Olympic medal drought to garner a new gold medal at the 1994 Games at Lillehammer. The achievement was all the more impressive since ski jumping in the meantime had gone through a virtual revolution in the shift to V-style.

## Appeal of Jumping

Why does ski jumping fascinate people? The attraction both to performers and to spectators has been the prospect of humans flying in the air. To watch a skier float through the air certainly is impressive, and for some viewers it represents the very height of skiing prowess. The risks mean that a certain amount of psychological strength is necessary to perform a decent ski jump. Hence, ski jumping, even in the countries of origin, never has been a large participant sport; the step from children's jumping on small and moderate hills to adult jumping on larger hills (70 meters [230 feet] and above) is extremely significant. Still, as a spectator sport ski jumping holds a firm grip on people and draws large crowds, especially in Finland, Austria, and Norway.

—Matti Goksøyr

**Bibliography:** Allen, E. John B. (1993) *From Skisport to Skiing.* Amherst: University of Massachusetts Press.

Bø, Olav. (1993) *Skiing throughout History.* Oslo: Det Norske Samlaget.

*FIS Bulletin* (journal of the Fédération Internationale de Ski, Bern, Switzerland).

Haarstad, Kjell. (1993) *Skisportens oppkomst i Norge.* Trondheim: Tapir Forlag.

*Revue Olympique* (Lausanne, Switzerland).

Vaage, Jakob. (1952) *Norske ski erobrer verden.* Oslo: Gyldendal Norsk Forlag.

# Skiing, Alpine

Alpine skiing developed in the European Alps in the late nineteenth century, following four to five thousand years of cross country skiing. Speeding down wooded mountain sides required different techniques for a safe descent, and the new alpine method, known as the Arlberg technique, soon spawned the varieties of skiing known as slalom and downhill. At first the new sport attracted primarily a wealthy clientele, and winter tourism, with its associated hotels, restaurants, and recreational facilities, spurred the development of posh ski resorts. But after World War II, travel by automobile and air made skiing increasingly available for the middle classes. With the big increase in the number of skiers came a flood of new resorts complete with lifts, grooming, and snowmaking equipment. Now environmentalists, particularly in Europe and the United States, regularly protest the overuse of the land.

Downhill and slalom, two alpine races, were sanctioned by the Fédération Internationale de Ski (FIS) in 1930 and have been part of the Olympic program both for men and women since 1936. Other varieties of alpine skiing have developed as well: freestyle, speed skiing, and snowboarding. Of the three, snowboarding appears likely to attract a large following.

## Origins

The name alpine derives from the Alps, but long before skiing was introduced to the Alps, Norwegians had skied fast down their own hills (see Skiing, Nordic—Origins). Norwegians, though, were used to their open, sloping highlands. When they visited the Alps in the late nineteenth century, they told their hosts that these mountains with their wooded and steep sides were no place to ski. Even so, a number of individuals in Germany, Austria, Switzerland, Italy, and belatedly in France, persevered and attracted a following of wealthy enthusiasts who crossed passes and even climbed mountains on skis. The exhilaration of the downhill rush was often commented upon by these early alpine skiers.

Even before World War I, the wealthy of Europe began to spend winter vacations in the mountains. They learned how to ski under instructors like Mathias Zdarsky (1856–1940), Georg Bilgeri (1873–1934) and Hannes Schneider (1890–1955), who experimented with a technique that originated in Austria. These three also instructed mountain troops during the war, and Schneider, particularly, developed the *Arlberg crouch*, with a lift and swing of the body, a method he taught to large numbers of beginner ski troops. After the war, he trained the wealthy

*The alpine ski environment has become standardized every-where. This high-tech-equipped skier could be from any-where and skiing at a ski resort anywhere there is snow.*

to ski in the same style. In the years between the wars, Hannes Schneider's Arlberg technique became both a way to ski and a way to teach skiing. The wealthy streamed from Germany, England, and the United States to St. Anton to learn the mysteries of the *stem turn* before mastering the *christie.* They also traveled to Murren, where Arnold Lunn (1888–1974) headed the development of the new alpine disciplines of *downhill* and *slalom,* originally intended to help mountaineers descend from peaks safely. From Schneider's and Lunn's ski schools, students dispersed around the globe, spreading the techniques they had learned to Australia, the United States, Japan, and India.

During the 1920s, most of the mountainous countries of Europe realized that winter tourism offered vast new economic opportunities.

Switzerland, with its stunning vistas, well-established health resorts, and summer tourist season, adapted easily. Germany popularized the Bavarian Alps successfully enough that the 1936 Olympic Games were staged at Garmisch-Partenkirchen. But with the exception of the towns of St. Anton and Innsbruck, Austrians showed surprisingly little interest in accommodating the new sport.

With the establishment of the exclusive new ski resorts, learning to ski became important socially, and a variety of national techniques—all variants of Schneider's Arlberg—taught by nationally certified instructors ensured vacationers a sure, safe climb to proficiency. But even more important, the variety of techniques provided skiers an excuse for hanging around the slopes during the fashionable ski schooling season. The best European instructors were in demand not only in the Alps but throughout the world. Otto Lang found himself teaching in Spain and the United States, Wendelin Hilty in Chile and the United States, and Ernst Skardarasy in New Zealand. Schneider himself traveled to Japan for the spring of 1930.

The Norwegians, long-time masters of cross country skiing, found it very difficult to accept the new alpine skiing. Not only was the graceful telemark turn eclipsed by the Arlberg crouch, but the whole *idraet* philosophy was undermined by alpine "hotel sport," and German-speaking instructors dominated the sport. One American instruction book written in 1935 listed eight foreign words "necessary for understanding a ski lesson." Seven were German. A Japanese tourist booklet (in English) extolling Hokkaido skiing listed the available *hutte* (huts) and took particular pride in the Okura *schantze* (jumps). Though the Norwegians complained about the canonizing of Schneider during the 1920s, his popularity soared with his films, *Wunder des Schneeschuhs* in 1926 and *Der weisse Rausch* with Leni Riefenstahl (1902– ) in 1931. Norwegians boycotted *Wunder des Schneeschuhs* and advertised their "Real Winter Sports," not to be confused with "circus sport" and money making.

When transferred to competition, the Arlsberg technique became downhill and slalom. These two disciplines had their genesis in the idea that following the conquest of a mountain peak, an accomplished skier cut a track straight down the

## Slalom Rules from 1924

Among the 18 rules for slalom were these:

1. A Slalom Race shall consist of a race in which Competitors are obliged to follow a course defined by flags or sticks.
2. A Slalom Race shall consist of two parts, the first part to be held on hard snow, the second part on soft snow.
3. Every Competitor shall be allowed one attempt at each part. No marks shall be given for style, but a Competitor's time shall be liable to be increased by penalties as follows:
   Ten seconds shall be added to a Competitor's time for a fall.
   Twenty seconds shall be added to a Competitor's time for a kick turn.
   A Competitor shall not be deemed to have fallen if he saves himself from falling with his hands, or if he stumbles. If a Competitor shuffles round to prevent his ski from sliding downhill by holding himself back with his sticks, he shall be deemed to have executed a kick turn.
4. A Competitor shall be disqualified:
   a) If he puts his two sticks together or if he puts both his hands on to a single stick.
   b) If neither of his skis passes between any pair of controlling flags.
   c) If he has a trial run round the course after the Judges have set the flags.

. . .

9. A Competitor is deeded to have finished when he breaks with his body, but not with his sticks or ski, the controlling tape which shall be affixed to the finishing post.

. . .

13. Two Timekeepers shall be appointed, to wit, an official Timekeeper and an assistant Timekeeper. The official Timekeeper shall announce audibly the time taken by each Competitor, and the times thus announced shall be checked by the assistant Timekeeper. No account shall be taken of minor discrepancies between the official Timekeeper's time and the times recorded by the assistant Timekeeper's watch.
14. Flag-keepers shall be appointed who shall stand by each pair of flags. It shall be the duty of each flag-keeper to direct competitors to his pair of flags and to ensure, as far as possible, that no Competitor shall be disqualified owing to failure to pass between the pair of flags for which he is responsible.
15. After the first Competitor has run down the Slalom course, no ski-runner shall be allowed on the course, and no attempts shall be made to improve the course by stamping out the snow or by filling up holes.

. . .

18. Competitors must use the same length of ski in both parts of the Slalom Race. No Competitor in a Slalom Race shall use skis that are not at least 10 per cent longer than the height of the ski-runner.

—E. John B. Allen

---

side of the mountain. These straight runs were possible above treeline and up to the end of the 1920s, races were often called straight races. "Taking it straight" was proof of dash. But once a skier reached the trees, straight running became impossible. Out of this problem grew the slalom, which Lunn named for the Norwegian *slalaam*, a race that required turning around natural obstacles. Lunn defined the downhill and slalom tracks with flags, put a premium on speed, and from 1922 on, rules were published for alpine events. Downhill courses have few gates, slaloms have a variety of different types of gates. Both races are won on time only.

The British Kandahar Ski Club was founded in 1924 to promote downhill skiing and lobby for its inclusion in international competition. By 1927 the Arlberg-Kandahar meet, founded by Lunn and Schneider, confirmed alpine events as prestigious races. The A-K has been run in Canada, the United States, Argentina, and France, in addition to Switzerland and Austria. Downhill and slalom events for men and women became official in 1931, when they came under FIS jurisdiction. Giant slalom, experimental as early as 1935, was sanctioned in 1972 and a Super-G in 1987. In giant slalom, the control gates for the coures (the poles the skiers must go around in fast turns) are spaced farther apart than on a slalom course. Giant slalom and Super-G combine elements of both downhill and slalom. Downhill is essentially a race down a mountain with control gates used only to check unsafe speeds or to guide racers around dangerous obstacles.

As World War II approached, the military in several countries sought to take advantage of their skiers' skills. Mussolini and Hitler aimed for total control of skiing in their respective countries. In Nazi Germany, skiing was managed by the bureaucracies of the Fachamt Skilauf, a division of the Deutscher Reichsbund fur Leibesubungen. In Italy, *dopolovoro* trips—Italian holiday weeks—took hundreds to the Dolomites. The winners of the men's and women's alpine events in the 1936 Olympics were both Germans, seeming proof that the "new order" was fit enough to conquer the world. In Finland, skiers defended their homeland against the Soviets at the start of World War II, a deed that spurred the formation of the ski troops of the 10th Mountain Division of the U.S. Army. The Finnish ski defense was accomplished entirely by cross country skiers, though, and the men who joined the American 10th were virtually all alpine skiers. But it hardly mattered, since very little fighting was done on skis in World War II.

After the war, alpine skiing became ever more popular, and wartime experiments with over-the-snow vehicles, cable lift construction, and strong, light metals and alloys were adapted to the slopes. Wooden skis gave way to more durable and faster metal skis, now designed specially for either downhill or slalom. Nylon and other new synthetic materials replaced cotton and wool in winter clothing—and at the same time created new opportunities for fashion designers. Many veterans of the 10th Mountain Division, upon demobilization, joined the ski business and entered the race to maximize skier visits and develop new resorts. Some of today's best-known destination resorts—Aspen, for example—were established during this period.

World travel changed in the 1950s. What had once been tourism by liner for the wealthy became tourism by airliner for the middle classes. Europe's alpine ski areas looked not only to European skiers for business but also sought to tap into the American tourist market and attract the middle classes from other industrialized countries. Package tours including flight, hotel, meals, and ski lift tickets became commonplace. And until the oil embargo of 1973, ski areas seemed to multiply endlessly. Eventually, though, environmentalists complained of overuse in the Alps and in the United States as well, on both federal and private land.

U.S. ski areas now vie with European alpine resorts in popularity. The British often come to ski the slopes in the northeastern United States, and the trail signs at Snowbird, Utah, are written in Japanese. Western Canada is well known for its helicopter skiing, and Australia and New Zealand now promote their winter joys during the northern hemisphere's summer, as South America once did as well.

But the ease of global travel also had a negative effect on alpine skiing. Though it is now quite possible for a skier of means to ski on three continents in one season, he or she will be disappointed to find that ski resorts everywhere are much the same—the lifts are all made by the same manufacturer, the ski equipment made by the same companies, and the clothing, food, drink, and even ski techniques are the same around the world. A rented condominium in Albertville or Zell am See is indistinguishable from a condo in Stowe or Sapporo. Only the accent of the skiers (who frequently speak in English) varies. Alpine ski development has urbanized and standardized the ski environment around the globe. In fact, the Japanese are about to open an indoor alpine ski slope in downtown Tokyo.

## Practice

The FIS governs international skiing and now has committees working on freestyle, speed skiing, and snowboarding. These three varieties of skiing, once marginal, have moved toward the center of the skiing program over the years. Freestyle skiing comprises two disciplines: mogul skiing and aerials. Since ski trails today are now groomed to carpet perfection, mogul skiing (skiing over bumps) has almost become a specialty. Most ski areas now deliberately create moguls on a designated trail or part of a trail. Aerials began with a somersaulting tradition dating back to before World War I but was made popular by the exhibitions of Stein Eriksen in the late 1950s and 1960s. The FIS sanctioned freestyle in 1994, and the event was on the Lillehammer Olympic program. Speed skiing began as the *kilometre lance* in 1931 in Switzerland, when Leo Gasperl achieved 136.319 kilometers (84.723 miles) per hour. After the war, speed skiing excited a flurry of interest. The 1960s witnessed a series of attempts to break the speed record in Portillo, Chile, and Cervinia,

Italy. By 1983 Franz Weber had reached 208.049 kilometers (129.303 miles) per hour and Kristen Culver 194.343 kilometers (120.785 miles) per hour. In the interest of safety, the FIS has now established a maximum speed of 229.3 kilometers (142.5 miles). Speed skiing appeals to only a handful of athletes and attracts few spectators.

Snowboarding, derived from skiing, skateboarding, and surfing traditions, has generated controversy in alpine skiing. Appealing initially to the young, snowboarding embraced a rebellious image. Some areas simply did not permit snowboards; others designated trails and provided specially constructed "half pipes" for the more acrobatic. Most ski areas now welcome snowboarders; they represent a growth segment in an otherwise flat industry.

—E. John B. Allen

**See also** Skiing, Freestyle; Skiing, Nordic; Snowboarding.

**Bibliography:** Allen, E. John B. (1993) *From Skisport to Skiing: One Hundred Years of an American Sport, 1840–1940.* Amherst: University of Massachusetts Press.

Arnaud, Pierre, and Thierry Terret. (1993) *Le reve blanc, olympisme et sport d'hiver en France: Chamonix 1924 Grenoble 1968.* Bordeaux: Presses Universitaires de Bordeaux.

Fanck, Arnold, and Hannes Schneider. (1925) *Wunder des Schneeschuhs.* Hamburg: Enoch.

*FIS Bulletin.* Oberhofen: Fédération Internationale de Ski.

Lloyd, Janis M. (1986) *Skiing into History 1924–1984.* Toorak, Victoria: Ski Club of Victoria.

Lunn, Arnold. (1927) *A History of Skiing.* London: Oxford University Press.

Palmedo, Roland, ed. (1937). *Skiing: the International Sport.* New York: Derrydale.

Polednik, Heinz. (1969) *Weltwunder Skisport.* Wels, Germany: Welsermuhl.

Ulmrich, Ekkehart, ed. (1992) *100 Jahre Skitechnik—40 Jahre Interski-Kongresse.* Planegg, Germany: Deutscher Skiverband.

Vaage, Jakob. (1979) *Skienes Verden.* Oslo: Hjemmenes.

Vida, F. (1976) *Storia dello Sci Italia, 1896–1975.* Milan: Milano Sole.

# Skiing, Freestyle

Freestyle skiing consists of four subdisciplines: mogul, ballet, aerial, and the combined. Evaluation of performances is done by a combination of quantitative measures and aesthetic criteria. As a form of skiing acrobatics, the sport has historical roots as long as leisure skiing itself. In its modern, standardized, and competitive form, the origins are to be found in the United States in the late 1960s. Due to its somewhat irresponsible "hot dog" image, and due to several serious injuries, freestyle skiing was not accepted by the skiing establishment until its inclusion in the International Skiing Federation (FIS) in 1979. Important steps in the development of the sport were taken as mogul skiing and the aerial events became Olympic events in 1992 and 1994 respectively. With its spectacular character and high entertainment value, freestyle skiing is perhaps the skiing discipline with the broadest appeal to sport fans in general.

## Origins

Acrobatics has been part of skiing from its very beginning. Historical roots of freestyle skiing can be found in Scandinavia and the European Alps, but it developed in North America.

Among the skiers of last century's Telemark, Norway, the ideal was to master a series of techniques: turning, jumping, and going straight downhill at high speeds. *Ville låmir* (wild courses), which were located in steep terrain, included tough turns, moguls, and steep jumps. During the 1930s, Norwegian ski champions, especially the famous Ruud brothers, especially Sigmund (1907–1994) and Birger (1911– ) used skiing acrobatics as part of their training programs. Their simultaneous somersault ski jumps were well-known exhibitions.

Pioneers of freestyle skiing are to be found in the European Alps as well. Mathias Zdarsky (1856–1940), who wrote a classic book on alpine skiing technique, was an excellent skier and gymnast. Simple acrobatic exercises were part of his skiing pedagogy. Other key figures were Ferdinand Oguey of Switzerland, who in the late 1920s and the 1930s practiced acrobatic jumps and mogul skiing, and, on a more theoretical level, the German medical doctor and figure-skating aficionado Fritz Reul, who in 1926 wrote a book on new possibilities in skiing technique.

In Europe, acrobatics was considered an acceptable part of a skier's training program but

*Only recently accepted by governing sports bodies, freestyle skiing includes jumps, ballet, and moguls, all done on skis. Ellen Breen of the United States demonstrates these skills at the 1993 World Championships.*

not a "real" competitive sport. The less traditional American skiing culture was to a larger extent open to alternative practices. In North America, skiing acrobatics had been part of professional ski shows since the turn of the century. Around 1950, skiing aces and skilled skiing acrobats like Stein Eriksen of Norway (1927– ), an Olympic champion, emigrated to the United States and revitalized the tradition, which was extended by people like the Arthur (Art) Furrer (1937– ) of Switzerland, a skier, author, journalist, and television personality.

Freestyle skiing found its form as a standardized, competitive sport in the 1970s. The first competition is said to have taken place in Waterville Valley, New Hampshire, in 1966. The first professional competition was held in 1971, and the first World Cup freestyle tour was staged in 1978. During the 1970s, national championships were arranged in several European countries. However, this was a time with organizational conflicts, economical instability, and bad injuries due to the lack of safety measures.

A decisive step in the sport's development was taken in 1979 when the FIS accepted freestyle skiing as an amateur sport. In 1986, the first official world championships took place in Tignes, France. Another important step occurred when freestyle skiing became a member of the Olympic family. During the 1988 Games in Calgary, Canada, freestyle skiing was included as a demonstration sport. In Albertville, France, in 1992, mogul skiing was part of the official Olympic program, and the 1994 Lillehammer, Norway, Games included both mogul and aerial competitions.

## Practice

Freestyle skiing consists of four subdisciplines: (1) aerial competition, (2) ballet, (3) mogul competition, and (4) the combined, which totals the scores of skiers who participated in the first three events.

First, the FIS defines an aerial competition as consisting of "two (2) different acrobatic leaps from a prepared jump(s), stressing take-off, height and distance (referred to as 'air'), proper style, execution and precision of movement (referred to as 'form') and landing." Performances are evaluated by seven (or five) judges on three components. Five (or three) judges evaluate "air," which accounts for 20 percent of the score, and "form," which accounts for 50 percent, while the two remaining judges evaluate the landing, which accounts for 30 percent. The scores are added and multiplied with a degree-of-difficulty factor (DD) defined for each jump. For example, the DD factor for the most advanced triple somersaults with twists is about twice the DD factor for a single somersault.

Aerial sites have to satisfy strict criteria set by the FIS. For safety reasons, the jumps have to be constructed out of earth (in the off-season) or snow. The size of the jumps vary with the age and quality of competitors, as do the difficulty of the jumps. For elite performers, the in-run is 55–65 meters (60–71 yards) long with a 20–25 degree pitch, the jump is about 3 meters (10 feet) tall with a 55–65 degree pitch, the landing slope, of which a part has to consist of softer snow, is about 30–35 meters (33–38 yards) long with a 34–39 degree pitch, and the finish area is about 30 meters (33 yards) long. A tower for the judges is placed on the left- or right-hand side of the site close to the jump. There are no restrictions on equipment other than that all competitors have to wear helmets and use safety bindings.

A second subdiscipline is called ballet, but will, according to official FIS decisions, change its name to acroski in the future. Ballet is described by some as "figure skating on skis." A ballet competition includes one run, which according to the rules has to consist of "jumps, spins, inverted movements and linking steps blended together with artistic and athletic aspects into a well-balanced program, performed in harmony with music of the skiers choice."

The area for ballet competitions must be evenly graded, smooth, and free of obstacles. The pitch is 11–15 degrees, the length of the slope approximately 150 meters (164 yards), and the width around 40 meters (44 yards). The tower for judges is placed on the right- or the left-hand side of the site close to the jump.

Again, seven (or five) judges are involved. And again, there is a split scoring system. Technical merit, which is evaluated by two judges, gives half of the score, while artistic impression, which gives the other half, is evaluated by five (or three) judges. Technical merit is evaluated on the basis of two criteria: degree of difficulty and execution. Only jumps (rotations around the vertical body axis) and flips (rotations around the horizontal body axis) are evaluated, and there is a minimum of three different jumps in a run. Artistic impression is judged on the basis of interpretation of the music, variety and creativity, and movement qualities such as carriage, control, fluency, and dynamic action.

In ballet, the length of poles and skis has significant influence on the difficulty of the performance. Consequently, there are restrictions here. Pole length cannot transcend body height. Ski length follows a defined table in which body length is multiplied by 81/100. For example, a competitor who is 150 centimeters (59 inches) tall can use skis with a minimum length of 121.5 centimeters (48 inches), while the minimum ski length for a competitor 180 centimeters (71 inches) tall is 145.8 centimeters (57.4 inches). No competitor is allowed to use skis more than 160 centimeters (63 inches) long.

In the third event, a run in a mogul competition is defined by the rules as "skiing on a steep, heavily moguled course, stressing technical turns, aerial maneuvers and speed." There is also the possibility for dual mogul competitions "using the same judging criteria as individual competition (except timing) with the winner of each round advancing to the next round." There is reason to believe that the dramatic and exciting dual mogul event will be the predominant subdiscipline in the future.

The mogul site must be uniformly covered with moguls and have a continuous fall line. The slope should not be overly concave or convex nor have any distinct changes in pitch, which is 24–32 degrees. The width of the slope is approximately 20 meters (22 yards) and the length is 200–270 meters (219–295 yards). The judges are situated at the bottom of the hill but no less than 300 meters (328 yards) from the start.

Turning technique gives 50 percent of the score, air gives 25 percent, and speed 25 percent. Five (three) judges evaluate turns (changes of direction of travel to either side of the fall line), which are supposed to be rhythmic and aggressive but at the same time controlled, whereas two judges evaluate air according to the form and difficulty of the jumps. Speed is simply the amount of time taken to complete the run. However, the speed of each competitor is evaluated according to a standard established by pacesetters (highly ranked mogul skiers) ahead of the competition. Times above a certain limit give lower scores whereas times below the limit earn higher scores.

For reasons similar to those in ballet, there are restrictions on ski length in mogul skiing. The minimum ski length for men is 190 centimeters (74.8 inches) and for women 180 centimeters (70.9 inches).

The fourth subdiscipline of freestyle skiing is the combined, which is open to competitors who have started in all three events. A combined skier's score in each event is divided by the score of the highest scoring combined skier in that event, and the result is then divided by ten, which gives that skier's event scores. When adding the three events, the skier with the highest score is declared the winner. Aerial, ballet, and mogul disciplines require very different skills from athletes, a fact that shows good combination skiers to be versatile athletes.

## Cultural Aspects

There is a general trend toward differentiation in modern sport. Traditional disciplines change, old traditions are revitalized, and new activities are created. To take some examples from skiing: Due to technological innovations and demands on entertainment value, cross-country skiing, ski jumping, and alpine skiing have radically altered over the last decades in technique and tactics and in the organization of competitions. The telemark turn, now more than 100 years old, was revitalized during the 1980s, and today, at least in Scandinavia, telemark skiing is growing both as a leisure activity and as a competitive sport. Other activities, such as snowboarding, which in December 1995 was approved as an Olympic discipline, have no clear historical roots but are the result of innovative technological development.

Freestyle skiing occupies a middle position in this picture. Skiing acrobatics and demands on aesthetic qualities of performance have a long history. At the same time, freestyle skiing carries the distinctive marks of a modern, materialistic sport culture with a basis in the norms and values of Western youth. Up to the 1990s, almost all competitors came from the United States, Canada, Western Europe, and Scandinavia. The sport focuses very strongly on entertainment and the spectacular and offers a great variety of experiential qualities. Aerial and mogul competitions express risk, speed, action, drama, and excitement. Ballet is built upon ideals like rhythm, harmony, and beauty.

The terminology of the sport and the framework within which the events take place offer clues to its cultural background as well. Jumps are given popular names such as Mule Kick, Daffy, Spread Eagle, Helicopter, and Back Scratcher, while ballet maneuvers are called Gut Flip and Rock and Roll. A terminological point of particular interest is the current change of name from ballet to acroski. The initiative came from the athletes themselves, who wanted to avoid the somewhat "feminine" image associated with the discipline. Moreover, in the rules of all subdisciplines, there are requirements that "rhythmic and engaging" music be played during the competition and that facilities be easily accessible to the public, even those who do not ski.

In its initial phase, freestyle skiing experienced a lack of acceptance in the established skiing milieu. This was due to a skeptical attitude in the conservative (European) skiing community and to the significant risk involved at unsupervised and commercially organized hot dog events in the 1970s. In fact, in 1972 and 1973, four U.S. skiers suffered severe spinal cord injuries. Lawsuits following these accidents resulted in trouble with insurance and economic guarantees of freestyle events, and to a banning of inverted aerials by the national ski area association in 1976.

Accepted by the FIS in 1979 and included in the Olympic Games in 1992, the sport has now become "clean." Today, safety precautions like good course preparation, rules on equipment, and limitations on jumps in the aerial events have decreased the risks involved. The main challenge today is to get a third subdiscipline, ballet, or acroski, on the Olympic agenda. However, due to somewhat limited commercial potential, this aim seems at present hard to realize. What might be another controversial topic today is the increased specialization. More and more competitors take part in only one event and the combined competition suffers. In fact, in Norway, the national championships have been without competitors in the combined since 1991.

Freestyle skiing is a sport in rapid development. The inclusion of aerial events and mogul skiing in the Olympic family represents an important step both in terms of expansion to new parts of the world and in terms of commercial potential. In the early 1990s, Eastern European athletes for the first time earned points in the World Cup. A Russian won the silver medal in the women's mogul event at the 1992 Albertville Games, while Lina Tsjerjazova from Uzbekistan won the gold medal in the 1994 Lillehammer Games' aerial competition. With its high entertainment value and its appeal to sports fans with little or no roots in traditional skiing cultures, freestyle skiing no doubt will experience growth and increased popularity in the future.

—Sigmund Loland

**Bibliography:** Heinrich, Fritz. (1978) "Wer hat das Trickskifahren erfunden?" *Leibesübungen-Leibeserziehung* 32, 1: 6–8.

Giel, Debra. (1988) "Freestyle Skiing: From 'Hotdogging' to Olympic Demonstration Event." *Physician and Sportsmedicine* 16, 2 (February): 189–190, 195–196.

International Skiing Federation. (1992) *FIS Freestyle. General Rules and Regulations. Rules for Specific Competitions.* Berne: International Skiing Federation.

———. (1993) *FIS Freestyle. General Rules for Scoring. Judging Manual.* Berne: International Skiing Federation.

# Skiing, Nordic

Nordic skiing—which includes cross country skiing and ski jumping—reflects a tradition of practical, day-to-day skiing over 5,000 years old. Written sources from China and Scandinavia tell of informal competition and the use of skis in war. It was not until the late eighteenth century, however, that the first organized competitions were held under the auspices of the Norwegian military. Civilian meets began in the 1840s, and within a generation, jumping had emerged as a special event. Norwegian immigrants in central Europe, the Americas, and Australasia spread the techniques of Nordic skiing worldwide. Thus the Norwegian way of skiing and the concept of *idraet*—the belief that vigorous outdoor sport would improve not only individuals but clubs and even the nation—formed the foundation of world skiing. Until the alpine skiing disciplines of downhill and slalom became popular in the 1930s, Norwegian attitudes and styles of skiing remained dominant. The Winter Olympic Games of 1932, held in the United States, were the last to be Nordic male only.

## Origins

The sport of Nordic skiing is modeled on the day-to-day skiing techniques of people who have relied on skis as transportation since prehistoric times. In Scandinavia and northern Russia, skis found preserved in bogs date back four to five thousand years. From the Norse Sagas and Icelandic Eddas, we also know of early informal competition.

The first modern, organized competitions took place in the Norwegian military, probably in 1767. Monetary prizes were awarded for shooting while skiing, for bushwhacking, for the fastest downhill run, and for running in full equipment. When the Norwegian ski troops disbanded in 1826, local civilian clubs took up the sport and organized races. The competition near Kristiania (which became the Holmenkollen) was first staged in 1879. By that time, Norwegians had emigrated throughout the world and taken their skiing style with them. In Australia and the Americas, they introduced locals to the use of skis for traveling, visiting, and for winter enjoyment. Gold fever also infected immigrants who knew how to ski, and in the deep mountain snows of Kiandra (Australia) and California (United States), skis became common in the mining camps. Skiing mail carriers there were often hailed as heroes.

In 1888 Fridtjof Nansen (1861–1930) crossed southern Greenland at latitude 64° on skis. When his book about the journey, *Paa Ski over Gronland*, was translated into German, it sparked an interest in skiing among the wealthy outdoorsmen of Europe. By 1900 Nordic skiing was "a rich man's

*Participants in the 5,000-year-old sport of cross country skiing get a workout in the snow-covered forest.*

passion" throughout Europe, and a number of skiing clubs were formed. Visiting Norwegians became club mentors and set up competitions with the jump as the centerpiece.

With the formation of clubs worldwide, administrative organizations were founded on the local, regional, and national levels to organize meets and establish rules. To retain control of 'their' sport, Norwegians called for an international ski congress in 1910 and held the secretaryship until the Fédération Internationale de Ski (FIS) was founded in 1924. The FIS is the world body governing ski competition. It makes rules for ski races, determines eligibility, approves courses for international competition, sanctions events eligible for FIS points, selects the sites for the biennial FIS world championships, and approves the courses for Olympic competition.

## Recreational Cross Country Skiing

Recreational cross country skiing was the only form of skiing until the 1920s and 1930s, when the alpine skiing craze put a premium on speed down a hill. The first major recreational use of skis was for winter trips into the mountains, and the more adventurous even attempted winter climbs on skis. The tradition continues today, as experienced Nordic skiers traverse the high mountains of the world—from the Karakorams (Pakistan) to the Caucasus (Russia), from the Atlas (Algeria) to the Wasatch (United States). The most committed—the "extreme" cross country skiers—have tested their skills against the Haute Route in Switzerland, the mountains of Patagonia, the rugged terrain of Greenland, and even on solo trips to the North and South Poles.

The majority of cross country skiers today, though, are less interested in a survival adventure than a 1900-style ski outing: a run across meadows and through forests. In 1900, though, such an excursion would have been a club outing. Today the ski party is more likely to be made up of families, or small, informal groups. And today's skier enjoys amenities unavailable at the turn of the century—lighted pathways in Nordmarka (just outside Oslo), machine prepared *Loipen* in the Alps, and marked loops in North America. All attest to the popularity of a form of winter recreation that costs substantially less than a day's "alpine" lift skiing.

Recreational Nordic skiing and ski equipment have been aggressively marketed in the United States, since World War II, possibly because the beginning of the country's fitness cult coincided with Bill Koch's (1955– ) unexpected Olympic silver medal for the 30-kilometer (18.6-mile) race at Innsbruck in 1976. Though several makes of skis were available in 1900, recreational skis were not developed specifically for cross country until a different sort of ski had been designed for alpine use. Wooden skis have now given way to synthetic materials requiring no waxing. The three pin binding designed to hold the front part of the boot firm while leaving the ankle and heel free has been replaced by click-in bindings requiring special boots, so the whole system must be coordinated. Poles made of bamboo and steel are now seen only in museums, replaced by high-tech poles with alloy shafts, small discs, and pointed davits. Fashion changes, too, have accompanied these developments.

Around the turn of the century, jumping was the high point of any ski competition. In Scandinavia and particularly in North America, local communities prided themselves on their jump. In Scandinavia many men continued jumping for recreation; in North America, only the experts continued and jumping became the great winter outdoor spectator sport. In Europe, it declined in popularity as skiing became a social activity, and though jumping was admired, it was no longer attempted by most skiers.

Telemark skiing is a style of turning first associated with peasant skiers from Telemark, Norway. In the late nineteenth century it was used both in cross country skiing and to turn and stop at the end of a jump. Now the telemark turn is often used in alpine settings as well. Special boots, special skis, and even special competitions are designed for the new breed of "tele skier."

## Competitive Cross Country Skiing

Cross country racing, first organized on national levels in Europe and America in the years before World War I, followed Norwegian rules. According to the Scandinavian *idraet* tradition, the purpose of outdoor sport was to produce an athlete who was not only fit but morally upright. The more optimistic proponents of the *idraet* believed that it could regenerate the nation, an especially

## Cross Country Racing in 1907

The first great cross country run ever pulled off in the United States took place starting from headquarters at 2 P.M., February 7.

It was a pretty sight to behold the uniformed members of Nor Ski Club, Chicago, starting from the headquarters with red, white and blue streamers to be posted along the nine mile course. A good natured and healthy looking lot of men, who would do honor to any regiment of infantry in Uncle Sam's army. The men were distributed along the course to watch at difficult passes, and report on any participant, who should in any way disobey the laws governing the contest. It is a very strict rule in Norway not to allow any participant in a cross country run to remove his skis during the contest, and this rule was adhered to in every detail. The skis could not be removed in jumping a fence or in clearing any other obstacle that might seem rather hard to overcome. The practical use of the ski is learned in runs of this nature, and it takes but a short time to get accustomed to handling the skis to advantage over obstacles of every description.

On a level surface, the Finns are the masters of the ski, while in a hilly and brushy country, the Norwegians cannot be beaten. The course of this run (the National Championship) was laid over a territory consisting of about four miles of hills and brush, three miles on the level and two miles on snow covered ice, thus giving the participating Finlanders a chance to gain on the level what their long skis naturally would lose through the brush, and the world famous Asarja Autio certainly knew how to avail himself of these level stretches as he practically flew over the snow as soon as the open availed itself, and he sustained his reputation by covering the distances two minutes ahead of the sturdy Norwegian runners, Elling Diesen and Gustav Bye, in the good time of 47 minutes and 30 seconds. The participants were in good condition, when they finished their hard run, and were well taken care of at headquarters. Warm milk was served as refreshments. It is of great importance, that the men posted along the course have a supply of bits of oranges or lemons to give the skiers as refreshments as they pass.

*Ely Miner* (22 February 1907): The ski race meet Sunday under the auspices of the Ely Finnish Athletic Club, was the best ever held in this city. There were twenty-three entries in the Men's race but out of that number only seven stayed to the finish. Asanias [*sic*] Autio won the first prize, covering the seven miles in 45 minutes and 45 seconds. Autio who resides in this city and claims to be the champion ski racer of the world, is anxious to meet anyone in the United States for a purse of $100 or over—the number of miles to be covered to be named by the party accepting the challenge.

—*National Ski Association Report* (7 February 1907)

important notion to Norwegians, who had just won their independence from Sweden in 1905.

The standard Norwegian races were 15 to 50 kilometers (24 to 80 miles) long, and the popular 50-kilometer (31-mile) race came to be known as the winter marathon. The true hero was not the winner of these races, though. He was the man whose combined points for cross country and jumping marked him as the best all-rounder. After World War II, specialization became increasingly apparent as men and, from 1952 on, women trained for specific distances. By the 1960s, cross country racing had become such a specialized sport that club and recreational skiers no longer even considered entering any competitions. In China, however, and in other countries where skiing did not become so specialized, cross country events continued as club activities.

One recent development that benefits the better amateur skier is the citizen race. These races are best known from the 13 marathons now held around the world. The Norwegian Birkebeiner and the Swedish Vasaloppet, commemorating military and national events from the thirteenth and sixteenth centuries, hold pride of place among the venues—7 in Europe, 2 in North America, and 1 each in Japan and Australia.

An offshoot of cross country skiing is the biathlon—a cross country race with target shooting at intervals—derived from the military ski patrol race. Before World War I, Western and westernized military leaders (in Sweden, Norway, Finland, Germany, Austria-Hungary, Italy, France, Switzerland, Russia, the United States, and Japan) all equipped a few military units as ski troops. International military ski competitions were held, sometimes under the eye of Norwegian officers. The Chasseurs Alpins (France) and the Alpini (Italy) were particular rivals. Patrols of four to six men in battle gear competed for the best time traveling between two points. During the war, troops on skis saw some duty on the major European fronts in the Vosges, Dolomites, and Carpathians.

After the war, the military patrol race was discussed in the Fédération Internationale de Ski

(FIS) which, in spite of its French title, was Scandinavian dominated, and by the International Olympic Committee (IOC). In 1909 proponents called for the inclusion of a military patrol race in the Olympic Games, but the biathlon remained a demonstration event until it became official at Squaw Valley (United States) in 1960.

Before World War II, women participated only peripherally in Nordic ski competition. Skepticism about the ability of women's bodies to withstand a race over distance prevented women from receiving serious consideration in Nordic ski racing, and jumping was quite out of the question for women. However, the two world wars opened opportunities for women. Competitive skiing for women in cross country became part of the Olympic program at Oslo (Norway) in 1952 with a 10-kilometer (6.2-mile) event. At Lillehammer (Norway) in 1994 there were women's events of 5, 15, and 30 kilometers (3.1, 9.3, and 18.6 miles) and a 4 x 5 kilometer relay, besides a 7.5 and 15 kilometer biathlon and a 4 x 7.5 kilometer relay. The 5-kilometer and 30-kilometer events were to be run in *classical stride*, the 15-kilometer event was to be run in the *free technique*, better described as the *skating step*.

## Style Controversies

The arguments between proponents of the classic technique and those who favored the skating step are about 20 years old. The skating step—one ski in a track and the other used like a skate to push off—was first introduced at the Holmenkollen 50-kilometer race in 1971, and the Engadine (Switzerland) marathon in 1975 was won by a skier using the skating technique. The method proved faster over flatter terrain, but it also cut up the prepared track, was derived from another sport, and seemed to place more emphasis on winning by use of a modern technique than on honoring the classic cross country stride. By the late 1970s, the skating stride was used so effectively by the Finns that it was called the *Finnstep*, or *Siitonenschritt*, after Pauli Siitonen. Today the classical and free technique are separate cross country disciplines.

Jumping styles, too, have changed over the past 100 years. At one time, a sort of squat position competed with the more upright position that is currently popular. Since the mid-1920s there has been an increasing interest in aerody-

namic styles. Jumping competitions are won or lost on the basis of two criteria: the distance achieved and the form or style of the jump based on positions at take-off, flight, and landing. Rules for awarding points have changed from time to time. Points were assigned to the crouch and the leap, which ideally produced the body aesthetically stretched and poised in the air with arms forward, back, or by the side to allow flight guidance and balance on landing. The lift during the flight was achieved by the parallel skis pointing straight out over the hill almost like the wing of a plane. In the late 1980s, Jan Boklov (Sweden) spread his skis in an outward "V" on taking off, and a hundred year old tradition was broken. Initially perceived as unaesthetic and marked down accordingly, the "V" style was given official sanction before the 1992 Olympics and has now taken over from the classic jumping form. In 1962 jumps were regulated at heights of 90 and 70 meters (295 and 230 feet), and *ski flying*, where distances of over 183 meters (600 feet) are attained, has been sanctioned by the FIS since 1972.

—E. John B. Allen

**See also** Skiing, Alpine; Ski Jumping; Snowboarding.

**Bibliography:** Allen, E. John B. (1993) *From Skisport to Skiing: One Hundred Years of an American Sport, 1840–1940.* Amherst: University of Massachusetts Press.

Berg, Karin. (1993) *Ski i Norge.* Oslo: Aventura.

Bomann-Larsen, Tor. (1993) *Den evige sne: en skihistorie om Norge.* Oslo: Cappelens.

*FIS Bulletin.* Oberhofen: Fédération Internationale de Ski.

Helly, Louis. (1966) *Cent ans de ski francais.* Grenoble, France: Cahiers de l'Alpe.

Lloyd, Janis M. (1986) *Skiing Into History 1924-1984.* Toorak: Ski Club of Victoria.

Luther, Carl J. (1926) "Geschichte des Schnee- und Eissports." In *Geschichte des Sports aller Volker und Zeiten*, edited by G. A. E. Bogeng. Leipzig: Seeman, 2: 497–557.

Mehl, Erwin. (1964) *Grundriss der Weltgeschichte des Schifahrens.* Stuttgart: Hoffmann.

Nansen, Fridtjof. (1890) *Paa Ski over Gronland; en Skildring af den Norske Gronlands-Ekspedition 1888–89.* Oslo: Aschehoug.

Nygren, Helge, Antero Raevuori, and Tarmo Maki-Kuuti. (1983) *Pitka latu: vuosisata suomalaista hiihtourheilua.* Porvoo: Soderstrom.

Palmedo, Roland, ed. (1937) *Skiing: the International Sport.* New York: Derrydale.

Vaage, Jakob. (1952) *Norske ski erobrer verden.* Oslo: Gyldendahl.

Vida, F. (1976) *Storia dello Sci Italia, 1896–1975.* Milan: Milano Sole.

# Skiing, Water

Water skiing is a sport in which a person is pulled along the surface of the water by a motorboat. In the basic style of the sport, the water skier wears a ski on each foot and holds a tow rope with both arms. As the boat moves forward, it pulls the skier at a speed that enables him or her to stand up on the skis and glide along the surface of the water. Variations include the use of only one ski, bare-foot skiing, and jumping off ramps, among others.

Water skiing combines elements of several sports, including boating and snow skiing, and it is a popular sport throughout the world. It has been estimated that approximately 30 million people participate in water skiing internationally. Most of these people water ski on a purely recreational, informal basis. In addition, many thousands of serious water skiers compete in organized events.

Water skiing appeals to people on many levels. It offers the opportunity to experience being on the water in a more direct sense than is possible in a boat, combined with the excitement of skiing along its surface at high speeds. The basic skills of water skiing can be learned quickly, and people with a moderate degree of physical proficiency can enjoy the sport on its simpler levels. Water skiing at more advanced levels is a very challenging sport that requires a great deal of physical skill and courage. Those who pursue the sport more seriously enjoy the opportunity to develop their skills, test their courage, and compete against other water skiers.

Water skiing is also a popular spectator sport in competition as well as in noncompetitive entertainment shows. The skiers can accomplish physical feats that are very impressive to watch, including intricate maneuvers on skis, high-speed runs, impressive leaps and flips in the air, and other demonstrations of prowess and courage.

The name can be spelled as two separate words (water skiing), as one word (waterskiing), or with a hyphen (water-skiing). The primary water skiing organization in the United States, the American Water Ski Association, spells it as two separate words.

## Origins and Development

Water skiing is a twentieth-century sport, with origins in the ancient principle of using the power of one moving object to tow another. Throughout history people have used animals to pull wagons on land or sleds on snow and ice. On the water, people used one vessel to tow a raft or attached boat containing cargo. In addition to harnessing this concept to accomplish tasks, people used it for recreational activities such as sledding.

Although it is believed that people attempted earlier forms of water skiing using sailboats, the sport originated in its modern form only after 1900 with the development of the motorboat, which provided sufficient power and speed to reliably pull people along the water's surface. As motorboats began to proliferate in the decades after 1900, people in various locations began to separately develop activities that evolved into the sport of water skiing, including towing sleds and other flat objects that people either sat on or stood up. These activities were popular on the French Riviera and other bodies of water in Europe. Count Maximillian Pulaski is believed to have devised an early pair of water skis in Europe in the early 1920s. In the United States, Ralph Samuelson invented and demonstrated a pair of water skis in 1922 on Lake Pepin, Minnesota. At approximately the same time, near New York City, Fred Waller also invented and marketed a style of water ski, and he also invented the bridle at the end of the tow rope that water skiers hold.

By the 1930s efforts were being initiated to organize and promote the sport more widely. In the United States an enthusiast named Dan Haines formed the American Water Ski Association (ASWA) in 1939. The organization held its first national championship at Jones Beach near New York City that year. Many of the pioneers of the sport came together under the umbrella of ASWA, and standardized rules and a structure of local clubs and competitions were established. Similar initiatives took place in other nations. In the late 1940s the World Water Ski Union (WWSU) was formed to coordinate the sport, sanction events and records, and formulate rules internationally. Tournaments and championship events were established throughout the world on regional, national, and international levels.

Water skiing also captured the public's attention as a spectator sport. Entertainment-oriented

*Water skiing lends itself to a variety of stunts and is popular as a spectator as well as a recreational sport.*

water shows became popular attractions that helped to boost the sport's visibility. These shows featured spectacular stunts, beautiful women performing choreographed dance routines, and other crowd-pleasing activities on water skis. One of the first of these water-sports shows was held in 1928 at the Atlantic City Steel Pier in New Jersey sponsored by entrepreneur Frank Sterling. In Florida, Dick Pope featured a ski-jumping demonstration that same year. Pope and his family became leading promoters of water skiing shows, especially after establishing a major ski show at Cypress Gardens, an aquatic theme park in Winter Haven, Florida. Similar attractions were established in many locations.

World War II inhibited recreational activities like water skiing that used fuel needed for the war effort. After the war, however, water skiing experienced steady and continued growth. It remained primarily an amateur sport, with trophies awarded more often than prize money. Many expert water skiers made a living by teaching, participating in shows, or holding other jobs connected to the sport. Professional competitive water skiing tours and events were eventually established, but the amateur emphasis remained. The distinction between amateur and professional aspects of the sport has been an ongoing debate.

Water skiing continued to grow and become more diverse in the decades after 1970. In part this reflected the overall popularity of the sport of powerboating. Enthusiasts continued to accomplish new speed and distance records and to perform ever-more-spectacular stunts. New variations of water skiing were also devised. These included activities that combined water skiing with elements of other sports such as hang-gliding and surfing. Both males and females participate in waterskiing on a recreational and competitive level. Tournaments and series often include categories for males, females, and mixed-gender events.

## Practice

In the basic form of water skiing, the skier uses two skis and holds a horizontal bar connected to the end of the tow rope, which is attached to the motorboat. The tow rope is typically 23 meters (75 feet) long, although the ropes vary in length depending on the particular activity. There are several basic ways to start a run. In a basic beach start, the skier crouches in the water with arms forward and knees close to the chest, with the lower legs placed so the ski tips are raised out of the water. As the boat moves forward, the skis are pulled and lifted straight onto the water's surface. The skier rises to a standing position and is pulled along. Variations include the dock-start, in which the skier begins by sitting on a dock and is pulled into the water as the boat starts forward.

The minimum sustained speed for water skiing begins at around 24 kilometers per hour (15 miles per hour). As water skiers become more proficient and confident, they can be towed at increasing speeds. In 1983, Christopher Michael Massey, an Australian, established a water-ski speed record of more than 230 kilometers (144 miles) per hour.

Once beginning skiers are able to maintain balance while riding straight behind the boat, they can progress to turning independently of the boat and making other movements. Water skiers control their runs in various ways, including how they bend their legs; lean forward, backward, and from side to side; hold and tug the tow rope; and shift their weight and position in other ways. One basic move is crossing the wake, which is accomplished by attaining the momentum to swing beyond the waves that fan out behind both sides of the boat. In a more exaggerated form, this is known as wake jumping. Water skiers may advance to using only one ski and to more difficult and specialized tricks, jumps, and other challenging activities.

The design of basic skis emphasize stability and ease of handling. They are often between 1.5 and 1.8 meters (60 and 70 inches) long and come in pairs, with a binding that holds the foot securely but releases quickly to protect skiers if they fall or lose control. There are many other variations and types of water skis for specific purposes. Advanced slalom skiers use single skis with two sets of bindings, one for each foot. Skis designed for stunts and other purposes may be shorter or more rounded. Other types of skis include the kneeboard, which is ridden in a kneeling position, and boards that are ridden without bindings (similar to a surfboard).

Many types of powerboats are used to tow water skiers. On a purely recreational level, a variety of general-purpose motorboats are suitable. However, certain characteristics are important. Boats should have an appropriate size, body design, and engine that has enough power to tow a person, but that does not create an excessive wake or overwhelm the skier in other ways. Certain powerboats are designed specifically for water skiing and are used by dedicated amateurs and in organized competitions and professional shows. The type of boat used is especially critical in competitions to ensure that the performances of individual skiers are based on their own abilities and are not the result of differences among towboats. The AWSA, for example, has very stringent criteria for boats that can be used in sanctioned events to ensure consistency, performance, and safety.

Safety is an important concern, especially in the more advanced aspects of the sport, in which skiers travel at high speeds and perform flips and other potentially dangerous moves. Flotation vests are encouraged for all skiers, and helmets and other protective gear are often used in addition. Water skiing clubs and events have strict guidelines for events to promote safety. Coordination between the driver and skier is crucial, and hand signals or verbal cues are often used to communicate. In many instances, a third person, or "spotter," also rides in the boat to watch the skier and make sure the driver is aware of his status.

Most often, water skiing has one person being towed by an individual boat. However, a boat may tow two or more people simultaneously. In water shows, for example, a team of performers may form a line with a single boat towing them. In 1986, the cruising vessel *Reef Cat* towed 100 water skiers simultaneously for one nautical mile in Queensland, Australia.

Individual competitions and overall rankings of competitive water skiers are based on age and gender, in addition to categories for specific events. Competitions are often organized by local clubs and are sanctioned and based on guidelines from national organizations and the WWSU. Traditionally, competitive water skiing tournaments feature three main competitions: slalom, tricks, and jumping.

In the slalom event, skiers maneuver back and forth on a course marked with buoys (usually six), while the boat follows a straight line down the middle. During the event the boat speed is increased and the tow rope shortened, which makes runs successively difficult. The ability of the skier to get as close as possible to all of the buoys during the run without missing one or falling is scored.

In trick skiing, the competitors ski on a straight course and perform as many stunts as they can within their designated time (usually two 20-second passes). A panel of judges scores their performance based on the difficulty of their routines and their skill in executing them. Trick skiing can include a wide variety of moves, such as twirling in the water, removing skis while in motion, and flipping out of the water.

In jumping, skiers go up an inclined ramp in the water, which launches them into the air. In addition to maintaining good form and control, skiers attempt to extend the length of the jump as far as possible before landing on the water. The standard ramp is approximately 1.8 meters (6 feet) high out of the water at its highest point for men's adult competition and 1.5 meters (5 feet) for others. During the history of jumping, the distance records have gotten progressively longer. In 1947, a distance-jumping record was set at 15 meters (49 feet). By the 1990s, skiers were achieving jumps of 60 meters (200 feet) and longer.

The sport also encompasses more specialized competitions. Freestyle jumping emerged in competition after the 1950s. In freestyle, jumpers add mid-air flips and other variations to the basic jump. Barefoot skiing was introduced publicly as a stunt at Cypress Gardens in 1947 and has since developed into a separate branch of the sport, with competitions and other events. In 1989, Scott M. Pellaton achieved a barefoot skiing speed record of almost 219 kilometers (136 miles) per hour. In 1978, Billy Nichols established a barefoot duration record by skiing for 2 hours, 42 minutes, and 39 seconds. In 1989, Steve Fontaine skied backward for just over 1 hour and 27 minutes. Barefoot skiing and jumping were combined into an event known as barefoot jumping, and competitors have made jumps of over 26 meters (86 feet).

In the 1950s water skiing shows began to feature a stunt in which a water skier was connected to a large kite, which created air currents that carried him aloft as the boat gained speed. This facet of the sport gained popularity in the 1970s. A cousin of hang-gliding and parachuting, it has been referred to by several names, including parasailing, paragliding, and kite skiing. Although safety and insurance-liability concerns inhibited its acceptance in sanctioned water skiing competitions in the 1980s, parasailing became popular among recreational water skiers. In the 1990s, a variation of this emerged in which water skiers attach tow lines to kites, which pull the skier along on the water.

In the 1980s and 1990s, a hybrid of powerboating and water skiing became popular that involved motorized craft known as personal watercraft, jet-skis, and other names. They are very small and are driven in a manner somewhat similar to water skiing, but they are self-propelled. Jet-skis are very fast and maneuverable. In some instances, when riders have acted irresponsibly, jet-skis have prompted concern and criticism about noise and other disruptions to other boats and the environments where they are used.

—John Townes

**Bibliography:** *Water Skier.* (1989) AWSA 50th Anniversary Edition (American Water Ski Association, Winter Haven, FL).

*A Profile of Water Skiing in the United States.* (1994) Winter Haven, FL: American Water Ski Association.

Overton, Kristi. (1995) "Kristi's Top Tips." *Motor Boating & Sailing Magazine* 173, 5 (May): 12.

Youngs, Jim. (1994) "Ultimate Ski Boat Test." *Popular Mechanics* 171, 11 (November): 48.

# Skittles

**See** Bowls and Bowling

# Sled Dog Racing

Sled dog racing is a sport in which harnessed dog teams compete. A team is controlled by a driver, otherwise known as a musher, and the primary goal is to maximize either the distance covered or speed. Frequently, as with Alaska's Iditarod, the challenge is a brutal combination of the two involving hundreds of kilometers of ice and snow trails to be covered in a period of days.

## Origins and Development

European racing originated in Scandinavia, where competitions can be traced back to the eighteenth century. In North America the history of sled dog racing is more recent, with the late nineteenth century witnessing the first races. It is entirely possible that early competition grew out of rival groups of gold prospectors or fur trappers challenging one another to see who had the fastest sled and the best team of racing dogs.

The sport was then, and continues to be, a minor one with limited international appeal. It obviously lends itself to polar and subpolar regions. The first organized, as opposed to informal, race was the 1908 All-Alaskan Sweepstake, a round-trip race between the townships of Candle and Nome in Alaska. The distance was 656 kilometers (408 miles). The Hudson Bay Derby was instituted in 1916, followed seven years later by the Banff Alberta Dog Derby. In 1936 the Laconia Sled Dog Club of New Hampshire organized the first World Championship Derby. The International Sled Dog Racing Association was launched in 1966, which led to the development of a racing circuit. The most famous of these races is the Iditarod, inaugurated in 1973, which begins in Anchorage, Alaska, and crosses the Alaska Range, turns west along the Yukon river and continues up the Bering Sea coast to Nome. The race takes approximately eleven days.

While far removed from a sporting context, the role of sled dog teams in exploration (in particular, the exploration of the Antarctic) is of major importance. The progress of the Norwegian Roald Amundsen (1872–1928) and the Englishman Captain Robert Falcon Scott (1868–1912) toward the South Pole in late 1911 was seen by their respective nations, and by the world's press, as a race to be the first to reach the South Pole. Amundsen was the victor, reaching the South Pole on 14 December 1911. Scott and his party died tragically on the return journey, victims of starvation and the intense cold. Scott relied on ponies and primitive motor engines early on dur-

*Tim Osmar starts off on the 1994 Iditarod, the world's best-known sled dog race.*

ing his trek, and at the end he and his exhausted team manhandled their own equipment. By contrast, Amundsen's whole venture was planned around the use of dogs and sleds. In his team he had four companions and four light sledges each pulled by thirteen dogs.

Although Eskimos used dog sleds for hunting, travel, and recreation in the precolonial period, regulated and institutionalized sled dog races did not appear until the late nineteenth century. A major figure in introducing these dogs, and indirectly their sleds, into the mainstream of American life was the writer Jack London (1876–1916). By the age of 20 he had held down a variety of jobs. He had been a sailor, a tramp, and a Klondike adventurer. His appreciation of and insight into the dramatic countryside of the Alaskan gold rush popularized the perception of the "man in the wild" constantly battling the elements and surviving in a tough world. With his novels *The Call of the Wild* and *White Fang,* London described a wild dog (probably a composite of Siberian huskies or malamutes that he had seen) and explored notions of a dog being tamed and yet never escaping from its savage origins.

The event that catapulted sled dog racing onto the front pages of newspapers around the world was a 1925 diphtheria outbreak in the Alaskan township of Nome. Hundreds of people were at risk and could not be reached by road or air because of ground conditions and severe weather, and the only way to get serum to them was by dogsled. This dramatic situation received worldwide media coverage and stimulated sled dog racing in Canada and in northern New England.

In 1928 the *New York Times* reported extensively on the events and performances in the St. Moritz Olympics. Sandwiched between columns on skating and ice hockey was a report of a somewhat different contest. The report described a three-day, 198-kilometer (123-mile) sled dog race in which Emile St. Goddard's of the Pas, Manitoba, defeated Leonard Seppala of Nome, Alaska. The race consisted of three separate sections, with one taking place each day. To give some idea of the closeness of the competition at the start of the third and final day, St. Goddard's lead over Seppala was a minuscule 40 seconds. As the race ended St. Goddard's margin of victory had increased to 3 minutes, 10 seconds. In light of the repeated successes by Iditarod female mushers in the 1980s and 1990s it is intriguing to see the newspaper report of the 1928 contest. The tenor of the piece is in keeping with the social climate of the time: a gentlemanly concern for the competitive female, liberally sprinkled with admonitions about the overwhelming nature of such physical challenges.

> "Mrs. Edward P. Ricker Jr. of Poland Spring, Maine, did not start the last day. She is the only woman who ever had courage or skill to enter this race against the best men drivers of the continent. Two of her dogs tired last night and she dropped out to save them" (*New York Times*, 23 February 1928).

## Practice

In recent years the Iditarod has become the most widely recognized of all sled dog races. Nevertheless, to see sled dog racing only through the medium of the Iditarod spectacular is erroneous.

## Susan Butcher: Living Dangerously

In 1989 the Public Broadcasting System in the United States produced a documentary entitled *Living Dangerously*. It examined the career of legendary sled dog racer Susan Butcher and explored the subculture of Iditarod mushers. Of particular relevance was a segment in which Butcher described her lifestyle, her commitment to her dogs, and how she trained them. She spoke of living in a compound with 160 dogs, of whom 60 were puppies. She describes a typical working day in which six hours must be devoted to watering and feeding her Alaskan huskies.

Butcher's success has frequently been attributed to her intensity and her ability to direct all of her energies toward one happening—the Iditarod. In Butcher's own words a great musher is one whose primary goal is "to relate to the dogs." For herself the passion of life is "dogs and the wilderness."

When her dogs are puppies Butcher rears them on long recreational cross-country rambles (walks). The philosophy is to give her dogs the thrill and excitement of being with her (and their teammates) as they explore unfamiliar ground. Her credo is to shape animals into a "race hungry" unit. With no snow on the ground in the summer and fall Butcher trains by getting her dogs to pull an all-terrain vehicle. She is constantly on the lookout for championship qualities: endurance, speed, and above all "character." "The great dog is all heart and will never give up," she says. In December she trains her dogs by trial sled dog journeys of 40 to 120 kilometers (25 to 75 miles) a day. By March Butcher has narrowed down her choices from 50 to 20 and has the nucleus of her Iditarod team.

The PBS documentary special captures the incredible demands on musher and dogs as the race nears its conclusion. The temperature is –40°F (–72°C), the faces of the mushers are caked with frozen snow, and they begin to stumble with the combination of fatigue and sleep deprivation. The dogs can grind out a pace of only 11 kilometers per hour (7 miles per hour), and the analogy at the end of the race is of mushers, and dogs, like boxers at the end of fifteen bruising rounds, in a nether world of pain and collapse at the very limits of human and animal endurance.

—Scott A. G. M. Crawford

In 1977-1978 there were 200 sled dog races worldwide for a total prize money of $250,000. For that year, the champion musher was a 44-year-old Athabascan Native American named George "Muhammad" Attla.

The most exciting contest in 1978 was the Iditarod. After more than two weeks of racing Dick Macky won by less than a dog's length over Rick Swenson, one of the most minute gaps ever between victor and vanquished. Sprints and horse races are frequently judged according to a photograph, but this takes place after activities that last only seconds or minutes. In the 1978 Iditarod, after nearly 15 days of racing the gap between first and second was one second! Many sled dog races count only periods of racing time and not rest intervals, so the musher and more importantly the dog teams are provisioned and rested. The World Championship Sled Dog Derby of 1978 (held in Laconia, New Hampshire) was based on unlimited teams and the time for three 28-kilometer (17.5-mile) runs, that is, a total distance of 84 kilometers (52.5 miles). The time of the 1978 winner was 3 hours, 13 minutes, 4 seconds.

Sled dog teams are traditionally composed of Siberian or Alaskan huskies. The numbers of dogs used varies, but it is common to see 7 or 9 in a team. With the Iditarod, as many as 16 may be used. While racing sleds are incredibly light they must be strongly constructed and able to carry equipment, provisions, or a sick or fatigued dog.

Sled dog race courses are marked red and green. Red flags indicate a turn. Green flags means that there is a straightway. Teams are inspected approximately 10 minutes before the start. Great attention is paid to make certain that the animals are neither sick nor injured and are "up to scratch" for the onerous demands of the competition. The International Sled Dog Racing Association, which governs the sport, has acknowledged the amazing metabolism of a racing husky: "A sled dog at rest in the summer needs about 800 calories per day. In the middle of a cold winter's long distance race the same dog may need up to 10,000 calories per day" (International Sled Dog Racing Association 1995).

—Scott A. G. M. Crawford

**Bibliography:** Brown, G., ed. (1979) *New York Times Encyclopedia of Sports—Winter Sports.* Danbury, CT: Grolier.

Cuddon, J. A. (1979) *International Dictionary of Sports and Games.* New York: Schocken Books.

Diagram Group. (1982) *Sports Comparisons.* New York: St. Martin's Press.

Hickok, R. (1992) *The Encyclopedia of North American Sports History.* New York: Facts on File.

International Sled Dog Racing Association. (1995) Various informational brochures.

*Living Dangerously.* (1989) Public Broadcasting System (documentary film).

Royal Norwegian Consulate General, New York. (1995) Various pamphlets and information documents.

Smith, N. L. (1979) *Almanac of Sports and Games.* New York: Facts on File.

Woolum, J. (1992) *Outstanding Women Athletes.* Phoenix, AZ: Oryx Press.

# Sledding

See Bobsledding; Luge; Sled Dog Racing; Tobogganing

# Snooker

See Billiards

# Snowboarding

Snowboarding, the art of standing upright on a board and maneuvering it across snow, is widespread in skiing regions throughout the world. It is even practiced in areas without mountains; in England snowboarders ride "dry slopes"—hills covered with plastic mats that replicate the characteristics of hard pack snow. However, bans on snowboarding remain in place in parts of Europe and North America, a legacy of the widespread prohibitions in the 1970s and 1980s. Snowboarding has influenced culture beyond the ski field through its distinct clothing and music.

Alternative youth subcultures and other boardriders shaped the development of snowboarding. The advent of snowboarding in the

*The daredevil sport of snowboarding combines elements of surfing and skateboarding. Preconceptions of these sports as "anti-social" has led to bans on snowboarding in certain ski areas.*

1960s saw the inculcation of a set of values and philosophies of the new leisure movement, a group of youths whose leisure was based around freedom, cooperation, fun, and hedonism. These values and philosophies, which attracted later youth subcultures to the activity, remain largely intact today and are at the center of controversies over snowboarding.

The first mass-produced snowboard came on the market in 1966. The snow surfer, or "Snurfer," was little more than a large skateboard. A hand-held rope provided steering and gave the rider some control over speed while the deck was covered with staples to give the rider's feet traction. While the Snurfer was sold as a toy, the new leisure movement of the 1960s saw its potential as serious recreational equipment. This movement involved individualistic, self-expressive, and cooperative activities that placed emphasis on fun and personal growth rather than winning.

Snurfers were notoriously difficult to control and consequently commercial ski fields banned the "dangerous" Snurfer. Snowboarding transferred to the backcountry, where it developed a cult following.

Surfers and skateboarders had considerable influence on snowboarding. Surfing's initial influence led to popular perceptions of snowboarding as a variant of surfing. Its close connection with surfing partly explains the ban on "snurfing." Surfers were viewed as social misfits and subversives, largely due to their carefree and hedonistic lifestyles. The counterculture and "soul-surfing" in the late 1960s and early 1970s further fueled negative perceptions of board riders. Snurfers were dangerous and restricted on ski slopes for good reason, yet while technological advances quickly overcame the limitations of the Snurfer in the mid-1970s, the ban remained in place.

In the late 1970s skateboarding began to affect snowboarding. At this time punk, an antisocial subculture involving extremes of fashion, music, and attitudes, adopted skateboarding. Punk "skaters" viewed ski slopes as the terrain of the yuppie. However, some professional skateboarders saw snowboarding as an appealing activity and promoted it to other skaters. Snowboarding simultaneously became "surfing on snow" and *the* winter activity for skaters.

In 1983 some ski areas began opening their slopes to snowboarders. The majority soon followed. Skiing had reached a growth plateau and snowboarding offered ski areas a new youth market and economic potential, although this meant tolerating the countercultural and punk dimensions of snowboarders. It is from this point that snowboarding became popular.

By the 1990s skateboarding and snowboarding had developed a close relationship. Snowboarders adopted skaters' aggressive riding styles and their distinct fashions and attitudes; the latter were designed to shock. Skating also brought to snowboarding the styles and politics of "hiphop," an urban black style of music and fashion. Skateboarding's influence dismayed many older snowboarders; they had worked hard to gain the public's—and particularly ski area operators'—acceptance and wanted to cast a better image of responsibility.

Complicating this tension was the fracturing of snowboarding into three distinct styles in the late 1980s: freestyling (influenced by skateboarding), alpine (largely influenced by skiing and surfing), and freeriding (a combination of both styles practiced on all slopes). The most noticeable tension among snowboarders is between freeriders and freestylers, and alpine snowboarders. The former dismiss the disciplined approach of alpine riders, referring to them as skiers on boards. In North America, freeriders make up around 40 percent of snowboarders, freestylers nearly 50 percent, and alpine riders less than 10 percent. In Europe, however, alpine riders make up around 40 percent. The absence of strong surfing and skateboarding traditions in Europe, combined with a stronger skiing tradition, probably explains the differences.

The debates within the snowboarding community spilled over into skiing. A small number of disruptive riders, exacerbated by a media frenzy, led several ski areas to re-ban snowboarding. However, the majority of ski area managements are trying to accommodate snowboarders and

reconcile both groups. Ski areas are caught between catering to the economic potential of snowboarding and the economic reality, which is that skiers are the main source of income.

Throughout the 1990s snowboarding has experienced phenomenal growth. This follows the commodification of an underground youth style called "grunge." Grunge youth oppose the high consumption and competitiveness of yuppie culture. Accordingly, they favor secondhand clothes and cooperative recreational games and activities such as snowboarding. Certain youth subcultures, such as grunge, act as "testing grounds" for new styles, which big businesses involved in the selling of youth styles then appropriate. This commercialization of grunge helps explain why snowboarding and skateboarding are so trendy.

The current rate of growth is such that even conservative projections suggest that snowboarders will outnumber skiers by 2012. At present snowboarders constitute just over 10 percent of ski area users in North America.

The dramatic growth of snowboarding in the 1990s has prompted the governing bodies of skiing to reappraise snowboarding. The Fédération Internationale du Ski (FIS) formed a snowboarding committee largely, it seems, to take advantage of snowboarding's popularity and its potential inclusion in future Winter Olympic Games. Battle lines were drawn when the International Olympic Committee recognized the FIS over snowboarding's own governing body—the International Snowboarding Federation (ISF). Most competitive snowboarders, and also many noncompetitive riders, support the ISF in what they consider to be a hostile takeover by skiers. Snowboarders fear the loss of their identity and want to remain independent of skiers. The struggle is ongoing. But the strong punk influence in snowboarding means that most snowboarders will probably follow their own path, ignoring competitive snowboarders, the ISF/FIS debate, and even the prospect of Olympic snowboarding.

—Duncan Humphreys

**Bibliography:** Humphreys, Duncan. (1996) "Snowboarders: Bodies out of Control and in Conflict." *Sporting Traditions,* forthcoming.

Werner, Doug. (1993) *Snowboarder's Start-Up.* Ventura, CA: Pathfinder.

# Snowshoe Racing

Snowshoe racing is of recent origin, although snowshoes themselves are ancient. It is clear that most snowshoeing has been of a utilitarian nature, enabling people to work and travel in snowy conditions. While informal racing is probably as old as the snowshoe itself, serious racing has only emerged within the past 30 years. Races are held either on groomed trails, as for most Nordic ski events, or on unbroken snow.

Future development of the sport will depend heavily on how courses are chosen. Snowshoe racing could become a sort of handicapped running event, over packed trails. On the other hand, it could create a form that preserves aspects of the traditional challenge the snowshoe was originally designed to address: how can humans most efficiently move across a naturally snow blanketed environment?

## Origins

It is not known precisely when the snowshoe was developed. This is not surprising, given that snowshoes until recently have been crafted out of wood, leather, and vegetable fibers: biodegradable materials that do not show up often in the archaeological record. The best evidence, though, is that snowshoes have been used for the past 6,000 years, primarily by Amerindian peoples. Although there is some evidence that the snowshoe was developed in Central Asia, it never gained any real popularity there.

Informal races have probably taken place for centuries, but for most of its historical career the snowshoe has had a primarily utilitarian life. The trappers, hunters, and explorers of North America all made use of snowshoes, and during the French and Indian wars, soldiers occasionally fought on snowshoes, or at least used them in moving from one camp to another.

## Development

As a form of recreation, snowshoeing in Canada came into its own with "snowshoe clubs." These clubs, some of them 200 years old, were popular among both French and English speaking populations, but more so among French Canadians. A number of the Quebec clubs are still active, though not as much as in the past. The clubs were originally tied to communities, churches, guilds, and military units; as these institutions have loosened their hold on social life, the role of the club has declined.

In 1907, the Canadian Snowshoer's Union was founded, a loose confederation of clubs. The union, though, never made a serious effort to transform snowshoeing from a recreation into a more competitive sport. Some snowshoe clubs, primarily among people of French ancestry, were formed in the United States and were found throughout New England and in New York. These, like the Canadian clubs, were primarily recreational, organizing only informal races.

In the 1970s, though, two things began to happen. First, the snowshoe went through a process of drastic redesign, which reduced size and weight and allowed for the use of a real racing stride. Second, athletes from other sports, primarily running and Nordic skiing, began to look for new ways to cross-train, keep fit, or enjoy themselves during the winter months. Snowshoeing was a natural option.

The long tradition of "social snowshoeing" continues in Quebec and New England, and racing in the east has taken on a more competitive edge since 1988, when the first "North American Snowshoe Classic" was run. The newest centers of snowshoe racing, though, are in Wisconsin and Minnesota and in Colorado and the neighboring mountain states. The races are increasingly more organized and competitive, which is not to say that they have no recreational qualities. The chief innovation has involved changes in the design of the snowshoe itself.

The traditional snowshoe was primarily a snow flotation device and, as such, not suited for high speed. Traditional snowshoes were as large as 36 by 122 centimeters (14 by 48 inches) and as heavy as 2.7 kilograms (6 pounds) apiece. Obviously, such shoes are not appropriate for the development of a racing movement, and even the smaller traditional shoes produce a tendency to waddle rather than stride over the snow.

Beginning in the middle 1960s, when aluminum and other alloy frames were introduced, weight has been reduced greatly, and the size of

*Women begin a sprint event during the two-day International Snowshoe Convention in Ottawa in 1948, an event attended by 4,000 snowshoers from New England and Canada.*

the shoe has become smaller as well. For racing, it is now generally accepted that a shoe can be no less than 20 centimeters (8 inches) wide and no shorter than 64 centimeters (25 inches) long. This size allows considerable flotation, yet it is small enough to accommodate a stride that is more like that of a modern runner than that of a heavily laden trapper. The new shoes have completely replaced wooden snowshoes in the modern races.

The deck of the racing shoe has also changed. It is no longer webbed but solid, and generally made from rubberized or other treated nylon. The deck is no longer attached to the frame with rawhide lacing, but riveted or clipped to it. This has the effect of preserving some of the flotation qualities of snowshoes while reducing overall

size. In fact, many modern racers hold that the traditional snowshoe was too massively constructed. It not only weighed too much at the start of a trek, but it was apt to weigh ever more as it picked up snow on the platform, particularly in fast and/or wet conditions.

Most modern shoes also feature a cleat at the toe or ball of the foot, and some are cleated at the heel as well. The overall result is a much lighter and smaller shoe, with improved climbing ability, that still allows a certain amount of controlled sliding on down slopes. All of this is anathema to the traditionalist, who appreciates the craftsmanship and beauty of the older shoes, with their steamed and bent wooden frames and woven decks. However, the inescapable fact is that the new shoes, while possibly less suited to the heavy utilitarian tasks traditionally asked of snowshoes, are better suited to racing. Binding, with the new shoes, seems to be still be in a state of evolution. Many of the best racers simply lace regular running shoes to the snowshoe.

Some of the main "modern style" races are the John Beargrease in Duluth, Minnesota—a marathon of 25 kilometers run in conjunction with a dogsled race of the same name—and the Birkebeiner in Northern Wisconsin, associated with the prestigious cross-country ski event. There is also an annual event now being run on one of the original sections of the famous Alaskan Iditarod. Obviously, these races are "piggy-backing" to some extent on other events and sports but increasingly, and especially in Colorado, snowshoe races are holding their own as competitive venues.

Colorado certainly offers much to the snowshoe racer. There is plenty of snow, on the one hand, and plenty of snowshoe history on the other. In the mountain town of Leadville, for instance, the name of Father Dyer, the "Snowshoe Preacher," is well known. In the late 1800s, Dyer became famous for making a weekly trek between Fairplay and Leadville over the 13,000 foot Mosquito Pass. Dyer's snowshoeing combined the utilitarian—he was also a mail carrier—with the spiritual—he preached in both towns. Now, it seems, folk in the Colorado Rockies are preaching the recreational—and competitive—aspects of the pastime.

There are several dozen races held in Colorado every year, most of them sponsored by local running clubs who have taken an interest or by snowshoe manufacturers. One of the questions about the future of such events has to do with the most appropriate course conditions. When the "modern" phase of snowshoe racing first began—and it is only some 12 to 15 years old—many races were run on groomed tracks. This led to the feeling, and not only among "traditionalists," that snowshoe racing might end up losing all its distinctiveness and become merely a sort of handicapped running activity.

On the other hand, races through unbroken snow were also problematic. When such races were staged, a typical strategy was simply to "hang back" while the leaders broke a more manageable path through the snow and then to capitalize on this in a sprint at the end. However, in an attempt to do away with this sort of "laggard's advantage," some recent races have featured a sequence of "primes," rather like in cycling races, to improve the ambitions of the pack. It is perhaps too early to tell, but for several years now there have been ten kilometer races over unbroken snow staged near Leadville, Colorado, and the ranks of both participants and spectators have grown.

At a recent conference held near Lake Saranac, New York, enthusiasts considered an Olympic future for their activity. Snowshoeing is clearly "North American," with eastern Canadians, generally, sticking to tradition and socialization—together with some of their U.S. neighbors—and western Americans working very hard to make the sport more competitive, perhaps even "professional." Thus far, little progress has been made in bringing together any sort of international campaign to popularize this as yet minor form of winter racing. On the other hand, American snowshoe companies report that sales of new-style shoes are picking up, not only in North America but also in Scandinavia and Japan.

—Alan Trevithick

**See also** Skiing, Nordic.

**Bibliography:** Bauer, Erwin A. (1975) *Cross-Country Skiing and Snowshoeing.* New York: Winchester Press.

Osgood, William, and Leslie Hurley. (1975) *The Snowshoe Book.* 2d ed. Brattleboro, VT: Stephan Greene Press.

# Soaring

Soaring—also called "gliding" by some people—dates from the 1800s. The two terms, however, are quite different. Both are practiced by individuals who either fly for the sheer personal enjoyment of powerless flight (gliding), or who compete as either individuals or members of teams in local, regional, national and international glider competition (soaring). Many pilots do both.

*The charm of soaring—gliding in an airplane with no engine—lies in taking advantage of existing air currents to stay aloft as long as possible. Updrafts are the "fuel" of gliders.*

## Origins and Development

The theory of soaring—and thus the sport itself—dates to the time man first saw birds flying without flapping their wings. Babylonian cave etchings and Greek mythology both tell tales of man's dream to fly. The papers of Leonardo da Vinci from the fifteenth century contain sketches and reflections on various kinds of flying apparatus, including parachutes.

While balloons were the first devices to provide man with the means to fly, it was in 1848 that Sir George Cayley, an eminent British scientist, is credited with having designed and built the first successful heavier-than-air device, a glider said to have carried a ten-year-old boy several yards after its launching from a hill. Although work of various kinds continued in the interim, from the 1890s onward, research and development of gliders, flying techniques, and similar subjects were being notably pursued in Germany, England, and the United States.

In the 1890s, Germany's Otto Lilienthal is reported to have made over 2,000 short duration and distance flights. He was the first man to fly a distance of over 100 meters (approximately 330 feet) in 1891. About that same time, Orville and Wilbur Wright in the United States and Percy Pilcher of England were working on similar glider developments. The little-known John Montgomery, living near San Diego, California, also conducted experiments during that period, and is purported to have even flown before Lilienthal. Montgomery is credited with a nine-minute unpowered flight that broke a record established earlier by the Wright brothers.

Lilienthal, Pilcher, and Montgomery all died in glider accidents during those early years. They and the Wright brothers were contemporaries of Octave Chanute, who at 60 years of age in 1896 took his first of a reported 2,000 flights without an accident. During the fall of 1902 alone, the Wright brothers are reported to have made over 1,000 glider flights, many involving turns and distances of over 183 meters (200 yards), before their first powered flight in 1903.

World War I brought a halt to glider development as the world's powers went to war. When it ended, however, the prohibition on powered flight in Germany by the Treaty of Versailles prompted enormous progress in the development of soaring flight. Three thousand German schoolboys are said to have been enrolled in glider instruction during 1928 alone. Throughout the 1920s and early 1930s, Germans dominated world gliding. Wolfgang Klemperer was the first to fly over 1,000 meters (1,094 yards) in 1920, and Robert Kronfeld set the world distance record of 100 kilometers (62 miles) in the late 1920s.

Richard DuPont of the United States held the world distance record of 248 kilometers (154 miles) in 1934. By the late 1930s the record was 557 kilometers (346 miles). The first world championships were held at Wasserkuppe, Germany, in 1937. Progress continued, but was slowed again during World War II when military applications of gliding forced sport flying into the background.

From then until now, the sport has flourished and several countries boast aggressive, healthy soaring programs. As of this writing, over 5,500 pilots throughout the world have earned diamond badges and over 150 have now flown flights farther than 1,000 kilometers (620 miles).

## What Makes a Glider Fly

Understanding the sport of soaring first requires basic comprehension of how a glider—an airplane without an engine—flies through the atmosphere. Air flows over the wings of a glider in much the same way as it flows over the wings of a powered airplane, which is propelled through the air by the force of its engine. A glider, however, has no engine. Glider flight can be achieved only by descending the glider, speeding it up, and causing air to flow around its wings and tail surfaces. In gliding flight, therefore, a glider (or sailplane, as it is often called) is always descending, usually at a rate of between 45 and 90 meters (150 and 300 feet) per minute in still air.

The acceleration of air over the wings of the glider produces a lifting force that counterbalances the weight of the glider and actually slows down its rate of descent. Were it not for the force of "lift," gliders would go straight down. Instead,

they follow predictable "glide ratios." Glide ratio is a measure of how far a sailplane will travel forward (horizontal distance) for each foot of altitude it loses (vertical distance). A 40:1 glide ratio, for instance, means that a glider could travel (in still air, with no updrafts or downdrafts) 40 kilometers over the ground for each kilometer of altitude above the ground. Depending on design and condition, modern sailplanes have glide ratios in the order of 20:1 to 60:1, or 20 to 60 meters forward for every one meter downwards. Older gliders generally have steeper glide slopes.

Glider pilots are taught to fly at very specific speeds to obtain the performance expected of their gliders. Flying at "best glide speed" will allow a glider to go the greatest distance possible over the ground. Flying at "minimum sink speed," usually *slower* than the best glide speed, allows the glider to stay in the air for the longest possible time—but not glide the farthest distance.

Even though some gliders are capable of loops, rolls, and other aerobatic maneuvers that enable them to climb for short periods—rather than to continually descend—it is important to remember that a glider, in gliding flight, is always descending.

## Soaring as a Sport

There is a difference between gliding and soaring—and that's what makes soaring a sport. Automobiles travel across continents and airplanes continue to fly by stopping periodically to refuel. What makes soaring a sport is the challenge to the pilot of finding and utilizing ascending air currents to keep the glider aloft—to cause it to climb faster than it is descending (which it always is)—so that height, distance, or flight durations can be achieved that are not possible in "still air." Updrafts are the fuel of gliders, so to speak.

The trick is for the pilot to "refuel" the glider along its route of flight, to find air currents that will enable the glider to stay up so that it can go farther, faster, and higher and fly longer than it otherwise could. Pilots who excel at being able to find and use the invisible ascending currents better than others are the champions and record holders. It is they who reap the full enjoyment of solitary soaring flight. They win contests because they make their aircraft perform better than their competitors.

# Classifications of Gliders

At the time of this writing, there are three classes of gliders generally recognized in world competition: Open, 15-meter, and Standard. A fourth type of glider, the so-called "World Class" glider, has been internationally classified but it has yet to be built or compete on any widespread basis.

## Open Class Gliders

The only specification that currently exists for this category of machine is that its maximum weight cannot exceed 750 kilograms (approximately 1700 pounds). Open class gliders typically have wingspans of about 25 meters (slightly over 87 feet) and a maximum glide ratio of about 60 feet forward for every foot down, or 60:1.

## 15-Meter Class

These gliders have maximum wingspans of 15 meters (almost 50 feet) and a maximum weight of 525 kilograms (slightly less than 1200 pounds). These gliders have control devices called flaps that enable them to fly a more controlled approach for landing and enhance performance in other ways, depending on design. The maximum glide ratio of most 15-meter Class gliders is about 45:1.

## Standard Class Gliders

Standard class gliders are similar to 15-meter class gliders except that their performance is more restricted. In particular, flaps are not permitted and standard class ships have a maximum glide ratio of about 42:1.

## World Class Gliders

Very recently, a "World Class" glider design has been approved by world gliding authorities. It is hoped that such a design will result in a simple, cheap, easy-to-fly glider that can be economically produced in many countries. Competition is planned for this glider in the 1997 World Air Games, scheduled to be conducted in Turkey.

# Methods of Launching Gliders

Only motorgliders have engines that enable them to take off under their own power. Other types of gliders are incapable of independently propelling themselves through the air with sufficient force to attain flying speed, normally 30–40 miles per hour. To create airflow over the wings, it is necessary to apply some outside initial force to get the glider moving at sufficient speed so adequate airflow passes around the wings to overcome the force of gravity and cause it to fly.

Many different methods have been used through the years to provide this speed. Among them have been: pushing gliders down the slopes of hills until airflow over the wings is sufficient to produce flight; dropping heavy weights on the ends of ropes to pull them into the air; pulling them with elastic-like ropes and "slingshotting" them to flying speed; pulling them into the air on long cables reeled in by engine-driven mechanical winches; pulling them into the air on ropes behind automobiles; and hooking them behind airplanes that take off and pull the glider to an altitude from which gliding flight can begin.

The Wright brothers launched their early gliders using the slopes of sand dunes near the Atlantic Ocean. There are even accounts of "shoulder launches" on occasions, where the speed of the wind approximated the flying speed of the glider as assistants held the machine aloft and ran with it into the wind until it flew!

Most gliding in the United States today starts with the glider being towed by a rope attached to a powered airplane. The technique is called "aerotow." An important skill required of glider pilots using this form of launch is the ability to fly safely and smoothly behind the towplane as it ascends until glider release altitude has been reached.

# Types of Gliding

Once a glider reaches sufficient airspeed and altitude to sustain itself, the glider pilot normally pulls a release handle in the glider cockpit, the towing rope is released, and the glider is in free flight. If sufficient "lift" to sustain flight is not found rather quickly, the glider will usually be forced to land within a matter of minutes.

The objective—and sport—for the glider pilot is to "soar" rather than to "glide." Soaring involves finding parcels of air going up at a greater rate than the glider is going down. As previously stated, most gliders naturally descend at between 45 and 90 meters (150 and 300 feet) per minute. There are several methods of remaining aloft. All involve pilot skill and knowledge in finding air currents rising at a greater rate than the glider's "built in" rate of descent. They are generally categorized as thermaling, ridge flying, mountain wave flying, and land and sea breeze flying. An additional source of life can be obtained by flying under or near newly developing cumulus clouds that owe their formation and sustenance to the updrafts found directly underneath them. In the early days of soaring, when little was understood about hazardous weather, pilots also used areas near (or inside) thunderstorms to propel themselves upward. That practice is recognized as extremely dangerous and little used in modern glider flying today. The safe rule is to avoid thunderstorms by a wide margin.

### Thermaling

Thermals or columns of rising air naturally occur at locations where the sun has heated surface geographical features to temperatures hotter than the surrounding terrain. Updrafts of warmer-than-normal air occur above these surface locations and parcels of air may be rising hundreds of feet per minute faster than surrounding air over these locations. This column of rising air is called a thermal. Sailplanes found in thermals will be lifted upwards, often thousands of feet. Entry into a thermal is normally indicated by an instrument in the glider that shows the speed of the rising air. The challenge of soaring in a thermal is to keep the glider in this narrow column of air by flying it in precise circles to maintain the greatest upward speed. The ability to repeatedly find these thermal updrafts, often extending thousands of feet up from the surface, allows skilled pilots to move from one thermal to another, increasing altitude with each thermal, thus enabling great distances, altitudes, and durations to be flown.

### Ridge Flying

Ridge flying entails pilots finding updrafts naturally produced when wind strikes the side of a vertical terrain feature such as a hill, mountain, or ridge line at an angle approximating 90 degrees. When that happens, updrafts are produced on the side of the obstruction from which the wind is blowing. A glider in these updrafts have flown in ridge "lift" without descending for hundreds of miles at great speeds. Flights of over 1,000 kilometers are not unusual in the strong ridge lift behind fast moving weather fronts.

### Mountain Wave Flying

Where strong winds are found near the world's great mountain ranges, strong lift is produced downwind of the mountains as they are struck by strong winds at near perpendicular angles. Gliders towed into these strong winds or which maneuver into them on their own frequently find strong lift. These winds can propel gliders tens of thousands of feet above the altitudes where they first encountered the mountain wave lift. Many world records have been produced, particularly in the United States where mountain wave phenomena exist and lend themselves to strong updrafts and great altitude gains. Attempts to fly in the mountain wave usually always entail special equipment such as heated clothing, supplementary oxygen and other high altitude precautions. Champion mountain wave flyers report there is nothing to compare with the views of a High Sierra or Rocky Mountain wave flight or the breathtaking views offered by the European Alps.

### Land and Sea Breeze Flying

Land and sea breezes are caused by wind changes near the shoreline that create differential temperatures of the land and sea at different times of the day. Glider pilots, like birds found gracefully gliding there, take advantage of these alternating sea and land breezes to soar into the headwinds they produce.

## Soaring Organizations

The world-wide popularity and prominence of air sports generally, and soaring specifically, has increased significantly in the last several decades. Some structure and uniformity in management was needed to promote development of the sport, foster progression of participants and devise accepted rules of competition among individual pilots and nations. As a result, most nations of the world in which any organized air sport is conducted have formed national Aero Clubs that represent their countries to the world ruling body for air sports, the Fédération Aeronautique Internationale (FAI), headquartered in Paris. Each sport has its own representation in the form of a group within the FAI made up of representatives from member nations participating in that sport. These groups make rules for their individual sports and administer their activities internationally. The representative group for soaring is the International Gliding Commission (IGC).

As the FAI's sole international agent for soaring, the IGC devises and publishes rules by which world soaring competitions are conducted, approves claims for glider world records, awards badges in recognition of skill and accomplishment by glider pilots, and otherwise administers international conduct of soaring as an air sport.

## World Competition

Each country involved in soaring, through its National Aero Club, the national soaring organization, local glider clubs, and commercial soaring enterprises, organizes and conducts local, regional, and national competitions to reward skill and select individuals to represent them in various levels of competition. Those who compete at the international level do so as representatives of their individual National Aero Clubs under the umbrella and sanction of the FAI.

The first world championship of soaring was conducted in 1937 at Wasserkuppe, Germany. No championships were conducted during World War II or shortly thereafter. In more recent times, during every odd calendar year, the FAI sanctions a World Gliding Championship for each of the three classes of gliders (Open, 15-meter, and Standard). The world contest is usually held over a three-week period, with the first week devoted to official practice and the last two weeks to actual competition. In 1995, 110 pilots from 25 nations competed at the world championships in New Zealand. Both individual and team champions were recognized in this world competition.

Individual phases of soaring competition are called "tasks." Each day at the world championship competition, for instance, pilots fly around a specifically assigned course comprised of carefully selected and clearly defined turn points on the ground. These turn points are the ends of airfield runways, prominent road intersections or other distinctly identifiable geographical landmarks over which competition pilots must precisely fly.

During world contests before 1995, pilots were required to photograph these turn points to prove they had flown the prescribed course. Beginning in 1995, however, pilots carried a "Data-Logger" that electronically recorded time, position and altitude, using signals received from satellites of the Global Positioning System (GPS).

When they are ready to begin the day's task, pilots fly over the landmark that defines the starting point. Then they fly each turn point, in order, until returning to the finish point. After flight, GPS data are downloaded into a computer for display, analysis, and scoring. The pilot with the fastest speed around the course is the daily winner. Other pilots are awarded points based on the ratio of their speeds to that of the winner. Points are accumulated over the course of the competition to determine the champion in each class: Open, 15-meter, and Standard.

Each team of participants represents the National Aero Club of its FAI member country. In 1995, team sizes varied from one to ten pilots. Each participating team has a manager who serves as team coach and leader. The more successful countries are those who are able to best fly as a team. After accounting for the differences in team sizes, performances are evaluated and national teams ranked in winning order.

## Levels of Accomplishment

The FAI has established international recognition for achievement of various milestones in glider flying. These are the Silver, Gold and Diamond badges, each signifying individual, documented and certified accomplishment for height attained, distance flown and duration achieved in soaring flight.

The FAI Silver Soaring Badge is the first level of international soaring recognition. Its accomplishment is intended to foster self-reliance in a new soaring pilot. The requirements for award of this badge are: completion of a flight of at least 50 kilometers (about 32 miles) over a straight course; an altitude gain of at least 1,000 meters (3250 feet); and a flight duration of at least five hours. The FAI Gold Badge requires: a distance flight of at least 300 kilometers (nearly 200 miles); an altitude gain of at least 3,000 meters (9,750 feet); and a flight duration of at least five hours. The highest of all FAI badges is the "Diamond

Badge." It is awarded for completion of three separate tasks: A flight, flown in designated turn point sequence, of at least 300 kilometers (almost 200 miles) over an out-and-return course; a flight of at least 500 kilometers (slightly over 320 miles); and an altitude gain of over 5,000 meters (16,250 feet).

The national soaring organizations of individual countries also have national awards given for specific accomplishments determined by each country. Awards may be made, for instance, to pilots who solo a glider, complete comprehensive written tests, perform accuracy landings to certain standards and perform to various prescribed levels in a variety of other skills. There may be other criteria as well.

—Walter D. Miller

**Bibliography:** Allen, R. C. Stafford. (1962) *Theory of Flight for Glider Pilots.* New York: Barnes & Noble.

Dank, Milton. (1977) *The Glider Gang.* Philadelphia: J. B. Lippincott.

Dixon, Peter. (1970) *Soaring.* New York: Ballantine Books.

Federal Aviation Agency. (1985) *Commercial Glider Pilot Practical Test Standards.* Washington, DC: Office of Flight Operations.

———. (1987) *Flight Instructor Practical Test Standards for Gliders.* Washington, DC: Office of Flight Standards.

———. (1987) *Private Glider Pilot Practical Test Standards.* Washington, DC: Office of Flight Standards.

Knauff, Thomas L. (1990) *Transition to Gliders.* Iceland: Prentsmidja Arna Valdemarssonar hf.

———. (1994) *Glider Basics from First Flight to Solo.* Iceland: Prentsmidja Arna Valdemarssonar hf.

Kronfeld, Robert. (undated) *Kronfeld on Gliding and Soaring.* London: John Hamilton.

Lowden, John. (1992) *Silent Wings at War.* Washington, DC: Smithsonian Institution Press.

McQuillen, John A., Jr. (1975) *American Military Gliders in World War II in Europe.* Ph.D. dissertation, St. Louis University.

National Aeronautic Association. (1995) *World and United States Aviation and Space Records.* Arlington, VA: National Aeronautic Association.

Piggott, Derek. (1977) *Understanding Gliding.* New York: Barnes & Noble.

Serjeant, Richard, and Alex Watson, eds. (1965) *The Gliding Book.* London: Nicholas Kaye.

Soaring Society of America. (1991) *SSA Membership Handbook.* Hobbs, NM: Soaring Society of America

Stewart, Ken. (1994) *The Glider Pilot's Manual.* UK: Airlife Publishing.

Weiss, J. Bernard. (n.d.) *Gliding and Soaring Flight.* London: Sampson Low, Marston.

Welch, Ann, and Lorne Welch. (1965) *The Story of Gliding.* London: John Murray.

Werner, Steve, and the editors of *Plane & Pilot* Magazine.

(1995) *The Plane & Pilot International Aircraft Directory.* Tabb Books.

Wills, Philip. (1974) *Free as a Bird.* New York: Barnes & Noble.

# Soccer

Soccer, or association football, may be called by many different names throughout the world—bollfoer in Finland, calcio in Italy, fussball in Austria, fútbol in Argentina, futebol in Brazil, labdarugó in Hungary, podosfairiki in Greece, soccer in the United States, and voetbal in the Netherlands—but the game remains essentially the same. In its organized form it is a game played between two teams of 11 players a side on a rectangular field not more than 110 meters (120 yards) long and usually 69–91 meters (75–100 yards) wide. Each side lines up in one half of the field facing each other, and the object of the game is to score a goal by kicking or heading (but not using the hands to propel) the ball over the opponent's goal line into a goal measuring 2.5 meters (8 feet) high and 7.3 meters (24 feet) wide. The team scoring the most goals wins. If the score is level, the result is a draw. The duration of the game is of two equal halves of 45 minutes. It is a simple game with only 17 laws, the most important of which deal with offside and the definition of and penalties for fouls and misconduct. Most of the laws evolved pragmatically in the last 40 years of the nineteenth century. Today, more men and women play and watch association football than any other sport. The world governing body, the Fédération Internationale de Football Associations (FIFA) has occasionally claimed more members than the United Nations. Its membership has increased from 7 in its foundation year of 1904 to 73 by 1950 and 170 in 1990. The World Cup, which FIFA organizes, is on a par with the Olympic Games as one of the world's most prestigious sporting events, televised in every country.

## Origins

Football games were found in most cultures, but the modern game was invented by the British in

*A midair collision between South Korea's Choi Soon-Ho and Argentina's Oscar Ruggeri as both attempt to head the ball during the 1986 World Cup competition in Mexico City.*

the nineteenth century. It was in Britain that the rules were codified, the first association football clubs were established, a regular calendar of fixtures was arranged, and competition was organized. The modern game was a by-product of the growth of the commercial, manufacturing, and professional middle class in Britain, especially that of the private secondary schools (known as public

schools) set up for the education of their sons. Organized games proved a way of providing discipline and identity among the boys via a system of houses such that, by the 1860s, team games in particular had become a defining characteristic of public schools, and the pursuit of physical fitness had become something of a cult. Games were also supposed to teach certain qualities of character, curbing rampant individualism in the cause of one's house and later school and, after that, club, region, and country. British public schools tended to develop their own unique forms of football. In order for interschool matches to be arranged and for the sport to be played at the university level and in the world outside education, there was need for a single rule book. This need began to be articulated by groups of young men in parts of the North of England, the Midlands, and particularly in London toward the end of the 1850s. Letters to sporting newspapers eventually produced a series of meetings in 1863, which led to the formation of the Football Association (FA). The aim of this organization was to produce a single game whose rules would be accepted by all, but arguments about how far to allow the use of the hands and whether hacking (kicking an opponent who was running with the ball across the shins) should be permitted could not be resolved. The adherents of those clubs that supported these "manly" features withdrew from the discussions and in 1871 formed the Rugby Football Union (RFU). The rest had formed the FA back in 1863. The FA and the RFU lie at the core of all modern football games.

Various forms of association football had been played by young men from most social classes since medieval times, usually on feast days and holidays. This fact may help to explain the speed at which the modern game grew, although it was slow at first partly because the FA was not representative of all parts of the country, partly because there was suspicion particularly in the north of an organization essentially run from London. An important moment came in 1871 when the FA introduced a knock-out cup.

The knock-out cup was copied from the house competition at Harrow School, probably on the prompting of the FA's new secretary, Charles Alcock (1842–1907), who had been a pupil at Harrow. In a knock-out cup, the names of the teams are put into a hat and drawn out in pairs. They play each other—that is a cup-tie—on the ground of the club whose name was drawn first. The winner goes through to the next round. Eventually only two will be left, and they will meet in the cup final.

This competition both reflected and stimulated the growth of the game especially in the provinces. Sheffield had been among the earliest towns to have a football club (1857), and there were soon

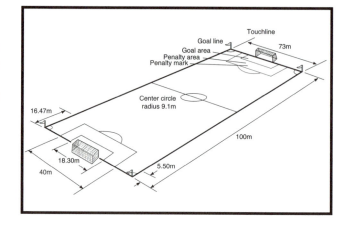

enough teams locally to set up their own Sheffield Football Association (SFA) in 1867. In 1871, the Sheffield FA actually played a match against the FA in London. In 1875, local clubs in Birmingham formed their own football association and soon, not only did most counties have one but so did Scotland (1873), Wales (1876), and Ireland (1880). Both they and the British counties were quick to organize cup competitions of their own.

It was this spread of association football away from London and especially to the Midlands, the North of England, and Scotland that changed the social class base of the sport. Young men from the well-established middle classes in London had set up the FA, but footballing activists in towns like Birmingham, Derby, Nottingham, and Sheffield and counties like Lancashire and Staffordshire included many lower-middle-class clerks, elementary schoolteachers, shopkeepers, and also young skilled workmen. The sport pushed out from these growth points until few parts of the country were unaffected by the 1890s. Many of the clubs that were to become the leaders of the British game (such as the 1995 Premier League champions, the Blackburn Rovers) were started by former public and grammar school (that is, selective state-run secondary school) boys, but many other clubs were grafted onto existing institutions supported by working-class young men, cricket clubs, public houses, workplaces, even churches and chapels.

Cup-tie football changed the nature of the game in Britain. City, county, and national cup competitions built on the traditional rivalries between local communities and provided opportunities for excitement and gambling. Newspapers were quick to notice and promote the new sport, which large crowds were prepared to pay to see. Money taken at the gate was used to recruit the best players. In 1883, a team of Lancashire working men called the Blackburn Olympic beat the Old Etonians in the FA cup final. It was a pivotal moment; no team of "gentlemen" amateurs would come close to winning the cup again. The competition also reflected the increasingly commercial nature of the sport: the players of the Blackburn Olympic had spent a week before both the semifinal and the final in special training at the seaside sponsored by a local manufacturer. Association football had become a craze in the urban and industrial centers of the Midlands, the North of England, and Central Scotland. Relatively high and regular wages, inexpensive transport both within and between cities, and the Saturday half-holiday all combined to make a fortnightly visit to a match well within the finances of working men. Many clubs began to pay their players, and there was a regular migration of young Scottish workers to English clubs. Professionalism in football was legalized in England in 1885 and in Scotland in 1893. In 1888, 12 leading clubs, all from towns in the Midlands or the North, banded together to play a regular schedule of home and away matches, at the end of which the club with the best record would be called champion. They called it the Football League (FL). Modeled on the County Cricket Championship, the league itself provided an exemplar first for many teams in towns and regions of the United Kingdom and later for those abroad. The FL and the Scottish Football League were the apex of the game in British popular culture. At the other end of the spectrum, association football was introduced into the curriculum of the elementary schools by teachers in the 1880s. The English Schools Football Association was founded in 1904, by which time most boys were introduced to the sport at school. The game had become a regular part of the subculture of working-class youth.

Modern association football in Britain had its own international dimension because it was not one country but four. England was economically, demographically, and politically the most powerful, but Ireland, Scotland, and Wales all had a clear sense of cultural distinctiveness that association football could represent. The first official international match was played between Scotland and England, in Glasgow, on 30 November 1872, and it was played annually, apart from the war years, until 1990. The four countries formed the International Board in 1882 to decide upon changes in the laws of the game and played a championship between them from 1883 to 1984.

## Development

### Football Spreads across Europe

Not surprisingly, the British played an important part in the spread of association football to the rest of Europe. In the late nineteenth and early twentieth centuries, Britain was a powerful country with a strong economy and a worldwide empire. Many young Britons who went abroad to buy and sell goods and services and to build modern facilities, such as railways and tramways, and to install gas and electricity generating and distribution systems took association football with them. Those Britons who went abroad to study did the same. The first club in Europe (outside of Great Britain) was probably the one set up by British students at the La Chatelaine School in Geneva, Switzerland, in 1869. In most countries the British were never numerous enough to play exclusively for long; thus they taught the sport to local young men. British influence worked in another way: European businessmen and students who traveled to Britain for education or training purposes were introduced to the sport, and they established their own clubs when they returned home. Britain and things British were fashionable and modern for a time and therefore attractive to local elites. There were groups of Anglophiles in most countries who adopted British sports and British titles for their clubs such as the Young Boys Berne (1898), Milan Cricket and Football Club (1899), and Go Ahead Eagles Deventer (1902). Association football, however, was not only a British export; it was often introduced to Southern Europe by Swiss, Austrian, or German nationals who had traveled as engineers or merchants. FC Barcelona, for example, was established (1899) by young Swiss, German, and British individuals who had learned to play the game at college. The other main club in Barcelona, Español (1900), was set up by Spanish students who did not like what they saw as the cosmopolitanism of FC Barcelona.

The spread of association football was not entirely uncontroversial. There was often opposition

## The Spread of Football 1863–1945

| Country | National Organization Set Up | Affiliation to FIFA | National League | Professionalism Introduced | First International Match |
|---|---|---|---|---|---|
| England | 1863 | 1905–20 1924–28 1946 | 1888 | 1885 | v. Scotland 30 Nov 1872 |
| Scotland | 1873 | 1910–20 1924–28 1946 | 1890 | 1893 | v. England |
| Denmark | 1889 | 1904 | 1913 | 1978 | v. France 19 Oct 1908 |
| Argentina | 1893 | 1912 | 1967 | 1931 | v. Uruguay 16 May 1901 |
| Switzerland | 1895 | 1904 | 1934 | 1933 | v. France 12 Feb 1905 |
| Belgium | 1895 | 1904 | 1896 | 1972 | v. France 1 May 1904 |
| Chile | 1895 | 1912 | 1933 | 1933 | v. Argentina 27 May 1910 |
| Italy | 1898 | 1905 | 1930 | 1929 | v. France 13 May 1920 |
| Netherlands | 1899 | 1904 | 1957 | 1954 | v. Belgium 30 April 1905 |
| Germany | 1900 | 1904–46 1950 | 1963 (WG) | | v. Switzerland 5 April 1908 |
| Uruguay | 1900 | 1923 | 1900 | 1932 | v. Argentina 16 May 1901 |
| Czechoslovakia (Bohemia pre-1918) | 1901 | 1906 | 1925 | 1925 | v. Hungary 5 April 1903 |
| Hungary | 1901 | 1906 | 1901 | 1926 | v. Austria 12 Oct 1902 |
| Norway | 1902 | 1908 | 1961 | | v. Sweden 12 July 1908 |
| Austria | 1904 | 1905 | 1911 | 1924–38 | v. Hungary 12 Oct 1902 |
| Sweden | 1904 | 1904 | 1925 | 1967* | v. Norway 12 July 1908 |
| Paraguay | 1906 | 1921 | 1906 | 1935 | v. Argentina 11 May 1919 |
| Romania | 1908 | 1930 | 1910 | | v. Yugoslavia 8 June 1922 |
| Spain | 1913 | 1904 | 1929 | 1929 | v. Denmark 28 Aug 1920 |
| United States | 1913 | 1913 | 1967–84 | | v. Canada 28 Nov 1885 |
| Brazil | 1914 | 1923 | 1971 | 1933 | v. Argentina 20 Sept 1914 |
| Portugal | 1914 | 1926 | 1935 | | v. Spain 18 Dec 1921 |
| France | 1918 | 1904 | 1932 | 1932 | v. Belgium 1 May 1904 |
| Yugoslavia | 1919 | 1919 | 1923 | | v. Czechoslovakia 28 Aug 1920 |
| Poland | 1919 | 1923 | 1927 | | v. Hungary 18 Dec 1921 |

*Amateurism abolished

from adherents to more traditional pastimes. In France, for example, association football seemed to some people not only foreign but crude. They preferred the more historic gymnastics, and there was also competition from cycling and, in the southwest of France, rugby. Opposition also flared in Germany, where the pioneers were white-collar workers and technicians. They set up the Deutsche Fussball Bund (1900), and by 1904 it had 200 affiliated clubs with 10,000 members. Nevertheless, vigorous opposition, especially from gymnastics enthusiasts, proved detrimental to the sport; it actually caused association football to be banned in Bavaria before 1913. World War I did much to encourage the popularity of the sport because it was used as entertainment and recre-ation for the German, French, and British armies. It did not become popular among the industrial working classes in the towns and cities of the Ruhr until the interwar years.

Association football's pattern of development differed not only from country to country but within countries. In northern and western Europe it often developed first in seaports, such as Genoa in Italy and Gothenburg in Sweden, and in particular regions such as northern and southeastern France before pushing out into other districts. France had three sports federations before 1914, which all had association football sections, and, although Frenchmen were crucial in the founding of FIFA in 1904, the French Football Association did not come into existence until 1918.

## The Spread of Football 1945–1995

| Country | National Association Formed | Affiliated to FIFA | National League | Professionalism Introduced | First International Match |
|---|---|---|---|---|---|
| USSR | 1922 | 1946 | 1936 | | v. Turkey 16 Nov 1924 |
| Turkey | 1923 | 1923 | 1959 | 1951 | v. Romania 26 Oct 1923 |
| Bulgaria | 1923 | 1924 | 1949 | | v. Austria 21 May 1924 |
| Greece | 1926 | 1927 | 1960 | 1979 | v. Sweden 28 Aug 1920 |
| Colombia | 1924 | 1936 | 1948 | 1948 | v. Mexico 10 Feb 1938 |
| Mexico | 1927 | 1929 | 1948 | 1931 | v. Spain 30 May 1928 |
| Peru | 1922 | 1924 | 1966 | 1931 | v. Uruguay 1 Nov 1927 |
| Egypt | 1921 | 1923 | 1949 | | |
| New Zealand | 1938 | 1963 | 1970 | | |
| Morocco | 1955 | 1956 | 1916 | | |
| Tunisia | 1956 | 1960 | 1921 | | |
| Algeria | 1962 | 1963 | 1963 | | v. West Germany 1 Jan 1964 |
| South Africa | 1892 | 1952–76 (suspended 1964–76) 1992 | 1971 | | |
| Zaire | 1919 | 1964 | 1958 | | |
| Zambia | 1929 | 1964 | 1962 | | |
| Nigeria | 1945 | 1959 | 1972 | | |
| Zimbabwe | 1950 | 1965 | 1963 | | |
| Ghana | 1957 | 1958 | 1957 | | |
| Côte d'Ivoire | 1950 | 1960 | 1960 | | |
| Cameroon | 1960 | 1962 | 1961 | | |
| Iran | 1920 | 1948 | 1974 | | |
| Japan | 1921 | 1929–45 1950 | 1993 | | |
| China | 1924 | 1931–58 1979 | 1953 | | |
| South Korea | 1928 | 1948 | 1983 | 1983 | v. Mexico 2 Aug 1948 |
| North Korea | 1945 | 1958 | | | |
| Iraq | 1948 | 1951 | 1974 | | |
| Saudi Arabia | 1959 | 1959 | 1979 | | |
| Australia | 1961 | 1963 | 1977 | | |

In other places the capital, usually the largest city, was the site of association football's early development, such as Copenhagen in Denmark and Vienna in Austria. By 1932, there were 25 teams in two divisions, but they all came from Vienna. It was 1949 before teams from outside were invited to take part in the Austrian League.

## Association Football Reaches South America

In South America association football was a mainly urban phenomenon taking root in the large cities of Buenos Aires, Montevideo, Rio de Janeiro, and São Paulo. The British were instrumental in starting the game in all of these places, especially in Buenos Aires, which contained a British community 40,000 strong by the late nineteenth century. The game was introduced in the British schools, which provided the impetus to set up the Argentine Association Football League with five clubs in 1893. By 1901, the league had expanded to four divisions. By June 1905, 52 teams (with 600 players), referees, and large crowds made it the biggest association football tournament outside Britain. Matches were reported in both English- and Spanish-language newspapers. British professional teams had begun regular visits, and those clubs that would become giants of the Argentine game had already been formed: River Plate (1901), Racing Club

949

(1903), and Independiente and Boca Juniors (1905). Anglo-Argentine and Argentine elites ran the game, and when the Argentine Football Association (AFA) was set up in 1903, it affiliated with the FA in London. In the same year, the rules of the game were drafted in Spanish, and the meetings were no longer conducted in English. Large-scale migration from Italy and Spain took over the sport, and in 1912 the AFA became the Asociación Argentina de Football—an Argentine institution.

A similar process occurred in the small neighboring republic of Uruguay, where young British engineers and managers founded cricket and rowing clubs in Montevideo in the early 1890s. The British schools that were set up also fostered association football, as did the regular contacts with players in Argentina. The Uruguayan Football Association (UFA) was formed in 1900. One of the British formations, the Central Uruguayan Railway Cricket Club (1891), added an association football section that was eventually taken over by local people who changed its name to Peñarol after the district in which its field was located. In 1899, local college students had formed the Naçional Club, and the Naçional and Peñarol have dominated Uruguayan football ever since. In 1905, the Uruguayan Association Football League was renamed the Liga Uruguaya del Football, marking its take over by Uruguayans.

The British also played a part in the birth of association football in Brazil. Charles Miller, born in Brazil of British parents but educated in Great Britain, took a football back to São Paulo and persuaded young men in the São Paulo Athletic Club to organize an association football section. This move was copied by Brazilian students at Mackenzie College in São Paulo in the late 1890s. When a group of young professional workers of various nationalities followed suit, a small league, the Liga Paulista de Football, was formed in 1901. A similar process was at work in Rio de Janeiro, where sons of local elites, educated in Europe, set up sports clubs including association football. The most notable was Fluminense, established in 1902. The America and Botafogo clubs followed in 1904, and Flamengo introduced an association football section in 1911. The "Fla-Flu" rivalry remains one of the most potent in Brazilian competition. The game did not remain an exclusive activity. Bangu (1904), set up by

British managers of a Rio textile factory, eventually allowed local workers to play, although it was the 1920s before poor blacks forced their way into the top teams, first in Rio and then in São Paulo.

Both Argentina and Brazil were large countries in which travel was difficult and expensive. The Argentine championship was a Buenos Aires tournament. No national league existed until 1967. In Brazil, Rio and São Paulo remained the most important association football centers for a long time. The sport did develop in other regions, notably Rio Grande Do Sul, Minais Gerais, even Amazonia, but there was no national championship on European lines until 1971. It was a popular spectator sport in the big cities and by the 1920s had shifted from a pastime for the elites to an opportunity for poor young men to win fame and fortune.

## International Association Football

If international association football began among the four nations of the United Kingdom, it soon spread to the European continent and South America. Uruguay and Argentina met for the first time in 1901 and initiated what was to become the most often played international fixture. Austria met Hungary for the first time in 1902, and France and Belgium in 1904. Some European players thought the game might be encouraged by the formation of an international organization. The British were the obvious leaders, but they were not interested, and when the Fédération Internationale de Football Associations (FIFA) was formed in 1904, the British were absent. Belgium, Denmark, France, the Netherlands, Spain, Sweden, and Switzerland were the founding nations, even though France, Spain, and Sweden did not have national football associations at the time. In fact, this international initiative stimulated their formation. The British did join FIFA in 1905 and stayed until 1920, when their refusal to play against Germany and her allies after World War I led to resignation. The British rejoined in 1924 but left in 1928 after their definition of *amateurism* was not accepted by other members. The British, however, did encourage the growth of association football overseas by sending coaches, clubs, and eventually their national team on tour. A team of amateurs representing Britain was beaten for the first time by foreign opposition—Denmark—as early as 1910, but the professional national team was unbeaten until May 1929, when Spain won in Madrid.

The first regional association football organization was not in Europe but in South America. A tournament had been organized by the Argentine Football Association (AFA) in 1910 as part of the centenary celebrations of the establishment of the first autonomous government in Argentina. Only Argentina, Chile, and Uruguay took part, but it was an important moment in the history of association football in that area. The idea of an organization for the region bore fruit in 1916, when the Confederación Sudamericana de fútbol (CONMEBOL) was set up and the first official South American championship was held in Buenos Aires. Uruguay won that competition and, along with Argentina, has dominated a tournament known as the Copa America since 1975.

The Netherlands and Belgium met twice a year, and there was a significant growth of international competition in the interwar years. A Scandinavian championship involving Denmark, Norway, and Sweden began in 1924, but it was the International Cup invented by the Austrian Hugo Meisl (1881–1937) that was an important marker for the future. The first tournament began in 1927, ended in 1930, and involved five countries—Austria, Czechoslovakia, Hungary, Italy, and Switzerland—playing each other home and away. Italy won the first tournament and triumphed again in 1933–1935, but Austria, Hungary, and Czechoslovakia also had victories, Czechoslovakia winning the final competition in 1956. Romania, Bulgaria, and Yugoslavia competed for the Balkan Cup in the 1930s.

It was also in Central Europe that a club tournament first crossed national boundaries. The Mitropa (short for Mitteleuropa, or Middle Europe) Cup was another Austrian invention. Every year, starting in 1927, the first two clubs in the national leagues of Austria, Czechoslovakia, Hungary, and Italy played each other in a two-legged knock-out. The Mitropa Cup captured the imagination of the publics of the participating countries and was probably the most glamorous interwar association football tournament. Among its winners were some of the area's most famous clubs—Sparta Prague (1927, 1935, 1938), Ferencvaros Budapest (1928 and 1937), Ujpesti Dózsa

Budapest (1929 and 1939), Rapid Vienna (1930), Fussball Klub Austria Vienna (1933 and 1936), and Bologna Italy (1932 and 1934). This competition encouraged the already existing enthusiasm for association football in the region. It would only lose its importance when its format was largely copied by the European Cup 1955–1956. The European confederation, Union des Associations Européennes de Football (UEFA) was formed in 1956, the same year that Stanley Matthews (1915– ) became the first European footballer of the year.

## The World Cup

With most association football remaining at the amateur level, the first tournament that might hope to produce a world's best national team was the Olympic Games. England won in 1908 and 1912, by which time 11 European countries had entered teams. After World War I, professionalism began to develop in places outside the British Isles. By the mid-1920s three of the strongest European footballing nations—Austria, Czechoslovakia, and Hungary—had professional leagues, which disqualified their best players from the Olympics. Britain's best were also professionals, and there was a good deal of suspicion that Uruguay, who had surprisingly but spectacularly won the Olympic football competition in 1924 and 1928, were also concealed professionals.

Jules Rimet, the French president of FIFA, and Henri Delaunay, general secretary of the French Football Association (FFA), proposed an open championship to be played every fourth year and organized by the FIFA. Uruguay was selected to stage the first, a strange choice because of its distance from Europe, where most of the leading football clubs and nations were located. Even though Uruguay had agreed to pay for the travel and accommodation of the other competitors, only Belgium, France, Romania, and Yugoslavia entered from Europe, and the Uruguay-Argentinian rivalry provoked great local interest. Uruguay's victory suggested that they were the best team in world association football. It was a remarkable success for a country with a population less than that of many cities, and it was a victory that would be repeated in 1950. Italy won in 1934 and 1938, but the continued absence of England and the political break-up of Austria in 1938 raised doubts about whether they were truly the best.

## The World Cup

| Year | Venue | Number of Entries | Winners | Runners-Up |
|------|-------|-------------------|---------|------------|
| 1930 | Uruguay | 13 | Uruguay | Argentina |
| 1934 | Italy | 31 | Italy | Czechoslovakia |
| 1938 | France | 30 | Italy | Hungary |
| 1950 | Brazil | 32 | Uruguay | Brazil |
| 1954 | Switzerland | 36 | Germany | Hungary |
| 1958 | Sweden | 48 | Brazil | Sweden |
| 1962 | Chile | 49 | Brazil | Czechoslovakia |
| 1966 | England | 70 | England | West Germany |
| 1970 | Mexico | 70 | Brazil | Italy |
| 1974 | West Germany | 92 | West Germany | Netherlands |
| 1978 | Argentina | 100 | Argentina | Netherlands |
| 1982 | Spain | 108 | Italy | West Germany |
| 1986 | Mexico | 113 | Argentina | West Germany |
| 1990 | Italy | 109 | West Germany | Argentina |
| 1994 | United States | 112 | Brazil | Italy |

Indeed, one of the intriguing aspects of the game is that the best team does not always win: Brazil failed in the final game in 1950, Hungary in 1954, and the Netherlands in 1974. The Hungarian team was one of the most outstanding of all time, losing only 3 matches out of 60 between 1949 and 1955, winning 12 in succession in 1951–1952, and being undefeated for four years until losing to Germany in the World Cup Final of 1954.

Brazil is the only country to appear in every championship between 1930 and 1994, winning a record four times. It has often been said that, after their own country, everyone supports the Brazilian team, mainly due to the skill and style that their players above all others have regularly brought to the sport. This extraordinary ability was particularly exemplified by the 1970 winning team including Pelé (Edson Arantes Do Nascimento, 1940– ). Although Brazil has few rich and many poor, the repute and success of the national association football team has provided something that all can share and politicians can try to exploit. Brazilians often say that the country is bad at lots of things, but at carnival, samba, and association football they are champions. In Brazil association football is a powerful source of national identity. Some Brazilians compared the third World Cup win in 1970 with Neil Armstrong's walk on the moon. Only the Olympic Games can rival the World Cup in terms of sporting prestige and interest. Television now ensures it reaches a world audience.

## New Football Worlds

### Russia

Association football had been introduced to Russia as a summer game by British, German, and other foreign workers in the 1890s. Russian students, clerks, and military cadets took it up, and soon there were thriving leagues in St. Petersburg and Moscow. A national association was established in 1912 together with a short-lived national championship, in which the teams were allowed not more than three Englishmen. The Russian Revolution changed Russian association football as it did much else. After the introduction of the New Economic Policy in 1921, competitive sport was criticized for its tendency toward commercialization and specialization and for turning the socialist masses into spectators rather than players. In the 1930s, as the Soviet Union was rapidly industrialized by Stalin's Five Year Plans, attitudes changed. Competitive sport in general and association football particularly now seemed ideal as recreation for urban workers. A national league was set up in 1936 partly in the hope that it would reinforce a sense of cohesion in the huge rambling country that was now the Soviet Union. Big matches were played on state holidays such as May Day or the anniversary of the October Revolution. By 1938, national league attendance averaged 19,000. The sport was also used to boost the morale of the people during the war. The Moscow rivalry between the Dynamo sports club (sponsored by the Ministry of the Interior) and the Moscow Spartak (sponsored by the workers' co-operative) was the big attraction, but there were also useful teams and large stadiums in Kiev, Leningrad, Odessa, and Tbilisi. The players were supposed to be amateurs, but in reality, despite holding jobs in the sponsoring organizations, they were given all the time necessary for practice and training. The Moscow Dynamo made a famous visit to Britain in 1945 and were undefeated in four matches. The Russians had not yet participated in the Olympics (first time was 1952) or the World Cup (first time was 1958), but the Dynamo tour helped the shaping of a new policy. Russia joined the Fédération Internationale de Football Associations (FIFA) in 1946, and, in 1949, a policy was launched to achieve world supremacy in major sports, partly to show off Soviet athletes in a friendly environment but perhaps more with the aim of demonstrating the superiority of the Soviet system. The use of sport for political ends was not new, but never had it been so well organized, and the Soviet model was extended to all the Eastern European members of the Warsaw Pact after 1950. Their insistence that their players were amateurs allowed these countries to dominate the Olympic Football Tournament between the Helsinki Games in 1952 and the Montreal Games in 1976. The Union of European Football Associations did not call the players of Czechoslovakia and Hungary professionals until 1988. Association football was the most popular game among the Eastern European workers and remains so in the unsettling period ushered in by the breakdown of the Soviet system. In the former Soviet Union there are 4.8 million registered players. Only the reunited Germany has more.

## The United States

Russian/U.S. rivalry became one of the features of the postwar sporting world but not in association football; the United States was the land without association football. Yet, the American Football Association (AFA) had been set up in 1884, the sport was played in several East Coast towns and cities, and the first international matches had been played with Canada in 1885 and 1886. The AFA had even affiliated with the Football Association (FA) in London. Herein lay the sport's major weakness. It came from Europe and still looked toward Europe. It has often been noted that the American elite, anxious about national identity in a land of so many newcomers, saw sport as a way of creating it and so favored games that were home grown, like baseball, basketball, and the native version of rugby, American football. Association football flourished largely among recent immigrants. It had no state support and was played in few schools or colleges. Like baseball in Britain, association football in the United States was always about to take off but never did. During the interwar years, the American Soccer League (ASL) flourished for a time, and teams like Bethlehem Steel and Fall River Rovers, often employing professionals from Britain who were provided with jobs in factories, gained a reputation for their vigor and skill. It was a working-class game, which suffered during the Great Depression. The ASL declined,

and, although it was temporarily reorganized, it never achieved national status.

After the war, the notorious 1950 World Cup win against England in Brazil had little or no effect on association football. It remained a sport tainted by ethnicity and seen by most good Americans as foreign until the 1960s, when it began to change from a working-class sport played by immigrants to a middle-class and suburban recreation played by the young in the better high schools and colleges. It also began to be developed as a game for girls and women. You did not have to be big to play it, and television brought the World Cup victories of England in 1966 and Brazil in 1970 to the attention of many Americans. The year 1967 saw the creation of a national league resembling those in Europe and South America, except that foreign teams were imported to represent U.S. cities. The popularity of the National American Soccer League (NASL) was enormously boosted when Pelé came out of retirement to play for the New York Cosmos in 1975. Yet ten years later the NASL had gone the way of all other U.S. association football leagues. Complacent Europeans blamed growth from the top rather than from the bottom and sneered at the NASL as a show and not a culture. Yet a sports-mad United States was awarded the 1994 World Cup by FIFA with the assurance that a national professional league would follow. It began its first season in the summer of 1996.

## Africa

The growth of association football in Africa has been one of the more remarkable features of the years since World War II, but its development continues to be hampered by economic and political upheavals. The colonial powers, especially Britain and France, took the sport to Africa, but before independence only well-to-do Africans were likely to get the chance to play. Until the coming of free education, association football was only for the African elite.

Association football developed earliest in North Africa, being closer geographically to Europe and containing countries with stronger social institutions and larger communities of Europeans than in most places south of the Sahara. Egypt, Algeria, Morocco, and Tunisia all had league association football from the 1920s and in French-occupied Algeria, Morocco, and

Tunisia there was a North African club championship from 1919 and a knock-out cup from 1930. Egypt had the Farouk Cup from 1922 and actually played in the 1934 World Cup finals. It was a sport for the capitals and second cities, with Cairo's Al Ahly and Zamalek dominating the postwar national league and drawing huge crowds when they met.

South of the Sahara, association football spread in a haphazard way. It was played by the colonial rulers, army soldiers, and students in what few schools and colleges there were. It began largely as an urban sport. As mining and industry developed in the south, migrating young males from the rural hinterland learned the game with their work and took it with them upon returning to their rural communities.

British settlers had formed association football clubs in the late nineteenth century, and Natal had a football association in 1882. Towns like Durban sprouted teams based on workplaces. On the goldfields around Johannesburg, the game flourished, encouraged by the Johannesburg Bantu Football Association (BFA), which was established in 1929. By the end of the 1930s, it administered nearly 500 junior and senior African clubs. With the coming of apartheid after the war, association football in South Africa became largely an African sport.

The year 1957 was an important year in the history of association football in Africa. There were still only four independent football associations—Egypt, Ethiopia, South Africa, and the Sudan—but in that year they set up the Confédération Africaine de Football and organized the first African Nations Cup in Khartoum. South Africa refused to send a multiracial team and withdrew until 1992. The African Nations Cup is held every two years in a different country with 16 (formerly 8 and then 12) finalists. The number of entries started increasing in the mid-1960s, following rapid growth in the number of independent states. Ghana with its Gold Coast Football Association (GCFA) of 1922, its national league of 1957, and its strong clubs such as Hearts of Oak (Accra) and Asante Kotoko (Kumasi), won four times between 1963 and 1982. After a slump in the 1980s, the Ghanaian under-17 team won three world youth championships in the 1990s. Cameroon played in three successive Nations Cup finals in the 1980s, winning two, and they

reached the quarter finals of the World Cup in 1990. They were the first African national team to play England at Wembley in 1991. The vulnerability of African association football to political change is illustrated by Nigeria. In terms of size and prosperity Nigeria should have long been a force in the sport, but Nigeria did not qualify for the Nations Cup finals until 1976. Civil war delayed the formation of a national league until 1972 and the club structure was weak. They finally won the cup in 1980 and in 1994, after being beaten finalists in 1984, 1988, and 1990. In 1996, after an impressive performance in the 1994 World Cup, Nigeria was withdrawn from the African Nations Cup by its government, but the team won the Olympic football tournament in Atlanta in 1966.

The top African players now head for Europe. Association football is one of the few paths to riches, social mobility, and status for young African men, and over 300 of them are currently playing in Europe. Eusebio Da Silva Ferreira (1942– ) from Mozambique was the first African to be voted European Player of the Year in 1965, and the Liberian George Weah (1966– ) became the second in 1995.

## Asia

European colonists brought association football to Asia too. Now it has half the world's population and also half the world's registered association football players, but it has struggled to gain a commensurate place within the world game. In 1966, 16 African and Asian countries withdrew from the World Cup because the FIFA offered them one place between them. One place became two in 1970, and the election of João Havelange from Brazil as the FIFA president in 1974 was partly due to his promise to double it again. (Half of the FIFA's membership by then was African-Asian.) Havelange also initiated world championships for under-seventeen and under-twenty teams to be staged in African-Asian countries; these competitions were established as part of general attempts to promote association football in those countries.

Association football is particularly popular in Bangkok, Hong Kong, Jakarta, and Kampala. Calcutta has the strongest league in India. South Korea has had an eight-team professional league since 1983 and has been a powerful force in the

## Patterns of Play

**Before 1925**

```
                  G

        RB                LB
   RH            CH            LH
   OR    IR      CF      IL  OL
```

**After 1925**

```
                  G

     RB           CH           LB
          RH                LH

        IR

     OR           CF           IL  OL
```

Asian Cup, played every four years since 1956, and in the Asian Games. In Japan, association football has always been a minority sport, but it was encouraged by the Olympic Games of 1964 and by Japan's bronze medal in the 1968 Mexico City Games, where their center forward, Konishige Kamamoto (1944– ), became a national hero. Japan saved the World Club championship, when Toyota started to provide sponsorship, allowing it to be played each December in Tokyo since 1980. Japanese business introduced a professional league in May 1993, importing players from Europe and South America, and South Korea and Japan will together stage the World Cup in 2002. Association football even has a long history in China. Although it has inevitably been affected by the economic and ideological upheavals of the last half century, by 1994 it had a national professional league.

### Australia and the Middle East

Even in Australia, where association football has never been the number one football sport in any state, it has grown in importance as a result of postwar immigration, particularly from Greece, Italy, Turkey, and the former Yugoslavia. For many native Australians, however, these immigrant athletes gave the sport a distinctly un-Australian image, especially when crowd trouble reflected interethnic tensions. Several unsuccessful attempts were made to rid the clubs of their ethnic identities and to replace them with spatial ones, especially after the formation of a national league in 1977. These clubs helped new immigrants to cope with life in a new country, providing cultural support and outside contacts as they have always done for urban newcomers. As European migration declines, the traditional support for ethnic clubs may also decline.

Association football is now the premier sport in the Middle East, particularly in the Gulf States where oil-rich conservative governments have promoted the game, importing Europeans and South Americans to teach and manage in modern stadiums, especially since the 1970s. The sport was illegal in Saudi Arabia in 1959; 35 years later its team did not look out of place in the 1994 World Cup finals. The wider context of these developments has again been economic growth and urban expansion. Association football has provided something to help integrate the influx of a migrant middle class and to provide some controlled modernization and Westernization. Its international context also fits neatly with government concerns about prestige and the building of national identity.

### Practice

Although association football was a team game in 1870, the emphasis on the individual was strong. Once in possession of the ball, the player tried to keep it by running forward and dribbling it toward the opposing goal. His teammates backed him up and tried to regain possession if he lost it. The first specialist position mentioned in the laws of the game was that of goalkeeper, but only as that player on the defending side who, for the time being, was nearest to his own goal. Some teams began to think about defense by keeping one player at the back and another halfway back, hence the term *halfback*. The big change came with the adoption of the passing game with the ball deliberately and systematically being passed between members of the same side as they moved toward the goal. This development was pioneered in the 1870s by the Royal Engineers in England and by Queen's Park in Scotland. It changed the form and shape of association football, opening up the field and allowing the players to become more spread out. This new style underlined what seems obvious today: that each team had a back, middle, and front section. In 1875, Queen's Park played a goalkeeper, two fullbacks, two half-backs, and three back-up players behind three forwards. The positions on the field became specialized with their own quiver of physical and mental skills.

By the early 1880s, a forward had been withdrawn to make room for a third halfback, and a 2-3-5 formation was established. This formation was to dominate world association football until well into the interwar years. Its main features included dribbling, long and short passing, shooting, crossing into the center, tackling, and heading. The British played a more physically vigorous game than most Europeans and South Americans, with the shoulder charge being one of their prominent plays.

There was no major change until 1925, when the offside law was relaxed in response to a decline in the number of goals being scored in the British professional leagues. Before 1925, a player had to have three opponents between himself and the opposition goal at the moment he received the ball, or he would be declared offside. The reforms reduced that number to two and for a time dramatically increased the number of goals. The reforms also prompted club coaches to think about strengthening the defense by withdrawing the center-half from midfield and converting him into a third fullback. To take his place in midfield, one of the inside forwards was also pulled back and a new formation was born (often called the WM). Herbert Chapman (1878–1934) has been given most of the credit for introducing the stopper center-half at the Arsenal club, but there was probably no single author.

Postwar changes in the patterns of play have also been largely connected with a determination to strengthen the defense. It is not clear who invented the 4-2-4 formation, but the great Hungarian team of the 1950s often played Zakarias next to center-half Lorant in the center of defense and operated with Boszik and a withdrawn Hidegkuti in midfield. It was the Brazilian team, which spectacularly won the World Cup in Sweden in 1958, who not only introduced Pelé but also played two center-halves, a double stopper of Bellini and Orlando, and two players in midfield. This strategy made conversion from defense to attack very quick, but it also made the two midfielders work very hard. England turned the 4-2-4 formation into the 4-3-3 in the mid-1960s by withdrawing an attacker to bolster the midfield. For the first time, the number of players whose primary duty was defense outnumbered those whose main role was attack.

Defense was increasingly considered the best form of strategy, particularly in Italy. During the 1960s, Italian teams began to play with five defenders, four who could either mark men or zones and one free player behind them whose role it was to intercept anything that came through. He was the libero—the "free" man or sweeper. This position was most likely invented by Karl Rappan, an Austrian who had coached Swiss teams in the 1930s. Then the formation had been called the bolt, but the Italians renamed it catenaccio, and Helenio Herrera (1916– ), coach of Inter Milan, was its chief disciple. It was a system that had as many detractors as supporters. In the 1970s, the Dutch reached two World Cup Finals by playing a system that was christened total football, emphasizing attack when in possession, defense when not and aiming to produce players with skills that would enable them to play in any position, thus undermining the old stereotypes. Most leading teams now play variants of the formations 4-4-2 or 5-4-1, but association football has remained a game of fluid, flexible systems, a game where the individual can shine, a game of continuous movement of ball and players rather than one of prearranged set plays. An obsession with defense can produce tedious spectacles for the neutral observer, but, for those who identify with the teams, association football retains its ability to seize the emotions.

—Tony Mason

**Bibliography:** Dizionario del calcio. (1990) *La Gazzetta dello Sport (Dictionary of Association Football)*. Milan, Italy.

Glanville, Brian. (1980) *The History of the World Cup*. London: Faber and Faber.

Golesworthy, Maurice. (1957) *The Encyclopaedia of Association Football*. London: Robert Hale.

Henshaw, Richard. (1979) *The Encyclopaedia of World Soccer*. New York: New Republic Books.

Mason, Tony. (1980) *Association Football and English Society, 1863–1915*. Brighton, UK: Harvester.

———. (1995) *Passion of the People? Football in South America*. London: Verso.

Meisl, Willy. (1956) *Soccer Revolution*. London: Phoenix.

Murray, Bill. (1994) *Football: A History of the World Game.* London: Scolar Press.

Oliver, Guy. (1992) *The Guinness Record of World Soccer: The History of the Game in over 150 Countries.* London: Guinness Publishing.

Radnige, Keir. (1994) *Ultimate Encyclopaedia of Soccer.* London: Hodder and Stoughton.

Soar, P., ed. (1984) *The Hamlyn World Encyclopaedia of Football.* London: Hamlyn.

Versi, A. (1986) *Football in Africa.* London: Collins.

Wagg, Stephen, ed. (1995) *Giving the Game Away: Football, Politics, and Culture on Five Continents.* London: Leicester University Press.

# Sociology

The sociology of sport is a fledgling subfield that has developed as an academic specialty only during the last 30 years. However, the formal sociological study of sport began at the turn the century. For example, Thorstein Veblen made a critical analysis of modern sport in his book *The Theory of the Leisure Class,* first published in 1899; and the *American Journal of Sociology* published W. I. Thomas's article on "The Gaming Instinct" in 1901 and George Elliot Howard's paper entitled the "Social Psychology of the Spectator" in 1912.

Although American sociologists are credited with the earliest sociological studies of sport, German scholars are acknowledged for first fostering the formal development of the field. Heinz Risse wrote a book titled *Soziologie des Sports* in 1921; and in the early 1950s U. Popplow ("Towards a Sociology of Sport" [1951]), and H. Plessner ("Sociology of Sport" [1952]) published programmatic papers about the need to develop this distinct field of study. By contrast, the first calls for the development of the sociology of sport as an academic specialty in North America were not made until the mid-1960s by Gerald Kenyon and John Loy, "Towards a Sociology of Sport" (1965) and Arthur Daniels, "The Study of Sport as an Element of Culture" (1966).

The emergence of the sociology of sport as a distinct field of study in the 1960s was further stimulated by the publication of the first contemporary text on the subject, *Sport in Society* by Peter McIntosh (1963), and the first anthology on the subject, *Sport, Culture and Society,* edited by John Loy and Gerald Kenyon (1969). In addition to these early published writings about the sociology of sport, an International Committee for Sport Sociology (ICSS) was established in June 1964. This organization was composed of worldwide representatives from both physical education and sociology.

## Development

The ICSS was instrumental for two early milestone events in the development of the sociology of sport. First, it sponsored the first international conference on the sociology of sport in Cologne, Germany, in 1966, attracting approximately 50 participants addressing the topic "Small Group Research in Sport." Second, it established the first journal for the field, namely, the *International Review for Sport Sociology.* This journal was published annually from 1966 to 1973, when it became a quarterly publication. In 1984 the title of the journal was changed to the *International Review for the Sociology of Sport.* In turn, the ICSS changed its name to the International Sociology of Sport Association (ISSA) in 1994. From its initial membership of 11 personal and 26 corresponding members in 1965, the ICSS/ISSA reached a membership of approximately 300 sport sociologists in 1995. Since its initial international seminar in 1966, the ISSA has sponsored many international conferences and workshops as well as sessions on the sociology of sport in conjunction with the world congresses of the International Sociological Association. It keeps its members abreast of the field with a newsletter called *The Bulletin,* first issued in January 1966.

The first North American newsletter for the sociology of sport, titled *Sport Sociology Bulletin,* appeared in 1972 under the editorship of Benjamin Lowe, but ceased publication in 1977. Benjamin Lowe was also responsible for the publication of the first sport sociology journal in North America called the *Review of Sport and Leisure,* which he founded in 1976.

A major benchmark in the development of the sociology of sport in North America was the establishment of the North American Society for the Sociology of Sport (NASSS) in 1978. The first

NASSS meetings were held in Denver in 1980, and they have been held annually in both U.S. and Canadian cities ever since. In the past 15 years, the NASSS membership has grown from slightly over 100 members to over 300 members. Like the ISSA, NASSS publishes both a newsletter and a journal. The first issue of its newsletter was printed in December 1978, and the first issue of its quarterly journal, the *Sociology of Sport Journal,* was published in 1984.

The membership of both the ISSA and NASSS, as well as that of other national societies for the sociology of sport, is predominantly composed of both physical educators and sociologists. The ICSS/ISSA is affiliated with both the International Council for Sport and Physical Education (ICSPE) and the International Sociological Association (ISA). And many members of NASSS also hold membership in the American Sociological Association (ASA) and/or the American Association for Health, Physical Education and Recreation (AAHPER). The ASA has hosted sessions on the sociology of sport at its annual meetings since 1968; and the AAHPER founded a Sociology of Sport Academy in 1976 to promote the sociological study of sport. Moreover, the research journals of both the ASA (the *American Sociological Review)* and the AAHPER (the *Research Quarterly for Exercise and Sport)* have periodically published influential articles related to the sociology of sport.

Throughout North America sociology of sport courses are offered in both departments of sociology and physical education (kinesiology) at both the undergraduate and graduate level. However, although many of the most noted sport sociologists hold appointments in departments of sociology, most graduate programs focused on the sociology of sport are found within departments of physical education (kinesiology). Two factors may account for this. First, sport sociology is not a prestigious subfield of study within sociology. Second, as George Sage notes, since the 1960s, "graduate emphasis in physical education shifted from the preparation of persons with a broad background in education to the preparation of young scholars whose training was linked to an established academic discipline and to the study of exercise and sport" (1996).

The content of early courses about the sociology of sport tended to focus on sport as a social institution and was largely based on the concepts, theories, and methods of sociology per se. Today, however, the content of such courses focuses on sports as sets of embodied social practices and draws more widely from all the social sciences, including the humanistic aspects of cultural, feminist, and media studies.

## Paradigms

Sport sociologists study the relationships between sport and society, both theoretically and empirically. They have studied these relationships in terms of three major theses or theories, which have progressively gained acceptance within the field as it has developed over the course of thirty years; these major theories are known as: the reflection thesis, the reproduction thesis, and the resistance thesis. In addition to theoretical analysis, sport sociologists have made empirical examination and observation of these relationships in terms of "categorical," "distributive," and "relational" analysis. As Donnelly (1996) has noted in the case of the study of social inequality in sport, although there is not a perfect correspondence between these theoretical and empirical trends, ". . . there is a temporal relation, and both typologies reflect the increasingly sophisticated level of interpretation and analysis in the sociology of sport."

The reflection thesis proposes that sport is a mirror or microcosm of society and, thus, reflects both the positive and negative aspects of society. Much of the early (ca. 1966–1975) work in the sociology of sport showed how sport reflects society at large in terms of economics, politics, and forms of social discrimination. Empirical research was largely descriptive and mostly categorical in nature, showing how degree and kind of sport involvement was related to different social identities such as age, class, ethnicity, sex, and race.

The reproduction thesis proposes that sport not only passively reflects but actively produces and reproduces social formations and actively reinforces social inequalities in society. This thesis was a primary focus of attention of sport sociologists during the second decade of sport sociology (ca. 1976–1985) and was often associated with distributive analyses of the kind and degree of opportunities and resources available to different categories of individuals. For example, studies of salary differentials between black and white professional athletes and scholarship differentials between male and female intercollegiate athletes were prominent during this period.

The resistance thesis proposes that sport situations are "contested terrains," wherein participants can actively engage in actions to change social conditions and social relations for the betterment of disadvantaged individuals and oppressed, subordinate groups. Within the last 10 years, work in the sociology of sport has increasingly shown how sport situations are sites of social struggle for resistance to dominant ideologies and practices, especially those regarding gender and race. The focus on resistance has directed attention to relational analyses of the complex sets of social relations among men and women, social classes, and racial/ethnic groups.

Twenty years ago Gunther Luschen (1975) stated that the sociology of sport could serve to (1) contribute to sociological theory, (2) contribute to the body of knowledge of physical education, physical culture (or sport science), (3) contribute to public policy problems, and (4) provide sport personnel with a better understanding of their own status and role within society. The development of the field during the last two decades gives evidence that with varying degrees of success these purposes have been fulfilled.

—John W. Loy

**Bibliography:** Coakley, J. (1987) "Sociology of Sport in the United States." *International Review for the Sociology of Sport* 22: 63–79.

Daniels, A. S. (1966) "The Study of Sport as an Element of the Culture." *International Review of Sport Sociology* 1: 153–165.

Donnelly, P. (1996) "Approaches to Social Inequality in the Sociology of Sport." *Quest* 48: 98–120.

Frey, J. H., and D. S. Eitzen. (1991) "Sport and Society." *Annual Review of Sociology* 17: 503–522.

Gruneau, R. (1978) " Conflicting Standards and Problems of Personal Action in the Sociology of Sport."*Quest* 30: 80–90.

Kenyon, G. S., and J. W. Loy. (1965) "Toward a Sociology of Sport." *Journal of Health, Physical Education, and Recreation* 36: 24–25, 68–69.

Loy, J. W., and G. S. Kenyon, eds. (1969) *Sport, Culture and Society: A Reader on the Sociology of Sport.* New York: Macmillan.

Loy, J. W., B. D. McPherson, and G. S. Kenyon. (1978) *The Sociology of Sport as an Academic Specialty: An Episodic Essay on the Development and Emergence of an Hybrid Subfield in North America.* Vanier City, Ontario: University of Calgary Press.

———. (1980) "The Emergence and Development of the Sociology of Sport as an Academic Discipline." *Research Quarterly for Exercise and Sport* 51: 91–109.

Loy, J. W., and J. O. Segrave. (1974) "Research Methodology in the Sociology of Sport." In *Exercise and Sport Sciences Reviews, Volume 2,* edited by J. H. Wilmore, 289–333. New York: Academic Press.

Luschen, G. (1975) "The Development and Scope of a Sociology of Sport." *American Corrective Therapy Journal* 29: 39–43.

Luschen, G. (1980) "Sociology of Sport: Development, Present State, and Prospects." Edited by A. Inkeles, N. J. Smelser, and R. H. Turne. *Annual Review of Sociology* 6: 315–347.

McIntosh, P. C. (1963) *Sport in Society.* London: C. A. Watts.

McPherson, B. D. (1975) "Past, Present and Future Perspectives for Research in Sport Sociology." *International Review of Sport Sociology* 10: 55–72.

Sage, G. H. (1979) "The Current Status and Trends of Sport Sociology." In *The Dimensions of Sport Sociology,* edited by M. L. Krotee. West Point, NY: Leisure Press, 23–31.

Sage, G. H. (1996) Sport Sociology. In *History of Exercise and Sport Science,* edited by J. D. Massengale and R. A. Swanson, 111–143. Champaign, IL: Human Kinetics.

Snyder, E. E., and E. Spreitzer. (1974) "Sociology of Sport: An Overview." *Sociological Quarterly* 15: 467–487.

———. (1979) "Sport Sociology and the Discipline of Sociology: Present Status and Speculations about the Future." *Review of Sport and Leisure* 4: 10–29.

# Softball

Since its invention in 1887, softball has captured the fancy of millions of people throughout the world. It was created as a variation on baseball and, since that memorable day in Chicago, has become a social sport as well as a physical game. While it was invented in Chicago, its popularity has spread worldwide. Today it is played in more than 90 countries and is one of the three most widely played team sports in the world.

People who play softball have a passion for it. Some play four to five nights a week, not counting weekends. Playing a couple of hundred games a year is nothing for the true softball aficionado. The sport is different things to different people. To some, softball is a good release from the everyday hustle and bustle of life. To others it is an obsession. In Austin, Texas, an enthusiastic

*As an amateur sport softball has a significant social component, but many players are dedicated athletes. Softball was on the Olympic program for the first time in 1996 at Atlanta.*

softball manager once camped out overnight in front of a local Parks and Recreation office to make sure he signed up his team for the season. Softball also has a social side; it offers an opportunity for people to meet and become friends or even married (some people play on coed teams).

Softball is also a business that many sporting goods companies have capitalized on, causing players to spend millions of dollars on equipment such as gloves, bats and balls, uniforms, and whatever else is needed to play "their" game.

## Origins and Development

George Hancock, a reporter for the Chicago Board of Trade, and 20 or so young men gathered inside the Farragut Boat Club at the edge of Lake Michigan in Chicago in the 3000 block of Lake Park Avenue, awaiting the results of the Harvard-Yale football game. It was cold outside on this Thanksgiving Day, 1887. Some friendly bets were made and once the score was announced (Yale 17, Harvard 8), it was time to pay them off. "Animal spirits came to fore. Horseplay was rampant" (Dickson 1994, 46–47). One of the Yale backers picked up a stray boxing glove and lobbed it across the gym at one of the Harvard fans. Seeing the glove coming, the Harvard booster grabbed a pole and smacked the glove back across the room over the Yalie's head. The batter let out a howl of approval. Watching this, Hancock said, "I've got it. Let's play ball." Taking the boxing glove, he tied its own laces together to resemble a ball and then mapped out a crude diamond on the gym floor. A broom with the handle broken off was used as a bat. Teams were selected and this "indoor version of baseball" was played for more than an hour. The new game could have easily died inside the gymnasium that day if Hancock had not decided to take it a step further, drawing up a set of rules and creating a bat and a ball. He painted permanent foul lines on the inside of the gymnasium and called his game "indoor baseball."

It quickly caught on in Chicago and by mid-winter was played in gymnasiums and lodge halls throughout the city. It filled the void between football and baseball and also alleviated the monotony of the exercise and calisthenics that were often held inside gymnasiums.

In the spring of 1888, Hancock moved his game outdoors. It was played on a smaller diamond and was called "indoor-outdoor." Sensing he had created something noteworthy, Hancock published the first set of indoor-outdoor rules in 1889. The popularity of the sport continued to rise, and in 1895 Lewis Rober, Sr., a fire lieutenant in the Minneapolis Fire Department, added to the legacy of softball by inventing a game that eventually became known as kitten ball. It is not known if Rober knew of Hancock's invention, because indoor-outdoor was generally played in the Chicago area and didn't attract much media attention in the Chicago papers.

What is known is that Rober wanted a game to occupy his men's idle time and to keep them in shape. The men of Engine Company No. 11 were on duty 24 hours a day, living on the second floor of the firehouse. There was a vacant lot adjacent to the firehouse, which Rober used for his playing field. It was half the size of a baseball field and the pitching distance was 10.7 meters (35 feet). The bats used were 5 centimeters (2 inches) in diameter and were turned out by a local woodworker. The ball was a small medicine ball that came from Rober's other pastime of making medicine balls as a part of promoting boxing matches. Rober's game caught on quickly and became popular as other fire companies and groups began playing it on city playgrounds.

Rober had moved to another fire company, Fire Company No. 19, in 1896 and had a new team to manage—the Kittens. A league was started by 1900 and included such teams as the Kittens of Engine House No. 19, the Rats of No. 9, the Whales of No. 4, the Salisburys, and the Central Avenues. That summer, Captain George Kehoe of Truck Company No. 1 named Rober's game kitten league ball in honor of Rober's team. Feelings ran high in these league games, with enthusiastic crowds of more than 3,000 attending. The name kitten league was eventually shortened to kitten ball, and, by 1913, it fell under the jurisdiction of the Minneapolis Park Board (MPB) and many leagues began to form.

Because Rober's game could be played in a small amount of space with minimal equipment, commercial businesses and athletic associations throughout the city began playing the sport. By 1920, the MPB had 64 men's teams in 11 divisions and 25 women's teams in four divisions. Feeling that the name kitten ball was not appropriate, the MPB changed the name of the game to diamond ball in 1922. The game could be played in one hour or less and was ideal for public parks and for blue-collar workers after a hard day of labor.

The basic game continued to spread to the Midwest and then the rest of the country, but with different rules, different names, and even different sized balls. Multiple organizations sprang up, each trying to take hold of this emerging sport and to stabilize it into a unified, cohesive recreational activity. In his 1940 book *Softball*, Arthur T. Noren best summarized softball in the 1920s and early 1930s: "Softball was being played in every hamlet, village, town, city and state in the nation, and in many foreign countries. A dozen sizes of balls were in use, as well as many different bat lengths, every conceivable base-length and bewildering array of variations in rules (54–55)."

Despite this variation, the game continued to grow in popularity. Two factors that contributed to the game's growth were daylight saving time and World War I. "In 1918 *Sporting Goods Dealer* magazine saw the potential of the sport and suggested retailers sponsor 'sunset' leagues to encourage men to play after work. Many large variations of the game were played during the War. This prompted the nickname 'Army Ball'" (Dickson 1994, 55).

Still, there was no national organization, which was needed to bring about a national cohesiveness. This situation got to the point where in 1932, the National Diamond Ball Association sponsored a tournament in Milwaukee with every one of the 40 teams from six states having a different set of rules. The game still did not have a proper name and had a variety of names ranging from playground baseball to kitten ball, softball, and twilight ball.

The numerous changes in the game also reflected the changes in the direction recreation in general was going in the United States. Foster Rhea Dulles, in his *A History of Recreation*, compared recreation in the United States to a river—

## Not Quite Cricket: Softball in Britain

Softball came to London with American film people in the early 1960s, when Great Britain was a land of tax breaks, cheap technicians, and character actors. The swinging Sixties were about to begin. Moe Frank and Norman Panama had written Bob Hope/Bing Crosby road movies, and the informal softball game they started in the spring of 1962 flourished. Frank produced the movie *A Touch of Class* and put London softball into the opening scene: the American character played by George Segal runs into Glenda Jackson while pursuing a fly ball.

After a spell in a Chelsea churchyard, the game settled in Hyde Park, near Harrods and the Knightsbridge apartments favored by visiting Americans. It became known as the Hyde Park International Softball and Canoeing Organisation (HYPISCO). (Team historians insist that no one ever went canoeing.) Movie and athletic stars played. Tony Curtis, Charles Bronson, Eli Wallach, David Hemmings, director Martin Ritt, American football legend Jim Brown, and Australian cricketer Ian Cappell were known to join the HYPISCO game.

Less-celebrated Americans, though, found HYPISCO to be as exclusive as some of the London clubs on Pall Mall a few miles to the east. It was almost impossible to get in a game unless you were an actor or a friend of someone's stockbroker. In 1972, Bob Fromer, a populist American and second baseman who had been snubbed once too often at HYPISCO, advertised for players in the weekly magazine *Time Out* and started another game, a people's game in which everyone, and anyone, would get to play.

They first played at Highbury Fields, then on Hampstead Heath, and finally moved to their present home on the edge of Regent's Park near the London Zoo. The late 1970s was the golden age of what became known as Regent's Park Softball. There were often two or three games played at a time. Women were allowed, even encouraged, to play. Paul Gambaccini, an expatriate American and disc jockey on a popular London radio station, was the resident celebrity.

The first HYPISCO vs. Regent's Park match was played in June 1979 in Hyde Park, amidst the mud and drizzle that characterize British sport. The annual game became the high point of every season for the now veteran players, and there was considerable hostility when Hyde Park consistently won by a single run. By the mid-1980s, however, the virtues of an open game became clear. HYPISCO, where an estimated 100 players participated between 1962 and 1990, was aging. Regent's Park, on the other hand, had welcomed close to 1,000 players between 1972 and 1990, including many British players. While a few die-hards clung to their bases, new blood and relative youth gave Regent's Park an advantage over their older rivals; by 1990, Regent's Park was winning most of the annual matches.

*Time Out* was crucial in pulling together London's softball community. In 1983, an ad in *Time Out* drew 40 women, mostly British, to a sunny spot in Regent's Park where they started the first women's softball league in Britain. The league that first summer included a motley crew called the Artful Dodgers and a highly capable team from northeast London who referred to themselves informally as the Hackney Dykes.

About the same time, representatives of the Hyde Park and Regent's Park teams, with some down-to-earth enthusiasts from the North of England, and the women's teams gathered to form the first British softball league, the South of England Softball Association (SESA).

A point of conflict between British and American players was always over the call to cancel a game. Americans saw rain pouring down at 7:00 A.M. and canceled without batting an eyelid. To the stalwart British, this was not cricket. And they, used to catching a cricket ball (similar in size and weight to a standard baseball) with bare hands, complained about wearing a large leather glove to catch the larger and softer softball. They liked the game, however: it was friendly, challenging but easy to pick up, and over quickly (unlike cricket, which takes 6 to 8 hours minimum), so there was plenty of time to go to the pub.

Today, there are dozens of softball teams in London and elsewhere in the country, and the leagues have sponsorship from U.S. beer companies. While "softball" is not yet a household word in Great Britain, and most players are American, Canadian, or Japanese expatriates, softball in the park has become part of the London summer.

—Karen Christensen

"its course adapting itself to the nature of the country through which it flows, the main stream continually augments by tributaries, and the river bend itself growing broader and deeper" (Dickson 1994, 59).

By 1933, the United States was experiencing the Great Depression. Ironically, it proved to be helpful to softball. Thousands of people were out of work and had idle time. Watching boys and girls playing playground ball, they became involved in the game and continued to play it once the job market improved.

Leo Fischer, a sports writer for *Chicago America*, saw these games and felt that it could be successfully promoted. Fischer and M. J. Pauley, a Chicago sporting goods salesman, envisioned a softball tournament at the Century of Progress Exposition, or the Chicago World's Fair. The two met, adopted a common set of rules, agreed on Walter Hakanson's name of softball, which had been accepted in Colorado in 1926, and approached the fair officials with their idea. The officials, however, were not overly enthused about the idea. Fischer and Pauley persisted, though, and finally in late August they were given the OK by the fair officials, who put up $500 for advance promotion and a playing surface on the fair grounds for the event.

At this point, Pauley and Fischer had ten days in which to drive throughout the Midwest trying to convince teams to participate. They succeeded in getting 24 teams, 16 men's teams and 8 women's teams from 16 states. Conditions were sparse, with teams living in tents and eating a diet of bread and bologna. Admission was free, and more than 70,000 people attended the first round of play, 350,000 during the entire event. There were separate divisions for fast pitch, slow pitch, and women.

With the event being so successful, Pauley and Fisher decided to go a step further and formed a national organization—the Amateur Softball Association (ASA)—of state and metropolitan organizations. Commissioners were appointed, and for the first time the sport of softball had a national organization to move it forward. The state and metro organizational structure is still used today by the ASA, which is located in Oklahoma City, Oklahoma.

While the formation of the ASA provided a foundation from which the sport could grow, the formation of the Joint Rules Committee on Softball (JRCOS) in 1934 brought a consistency on the field and throughout the United States as the game continued to grow in popularity. The JRCOS remained in existence until 1980, at which time the ASA took over the responsibility for the official rules of softball.

During the Depression, softball games were played in the afternoon. Once economic conditions improved and people went back to work, the workers did not discontinue playing softball. They played after work, with industrial leagues forming and companies often hiring top players to work. The sport served as a morale booster for the blue-collar workers.

The year 1936 proved to be an important year in the development of the sport because of the provisions of President Franklin D. Roosevelt's New Deal; 3,026 athletic fields were built from 1936–1940 in an attempt to boost the U.S. standard of living through recreation. Many of the fields included lights, making them ideal for evening games. Softball emerged as a new type of leisure that appealed to the masses and all classes of people, and it put people back to work in a time when work was needed.

Softball got yet another boost from World War II, with the game being played at just about every camp or base of any size in the world. The intensity of softball increased after the war, and Fischer told the ASA that an "estimated 2,000 fenced-in fields existed throughout the United States, Canada, Mexico and other North American nations" (Dickson 1994, 86).

In the 1930s and 1940s, fast-pitch softball was the dominant game played, and pitchers of both teams would have double-digit strikeout totals. The JRCOS eventually changed the rules of the game to offset the balance between the batter and the pitcher by increasing the pitching distance from 11.5 meters (37 feet, 8 $\frac{1}{2}$ inches) to its present distance of 14 meters (46 feet) in 1950. The women's pitching distance also kept pace and was increased to 12.2 meters (40 feet) in 1965. In U.S. colleges women pitch from 13.1 meters (43 feet.)

Slow pitch, softball's other form, had been part of the 1933 World's Fair, but did not develop further until it was added to the ASA's championship program in 1953. Lakewood, Ohio, had formed a slow-pitch league in 1935 with four teams composed of city employees. In Cincinnati, members of the fire department played slow pitch to keep in shape, and, by 1958, industrial leagues and city recreation departments were playing this version of the game.

By 1960, slow pitch had surpassed fast pitch in popularity. Several reasons contributed to this phenomenon: more players were involved, older players could play, there was often more action for the spectator's enjoyment, and games could be played in less than one hour. That was in the early days of slow pitch. Today, games in the men's super slow-pitch division can take three to four hours, while recreational softball games still have one hour time limits because of the volume of teams and local ordinances prohibiting play past a certain hour.

With the popularity of slow pitch came different divisions of play, national tournaments of every size and shape, and various softball organizations, although the ASA remains the largest and the national governing body of the sport in the United States. With people of varied abilities, classification of teams became paramount throughout the United States in order to regulate fairness.

From its two national tournaments in 1933, the ASA has expanded to include more than 60 national championships, ranging from super slow pitch for men to coed slow pitch. Modified pitch, a variation of fast pitch, was added to the ASA program in 1975 and today accounts for more than 3 percent of the ASA total registration. Coed slow pitch is growing even faster since it was added to the ASA program in 1982 and represents 13 percent of the total membership of more than 260,000 teams.

Unlike most sports, where people have to stop playing at a certain age, softball is a lifetime sport, allowing people to remain active despite getting older. Classifications now exist for people from 50-and-over to 75-and-over.

Softball was on the Olympic program for the first time in 1996. Teams from eight countries—Australia, Canada, China, Chinese Taipei, Japan, the Netherlands, Puerto Rico, and the United States—entered the competition. Softball was officially approved by the International Olympic Committee on 13 June 1991.

Softball is now played in more than 90 countries, according to the International Softball Federation (ISF), the sport's international governing body. It has the potential to become one of the great global sports of all time. While the majority of participants who play in the United States are men, women outnumber men internationally, playing fast pitch rather than slow pitch. Some of the top female players in the United States often end up on college teams with a softball scholarship; thus, there is an incentive to play beyond the passion of the game.

People from all walks of life and all socioeconomic groups have this common thread that runs through them: they enjoy playing softball. Softball is amateur, for those people who will not play professional baseball but who can still tingle at the idea of hitting a single in the bottom of the seventh to win the game or making a game-saving catch for the last out. Softball is for young athletes on the way up the athletic ladder who just enjoy playing for their local team or college. It is also the "ultimate class equalizer," says ASA Cincinnati Metro Commissioner Dan Saylor. "You can be a nobody and a star in softball or be a Ph.D. and go 0-for-4. No matter how good or bad you are, there's a league for you."

Softball is the United States' Number 1 team sport and favorite pastime. It is a sport for people and for generations. It's played at just about every level possible by people from all walks of life—doctors, lawyers, insurance agents, accountants and whoever else finds time to play. After playing, there also is time to discuss the game and why the team won or lost. According to *USA Softball* magazine, "At any level, the game whispers of anticipation—the double play, the force out, the grand slam. These are plays that become famous as they are retold the next day at work." For the millions who play softball, it's easy to play but hard to forget.

—Bill Plummer III

**Bibliography:** Bealle, Morris A. (1962) *The New 1962 Compact Edition of the Softball History.* Washington, DC: Columbia Publishing.

———. (1957) *The Softball Story.* Washington, DC: Columbia Publishing.

Claflin, Edward. (1978) *The Irresistible American Softball Book.* New York: Dolphin Books.

Dickson, Paul. (1994) *The Worth Book of Softball.* New York: Facts On File.

Fischer, Leo H. (1939) "Softball Steps Up." *Reader's Digest* (June).

Fischer, Leo H. (1940) *How To Play Winning Softball.* New York: Prentice-Hall

Lee, Mabel. (1983) *A History of Physical Education and Sports in the U.S.A.* New York: John Wiley and Sons.

Meyer, Robert G. (1984) *The Complete Book of Softball: The Loonies Guide to Playing and Enjoying the Game.* New York: Leisure Press.

Michener, James A. (1976) *Sport in America.* New York: Random House.

Noren, Arthur T. (1940) *Softball.* New York: A. S. Barnes.

Oetgen, Albert. (1986) "Softball Ranks as American Religion for Some." *Knight-Ridder Newspapers* (1 June).

Sullivan, George. (1965) *The Compete Guide to Softball.* New York: Fleet Publishing.

Thomas, Lowell, and Ted Shane. (1940) *Softball: So What?* New York: Frederick A. Stokes.

Zolna, Ed, and Mike Conklin. (1981) *Mastering Softball.* Chicago: Contemporary Books.

# Spectators

Although many people regard it as trivial or simply take it for granted, sports spectatorship is an important social phenomenon. Take the case of association football, or soccer as it is widely known. It is the world's most popular team sport and has been described by Kitchin (1966) as "the only global idiom apart from science." By this, he means that soccer serves as a means of communication that unites people all over the world in a common interest despite the linguistic, sociopolitical, socioeconomic, and other ways in which they are culturally divided.

A measure of the fact that soccer has become a "global idiom" is provided by the fact that just under 2.6 million spectators paid around £85 million ($127.5 million) to watch the World Cup finals in Italy in 1990. When account is taken of the fact that "Italia-90" was also watched by some 31 billion television viewers worldwide and that an estimated 32 billion watched the 1994 World Cup finals from the United States on television, you get an idea of how big soccer has become internationally, not simply as a participant sport, but, more crucially, as a spectator sport as well.

What holds for soccer also holds for sport more generally. The multisport Olympic festivals attract large numbers of spectators and TV viewers worldwide, too. So do boxing and many other sports that, so far, have spread less globally, such as American football, baseball, basketball, rugby, and cricket. If one moves to a higher level of generality and focuses on what all these activities have in common as modern sports—international or national organizations concerned with formulating and enforcing common rules and a commitment to high levels of achievement tempered by dedication to a spirit of "fair play"—one can hazard the suggestion that it is not just soccer but sport in general that has come in the present-day world to form a global idiom.

The fact that many people in today's divided world are united by their interest in watching sport is on the face of it rather surprising. Some might be tempted to say that what unites them is a form of "voyeurism." Interestingly, the negative connotations of such a word are nothing new.

## History

Sports spectatorship has been a source of puzzlement and scorn for centuries. As early as the second century C.E., Lucian of Samosata constructed an imaginary dialogue between Solon and Anacharsis, a visitor to Athens whom Solon was conducting around the Lyceum, the famous gymnasium. Parts of the dialogue run as follows:

> Why do your young men behave like this, Solon? Some of them grappling and tripping each other, some throttling, struggling, inter-twining in the mud like so many pigs wallowing. . . . I don't know what comes over them. . . . I want to know what is the good of it all. To me it looks more like madness than anything else.

Anacharsis was probably referring here to the *pankration*, described by Finley and Pleket as " a combination of wrestling and judo with a bit of boxing thrown in" (1976, 40). It was a violent activity and one of the most popular events in the ancient Olympics. Solon went on to justify it by reference to the popularity of the Games and the honor and glory brought by victory. This led Anarcharsis to become even more bewildered:

> Why, Solon, that's where the humiliation comes in. They are treated like this not in something like privacy but with all these spectators to watch the affronts they endure, who, I am to believe, count them happy when they see them dripping with blood or being throttled. . . . However, though I can't help pitying the competitors, I'm still more astonished at the spectators. You tell me the chief people from all over Greece attend. How can they leave their serious concerns and waste time on such things? How they can like it passes my comprehension—to look on people being struck and knocked about, dashed to the ground and pounded by one another (quoted in Finley and Pleket 1976, 128–129).

Although Lucian's descriptions were of "sports" at a lower level in a "civilizing process" (Elias 1939, 1994) than is the case with the majority of their present day counterparts, his questions retain their relevance today. Why do some people

*Umbrellas are the order of the day as the crowd assembles at the ninth hole in front of the Shinnecock Hills Golf Club during the first round of the 1986 U.S. Open.*

apparently derive enjoyment from watching two men pummeling each other in a boxing ring? What sorts of satisfactions are obtained by the mainly male crowds who flock to see twenty two people kicking a soccer ball about? Why should it be of interest to watch, either directly or on television, to see who can run fastest, jump highest or longest, or propel a hammer or javelin the furthest distance? In order to move towards an answer to these questions, I shall start by examining aspects of what is known about the history of sports spectatorship.

There is a tendency both in academic discourse and popular mythology to look on the "sports" of Ancient Greece as representing a pinnacle of civilized sporting achievement. By contrast, the "sports" of Ancient Rome are commonly viewed as a regression into barbarism. There is no need to deny what was, from the standpoint of people who consider themselves "civilized" today, the undoubted cruelty of the "sports" of Ancient

Rome. The brutality of the gladiatorial combats, the mock battles and the massacres, and the blood lust of the crowds who flocked to see them are well established. Sociologically, these "sports" are indicative of an attitude to life and death which was very different from that which dominates in the contemporary West (Auguet 1972). It probably reflects the fact that Ancient Rome was based on slavery. Probably less well known is the fact that the violence of the Roman games was not restricted to events in the arena: crowds throughout the empire behaved violently as well. Take the "circus factions" at the chariot races. They were divided principally into "the Blues" and "Greens," and an indication of how violently they sometimes behaved is provided by the fact that, in Constantinople in C.E. 491, 498, 507 and 503, they set the wooden hippodrome on fire, leading the emperor Justinian to invest in a marble stadium By far the worst of these circus riots occurred in 532 when the Blues and Greens joined forces, rescued prisoners who were about to be publicly executed, and were eventually put down by troops at an estimated cost of 30,000 lives (Cameron 1976; Guttmann 1986).

What about Ancient Greece? Lucian's account suggests that "sports" such as the *pankration* would offend the conscience of people today who consider themselves to be "civilized." The surviving evidence suggests that Ancient Greek spectators were less civilized as well. The *hellanodikai*, the managers of the Olympics employed two classes of assistants: the *mastigophoroi* or whip bearers, and the *rabdouchoi* or truncheon bearers. Their task was to keep both competitors and spectators under control (Guttmann 1986). The need for functionaries of this kind is indicative of crowds that must have frequently been unruly and which required a strong measure of externally imposed physical restraint. One measure of their unruliness is provided by the fact that drunken rowdiness was apparently such a recurrent problem at the Pythian Games at Delphi that spectators were forbidden to carry wine into the stadium (Guttmann 1986).

Besides the mythical belief that the "sports" of Ancient Greece were highly civilized, it is also commonly assumed, perhaps especially by adherents to the present day ideology of "Olympism," that there is a direct line of descent between ancient and modern sports. That is another myth. The Dutch historian/philosopher, Huizinga, has shown that England in the eighteenth and nineteenth centuries formed "the cradle and focus of modern sporting life" (Huizinga in Dunning 1971). In fact, many modern sports are descended from the folk games of medieval England. In common with other European countries in the Middle Ages, there were in England four main equivalents of modern sports: tournaments, hunts, archery contests, and folk games. Tournaments and folk games are the most interesting from the standpoint of spectator behavior.

The earliest surviving records of tournaments date from the twelfth century and are indicative of a very violent type of "sport." "The typical tournament," we are told, "was a mêlée composed of parties of knights fighting simultaneously, capturing each other, seeking not only glory but also ransoms" (Guttmann 1986; Barber 1974). Significantly, between the twelfth and sixteenth centuries, the tournaments underwent a civilizing process in the course of which they were transformed increasingly into pageants involving "mock" rather the "real" violence. That is, they became centrally concerned with spectacle and display, and as this process unfolded, the role of spectators, especially upper class females, grew in importance. As a leading authority has expressed it:

The presence of upper-class women at tournaments plainly signals transformation in function. The perfection of military prowess became ancillary and the tournament became a theatrical production in which fitness to rule was associated with fineness of sensibility (Guttmann 1986, 41).

This is consistent with what Elias (1939) called "the courtization of the warriors" (*die Verhöflichung der Krieger*) and with the part he attributed to the growing power of females in that process. Despite the taming of the tournaments, however, spectatorship continued to be a hazardous affair and stands are reported as having collapsed in London in 1331 and 1581 resulting in numerous injuries and, on the latter occasion, loss of life as well (Guttmann 1986). Disasters such as these can be regarded as medieval precursors of recent events such as the Hillsborough tragedy in 1989 when 95 fans at a soccer match in Sheffield, England, were crushed to death.

The largest attendance at the tournaments seems to have been around two thousand, minuscule in comparison with the 200,000 who, we are told, regularly attended chariot races in the ancient world (Guttmann 1986) and clearly a consequence of the smaller size of urban settlements in medieval Europe. Spectator attendance at the folk games was even smaller. We learn, for example, that in twelfth century London on Shrove Tuesday, "the older men, the fathers and the men of property" would ride on horseback to watch their juniors play "the famous game of ball" (*ad ludum pilae celebrum*) (Marples 1954). More interestingly, the evidence suggests that the kind of strict separation between players' and spectators' roles that we are accustomed to today—and that breaks down in the context of invasions of the playing area that are designed to affect the outcome of a contest—was often entirely lacking. For example, in an early seventeenth-century account of a folk game called "knappan," we are told:

Neyther maye there be anye looker on at this game, but all must be actours, for soe is the custome and curtesye of the playe, for if one that cometh with a purpose onlye to see the game . . . beinge in the middest of the troupe is made a player, by giveinge him a *Bastanado* or two if he be on horse, and by lending him halffe a dozen cuffs if he be on foote, this much may a stranger have of curtesye, although he expecte noethinge at their handes (Owen 1603, 270–282).

This was possible, of course, because these folk games were played across country and through the streets of towns rather than in a stadium on a specifically demarcated playing field or "pitch."

Folk games such as "knappan"—other local names included "hurling," "camp ball," "trap ball," "tip cat," and "dog and cat," and somewhat more generally various spellings of "football"—were the ancestors of such modern games as soccer, rugby, American football, hockey, baseball, and cricket. The evidence suggests that they began to take on their modern forms in two main overlapping phases: a phase that began in the eighteenth century in which members of the landed aristocracy and gentry were predominant, and a phase that began in the nineteenth century when members of the ascendant urban middle classes joined the landed classes in taking the lead. More particularly, the eighteenth century saw the emergence of more regularized and civilized and, in that sense, more "modern" forms of boxing, foxhunting, horse racing, and cricket, while the nineteenth century saw the emergence of more regularized forms of track-and-field athletics and water sports and, above all, the development of more civilized ball games such as soccer, rugby, hockey, and tennis.

The principal social location of the eighteenth-century phase was the estates of the landed aristocracy and gentry, and it took place largely in conjunction with what Elias (Elias and Dunning 1986) called "the parliamentarization of political conflict." That is, members of the landed classes began simultaneously to develop less violent rituals through which to conduct their political affairs and less violent ways of comporting themselves in their leisure. The principal social locations of the nineteenth-century phase were the elite boys' boarding schools that are called "public schools" in Britain, together with the universities at Oxford and Cambridge. This phase,

too, took place largely in conjunction with a "civilizing" shift, this time involving social relations in the public schools (Dunning and Sheard 1979).

The eighteenth-century phase also involved the activities of entrepreneurs who sought to make money by running "boxing academies," putting on boxing shows and general displays of "martial arts," and charging admission to cricket grounds they owned. However, this phase is principally interesting for present purposes because the main actors were members of the aristocracy and gentry, and they seem to have had few objections to performing in front of large crowds or playing together with lower-status men—often their servants or retainers—who were paid for playing. Presumably their status was so secure that they were not seriously threatened by the possibility of performing badly in public or being beaten in sporting competition by their social inferiors. The status of the middle-class groups who became increasingly dominant in sport and British society as the nineteenth century progressed, however, was less secure, and one of the consequences of this was the development of a socially exclusive amateur ideology in terms of which sports should be for players only. Spectators came to be viewed as anathema. For example, H. H. Almond, headmaster of Loretto Academy, the Scottish public school, wrote in 1892 that

> no idle spectators should be allowed to stand looking on at school sides. The very sight of loungers takes the spirit out of players, and the loungers should be doing something else if they are too feeble for football. "Spectating" is . . . the greatest of all football dangers (Dunning and Sheard 1979, 162).

As late as 1929, Sir Cyril Norwood could write:

> The wrong view, the un-English view, of sport, prevails widely, and is cutting deep into the national mind. It is the view that all sport is competitive, designed to be a spectacle of gladiatorial character, and to demonstrate the one team or individual who may be acclaimed as the best. It is the spirit which gloats breathlessly over international contests, and sees the signs of national decadence if England does not win every championship and every game (Ibid.).

These elite public-school amateurs evidently identified their own ethos with that of the English nation as a whole. According to them, sports participation is physically and morally beneficial—in building "character" and fostering "team spirit," for example—but spectatorship has no such desirable effects and can even be morally harmful. However, these elite amateurs' dislike of spectator sports did not rest solely on moral grounds but was also firmly rooted in the fact that spectatorship was increasing mainly among the working classes and involved the congregation of large crowds who behaved in an openly excited manner. This not only ran counter to their sports ethos, with its stress on the controlled expression of emotion, but was also perceived as a threat to public order.

In Britain, a long and unsuccessful rearguard action was fought by the devotees of amateurism against professional, spectator-oriented forms of sport. Impressed by the British amateur ideology, Baron de Coubertin sought—again in the long term unsuccessfully—to instill it in the Olympic movement. In the modern world, top-level sport has become increasingly commercialized, professional, and oriented toward the production of crowd-pleasing spectacles. It has become, that is, fundamentally capitalist in structure and orientation. However, a necessary precondition for explaining how that has come about is an understanding of what it is that people get out of watching sport.

## Meanings

Writing with American football primarily in mind and from the "poststructuralist" viewpoint associated with the French philosopher Michel Foucault, Fiske suggests that "one reason for the popularity of sport as a spectator activity is its ability to slip the disciplinary mechanism of the workaday world into reverse gear (1991)." Spectator sport, argues Fiske, is an "inverted panopticon" where fans who are monitored at work themselves become the monitors. This argument is perceptive. However, it is limited because "controllers" and not only those who are "controlled" are often "mad" on sports, a fact that suggests that sports "fandom" in modern societies may not be class specific in quite the way that Fiske implies. In fact, it is reasonable to suppose that,

independently of class, gender, and "race," one of the main functions performed by watching sports is that it enables people to engage in a "quest for excitement" (Elias and Dunning 1986). As such, it serves as a counter to the external and internalized controls and routines that have become ubiquitous in modern societies and that tend to be conducive to the regular generation of feelings of boredom and emotional flatness. In a word, sports spectatorship appears to be about the playful and pleasurable arousal of affect. Of course, blended with affect are the aesthetic pleasures that can be derived from witnessing the skillful and graceful execution of a sports maneuver, and the cognitive satisfactions that can be obtained from discussing sports strategies. Maguire (1992) writes cogently of "a quest for exciting significance" in this connection.

Sports can also be said to be a form of non-scripted, largely nonverbal theater, and at the top level sports such as soccer, rugby, and American football can have a ballet-like quality. Emotional arousal can be enhanced by spectacular presentation and the emotional "contagion" that derives from being part of a large, expectant crowd. However, to experience excitement at a sports event one has to *care.* In order, as it were, for the "gears" of one's passions to engage, one has to be *committed* both to the sport itself and to one or another of the contending teams or individuals one is watching and to want to see them win. Questions of identification and commitment are of critical importance both for the routine functioning of spectator sports and for some of the problems such as spectator hooliganism that are recurrently generated in connection with them.

The people most committed to sport are commonly called "fans," an abbreviation of the term "fanatic." For the most committed fans, and perhaps for others besides, sport can be said to function as a kind of "surrogate religion" (Coles 1975). Indications of this are provided by the reverential attitudes of many fans toward their teams and by their idolization of particular players. Indeed, it is not uncommon for such fans to turn their bedrooms into shrines. Of course, unlike the major world religions, sport does not have an elaborate theology. Nevertheless, to the extent that sports fans can be said, through their involvement with a particular team, to "celebrate" or "worship" the collectivity that it represents, the sports in question can be said to possess some of the principal characteristics of a religion in Durkheim's (1912) sense of the term. In fact, according to Carl Diem (1971), all sports were originally cultic. More to the point, Durkheim's analysis of the "collective effervescence" generated in the religious rituals of the Australian aborigines, which he saw as the root of the experience and concept of "the sacred," can be transferred, *mutatis mutandis*, to the feelings of excitement and collective celebration that constitute a peak experience in the context of a modern sport. It may even be that part of the explanation for the growing social significance of sport today lies in the fact that it has come to perform some of the functions assigned to religion in earlier societies. That is, it may in part be catering to a type of need that for growing numbers of people is not being met elsewhere in the increasingly secular and scientific societies of our age.

—Eric Dunning

**See also** Violence.

**Bibliography:** Auguet, Roland. (1972) *Cruelty and Civilization: the Roman Games.* London: Allen and Unwin.

Barber, Richard. (1974) *The Knight and Chivalry.* Ipswich, UK: Boydell Press.

Cameron, Alan. (1976) *Circus Factions.* Oxford: Clarendon Press.

Coles, Robert. (1975) "Football as a Surrogate Religion." In *A Sociological Yearbook of Religion,* no. 3, edited by Michael Hill.

Diem, Carl. (1971) *Weltgeschichte des Sports.* 3d ed., 2 vols. Frankfurt: Cotta.

Dunning, Eric, ed. (1971) *The Sociology of Sport: A Selection of Readings.* London: Cass.

Dunning, Eric, and Christopher Rojek, eds. *Sport and Leisure in the Civilizing Process: Critique and Counter-Critique.* London: Macmillan.

Dunning, Eric, and Kenneth Sheard. (1979) *Barbarians, Gentlemen and Players.* Oxford: Martin Robertson.

Durkheim, Emile. (1961 [1912]) *The Elementary Forms of the Religious Life.* New York: Collier.

Elias, Norbert. (1939) *Über den prozess der zivilisation.* 2 vols. Basle: Haus zum Falken.

———. (1991) *The Symbol Theory.* London: Sage.

———. (1994) *The Civilizing Process.* Oxford: Blackwell.

Elias, Norbert, and Eric Dunning. (1986) *Quest for Excitement: Sport and Leisure in the Civilizing Process.* Oxford: Blackwell.

Finley, Moses I., and H. W. Pleket. (1976) *The Olympic Games.* New York: Viking.

Fiske, John. (1991) "Bodies of Knowledge: Panopticism and Spectatorship." Unpublished keynote address at the annual meetings of the North American Society for the Sociology of Sport, Milwaukee.

Foucault, Michel. (1979 [1977]) *Discipline and Punish.* Harmondsworth: Penguin.

Guttmann, Allen. (1986) *Sports Spectators.* New York: Columbia University Press.

Huizinga, Johan. (1971) "The Play Element in Contemporary Sport." In *The Sociology of Sport: a Selection of Readings,* edited by Eric Dunning. London: Cass.

Kitchin, Lawrence. (1966) "The Contenders." *Listener* (27 October).

Marples, M. (1954) *A History of Football.* London: Secker and Warburg.

Maguire, Joseph. (1992) "Towards a Sociological Theory of Sport and the Emotions." In *Sport and Leisure in the Civilizing Process,* edited by E. Dunning and C. Rojek. Toronto: University of Toronto Press.

Owen, George. (1603) *The Description of Pembrokeshire.* Edited by H. Owen. Cymmrodarian Society Record Series 1 (1892).

# Speed Skating

**See** Skating, Speed

# Speedball

## History

Speedball was originated in 1921 by E. D. Mitchell, the director of intramural sports at the University of Michigan, to fill the need for a fall sport that was not as dangerous as football and that would interest students of average athletic ability. There was basketball in the winter and baseball in the spring as games of interest and suitable for average players, but the fall lacked a game in which everyone could safely participate.

Speedball is an ideal intramural game because it is safe and inexpensive, doesn't take a great deal of training or skill, is excellent exercise for the entire body, and holds a large element of interest because of the different ways to score points. The facilities are also simple because a soccer (association football), hockey, or football field can be used. One need only add goalposts.

Speedball was successful from its inception. It had widespread use in the intramural departments of colleges and universities throughout the country but primarily in the Midwest. It was used extensively in physical education activities in secondary schools. It even found its way into industrial recreation programs as sponsored by city departments of recreation in the 1930s. It lost favor with men's recreational programs by the end of the 1930s, and was no longer included in the intramural college programs of men by the 1950s. It also died in the high schools for men by the end of the war. Many more schools started to play flag football or soccer, and speedball was a forgotten sport.

By the 1930s, however, the game had proved itself to be particularly suitable for girls and probably had a larger following among women players than among men. By the 1950s it had become a very popular sport for girls and women in colleges and high schools throughout the Midwest. California used it in all its high school programs (at least until some places in California turned to speedaway as a team sport). In the East, however, private high schools and colleges played field hockey in the fall and moved directly to soccer later. Speedball remained an important game for girls and women until the 1960s when soccer took over.

## Practice

The game combines soccer, basketball, and football skills, using the catching and passing skills of basketball, the kicking and punting tactics of soccer and football, and drop-kick skills. The new skill needed is kicking a grounded ball up into the air. The player can kick the ball either to him- or herself or to another player. A ball kicked into the air from a kick-up is called "fly" ball; when it is started on the ground, or bounced on the ground without a kick-up, it is called a "ground" ball.

The game, played with 7 to 11 players, has incorporated the most desirable feature of soccer, the kicking element, and combined with it the passing aspects of basketball as well as allowing one dribble step. Touchdowns are scored by catching forward passes in the end zone. Players can't run with the ball. A player is not permitted

*Combining elements from football, soccer, and basketball, speedball was initially popular with both men and women, but by the 1930s it had become an almost exclusively female sport. Rules for men and for women differ.*

to touch a ground ball with his or her hands and must play it as in soccer. A fly ball, defined as one that has risen into the air directly from the foot of a player, may be caught with the hands provided the catch is made before the ball strikes the ground again. A bounce from the ground may not be touched with the hand in that it has touched the ground since being kicked and consequently dribbling as used in basketball is not permitted. In advancing the ball, the player may use one overhead dribble, that is, may throw the ball in the air ahead and run forward and catch it before it strikes the ground.

The rules of the game were standardized soon after the origin of the game in 1920s. The women physical educators appointed a committee for the standardization of speedball rules for women. These rules appeared in the Women's Soccer and Speedball Rulebook of 1935.

As with other sports played at different level of competition, the rules vary for high school versus college and intramural versus varsity competitions. Since the beginning, there have also been different rules for men's and women's games. Regardless of specific rules, however, the game is played in four periods of 10 minutes each (8 minutes at the high school level), with the object being to score points by kicking the ball into the goal or though the goalposts, catching it in the end zone, or kicking out of the end zone. The standard field for men is 360 feet (110 meters) long by 160 feet (49 meters) wide; for women the field length is cut to 300 feet (91 meters). Each

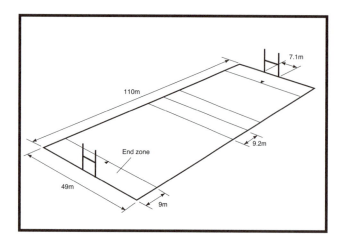

team has 11 players aligned across the field as forwards, backs, guards, and a goalkeeper. Free substitution of up to 5 players is allowed. A soccer ball is usually used, although a basketball is sometimes used on smaller fields. Play involves moving the ball toward the other team's end zone and scoring points by kicking and hand passing. Running with the ball is not permitted. Contact between the players is not allowed, although players may guard each other and try to kick the ball away from the offensive player.

There is a key distinction between ground balls and aerial or fly balls. A ground ball is one that has touched the ground and is stationary, rolling, or bouncing. It may be played by kicking, heading, or playing off the body. It cannot be touched with the hands. A ground ball may be made an aerial ball by passing to oneself (kicking the ball into the air and catching it). This play is unique to speedball and swift, smooth conversion of a ground ball to an aerial ball is a skill that distinguishes the best speedball players. An aerial ball is one that is in the air and it may be played by catching it and by then drop kicking, punting, or dribbling in the air (throwing it in the air then running to catch it).

The three types of kicks allowed are punting (kicking the ball while it is in the air), drop kicking (kicking the ball after one bounce), and place kicking (kicking the ball while it is stationary). Scoring differs slightly for men and women: field goal (kicking a ground ball beneath the crossbar and between the upper rights of the goal) is 3 points for men and 1 point for women; drop kick (kicking a dropped ball through the uprights and above the crossbar from outside the opponent's end zone) is 2 points for men and 3 points for women; touchdown (catching a ball in the opponent's end zone is 1 point for men and 2 points for women; penalty (kicking the ball into the goal following a foul by the opponent) is 1 point for men and 1 point for women; and end kick (kicking a ground ball from within the opponent's end zone over the end line) is 1 point for both men and women.

Today, speedball as a sport for women has largely disappeared, replaced by soccer, basketball, softball, hockey, and other formerly mostly or exclusively male sports.

—Joan Hult

# Squash Rackets

Squash rackets developed in exclusive English boarding schools (known as public schools) in the 1800s and a century later has become a global sport.

## Origins

The first recorded reference to the game of squash rackets, more commonly known as squash, appeared in 1890 in the *Badminton Library of Sports and Pastimes*. As the story goes, schoolboys at England's Harrow School occupied themselves while waiting their turns for the rackets court by hitting a hard rackets ball around the courtyard, often breaking windows. They were told that this practice could only continue if they used a soft or "squashy" ball to prevent unnecessary noise and damage to school property. Thus, the game was born. Squash was later used as a basis for learning to play tennis and rackets.

Nearly every boarding house at Harrow had a miniature racket court in which students played squash with the soft India rubber ball. The courts were inexpensive and simple to construct, requiring only two smooth walls running at right angles to each other and an area of asphalt. The game soon became very popular as players learned to handle a racket and judge the flight of the ball

# Squash Rackets

*Squash players now number over 10 million worldwide; here European players compete in the 1993 Dubai Squash Classic.*

before proceeding to the regular rackets hard-ball court, having gained valuable playing experience.

With increased popularity, other designs for squash's play area were introduced, eventually culminating in four walls of varying size. There was no standardization of courts, but the early ones were constructed of wooden planks for both walls and floor, since wood was easier on the feet than asphalt. During the 1890s more elaborate courts were attached to private houses. Records show that the early courts were slightly wider and considerably longer than their present-day counterparts. The width of three known courts in the English towns of Norwich, Watford, and Weybridge was 7.1 by 12.2 meters (23 feet, 4 inches by 40 feet). These courts were 5.5 meters (18 feet) high and the service boxes and other floor markings were similar to today's courts.

Eustace Miles, a world champion rackets and tennis player, wrote the first book on the game of squash in 1901. Prior to that date, squash had no literature of its own. In fact, there were no press reports on or results for the game until 1899. In his book, Miles reported that there had never been a squash championship and only a few squash competitions, while there were no professionals devoted to the game. He stated that squash was played and enjoyed by many people in various parts of the world, although only in England was the game part of school and university activities. By now, there were courts in private houses in the United States as well as England, and many U.S. athletic clubs were constructing courts. Americans favored the use of the hard lawn tennis ball and a small lawn tennis racket for their long, narrow courts. The English courts, however, were better suited to the small ball and light rackets. It was not until the 1980s that Americans and Canadians started to convert to the internationally standardized courts.

Miles offered coaching tips in his book, although he felt that squash was generally a "selfish" game unless played as doubles in a larger court. Nevertheless, squash was considered good for the development of the body, health, mind, and character, and was regarded as a "grand game" for ladies, unlike many others of the period.

## Development

The first recognized squash championship was the American National in 1907. In 1920, the first Professional Championship of the British Isles was played between the only two entrants. There was no Squash Rackets Association (SRA) at that time and no standard courts, rackets, or balls. The next championship, between the same two players, did not take place until 1928. In 1921, Joyce Cave had the honor of becoming the first British amateur champion of either sex.

Charles Arnold (1884–?), London's Bath Club professional and a coach who included the Prince of Wales among his pupils, wrote the first English coaching manual for squash. Produced in 1924 by the Tennis and Rackets Association, it included the first set of rules on the soft-ball version of squash rackets. Thanks to this book, court and racket sizes began to be standardized. Meanwhile, long, flannel trousers were replaced by shorts, court walls were being plastered, and team squash came into favor.

It has always been easier for soft-ball players to adapt themselves to the hard-ball game than vice versa. In his manual, Arnold stated, "The ball is a very vexed question in Squash Racquets even to this day, and I should not be surprised if the present standard were again to be superseded by another in the very near future!"

The English SRA was founded in 1928 to act as the game's central authority and to formulate, add to, and alter the rules. It was this body that decided to use the English spelling of "rackets" (as opposed to the French "racquets") and to reduce the number of squash balls to three varieties of hollow, black rubber.

As far as etiquette was concerned, squash champion Charles Read (1889–?), said in his 1929 book on the sport: "Modesty is essential to gentlemanly play, and modesty forbids any display of temper. Even if your opponent drives the ball into one of your most tender parts, smile, accept his apology as you would accept a fat legacy, and remember that the last thing the opponent intended was to hurt you. If you suspect otherwise, don't play with him again."

South Africa held its inaugural championship in the 1929–1930 season as the British Army instituted its venerable championship of India. By 1931, Egypt, Australia, and New Zealand had formed organizing bodies for the sport. The great Egyptian player F. D. Amr Bey (1910–198?) won the first of his five British Open Championships in 1932, in addition to his six amateur victories. He retired undefeated in 1937 as perhaps the greatest exponent of the game in its history.

The International Squash Rackets Federation (ISRF) was founded in 1967 as the game became a worldwide sport. The ISRF's founding members were Australia, Egypt, Great Britain, India, New Zealand, Pakistan, and South Africa. Canada and the United States were also represented, although at the time they played a different version of the game. In addition, regional associations were being formed. The European Squash Rackets Federation was founded in 1973, followed by the Asian Squash Rackets Federation and others.

The British Open Championship was regarded as the world championship until the ISRF inaugurated world championships in 1967 for teams and individuals. England's Jim P. St. G. Dear (1910–1981) won the British Open in 1939 after losing in the three previous finals to Amr Bey. Dear was the major link between prewar and

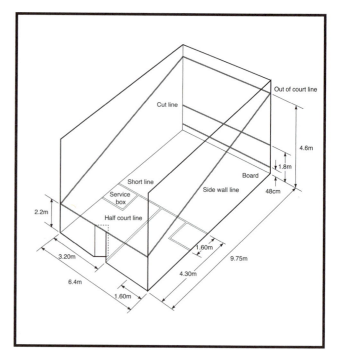

postwar players. Although he was past his best in 1947, it took new Egyptian champion Mahmood Karim (1912– ) five games to beat Dear in the last of the "challenge" system of the British Open Championships. Karim won four Opens in a row, a feat that eventually yielded to the Khan family's domination of the game.

The women's championships were dominated by British players until 1962. Among the game's most famous women players were Janet Morgan (1921–1990), who won the women's world championships ten times, and Australia's Heather McKay (née Blundell) (1941– ), who won her 16th consecutive title in 1977.

A 1950 report from the newly founded Pakistan SRA mentioned for the first time a player destined to change the history of the game. This "tough young player," who had a number of championships to his credit in prepartitioned India, was Hashim Khan (1915– ) of the Royal Pakistan Air Force in Peshawar. On his first visit to Britain in 1951, Khan won every match—a pattern that continued until 1956. He won the British Open final against Karim to become unofficial world champion at his first attempt and without losing a game. This was a truly remarkable performance for a man nearly 35 years of age. Khan lost the 1957 British Open final to his cousin, Roshan Khan (1928– ) before winning his seventh title over his brother, Azam Khan (1920– ) in 1958.

Azam Khan won four titles until his run was stopped by fellow Pakistani Mohibullah Khan (1937– ) in 1963. This preceded three years of Egyptian domination by Abdelfattah Abou Taleb (1939–1983). However, there was no fitter player than Ireland's Jonah Barrington (1941– ), who won the British Open in 1967 and 1968 and from 1970 to 1973. Australian Geoff Hunt (1947– ) won in 1969 and 1974 and from 1976 to 1981.

Then, problems with amateur status in sport resulted in the once exclusive game being opened to all players. Hunt won the first World Open Championship in 1975 and in 1976 McKay won the first Women's World Open Championship. Pakistan again dominated the championships for men with Jahangir Khan (1963– ) winning the British Open from 1982 to 1991 and Jansher Khan (1969– ) from 1991 until 1995. Australian and New Zealand women won the British Open, with Susan Devoy (1964– ) gaining seven titles. Australia and Pakistan continued to win world team titles for men, and England and Australia gained most women's team titles.

## Practice

Squash rackets is a ball game much like rackets, from which it was developed. The main differences are that squash rackets—usually called squash—is played in a smaller court using a somewhat shorter racket and a hollow ball of black or colored rubber. The court has four walls and is 9.75 meters (32 feet) long and 6.40 meters (21 feet) wide. Most courts are indoors with wood floors, but in countries with mainly sunny climates there are outdoor courts with concrete floors. Along the front wall of the court is a wooden or metal board or tin, its upper edge .43 meters (19 inches) from the ground.

The object of the game is to keep the ball in play, above this board. The two players ("singles") or four players ("doubles") take turns striking the ball. The ball may not bounce more than once before it is struck, although it may be volleyed (hit before it touches the ground). The ball need not be hit directly to the front wall, but may be hit via a side or back wall on to the front wall.

The players spin a racket to determine who serves first and the winner selects the side from which to serve. The service is from a space marked on the floor by lines called the "service box." The ball must be served onto the front wall above a line marked on it 1.8 meters (6 feet) from the floor so that it rebounds into the opposite rear quarter of the court. A "rally" (series of hits) continues until one player fails to return the ball above the board. Points are scored by the server on winning rallies, but on losing a rally the receiver becomes the server. The player who first scores nine points wins the game, except if both players reach eight points ("eight-all"). At this point, the player who first reached eight may choose to "set one" or "set two." In the first case, the game ends when one player reaches nine points. In the second case, the game ends when the first player reaches ten points.

## Outlook

Squash is now played by more than 10 million people in 120 countries and has become internationally known and accepted. The game is enjoyed in Africa, Asia, Europe, and Oceania and in North, South, and Central America. Membership in the ISRF, now known as the World Squash Federation, exceeds 100 countries.

Technical developments have kept pace with the sport's popularity—equipment is well designed and courts and clubs are built to high specifications. Inside the clubs, the use of glass to form one or more walls of the squash court has been a major development in the last 20 years. This has led to exciting spectator squash and the development of the game for television. In addition, side and front walls are now manufactured for either permanent or portable courts.

—Ian D. W. Wright

**Bibliography:** Beaufort, Duke of. (1890) *The Badminton Library of Sports and Pastimes.*

Miles, Eustace. (1901) *The Game of Squash.* New York: E. P. Dutton & Co.

Read, Charles. (1929) *Squash Rackets.* London: Heinemann.

# Steeplechase

**See** Horse Racing, Steeplechase

# Stickball

Stickball is an urban form of baseball. The game developed in New York City immigrant communities in the late 1800s and flourished as a local sport until the end of the immigrant era in the 1920s. It was a small though continuing part of the assimilation process, and many young men from Eastern European nations took pride in playing their own street variety of American baseball.

The game was ideally suited to urban life. It required only two pieces of equipment: a bat made from a cut-off broom or mop handle and a ball—ideally a high-bouncing spaldeen, a pink, rubber ball manufactured by the Spalding sporting goods company and sold in local candy and five-and-dime stores. The playing field was a city street, with a "sewer" (actually a man-hole cover) serving as home plate and virtually anything else—other sewers, lamp posts, chairs, boxes serving as the bases. Pitches were delivered on a single bounce (as in cricket), with only one strike per out. Pitching expertise was based on a combination speed and curving, or putting spin on the ball to make it jump or move left or right as it crossed the plate. All foul balls were outs, although any ball that ultimately landed in bounds even after bouncing off buildings was fair and in-play. Balls hit over rooftops were also outs to discourage losing balls, which were expensive.

Because of the narrow playing field, stickball did not require nine players and as few as four could play, with the at-bat team providing the catcher and the team in the field having a pitcher and one outfielder. A batter's reputation was based on the number of sewers he could reach, with two considered good and three legendary. Claims that some batters could reach four sewers seem to be more myth than fact.

The game began to decline in the 1920s, but has enjoyed a recent revival, particularly in retirement communities in Florida and Southern California, where older men who played the game as young men are again playing and are encouraging local youths to play as well. An official stickball bat can now be purchased for about $12.

While this form of stickball has drawn the most attention, other forms of stickball are also

Hotel employees take a break to play a game of stickball on 42d Street in New York City in January 1943. A temporary ban on driving enabled the game to take place, but play was occasionally halted while a trolley traveled the normally crowded thoroughfare.

played in U.S. cities. The most popular form is played in schoolyards or empty lots, and as with traditional stickball requires only a stick and a rubber ball. As spaldeens are now longer manufactured, tennis balls are often used instead. There is no home plate, but instead a rectangular batter's box drawn in paint or chalk on the building wall. A pitch in the box is a strike, one outside the box is a ball. Like baseball, the rules call for three strikes and four balls per at-bat. A foul ball is not an automatic out, although sometimes a second consecutive foul ball is. There are no bases and instead hits are marked by distance—past the "pitcher's mound" on the fly a single, to the schoolyard fence a double, hit the fence a triple, over the fence a home run. With the field and these rules, the game can be played by two individuals, and more than four are not needed. Related to this version of stickball is stoopball in which the "hitter" bounces the ball off the edge of a stoop or stairs on the front of a house. The fielder must then catch the ball before it hits the ground for an out. Again, there are no bases or base running, and the distance reached marks the number of bases.

The commonality among all of these varieties of stickball is the urban setting and the accompanying lack of space for a full baseball game, the absence of money and institutional support for all the equipment required, and the need to have flexible rules that allow the game to be enjoyed in a crowded conditions in which playing conditions might vary from street to street.

—David Levinson

**See also** Baseball, North American.

# Stock Car Racing

Stock car racing events routinely are the largest professional spectator sports events each year in the United States in terms of attendance. Typically, more than 100,000 spectators turn out for each of the major Winston Cup races held in the southern states each year, while tens of thousands more watch the preliminary contests. Although attendance at other races is much less, the presence of more than 500 tracks hosting stock car races scattered around the nation reflects the broad popularity of this sport, which is largely ignored by the traditional sources of sports news coverage. Unlike most professional sports, however, stock car racing evokes strong feelings in the American public; hardly anyone is neutral about this activity.

These strong feelings probably stem from the belief by many that its participants, and to a degree its spectators, are composed of the lowest levels of society. In some respects, the devotees of the sport themselves have encouraged this belief by creating "moonshining" and other mythologies of the early days of southern racing. Early driver and now car owner Junior Johnson (1930– ), for example, became a legend in the early days of his career in regaling the press and fans

alike with his tales of transporting moonshine (illegal homemade whiskey) in the mountains of North Carolina. Although these images of stock car racing are changing as a result of expanded television and journalistic coverage, many of the myths about the sport's beginnings continue.

It is true that the demographics of the sport's typical spectator suggest that the most ardent followers tend to have less income and less education, and are less urban than the population as a whole, but even a casual visit to a short track event would dispel the rumors of rowdy, inebriated crowds of troublemakers. The low ticket prices and rural nature of the sport tends to make most short track racing a family outing with little of the antisocial behavior often assumed to characterize these events.

Why this sport is so identified with the nation's rural underclass is unclear. Some suggest that this support stems from the alienation of these fans from traditional collegiate affiliations, a lack of experience with most team sports, and a rural/small town association that makes "big city" professional athletics anathema to their lives. Others suggest that its fans can identify with the Chevrolets, Pontiacs, and Fords on the major league circuits. The outsider, however, is mystified at this latter explanation as the Winston Cup circuit vehicles clearly represent some of the most sophisticated automobile race cars in the world. Originally defined as "stock" automobiles outfitted with only parts that could be purchased directly from the manufacturers and available to the general public, superspeedway stock cars are not and have not been "showroom" vehicles for more than a generation. No fan believes that if he or she were to go to Elliott Ford in Dahlonega, Georgia, and purchase a Thunderbird from the showroom floor that even a single component of that car would be found on the Thunderbird raced by Bill Elliot (1955– ) on the Winston Cup circuit. The engine, electronics that run the engine, suspension, and other speed elements are obviously different, but even the body itself is a fiberglass and aluminum replica only generally resembling the showroom vehicle.

American stock car racing thus is at best a misnomer and at worst a prevarication. No American professional automobile race today is conducted with a strictly stock vehicle, with the possible exception of the increasingly popular vintage automobile races. Those racing automobiles closest to showroom condition are not classed as stock cars at all, but are sports cars raced in the strictly showroom class of the Sports Car Club of America. Even these automobiles, however, are allowed to have altered tires, wheels, and suspensions. Among stock cars, the racing automobiles closest to original manufacturers' equipment specifications are the lowly hobby divisions of the various sanctioning organizations, the entry level in automobile racing. Restricted in dollar value and size, even these "junkyard" racers generally have rebuilt engines, new electronics (if they are modern enough to possess electronic ignitions), safety gas tanks, and tubular steel safety cages, while most superfluous equipment has been cast aside.

## Origins

The first automobile race in America was sponsored by the Chicago *Times Herald* in November 1893. Two races were ultimately held because of mechanical problems of the contestants' vehicles. First a match race featuring Oscar Mueller (1871–1941) and J. Frank Duryea (1869–1967) racing from Chicago to Evanston, Illinois, was held on the advertised date followed by a race between all of the competitors in a howling snowstorm on Thanksgiving day. The first track race was held in 1894 at the Rhode Island State Fair before 50,000 spectators. These cars were raced in sprint heats over several days to eventually determine the winner. Early automobiles were so unreliable that most contests during the early decades focused upon time trials, achieving top speeds under ideal conditions, or were endurance contests to demonstrate automotive reliability.

The first paved automobile racing track was the Indianapolis Motor Speedway, which was covered with more than 3 million bricks—hence the sobriquet "brickyard." The first race on the paved surface was in 1909, while the now famous 500-mile race on Memorial Day, the Indianapolis 500 as it is now known, followed two years later in 1911. The concept was great, but execution was something else again. Tire problems plagued that race, as they did all early paved track races, until new tire designs could be developed. Stock cars (all cars were "stock" when racing began) were

*Like other popular spectator sports, stock car racing has become big business, with commercial sponsorship of cars and races in traveling circuits at large paved tracks.*

banned from the Indianapolis 500 in 1919, but stock car racing continued in the Midwest. The American Automobile Association was the most important automobile racing sanctioning and promoting organization in the nation until numerous fatal wrecks forced them to retreat from the sport after World War II. In one sense these new, higher speeds and resultant fatal wrecks were the rescuer of the sport as engineers thereafter worked harder developing automobiles that could withstand virtually any possible collision.

## Practice

There are essentially two quite distinct types of stock car racing in the United States today. The highest level, in terms of prize money, quality of competition, and fame, are several sponsor-driven traveling circuits of competitors similar to those traveling contests that dominate golf and tennis competition. The Winston Cup circuit is the most prestigious and well known of these race series. It is the modern outgrowth of the strictly stock division of the National Association for Stock Car Automobile Racing (NASCAR) sanctioning organization. Thirty-one races at 18 tracks were held in 1995. More than 3 million dollars in prizes was awarded in the Winston Cup series.

Public knowledge of stock car racing has become increasingly focused upon the traveling race circuits, as these events are the most likely to be televised and receive newspaper coverage. Perceiving the value of these competitions, promoters have begun expanding the traveling series to other types of events. NASCAR, for example, now has pickup truck racing and several levels of circuit racing, while other sanctioning organizations have also entered this crowded competition for television coverage.

Circuit races typically are held at the nation's largest paved tracks. The Winston Cup series in the current season included contests at tracks both dedicated to stock car racing, such as Talladega Superspeedway and Darlington Raceway, and general purpose tracks such as Watkins Glen and Daytona International speedways. To suggest the complexity of the contemporary race scene in 1995, the Winston Cup circuit was supervised by NASCAR, it was sponsored by the R. J. Reynolds Tobacco Company, and individual races were in turn sponsored by other companies. Thus, the NASCAR Winston Cup November race at the Atlanta Motor Speedway is the Hooters (a restaurant chain) 500 while the second race each year at Charlotte is the First Union (bank) 400. Simultaneously, 15 additional award programs were also conducted in 1995. These ranged from the Busch Pole Awards, for the driver who started at the pole (fastest qualifying time for the race) most often, to the Mayflower-NASCAR Truck Driver Challenge, for drivers of the trucks hauling the Winston Cup cars between races. This latter competition is held between the truck drivers in the pits and parking lots before the races to demonstrate their extraordinary ability to handle their trucks.

Most stock car racing, however, takes place in weekly competitions at isolated short tracks featuring local part-time and semiprofessional drivers. Track promoters typically join sanctioning organizations such as NASCAR or IMCA (International Motor Contest Association) who define the classes of competitors, keep track of records, and make safety rules. Track promoters hold weekly races in each of the classes they support and most also have seasonal "track" champions in each class to help develop a sense of continuity among the fans. Contesting vehicles are placed in classes based on size, body style, and engine displacement. The classes range from the entry-level "hobby division," which utilizes the smallest vehicles, to the super-modified division, which has the most powerful and most visually modified vehicles.

These race tracks typically range in length from 0.4 to 1.0 kilometers ($\frac{1}{4}$ to $\frac{5}{8}$ mile). Most tracks are banked dirt ovals with concrete grandstands on one or more sides and an interior pit area that is open to anyone willing to pay the higher admission price. Some promoters began paving their short tracks during the 1980s in an attempt to emulate the "big leagues." Acceptance of these tracks, however, has been mixed. Drivers and owners are concerned about the increased cost of competition as tire wear increased dramatically on the harder pavement, while collisions with the outside containment wall cause more body damage. Spectators also often seem to prefer the dirt surfaces, which allow for more spectacular driving as the cars slither around the tracks. IMCA, the nation's largest sanctioning organization of small tracks currently has about 85 percent dirt tracks and 15 percent paved tracks. A number of dirt tracks around the nation that paved their racing surfaces in the 1980s are now beginning to remove these asphalt surface because of negative driver and spectator response.

Short track racing continues to be highly regionalized with little interaction between competitors. NASCAR is the best-known of the stock car racing bodies and sanctions races at all levels of competition. NASCAR began on 14 December 1947 in Daytona Beach, Florida, with several name changes before settling on its current appellation in 1948. The new racing organization created three classes of cars: strictly stock, modified stocks, and roadsters. No strictly stock car races (the progenitor of the Winston Cup series) were held in the 1948 season because new automobiles were in short supply in those early postwar years and the racing association was concerned about upsetting fans by destroying these hard to find vehicles. The first strictly stock race was a marathon 150-mile (241 kilometer) contest held on Charlotte's three-quarter-mile (1.2 kilometer) dirt oval on 19 June 1948. The race, which featured a purse of 5,000 dollars, was open to all comers who owned a full-size American passenger car.

The race attracted drivers from all over the nation and some of these drivers were to become the cream of the early NASCAR circuit including: Curtis Turner (1924– ), the Flock Brothers, Buddy

Baker (1941– ), Lee Petty (1914– ), Sara Christian, and 26 others. Nine different makes of cars were represented, including four Hudsons, a Kaiser, and even a Cadillac. Possibly the most memorial event of the day occurred when Lee Petty (Richard Petty's father and Kyle Petty's grandfather) gained eternal fame after his family Buick tumbled end over end to land on its wheels. Getting out dejectedly he sat on the edge of the track and told an inquiring passerby, "I was just sitting there thinking about having to go home and explain to my wife where I'd been with the car."

Though most associated with the South, NASCAR is the most nearly national of the sanctioning organizations, with eight regional short track circuits covering every region in the nation. Almost 100 short tracks were affiliated with NASCAR in 1995, each operating independently and in some cases also conducting non-NASCAR events. This organization is weakest in the Midwest, home base of its historic competitors.

IMCA was the largest sanctioning organization in 1995, with races at 212 tracks. This organization was founded in 1915 in Pennsylvania, but today is headquartered in Vinton, Iowa. While sanctioning tracks in 28 states, most of its racing venues tracks are found in a band stretching from the northern Midwest southward to Texas.

A variety of smaller sanctioning organizations are regionally important. The American Speed Association (ASA) is strongest in the Midwest, while other groups, such as the Modified Owners and Drivers Corporation for the Advancement of Racing (MODCAR) and DIRT, are important in the Northeast. A more difficult question in defining stock car racing is the sanctioning activities of organizations such as the International Motor Sports Association (IMSA). IMSA and several other organizations sanction race series featuring a number of popular American production cars such as Camaros, Oldsmobile Cutlasses, and Corvettes, which purists would not consider stock cars, but most Americans would.

## Outlook

American sports dramatically changed after the establishment of ESPN, the cable television sports channel. The appetite of ESPN for sports programming was insatiable. Automobile racing was a natural to this largely male audience. Vir-

tually banned from the public airwaves after the numerous deaths and severe injuries that accompanied increasing speeds of the 1960s, stock car racing was again ready for mass consumption after the introduction of numerous safety measures in the 1970s and 1980s. ESPN race coverage soon encouraged the broadcast networks to cover the sport as well. Like other sports, the deluge of television contract money increased prize money and incentives for advertisers to sponsor cars and races, especially those products, such as smokeless tobacco, often favored by the typical racing spectator which were banned from traditional advertising avenues.

The massive infusion of money also financed increased competition as it became a multimillion-dollar business. Gone today from the Winston Cup series are the teams supported by local car dealerships and independent drivers financed by their business friends. (The older Skoal Bandit, Kodiak [both smokeless tobacco products], and Budweiser teams have recently been joined by cars sponsored by Tide [detergent], Coca Cola, and McDonalds.) Gone too is the casual character of stock car racing in the upper echelons as car ownership has become big business. Room for the hell-raising drivers of the past is gone. Too much money is involved for the old practices to continue.

The changing character of the stock car elite has also been felt at the lower levels as well. The lure of television money has encouraged the development of additional racing circuits. The Havatampa series, for example, features dirt short track racing throughout the South and is broadcast on the TNN cable network. Increased potential rewards on the senior circuit has both encouraged sponsors to support more lower level teams while encouraging more drivers to compete full time in the hope that they could rise in the racing hierarchy. This infusion of potential rewards and sponsorship has increased the quality of short track racing generally.

Stock car racing stands at the brink of great change. Superspeedway racing has become a major sport with traditional mainstream sponsors. The best drivers are millionaires; team owners and car builders now operate complex business empires that typically extend into automobile dealerships and other related automotive activities. The costs of short track racing have increased and so have the potential rewards. One rarely sees cars driven off the used car lots with duct tape numbers on their sides in competition. Even the audiences have changed as stock car racing has received increased respectability. Simultaneously, part of the traditional appeal of the sport, its "outlaw" image, is rapidly fading. Will fan support continue or increase as the character of the sport changes, or will this sport lose its early regional and social identities and become just another time slot on the television sports machine?

—Richard Pillsbury

# Sumo

Since wrestling of one kind or another is practiced as a sport in all known cultures, some historians have used archaeological evidence, such as the terra-cotta figures known as *haniwa*, to claim prehistoric origins for sumo. Others have seen the beginnings of sumo in the mythic hand-to-hand unarmed combats recorded in the eighth-century *Kojiki* ("Record of Ancient Matters"). In fact, sumo can be reliably traced no farther back than 821, when sumo matches constituted one of the three great annual tournaments of the imperial court, recently moved from Nara to Kyoto. (The other tournaments were archery on the seventeenth day of the first month and equestrian archery on the fifth day of the fifth month.)

## Development

The sumo tournament was held on the grounds of the imperial palace. An area behind the *Shishinden* ("Hall for State Ceremonies") was strewn with white sand for the ceremonial occasion. Thirty-four wrestlers, drawn from the "right" and "left" imperial bodyguards, entered the garden to the accompaniment of two drums and two gongs. They were followed by officials, musicians, and dancers. Then came the emperor and his courtiers. The "left" team wore paper hollyhocks in their hair, the "right" wore calabash blossoms. Matches were decided by falls or when

a helpless wrestler was dragged by his opponent to the tent that housed his team. (In today's matches, winning and losing are determined in almost the same way: the winner is the wrestler who throws his opponent to the ground or forces him out of the ring.) After each match, the musicians beat their drums, struck their gongs, and performed a ritual dance. The results were recorded by arrows thrust into the sand.

These annual tournaments were suspended from 1120 to 1156, sporadically revived until 1185, and then discontinued. Sumo, however, persisted in other forms—as *no sumo* (field wrestling) and *kusa sumo* (grass wrestling) or as *shinji-zumo* (wrestling in the service of the gods). The most famous version of the last was *karasu-zumo* (crow wrestling). It took place at the Kamo Shrine in Kyoto, where boys who represented the god Takemikazuchi wrestled against other boys who represented the secular world. There was also *onna-zumo* (women's wrestling), which seems to have been arranged for men's titillation.

Modern sumo can be traced to the early eighteenth century, when Yoshida Oikaze and a number of other *toshiyori* (elders) codified the sport and introduced a number of the rituals that make sumo a distinctively Japanese form of wrestling. Matches were staged for the pleasure of the shoguns who, until the Meiji Restoration of 1868, wielded far greater political power than the emperors. According to P. L. Cuyler's *Sumo: From Rite to Sport* (1979), "Shogunal sumo lifted the sport out of the vulgar world of entertainment and imparted to it a sense of ritual that later became its major characteristic."

## Practice

The administration of the sport, even today, is a complex mixture of traditional and modern elements. All sumo wrestlers are members of a *heya* (room), the equivalent of a stable in horse racing. The most famous of these *heya* were established in Edo (modern Tokyo) between 1751 and 1781. The elders who ran them received official recognition by the shogun in 1773 and by the emperor in 1885. At that time, there were 105 elders. The organization was restructured in 1926 when *heya* from Tokyo joined those from Osaka to form a more nearly national organization. In 1958, this organization, frequently reformed and renamed,

*U.S. sumo wrestler Tyasokichi Konishiki, the world's heaviest at 229 kilograms, challenges Japan's Setsuo Terao—only 111 kilograms—at a series of exhibition matches in Paris in 1986. The heavier man emerged triumphant.*

became the *Nihon Sumo Kaikyo* (Japanese Sumo Association). In 1989, there were 41 *heya* informally organized into five great families. The Yoshida family, which claims to have been involved with sumo since the thirteenth century, was so dominant in the administration of the sport that it was not until 1951, after a 17-year-old became the official head of the family, that the

Yoshida finally agreed to let the official sumo organization decide which wrestlers should be elevated to the top rank.

The pyramid of ranks is extremely complicated. Beginners enter the system as *maezumo* (before sumo). They receive room, board, and a small allowance. They are also given new names, which are invariably written in *kanji* (Chinese

## The Pyramid of Sumo Ranks

Yokozuna

Ozeki

Sekiwake

Komusubi

Maegashira

Juryo

Makushita

Sandamme

Jonidan

Jonokuchi

Maezumo

characters). (Baseball players, by contrast, not only keep their own names; on the players' uniforms, these names are spelled in the Latin alphabet.) If the *maezumo* are successful in the six annual 15-day tournaments, they rise to become *jonokuchi*, who are given individual rankings. Further successes mean promotion to the *jonidan, sandamme, makushita,* and *juryo* ranks. Only about 1 in 60 wrestlers rises to *juryo* status. If they reach this rank, they are classified as *sekitori* and allowed to change from black or dark blue loincloths to white ones and to participate in the ring-entering ceremony. They wrestle daily during the tournaments, receive a regular salary in addition to their winnings, and have apprentice wrestlers to assist them. When they are not actively engaged in the sport, they are also allowed to wear kimono and *haori* (a man's light coat).

The five ranks above *juryo*—the *maegashira, komusubi, sekiwake, ozeki,* and *yokozuna*—comprise the *makuuchi* division. Wrestlers of this elevated status are allowed four minutes for *shikiri,* the crouching, stamping, and glaring that precedes the actual combat (which usually lasts only a few seconds). *Juryo* are allowed only three minutes of *shikiri* and *makushita* have to be satisfied with

two. The others must enter the ring and move directly into competition.

Election to the eleventh and highest rank—that of the *yokozuna*—is a great honor that is bestowed on very few wrestlers. From all other ranks, one can be demoted after a number of losses. A *yokozuna* cannot be thus humiliated. (If his powers begin to wane, he is expected to retire.) A series of successful tournaments will raise a gifted wrestler to the *ozeki* rank, but promotion to *yokozuna* is granted only to wrestlers who are deemed by the elders to have *seishin* (spirit). Although a few foreigners have become *ozeki,* it is all but impossible for them to become *yokozuna.* When Hawaii-born Jesse Kuhaulua retired in 1976, the elders ruled that foreign-born wrestlers not be allowed to achieve elder status. The elevation of the American Chad Rowan ("Akebono"), however, may signal a shift in Japanese attitudes.

Westerners who attend a sumo tournament are struck not only by the huge size of the wrestlers, some of whom weigh over 182 kilograms (400 pounds), but also by the many rituals that characterize the sport. Among the ritual elements is the design of the *doyo* (the ring), which consists of a circle inscribed in a square. The *doyo,* which dates from the middle of the seventeenth century, is flanked by four pillars that stand at the four corners of the rectangular "ring." These pillars are painted blue for the god of spring, red for the god of summer, white for the god of autumn, and black for the god of winter. At some moment in the eighteenth century, it became customary for four elders to lean against these four pillars in order to assist the referee in his decisions. They were known as the *naka aratame* (middle determiners). The circle within which the wrestlers grapple is formed by 20 bags of rice straw stuffed with earth. The ring is approximately 50 centimeters (20 inches) high and has a diameter of 4.545 meters (14 feet, 11 inches). Before each bout, the *doyo* is purified by handfuls of salt. The *shimenawa,* or ropes that the *yokozuna* wear wound about their waists, represent the ropes that adorn Shinto shrines. These ropes date from the sixteenth century.

Some of sumo's many traditions are very old, but others can be traced back only to the eighteenth century. Yoshida Oikaze, for instance, introduced the ring-entering ceremony in 1791 when sumo was staged for the Shogun Ienari and something suitably ceremonial was in order.

Today, all *sekitori* participate in the ceremony, which includes an entrance by means of the *hanamichi* (path of flowers). The wrestlers circle the ring, face inwards, clap their hands, raise their arms, lift their aprons slightly, and file out. For the *yokozuna*, the ceremony is slightly different. He appears with a *tsuyu harai* (dew sweeper) and a *tachi mochi* (sword-bearer). He wears a thick white rope over his apron. After his hand movements, he goes to the center of the ring, stamps his feet, lies down, rises, stamps again, and repeats his hand movements. The stamping is intended to drive away demons. (The salt that the wrestlers strew upon the *doyo* has the same function.) The *yumitorishiki* (bow dance) first occurred at this time, when the shogun expressed his pleasure by handing one of the wrestlers, the great Tanikaze Kajinosuke, a bow. Tanikaze's dance was an expression of his gratitude.

Unlike most sports, sumo has not undergone a steady process of secularization to rid it of its religious elements. On the contrary, sumo has been characterized less by modernization than by "traditionalization," by a conscious effort to introduce religious elements into a previously secular institution and to link the sport more closely to the culture of medieval Japan. The referee's hat, which looks like the headgear of a Shinto priest from the Heian period (794–1185), was adopted in 1909. His colorful kimono, which mimics Heian courtly attire, also dates from this period of nationalistic fervor. The roof that is suspended above the *doyo*, for indoor matches as well as outdoor ones, was originally shaped like the roof of a traditional Japanese farmhouse. In 1931, in the midst of another highly nationalistic period, the roof was redesigned to resemble the roof of the Ise Shrine, the most sacred of all Japanese religious sites. In other words, much of the religious symbolism that the naive observer assumes to date back to the Heian period, when the *Genji Monogatari* and other classics of Japanese literature were written, is actually an instance of what Eric Hobsbawm has called "invented tradition."

The elders who "traditionalized" twentieth-century sumo were quite successful. Sumo flourishes today as baseball's only serious rival among spectator sports. Together, the two sports aptly symbolize Japan's desire to be, simultaneously, a traditional and a modern society.

—Allen Guttmann

**Bibliography:** Cuyler, P. L. (1979) *Sumo: From Rite to Sport.* New York: Weatherhill.

Kuhaulua, Jesse. (1973) *Takamiyama.* Tokyo: Kodansha International.

Thompson, Lee. "The Modernization of Sumo as a Sport." Ph.D. dissertation, Osaka University, 1989.

# Surfing

Surfing, the art of standing upright on a board and guiding it across the face of a breaking wave, exists today as both a hedonistic pastime or subculture and a highly disciplined professional sport. Two sets of conditions frame the social history of modern surfing: (1) the cultural contexts in which surfing developed as a hedonistic pursuit and a competitive sport and the various attempts to reconcile the respective philosophies of these two forms and (2) the development of surfboard technology and its influence on riding styles and the codification of surfing.

## Origins

Polynesians surfed in premodern times. Early European explorers and travelers in the Pacific wrote highly of their skills, especially those of the Hawaiians. U.S. missionaries in Hawaii, however, took a different view. They considered surfing an "evil and immoral activity," allowing as it did unrestrained intermingling of the sexes. They banned surfing, and by the end of the nineteenth century only a few dozen Hawaiians surfed. Young *haole* (European-American) Hawaiians "rediscovered" surfing early in the twentieth century. Surfing's reemergence coincided with a new culture of pleasure sweeping the Western world, which cast it as a healthy, thrilling, and acceptably hedonistic pastime. Surfing diffused to the Pacific Rim following its "rediscovery." Instrumental in this trend were Hawaiian surfers George Freeth (1883–1919) and Duke Kahanamoku (1890–1968). The latter gave exhibitions in Los Angeles, Sydney, Wellington, and Christchurch.

*Associated with the counterculture in the sport's three hotspots, California, Australia, and Hawaii, surfing has nonetheless also developed as a competitive sport.*

## Development

Distinctive beach cultures in Hawaii, Australia, and California shaped the growth of surfing. The Hawaiian beach, especially Waikiki, symbolized early twentieth-century hedonism. It was the archetypal paradise with grass skirts, *leis* (flower necklaces), the *hula* (a "suggestive" dance), and surfing. In Waikiki beach boys and *wahines* (beach girls) preserved Hawaii's relaxed, casual, and hedonistic culture. Charles Paterson, president of the Australian Surf Life Saving Association (SLSA), described Waikiki in 1927 as "a riot of colour." Unlike Australia and California, where men who bared their chests and women who wore "backless" swimsuits risked prosecution, no restrictions on bathing costumes existed in Waikiki. "People wear what they like" in Waikiki,

Paterson complained: "some roll [their costumes] down to the waist—men and girls both" (Surf Life Saving Association 1928). Surfing was an integral part of Waikiki culture where Paterson observed beach boys giving surfing exhibitions and lessons.

In contrast, Australian surfing developed within the SLSA's peculiar cultural milieu of militaristic athleticism. In return for safety and rescue services for beachgoers, local councils and shires ceded control of beaches to SLSA clubs, which cast a shadow of discipline over local beaches. The typical Australian surfer was a duty-bound lifesaver who had little time to ride waves for pleasure.

California was the early center of technical and cultural developments. Traditional Hawaiian *alaia* (long) boards were solid wood 2 to 3 meters (6 to 9 feet) long. They weighed 41 to 45 kilograms (90 to 100 pounds), were flat-bottomed and highly unstable, and hence extremely difficult to maneuver. The cumbersome boards slid down the face of waves, and surfers changed direction by dragging one foot in the water. In the 1920s, Californian Tom Blake (1900–?) developed lighter "hollow boards" and added a fin. His first versions were solid timber with large holes drilled between the deck (top) and underside. He "sealed" the boards with a thin layer of timber on each side. Later, he made boards using box-frames covered with thin redwood. Although Blake's hollow boards were long (5 to 5.5 meters [16 to 18 feet]), they were relatively light (18 to 27 kilograms [40 to 60 pounds]), stable, and maneuverable. Surfers could now "trim" (set their boards to run at the same speed as the wave) and change direction by leaning and shifting their weight and by bending their knees and pushing. More stylistic body movements—bent knees, arched backs, outstretched arms—accompanied finned hollow boards; grace and deportment replaced the rigid, upright statue-like stances associated with the *alaia* boards.

In the late 1940s and early 1950s, Californians Bob Simmons (?–1954) and Joe Quigg ushered in a second revolution in board technology. Simmons placed styrofoam between plywood and balsa wood and experimented with resin-soaked fiberglass cloth to seal his "sandwich boards." Quigg developed the short (approximately 3 meters [9 to 10 feet]), lightweight (11 to 13 kilograms

[25 to 30 pounds]), and highly maneuverable malibu boards, named after the California beach where they first became popular. Quigg made his malibus from balsa wood wrapped in fiberglass. Wooden boards "died" in 1958 when polyurethane and improved catalysts (used to harden the fiberglass resin) became commercially available. The first to work with the new materials were Hobie Alter, Dave Sweet, and Gordon Clark.

Unlike surfers in Hawaii and Australia, where limited transport and a more formal club environment confined devotees to "local" beaches, more affluent California surfers traveled in search of better waves. Cheap air travel in the late 1940s took many Californians back to Hawaii where they had observed idyllic conditions on Oahu's North Shore during wartime postings. "The search," or "surfari," became synonymous with escapism; combined with "the warm *aloha* of Hawaii," which pioneer California surfers took back to the mainland, it became the foundation of a distinctly hedonistic lifestyle and subculture. Surfers adopted their own argot, humor, rituals, and dress.

Surfing subculture burgeoned in California in the late 1950s. It spread internationally through Hollywood-produced surf films, notably *Gidget*, "pure" surf films made by devotees, including *Slippery When Wet, The Big Surf,* and *Surf Trek to Hawaii*, and specialist surfing magazines such as *Surfer* and *Surfing*. Surfing subculture challenged accepted limits of social tolerance. The "brown eye" (exposing the anus to public view from a passing vehicle) was a popular antisocial act among surfers in California. Such behavior, as well as concerns about the utility of "the search," which conjured images of subversive "itinerants," "nomads," and "wanderers," fueled a social backlash against allegedly undisciplined surfers. *Surfer* became a dirty word. Newspaper editorials in the United States, Australia, New Zealand, and South Africa condemned surfers. Some local authorities closed beaches; others banned surfboards.

In 1954, the Waikiki Surf Club organized the first International Surfing Championships at Makaha, Hawaii. Judges awarded points for length of ride, number of waves caught, skill, sportsmanship, grace, and deportment. The Makaha championships founded a new sport. Although the event, like embryonic competitions elsewhere, resembled fraternal social gatherings, surfers were divided on the issue of competition. Renowned big wave rider, Australian Bob Pike, articulated the sentiments then held, and still held, by many surfers when he said that "competitions are against the spirit of surfing which is supposed to be a communion with nature rather than a hectic chase for points" (Australia's Fifty Most Influential Surfers 1992, 88). The development of competitions sparked an internal debate over the meaning of surfing. Some surfers defined themselves as pleasure seekers, others as disciplined athletes.

Social antagonism toward hedonistic surfers provided the impetus for them to organize regional and national associations around the world in the early 1960s. At the first World Surfing Championships (1964) in Manly, Australia, representatives of national associations formed the International Surfing Federation. Surfers recognized that organized competition was essential for public acceptance. Hoppy Swarts, the inaugural president of the United States Surfing Association, noted, "Competition helped develop a new image with the public—the public has come to respect our surfers in the same way as they respect other athletes" ("The Competition Scene" 1968, 27)

Codification of the sport proved to be a difficult matter. The malibu ushered in "hot-dog" surfing, a style based on maximum turns and tricks (stalling, walking the nose, dipping the head into the wall of the wave). In the late 1950s, surfing styles reflected regional variations. Californian and Australian surfers introduced creative maneuvers such as "cut backs" and "nose riding," trying to preserve the poise that had characterized surfing since the introduction of the hollow board. The Hawaiians resisted the new style as evidenced by the fact that it was not until 1962 that an "outsider"—Australian Bernard "Midget" Farrelly (1944– )—won at Makaha. (He also won the inaugural men's World Surfing Championship in Manly in 1964.) As Farrelly caustically put it, "The Hawaiian idea is, stand on the center of your board and look like a man, if possible against the setting sun" (McGregor 1968, 287). But the most intense debate over style was between Californians and Australians.

In 1966, *Surfing World* (Australia) published an interview with local champions Bob McTavish and "Nat" Young (1947– ) in which the pair boldly announced a "new era." In the same edition, staff writer John Witzig described the passing of the old era. The aesthetic grace and poise of modern surfing, he wrote, has been swept away by "the onslaught of impetuous youth" and replaced with aggression, power, and radical (creative) maneuvers on short boards (Witzig 1966, 37–41). Californians ignored Australian derogatory pronouncements and hailed the emergence of Californian "high performers." The entire sport, Bill Cleary wrote in *Surfer* magazine, is following the "relaxed creativity" of David Nuuhiwa, a Hawaii-born California resident (Cleary 1967).

Debate over style had major ramifications for the development of competitive surfing. It fueled dissension over judging methods and scoring and led to accusations of corruption, cronyism, nepotism, and bias. Competitive surfing declined in the late 1960s under these conditions. *Surfer* magazine summed up the malaise: "More and more . . . contest results, in the eyes of most surfers, are getting further away from what surfers feel is really happening. . . . bias and ignorance must be removed from the scene before the contest system in surfing can ever hope to reach maturity" ("Those Who Sit in Judgment" 1968, 41). Codification stalled as debate raged over style.

Style, however, was not the sole cause of the decline in competition. The counterculture, an amalgam of alternate lifestyles (typically utopian) and political activism, also penetrated surfing. Soul-surfing (surfing for "the good of one's soul") became an oppositional cultural practice symbolizing the counterculture's idealism. Soul-surfers applied increasingly esoteric interpretations to surfing: waves became dreams, playgrounds, podiums, and even asylums, and the search for perfect waves became an endless pursuit. Surfing signified escape, freedom, and self-expression. Most importantly, soul-surfers scorned competitions.

The counterculture's anticompetition ideals delayed professional surfing by perhaps a decade. It only developed apace after the counterculture, unable to reconcile alternative independence in an interdependent society, waned in the early 1970s. As pervasive as the counterculture was, it never totally subsumed the sport. Not all surfers embraced its alternate philosophies; its disjointed tenets made absolute subscription impossible anyway. For example, neither *kamaaina haoles* (nonindigenous Hawaiians born on the islands or residents there for a lengthy period) nor indigenous Hawaiians welcomed soul-surfers. They viewed them as a threat to paradise. *Kamaaina haole* Fred Hemmings, the 1968 world surfing champion, denounced soul-surfers for impairing surfing's potential as a competitive sport. Nonetheless, the counterculture also had a positive impact on professionalism. Its work-is-play philosophy enabled a group of perspicacious Australian surfers to reevaluate competition. They recognized that professionalism could offer competitors, administrators, and a host of small business people an avenue to eternal hedonism.

The 1968 Duke Kahanamoku contest in Hawaii marked a turning point in the development of professional surfing. Although amateurism never encumbered surfing (surfers endorsed and advertised products, wrote newspaper and magazine columns, made their living from associated industries, and from the early 1960s won money prizes), organizers of the fourth Duke offered the first substantial prize money of $1,000. They also proposed the formation of the International Professional Surfers' Association (IPSA). The objective, said surfer Fred Van Dyke, was to establish a professional circuit and a surfers' association to govern the sport and give it credibility.

IPSA failed to address concerns about judging and merely exacerbated tensions. IPSA officials, such as Fred Hemmings, were entrepreneurs who invited participants to compete in their tournaments on the basis of "reputation"— the antithesis of sporting objectivity. IPSA never matured into a surfers' association; it simply organized and promoted contests such as the Smirnoff (Vodka) World Pro-Am Surfing Championships (considered the unofficial World Championship until 1976) and the Duke Kahanamoku and Pipeline Masters contests. Cash prizes signaled new economic possibilities for surfers, but the tournaments suffered from poor administration and direction: "reputation" continued to decide participation, rules varied between contests, judging appeared inconsistent and biased, and Hemmings' close relations with sponsors prompted suspicions about his motives.

In 1975, several Australian surfers, including Ian Cairns, Peter Townend, Graham Cassidy (a Sydney journalist and contest promoter), and Doug Warbrick (proprietor of Rip Curl, manufacturers of assorted surfing products), established the Australian Professional Surfers Association. The following year, Hemmings formed a new body—the International Professional Surfers (IPS). Both organizations claimed to represent surfers' interests and produced ratings systems, based on placings and prize money respectively, to decide the world champion. While Cairns and Hemmings worked together late in 1976 to develop the grand prix format, their respective associations merely co-existed.

The IPS still left surfers dissatisfied, and in 1977 Cairns and Townend formed a surfers' union— the Association of Surfing Professionals (ASP). Hemmings protested that the IPS was a marketing body designed to serve the entire surfing industry, and he changed the name to International Professional Surfing. He outmaneuvered Cairns and Townend by securing sponsorship from Pan-Am in 1978. With sponsorship the IPS won fresh support from surfers.

Two other factors contributed to the ASP losing support: arrogance and pretentiousness. Australian surfers dominated Hawaiian contests in 1975–1976, and they left no doubt about their feelings of superiority. In a provocative article, reminiscent of the "new era" challenge, professional surfer Wayne Bartholomew claimed that the Hawaiian surfing establishment discriminated against Australians whose only option was to "come through the back door to get invitations" to professional contests (Bartholomew 1976/1977, 74).

"War" erupted when Australian surfers returned to the North Shore the following season. Bartholomew was assaulted; Cairns felt sufficiently intimidated to barricade himself in his hotel; threats were made to burn down Cairns's house; and Hawaiian surfers exerted pressure on local board manufacturers not to supply Australians. Tensions only eased after respected Hawaiian elder surfer Eddie Aiku intervened. Calm would only return, he said, when "you Aussies learn to be humble."

Australian surfers also shied from the ASP because of Cairns's and Townend's brazen attempt to advance professional surfing through an os-

tentatious marketing venture known as the Bronzed Aussies. The counterculture may have waned by the mid-1970s, but that did not mean that the time was ripe for the crass hype and glitter adopted by the Bronzed Aussies.

Hemmings's "victory" was shortlived. He resigned when the IPS could not find a successor for Pan-Am, which withdrew its sponsorship after one season. Hemmings could not reconcile his dual positions as an IPS director and a contest promoter. Surfers took over the IPS, comprised of a 24-member board made up of an equal number of contest directors and professional surfers. The structure was too unwieldy, however, and the IPS failed to secure an umbrella sponsor.

In 1982, Cairns announced that Ocean Pacific (manufacturers of surfwear) would underwrite an ASP grand prix circuit for three years in return for licensing rights to the ASP logo. Cairns would be the new executive director. It was another short marriage: Ocean Pacific withdrew after two years, again leaving the ASP without sponsorship. Cairns had moved the ASP headquarters to Los Angeles in the mistaken belief that California would carry professional surfing into its golden era. The golden era never dawned, and Cairns retired in 1986.

Under Cairns's leadership the ASP reorganized the surfing calendar. Instead of climaxing in the giant surf of Hawaii at the end of the calendar year, the ASP shifted the season from June to April, beginning in South Africa and finishing in Australia. The ASP argued that Hawaii was geographically isolated and that the Hawaiians had failed to promote the sport, had not attracted sponsors from the mainland, and did not give surfers their due recognition. Indeed, political activism among indigenous Hawaiians, aimed at ridding the islands of foreign culture including professional surfing contests, has undoubtedly retarded surfing's development there. But most professional surfers opposed the ASP's decision, and in 1988 the ASP reorganized the circuit to finish in Hawaii. When Graham Cassidy replaced Cairns as the ASP's executive director, he moved the headquarters to Sydney, "the real money base" of professional surfing.

In 1993, the ASP finally secured another umbrella sponsor—Coca Cola. With the sponsorship came another reorganization of the calendar. As Cassidy explained, "the best possible spotlight on the year end season . . . can't be achieved in Hawaii" where "they tend to treat [surfing] as a lifestyle thing rather than a serious sport." ("Finale of World Tour" 1994) Increasingly, more professional surfers are concurring with Cassidy, despite their earlier insistence that the circuit conclude in Hawaii. Professional surfer Australian Gary Elkerton conceded the realities: "The ultimate is to have three events that finish off the tour in big surf in Hawaii," but "because of the locals and the politics you can't do that." ("Oh Good" 1993, 36)

The early 1970s witnessed the beginning of a third revolution in board technology. Tom Hoye and other Californians developed "twin-fin" boards, which allowed radical maneuvers anywhere on the face of the wave. Twin-fins, however, were slower than single fins and tended to "slip." In 1980, Australian professional surfer Simon Anderson introduced the "thruster"—a design utilizing three fins, one set on the midline and one on each side. Three fins gave surfboards more "thrust" (power and speed) when turning and solved the instability problem associated with twin-fins. Although polyurethane and fiberglass still remain the principal materials of construction, surfboard shapers continue to experiment with thinner, lighter, faster, and more maneuverable boards. These boards, combined with the intense competition of professionalism, have progressively transformed surfing into a more "gymnastic" activity. In the mid and late 1990s, professional surfers' repertoires include "tailslides" (withdrawing the fins from the wave and allowing the board to slip down the face of the wave); "floaters" (floating the board along the top of a breaking wave); "reverses" (making a rapid change of direction); "360s" (turning the board 360 degrees on the face of the wave); and "air" (flying above the face of the wave).

## Practice

Competitions on the Men's World Championship Tour consist of three preliminary rounds and three finals. Round one consists of 16 three-man heats with the winners progressing to round three. Round two comprises 16 two-man heats with the winners advancing. Round three pits the winners of round one against the winners of round two in man-on-man heats. The finals are all man-on-man

format with winners progressing. There are four quarterfinals, two semifinals, and one final.

Heats in preliminary rounds are generally 20 minutes; judges may extend the finals to 40 minutes. Surfers can catch a maximum of ten waves but only the best four waves count toward the surfer's total score. Five international judges adjudicate all heats and finals. Judges score each wave on a scale of ten, with poor rides 0–2 points, fair rides 2.1–4 points, average rides 4.1–6 points, good rides 6.1–8 points, and excellent rides 8.1–10 points. Computer software eliminates the highest and lowest score and averages the three remaining scores to produce a wave score. Judges look for "the most radical controlled maneuvers" performed with "speed and power in the most critical section of a wave."

## Outlook

Professional surfing has undergone remarkable growth since the first year of the circuit when men contested 14 events for less than $78,000 prize money and women competed in five events for under $20,000. In 1990, men met in 21 events for nearly $2 million, while in 1992 women competed in 15 events for $320,000. The ASP restructured its grand prix circuit in 1992 and introduced a two-tier structure—a World Championship Tour and a "feeder" World Qualifying Tour. In 1995, the former comprised 10 events for men worth $1.15 million, while the latter included 60 men's events worth $1.5 million. There is only one professional surfing circuit for women. The 1996 Women's World Tour comprises 15 events worth $320,000.

Despite growth and restructuring of the circuit, several factors constrain professional surfing. First, unlike stadium sports, corporate advertisers have free access to ocean, wave, and surfing imagery, allowing them to create images at little cost to themselves. Second, official associations cannot manufacture the conditions that can make surfing a dramatic spectator sport. Lastly, most surfers still aspire to a peculiar hedonistic life-style rather than a competitive sport. As professional U.S. surfer Jamie Brisick puts it, "I surf for the same reason I perpetually flog myself to the heights of orgasmic pleasure—because it feels good" ("Surfers on Why They Surf" 1991, 81).

—Douglas Booth

**Bibliography:** "Australia's Fifty Most Influential Surfers." (1992) *Australia's Surfing Life* 50: 88.

Bartholomew, Wayne. (1976/1977) "Bustin' down the Door." *Surfer* 17, 5: 74.

Booth, Douglas. (1991) "War off Water: The Surf Life Saving Association and the Beach," *Sporting Traditions: Journal of the Australian Society for Sports History* 7, 2: 135–162.

———. (1994) "Surfing '60s: A Case Study in the History of Pleasure and Discipline," *Australian Historical Studies* 26: 262–279.

———. (1995) "Ambiguities in Pleasure and Discipline: The Development of Competitive Surfing," *Journal of Sport History* 22, 3: 189–206.

Carroll, Nick, ed. (1991) *The Next Wave: A Survey of World Surfing.* Sydney: Angus and Robertson.

Cleary, Bill. (1967) "The High Performers." *Surfer* 8, 1: 38–49.

"The Competition Scene." (1968) *Surfer* 9, 2:27.

"Finale of World Tour Is back at Home." (1994) *Sydney Morning Herald* (3 January).

Finney, Ben, and John Houston. (1966) *Surfing: The Sport of Hawaiian Kings.* Johannesburg: Hugh Keartland Publishers.

Irwin, John. (1973) "The Natural History of an Urban Scene," *Urban Life and Culture* 2, 2: 131–160.

Lueras, Leonard. (1984) *Surfing the Ultimate Pleasure.* New York: Workman Publishing.

McGregor, Craig. (1968) *Profile of Australia.* Chicago: Henry Regnery.

Noll, Greg, and Andrea Gabbard. (1989) *Da Bull: Life over the Edge.* South Laguna, CA: Bangtail Press.

"Oh Good, an Umbrella Sponsor." (1993) *Australia's Surfing Life* 63: 36.

Pearson, Kent. (1979) *Surfing Subcultures of Australia and New Zealand.* St. Lucia: University of Queensland Press.

Surf Life Saving Association. (1928) *Twentieth Annual Report 1927–1928.*

"Surfers on Why They Surf." (1991) *Tracks* (October): 81.

"Those Who Sit in Judgment." (1968) *Surfer* 9, 5: 41.

Timmons, Grady. (1989) *Waikiki Beachboy.* Honolulu: Editions Limited.

Witzig, John. (1966) "An End to an Era." *Surfing World* 8, 1; 37–41.

Young, Nat. (1983) *The History of Surfing.* Sydney: Palm Beach Press.

# Swimming, Distance

Long-distance swimming demands all of the standard physiological and psychological attributes that are found in, for example, Olympic swimming, in which events range from 50 meters to 1500 meters. The colossal difference, however, is that in long-distance swimming good technique must be maintained for many hours, over many miles, and in the face of awesome levels of pain, tiredness, and exhaustion. Pat Besford notes some of the additional problems: "Long distance swimming requires courage . . . to go through a pitch black night, fog, weed, flotsam, occasional oil fuel patches, swarms of jellyfish and maritime traffic."

In antiquity there were the chronicles of Leander swimming the Hellespont to meet Hero, a distance of two and one-half miles round-trip. In the nineteenth century, Lord Byron, who popularized pugilism, did the same thing for long-distance swimming with a series of distance swims in the Mediterranean Sea. The father of long-distance swimming was Captain Matthew Webb, who conquered the English Channel in 1875.

As with all types of swimming, performances get better and better as the years pass. For example, in 1911 James Foster finished the Lake Windermere, England, swim in a record time of 11 hours, 29 minutes. By 1968, the time had dropped to 4 hours, 7 minutes (Besford 1971).

In the history of long-distance swimming, the blue ribbon has been, and continues to be, the English Channel. The traditional route (the one taken by Gertrude Ederle in her 1926 swim) is from Cape Gris Nez, France, to Dover, England. While the distance is only 32 kilometers (20 miles), currents, tides, drift, and weather conditions can add several miles to the actual distance swum.

There is a claim that the first English Channel crossing took place in 1815 when Jean-Marie Saletti, a French soldier, escaped from an English prison hulk in Dover and swam to Boulogne. While he certainly escaped by sea, it is more than possible that he used a raft or small boat. As with sea-borne escapes from Alcatraz Prison in the San Francisco Bay area, legends and fables perhaps outstrip hard facts.

The first authenticated swimming of the English Channel took place 24–25 August 1875, by Captain Matthew Webb. Webb is regarded as the founding father of long-distance swimming, and to this day he reigns supreme as the greatest showman in the history of the sport. Just as Esther Williams glamorized swimming and Johnny Weissmuller gave the sport a macho muscular image with his Tarzan movie roles, Captain Webb

*A greased-up Gertrude Ederle approaches the water on her way to becoming the first women to swim the English Channel.*

transformed long-distance swimming venues into a three-ring circus, one part carnival, one part festival, and one part rip-roaring recreational vacation spot. Webb was no mere athletic braggart. He was possessed of enormous athletic skill and limitless courage. It is thought that Webb may have zig-zagged as many as 28 miles (45 kilometers) in order to cross the 20-mile Dover Strait (Willoughby 1970).

Following Webb's 21 hour, 45 minute swim from Dover to Calais (as freestyle was not yet invented, Webb's only source of propulsion was alternating cycles of breaststroke and sidestroke), he capitalized upon his folk hero status and became a touring professional. He took part in stunts, challenges, and all manner of swimming feats. The ingenious Captain Webb and his management entourage were willing to arrange, promote, and charge admission to all types of swimming events.

The memoirs of journalist Robert Patrick Wat-

son paint a gruesome picture of Webb, ecstatic following his channel swim, eventually ending up as an enfeebled professional athlete desperately trying to drum up public support for a succession of swimming stunts. His health declined and his spirits suffered. In 1883, Webb met with Watson, who told him of the dangers of trying to catch a crowd, make a fortune, and swim the Niagara Falls rapids in the United States. Watson cautioned Webb, "From what I hear you will never come out alive." The tragic reply was, "Don't care. I want money and I must have it." On 24 July 1883, Webb drowned in the Whirlpool Rapids below Niagara Falls. Watson writes a telling lament on the ills and abuses of the life of a professional athlete who falls from grace.

As we stood face to face I compared the fine handsome sailor, who first spoke to me about swimming in Falcon Court, with the broken-spirited, and terribly altered appearance of the man who courted death in the whirlpool rapids of Niagara. I pictured him in his suit of serge, and called to mind the happy hours we once spent in the New Cut, Lambeth, over many a frugal meal of fried fish, bread and cheese, washed down with old ale. Then my thoughts wandered to gilded hall, champagne dinners, fast life, and high-class Bohemian society, the society that kills, and knows no cure.

It was not until 1911 that the next successful English Channel swim took place. Edward Temme was the first swimmer to cross the channel in both directions—but not consecutively. He swam from France to England in 1927 and seven years later swam from England to France.

There is no agreement as to who is the greatest long-distance swimmer in terms of distance covered. Pedro Candiotti of Argentina in 1935 swam 281 miles (450 kilometers) from Santa Fe to Zarate, Argentina. It took him 84 hours. The *All Sports Record Book* lists the feat of John V. Sigmund of St. Louis, Missouri, who swam nonstop down the Mississippi River from St. Louis to Caruthersville, Missouri, a distance of 292 miles (467 kilometers). The swim took 89 hours, 48 minutes, and ended on 29 July 1940.

Channel swimming is one of sport's most taxing challenges, with very high rates of failure.

## Gertrude Ederle (1906– )

In 1922, at the age of 15, Gertrude Ederle took part in a three-mile swim in New York Bay for the J. P. Day Cup. Up until that time her longest race had been only 220 yards. She won the cup and was convinced that long distance swimming could be her forte. Nevertheless, she remained an amateur until the 1924 Paris Olympics, where she won bronze medals with the 100- and 400-meter freestyle relay teams. During her amateur career she broke nine world records in distances ranging from 100 to 500 meters. In 1925, following her triumph in taking six national outdoor swimming titles, she turned professional.

In 1926, she became the first woman to swim the English Channel. Her time of 14 hours, 34 minutes from Cape Gris Nez, France, to Kingsdown, England, was faster than any man before her, nearly two hours faster than the France-to-England record of 16 hours, 33 minutes set on 11 August 1923, by the Italian Enrique Tiraboschi.

The *New York Times* of 7 August 1926, offers an amazing Ederle tapestry with literally thousands of words on her background, training, and the swim itself. The *Times* commented: "The record of her 19 years shows her to be courageous, determined, modest, sportsmanlike, generous, unaffected and perfectly poised. She had, in addition, beauty of face and figure and abounding health."

The newspaper then went on to describe her ethnic background and her first-generation immigrant status as a child of New York's sidewalks: "Miss Ederle's father is a German butcher and her mother is of the sturdy German housewife type. Some of the qualities of endurance and stamina which have been displayed by Miss Ederle were inherited from her parents and improved by the girl's life and training."

Twice during the epic swim her trainer/coach asked her to give up, but her father and sister urged her to keep going. Ederle declared that she was powerfully motivated by two things. First her father read to her from the support boat a series of encouraging telegrams that were wired from her mother in New York. Next, her father promised her that if she succeeded she could have the "roadster" (sports car) of her choice.

Some of the sportswriting about that swim was memorable. British swimming expert Alec Rutherford wrote about a plucky swimmer, "a pretty, tiny atom of humanity" battling for fourteen hours against merciless elements and looking fragile yet determined in a red "bathing dress" and motorist's goggles: "The swim came to an end in what might be described as a blaze of glory . . . huge bonfires were kept burning along the beach, lighting up the waters, so that those ashore could see the strong, steady strokes which Miss Ederle kept until she was able to touch bottom and walk ashore."

On her return to the United States, New York lavished Ederle with a two million people ticker-tape reception. Sadly, as she found herself swept along by the hoopla surrounding her celebrity status, various vaudeville tours of North America and Europe took a severe physical toll on her health. In 1928, she suffered a nervous breakdown but, after her recovery, she taught swimming to deaf children—physical trauma, as a result of her Channel swim, had caused her to become deaf.

—Scott A. G. M. Crawford

---

The fact that less than 7 percent who attempt to swim across the English Channel complete the trip is a testament to the difficulty of the task. Only the very strong succeed.

Two-way English Channel swims originated in 1961, when an Argentinian, Abertondo, swam the channel in both directions in a combined time of 43 hours, 5 minutes. In such swims a five-minute intermission is allowed at the changeover point. Two 14-year-old Americans have swum the English Channel; the youngest to have succeeded is a 13-year-old Egyptian. In 1964, a spastic and a polio victim completed the swim. At the 1972 Olympics, when Mark Spitz of the United States won seven gold medals in swimming events, his coach was James "Doc" Counsilman of Indiana University. Counsilman celebrated his sixty-fifth birthday by swimming the English Channel. The fastest crossing of the English Channel was completed by an American woman, Penny Dean, on 29 July 1978. Her time was 7 hours, 40 minutes.

Many other courses and areas are used for long-distance swimming. Today the crossing of the Cook Strait from the South Island to the North Island of New Zealand is considered a more severe challenge than that posed by the English Channel. The fastest swim around Manhattan Island in New York City was 5 hours, 53 minutes, by American Kris Rutford on 29 August 1992.

Long-distance swimming is now recognized by the American Athletic Union and there is now a one-hour swim championship that measures how far one can travel in one hour. At the 1978 championships in the men's 25–29 and 75–79 divisions, the leading distances were 5,240 yards

(4,793 meters) and 3,260 yards (2,982 meters), respectively. In the women's 25–29 and 75–79 divisions, the leading distances were 4,235 yards (3,873 meters) and 1,575 yards (1,441 meters), respectively.

The International Swimming Hall of Fame is located in Fort Lauderdale, Florida. It has a library with 5,000 volumes and has honored more than 200 inductees. Among these are a number of long-distance swimmers, including George Breen, Florence Chadwick, James "Doc" Counsilman, Penny Dean, Gertrude Ederle, and Captain Webb. One unusual and especially fascinating member is U.S. statesman and inventor Benjamin Franklin, who was also an outstanding long-distance swimmer.

The golden era of long-distance swimming as a major spectator sport was relatively short but, as Judith Jenkins George, has observed:

Thousands of spectators were drawn to the oceans, lakes and pools to observe the swimming marathons of the 1920s and 1930s. The fad of endurance swimming lasted less than a decade yet during this time, it captivated the public's interest and the athlete's imagination as a test of courage and stamina.

—Scott A. G. M. Crawford

**Bibliography:** *Amateur Athlete Yearbook.* (1978) Indianapolis: Amateur Athletic Union.

Besford, P. (1971) *Encyclopedia of Swimming.* New York: St. Martin's Press.

George, J. J. (1995) "The Fad of North American Women's Endurance Swimming during the Post–World War I Era." *Canadian Journal of History of Sport* 26, 1 (May): 52–72.

Hickok, R. (1992) *The Encyclopedia of North American Sports History.* New York: Facts on File.

Matthews, P., ed. *Guinness Book of Records—1994.* New York: Facts on File.

McWhirter, N. (1979) *Guinness Book of Women's Records.* New York: Sterling Press.

Menke, F. G. (1950) *The All Sports Record Book.* New York: A. S. Barnes.

*New York Times.* (1926) Various accounts of Ederle's swim (7 August).

Watson, R. P. (1899) *Memoirs of Robert Patrick Watson: A Journalist's Experience of Mixed Society.* London: Smith, Ainslie and Company.

Willoughby, D. P. (1970) *The Super Athletes.* New York: A. S. Barnes.

# Swimming, Speed

Speed swimming as a competitive sport has been performed in oceans, rivers, lakes, and pools throughout the world for centuries. Speed swimming is defined as sprints and middle distances, up to 1,500 meters (1,640.42 yards), which is currently the longest distance in international competitions in pools. It includes freestyle, backstroke, breaststroke, and butterfly. Throughout the twentieth century it has developed into a popular sport for both participants and spectators. Swimming events at the Olympic Games and the Federation Internationale de Natation Amateur (FINA) World Championships are feature events and attract television audiences internationally. However, the most successful participants in this sport come from those Western nations closely associated with its early development.

## Origins

Swimming was practiced throughout the ancient world for utilitarian and health reasons. The Egyptian hieroglyph for swimming depicted a man's head and one arm forward and the other back, and in Greek the phrase for the fundamentals of education was "the alphabet and swimming." The recurrence of the Latin words *iactare* and *alterna*, which indicate raising the arms alternately above the surface of the water, and other pictorial and literary sources provide evidence that the common swimming stroke was some form of crawl. Greek historians Herodotus (485–425 B.C.) and Thucydides (484–425 B.C.) wrote about the significance of swimming, but it was Pausanias (second century A.D.) who recorded that swimming races were held in honor of the Greek god, Dionysus. In the Middle Ages, books on the art of swimming were published throughout Europe; one of the first in England was written in 1587 by Everard Digby, who recorded that the art had been much neglected, "specially among noble men." In Japan in 1603, an imperial edict made swimming an integral part of the curriculum, thereby promoting interschool competition which inevitably led to nationally organized swimming races.

## Development

Not until the nineteenth century did regular, organized speed swimming events begin to develop. Swimming baths were opened in Liverpool, England, in 1828 and other cities soon followed; by 1837 the city of London had six pools in which speed swimming contests were conducted. Swimming clubs were soon established, with the Serpentine Club claiming to be the oldest. After the formation of the Metropolitan Swimming Club Association (MSCA), on 7 January 1869, T. Moriss won the first championship, swimming 1 mile (1,609 meters) downstream on the Thames River, between Putney Aqueduct and Hammersmith Bridge.

On the opposite side of the world in Sydney, Australia, there were similar developments in competitive swimming. In Woolloomooloo Bay on 14 February 1846, a 440-yard (402.3-meter) open race and a 100-yard (91.4-meter) race for juveniles were held in floating baths. The first "world championship" is also believed to have been held in Australia; on 9 February 1858, Joseph Bennet from Sydney beat an Englishman, Charles Steedman (1830–?), in a 100-yard event at St. Kilda, a Melbourne suburb.

In North America, the sports newspaper, *Spirit of the Times,* lamented in 1863 that New York had so few swimming clubs compared with Europe. The Dolphin Swim Club in Toronto was not formed until 1876 and a year later seven swimmers competed in that city for the governor-general of Canada's silver medal. The first major race in the United States, billed as the national championship, was held by the New York Athletic Club in 1883.

In continental Europe, European championships were conducted in 1889 by the Erste Wiener Amateur Swim Club in Vienna; the only two events were over 60 and 500 meters (65.62 and 546.81 yards). The success of swimming races in Britain from the mid-nineteenth century led to a proportional increase in the prizes, which were usually won by "professional swimmers," who were swimming teachers involved in giving lessons in return for money. Interclub swimming competition soon led to the formation of associations. In 1837 the National Swimming Society (NSS) was formed to define and organize races which were promoted by the weekly sporting

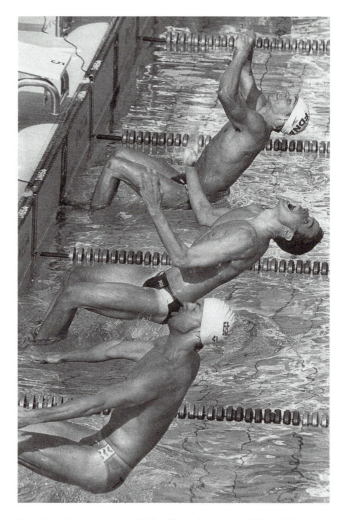

*Backstroke swimmers kick off at the start of the 100-meter heat at the 1986 World Swimming Championships in Madrid. In the center is Daniel Veatch of the United States, who qualified for the final.*

periodical, *Bell's Life.* In 1840, members of the NSS were responsible for teaching more than 3,000 Britons to swim and local committees organized speed swimming competitions in many regions.

Toward the end of the nineteenth century the distinction between "amateur" and "professional" became a significant issue in many sports. After the formation in 1886 of the Amateur Swimming Association, teachers of swimming in Great Britain were excluded from racing. Since that time the development of speed swimming, both in that country and internationally, has been predominantly through the efforts of amateur swimming organizations. For example, the New South Wales Amateur Swimming Association (NSWASA) was formed in 1892, and two years later this body staged the initial Australasian championships in New Zealand, in conjunction with the New Zealand Amateur Swimming Association (NZASA).

The modern Olympic Games were introduced to foster amateurism internationally and swimming events were held in Athens at the inaugural Olympic Games of 1896. Three events, the 100, 500, and 1,200 meters (109.36, 546.80, and 1,312.32 yards), were conducted in the Bay of Zeas near Piraeus; Arnold Guttman (1878–1955), known by his swimming pseudonym as Alfred Hajos, of Hungary, won both the 100 (1 minute, 22.2 seconds) and 1,200 meters. The events at the Olympic Games of 1900 (Paris), 1904 (St. Louis), and 1908 (London) were decided by the respective organizers. Immediately after the London Olympics, on 19 July 1908, at the Manchester Hotel in London, representatives of Belgium, Denmark, Finland, France, Germany, Great Britain, Hungary, and Sweden met and formed the Fédération Internationale de Natation Amateur. FINA's main roles were to establish rules for swimming events and international competitions, to verify and monitor world records, and to organize the swimming programs of the Olympic Games. FINA retained the swimming events held at the 1908 Olympic Games (100, 400, and 1,500 meters [109.36, 437.40, and 1,640.42 yards] freestyle; 100 meters backstroke; 200 meters [218.72 yards] breaststroke; 4 x 200 meters freestyle relay) until 1964, with the addition of the 200 meters butterfly in 1956.

FINA was also instrumental in the International Olympic Committee's (IOC) decision to introduce swimming for women at the 1912 Olympic Games in Stockholm. Throughout the latter half of the nineteenth century, most swimming for females was confined to pleasure bathing, but Australian Annette Kellerman (1886–1975) did much to influence societies throughout the world that speed swimming was an appropriate sport for women. Kellerman is acknowledged as having set the first world record for women over 100 yards (91 meters) when she swam 1.22.0 in 1902. More important, her exploits as swimmer, diver, entertainer, and movie star in "aquacades" throughout Europe and North America from 1906 to the 1930s greatly influenced the development of competitive swimming for women. Kellerman's life story was

portrayed on film by Esther Williams (1923– ), who was the U.S. 100-meter freestyle champion in 1939. Williams became the female lead opposite Johnny Weissmuller in the 1940 San Francisco World's Fair Aquacade and went on to star in "swimming" movies in the 1950s.

Another Australian, Sarah "Fanny" Durack (1889–1956), won the only individual swimming event for women, the 100 meter, at the 1912 Stockholm Olympics. Durack and her compatriot, Mina Wylie (1892–1984), who was the silver medalist, assisted in the promotion, development, and establishment of competitive swimming for women throughout the world. The New South Wales Ladies Amateur Swimming Association (NSWLASA), formed on 8 February 1906, had a rule that prohibited members from swimming when males were in attendance. However, when it was clear that both Durack and Wylie deserved selection for the 1912 Olympic Games, there was much debate over this rule. "Natator," writing in the Sydney sports weekly, *The Referee*, reported in February 1912 that "whenever carnivals are held by affiliations of the NSWLASA it is writ large over the gates and clinched by the strong rivets of unwavering firmness 'no man shall enter here.'" Eventually, in a clandestine gathering at which the NSWLASA president was not present, the rule forbidding men attending carnivals that included NSWLASA swimmers was rescinded, thereby facilitating Durack's and Wylie's participation in the Stockholm Olympics.

The keeping of world-record times has been a significant aspect of speed swimming, and a race against the clock is regarded as an important element of the "spirit of sport." However, there are many factors that need to be considered, such as regulations pertaining to clothing and the technological development of pools, when comparing times in speed swimming. Both the style and materials of men's and women's costumes were governed by social acceptance and official regulations and the neck-to-knee costumes worn into the 1930s were made of a wool or heavy cotton which retained much more water than nylon, which was introduced in the 1950s, or the brief Lycra costumes of the 1980s.

The swimming events at the first few Olympic Games were conducted in various water environments: the sea at the inaugural Games in Athens in 1896, the Seine River of Paris in 1900, an artificial lake built for the St. Louis World's Fair in 1904, and in a specially built 100-meter-long swimming tank in the main stadium in London in 1908. Bronze medalist in the 1,500 meters in 1908, Frank Beaurepaire (1891–1956), stated he could not see where he was going in the black water. It was not until the 1924 Olympics in Paris that events were held in a stadium constructed especially for swimming and divided into lanes separated by floating markers.

## Practice

In 1873, John Arthur Trudgen, an English amateur swimmer, introduced an alternate overarm stroke, also known as the double overarm stroke, with a breaststroke kick he had seen performed in South Africa. This stroke became widespread and was named the Trudgen. The Cavill family in Australia developed the crawl into the classic stroke for both sprints and middle distances. English-born "Professor" Frederick Cavill (1839–1927), who taught swimming in Sydney, had a family of nine children, six of them boys who all became swimming champions. Dick "Splash" Cavill (1884–1938) had seen Alick Wickham from the Solomon Islands swim the stroke with leg kick. He eventually developed it, with the help of his brother Arthur (1877–1914), to a stage where he could swim the crawl for the entire distance, unofficially breaking the world 100 yards record (unofficially, because it was a handicap race) in Sydney in 1902. The crawl had many names: the flutter kick, Cavill splash stroke, Australian crawl, and Australian splash.

The flutter kick was tiring and, for many years, swimmers in longer distances used a combination of scissors and flutter kicks which became known as the crawl Trudgen. Some successful distance swimmers at the Olympic Games of this era who pioneered the evolution of the various styles of crawl in the first few decades of the twentieth century include: Australians Frederick Lane (1880–1969) and Andrew "Boy" Charlton (1909–1975); Americans Charles Daniels (1885–1973), Norman Ross (1896–1953) and Johnny Weissmuller (1904–1984); Canadian George Hodgson (1893–1983); and Swede Arne Borg (1901–1987).

One of the major developments was the American kick. Duke Kahanomoku (1890–1968) from

## International Swimming Hall of Fame

The citizens of Fort Lauderdale, Florida, raised more than 1 million dollars to pay for the erection of a huge building and a 50-meter (54.68-yard) swimming pool, which has become the International Swimming Hall of Fame (ISHF). Supported by more than 100 countries that agreed to give it international status, the ISHF is operated by a chartered nonprofit organization that is responsible for the annual induction of famous swimmers and coaches. When the honor ceremonies take place at the annual festival at Christmas, the ISHF is visited by many of the world's great competitors. An 11-million-dollar expansion in 1988 enhanced the facilities and resources for the presentation of displays and utilization of the library comprising more than 5,000 volumes, films, and videotapes pertaining to aquatic sports.

—Ian Jobling

the Hawaiian Islands, and later Johnny Weissmuller, epitomized this style by swimming in the hydroplane position which enabled the kick to start at the hip and thereby obtain maximum efficiency from the legs as only the flat of the foot broke the surface. Both Kahanomoku and Weissmuller were two-time 100 meters Olympic Games gold medalists in 1912 and 1920, and 1924 and 1928, respectively. Since that time there have been many variations of leg kick in the crawl, many of them cyclical.

The rules and techniques of breaststroke are not designed for speed. Swimming on the breast with the head out of the water and symmetrical leg and arm movements under the water was well known in antiquity. In deference to its popularity in Europe throughout the latter decades of the nineteenth century, the organizers of swimming for the 1904 St. Louis Olympic Games introduced a 440-yard (402.34-meter) event. The arm action of early breaststrokers was a wide stroke of "oars" parallel and close to the water's surface which continued until in line with the shoulders; the leg action was a wide lurch preceded by a bending of the knees, which were pointed outward. Erich Rademacher (1901–1979) changed this technique in 1924, and 1928 Olympic gold medalist Yashiyuki Tsuruta (1903–1986) of Japan introduced another modification that produced a fast, nonjerky stroke that basically remained until 1956.

Since the beginning of the 1950s, surface breaststroke improved remarkably because of a greater importance being placed on the power from the arm movement, thereby modifying the traditional belief that the legs provided primary propulsion. American Chet Jastremski (1941– ) established world records in the 100 and 200 meters by totally eliminating the legs for the rotating action of the arms. Most of the place-getters in breaststroke at the Tokyo Olympic Games in 1964 used this action. Since that time, minor modifications by Russian, U.S., and Australian swimmers have seen breaststroke develop into a most interesting event. and the times have been significantly reduced over all distances.

Swimming breaststroke under the water was faster than the surface style; this was the reason many of the successful breaststrokers swam longer underwater on starts and turns. Japan's Masaru Furukawa (1936– ) broke world records on several occasions, the most remarkable being on 1 October 1955. In a 25-meter ((27.34-yard) pool, Furukawa surfaced only 20 times when he swam 200 meters in 2.31.0. Furukawa won the 1956 Olympic gold medal in the 200 meters, but underwater breaststroke was banned after 1957 because it gave a distinct advantage and detracted from the spirit of the stroke; spectators wanted to see swimmers on the surface of the water, not under it.

Despite protests in 1926 when German Erich Rademacher recovered his arms by bringing them over the surface, thereby reducing the braking effect of the water, the rules of breaststroke at that time did not stipulate that a swimmer had to keep the arms underwater while bringing them forward. This style, known as breaststroke butterfly to distinguish it from the traditional classic breaststroke called orthodox hand-over-hand, recurred periodically (e.g., Australian John Davies (1929– ) won the 200-meter breaststroke event at the Olympic Games in Helsinki in 1952 using a butterfly arm stroke and a frog kick) until the butterfly became an official stroke in its own right in 1953.

The rules of butterfly stipulate that it is a double-crawl with simultaneous movements of the arms and legs. The best butterfly swimmers have used the dolphin kick, which was banned in breaststroke events because it did not comply with the strict rules of the stroke that required a symmetrical sideways and backwards movement. On the inaugural occasion for the butterfly event in the 1956 Olympic Games in Melbourne, the dolphin kick had progressed from a series of immersions and emersions to a much flatter position on the water, facilitating faster times.

Backstroke speed swimming is a relatively recent phenomenon, not having been recorded until the beginning of the twentieth century. The 1900, 1904, and 1908, Olympic champions all used an arm-over-arm technique, but the back-crawl method used at the 1912 Olympic Games by Harry Hebner (1989–1968) has dominated. Japanese male backstrokers, using a kick based on an ascending movement of the extended leg, took the first three places in the 100 meters in the 1932 Olympic Games. The great American coach, Louis de B. Handley (1874–1956), observed the new technique of the Japanese, and coached Eleanor Holm (1913– ) to the gold medal using that technique in the 100 meters at those Olympics. Several modifications occurred over the next twenty years but when the men's Olympic backstroke distance changed to 200 meters at the 1964 Olympic Games in Tokyo, the major changes have been a greater emphasis on the speed of the arm action. Both male and female U.S. swimmers have been dominant in the backstroke.

Speed swimming is a popular sport throughout the world, but international success has been concentrated among Western nations. At the Olympic Games from 1896 through 1992, U.S. male and female swimmers have dominated in all strokes, winning 266 gold, silver, and bronze medals. The combined total of Germany, both East and West (110 medals), Australia (85 medals), and the Soviet Union (47 medals) does not reach the U.S. figure. Japan, which had several successful freestyle and breaststroke swimmers (41 medals), is the only Asian country that has won more than 2 medals; other countries to have achieved that distinction are Hungary (34), Netherlands (18), Sweden (20), Canada (19), Great Britain (17), France (13), Denmark (8), Austria (7), Belgium (5), Greece and New Zealand (4), and Brazil, Bulgaria, Italy, and Spain (3). Of the 315 medals won by women, more than two-thirds were won by Americans (104), Germans (74), and Australians (30); the only non-Western nation to have gained medals in women's swimming are Japan (7), Argentina (1), and Mexico (1). The 1996 Olympics showed some potentially changing trends: China won 6 medals, Ireland 4, Brazil and South Africa 3, and Cuba 2. The U.S. total of 26 medals did not exceed the combined total of the three top scorers: Australia (13), Germany (12), and Russia (8). Still, it is clear that many countries do not participate successfully in international speed swimming competition; this may reflect religious and societal values in many of those societies.

—Ian Jobling

**Bibliography:** Besford, Pat, editor. (1971) *Encyclopedia of Swimming.* New York: St. Martin's Press.

Brasch, R. (1970) *How Did Sports Begin? A Look at the Origins of Man at Play.* New York: David McKay Company.

Carlile, Forbes. (1963) *Forbes Carlile on Swimming.* London: Pelham.

Colwin, Cecil. (1992) *Swimming into the Twenty-first Century.* West Point, NY: Leisure Press.

Counsilman, James, and Brian Counsilman. (1994) *The New Science of Swimming.* Englewood Cliffs, NJ: Prentice-Hall.

Dyer, Ken. (1982) *Challenging the Men: The Social Biology of Female Sporting Achievement.* St. Lucia: University of Queensland Press.

Harris, H. A. (1972) *Sport in Greece and Rome.* Ithaca, NY: Cornell University Press.

Henning, H. N. (1983) *International Swimming and Water Polo.* Budapest, Hungary. Part 1, 2–7; Part 2, 2–7, 49–51, 57–59, 65–67.

Kellerman, Annette. (1918) *How To Swim.* London: William Heinemann.

Kenney, Karen. (1982) "The Realm of Sports and the Athletic Woman, 1850–1900." In *Her Story in Sport: A Historical Anthology of Women in Sports,* edited by Reet Howell. West Point, NY: Leisure Press, 107–140.

Mallon, Bill. (1988) *The Olympic Record Book.* New York: Garland Publishing Company.

McDonald, John. (1993) *The First 100: A Century of Swimming in Victoria.* Melbourne: Swimming Victoria.

Oppenheim, Francois. (1970) *The History of Swimming.* North Hollywood, CA: Swimming World.

Orme, Nicholas. (1983) *Early British Swimming, 55 BC–AD 1719, with the First Swimming Treatise in English, 1595.* Exeter: University of Exeter.

Spears, Betty. (1976) "Women in the Olympic Games: An Unresolved Problem." In *The Modern Olympics,* edited by P. J. Graham and H. Ueberhorst. New York: Leisure Press.

Terret, Thierry. (1995) "Professional Swimming in England before the rise of Amateurism, 1837–75." *International Journal of the History of Sport* 12, 1 (April): 18–32.

# Swimming, Synchronized

Synchronized swimming—"The sport that took 40 years to travel from Hollywood to Los Angeles [Olympics]" (McDonald's placemats 1984)—refers to the aquatic activity that some think was born with the Los Angeles Olympics, but will actually celebrate 50 years of U.S. national championship competition in Atlanta in 1996.

Competitive synchronized swimming, often called "synchro," is similar to both figure skating and gymnastics, with routines performed to musical accompaniment. Routines are composed to "synchronize" with and interpret the music in the performance of a variety of swimming strokes and complex body actions. Routines may be performed as solo, duet, or team (up to eight members). The combination of swimming and gymnastic-type movements produces an athletically demanding sport that demonstrates technical and physical skills with artistry and showmanship.

Synchronized swimming has a special appeal for children in building upon the natural tendencies to play imaginatively, to dance, to act, and to enjoy rhythmic activities. Synchronized swimming puts all these into the water and adds competition. The sport meets a need for a physically demanding activity that provides a balance of strength and aerobic development while encouraging grace, expanding mental skills, stimulating cooperative and group outlooks, enhancing creativity and poise, and furthering musical awareness.

## Origins and Development

The elements of synchro—swimming strokes, figures, sculling, and floating—are as old as swimming itself. A bas relief from the Assyrian palace of Nimroud, about 880 B.C.E., portrays underwater swimmers, and old Japanese wood-block prints show men performing figures such as somersaults and demonstrating a position much like modern synchro's "ballet leg." "Scientific and Ornamental Swimming" for men was found in 1892 in England, with Canada beginning, in 1898, a similar men's competition, "Stunts and Strokes."

# Swimming, Synchronized

*The combination of swimming and gymnastic-style movement in synchronized swimming makes it an athletically demanding sport, but also produces a spectacle of grace and beauty that kept "synchro" from being taken seriously as a sport. It did not achieve Olympic status until 1984, after almost 40 years of competition.*

At the turn of the century, women had floating pattern groups in Germany, Belgium, the Netherlands, and France.

Water show activities, though, did underlie the development and popularization of synchro, beginning in 1907 with exhibitions by Annette Kellerman (?–1975), who performed in a glass tank in countries around the world, and later in the film *Neptune's Daughter,* in which her life was portrayed by MGM's aquatic star, Esther Williams.

Katharine Curtis (?–1980), the "mother of synchronized swimming" in the United States, experimented, in 1915, with water figures and added music. She extended this, in 1923 for her University of Chicago classes, to combinations of various "tricks," strokes, and floats that were finally "synchronized" to musical beats and measures, "just as in dancing." Her students appeared, as the "Kay Curtis Modern Mermaids," in the 1933–

1934 Chicago "Century of Progress" Fair, performing three times daily for audiences of up to 10,000. The term "synchronized swimming" was coined by announcer Norman Ross to describe those shows. Those successes inspired showman Billy Rose's water extravaganzas, leading to Aquacades at both the 1939 New York World's Fair, starring Eleanor Holm, the 1936 U.S. Olympic backstroker, and the 1940 San Francisco World's Fair, starring Esther Williams, 1939 100-meter freestyle national champion. Williams went on to make a series of Hollywood films featuring water spectaculars that brought world attention to "water ballet."

Meanwhile, competitive development was spurred by Frank Havlicek, a student in Curtis's class at Chicago's Wright Junior College, who suggested in 1939 that the collegiate routines could form the basis for competitions between colleges. Rules were drawn up, leading to the first known competition, a dual event between Wright Junior College and the Chicago Teachers College, in May 1939. Amateur Athletic Union (AAU) swimming committee member, David Clark Leach (?–1977), took interest and championed its adoption as a sport sanctioned under the AAU in 1940. He became the first chairman of AAU Synchronized Swimming. The first national championship was delayed by World War II until 1946. When all U.S. sports became independent of the AAU in 1978, United States Synchronized Swimming, Inc., was formed to govern the sport. The headquarters is Indianapolis, Indiana.

Canada concurrently developed competitive forms of synchro, beginning in 1951. Both Canada and the United States helped spread the sport worldwide through international exhibitions during the 1950s. Synchronized swimming became an official world sport in 1954 when the Fédération Internationale de Natation Amateur (FINA) accepted it as a swimming "discipline."

The first truly international competition, held under FINA auspices, was the Pan American Games of 1955 in Mexico City. Synchro was included in the World Aquatic Championships in 1973 in Belgrade, Yugoslavia. Its Olympic debut came in Los Angeles, California, in 1984. Of this event, the *Los Angeles Examiner* wrote, "For millions of viewers, a star is born. I'm not talking about any individual athlete, but a whole sport—synchronized swimming, a bizarre meld of figure skating, gymnastics, and Busby Berkeley musicals, which takes place in the water. It truly resists comparison with any other sporting event."

## Practice

Internationally, competition is held in senior class, junior class (ages 14–17), and by age groups (12 and under, 13–14, and 15–17), as well as in masters programs for adults 25 and over.

Competition in synchro includes three events: figure competition, technical program, and free routine. The figure competition is similar to a diving competition, where each competitor performs a set of closely prescribed movements for one judging award. The scores for each of the four figures are added for a total. The technical routine is set to music and contains compulsory actions, similar to the technical program in ice dance competitions. The free routine is longer

## **Sport or Theater?**

While a complex, rapidly developing sport may be expected to generate many internal problems, synchro's main controversy, "sport or theater," is generated externally, by media that are unwilling to consider as "sport" anything not meeting the "swifter, higher, stronger" standard. But even *Sports Illustrated*, despite normally less than flattering reviews, admitted in its report on the 1984 Los Angeles Olympics, "Synchronized swimmers may look like cupcakes, but they're tough cookies, half the routine is performed upside down in a pool." Its water-show beginnings still haunt it. The idea that water ballet is show, while synchronized swimming is sport, has been hard to sell to swimming officials, the public, and the media. Its acceptance into the Olympic Games came only after Lord Killanin, then chair of the International Olympic Committee, saw it for himself at the third World Aquatic Championships. "I am very impressed. I saw synchronized swimming for the first time today. It is a very elegant sport."

Synchro enjoys more popularity and acceptance as a sport in parts of the world outside the United States. In every Olympic competition, 1984 through 1996, it has been one of the first sports to sell out all audience tickets.

Another issue is male participation. Interestingly, at the turn of the century competitions in the equivalent of figures were for males. Then the beautiful spectaculars of aquacades and films accented the female attraction. Early U.S. competitions included male championships, but they were never popular. Neither U.S. nor international rules prohibit male participation except for the Olympic Games and the World Aquatic Championships. Presently, male participation is greater in Europe than in the United States and Canada. Indeed, in 1991, the French national champion duet was a mixed pair and a junior male qualified, in 1996, to be part of the U.S. National Junior Team and will compete in competitions that allow males. Men are included in the U.S. masters program.

—Dawn Bean

and the athlete has complete freedom in choosing actions to perform. A competition must include at least two of the three events. When all three are conducted, the final score is 50 percent of the free routine and 25 percent each for the technical routine and figures. World, Regional, and Junior Championships may include all three events, or just the free routine (65 percent) and figure competition (35 percent).

In each routine event, two scores—for technical merit and artistic impression—are awarded by panels of 5 to 7 judges. Technical merit includes execution, synchronization, and difficulty and counts for 60 percent of the routine's score. Artistic impression, which counts for 40 percent, includes choreography, music interpretation, and manner of presentation.

In figure competition, each athlete is judged individually on four separate figures. Each figure consists of complex body movements in a specified sequence and design. Actions include spins, twists, somersaults, and many other special movements that are named for identification. Five to seven judges assess each swimmer's conformation to the action description and on the demonstration of height, strength, and control.

Different countries vary the international rules according to their own needs and perceptions for their internal competitions. Competitions in the United States, for example, may include a trio (three-swimmer) event and also a 10 and under division. U.S. competitions currently include a free routine and figures.

## Major Events and Competitors

Synchronized swimming is now practiced on every continent in the world, with more than 60 nations conducting national programs. World championship and Olympic Game competitions have included 20 to 35 entries. The 1992 world coaches seminar in Greece brought 104 participants from 57 countries, while the 1994 world judges conference in Canada included judges from more than 60 nations.

The top international competitions, each held every four years, are the Olympic Games (restricted in 1996 to team events only), the World Aquatic Championships (including solo, duet, and team events), and the Goodwill Games (solo and duet only). The FINA World Cup and Junior World Championships are held every two years. Regional championships—European, Asian, Pan American, Pan Pacific, Coman (Mediterranean), Central American, and South American Games—are held every four years. Numerous international "open" competitions are held in conjunction with various national championships. The American Cup for Juniors is held every two years.

The United States has had the singular distinction of being the first winner in most of the major competitions. Tracie Ruiz (solo and duet) and Candy Costie (duet) became the first Olympic champions in 1984 in Los Angeles. Kristen Babb (solo), and Sarah and Karen Josephson (duet) won the first Goodwill Games in 1990 in Seattle, Washington. Becky Dyroen (solo and duet) and Jill Sudduth (duet) and the U.S. Junior Team won the first Junior World Championships in 1989 in Cali, Colombia. Teresa Andersen (solo and duet) and Gail Johnson (duet) and the Santa Clara, California, Aquamaids (team) won the first World Aquatic Championships in 1973 in Belgrade. Beulah Gundling (solo), Connie Todoroff and Ellen Richard (duet), and Oakland, California, Athens Club (team) won the first international competition in the 1955 Pan-American Games in Mexico City. The 1979 World Cup in Tokyo, Japan, was the only exception to all the U.S. firsts. The U.S. National Team won the team event, but the solo and duet events went to Canadians Helen Vanderberg (solo and duet) and Kelly Kryczka (duet).

World events have been dominated by the United States and Canada. Japan, a perennial bronze medalist, took the silver medals in solo and duet at the 1994 world championships. Russia moved into bronze-medal places in all three events at the 1995 FINA World Cup. Currently, the top eight synchro powers in the world are the United States, Canada, Russia, Japan, France, People's Republic of China, Italy, and Mexico. Korea, Great Britain, Switzerland, the Netherlands, Ukraine, Brazil, Australia, and the Czech Republic all competed in the 1995 Olympic qualifying competition.

In the United States, the U.S. National, U.S. Open, U.S. Junior, Collegiate National, Masters National, and National Age Group and National Junior Olympics are the major competitions. Senior and junior championships are also held in four geographic zones, 15 age group regions, and 58 local associations. The main participants are females from the age of 8 through the early twenties. Current U.S. team champion is Santa Clara, California. The collegiate champion is Ohio State University.

—Dawn Bean

**Bibliography:** Bean, Dawn, ed. (1979–1992). *Synchro*. Santa Ana, CA.

———. (1963–1978). *Synchro-Info.* Santa Ana, CA.

Chiefari, Janet, and Nancy Wightman. (1981) *Better Synchronized Swimming for Girls.* New York: Dodd, Mead.

Davis, Charlotte, and Dawn Bean. (1988) *Three Month Curriculum for Synchronized Swimming.* Indianapolis, IN: U.S. Synchronized Swimming.

Fédération Internationale de Natation Amateur. (1946– ) *FINA Handbook.* Lausanne, Switzerland: Fédération Internationale de Natation Amateur

———. (1995) *Synchronized Swimming Judges' Training Manual.* Lausanne, Switzerland: Fédération Internationale de Natation Amateur

Gray, Jennifer. (1993) *Coaching Synchronized Swimming Figure Transitions.* Maidenhead, Berkshire, UK: Standard Studio Publishers.

Gundling, Beulah, and Jill White. (1988) *Creative Synchronized Swimming.* Champaign, IL: Leisure Press.

Gyarfas, Tamas, ed. (1977– ) *International Swimming and Water Polo.* Belgrade, Yugoslavia.

Heath, Fran. (1989) *Synchronized Swimming Routine Choreography.* Edmonton: Synchro Swim Alberta.

LaMarca, Laura, ed. (1993– ) *Synchro USA.* Indianapolis, IN: United States Synchronized Swimming.

Lundholm, Jean K., and Mary Jo Ruggieri. (1976) *Introduction to Synchronized Swimming.* Minneapolis: Burgess Publishing Co.

Rackham, George. (1968) *Synchronized Swimming.* London: Faber & Faber.

Swan, Margaret, Donald Kane, and Dawn Bean. (1984, 1989) *Coaching Synchronized Swimming Effectively.* Champaign,. IL: Human Kinetics.

U.S. Synchronized Swimming. (1944– ) *Official Synchronized Swimming Handbook.* Indianapolis, IN: U.S. Synchronized Swimming.

Van Buskirk, Kim, ed. (1987) *Coaching Intermediate Synchronized Swimming Effectively.* Champaign, IL: Human Kinetics.

Wenz, Betty, ed. (1980) *Sports Medicine Meets Synchronized Swimming.* Reston, VA: American Alliance for Health, Physical Education, Recreation and Dance.

# Table Tennis

**See** Tennis, Table

# Tae Kwon Do

Tae kwon do ("the way of kicking and striking") is a Korean martial art practiced by more than 20 million students in over 140 countries. Like other martial arts, tae kwon do emphasizes physical and mental discipline, obedience, and respect as a path to self-mastery. As they demonstrate increasing skills, students move gradually up a hierarchy symbolized by differently colored belts. The use of special etiquette and forms of address, wearing of uniforms ("dobuks"), recital of the oath and tenets, and learning about Korean culture and history are all part of its practice. Tae kwon do's distinctiveness arises from its emphasis on kicking, especially powerful flying kicks, as its main weapon.

## Origins

Most commentators suggest three possibilities for the early development of tae kwon do. One account traces tae kwon do to Korea's three-kingdom era (50 B.C.E.), when Silla Dynasty warriors, the Hwarang, spread a traditional martial art, tae kyon ("foot-hand"), throughout Korea. A second idea is that tae kwon do began as a form of Chinese boxing established at Shaolin Temple in 520 C.E. by Bodhidharma, the legendary Indian monk and founder of Zen Buddhism. A third suggestion is that tae kwon do is an offshoot of Japanese or Okinawan karate, which it resembles. There is no way to decide which of these is the most authentic or how substantial a contribution each may have made to the whole. Overall, it is probable that tae kwon do represents an overlay of other Asian martial arts on a native Korean form of punching and kicking.

## Development

For practical purposes, modern tae kwon do history begins in the twentieth century: Japanese prohibited the local practice of martial arts ("Subak") when they occupied Korea in 1909. Present-day Korean martial artists argue that the Japanese interdiction inspired a conscious struggle to establish a patriotic martial arts culture. At the end of World War II, a number of Korean martial arts schools ("kwans") claimed involvement in resistance activities as a credential for their authenticity.

The international police action of the early 1950s seems to have increased the visibility and prestige of Korean martial arts, since many Korean soldiers had been formally trained in tae kwon do. As well, Korean martial arts were brought to the attention of U.S. troops for the first time in much the same fashion as Japanese martial arts became familiar during the U.S. occupation of Japan. In 1955, a conclave of the leaders of Korean martial arts schools attempted to identify an authoritative style of martial art that could be promoted both nationally and internationally. Tae kwon do was ultimately chosen as the name of this style. A general of the Korean armed forces, Hong Hi Choi, was designated the official founder of tae kwon do; he has subsequently published a multivolume encyclopedia of tae kwon do that currently serves as its approved doctrine.

By 1973 the Korean government had recognized the World Tae Kwon Do Federation (WTF) as the sole legitimate organization that sets international standards and awards world titles for tae kwon do performance, as well as national titles through its affiliates. Tae kwon do is now vigorously supported by the Republic of South Korea through its public schools and armed forces.

The International Olympic Committee admitted the WTF as a member organization in 1980, and named tae kwon do a demonstration sport in the 1988 Seoul Olympics, ensuring worldwide media attention. The increase of tae kwon do's popularity in the 1990s has in its turn contributed to tae kwon do's elevation to the status of a regular Olympic event.

## Techniques

Tae kwon do teaches an immediate physical reaction, unmediated by mental response, that directly

*Grandmaster Jae Kyn Lee breaks ten bricks, a demonstration of the focus and power of the tae kwon do practitioner.*

meets the opponent's force. It uses both quick linear movements, like karate, and circular flowing movements, like tai chi chuan. Tae kwon do distinguishes itself from other Asian martial arts by its emphasis on powerful kicking techniques. This feature makes tae kwon do more accessible to children and women, whose flexibility and lower body strength provides them an advantage in this martial art by contrast to more male-oriented systems, such as kendo, that depend heavily upon upper body strength.

The techniques of tae kwon do teach rhythm, timing, balance, agility, and breath control. Tae kwon do students learn to defend against attacks from all directions, using both sides of their body and all arms and legs. Self-mastery is achieved through regular, frequent repetition of physical techniques.

All movements fall into four elementary categories: kicks, strikes, stances, and blocks. Kicks rely on the leg's musculature and reach to deliver great force and keep an opponent at a distance.

Like leg kicks, arm strikes are retracted rapidly to permit multiple blows and prevent an opponent from grabbing a limb. Stances are upright and fluid, requiring careful attention to placement of the hips, waist, and pelvis. Blocks protect specific areas of the body, but are not developed to anticipate particular forms of attack, since tae kwon do teaches spontaneous responses to a wide variety of threatening situations.

Forms, sparring, and breaking, the three main categories of training and competition, require coordinated combinations of these basic movements. Each rank has its own form, kicking combinations, sparring, and defense moves to be learned. Free sparring allows students to devise their own combinations of kicks and strikes spontaneously; protective gear is worn to ensure safety. Breaking of boards and bricks demonstrates the focus and power of a student.

The introduction of tae kwon do as an Olympic event has widened a division between schools that focus on physical performance, competition, and winning (sport tae kwon do) and schools that combine the study of physical technique with a philosophical orientation (traditional tae kwon do). It seems likely that this difference between sport tae kwon do and traditional tae kwon do will continue to grow.

## Philosophy

Tae kwon do, like many other Asian martial arts, probably spread as part of the ascetic training practices of monks and warriors. Thus for historical reasons tae kwon do shares a philosophical background allied with the Chinese Tao or Japanese Zen. Indeed, the common Asian term for life force ("ki") is used in tae kwon do, as is the term for path or way ("do"), though modern Western practitioners are usually vague about the more general significance of such ideas. For the most part, modern tae kwon do is taught in urban settings to students with diverse religious and cultural backgrounds. Its philosophy, therefore, is usually expressed more often in routine training exercises or etiquette than in an extended study of specific beliefs. For instance, training sessions typically begin and end with meditation; instructors deliver occasional brief lectures on proper attitude and conduct; lower ranks bow to senior ranks; students employ respectful forms of

## Children's Home Rules

1. Children must show respect to their parents and family members at all times.
2. Children shall greet their parents when they enter the home and tell them goodbye when they leave.
3. Children will be truthful at all times.
4. Children will maintain a good relationship with their brothers and sisters.
5. Children must help with household chores.
6. Children will keep their own room neat and clean.
7. Children must keep their body, hair and teeth clean at all times (every day).
8. Children will not interrupt adult conversations.
9. Children will study their school work at school and at home.
10. Children must show respect for teachers and peers at all times.

Children who do not obey their parents may be reduced in rank.

address to their masters; and groups recite the tae kwon do oath and tenets at each session:

**Tae kwon do Oath**
I shall observe the tenets of tae kwon do.
I shall respect the instructors and seniors.
I shall never misuse tae kwon do.
I shall be a champion of freedom and justice.
I shall build a more peaceful world.

**Tae kwon do Tenets**
Courtesy
Integrity
Perseverance
Self Control
Indomitable Spirit

The emphasis on different aspects of tae kwon do philosophy differs from one part of the world to another, as masters change it to suit new circumstances. Traditionally, for instance, Korean men learned tae kwon do in military and public educational contexts, and accepted the strict obedience and discipline associated with such institutions. In the United States, by contrast, most students purchase lessons from a private school ("do jang"), and many pursue tae kwon do training for individual self-improvement and personal fitness. A significantly increasing number of American women, children, and the differently abled have been attracted to tae kwon do as do jangs have publicized its benefits for self-confidence and protection against street crime. Most recently, Americans have attended classes as a family activity, leading to the adoption of the children's home rules as part of their training.

## Outlook

The very diversity of tae kwon do continues to be a matter for considerable controversy, since the styles and organizations that are officially approved are vastly outnumbered by new ones that are continually appearing. For instance, the other traditional Korean martial art, hapkido, has recently borrowed many tae kwon do techniques in an effort to broaden its appeal. To take another example, there are at least a dozen tae kwon do organizations in the United States alone that claim national or international status in addition to those formally recognized by the Korean government and the International Olympic Committee. The standardization of tae kwon do performance in the Olympics is likely to promote further the dominance of "authorized" styles and associations. Nevertheless, independent organizers and business owners have a strong incentive to present innovative services to satisfy local consumers, which will limit such tendencies towards uniformity.

—Margaret Carlisle Duncan

**Bibliography:** Choi, Hong Hi. (1993) *Taekwon-do: The Korean Art of Self-Defence.* 3d ed. 15 vols. Mississauga, Ontario: International Taekwon-Do Federation.

Corcoran, John, and Emil Farkas. (1983) *Martial Arts: Traditions, History, People.* New York: Gallery Books.

Donohue, John. (1991) *The Forge of the Spirit: Structure, Motion, and Meaning in the Japanese Martial Tradition.* New York: Garland.

———. (1994) *Warrior Dreams: The Martial Arts and the American Imagination.* Westport, CT: Bergin & Garvey.

Farkas, Emil, and John Corcoran. (1985) *The Overlook Martial Arts Dictionary.* Woodstock, NY: Overlook Press.

*Journal of Asian Martial Arts* (1992– ). Erie, PA: Via Media.

Park, Yeon Hee, and Jeff Liebowitz. (1993) *Taekwondo for Children: The Ultimate Reference Guide for Children Interested in the World's Most Popular Martial Art.* East Meadow, NY: Y. H. Park.

———. (1993) *Fighting Back: Taekwondo for Women.* East Meadow, NY: Y. H. Park.

Park, Yeon Hee, Yeon Hwan Park, and Jon Gerrard. (1989) *tae kwon do: The Ultimate Reference Guide to the World's Most Popular Martial Art.* New York: Facts on File.

Reid, Howard, and Michael Croucher. (1983) *The Fighting Arts: Great Masters of the Martial Arts.* New York: Simon and Schuster.

*tae kwon do Times* (1982– ). Davenport, IA: C. K. Publications.

Wiley, Carol, ed. (1992) *Women in the Martial Arts.* Berkeley, CA: North Atlantic Books.

# Tai Chi

Taijiquan or Grand Ultimate Boxing, often simply called *taiji*, or taichi in the anglicized version, is a Chinese martial art of the *Neijia* or soft/internal school. Like other arts of that school, such as *Baguazhang* and *Xinyiquan*, taijiquan is intrinsically linked to the Daoist (Taoist) philosophical, meditative, and medical tradition. The soft, slow movements of the popular Yang style of taijiquan are often performed by invalids and the elderly in the Chinese world to strengthen the constitution generally and to promote longevity. Disciplined daily practice of the art is said to enhance the quality and circulation of *qi* (ch'i) or vital energy within the body, tone all the muscles, improve all bodily functions, and engender a calm and relaxed mental attitude. The vast majority of the many millions of people who practice taijiquan in China and elsewhere do so for these health and psychological benefits, but taijiquan is a premier martial art as well, and one that can be utilized effectively even very late in life.

## Origins

The links among martial arts, internal exercises, and Chinese traditional medicine antedate accurate historical knowledge. Chinese legendary history attributes taijiquan's origin to Zhang Sanfeng, a Daoist adept who was canonized in 1459, but taijiquan enters recorded history centuries later as a tremendously effective martial art practiced esoterically by the people of Chenjiagou (Chen village) in Henan Province. A form of the art was first demonstrated and taught in public in Beijing by Yang Luchan (1799–1872), who had learned it in Chenjiagou. Yang is said to have accepted all challenges from the many Beijing martial arts masters, never to have been bested, and never to have injured an opponent seriously. He became known as "Yang the Invincible" and was appointed martial arts instructor to the Imperial Court. Yang Luchan taught the slow and soft performance of a lengthy sequence of named techniques or patterns publicly, but transmitted a much larger and more varied corpus of lore to his private students, a practice quite in keeping with martial tradition. It is Yang's and his successors' publicly taught form from which popular conceptions of taijiquan as an only vaguely martial, though particularly beneficial, health and longevity exercise are drawn. This continuing process of softening and simplifying the form has made the art accessible to many more people than would otherwise be the case. However, the more obviously martial and physically very strenuous Chen style continues to be practiced, as do the derivative Wu, Hao, and Sun styles.

## Practice

As a martial art taijiquan employs a cultivated subtlety of touch to sense an opponent's strength in order to instantly redirect his or her motion so that one's defensive movement effectively neutralizes it and becomes a counterattack as well. In describing this capacity such phrases as "when the opponent is still, be still; when the opponent moves, move first," and "use four ounces to deflect a thousand pounds" are employed. The technique depends upon the ability to maintain gentle physical contact with the opponent without resisting, i.e., to "never meet force with force." The taijiquan player's counter to the aggressive move, once the instant has been seized and the movement's force captured, can be any of a number of techniques. Most simply and most benignly, the taijiquan player can accelerate or redirect the opponent's motion, sending him or her many feet away. Alternatively, any of a variety of in-fighting techniques ranging from low kicks to punches to open-hand strikes and grappling techniques can be employed singly or in combination, practically simultaneously with the blending with the opponent's force. The initial contact is said to be as soft as cotton, the counter that it becomes, as springy as steel.

*This student is attempting to use the subtle techniques of taijiquan, or tai chi, to unbalance his teacher.*

The sensitivity, skill, strength, and mental attitude necessary to perform such feats spontaneously and without effort are cultivated partly through the practice of solo forms, or sequences of patterns, and partly by other means. Forms vary in length and in their composition and sequence of techniques; they can be practiced at different speeds with larger or smaller patterns and in higher or lower stances. In some forms the tempo is even; in others it varies. Forms should be practiced with the continuity of one "reeling silk from a cocoon." In appearance form practice should resemble an eagle in flight; the attitude should be that of "a cat when about to pounce on a mouse." Form practice is a form of meditation in motion and requires great concentration without tension. Paired practice routines in which one works with a partner to simulate martial encounters exist in varying degrees of formality, ranging from duo form sequences to freestyle sparring.

The full range of taijiquan skills includes the use of weapons as well; the sword, broadsword, spear, and staff are used according to the principles of the art. In some schools auxiliary exercises are practiced to facilitate the development of the physical conditioning, skills, and mind set appropriate to taijiquan; in others taijiquan itself is considered the only necessary exercise. In either case the expectation is that the player will gradually learn to direct and augment the flow of vital energy within the body with his or her mind in harmony with the breath and that bodily functions will be enhanced as the body is renewed by the improved circulation of the *qi*. Through this internal aspect of the art the body is expected to become limber and supple as well, which is essential both to good health and to proper performance of the art.

The mechanical principles of taijiquan involve natural erect stances that combine great stability with nimbleness of foot. Movement begins at the *dantian*, an anatomical point at the body's center of gravity, just below the navel. With no tensing of muscles and with remarkable mechanical efficiency and relaxed precision, the weight is shifted and energy transmitted via the waist to the hands. In effect the legs, spine, and arms become like five bows, resulting in springy whole-body strength to be applied at the optimum instant. Footwork should be comparable to the tread of a cat. Taiji sport competition involves solo form performance and sometimes *tuishou* or push-hands, a more or less structured demonstration of mastery of the principles inherent in the art.

From a Chinese cultural perspective the medical and psychological value of the art as well as its martial potential are quite reasonable expectations. Both are in harmony with Daoist philosophical principles believed to be universally valid. The Daoist classics, i.e., the *Daodejing (Tao Te Ching)* and the *Yijing (I Ching)*, promulgate the principles, the balance and interplay of opposites that taijiquan embodies. Taijiquan, then, can be seen as intrinsically an art of harmonization with nature that includes the ability to harmonize with an opponent's attack and nurturance of the *qi* that animates every living thing in the universe. This is to say that it is considered a spiritual discipline as well.

During the Cultural Revolution taijiquan was under political attack in the People's Republic of

China, but the situation is now quite different. It has been reinstated as a national treasure and a uniquely Chinese form of art and sport. Basic Taijiquan is now taught there publicly in parks and other suitable places, as it is in other parts of the Chinese world. Advanced instruction is available and form competitions are held frequently. Lacking knowledge of Chinese philosophy and its implications for medicine and self defense, westerners have generally been drawn to flashier martial arts instead. However, that situation is changing too; gradually taijiquan is becoming better known in the West as well. It is of growing interest to the international medical research community and to martial arts scholarship, but taijiquan is still best known in the West as a health and longevity exercise of particular benefit to seniors.

—Michael G. Davis

**Bibliography:** Cheng, Man-ching. (1956) *Tai Chi Chuan: A Simplified Method of Calisthenics for Health and Self Defence.* Taipei: Shih Chung Tai-chi Chuan Center.

De Marco, Michael A. (1992) "The Origin and Evolution of Taijiquan." *Journal of Asian Martial Arts* 1, 1: 8–25.

Draeger, Donn F., and Smith, Robert W. (1980) *Comprehensive Asian Martial Arts.* Tokyo: Kodansha International.

Holcombe, Charles (1993) "The Daoist Origins of the Chinese Martial Arts." *Journal of Asian Martial Arts* 2, 1: 10–25.

Jou, Tsung Hwa. (1983) *The Tao of Tai-Chi Chuan: Way to Rejuvenation.* Edited by Shoshana Shapiro. Warwick: Tai-Chi Foundation.

Liang, T. T. (1977) *T'ai Chi Ch'uan for Health and Self Defense: Philosophy and Practice.* New York: Vintage Books.

Smith, Robert W. (1995) "Cheng Manqing and Taijiquan: A Clarification of Role." *Journal of Asian Martial Arts* 4, 2: 50–65.

Sutton, Nigel. (1991) *Applied Tai Chi Chuan.* London: A. & C. Black.

Tek, Peter Lim Tian. (1995) "Principles and Practices in Taijiquan." *Journal of Asian Martial Arts* 4, 1: 65–72.

# Taijiquan

**See** Tai Chi

# Takraw

Various forms of takraw—the word is Thai for ball—are played throughout Southeast Asia in Thailand, Malaysia, Singapore, Burma, and the Philippines. Other names include sepak takraw, sipa, ching loong, kator, and tago. All are team games, all are played with a rattan or, increasingly, a plastic ball, and all prohibit players from touching the ball with their hands. Takraw has been called by some "the international ball game of Southeast Asia," and it has been played for some 30 years between national teams (primarily Malaysia, Singapore, and Thailand). It has grown enormously in popularity in recent years and may be poised to assume a genuinely international character in the currently very competitive global sports market.

## Origins

The precise origins of takraw, as is the case with most ancient sports, are obscure. A takraw-like game, kemari, was played in Japan from perhaps the seventh century, and a similar sport was in evidence in south-central China, in what is now Yunnan province. However, it is in Southeast Asia that the game truly came into its own. All of the Southeast Asian countries where the game is currently played offer some "national origin" myths for the creation of the sport, but none of them offer incontrovertible proof that takraw has one and only one specific birthplace.

In whatever form, the most important physical skills in takraw are the various striking movements. Team skills, however, are also vital to success. Players compare the required teamwork to that seen on the best volleyball or soccer (association football) teams.

In Southeast Asia, where takraw-like games have achieved their most distinctive forms, evidence of the sport dates from the eleventh century, particularly in the areas comprising modern Malaysia and Sumatra. These games were apparently very much like the game now called sepak raga (which in Malay translates as kickball) and were played frequently in royal courts. Indeed, some link between aristocracy and takraw seems

*All forms of takraw involve keeping a ball (traditionally of rattan) aloft by using anything but the hands. Eric Bartholomay of Team USA hones his technique.*

clear, but this could well be a reflection of the fact that it is only royal records that provide any surviving accounts of earlier times. However, if takraw was not purely a sport of the royal classes, it was at least played seriously by them. For instance, in a record of the Malay rajahs, it is claimed that an heir to the sultanship of Malacca was insulted when his royal headgear was knocked off and that the hapless offender was executed. In the same chronicles, Sultan Mansur is described as kicking the ball more than 100 times before passing it on to the young nobles with whom he played sepak raga, or kicking the ball for as long as it would take to cook "many pots of rice."

According to another legend, a second Malay chief managed to keep a ball in the air for over 200 kicks off of the royal foot without letting it touch the ground. Others are said to have kept the ball aloft for hours at a time, impressing their retainers and rivals with their athletic skill. The game was clearly associated with the aristocracy and royal competitions were played as early as the fifteenth century.

In the Philippines, a takraw-like game called kasipa or sipa was being played prior to 1380, much in the manner of the Malay principalities. It is thought to have been, prior to the Spanish colonization, an important activity during coronation celebrations and remained, throughout the Spanish and American periods, a popular pastime at wedding celebrations and village fiestas. In Thailand, very early literature has not come to light, but it is clear from references in the poetic works of King Rama II (1809–1824) that the game was of considerable antiquity.

The ball that is used in takraw and related games is of considerable interest in itself. It is traditionally woven of rattan (*rottan* in Malay)—a tough vegetable material from the climbing palm creeper of the genus Calamus—and this, though it does not point to any particular place of origin, may according to some authorities hint that the game is quite ancient. Rattan, used throughout the region for the manufacture of everything from baskets to huts, was clearly central to ancient Southeast Asian technology.

Although rattan generally disappears very quickly and very completely from the archaeological record—as does all vegetable material—traces of woven hexagonal patterns left in ceramics indicate that rattan was used from neolithic times. Thus, while there is no direct evidence for the deep antiquity of takraw, the traditional rattan construction of the ball—in either hexagonal or pentagonal patterns—shows that the game may be very old.

Unfortunately for national origin theorists, none of this helps to pinpoint a specific birthplace for takraw. Balls from Malaysia, Thailand, and Burma that have been preserved in the British Museum and other European museums seem very similar to one another. Because rattan is a tough material with a very hard surface, various techniques have been used to render the ball soft and more responsive. Applications of coconut or other oils are used to produce a ball that is more pliant and less likely to blister a bare kicking foot. Again, though, none of this seems likely to "solve" the problem of origins.

Takraw-like games may have had a variety of origins, and, certainly, the number of versions of takraw that are played may indicate multiple origins. In what follows, descriptions are given of sepak raga, hoop takraw, flag takraw, and "in-carrying takraw," just a few of the "traditional" versions, and of sepak takraw, the increasingly internationalized and competitive form of the game.

## Types of Games

Sepak raga, the traditional Malay game, is played by a six- or seven-man team. The men form a circle some 15 meters (50 feet) in diameter and kick or head the ball to one another in a continuous round, the goal being simply to keep the ball from touching ground. As in all forms of takraw, feet, knees, shoulder, elbows, and head—everything but the hand and the forearm—can be used. The winning team is the team that keeps the ball aloft for the required period of time—usually about 30 minutes—with the most kicks. A similar game is played in Thailand.

In hoop takraw, which is very popular in Thailand, three large hoops are suspended over a circular court some 16 meters (52 feet) in diameter, and the players are required to put the ball through them as often as possible. The hoops, each with a radius of about 20 centimeters (8 inches), are made of metal, rattan, or wood and suspended from a high, tight rope so that the bottom of the rims are about 6 meters (20 feet) off the ground. The team, usually of seven, is cooperative, attempting to keep the ball "alive"—off the ground—and flying through the hoop as often as possible during a 30-minute period.

Style counts in hoop takraw: simple shots score lowest and more difficult ones higher. For instance, a plain kick through the hoop is the most humble approach and thus a low scorer, but firing the ball off the knee, elbow, or shoulder scores higher. The fanciest shots, naturally, score the most. The top-scoring shot is an amazing accomplishment: the player stands facing away from the hoop, both feet together, then jumps up, executing a "tandem back-kick" which directs the ball upward through a loop formed by his arms—joined at the fingers behind his back—and, finally, through the suspended hoop.

Hoop takraw was developed in Thailand in the late 1920s. It appears that early versions of the game were played with hoops of different sizes, with shots scoring differentially depending of which hoop they through.

Another Thai form of the game is called "flag takraw." This requires the player to move as quickly as possible along a narrow track some 50 meters (55 yards) in length, all the while keeping the ball aloft through kicks of the foot and jerks of the head and elbows. The game, often played during village festivals, is won by the contestant who reaches the end of the track without either dropping the ball or veering off the path.

Yet another Thai takraw game, sometimes called "in-carrying takraw" requires a single player to catch and carry as many balls as possible without using his hands. This game, which seems more a form of juggling performance, calls on the "player" to be rather ingenuous about holding onto the caught balls: he may hold them with his teeth, or under an arm. Twelve balls is the standard goal, but as many as seventeen have been caught and held by expert practitioners.

Sepak takraw, one form of which is sometimes

called "net takraw," is the game that has achieved the most "international" status, being played by amateur and semiprofessional teams throughout the region. Sepak takraw is played on a rectangular court that is 13.4 by 6.1 meters (44 by 20 feet). The court is divided by a centerline at either end of which is marked a half-circle with a radius of 0.9 meters (3 feet). Across the centerline is stretched a net that is 1.52 meters (5 feet) from the ground. In each half-court a "service circle" is drawn, the center of which is 2.45 meters (8 feet) from the back line and 3.04 meters (10 feet) from either side.

The game is played between two squads—called regus—of three players each. Each team enters three regus in the course of a formal competition, and the winning team is that which hosts two out of three winning regus. A regu wins the set with 15 points. As in volleyball, each team is entitled to hit the ball three times before sending it across the net, but the three hits can come from the same player. Points are won or lost when the ball touches the ground in or out of the court, or does not cross the net after being played three times by the offensive regu.

A game of sepak takraw begins when the ball is thrown by either the "left inside" or "right inside" player, standing in one of the quarter-circles at either end of the service line, to the "back" player. The "back," who stands with one foot inside and one outside of the serving circle, is required to kick across the net. As soon as this service has taken place and the ball is over the net, all players are allowed to move about anywhere in their respective half-courts.

Faults during service can be called against the serving side for a number of reasons, including movement out of the quarter- or serving-circle prior to play or overly artistic delays on the part of the "inside" player in throwing the ball to the "back" for service. During actual play, faults include stepping on the center line, crossing the net with any part of the body either over or under the net, "holding" the ball in any way—under the arm, for instance, or between the legs—and, of course, touching the ball with the hand. Faults committed during course of play result in a point being awarded to the opposite regu.

The net used in modern sepak takraw was introduced only in the 1920s, and in general the game was played according to various local rules for many years. In fact, it seemed for a time that

no form of takraw would survive to compete with the various Western sports that were being exported to all parts of Asia. However, in Singapore before World War II, the main Malay form of the game was included in high school variety programs, and after the war an association called the Singapore National Body of Sepak Takraw (PARSES) was formed.

PARSES, together with the emerging takraw organizations in Malaysia and Thailand agreed, in 1965, on a uniform set of regulations and on the name sepak takraw. This was the culmination of negotiations that had started in 1958, during the course of the third Asian Games in Tokyo. There, representatives from Thailand had invited officials from Burma and Malaya (now Malaysia), as well as Laos, to consider the benefits of holding small regional events. These events, held more frequently than either the Asian Games or the Olympics, would allow athletes to hone their skills for the more global competitions and would also advance the cause of regional cultural interaction. They would also allow interested countries to pursue "traditional" sports—like takraw—that were virtually unknown in sports networks that were oriented purely to the "Western" and "Olympic" standards.

The final outcome of regional negotiations was the formation of the Southeast Asian Games Federation, which sponsors competitive events such as the games in Bangkok in 1965, the first to feature what could be called "world-class" takraw. Since the mid-1960s, takraw has been a major competitive international sport in the Southeast Asian region.

## Outlook

Wider acceptance for the sport outside of Southeast Asia has been slow but steady. The Asian Sepak Takraw Federation (ASTAF) proposed in 1967 that the sport be included in the Asian Games, and it was, but only as an exhibition, played in the sixth (Bangkok) and ninth (New Delhi) events. In 1984, ASTAF proposed that the sport be accepted as a regular competition but was rebuffed, with officials citing both lack of popularity and lack of preparation.

Then, in 1988, ASTAF reorganized itself as the International Sepak-Takraw Federation (ISTAF) and began to campaign more vigorously for wider global acceptance of the sport. This came, in 1990, when sepak takraw was included in the eleventh Asian Games in Beijing. Clearly, this move was facilitated by the games' Chinese hosts, who displayed their confidence in the international future of the game by supporting 19 teams of its own and sending Chinese takraw players to train in Singapore and Malaysia.

With internationalization comes standardization, and, if sepak takraw continues to grow, the hand-woven rattan ball—one of the game's most distinctive features—may become a thing of the past. The handcrafted ball, unfortunately, varies considerably in circumference and weight and is difficult to produce even within the flexible official guidelines—between 40 and 42.5 centimeters (15 3/4 to 16 3/4 inches) in circumference and 160 to 180 grams (5 2/3 to 6 1/3 ounces) in weight. Trivial though such differences may seem at first, they are clearly a challenge to the sorts of replicable criteria that increasingly mark "modern" sports. Not surprisingly, then, a company in Singapore has taken to manufacturing absolutely standard takraw balls, woven in the traditional pattern to be sure, but of precisely milled plastic strips and not of rattan: the Thais are already playing competitively with such balls and the acceptance of plastic seems all but inevitable.

With the traditional rattan ball on its way to the museum, with agreed-upon international rules and recognized venues, sepak takraw seems securely established on the international sports scene. Longtime popularity in Southeast Asia and more recent Chinese patronage of the game ensure its survival as a major competitive sport. Whether or not it can move beyond its present level of popularity will depend more on commercial considerations and communications than on purely "sporting" values.

—Alan Trevithick

**See also** Footbag.

**Bibliography:** Dunsmore, Susi. (1983) *"Sepak Raga" (Takraw): The Southeast Asian Ball Game.* Occasional Paper No. 4. Sarawak: Sarawak Museum.

Singapore Amateur Sepak Takraw Association. (1978) *Status Report on Sepak Takraw in Singapore.*

Thailand, Government of. (1968) *Thai Games and Festivals.* Bangkok: Public Relations Department of Thailand.

Wagner, Eric A. (1989) *Sport in Asia and Africa: A Comparative Handbook.* New York: Greenwood Press.

# Technology

Technologies have historically played significant roles in the sporting practices of human cultures. Certain technologies have been used as essential ingredients in athletic games. Other technologies have been adopted to enhance athletic performance. Some technologies have created opportunities for spectators to watch sporting contests. In addition to employing technologies to play games, increase athletic achievement, and provide opportunities for public viewing of sporting events, some cultures have considered sport itself a social technology designed to reform communities.

Hunting and gathering peoples created athletic games that employed the technological kits with which they wrested a living from the environment and engaged in warfare. Those cultures used *atl-atls*, spears, bows and arrows, and other such implements in some of their games and sports. Many of the original human athletic games employed familiar tools as basic ingredients in competitions. Sport and technology have been interconnected throughout human history.

The technological developments that sparked the agricultural revolutions that gave rise to the first urban civilizations also generated new sporting technologies. Ancient civilizations around the globe constructed monumental architectural sites for sports. Ancient Greeks built stadiums, hippodromes, gymnasiums, and palestras throughout the Peloponnesus. During the Hellenistic period Greek sports and Greek athletic architecture spread around the Mediterranean world. In the centuries that followed, Roman coliseums sprouted in the vast lands that fell under the sway of their empire.

At least 1,500 years ago, Amerind cultures in the Americas built massive courts with stone walls that served as the locations for ball games. Those ball courts spread over a huge geographic range. The archeological record documents ball courts as important parts of the material culture of peoples from the northern edge of South America's Chacoan desert through the Andean highlands into Mesoamerica and extending to the northern reaches of modern Mexico and the contemporary Southwestern United States. Amerind peoples engaged in elaborate ball games on technologically

*New technologies are constantly changing sports. The photo finish was an important refinement in horse racing, shown here at an exciting 1963 race in which seven horses finished within a length of the winner.*

sophisticated courts until contact with European cultures in the 1500s and 1600s C.E. destroyed indigenous traditions.

In the post-antiquity period, monumental architecture devoted to sports declined markedly in Europe and the Middle East. However, in medieval and early modern times Western cultures frequently organized sports around military technologies. Medieval jousting and melees, archery, fencing, and shooting contests taught familiarity with weapons and warrior talents. Native American, Asian, and African cultures also cultivated martial skill through sports that used weaponry. Skilled artisans produced "tools" for other elite and folk recreations such as tennis, golf, and early forms of cricket, baseball, and football.

The technological dynamism of the Industrial Revolution radically changed the nature of society and sports. A wide variety of technological advances amplified athletic games and pastimes. During the nineteenth century, and especially in Great Britain and the United States, innovations such as the process for "vulcanizing" rubber altered golf, tennis, and other athletic balls and the games in which they were employed. New machines such as the bicycle created new sports and recreations. Athletes in industrialized nations became enamored of new and specialized devices that allowed for greater achievements and higher standards of play. That dynamic and evolutionary process produced the later "hi-tech" athletic shoe industry, a multibillion dollar business selling the notion that technology does indeed enhance sporting performance.

During the nineteenth and twentieth centuries modern sport became a central feature in the mass cultures created by the new technological civilizations. Monumental architecture devoted to sport reappeared. Giant stadiums sprang up in industrial cities. Spectators by the thousands filled those stadiums to witness amateur and professional sports. The selling of sports and sporting equipment became a big business in which technological innovations often produced significantly larger market shares. Modern sport became enmeshed with industrialism. A thriving sports industry sold athletic goods and knowledge to consumers.

The organizational revolution that characterized late nineteenth- and twentieth-century industrial societies—highlighted by centralization, nationalization, and bureaucratization—gave athletics a distinctively modern shape as clubs, collegiate teams, and professional leagues followed the patterns typical of most modern social institutions.

The transportation and communication revolutions that underpinned the Industrial Revolution also transformed the sporting cultures of first European and North American nations and then those of much of the rest of the globe. The railroad facilitated the rise of professional baseball and college football in the United States, engendering rivalries between cities and colleges. It was more than a coincidence that in 1869 Americans witnessed both the completion of the transcontinental railroad and the first transcontinental tour of a baseball club, Cincinnati's famed Red Stockings. Technologies were instrumental in transforming folk recreations into national pastimes.

The development of national presses in industrialized nations made reading the sports pages a daily habit for millions of newspaper subscribers. Sports pages crowded mass circulation dailies, while articles and essays on athletics appeared regularly in magazines. New international media promoted sporting rivalries between nations. The re-creation of the Olympic Games in 1896, facilitated by communication and transportation technologies that allowed athletes from around the world to compete and spectators from around the world to witness the results, created one of the most important spectacles for modern global technological civilization. Indeed, it was no mere coincidence that two of the first three Olympic Games, the Paris Games of 1900 and the St. Louis Games of 1904, were held in conjunction with

technological civilization's primary celebration of modern machinery—the World's Fair.

In the twentieth century, technological innovations led to new games, superior performances, and enhanced access by spectators to the burgeoning global sporting culture. From airplane races to Ultimate Frisbee, new gadgets spawned new sports. New technological advances in athletic tools, from shoes to golf clubs, changed performance standards for nearly every modern athletic game. Innovations such as artificial turf, synthetic tracks, artificial climbing walls, and fiberglass vaulting poles radically changed the ways in which some games were played and certain sports were performed.

Modern technological developments also raised aesthetic and ethical dilemmas for sport. Did aluminum baseball bats produce pleasing sounds? Did they confer unfair advantages on batters? Did graphite tennis rackets with larger string surfaces distort the fundamental nature of tennis? Should biomedical advances, from the development of anabolic steroids to blood-doping techniques designed to enhance the oxygen-carrying capacity of distance runners, be applied to athletic performances? If better athletes could be made, should they be made?

Perhaps the most important technological changes impacting sport came from the development of new transportation and communication systems. Passenger airlines transformed competitive sport in industrial nations and made international contests more frequent and more practical. Electric lighting systems and artificial grass altered the style of monumental athletic architecture. Electronic communication systems, first radio and then television, instantaneously brought athletic contests from around the world into the homes of fans, forever altering the nature and meaning of spectatorship.

The technological developments of the twentieth century sparked the development of powerful national sporting industries in nearly every nation in the world. They also spawned a global sporting culture centered around the Olympic Games and World Cup soccer matches. In the so-called "global village" created by the electronic media there always seems to be a sporting contest going on somewhere that everyone can watch.

In modern industrialized cultures, and particularly in the United States since the late nineteenth century, sport itself has been understood as a technology. While such a conception might at first seem odd, it is important to remember that technologies are not just machines and "made" things—inanimate objects. Technologies are also organizations of human energy designed for problem solving. Historically, armies and navies have been important human social technologies. More recently, public schools have been employed as social technologies. When the advocates of modern sporting ideologies promise that sport will teach people the value of team play and cooperation, assimilate immigrants and colonized peoples, prevent crime and behavioral deviance, inculcate the values of fair play and regulated competition, spark nationalistic sentiment, ameliorate race, class, and gender divisions, and rescue the inhabitants of technological civilization from the artificial sterility of the machine process, they believe that sport is a social technology. Whether or not they overestimate the power of sport to change society, many of the late nineteenth- and twentieth-century promoters of athletics consider sport the single most significant social technology for shaping modern cultures.

Thus sport itself was transformed into a technological system by the inventors of modern athletic ideas and institutions. Technology shapes not only the kinds of athletic games that modern peoples play, not only the way they play those games, not only the level of their achievement in those games, but the very meanings and purposes of sport. Sports themselves have become accepted as technologies designed for making social changes.

—Mark Dyreson

**See also** Modernization.

**Bibliography:** Baker, William. (1982) *Sports in the Western World*. Totowa, NJ: Rowman and Littlefield.

Betts, John R. (1974) *America's Sporting Heritage, 1850–1950*. Reading, MA: Addison-Wesley.

Brohm, Jean-Marie. (1978) *Sport—A Prison of Measured Time*. Trans. by Ian Fraser. London: Ink Links.

Carter, John Marshall. (1988) *Sports and Pastimes of the Middle Ages*. New York: University Press of America.

Guttmann, Allen. (1978) *From Ritual to Record: The Nature of Modern Sports*. New York: Columbia University Press.

———. (1986) *Sport Spectators*. New York: Columbia University Press.

———. (1994) *Games and Empires: Modern Sports and Cultural Imperialism*. New York: Columbia University Press.

Harris, H. A. (1972) *Sport in Greece and Rome*. London: Thames and Hudson.

Hoberman, John. (1984) *Sport and Political Ideology*. Austin: University of Texas Press.

Holt, Richard. (1989) *Sport and the British: A Modern History*. Oxford: Clarendon.

Katz, Donald. (1994) *Just Do It: The Nike Spirit in the Corporate World*. New York: Random House.

Kyle, Donald. (1987) *Athletics in Ancient Athens*. Leiden: E. J. Brill.

Rader, Benjamin. (1984) *In Its Own Image: How Television Has Transformed Sports*. New York: Free Press.

Rushin, Steve. (1994) "How We Got Here." *Sports Illustrated* 81 (August 16).

Sansone, David. (1988) *Greek Athletics and the Genesis of Sport*. Berkeley: University of California Press.

Stern, Theodore. (1949) *The Rubber Ball-Games of the Americas*. Seattle: University of Washington Press.

Todd, Terry. (1987) "Anabolic Steroids: The Gremlins of Sport." *Journal of Sport History* 14.

# Tennis

Tennis is among the most thoroughly international of competitive sports. Women from 61 different countries were among the 950 players included in the official year-end world rankings for 1992 produced by the Women's Tennis Association; men from 19 different countries appeared among just the top 100 in the world in the rankings for the same year produced by the Association of Tennis Professionals. But the game has not always been so broadly based. Following the invention of modern tennis in the 1870s, the competitive game was initially organized and played predominantly by wealthy Englishmen and Americans. Thus the championships at Wimbledon were won exclusively by British men for the first 30 years of the competition's existence, and only U.S. and British men won the first 45 national championships of the United States. In contrast, in recent years the champions of the sport's major tournaments have come from a wide variety of countries. In just the ten years from 1985 to 1994, for example, Wimbledon was won by men from Germany, Australia, Sweden, and the United States, and the U.S. Open was won by men from Sweden, Germany, Czechoslovakia, and the United States.

During the twentieth century, the game has also undergone many other changes, and the pace of these has accelerated in the past three decades. The evolution has been dramatic. In little more than a century tennis has changed from a pastime played by wealthy English aristocrats on the lawns of country estates and exclusive private clubs to a mass-market sport played on asphalt courts by tens of millions of people around the world. The game's leading players, once children of socially prominent families who learned the game as students at Harrow, Eton, Harvard, and Princeton and played it as an enjoyable form of weekend recreation, are now full-time professionals who travel with entourages of coaches, trainers, and business agents and who leave school in their teen years to get an early start on the pursuit of the millions of dollars paid out annually in prize money and commercial endorsements. These and other changes can be understood by looking at the changing role of tennis in society, as shifts over time in its geographic extent and economic rewards have been caused by fundamental innovations in the way competitive tennis is organized and played.

## Practice

Tennis is a game played by two persons (singles) or by two teams of two persons (doubles). It is played outdoors on surfaces of grass, clay, or asphalt, and indoors on a variety of surfaces, including asphalt and carpet. For singles, the court measures 24 by 8.2 meters (78 by 27 feet), and in doubles the sidelines are extended to make it 24 by 11 meters (78 by 36 feet). The court is divided in half by a net 0.91 meters (3 feet) high at the center and 1.1 meters (3 feet 6 inches) at the sides. Each half of the court is divided into a service court 6.4 by 4.1 meters (21 by 13 feet 6 inches) and a backcourt 8.2 by 5.5 meters (27 by 18 feet). A 1.4-meter (4 foot 6 inch) alley runs along the outsides of the court perpendicular to the net and is used only in doubles play. The ball is an inflated, felt-covered rubber ball about 6 centimeters (2.5 inches) in diameter. The oval-headed rackets are 69 to 74 centimeters (27 to 29 inches) long, with the hitting surface strung with nylon or other materials.

The player's goal is to hit the ball into the prescribed area of the court in such a way that it cannot be returned. A player serves an entire game and is allowed two service attempts for each point. The ball is served diagonally from behind

*Boris Becker makes a leap for the ball on his way to the 1985 Wimbledon singles championship.*

the baseline (the far end of the backcourt) and must bounce in the opposite service court beyond the net. If the ball fails to do this on two consecutive attempts, the receiver is awarded the point by double-fault. Stepping on or over the baseline during service also makes the serve invalid by foot-fault.

After the serve, the ball may be returned into any area of the opponent's court and may be hit by forehand or backhand groundstroke (after one bounce) or by volley or overhead (before it bounces). The point is lost by the first player who hits the ball into the net, beyond the opponent's baseline (long), beyond the opponent's sideline (wide), or who allows the ball to bounce more than once in his own court. Points may be won by either the server or receiver. The first point won by a player in a game gives a score of 15, the second 30, and the third 40. Winning a fourth point gives the player the game, unless the players are tied at 40 each (deuce), in which case a player must win two

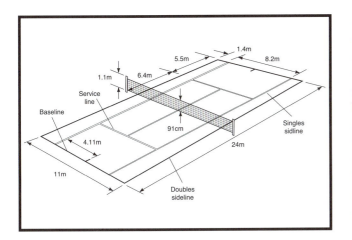

consecutive points to win the game. A set is won by the first player to win six games while leading by at least two games; if neither player gains a winning margin, today a tie-breaker is normally played at 6–6. The tie-breaker (and the set) is won by the first player to win 7 points while leading by at least 2. In championship play, women's matches are normally won by taking two of three sets, and men's either two of three or three of five sets.

## Origins

The origins of the modern game of tennis are usually traced back to 23 February 1874, when the British patent office issued a provisional license to Major Walter Wingfield for "A Portable Court of Playing Tennis." Wingfield's game of lawn tennis was a descendant of the much older game of court tennis, as well as other racket games, but Wingfield was the first to codify the outdoor game and market it commercially. The game immediately achieved considerable success, as within a year of receiving the patent Wingfield had sold numerous sets for his game, which came in a box containing "poles, pegs, and netting for forming the court, 4 tennis bats . . . a bag of balls . . . and *The Book of the Game*" (Collins and Hollander, 1994); purchasers in that first year included Russia's royal family, the Prince of Wales, and 42 members of the English House of Lords. The game became popular at English country houses, for it provided exercise for men and women of all ages, and courts could readily be set up on croquet lawns. The game also soon came to be played at London's sports clubs.

In the spring of 1877 the All England Croquet Club, located in the London suburb of Wimbledon,

decided to hold a tennis tournament. For the occasion, the club had a committee of its members draw up new revised rules for the game. These rules became the basis for the modern game. A rectangular court measuring 24 by 8.2 meters (78 by 27 feet) replaced the hourglass court shape used earlier by Wingfield. The scoring system was also changed. In competition the players would serve alternate games. A game was won by the first player to win four points, provided he led by at least two points. The point score within games was now referred to not as 1, 2, 3, but as 15, 30, 40; a tie at 40 was referred to as "deuce," while a score of no points was referred to as "love." The first player to win six games while leading by at least two would win a set; if neither player led by two games, the set was extended until a margin of two games was achieved. Matches were to be won by the first man to win three sets. (This best-of-five set format continues today for men's competition at Wimbledon and other major men's tournaments; women's tournaments, and lesser men's tournaments, use a best-of-three set format.)

The tournament of 1877—the first Wimbledon—attracted 22 entrants, and its success led the All England Club to make the championships an annual fixture. Over time Wimbledon became the most important tennis tournament in the world, and its innovations often led the way for other competitions. A number of changes were introduced at Wimbledon within a few years. For several years the tournament referee adjusted the height of the net and the distance of the service lines from the net in view of the numbers of points won and lost on service, but in 1882 the net height and the service lines were fixed at today's standards. Wimbledon added a women's singles competition to the championships in 1884, as well as a men's doubles event; the other two major events of the tournament, women's doubles and mixed doubles, were added in 1913. In 1885 a system of first-round byes was introduced; this prevented three players from arriving in the semifinals, as happened at the first Wimbledon. A number of sequences for changing ends of the court were tried until the system in use today was introduced in 1890, in which players change sides after each odd game of each set.

Several other significant rule changes were made during the 1920s. Initially Wimbledon used a challenge round format, in which the champion stood aside the following year, waiting for a challenger to be determined by the elimination tournament. Wimbledon discarded this format in 1921, nine years after it had been eliminated from the U.S. national championships. Seeding, the deliberate placing of designated strong players so they would not meet in the early rounds of a tournament, was introduced into competitive tennis at Wimbledon in 1924, and soon became standard in all tournaments.

Perhaps the most important recent change in the basic rules of tennis competition came with the adoption of the tie-breaker. First used in a major tournament at the U.S. national championships in 1970, and soon thereafter throughout competitive tennis, the tie-breaker was invented by Jimmy Van Alen, founder of the tennis Hall of Fame. Played when the score reached 6 games all, in its original version the tie-breaker was won by the first player to win 5 points, who thereby won the set by a score of 7–6. Many players objected to the sudden death nature of this version, in which a single point could determine the outcome of a set in favor of whichever player won it when the tie-breaker score stood at 4–4, and it was subsequently changed. The version in use today awards the set to the first player to win 7 points, while leading by at least two. Tie-breakers are now universally used in competitive tennis, except at Wimbledon and the French Open, where they are not used in the third set of women's matches, or the fifth set of men's matches.

## Development

The All England Club became the major organization in the early history of tennis, and it has remained a powerful presence to date. But its preeminent position would not last indefinitely. In part this devolution was voluntary, for in 1884 the Club agreed to the founding of the Lawn Tennis Association, which would share the profits produced by the Championships. In part, however, the reduction in the All England Club's dominant role in tennis was an inevitable result of the spread of the game to other countries.

Tennis arrived in the United States within months of Major Wingfield's patent. A first tournament was held in Nahant, Massachusetts, in 1876, and in 1880 a national tournament was played at the Staten Island Cricket and Baseball Club. Disputes over proper procedures led to the formation in 1881 of the U.S. National Lawn Tennis Association (USLTA, later simply the USTA), which became the country's governing tennis body. Under the direction of the new association, the first official national championship tournament for men was held at the elegant Casino in Newport, Rhode Island, in 1881; a women's tournament was added in 1887. As in England, private clubs became the major venues for tennis in the United States. The first tennis club in the United States was founded in New Orleans in 1876, but in the next few years the eastern clubs that would control the competitive game for many decades began to emerge, as the Longwood Cricket Club in Boston adopted tennis in 1878, the Merion Cricket Club in Philadelphia did the same in 1879, and the Orange Lawn Tennis Club in New Jersey was founded in 1880.

Lawn tennis also spread quickly to many other countries. Clubs were founded in Scotland, Brazil, and India in 1875, and in 1877 the first clubs were founded in Ireland and France. The first tournament in Australia was played in 1879, and South Africa had a championship in 1891. The game was also played in Denmark, Switzerland, the Netherlands, Greece, Turkey, Lebanon, Egypt, and Finland by 1890. Yet although the game was played all over the world, during its early history competitive tennis was dominated by a mere handful of countries. From its inception through 1950, the men's singles at Wimbledon, generally considered the game's single most important event, was won by men from only five different countries: England, the United States, France, Australia, and New Zealand. Through 1950 the men's championship of the United States was won by men from only three countries: the United States, England, and France. The third of the tennis world's most important events, the national championship of France, was only a bit less exclusive. Open only to French nationals until 1925, the men's singles champions from 1925 to 1950 included men from six countries: France, England, the United States, Australia, Germany, and Hungary. The early domination of tennis by a few countries is also apparent in the history of the Davis Cup, the sport's major international team competition. The cup was created in 1900, with a format in which national teams of at most four men play matches over three days, with a best-of-five matches result determined by four singles and one doubles. From the first competition in 1900 through 1973, the cup was won by only four different entrants: the United States, England, France, and Australia/New Zealand (the latter two competed as one team to 1923). Remarkably, for one stretch from 1937 through 1973, the cup was won only by Australia and the United States.

Prominence in competitive tennis has become much more widely diffused geographically in more recent times. Several of the early dominant countries have declined in importance. No Englishman has won the English, U.S., or French championships since 1936, and no French man has won the English or U.S. titles since 1946. After winning the Davis Cup nine times from 1900 to 1936, England has not won the cup since; after six consecutive victories between 1927 and 1932, France has won the cup on only one more occasion. But a much wider range of countries has produced champions since 1950 than before that date. Wimbledon has had men's singles champions from 7 different countries since 1950, as men from Czechoslovakia, Peru, Spain, Sweden, and Germany have won the title, in addition to champions from the older powers of Australia and the United States. Men from 9 different countries have won the U.S. title in the same period, as champions from the United States and Australia have been joined by others from Mexico, Spain, Romania, Argentina, Czechoslovakia, Sweden, and Germany. The French men's championship has been won by men from 11 different countries since 1950 as champions from France, the United States, and Australia have been joined by men from Sweden, Italy, Spain, Romania, Argentina, Czechoslovakia, Ecuador, and Austria. After having only four different winners between 1900 and 1973, the Davis Cup has had eight different holders since then, as South Africa, Sweden, Italy, Germany, and Czechoslovakia have all become holders of the cup, joining the United States, Australia, and France.

Of the four countries that were most important in the early decades of competitive tennis, two—England and France—declined to minor status prior to World War II, and have never regained their early prominence. Australia enjoyed some success early in the history of tennis, and a posi-tively dominant position in international competition during the period of leadership of its national program by Harry Hopman, with a succession of champions during the 1950s and 1960s. Yet after winning the Davis Cup fifteen times during Hopman's reign as captain from 1950 to 1969, Australian tennis faded after Hopman's retirement. So, for example, Australia won the Davis Cup only four times from 1970 to 1994, and Australian men won Wimbledon in only three years, and the U.S. title in only two years, during that time. Of the early tennis powers, only the United States has remained an important source of champions throughout the sport's history.

The wider geographic extent of competitive tennis has many sources, but one important factor has been fundamental changes in the organization of the sport. From the origins of tennis through the 1960s, the sport's major competitions were organized by national associations, as well as by the International Lawn Tennis Federation, which included the national associations as its members. The administrators who controlled these organizations, and therefore dominated the management of competitive tennis, were volunteers, wealthy men drawn from the membership of the private clubs that served as the sites for the sport's major competitions. Very early in the history of tennis, the sport's governing associations decided that their competitions would be open exclusively to amateurs. Not only did players consequently win no money in the major tournaments, but they were forbidden to earn money for endorsements, for teaching tennis, or for any other activities related to the game. This amateur regime was challenged periodically by professional promoters and by players who wished to earn money from the game. As early as 1926 a small group of players left amateur tennis to tour as professionals, and over the next four decades many of the sport's greatest champions followed their lead, turning professional and traveling in small groups. Thus after Suzanne Lenglen of France became the first great champion to tour professionally during the 1920s, she was followed in later years by such stars as William Tilden (who turned professional in 1931), Ellsworth Vines (1933), Fred Perry (1936), Don Budge (1939), Bobby Riggs (1941), Frank Kovacs (1941), Jack Kramer (1947), Pancho Segura (1947),

Pancho Gonzalez (1949), Frank Parker (1949), Ken Rosewall (1957), Lew Hoad (1957), Andres Gimeno (1961), and Rod Laver (1962). Some of these players earned respectable incomes for their efforts, but their matches were often regarded as exhibitions rather than genuine competitions, and they did not generate sustained public interest comparable to that produced by Wimbledon, the U.S. championships, the Davis Cup, and the other major amateur competitions. Thus for example Don Budge turned professional in 1939 after becoming the first player ever to win the Grand Slam—the singles titles of Australia, France, England, and the United States—the previous year. He later commented, "By the time I signed, Tilden, Vines, and Perry had also all turned professional, but pro tennis then, as right up to 1968, had to struggle with talent and showmanship, but without tradition and honor."

## The Open Era

This situation changed dramatically during the 1960s. Faced by a new challenge from World Championship Tennis, a venture funded by Texas oil millionaire Lamar Hunt, that threatened to lure more and more of the top amateurs into professional competition, English tennis officials announced that in 1968 Wimbledon would be open to all players regardless of their status. The other national associations quickly followed the lead of the English, and 1968 initiated the era of Open tennis. Men began to compete for prize money at Wimbledon and elsewhere in that year. In 1970, under the leadership of Gladys Heldman, founder and editor of *World Tennis* magazine, and of former Wimbledon and U.S. champion Billie Jean King, the women organized their own professional tour. Once Open tennis was established, the prize money grew rapidly. From a total of $250,000 in 1971, prize money on the women's pro tour increased to $7 million in 1980, to $23 million in 1990, and to $33 million in 1993. Rod Laver, the top male player, won $124,000 in prize money in 1969, the first full year of Open tennis; in 1979 Bjorn Borg and John McEnroe became the first two men to win $1 million in one year; in 1982 Ivan Lendl became the first to win $2 million, and in 1993 Pete Sampras became the first to win $3 million. Both Ivan Lendl and Martina Navratilova won total prize money of more than

---

## Tilden on Centre Court

To Tilden the Centre Court [at Wimbledon] was a real and a true inspiration. When he first trod its velvet sward and hurled the ball to the place his strategic brain saw to be the right one, he was no mere earthbound mortal playing a match as he had played hundreds before. The untoward features of the classic rectangle irked him not; to him they were almost non-existent. He was not aware of the gloominess, the cramped, cribbed and confined nature of his supreme battles; nor did it trouble him that the magnificent distances of the Forest Hills and Newport courts, and their freedom of movement and ideal conditions of light and air, were lacking. What he said to himself was something like this:

"Here am I, America's representative, given the opportunity, the fates being kind, to do what no other American has yet done. Under my feet is the turf which the giants of all lawn tennis time have trod. Looking on are the shades of the Renshaws, the Baddelys, the Dohertys, and scores of others almost equally great, watching my strokes, noting my strategy and tactics, nodding, approvingly or the reverse, as they envision my bearing and take cognizance of my every action. Around me, filling every available bit of space, are the men and women who compose the most distinguished and critical gallery in all the lawn tennis world; even royalty has come to view the scene and add luster and éclat to it. 'Twould ill become me to do aught but acquit myself well, to justify my selection as one of the representatives of my country. I must act worthily, as beseems the game and its followers. And may the best man win."

—"A Little Story" in *ALT*, 1921, reprinted in Wm. T. Tilden II and Stephen Wallis Merrihew, *Match Play and the Spin of the Ball* (New York, 1925).

---

$20 million during their careers. And prize money is of course only part of the earnings of today's professional tennis players. Considering earnings from endorsements and other sources, in 1991 *Forbes* magazine placed nine tennis players on its list of the world's forty highest-paid athletes, and estimated that five of these tennis players had total annual incomes of more than $7 million (Newcomb 1991).

The rising earnings of players have produced considerable changes in the balance of power in the control of the game. In 1972 the Association of Tennis Professionals (ATP) was founded as a union for male professionals, and the Women's Tennis Association (WTA) was founded in 1973 as a union for women pros. By 1990, the ATP had succeeded in bringing all men's professional tournaments (except the Davis Cup and the national championships of England, the United States, France, and Australia) under their control, and the WTA had done the same for women's professional tournaments. Unlike in the amateur era, when competitive players officially received only their expenses, and labored under the control of volunteer officials in whose appointment they had no say, in recent years tennis professionals have joined the ranks of the highest-paid professional athletes in the world and have a substantial voice in governing their sport. In the amateur era, the financial benefits from tennis's popularity were captured by the national associations that ran the game and the private clubs that sponsored its tournaments. Davis Cup players, or stars who increased tournament attendance, were rumored to receive illegal payments from their national associations or individual tournaments, leading to characterizations of the system as "shamateurism," but these payments were probably not great in most cases, and they were given or withheld at the whim of tennis officials. Jack Kramer, a Wimbledon and U.S. champion of the 1940s who later played and promoted professional tennis, pointed to both the absence of fair economic rewards for players and their lack of voice in the game's direction in describing the old amateur regime as "immoral and evil." In contrast, during the Open era players have been largely free to play when and where they choose, under economic arrangements subject to their voluntary agreement.

The economic rewards of the Open era have clearly been an important factor in the spread of competitive tennis around the world, for tennis is one of the few sports played professionally in virtually every country. In some countries, including the United States, boys who want to follow careers in professional sports have a considerable number to choose from, but the number of professional sports is considerably smaller in many other countries. And the number of sports in which women can earn a living is not great anywhere. That there has been a steady increase during the Open era in the number of countries that have produced world-class tennis players is therefore not surprising.

## International Play

Tracing the popularity of tennis around the world is a difficult task, for systematic evidence on participation is lacking. Yet the general outlines of the sport's evolution are broadly reflected in the sport's history in the United States. From early in the game's history, the United States has not only been the largest single producer of world-class players, but it has also been the largest commercial market for the sport and has had many more recreational players than any other country. As noted above, in its early years tennis was played primarily in private clubs on the East Coast. Its competitions were organized by wealthy club members, and the earliest U.S. competitive players were predominantly Ivy League graduates, drawn from prominent New England society families. Thus for example of the 13 men who represented the United States in the Davis Cup in the first ten years of that competition after its establishment in 1900, seven were Harvard graduates, two had attended Princeton, one Yale, and one Cornell. From 1881 until 1914, the national championships were held in Newport, Rhode Island, "the center of the Smart Set of gay summer days," in the words of sportswriter John Kieran, "with high society looking on and the vulgar barred by mutual consent as well as by the scarcity of seats in the sacred enclosure and the high price of tickets. There was an aura of aristocracy, a touch of hauteur, to the game in those days. The courts of the class-conscious Casino were not to be profaned by the common herd." From its precious New England origins, American tennis gradually spread more widely, both in geographic and social extent. The geographic shift has been the more thorough, as the temperate parts of the country—most notably Florida, Texas, and California—have become the centers of the sport. The shifts of the national championships, first in 1914 from the Newport Casino to the grass courts of the private West Side Tennis Club in New York, and later, in 1978, to the asphalt courts of the public National Tennis Center in New York, serve to symbolize not only the early end to New England's role in American tennis, but also the longer-term decline of the aristocratic trappings that surrounded the game in its early days. But the geographic shift in American tennis is readily apparent in other ways. A clear example is afforded by college tennis. From the inception of the National Collegiate Athletic Association (NCAA) tennis championship in 1883 through 1922, 37 of 39 men's singles champions were from Ivy League colleges. In addition, every doubles championship from 1883 through 1921 was won by Ivy League teams. In contrast, no Ivy Leaguer ever won the singles championship after 1922, and only one Ivy League team won the doubles after 1921. Since the first singles victory by a California college player in 1921, players from California schools have won the singles title 36 times, followed by those from Texas schools with 9 championships. In one stretch of 24 years (1958–1981), the men's college singles championship was won exclusively by players from California and Texas schools.

The social shift in tennis's orientation has been more limited, for although tennis is no longer dominated by the wealthy, and public courts have gained importance relative to private clubs as training grounds for young players, tennis remains an expensive game to learn and play, and most competitive players come from middle-class families. Some social barriers that existed in the past have disappeared. Jewish players, for example, rarely played competitive tennis before the 1960s. This was probably in part a result of anti-Semitism at the private clubs that dominated American tennis for most of the amateur era; Jews could never be admitted to these clubs as members, and Jewish players were often refused entry into many of the major tournaments sanctioned by the USLTA. Such discrimination has greatly diminished, and there have been a number of successful Jewish players in the United States since the 1960s. Yet other barriers have been more persistent. Poverty is a clear example. Occasional champions from poor families have appeared in American tennis, including several cases in which children from impoverished immigrant backgrounds became outstanding players. The number of competitive U.S. players from poor or lower-class families has never been great, however, and has not clearly increased over time.

A persistent feature of American tennis has been the small number of blacks who have become competitive players. For many years this was clearly due in part to the actions of tennis officials. Racism was a hallmark of the exclusive private clubs that served as the breeding grounds for tennis officials, and the officials carried this policy of exclusion over to their associations. In 1950, Althea Gibson became the first black allowed to play in the U.S. championships, but the color line did not simply fall thereafter. Arthur Ashe, who grew up in Richmond, Virginia, and played there as a junior until 1960, was never allowed to enter junior tournaments sanctioned by the Mid-Atlantic Tennis Association, the local subdivision of the USTA. But even later, in an era of diminishing official racial discrimination, blacks have not been attracted to tennis in large numbers. The triumphs of Gibson (U.S. and Wimbledon champion in 1957 and 1958) and Ashe (U.S. champion in 1968 and Wimbledon champion in 1975) have not served as inspirational examples that would result in the systematic entry of large numbers of young blacks into competitive tennis. In 1993, for example, there were five blacks among the 45 women nationally ranked by the USTA, and only two blacks among the 75 nationally ranked men. The expense of learning the game must again be a major factor in explaining these modest numbers, but a lingering perception of tennis as a sport for privileged whites may also lie behind the general lack of interest shown by blacks in the game.

Competitive tennis has produced a number of different styles of play. One basic contrast has been between baseliners—players who remain in the backcourt and rely on the consistency of their groundstrokes—and serve-and-volleyers, who rush the net to volley behind powerful serves. Baseline players are generally more effective on clay courts, where the slower and higher bounce gives them more time to prepare for their groundstrokes, while serve-and-volleyers have thrived on grass and to a lesser extent on hard courts, where the lower and faster bounce makes the power and speed of their attacking games more effective. In consequence, although there have been exceptions, baseline players have been more common among continental Europeans and South Americans, who play more often on clay courts, while serve-and-volleyers have traditionally come from Australia and the United States, where more players were trained on grass or hard courts. The serve-and-volley game has also been rarer among women than men. The relative popularity of these two styles has gone through cycles in the history of tennis, but neither has come to dominate competitive tennis completely. In part this is because the competitive game has never been restricted to a single type of surface. Grass was originally the most important competitive surface: it was used not only at Wimbledon, but also at the national championships of the United States and Australia, and at many lesser tournaments in these two countries as well as England. The French championships have always been played on clay, as have most tournaments in continental Europe and South America. Grass has declined sharply in popularity over time: although it remains in use at Wimbledon, it was abandoned in the U.S. for championships in 1975, and in Australia in 1988. The U.S. nationals briefly switched to clay, but since 1978 the tournament has been held on asphalt courts, as are the Australian championships. The great majority of professional tournaments, indoor as well as outdoor, are now held on hard courts, with a significant minority on clay, and only Wimbledon and a few of its warm-up tournaments on grass.

## The Effect of Technology

Perhaps the most systematic change in the way competitive tennis is played, which has affected virtually all players, has been the recent trend toward the use of greater power. This has been due in large part to technological change in the design and construction of tennis rackets. From the origins of tennis until the 1960s, the best rackets were made of wood. This first changed with the invention of the steel racket by former French champion Rene Lacoste, introduced into competitive play in 1967. Other innovations involving new materials soon followed; aluminum rackets appeared in 1968, and graphite and fiberglass rackets during the 1970s. During the early 1980s wood and metal rackets gave way altogether to new synthetic materials. Most rackets in production today are composites, made of graphite, fiberglass, and such new materials as boron and Kevlar. These composites are considerably stronger than wood or metal, and the rackets can consequently be lighter than traditional rackets; some current models weigh less than 284 grams (10 ounces), compared with the 354 to 369 grams (12.5 to 13 ounces) of wood or metal rackets.

Another major change in racket design occurred in 1976, when Prince Manufacturing introduced a racket with a wider and longer face that had a surface area more than 50 percent larger than conventional designs. The inventor, Howard Head, had intended only to increase the racket's effective hitting area, but he discovered that enlarging the head also had the unanticipated benefit of increasing the power generated by the racket. By the 1990s, conventional head sizes had disappeared in favor of oversized and new intermediate, mid-sized heads; today's rackets have heads 25 to 60 percent larger than those of conventional rackets.

The most recent significant innovation in racket design appeared during the late 1980s. Called the "widebody" because of the extreme thickness of the racket head, the new design is stiffer and generates even greater power than earlier designs. The widebody, which quickly became popular among recreational players, has not yet gained wide acceptance among professional men players, but is almost universally used by professional women players.

By producing lighter rackets that make it possible to hit harder with less effort than older wood or metal rackets, the changes in racket design and construction of the past three decades have systematically rewarded the use of greater power. The two-handed backhand, used sporadically in earlier times, but popularized during the 1970s by Bjorn Borg, Jimmy Connors, and Chris Evert, proved to be ideally suited to the new, larger racket heads; the larger effective hitting area allowed players to produce more topspin that provided control for the greater power generated by the two-handed stroke. The two-handed backhand has become a staple of the competitive game: in 1970 none of the world's top 10 men or women used the stroke, while in 1992 5 of the top 10 men and 6 of the top 10 women normally did. The serve has of course also been affected by the new rackets, as today's game places an even greater emphasis on power serving than was the case in the past. Although opinions differ enormously on the desirability of recent changes in competitive tennis, there is virtually unanimous agreement among both defenders and critics of today's game that the new racket technology is responsible for a much greater reliance on power in all areas of the game than was ever true in the past.

The ages of competitive tennis players have attracted considerable attention in recent years. A succession of women players has become successful at very young ages: Tracy Austin reached the world's top 10 in 1978 at 16, Andrea Jaeger in 1980 at 15, Steffi Graf in 1985 at 16, Gabriela Sabatini in 1986 at 16, Monica Seles in 1989 at 16, and Jennifer Capriati in 1990 at 14. In addition, between 1985 and 1990, the three most important tournaments in men's tennis, each more than a century old, all had their youngest singles champions, as Boris Becker won Wimbledon in 1985 at 17, Michael Chang the French Open in 1989 at 17, and Pete Sampras the U.S. Open in 1990 at 19. Many observers have concluded that competitive tennis players are now maturing earlier, and retiring earlier, than in the past. In 1992, comparing the current regime to that at the beginning of her professional career in the mid-1970s, Martina Navratilova, winner of nine Wimbledon singles championships, observed: "Players are better at an earlier age, but then they quit earlier as well" (Higdon 1992, 20). Monica Seles, the world's top-ranked woman player in 1991–1992, compared women's tennis to another sport dominated by young athletes: "I think what's happening in tennis is what's happening in gymnastics. The players are getting younger and younger"(Berry 1992). Navratilova and others have attributed this trend to improvements in both coaching and equipment. The more powerful rackets available today can compensate for young players' lack of size and strength, while the increasing speed of the game rewards the faster reflexes and greater foot speed of these players. The increasing popularity of tennis during the 1970s produced larger numbers of junior competitions and training programs. The greater financial rewards available in professional tennis have also spurred the establishment of tennis academies, where children can live and train year-round. The most prominent of these was started during the 1970s in Florida by Nick Bollettieri (the Nick Bollettieri Tennis Academy) and has already trained such champions as Andre Agassi and Jim Courier, both of whom have held the top ranking in the world. This record has attracted many more hopeful juniors, as well as stimulating other entrepreneurs to try to emulate Bollettieri's financial success. As a result of these and other changes, journalist Peter Alfano concluded in 1989 that "the primary age of a tennis pro is being lowered."(Alfano 1989)

Although evidence has not been analyzed for all world-class players, recent analysis of the careers of U.S. men and women nationally ranked by the USTA from 1960 through the early 1990s contradicts Alfano's conclusion. Prior to Open tennis, competitive players were typically young. Few players in the amateur era could afford to play full-time for more than a few years after leaving college because of the difficulty of earning a living as a tennis player under the rules governing amateur status. So for example the mean age of all nationally ranked U.S. women was below 20 in five different years during the 1960s; the mean age of nationally ranked men was below 23 in nine of ten years during that decade, and in one year was below 22. With the advent of Open tennis, the mean age of competitive players rose sharply, as many found they could earn more money playing tennis than in other careers. The mean age of nationally ranked women has never fallen below 20 during the Open era and has risen over time, falling below 22 only once since 1977, and rising above 23 in 1987 and 1992. Similarly, the mean age of nationally ranked U.S. men never again fell below 23 after 1970; it has been above 24 in every year since 1973, and in three years since 1981 it has been above 25. As these trends imply, the length of competitive players' careers has increased substantially in the Open era. U.S. men ever ranked in the U.S. top 20 who retired during the 1960s had been nationally ranked for an average of six years during their careers, while those who retired during the late 1970s and early 1980s had been ranked for an average of more than twelve years. Similarly, women ranked in the top 20 who retired in the early 1960s had been ranked on average for less than five years, while those who retired in the late 1970s and 1980s were ranked on average for more than eight years.

The examples cited above of the recent successes of young players stand as exceptions to this trend. Occasional players of exceptional ability at extremely young ages have long been a striking feature of competitive tennis, and the recent advances in equipment and training techniques may have made it possible for these gifted players to achieve success in adult competition at even younger ages than in the past. And recent years appear to have seen particularly large numbers of these exceptionally gifted players in the wake of the U.S. tennis boom of the 1970s. The number of Americans who played tennis annually mushroomed from an estimated 10 million in 1970 to more than 30 million annually during 1974 and 1978. The most talented of the children who began playing tennis during the 1970s began to enter adult competition during the 1980s, and the larger numbers of players in this cohort meant that there would be more of these talented players than in earlier times. So for example the mean age of the top 10 U.S. women fell from 24 in 1975 to 20 in 1981, and 21 in 1983; even more dramatically the mean age of the top 5 U.S. men fell from over 27 between 1985 and 1987 to 20 in 1991. But the popularity of tennis during the boom of the 1970s gave way to a bust during the 1980s, and the next cohort contained fewer gifted players. The mean age of the top 10 U.S. women rose above 25 in 1992–1993, and the mean age of the top 5 men rose above 22 in 1993.

The evidence for U.S. competitive players therefore indicates that generalization from the experience of a small number of stars to the careers of all competitive players is not appropriate: although the very youngest successful players have been younger than in the past, the ages at which tennis players typically enter and leave adult competition have not declined over time. For both men and women, the most important long-run demographic change during recent decades has been an increase in the mean ages of competitive players, with lengthening careers that have clearly been produced by the prize money of Open tennis.

—David W. Galenson

**Bibliography:** Alfano, Peter. (1989) "The Oversized Generation." *International Herald Tribune* (27 June): 15.

Baltzell, E. Digby (1995) *Sporting Gentlemen: Men's Tennis from the Age of Honor to the Cult of the Superstar.* New York: Free Press.

Berry, Eliot. (1992) *Tough Draw.* New York: Henry Holt.

Collins, Bud, and Zander Hollander, eds. (1994) *Bud Collins' Modern Encyclopedia of Tennis.* Detroit: Visible Ink Press.

Galenson, David W. (1995) "Does Youth Rule? Trends in the Ages of American Women Tennis Players, 1960–1992." *Journal of Sport History* 22, 1 (Spring 1995): 46–59.

———. (1993) "The Impact of Economic and Technological Change on the Careers of American Men Tennis Players, 1960–1991." *Journal of Sport History* 20, 2 (Summer 1993): 127–150.

Higdon, David. (1992) "Martina." *Tennis* (March): 20.

Hart, Stan. (1985) *Once a Champion: Legendary Tennis Stars Revisited.* New York: Dodd, Mead.

Mewshaw, Michael (1993) *Ladies of the Court: Grace and Disgrace on the Women's Tennis Tour.* New York: Crown Publishers.

Monsaas, Judith A. (1985) "Learning To Be a World-Class Tennis Player." In *Developing Talent in Young People,* edited by Benjamin S. Bloom. New York: Ballantine Books.

Newcomb, Peter. (1991) "Madonna Is the Model." *Forbes* (19 August): 80–84.

# Tennis, Paddle

Paddle tennis is a version of tennis that is played on a smaller court. Players use solid light paddles and balls that are less pressurized than tennis balls. It is sometimes confused with platform tennis, because they have similar equipment and other common characteristics. However, they are distinct games. In platform tennis, players may hit shots bounced off the screens. In paddle tennis (as in standard court tennis) that is not allowed. Both games are also different from paddleball, which is played against solid walls.

Paddle tennis was invented in Michigan in 1898 by Frank P. Beal, a minister who developed it to train young people for standard court tennis. To make the adult version more manageable for children, he established a smaller court, 39 feet (11.9 meters) long by 18 feet (5.49 meters) wide and devised short, light solid paddles and a slower ball.

Beal moved to New York City in the 1920s, and the game became a popular playground game there. It also spread to other parts of the United States, especially California. Adults also had begun to play paddle tennis, and in 1923 the American Paddle Tennis Association was formed. A number of tennis champions were paddle-tennis players in their youth, including Althea Gibson (1927– ).

Although the game had many enthusiasts, there were disagreements about how it should be played. Critics said the use of overhand serves and small court made it too easy to overpower an opponent with fast serves and shots slammed from the net area. The court was enlarged to 44 feet (13.4 meters) by 20 feet (6 meters), but many players still believed it was too small. Different versions of the game and courts developed, which made it difficult to organize tournaments on a national basis.

In 1959, the courts were enlarged to a standard

*Paddle tennis was originally developed to help teach the adult game to children.*

size of 50 feet (15.2 meters) by 20 feet (6 meters), divided into two service areas on each side, and a net in the center of the court 31 inches (0.7 meters) high. In the rear, a 3-foot (0.9-meter) lob or service area was added on each side. To discourage low, fast shots, the ball must be hit at least 10 feet (3 meters) off the ground if it lands there. The methods of service were also changed, including the addition of a one-serve-only rule. Also adopted were rules requiring that the ball bounce once on the other side before a volley. Although these changes eased some of the disagreements, there were still differences in the way the game was played, especially between the East and the West. Further progress was made toward a consistent form of the game in the early 1980s, when regional organizations on each coast merged and adopted more standardized rules.

—John Townes

**See also** Tennis; Tennis, Platform.

# Tennis, Platform

Platform tennis is a form of tennis that was originally designed to be played outdoors in winter on courts built on raised platforms that could be cleared of snow and ice. The game combines elements of court or lawn tennis with several other sports, including squash, racquetball, and paddle tennis. Players use short, solid paddles to hit a ball back and forth over a net in the center of the court, which resembles a tennis court but is smaller. The goal is to make shots that the opposing players cannot return.

Platform tennis is sometimes confused with paddle tennis, not surprising since the two games resemble each other in certain respects and platform tennis is also called paddle tennis. However, they are actually two separate sports. Both are distinct from paddleball, which is played against walls.

## Origins

The game of platform tennis originated in Scarsdale, New York, in 1928. Two tennis players, Fessenden S. Blanchard and James K. Cogswell, wanted to develop an outside court they could use for tennis, badminton, and similar games in the colder weather. The court they built and the weather were not suited to traditional tennis or other games. Instead, the two men developed a version of tennis that was suited to the site. They used the wooden paddles and rubber balls that were already being used in paddle tennis and devised rules that were based on tennis but that accommodated the smaller size of the court.

The game became popular among their friends. In 1931 the nearby Fox Meadow Tennis Club installed a platform tennis court. It became a popular activity there, and eventually more courts were added and tournaments organized, which developed into annual national championships at Fox Meadow. Other tennis clubs adopted the sport, and in 1934 the American Paddle Tennis Association was formed. The name was changed to the American Platform Tennis Association in the early 1950s to avoid confusion with the original form of paddle tennis and its related organizations. Originally, platform tennis was primarily a sport for the affluent, because most courts were located in private clubs. It became more widely popular in the 1960s and 1970s, however; courts were built in parks, resorts, and on other sites, and it was played in warmer seasons and climates.

## Practice

Platform tennis is played on a court surrounded by a 12-foot (3.6-meter) tall wire-mesh fence. The

*Platform tennis courts are elevated to keep them clear in bad weather.*

court surface is divided by markings that indicate the baselines and other areas of play. The layout is similar to tennis courts but with smaller proportions. The standard platform-tennis court is 30 feet (9.14 meters) wide and 60 feet (18.28 meters) long, with a playing area of 20 feet (6 meters) by 44 feet (13.4 meters) for doubles. Platform tennis balls are made of rubber and are close in size to a tennis ball. The paddle has a large, relatively flat oval head with a short handle. Unlike the strings of a tennis or squash racquet, the surface of a platform tennis paddle is solid, with a grid of smaller holes cut into it. Paddles are made of wood, plastic, aluminum, and other materials. The paddles are generally about 17 inches (43 centimeters) long, weighing from about 14 ounces to 18 ounces (0.3 to 0.5 kilograms).

The basic rules of platform tennis are based on court tennis. Although platform tennis can be played by two opponents as a singles game, it is more often played by four people as doubles. Competitive matches and tournaments are doubles matches. Platform tennis players also use many of the movements and strategies of tennis, such as forehand and backhand shots. A player scores a point when he or she serves or hits the ball into the marked playing areas on the other side of the net and the opponent is unable to return the shot or hits it out of the playing boundaries.

Games are scored in the same way as tennis. The side who first receives four points (or who wins two points over deuce) is the winner. Platform tennis has similar terms for scoring and a similar division of overall sets and games as court tennis. The rules for platform tennis differ from court tennis in two basic ways. Unlike tennis, where the server is allowed two chances to make a good serve before losing a point, platform tennis allows only one serve per point. If the first serve goes out of bounds or is disqualified for other reasons, the point is given to the other side. A serve that hits the net but lands within bounds, or is interfered with in other ways, is a "let" and is taken over. The other major difference is that the ball remains in play if it lands within the area of play, but then bounces up and hits the side or back screens. In that respect, platform tennis is similar to squash and racquetball. A player may return a serve or shot after it hits the screen on his or her side, as long as the ball does not hit the ground and bounce a second time.

These differences give platform tennis its unique characteristics. Although platform tennis can be played at a fast and strong pace, it is less oriented to rapid, powerful shots than tennis. Strategy in placing shots and the use of the screens to carom the ball at appropriate angles are especially important. Accuracy is especially crucial for the server because there is not a second opportunity to make up for a bad one. Volleys can last longer than in court tennis because there is more opportunity to return shots. It is also more difficult to overpower an opponent with fast serves than it is in court tennis. Platform tennis players must maintain their concentration and determination during long volleys. Many young people play platform tennis, but the game is also popular among older players because although it is demanding it does not necessarily require the same amount of running, speed, and exertion as tennis.

The courts are made of wood or other materials. The surface is generally treated with a material that balances the need for traction with smoothness. Traditionally, the courts were built on raised platforms to elevate them above the snow. However, courts can also be built at ground level in warmer climates or other situations.

Because of its background as an outdoor, cold-weather sport, the dress code of platform tennis is very relaxed. Players dress for comfort and movement. Platform tennis started in the U.S. Northeast, where it remained most popular for many years. However, it subsequently experienced growth in other regions of the United States and in other countries, especially in the 1970s. It is often played by people who are also active tennis players. While it is primarily an amateur sport, platform tennis tournaments and circuits with prize money have also been organized.

—John Townes

**See also** Tennis; Tennis, Paddle.

**Bibliography:** Squires, Richard C. (1969) *How To Play Platform Tennis.* New York: Devin-Adair Company.
———. (1978) *The OTHER Racquet Sports.* New York: McGraw-Hill.
Sullivan, George. (1975) *Paddle. The Beginner's Guide to Platform Tennis.* New York: Coward, McCann & Geoghegan.

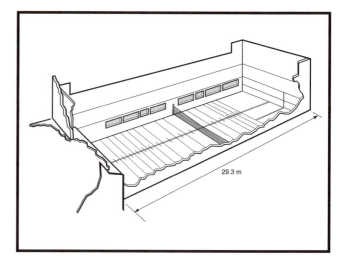

29.3 m

# Tennis, Real

## Origins

Real tennis, the ancestor of modern (lawn) tennis, is the descendant of a ball game that presumably originated in the north of medieval France. The game is first alluded to in the *Dialogus miraculorum* (1219–1223 C.E.) by Caesarius of Heisterbach, a German Cistercian monk who tells the story of a young clerk in holy orders from Paris whose soul was abducted to hell and abused as a tennis ball by a band of demons. Because the authenticity of the young man has been ascertained, the incident can be dated fairly precisely to around the middle of the twelfth century.

The name *real tennis* was coined in the latter part of the nineteenth century when adepts of the game, filled with deep misgivings about the apparent success of the newfangled lawn tennis, stubbornly called their brand the *real* tennis. In the United States, real tennis is referred to as court tennis; in Australia it goes by the name of royal tennis. In France, it has preserved one of its many medieval names, *jeu de la paume,* literally "game of the palm [of the hand]"; in French, this term must be distinguished from *jeu de paume,* which denotes the facility or court. Today, the

distinction between *jeu de la paume* (the game) and *jeu de paume* (the facility) is not always made; that is why the sport is now officially known as *jeu de courte paume,* where the adjective is used to differentiate it from a variant evolved from it and played in the open, *jeu de longue paume.*

There are good reasons for the assumption that tennis was at the outset a goal-game, a variety of medieval football played by clerics in the cloisters of their monasteries. This explains the architecture of the real tennis court, which features three penthouses with slanting roof and a hazard called the grille. Penthouse and grille were apparently adapted from the arcaded walks of the cloisters and the lattice window of the locutorium respectively. The walls of the court have been black at least since pictorial representations by Flemish painters around the middle of the sixteenth century. The oldest courts in existence are those of Hampton Court, erected under Henry VIII in 1532–1533 (rebuilt in 1625), and Falkland Castle in Scotland, built by James V in 1539. The latter is unique in that it belongs to the type of the *jeu quarré* that characteristically lacks a *dedans* and a *tambour* (see below for explanation of these terms) and has four openings in the wall at the service end.

## Practice

Played with the palm of the hand (and the feet) by its inventors, real tennis has made use of the sheepgut-strung racket since about 1500 C.E.. The asymmetrical shape of the modern racket made from ash is said to facilitate taking balls near the floor. It also enables players to impart sufficient

*This thirteenth-century ancestor of lawn tennis is played in an enclosed court and utilizes the walls.*

backspin on the ball, which prevents its rebounding too far from the rear wall, this resulting in a bad chase (see below for an explanation of this term). Stuffed with animal hair originally, the still solid balls now consist of strips of heavy cloth tape wound into a ball, tied with twine, and covered with white felt. They are still sewn by hand by the club professional.

The courts vary in size, standardized playing fields being a feature of modern sports since the nineteenth century only. Real tennis courts are about half the length of a lawn tennis court and slightly wider, with average measurements of 29.3 meters by 9.8 meters (96 feet by 30 feet).

Real tennis is played in much the same way as lawn tennis: the ball must be struck after its first bounce or on the volley. The distinctive features of the game are due to the fact that the medieval player, more attracted by the gambling than the athletic potential of his game, put to good use the peculiarities of the original court. The ball can always be hit hard, with the undercut stroke characteristic of the game, since the surrounding walls will prevent it from getting out of play. Indeed, one of the game's chief attractions is balls ricocheting off the walls, an effect enhanced by the contrivance of the *tambour,* a projection in the sidewall deflecting the ball unpredictably. A particularly intriguing feature is the service, for which the ball is sent onto the roof of the side penthouse. The serve is always performed from the so-called *dedans* or service side (as distinct from the hazard side)—that side of the court featuring a rectangular netted opening in the wall to the rear of the server. Possession of the service is important, because, by availing him- or herself of the opportunities offered by the court, the clever server can often make his or her balls unreturnable. The railroad serve, for instance, cuts the ball back into the sidewall, whereas the high sidewall serve can be executed in such a way as to make the ball drop back into the court parallel (and very closely so) to the hazard back wall. Points can be scored outright by sending the ball into the dedans (on the service side) or into the grille and the winning gallery, the last netted opening on the hazard side. The rule deviating most from lawn tennis is the so-called chase rule. It has been a feature of tennis since the earliest times. Whereas in lawn tennis the ball is dead if it bounces a second time, in real tennis the spot of the second impact (known as "the chase") is marked. Whenever the score is within a point of winning the game (the scoring method is the same as in lawn tennis) or whenever two chases have occurred, the players change ends to contend the chase or chases. In order to do this, the player who made a chase in his opponent's court has to "defend" it, by preventing the ball of his opponent from landing, if it bounces a second time, closer to the rear wall than in the case of his own chase. Yard and half-a-yard lines on the floor enable the marker to mark chases with precision. Typical phrases are "chase better than half a yard," "chase the line," and "chase nearly a yard worse than last gallery," of which the first and the second describe the best and the worst chases possible, and the last points out the fact that chases are also made if a ball enters any of the galleries (except the winning gallery).

## Social Background

A pastime of the medieval clergy originally, real tennis seems at an early date to have been adopted by the young noblemen receiving their education from them. It continued to be the favorite exercise of the aristocracy for many centuries and was known as the "Game of Kings" accordingly. Francis I and Henry IV of France, and Henry VIII and Charles II of England were particularly keen and noted tennis players. From the late-sixteenth century on, tennis increasingly became a prerogative of university students, too, notably in Germany, where the game formed part of the curriculum in the so-called *Ritterakademie* (knights' academy) where courtiers were trained after the model of the French *galant homme*. In addition, commercial courts existed in almost every important town of Europe. However, tennis was also soon appropriated by townspeople and the medieval peasantry. The former appended smaller roofs to the gables of their houses, and the latter resorted to makeshifts such as stone slabs or corn sieves in order to execute the service properly (on the peculiar service see above).

The games played by the townspeople and peasantry have spawned many traditional or folk games the world over: the now-extinct Saterlandic game in Germany; the Gotlandic game of *pärk* in Sweden; Frisian *keatsen* in Holland, and *kaatsen* or *jeu de balle* in the Flemish- and French-speaking parts of Belgium respectively; the *jeu de tamis* and the *jo de paumo* in the former French provinces of Picardy and Provence; the Basque *pelota* games of *bote luzea* and *lachoa;* the Tuscan game of *palla* in Italy; the game of *pelotamano* on the Spanish island of Lanzarote; and in the Americas the *pelota Mixteca* in Mexico and the *juego de la chaza* in Colombia and Ecuador. These games are characteristically played by the lower strata of society and minorities, and in the latter case has not infrequently become a means of preserving ethnic and cultural identity.

Despite a reference in 1427 to Margot, an excellent female player from Hainault, and to tennis-playing women in late sixteenth-century France, women have been notably absent from real tennis courts until very recently. As late as 1903, J. M. Heathcote could write: "We may not wish to encourage our wives and daughters to emulate . . . Margot . . . and to compete with us in an exercise fatiguing to all, and to them possibly dangerous, but we accord to them a hearty welcome when they honour the 'dedans' (as spectators) with their presence."

## Real Tennis Today

Recent years have seen a revival of real tennis, especially in Australia, and possibly owing to the game's snob appeal, this revived interest is likely to continue.

There were nineteen real tennis clubs in the United Kingdom, three in Australia, three in France, and nine in the United States in 1993. The sport has six national governing bodies: The Tennis and Rackets Association (United Kingdom; founded in 1907; headquarters at The Queen's Club, London; membership 2,100 in 1993); the Australian Royal Tennis Association (Richmond, Victoria); the Canadian Real Tennis Association (Toronto, Ontario); the Comité Français du Jeu de Courte Paume (Fédération Française de Tennis) (Mérignac); the United States Court Tennis Association (Bedminster, New Jersey); and the Dutch Real Tennis Association (The Hague, Netherlands). There have been world championship games since ca. 1750 (when the championship was held by a certain Clergé of France). From 1928–1955 (!) the title was held by the legendary Pierre Etchebaster of France. The administration of the world championship title is now managed by the association of the country of which the champion is a national citizen or in which he resides (at present the Australian Royal Tennis Association, owing to Australia's Robert Fahey's defeating his compatriot Wayne Davies in 1993). The governing association is required to accept a challenge from any winner of the Australian, British, U.S., or French Open Championships.

—Heiner Gillmeister

**Bibliography:** Aberdare, The Rt. Hon. Lord. (1980) *The Willis Faber Book of Tennis & Rackets.* London: Stanley Paul.

Bonhomme, Guy. (1991) *De la paume au tennis.* Paris: Gallimard.

Butler, L. St.J., and P. J. Wordie, eds. (1989) *The Royal Game.* Fordhead, Kippen, Stirling, UK: Falkland Palace Real Tennis Club.

de Bondt, Cees. (1993) *"Heeft yeman lust met bal, of met reket te spelen . . . ?" Tennis in Nederland 1500–1800.* Hilversum: Uitgeverij Verloren.

Garnett, Michael. (1983) *A History of Royal Tennis in Australia.* Mt. Waverley, Victoria: Historical Publications.

———. (1991) *Royal Tennis for the Record.* Romsey, Victoria: Historical Publications.

Gillmeister, Heiner. (1990) *Kulturgeschichte des Tennis.* Munich: Wilhelm Fink Verlag.

Heathcote, J. M., et al. (1890; rpt. 1903) *Tennis. Lawn Tennis. Rackets. Fives.* London: Longmans, Green.

Marshall, Julian. (1878) *Annals of Tennis.* London: "The Field" Office; reprint. Baltimore: Racquet Sports Information & Service, 1973.

Mursell, Vernon. (1986) *An Introduction to Royal Tennis* (video). Melbourne: Royal Melbourne Tennis Club.

Noel, E. B., and J. O. M. Clark. (1924) *A History of Tennis.* London: Oxford University Press; reprint. London: Gerald Duckworth & Co., 1991.

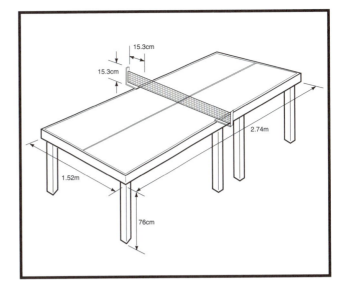

# Tennis, Table

After having been looked upon in the late nineteenth century as an extension of an entertaining board game, an after-dinner social diversion among the English upper classes, table tennis began to find mass acceptance at the turn of the century. Because of its universal appeal—it has been played and continues to be played recreationally, often under its trademark name "Ping-Pong," by millions of people the world over—it quickly spread to every continent.

The game became a competitive athletic sport in 1926 under the auspices of the newly formed International Table Tennis Federation (ITTF). Clearly, it had penetrated deep into the masses, even in the Orient. Edward Bilinski, for instance, in the May–June 1992 issue of the official United States Table Tennis Association's publication *Table Tennis Topics,* wrote of his interview with a 71-year-old man who spoke of how he'd won a small 1932 tournament in Xizhou, a city of then 300,000 in the same province as Shanghai. The conditions were extremely primitive: just one table with a net but without a white center line for doubles play; a single 40-watt bulb; a poorly glued celluloid ball, wobbly because of the sand and grist that had gotten into the openings on its seams; and nailed boards shaped into rackets.

This account suggests that, given the chance, players in China might one day be enthusiastically prepared to take the sport very seriously.

Japan and then China's dominating expertise did not become manifest to the West, however, until Asian players, using the supposedly outdated penhold grip (European players used the shakehand grip), began winning ITTF world championships in the 1950s.

World championships were begun in 1926, and the ITTF, composed of associations from 170 or more countries, continues to supervise these and other world title events, including even a biennial World Veterans event (for those 40–80 years of age; the 1994 version in Australia drew over 1,800 participants from all over the world). In 1995, 550 elite players participated in the forty-third world championships. Also, beginning in 1988, table tennis became part of the Olympic Games.

During the seven decades of serious tournament play, there have of course been controversies—over, for example, the use of various illegal serves (still a bone of contention today) or over nonattacking, interminably slow play—and consequently there have been necessary rule changes, including, initially in 1936–1937 U.S. tournaments, the lowering of the net from 17.1 to 15.3 centimeters (6 3/4 to 6 inches). Nothing has been more disputed than the coming into prominence of the sponge rubber rackets of the 1950s, with which the Japanese began to win world championships, and the consequent change and proliferation of the sponge-based racket surfaces that have evolved since.

*Originally popular with the British upper classes as after-dinner entertainment, table tennis quickly evolved into a fast-paced, aggressive, and highly competitive sport played around the world. Kjell Johansson (Sweden) beats Dragutin Surbek (Yugoslavia) in the semifinals of the 1973 World Championships.*

Indeed, it is fair to say that there is table tennis before sponge, and table tennis after sponge. They are almost two different games. Players may use the shakehands or penholder grip down through the years (and which is best is a seemingly never-ending controversy itself), but with regard to the sport's essential characteristics of speed and spin, and the new athleticism that serious play requires, the technological changes in the racket coverings in the last 40 years have brought about profound changes.

Meanwhile, the best table tennis players—most recently, the Chinese and Swedish men and the Chinese and South Korean women—continue to thrive, as do their lesser counterparts, in professional leagues and increasingly larger prize money tournaments in both the East and West.

The ITTF continues to function as a miniature United Nations, and in 1991 it enabled a combined North and South Korean team to participate in the world championships. The year 1996 marks the twenty-fifth anniversary of the famous "Ping-Pong Diplomacy" visit of the U.S. table tennis team to a China that would forever after be changed.

## Origins

Table tennis—often known by the English Jaques and the U.S. Parker Brothers onomatopoetic trade name of "Ping-Pong"—is generally considered to be of English origin. Miniature "tennis" was played indoors in England in the 1880s and 1890s, largely among the formally dressed gentlefolk as a mixed-company after-dinner diversion (Gurney n.d.). The table was invariably set up in a dining room or more roomy parlor. Nets were sometimes improvised of woven fabric, taut towels, stringed bottles, or books. Eventually, long-handled, hollow, vellum battledore rackets were replaced by short-handled wooden ones covered variously with sandpaper, cork, and, as the game flourished in the first years of the 1900s, pimpled rubber—the pips-out rubber offering more ball-grabbing opportunities for spin and control. In progressing from batting about tipsily angled balls carved out of champagne corks, ladies and gentlemen players came to prefer manageable celluloid balls.

## Development

By the beginning of the twentieth century, table tennis had moved out of the drawing-room confines of the British upper classes and their servants and was being enjoyed by people from every walk of life. Indeed, from 1900 to 1902 a table tennis craze developed in both Britain and the United States. The game was inexpensive and athletic and provided wholesome family entertainment. Ping-Pong postcards, party invitations, and even musical pieces were the order of the day. There was a huge demand for equipment, and boxed sets flourished. In England, a great many table tennis clubs were formed, and tournaments, some offering prizes valued at £100, were held.

England's Arnold ("Ping-Pong") Parker (? – 1954), no relation to Parker Brothers, the game manufacturers who in 1928 would patent the trade name "Ping-Pong" in the United States, was a turn-of-the-century star player and authority on the game. He formulated some much needed laws, one of which championed the "double-bounce" serve. Of course this two-bounce serve is now the norm, but, despite Parker's influence, it wasn't always so.

Though table tennis carried over much from lawn tennis (even perpetuating for a time lawn tennis scoring or variations in court-dividing line-markings), it was immediately apparent that some modification had to be made to the "single-bounce" tennis serve (where the server's ball could not bounce until it was on his opponent's side). Obviously, since serving overhand would be viciously absurd, a quite early rule that had been popularized demanded an underhand one-bounce serve. As the server struck the ball from behind and within the end lengths of the table,

perhaps even from a line drawn behind the table, only the handle of his racket could be above his waist. No wonder then that in the late 1920s in the United States many players were using the forehand-favoring, blade-down penholder grip rather than the double-winged shakehands tennis grip.

Strangely, as incredibly fashionable as table tennis, or ping-pong, had become in England and the United States for those few years at the beginning of the century, it just as incredibly became unfashionable. In 1922, however, a Cambridge University student, Ivor Montagu (1904–1984), began to interest himself in codifying the laws of the game, including the retention of the double-bounce serve. In January 1926, England's Montagu, along with representatives from four other countries—Austria, Germany, Hungary, and Sweden—held a historic meeting in Berlin. With Dr. Georg Lehmann, president of the Deutscher Tischtennis-Bund, taking the initiative, the International Table Tennis Federation (ITTF) was organized with Montagu as its first and longest-serving president (1926–1967).

In December 1926 the ITTF held its first world championship in London. Lady Swaythling, Montagu's mother, donated a cup for the men's team matches, and six European countries and India competed for it. Of course there was a men's singles (with 51 players) and a men's doubles championship as well. Women's doubles would not be introduced until 1928, and women's team matches for the Marcel Corbillon Cup not until December 1933 in Paris. In 1926, however, the women had their own singles championship (14 players) and also mixed doubles to play. Contrast this beginning world championship with the forty-third one, held in Tianjin, China, in 1995: 77 men's teams, 71 women's teams, 322 participants in men's singles, 227 in women's singles.

Back in the early 1920s, Montagu and his Cambridge friends, with the help of a leading manufacturer, Jaques, had reestablished an English Ping-Pong Association, but when Jaques insisted that all players in that association use Jaques equipment, Montagu's group promptly changed their name to the Table Tennis Association. Very much the same thing happened almost a decade later in the United States when players balked at using only Parker Brothers equipment in Parker

Brothers-sponsored American Ping-Pong Association (APPA) tournaments. Though the 1930 Metro and then the 1931 First National APPA Championships, both held in the Pennsylvania Hotel in New York City, were quite successful, New York area players, wanting to preserve their independence, broke away from the APPA to form the New York Table Tennis Association (NYTTA) and to hold their own national championships. By 1935, APPA players had joined, as the NYTTA players did earlier, the United States Table Tennis Association (USTTA). On its formation in 1933, this association (in 1993 renamed at its Colorado Springs Olympic Headquarters as USA Table Tennis or USATT) immediately affiliated with the ITTF.

From the initial APPA tournaments in New York City that each drew over 300 entries (men only; women were soon to follow), one could see that the sport was a great social leveler and that the immigrant influx was strong. Evelyn Seeley, writing in 1930 in the *New York World-Telegram*, spoke of "an amazing miscellaneous group" of participants. "Bankers and brokers . . . office boys and clerks, yachtsmen and Y.M.C.A. boys." A number of players, she said, "spoke in Continental accents," and, she might have added, they were sometimes shamelessly hyped as the "champion" of this or that European city or even country.

The multiethnic, multicultural appeal of table tennis remains strong today as can be seen from the 80 ITTF member-countries that sent players to the 1995 Tianjin, China, world championships. In 1995, of the top 10 men and top 10 women players in the USATT, half were from China, another 5 from the vastly different countries of Vietnam, Yugoslavia, Nigeria, South Korea, and Romania, and only 5 were native-born (Dunn 1995).

In the beginning, Hungarian players dominated the world championships—particularly five-time world champion Maria Mednyanszky (1901–1974), two-time world champion Anna Sipos (1908–1972), and the "Three Musketeers," Victor Barna (1911–1972), Miklos "Mike" Szabados (1912–1960), and Laszlo "Laci" Bellak (1911– ). Among other famous European world champions prior to the Asian ascendancy in the 1950s are Czechoslovakia's Marie Kettnerova (1911– ) and Bohumil Vana (1920–1989), Hungary's Gizella "Gizi" Farkas (1925– ), Romania's

Angelica Rozeanu (1921– ), England's Johnny Leach (1922– ), and Hungary's Ferenc Sido (1923– ).

Victor Barna (born Berna) is perhaps the most famous name in table tennis. Known more than any other player for a signature stroke, his backhand flick, he won 20 of his 22 world titles before he broke his playing arm in a car accident at age 23. That arm was said to be insured for $10,000, but, as Barna himself said, "with that crash went a part of my game never to return." After his first (1934–1935) Exhibition Tour of the United States, Barna was the first player to warn the ITTF of the havoc fingerspin services could cause. As skillfully practiced by the 1930s U.S. singles and world doubles champions Jimmy McClure (1916– ) and Sol Schiff (1917– ) and to a lesser degree by Europeans, these serves eventually forced a service rule stating that the ball must initially rest on the flat open palm and be thrown up without any fingerspin. Otherwise, players would cause consternation among their opponents: they'd rub the ball against the racket and let it fly; or with index and middle finger throw the ball viciously in a wheellike motion at different positions on the racket to have it bounce crazily here and there; or shoot the ball off like a wobbly marble, snapped from a sometimes already swollen thumb; or even nick the at that time not too hard celluloid ball with a fingernail that would cause it, as it landed on the dent, to hop like a Mexican jumping bean. Often, if the poor opponent was lucky enough to get the ball back, it would present a set-up, an easy point-winning follow for the server.

In the 1940s, after such U.S. stars as Leah Neuberger (1915–1993) and Thelma Thall (1924– ), Lou Pagliaro (1919– ), Marty Reisman (1930– ), and Dick Miles (1925– ) had been more or less just putting the ball into play (to them, as well as the Europeans, the server's advantage was in Miles's words "minimal"), the Asian players, about to become the world's best, would aim to win the point as quickly as possible. Ichiro Ogimura (1932–1994), the Japanese 1954 and 1956 world champion and, later, successor to Montagu and Roy Evans as president of the ITTF, though using open-palm serves, was still able to get an immediate advantage by squatting and, with a scimitar swipe of the racket, spinning (or deceptively not spinning) the ball; he would then look to sock

## How Sponge Technology Has Changed Play

Whereas from the 1920s into the 1950s serious players used to play with just the uncovered wooden blade, then preferred a sandpaper, or cork, or hard-pimpled rubber covering, now these rackets are passé. Gone, too, is the old sound of the game. When Japan's Hiroji Satoh won the 1952 world championships with a thick sponge rubber racket, the sport was forced to absorb a great controversy. Should the new "soundless" racket be banned, or not? After much debate it was not—but the thick sponge of the 1950s has been replaced by a plethora of thinner, far more sophisticated sponge coverings. Today's rackets, after some standardization in 1959, have easily removable sheets of sponge-based pips-out or inverted pips-in rubber with varying properties that greatly increase the speed and spin a player can put on the ball and that in some cases allow him to be quite strategically deceptive.

Because some players began using combination rackets that, to judge by the color, appeared to have the same kind of sponge sheet on both sides but really didn't—that is, one side may have had an antispin sheet that provided a dead return and the other, just the opposite, an inverted sheet that gave off a lively return—opponents were confused, their timing thrown hopelessly off, when the user twirled the racket in play to deceive them. So to combat this bit of trickery, deemed unfair, the ITTF passed a rule that one side of the racket had to be colored black, the other red, whether both sheets of sponge rubber were identical or not.

Another matter of concern to the ITTF is the length of the pimples on a racket, for how they bend or don't, and how the ball comes off such a covering, is of great importance to competitors. Even the glue that a champion player uses to repeatedly affix a new sheet of sponge rubber to the blade (likely after every match) is important, for its fresh application likewise helps to increase his powerful play.

As a result of this technological advance, there are few defenders left in the sport, for neither by chopping, that is, by imparting heavy backspin, or by lobbing, that is, by arcing the ball, badminton-like, to bounce back uncomfortably high, can they repel the force of the topspin attack. Instead, beginning with the serve, and the return of serve, both of which over the years have become of primary importance, each player seeks as best he can to quickly get ball control over his opponent and to end the point immediately or as soon as possible. Aggressive positional play with often risky follow-ups, and certain racket coverings that tend to give off "unreadable" spin, produce points that in the opinion of many are over much too quickly. So, though many rallies, especially by top players using sponge sheets that are most predictable, are more counter-attacking spectacular than ever before and bring exciting roars of approval from spectators, discussion continues about whether to try to slow down the game and, if so, how to do it (ban the rubbers that are most unpredictable, make the ball lighter to reduce its speed, or raise the height of the net).

—Tim Boggan

away the return (in what is called a third-ball attack) or maneuver to sock away the next return (in what is called a fifth-ball attack).

By the mid-1970s, after three-time world champion Zhuang Zedong (1942– ), his perennial runner-up Li Furong (1943– ), and long pips initiator Zhang Xielin had established Chinese supremacy, other players coming to the fore after the Cultural Revolution showed further inventiveness: Hsu Shao-fa, by tossing the ball up 6 meters (20 feet high), then pivoting into the drop, found new spins and new deceptions, and Huang Liang (1954– ), taking advantage of technology, used still unfamiliar long pips-out rubber to terrorize opponents with unreadable spins.

On into the 1980s and 1990s, players and officials have had to wrestle with behind-the-back illegal serves or players who are adept at legally "hiding the ball" on service. Deception remains an integral part of the sport. Players must learn how to "read" not only the spin on the ball but the movements of the opponent as well and to anticipate very quickly how best to instantaneously react to them.

Another 1930s problem—seldom applicable today given the change from the old hard rubber days of attack versus defense to the new sponge rubber days of attack versus attack—had to do with the interminably long play that would occur when two inveterate defenders met and played a match in which both simply "chiseled," that is, pushed the ball passively back and forth, waiting for the other to miss. One infamous point at the world championships in 1936 lasted over two hours! Naturally, a rule to expedite play had to be agreed upon, and variations were not always to a player's liking.

The U.S. team was not too happy when defending world women's singles champion Ruth Aarons (1918–1980)—to date its only world singles champion ever—was disqualified from defending her title in the 1937 final, along with her Austrian opponent Gertrude "Trude" Pritzi (1920–1968), for not being able to finish their match in the allotted time. Not so long after that, the great four-time world champion, the Austrian turned naturalized Briton, Richard Bergmann (1919–1970), reportedly put three alarm clocks under the playing table. Why? Because a new rule mandated that if a game wasn't finished in 20 minutes, whoever was ahead would be awarded that game. So proud, iconoclastic defender Bergmann set his clocks to go off at intervals to warn him of his used-up playing time. Of course the disrupting clocks were soon banned.

Today the standardized "Expedite Rule" stresses a 15-minute time period for any one game, then, if the game isn't finished, players must alternate services for the rest of the match, with the stipulation that if the server's opponent successfully returns a thirteenth ball he automatically wins the point.

However, by the 1970s and the super-topspin game of the Hungarians Istvan Jonyer (1950– ), Tibor Klampar (1953– ), and Gabor Gergely (1953– ), who, if forced to their far forehand side, could loop the ball around the table net posts with the precision of a bowler spinning strikes into a pocket, there wasn't much likelihood of slow, boring play. Likewise with the often fast at-the-table attack of not only the Chinese but the Swedish world champions of the 1970s, led by Hans Alser (1943–1977), Kjell Johansson (1946– ), and Stellan Bengtsson (1952– )

From 1956 through 1969, Japanese women won six out of seven world women's singles titles, with two-time winner Kimiyo Matsuzaki (1940– ) leading the way. Japanese men were also spectacularly successful after Hiroji Satoh's (1927– ) unexpected world championship win in Bombay in 1952. For the last 25 years, however, the Japanese women and for the last 15 years the Japanese men have been unable to match the achievements of their Chinese and Korean neighbors. In his book *Songs of International Friendship,* Hikosuke Tamasu (1920– ), the well-known "Butterfly" table tennis manufacturer, says that at a Japanese training camp back in the 1960s players were not permitted to go to bed until they had hit 1,000 forehands in a row without missing; now, 30 years later, he says, players not only lack what

technology has made ever more indispensable, paid professional coaching, but dedication and love for the game. Of course, in the last quarter of a century only Pak Yung Sun (1957– ) of North Korea and Hyun Jung Hwa (1969– ) of South Korea have been able to break the Chinese world women's singles hegemony; and no Korean man has ever been able to win a world singles, though South Korea's Yoo Nam Kyu (1964– ) did win the 1988 Seoul Olympics over his compatriot Kim Ki Taek (1962– ).

In 1971, after emerging from their Cultural Revolution, the Chinese coined the diplomacy phrase, "Friendship first, competition second," and proceeded to reacquaint the world, especially the so-called "Third World" of Asian, African, and Latin American countries, with their table tennis expertise . . . and their friendly propaganda. Only once in the 1970s did they have a world men's singles champion: Hsi En-ting (1945– ), as one of the sport's historians, Zdenko Uzorinac, tells us, "tattooed" his nonplaying hand "with thoughts of great thinkers." Said Hsi, "I played with both hands, the one in which I held the racket and the other which inspired me with wise sayings that led me to victory."

China's diplomacy went so far as to sometimes allow Chinese players to take it easy on their opponents, even, it was thought, in major championships. Could this account for a number of European teams winning world doubles titles? Perhaps—but given the opportunity, standout stars like Romania's Maria Alexandru, Russia's Stanislav Gomozkov (1948?– ), France's Jacques Secretin (1950– ), Yugoslavia's Dragutin Surbek (1946– ), and Germany's Jorg Rosskopf (1960– ) were certainly capable of rising to the occasion.

In the 1980s and early 1990s, a new wave of Swedish athletes—Jan-Ove Waldner (1965– ), Mikael Appelgren (1961– ), Erik Lindh (1964– ), Jorgen Persson (1966– ), and Peter Karlsson (1969– )—wrested away championships that had seemed second nature to the Chinese. These victories illustrated what a country—with a total population less than any one of China's three major cities—could do, at least for a generation or two, with a superb table tennis development program, a unifying team spirit, and a will to win.

Today, however, the Chinese, have come back, as they did in 1981, to capture all seven 1995 world championship titles in team, singles, and doubles play. There are good reasons for this. The Chinese have strong veteran players—Wang Tao (1967– ), for example, who, partnered with Liu Wei (1969– ), has won the world's mixed doubles three straight times, and who, with Lu Lin (1970– ), has won the world's men's doubles twice in a row as well as the men's doubles in the 1992 Olympic Games. The Chinese also have Deng Yaping (1973– ), just approaching her mid-twenties and already twice world and 1992 Olympic women's singles champion. And, most importantly, the Chinese have exceptional young players—both 1995 world men's singles champion Kong Linghui (1975– ) and runner-up Liu Guoliang (1976– )—who are just out of their teens.

Since their chief rivals have no comparable up and coming players, not even a few to China's many, perhaps the old problem faces the Chinese anew: with their strong sense of national pride, their enormous pool of past and present top players and coaches, and their strictly professional approach to table tennis perfection, who can beat them? Are they perhaps too good for the sport's own advance?

—Tim Boggan

**Bibliography:** Barna, Victor. (1962) *Table Tennis Today.* London: Arthur Barker.

Bellak, Laszlo. (1990) *Table Tennis: How a New Sport Was Born.* (Self-published.)

Bergmann, Richard. (1950) *Twenty-One Up.* London: Sporting Handbooks.

Bilinski, Edward. (1992) "When Table Tennis Was 'Ping-Pong' in China." *Table Tennis Topics* (May–June): 37.

Boggan, Tim. (1976) *Winning Table Tennis.* Chicago: Henry Regnery.

Clark, Coleman. (1933) *Modern Ping-Pong.* New York: John Day.

Craydon, Ron (1995) *The Story of Table Tennis—The First 100 Years.* Hastings, UK: English TTA.

Dunn, Ashley. (1995) "Table Tennis Anyone?" *New York Times* (17 August).

Gurney, Gerald N. (n.d.). *Table Tennis: The Early Years.* St. Leonards-on-Sea, East Sussex, UK: International Table Tennis Federation.

Miles, Richard. (1968) *The Game of Table Tennis.* Philadelphia: J. B. Lippincott.

———. (1970) "Miles on Bergmann." *Table Tennis Topics* (July–August): 1

Montagu, Ivor. (1936) *Table Tennis.* London: Sir Isaac Pitman and Sons.

Neale, Denis. (1970) *Table Tennis: The Way to the Top.* London: Arthur Barker.

Reid, Philip. (1974) *Victor Barna.* Lavenham, Suffolk, UK: Eastland.

Reisman, Marty. (1974) *The Money Player.* New York: William Morrow.

Schaad, Cornelius G. (1930) *Ping-Pong: The Game [and] Its Tactics and Laws.* Boston: Houghton Mifflin.

Schiff, Sol. (1939) *Table Tennis Comes of Age.* New York: Henry Holt.

Seeley, Evelyn. (1930) "Here in the Small, Closed Spaces." *New York World-Telegram* (25 March).

Tamasu, Hikosuke. (1993) *Songs of International Friendship.* Tokyo: Kimihiko Tamasu.

Uzorinac, Zdenko. (1981) *From Sarajevo to Novi Sad.* Zagreb: Graficki zavod Hrvatske.

# Thoroughbred Racing

**See** Horse Racing, Thoroughbred

# Toboganing

Toboganing is a popular traditional winter recreational pastime in many countries, especially where there is plenty of snow and winter is long. It is well suited to childhood or family recreation. Quite simply, toboganing involves sliding down an ice- or snow-covered slope on a small sled. The original wooden toboggan was designed and used by Native Americans. From this original design, three primary types of toboggans emerged: the skeleton or Cresta Run toboggan, the luge toboggan, and the bobsleigh or bobsled. The main focus of this entry is skeleton or Cresta Run toboganing, in which the rider assumes a head first, prone position upon the toboggan.

## Origins

The term "toboggan" has been traced back to the French-Canadian word *tabaganne*, which was originally derived from an Algonquian word *odabaggan*, meaning sled. The Algonquian term has a Micmac variation, *toba (a·) kun*, and an Abnaki variation, *udabagan.*

The origin of the toboggan is ascribed to the Native American people who inhabited the snow-covered northern forests of present-day Canada. Native Americans fashioned a simple, highly functional sledge or sled from long thin strips of birchwood poles or slats with turned-up ends, fastened together with deer leather thongs. These toboggan sleds were first used to transport items across the frozen northern terrain of various lake and river systems. The narrow design of the toboggan permitted it to "float" easily on the trail packed down by a snowshoer who pulled it along behind him or her. On downhill stretches, the rider sat upon and steered the toboggan with sticks.

## Development

In modern times, the toboggan became popular, transformed from its original practical use of transporting goods into a craft designed for winter recreational pastimes and competitive sport. For example, in North America, in addition to using the toboggan for pulling supplies and as a means of transportation, the French-Canadian *coureurs de bois* (sledge with wooden runners) was used for informal recreational racing and amusement. The modern origins of tobogganing as a sport began on the slopes of Mount Royal near Montreal, Canada, during the nineteenth century.

In Europe, the use of toboggans for winter recreational purposes was recorded in documents as far back as the sixteenth century. In 1520 Hans Sachs reported his delight in tobogganing. Also, Conrad Schwartz wrote a paper in 1530 in which he referred to the toboggan with the German term *rodel*.

During the 1860s, Dr. Alexander Spengler, a German émigré, noticed that tuberculosis was absent from the Swiss Alpine village of Davos. Concluding that this healthfulness was due to the clean Alpine air, Spengler published his theory in 1869. Soon after, word of his theory became popular and attracted visitors who sought relief from their chronic lung diseases. Tobogganing was introduced by visitors from Great Britain and the United States at the Alpine recuperative centers in Davos and St. Moritz, Switzerland, and the sport soon became popular among tourists in the snowclad Swiss Alps region during the winter.

*Native Americans of northern Canada were the first to use the toboggan. Originally a mode of transportation, it developed into a competitive and recreational activity.*

Tobogganing was considered to be an excellent form of recreation for people with disabilities, since it could be done while sitting in an upright position.

Much experimentation in the design of both toboggans and runs took place during this period. In 1879 two toboggan runs were designed and constructed at Davos, Switzerland. Shortly thereafter, in 1881, national toboggan competition began on a course located between the hamlets of Davos and Klosters in Switzerland. The Davos Tobogganing Club was formed in 1883 and began to sponsor races among teams from different local luxury hotels-cum-sanitariums. By March 1883 international competitions were being held in Switzerland on the Davos-Klosters toboggan run, which was over 3,000 meters (3,281 yards) in length. In the later part of that decade, tobogganing became popular in Canada, Switzerland, Germany, Austria, the United States, and Russia, with toboggan runs built in each of these countries.

Toboggan runs were designed and engineered to provide a directed curving, downhill course (or chute), which increased the speed, skill requirements, and competitive appeal of the activity for both participants and spectators alike, while minimizing the hazards and mishaps associated with natural or ill-conceived courses. Tobogganing does not require great physical strength, but rather agility and good reaction skills—therefore, it was considered an ideal sport for both genders and people of all ages and conditions.

During the period of rising participation and popularity as a winter sport (1880s), tobogganing evolved and branched into the three main forms of skeleton or Cresta tobogganing, lugeing (which developed from the one-person toboggan), and bobsledding (dubbed the "bob-sleigh" because the early riders leaned back and then "bobbed" forward to increase speed on the straightaway sections). Skeleton or Cresta tobogganing is the original sliding sport from which the other two forms of sliding sport were developed. In 1964 luge became an Olympic event and replaced skeleton or Cresta tobogganing as a competitive sport. At this juncture, luge tobogganing emerged from the shadow of bobsledding events, which had already attained Olympic status in 1924.

## Practice

Skeleton or Cresta tobogganing began in 1884 in St. Moritz, Switzerland, when the Englishman Major W. H. Bulpetts designed a toboggan run in the Cresta Valley as an alternative to the first run constructed down Klosters Road near Davos, Switzerland. (The term "skeleton" refers to the simple, skeleton-like outline of the toboggan frame, originally crafted from steel, wood, and canvas or leather. Today, the skeleton toboggan is constructed of steel or fiberglass.) On 18 February 1885, the first major competition, the Grand National, was held on this newly created course between a team from Davos and a team from St. Moritz, Switzerland. Tobogganists in this race assumed a face forward, sitting position on the toboggan and used their hands and feet to brake the craft. The team from Davos won, for the Davos team was prudent in navigating the course, while the St. Moritz team took many chances and could not stay on the run.

The St. Moritz Tobogganing Club (Switzerland) was formed in 1887, and this organization led to the further development and improvement of the Cresta toboggan run. Major Bulpetts was one of the founding members of the club, which has a rather exclusive membership and fee schedule, with numerous members from Great Britain, Switzerland, and the United States. Women have been club participants from its early days, including riding the races at the Cresta Run.

The Cresta run was composed of packed snow upon which water was sprayed to form a smooth ice surface. The Cresta course is 0.9 kilometers (three-quarters of a mile) long, descends 157 meters (514 feet) from top to finish, and covers a varied snowscape wherein no two curves or slopes are alike and there is no straightaway section; several of the curves are configured almost as right angles with high banks. Improvements to the course led to tinkering with and reengineering the toboggan itself, altering materials, height, weight, runners, and the way it was ridden. A man named McCormick redesigned and tested his "skeleton" toboggan on a trial run down the Cresta course in 1888. A news report in the *Alpine Post* in 1888 mentioned that McCormick traveled the run in 2 minutes and 8 seconds. McCormick captured people's attention because during this test run he became the first person to ride the toboggan in the face forward, prone position, rather than lying upon his back as in luge. Several other design improvements were made to the toboggan. In 1901 a man named Bott developed the sliding seat. By 1903 a snub-nosed toboggan was introduced. Ball-bearings were later used to improve the sliding seat apparatus. Since this period, the design of the skeleton toboggan has remained essentially the same.

### Rules of Play and Equipment

The Cresta run is an extremely winding and challenging course with steep banks rebuilt each year by the St. Moritz Toboggan Club in Switzerland. This channel of ice is 1,212.25 meters (1,325.7 yards) in length and has an average slope of 1:7.7. Straight channel sections are 2 meters (6 feet 7 inches) wide and corner banks range up to 4 meters (13 feet) high. Races typically begin from either the top or from junction to the finish. Top to finish represents the full length of the course. The section from junction to finish covers three quarters of the course, a distance of 890.20 meters (973 yards) with a declivity of 1:8.

Various sections of the course have been given special names (e.g., Battledore, Thoma, Shuttlecock, Bulpetts, Brabazon) after prominent Cresta personalities or special features of the course. The Shuttlecock section has the infamous distinction of being the most demanding of the nine corners on the Cresta course. Shuttlecock presents the rider with a right-angled corner encased in a 3-meter (10-foot) high bank of ice, which slings the rider into a sharp left exit. Riders who do not successfully negotiate the Shuttlecock corner may find themselves in a pile of straw placed up and over the bank to soften their landing. Shuttlecock retains a uniquely challenging characteristic, since course planners modify it each year.

The prime Cresta toboggan competition occurs during the subzero temperature season between January and February, when 50 events are often scheduled. The St. Moritz Tobogganing Club drafts and oversees the rules governing the races. Approximately 50 cups and trophies are competed for during a season: half of them for races begun at top and the other half for races started from junction. Cresta course races are composed of three heats; the winner is the person with the shortest cumulative time from the three runs. Since the course conditions may vary based upon the time of day or the day of the heats, the order in any run is determined by drawing lots. Tobogganists who arrive late for their heat are automatically eliminated. The runners on the toboggan may not be heated. In contrast to luge or bobsledding competitions, in which the size and weight of the craft are regulated, toboggans used in the Cresta run may be any size, shape, or weight, with speed and stability being the guiding design factors. A critical selection factor for competitors is that the toboggan dimensions must be a "good fit" for the user in terms of length, width, height, and weight. Mechanical brakes and steering components, however, are not allowed on the toboggan.

The type of toboggan preferred on the Cresta course is known as the "steel skeleton." The Swiss-German word for the skeleton toboggan is "Schlitten." One person rides upon the skeleton toboggan. The original dimensions of the basic steel skeleton tailored for a person 1.8 meters (5 feet 11 inches) tall were as follows: a top platform

## Tobogganing and Character Development

Tobogganing became popular during the Victorian era (1830–1900), a period associated with the rise and modernization of sport. The doctrine of the Muscular Christianity Movement was popular in the last half of the nineteenth century: it lauded leisure pursuits that contributed to the development of moral character, as well as one's physical prowess (a sound mind in a sound body). A concurrent influence during this period involved the application of Darwin's evolution theory into the social sphere of life (Social Darwinism). Participation in sports was encouraged, since the skills of discipline, competition, accountability, specialization, team play, self-restraint, and fair play were viewed as "civilizing," transferable, and necessary for success in the world of business:

> Now, what are the qualities of a good tobogganer? To quote Mr. Gibson, "Tobogganing is a sport which appeals to all Englishmen, as it calls into play all those qualities for which England as a nation is famous. The decision quickly called for and instantaneously carried out, the opportunity of exercising pluck, nerve, resource, and activity, the quick eye for a curve, the necessity for hand and eye to work exactly together" (Topham 1898, 472).

—Katharine A. Pawelko

or chassis about 1.2 meters (4 feet) long that had a sliding seat; a height of about 10 to 12 centimeters (4 to 5 inches); steel runners which are 1 to 1.2 meters (3 feet 6 inches to 4 feet) long, which ideally have about 10 millimeters (0.4 inches) of spring in them; these steel runners are placed 45.6 centimeters (18 inches) apart, with each runner being 16 millimeters (0.6 inches) wide. The steel skeleton weighs approximately 36.2 kilograms (80 pounds). The basic design of the contemporary skeleton toboggan, according to the United States Bobsled and Skeleton Federation, measures 3 feet in length, 16 inches in width, and weighs between 70 and 115 pounds. "Raking" equipment, composed of steel spiked toe pieces screwed into the boots worn by tobogganists, is applied to the run for steering and braking purposes.

Cresta run safety equipment is similar to that used in luge events: an approved design crash helmet with goggles, a face shield or visor, and a

## Hesta of the Cresta

This poem illuminates the legendary female tobogganing pioneer, Hesta, who as the poem attests, rode down the Cresta Valley three years before the run was officially constructed:

Now Hesta rode the Cresta
Midst the snows of '82
Tho' her mother had impressed her
It was *not* the thing to do.
She said "It's nice,
I like the ice,
It thrills me thru' and thru'."
In defiance of her mummy
She slid upon her tummy.

Unfortunately, folk heroine Hesta lost control at what is known as the Shuttlecock curve and wound up in a hospital, like many of her real-life male and female contemporaries.

Early women tobogganists rode the course in the requisite attire of their day: skirts. In spite of this hindrance, some women riders turned in very respectable performances. Women riders were also resourceful and developed techniques such as wrapping a band of elastic around their skirts above the knees to keep them from flapping on a run. Women toboggan pioneers such as Mrs. J. M. Baguley drew attention in 1919 as she placed in the last eight competitors of the Curzon Cup. She finished ahead of her husband by one-eighth of a second aggregate time in the first half of a race over three heats. Some women participants risked the label "fast" when they chose to wear breeches on the runs during this era. Mrs. J. M. Baguley set a course record on 14 February 1921, when she rode from junction to finish in 48.9 seconds. This time would have put her in the top 10 finishes at the 1948 Olympics. Due to some bad spills on the course among women tobogganists, a heated debate arose in the 1920s concerning their participation in the sport. Ultimately, women were banned from, or granted only limited access to, the course, due to several incidences of female mishaps on the course run. Women associate club members may ride the course only on the last day of the Cresta season from junction to finish.

—Katharine A. Pawelko

chin guard; padded gloves with an outer covering of glove studs or gauntlets (i.e., metal knuckles) to prevent "Cresta hand" (scraping one's knuckles on the ice); leather elbow pads; and leather kneepads. The Italian Edi Bibbia (cousin of Cresta tobogganing great Nino Bibbia) has been the St. Moritz Tobogganing Club's expert outfitter of tobogganing gear.

## Racing Strategies

Good judgment gained through experience is necessary for both selection of the most appropriate toboggan and appropriate strategies and techniques for the course. Tobogganists wear spiked shoes to help them gather initial momentum during a 50-meter sprint start, which is accomplished in a bent-over position by pushing the skeleton toboggan along the track. Once they achieve the desired momentum, riders lunge smoothly onto the sled. To negotiate corners or prevent slipping on iced banks, sledders use a technique called head steering: the rider shifts position so the body weight is primarily to the rear of the toboggan, which has deeply grooved runners. This arrangement permits the front of the toboggan to be steered by swinging or jerking it from side to side. The technique requires quite a bit of mastery to perform well. On straighter sections of the course, a rider distributes his or her weight along the full length of the toboggan or shifts the weight on the sliding seat towards the front part to keep the grooves at the rear end of the runners from digging into the course and slowing the pace. Changes in direction may be initiated by slightly tilting the head. While the feet are seldom used, they may be sparingly and judiciously applied to help steady, steer, and control the pace on banks or corners. Steel "rakes" or teeth attached to shoe toecaps are utilized for this purpose. A good run down the Cresta course may be made in under 75 seconds, with speeds over 112 kilometers (70 miles) per hour in various sections. Skilled tobogganists beginning at top achieve speeds of 80 kilometers (50 miles) per hour and accelerate to nearly 145 kilometers (90 miles) per hour at finish.

## Major Competitions and Players

After the Grand National toboggan competition, the Ashbourne Cup (now known as the Curzon Cup) was inaugurated in 1910. The Cresta Run was included in the 1928 and 1948 Olympic Games. During the early era of organized toboggan competitions (1885–1939), noteworthy tobogganists included Captain Dwyer, a two-time Grand National and Ashbourne Cup winner in the 1890s; Gibson, Dwyer's chief rival, won the Grand National title once and the Ashbourne Cup twice; Bott, a five-time Grand National and a three-time Ashbourne Cup winner; Thoma-Badrutt, a one-time Grand National and five-time Ashbourne Cup winner; Jennison R. Heaton, the Olympic Games gold medalist in 1928; and Lord Brabazon of Tara, who won the Curzon Cup three times (and for whom a curve at Cresta Run is named). After World War II, the Italian Nino Bibbia (1924– ) dominated Cresta tobogganing by capturing the gold medal at the 1948 Olympic Games (held at St. Moritz), eight Grand National titles, and eight Curzon Cups.

In 1930 Jennison R. Heaton set a Cresta course record time of 58.4 seconds while traveling an average speed of 124.5 kilometers (77.3 miles) per hour. By 1970 Nino Bibbia ran the Cresta in 54.67 seconds and was clocked at 137 kilometers (85 miles) per hour at finish. Franco Gansser set a new club course record in 1987, traveling the course from top to finish in 50.91 seconds.

## Governing Bodies

The St. Moritz Tobogganing Club administers the Cresta run course from its headquarters in the Kulm Hotel (St. Moritz, Switzerland). The Fédération Internationale de Bobsleigh et Tobogganing (FIBT) was originally founded in 1923 and governed bobsledding, tobogganing, and luge international rules and events. Luge separated from bobsledding and tobogganing into an independent organization (i.e., Fédération Internationale de Luge de Course (FIL) ) in 1955. The Fédération Internationale de Bobsleigh et Tobogganing was reorganized in 1957 as the official international governing body for bobsledding and skeleton tobogganing. The chief administrator of tobogganing in the United States is the United States Bobsled and Skeleton (Toboggan) Federation.

## Tobogganing Variations

Other variants of the original snow tobogganing format include marine tobogganing and cabogganing. Marine tobogganing was adapted from its popular winter sport cousin in 1887 by C. J. Belknap of Bridgeport, Connecticut, as a summer pastime. Belknap built a high chute 54.3 meters (178 feet) long, 0.51 meters (20 inches) wide, and 9.8

meters (32 feet) high for marine toboggans to zoom over a conveyor of 725 wheels down into Long Island Sound. The marine toboggans were reported to shoot off the long slide and skip across the waters of the sound like a smooth, thin pebble for about 23 to 53 meters (75 to 175 feet). Once momentum was lost, participants swam to shore, hauling their toboggan behind them. A modern version of this water toboggan concept is available at Walt Disney World's newest waterpark, Blizzard Beach. Melting snow, aerated water, and oscillating water jets are used to produce tall, fast, enlivening, and challenging ski and toboggan runs.

A more recent winter sport spin-off, cabogganing is a combination of tobogganing and canoeing. It is essentially winter downhill canoe racing and has been offered in the Midwest at Wild Mountain Ski Area in Taylor's Falls, Minnesota. Caboggans travel down snow chutes about 1 meter (3 to 4 feet) deep, which are just a bit wider than a canoe and about 183 meters (200 yards) long. Caboggans may travel at speeds up to 64 kilometers (40 miles) per hour and have less stability and steering capacity than toboggans. A caboggan crew is composed of two persons: a ballast and a pusher. The ballast member lies flat down in the bottom of the canoe so as to distribute the body weight and reduce air resistance. The pusher puts on soccer shoes, pushes the canoe from the starting line, and then as momentum builds, hops into the end of the caboggan before it slides away. Hay strewn at the end of the chutes serves to slow the caboggans to a stop. Qualifying heats are held in both the morning and afternoon to account for changes in course conditions. The top three qualifiers from the morning and afternoon heats move into the finals competition.

Several U.S. communities have begun to sponsor winter carnivals or snow bowls. One example of these occurs at Ragged Mountain at Camden, Maine. This is where the U.S. National Tobogganing Championships are held on New England's newly restored and longest toboggan slide (134 meters, or 440 feet, long). Participants ride the ice-coated wooden chute on traditional ash or maple sleds.

—Katharine A. Pawelko

**Bibliography:** Arlott, John, ed. (1975) "Tobogganing," in *The Oxford Companion to World Sports and Games.* London and New York: Oxford University Press, 1034–1039.

Bass, Howard. (1968) *Winter Sports.* South Brunswick, N.J.: A. S. Barnes.

Brabazon of Tara, Lord. (1966) "Tobogganing." *Winter Sports.* London: Lonsdale Library.

Bernstein, Jeremy. (1988) "Raking (Cresta Run in St. Moritz)." *New Yorker* 64 (28 March): 88–90, 93–98.

Caskey, George B., and David G. Wright. (1966) "Coasting and Tobogganing Facilities: A Manual and Survey on Construction and Operations." *Management Aids* 62. Wheeling, WV: National Recreation and Park Association.

Conover, Garrett, and Alexandra Conover. (1995) *A Snow Walker's Companion: Winter Skills from the Far North.* Camden, ME: Ragged Mountain Press.

Cook, T. A. (1894) *Notes on Tobogganing at St. Moritz.* New York: Scribner.

Cross, Gary. (1990) *A Social History of Leisure since 1600.* State College, PA: Venture.

"50 and 100 Years Ago: Toboggan Slide." (1988) *Scientific American* 259, 1: 12.

Hickok, Ralph. (1992) *The Encyclopedia of North American Sports History.* New York: Facts on File.

Seth-Smith, Michael. (1976) *The Cresta Run.*

St. Moritz Toboggan Club. *Cresta Magazine.*

Topham, Harold W. (1976 [1888]) "Tobogganing." In *The Encyclopedia of Sport, Volume 2,* edited by Henry Charles Howard, Hedley Peek, and Frederick George Aflalo. Detroit, MI: Gale Research Company.

Turner, Al. (1995) "The Big Freeze." *Leisure Management* (August): 58–59.

Westover, Craig, and Tamara Westover. (1979) "Caboganing." *Canoe* 7, 1: 60–61.

# Tractor Pulling

**See** Truck and Tractor Pulling

# Track and Field, Decathlon

The decathlon is a standard men's track and field event contested over two days. Its menu tests an individual's speed, strength, skill, and personality. The 100-meter (109.36-yard) dash, long jump, shot put, high jump, and 400-meter (437.44-yard) dash are held on the first day. The 110-meter (120.30-yard) hurdles, discus throw, pole vault, javelin throw, and 1,500-meter (1,640.42-yard) run make up the second day's schedule. A scoring table awards points for individual performances and the athlete with the highest score after ten events is the winner. The women's counterpart is the seven-event heptathlon.

Today's modern decathlon (from the Greek *deka* for "ten" and *athlos* for "contest") has an ancient Greek heritage and was added to the modern Olympic program in 1912. Native American Jim Thorpe of the Carlisle Indian School won the initial Olympic title but was subsequently stripped of the honor. Eight other Americans have won Olympic decathlon championships.

A variety of scoring tables has been employed to determine the decathlon or all-around winner and the rules are similar to those of other track and field events. Patience, a rigorous training regime, and long-term goals are necessary for multi-event success. Sponsorship by VISA, U.S.A. Inc., and a Reebok advertising campaign featuring a pair of U.S. decathletes has renewed interest in the event in recent years.

## Origins

Unlike the ancient Greek pentathlon (discus, jump, javelin, sprint, wrestling), which was presumably first contested at the eighteenth Olympiad in 708 B.C.E. but whose origins are shrouded in myth, the modern decathlon is a twentieth-century phenomenon. The ancient Olympic Games were banned by Emperor Theodosius I in 393 C.E. The pentathlon had lasted more than 1,100 years but disappeared until the mid-nineteenth century. At the turn of the century, Scandinavian nations (Sweden, Denmark, Finland) experimented with multi-event competition. The Danes called theirs a "decathlon" and offered a national decathlon championship as early as 1900.

It is here that Swedish efforts are spliced into modern Olympic history. Several nations had conducted multi-event competitions in the nineteenth century (most notably the American All-Around, a ten-event, single-day competition), but when the modern Olympic Games were reinstituted in 1896, multi-events went unscheduled. A "pentathlon" (consisting, peculiarly, of four events) was planned for the 1900 Paris Olympic

Games but was never contested. The 1904 St. Louis Olympic Games used the American All-Around and the 1906 (tenth-anniversary) Games in Athens offered men an ancient pentathlon (with wrestling!). No multi-event contest was tendered by the British at the dismal 1908 Games in London, but the Swedes proposed a pair of multi-event contests for men, a pentathlon (substituting the 1,500-meter run for wrestling) and a decathlon. In Stockholm in 1912, Sauk Indian Jim Thorpe (1888–1953) gave the event mythology and lore. So dominant was Thorpe (he won both pentathlon and decathlon by huge margins) that during the awards ceremony Sweden's King Gustav declared him the "world's greatest athlete"—the title accorded Olympic decathlon champions and world-record holders ever since.

In 1913, as a scapegoat for amateur AAU rules (Thorpe played a few games of minor league baseball while on summer break) Thorpe was divested of his medals, and the sad controversy over an Indian athlete being harshly punished for a common transgression played for the next 70 years, giving the decathlon additional lore. In 1982 the International Olympic Committee (IOC) restored the medals, returning them to his family; Thorpe had died penniless in 1953.

*Dan O'Brien pole vaults his way to a world record in 1992 during this ten-event two-day decathlon competition in France.*

## Decathlon Champions

Normally the event realizes notoriety only during Olympic years, and its champions have gained a special place in the pantheon of sporting heroes. Norwegian soldier Helge Lövland (1880–1984), Illinois osteopath Harold Osborn (1899–1975), and Finnish farmer Paavo Yrjölä (1902–1980) were early Olympic winners. When Kansas football star James Bausch (1906–1974) captured the Olympic title in Los Angeles in 1932, he began a U.S. winning streak that lasted until 1964. Glenn Morris (1912–1973), a Denver car salesman, blossomed to win in Berlin in 1936. World War II claimed the next pair of Olympiads. Then, in 1948, 17-year-old Bob Mathias (1930– ) of Tulare, California, became the youngest Olympic track and field winner ever. He repeated in 1952 with a world record.

Victories by Americans Milt Campbell (1933– ) in 1956 and Rafer Johnson (1935– ) in 1960 were followed by the Europeans and Americans trading Olympic wins. German student Willy Holdorf (1940– ) won in 1964 in Tokyo while American Bill Toomey (1939– ) was victorious in 1968 in Mexico City. It was during the 1960s that the Germans (both West and East) and the Soviets began to search for decathlon talent and promote the event. Even Bill Toomey trained in Germany with its renowned coach Friedel Schirmer (1926– ). Estonia's great coach Fred Kudu (1917–1987) developed Nikolay Avilov (1948– ), a Ukrainian Jew, who won in Munich in 1972, just two days after the Israeli team massacre. American winner Bruce Jenner (1949– ) thumped the world record in Montreal in 1976. A President Carter–led U.S. Olympic boycott in 1980 resulted in a dip of decathlon interest and an eight-year gap in U.S. Olympic participants. While U.S. fortunes sagged, Britain's Daley

Thompson (1958– ) became only the second double decathlon winner: 1980 in Moscow and 1984 in Los Angeles. Thompson was also fourth in 1988 in Seoul, but Eastern Europeans secured the next crowns: East Germany's angular Christian Schenk (1965– ) in 1988, and Robert Zmelik (1969–) of the Czech Republic in Barcelona four years later. The United States' Dan O'Brien (1966– ) captured the title in 1996. In all, Americans have won 11 of the 19 Olympic titles.

## The Role of Scoring

The first official multi-event scoring tables, using 1908 Olympic records as a basis, were provided in the spring of 1912 by the Swedes. These tables were immediately revised after the 1912 Stockholm Games and have been revised by the International Amateur Athletic Federation (IAAF) four times since (1934, 1950 [minor modifications in 1952], 1962, 1985). The IAAF alters the tables to take into consideration technical improvements in the events (e.g., fiberglass vaulting poles), new techniques (e.g., the Fosbury Flop style in the high jump), as well as improved performances. Most experts agree that the 1962 tables, prepared by Sweden's Axel Jörbeck, have been the fairest yet. The current (1985) IAAF decathlon scoring tables were widely regarded as hastily prepared and lacking in both statistical and scientific foundation. The functions have been merely sketched.

Since 1912, world decathlon records have been set on the different tables on 37 occasions, eight of them at Olympic Games. Thorpe's 8,412.955 points (on the 1912A tables) and Morris's 7,900 points (on the 1934 tables) lasted the longest; ironically, both lasted exactly 13 years, 326 days. Only once, on any set of tables, has 9,000 points been exceeded. In 1963 UCLA's C. Y. Yang (1933– ) of Formosa scored 9,121 points on the 1950 / 1952 tables) at the Mount San Antonio Relays in Walnut, California. The IAAF then changed the scoring tables just before the 1964 Olympic Games in Tokyo, leaving Yang with little time to strengthen point-weakened events. Disappointed and injured, he went from being the Olympic favorite to "also ran," ultimately placing fifth.

The scoring tables have always contained a degree of subjectivity. When earlier decathlon performances are rescored on more recent tables, we find a few surprising shifts of fortune. Finland's

Akilles Järvinen (1905–1943), the Olympic silver medalist in both 1928 and 1932, had a higher score on later tables than either of his world record–setting conquerors. For great champions, including Daley Thompson, Bob Mathias, Bruce Jenner, and more recently, American Dan O'Brien, the tables are incidental. No set of tables could keep them off the winner's podium. The current world record of 8,891 points by O'Brien was set in 1992 in Talence, France.

## Conventions and Rules

The order of decathlon events has remained unchanged since the first experimental modern decathlons contested in 1911. Only at the 1912 Stockholm Games, because of the unexpectedly large number of entrants (each nation was allowed up to 11 decathletes!) was the event contested over three days with the hurdles and discus swapped. Since then it has always been a two-day event except in the 1920s when, on a few occasions, American AAU officials conducted one-day affairs.

The decathlon rules are somewhat different from those for other track and field events. Two false starts are permitted before disqualification for running events, as opposed to open running events where one is allowed by the IAAF and none by the NCAA. Decathlon records are sanctioned with winds of not more than 4 meters per second (8.95 miles per hour) while individual events use 2 meters per second (4.47 miles per hour) as the cutoff. Only three attempts are allowed in the long jump and throws. In the rare event of a tie score after all ten events, the competitor who has outscored the other in a majority of events is the winner (similar to the ancient pentathlon). If the tie remains, the winner is he who has scored the highest number of points in any single event. The NCAA does not break ties.

The decathlon is the singular track and field event in which the world record has been held by someone from each major race (white, African American, American Indian, and Asian). Nevertheless, acceptance and success in the decathlon has been largely confined to North America and Europe, leading some to conclude that the Olympic decathlon is an Europe versus North America contest. Of the 54 Olympic decathlon medals awarded since 1912, North America has claimed 21 and Europe 32, with only one (that of

# Lost Opportunities

The decathlon has an official history. It is the account of those exceptional athletes who answered to the title of World's Greatest Athlete. Icons such as Jim Thorpe, Bob Mathias, Rafer Johnson, and Daley Thompson deserved the billing. All were Olympic champions. But the sport also has a counter-history, the saga of the forgotten, lost, and ignored. Sometimes talented athletes who would have been decathlon favorites or co-favorites never made it to the Olympic starting line. Wars, boycotts, political chicanery, injuries, and amateur policy all intervened to relegate them to historical footnotes.

Two such athletes were World War II victims. Big Bill Watson, an all-around talent from the University of Michigan, won the USA Amateur Athletic Union title in 1940 with 7,523 points, 400 points higher than anyone else in the world that season. Watson was a world-class shot-putter and long-jumper and a very adequate sprinter, hurdler, and vaulter. His place in decathlon history was virtually assured until the 1940 Games, originally awarded to Tokyo, were canceled.

Watson won a pair of national titles and some observers believe he would have won the 1944 Olympic crown as well. Yet those Olympic Games were also canceled by the War. By the time the 1948 London Games were contested, Bill, who became a Detroit policeman, had retired. He suffered from severe depression in later years because of his lost Olympic opportunity. His melancholy life ended in 1973 when he was gunned down on a Detroit street.

Heino Lipp's parable has a happier ending. A giant at 1.93 meters and 100 kilograms (6 feet, 4 inches and 220 pounds), the Estonian Lipp grew up while Adolph Hitler and Joseph Stalin bitterly fought over his Baltic homeland. Estonia passed to the Soviet sphere and the USSR declined an invitation to compete at the 1948 London Olympic Games. Several days after 17-year-old Bob Mathias astonished the track world, Lipp topped his winning London score by 445 points. *Track and Field News* ranked Lipp first in the decathlon world for the 1948 season.

The Lipp family was noted for wartime activities promoting Estonian sovereignty. Heino was periodically captured and jailed as a political prisoner by Soviet authorities. For several seasons after the war, in spite of being the world's top decathlete and Europe's best shot-putter, Lipp was never allowed to leave the Soviet Union. On several occasions he just missed breaking Glen Morris's world decathlon standard. When the Soviets did join the Olympic family for the 1952 Games held in Helsinki, just across the Bay of Finland from Lipp's home in Estonia, Lipp was denied an opportunity to compete.

Forty years later Heino Lipp did have an Olympic moment. A year after Estonia gained its autonomy from the Soviets, he became its flag-bearer at the 1992 Barcelona Olympic Games. Natives wept as their greatest hero—with the blue, black, and white flag in his clutch—led his country back into the Olympic arena during opening ceremonies.

—Frank Zarnowski

C. Y. Yang, who trained in the United States) going to the rest of the world. Few Asian and no South American nor African decathletes have attained worldwide success. Indeed, multi-event athletic contests cannot be found in the sporting histories of many nations. A check of ancient Celtic, Chinese, and American Indian cultures reveals no multi-event contest designed to settle on an all-around or general winner. It was up to the Scots-Irish, Germans, Americans, and Scandinavians in the late nineteenth and early twentieth centuries to invent, develop, and refine the ancient Greek pentathlon idea.

It is often thought that decathletes are mediocre athletes, generalists who can accomplish little else. But this view is surely erroneous. The decathlon itself is a specialty whose constituent athletes are fascinated by versatility; decathletes *prefer* doing well at ten sports rather than superbly at one. They are the Renaissance men of sport.

The event requires ample training. Few decathletes, for example, ever trained harder than Bruce Jenner, who was known to devote seven hours per day to workouts. Such a regimen is not recommended for the novice or anyone not in terrific shape. Training routines must attempt to enhance speed, strength, agility, and endurance. Off-seasons usually stress conditioning, weight training, and endurance runs, while the competition season features speed and technique training.

No decathlete can rely on a few competent individual performances to win. The scoring tables reward balance and consistency and no contest is won with a single great mark. Yet a decathlon is easily lost with a single weak event. This forces the decathlete into a physical cost/benefit analysis. The athlete must decide, for example, whether to put more emphasis on the shot put at the expense of running training. The additional points gained by a better throwing effort can be offset by points lost for lack of speed. And, because each athlete brings a different set of skills to the sport, training regimes vary. They have in common only the high volume of time and effort. Injuries are common, even presumed, and many decathlon men compete with some sort of injury. Again, a balance must always be struck between training and rest.

Mental factors play a bigger role in the decathlon than they do in other events. The main challenge is maintaining concentration and focus throughout the ten events. Decathletes must warm up physically and mentally for each effort. Frantic struggles against antagonistic opponents are rare; contestants compete against themselves and the scoring table. The adversaries are time, distance, fatigue, and the fear of failure. Other competitors are fellow competitors, helpful motivators, and often good friends. It is the most social of track events and promotes a strong sense of camaraderie among contestants.

Most really good decathletes are remarkably similar in size. Although world-class decathletes have been as small as 1.73 meters (5 feet, 8 inches) or as tall as 2.06 meters (6 feet, 9 inches), as light as 68 kilograms (150 pounds) and as heavy as 105 kilograms (230 pounds), most are in the 1.83–1.93 meters/82–95 kilograms (6 feet, 0 inches–6 feet, 4 inches/180–210 pounds) range. Today's average height/weight for world-class decathletes is 1.88 meters/88 kilograms (6 feet, 2 inches/195 pounds), exactly Bruce Jenner's statistics.

The sport is not without its controversies. Periodically a decathlete is suspended for anabolic steroid use. Evidence since the fall of the Berlin Wall reveals a good deal of "better performances through chemistry" in what was formerly East Germany.

Officiating snafus have been known to bring the decathlon to the front page. When officials called a third foul on American Dave Johnson (1963– ) in the 1992 Barcelona Games shot put, a protest ensued. Officials had not measured his efforts and he was subsequently accorded a fourth throw, "the shot heard 'round the world." Johnson's extra toss was a lifetime best and he went on to win the bronze medal, amid protests of several other decathletes. Johnson made up one-half of the $25 million "Dave and Dan" 1992 Reebok advertising campaign. Dan O'Brien had failed to make the U.S. Olympic team earlier in 1992 when, competing with a stress fracture, he zeroed

in the pole vault at the U.S. trials. A public outcry spotlighted the U.S. Olympic team's cutthroat selection system. O'Brien was the reigning IAAF World Champion, with a stress fracture likely to heal in a few weeks. Yet he was forced to try out for the U.S. team. Three weeks after the Barcelona Games, O'Brien set the world record and defeated the Olympic champion, Robert Zmelik, by more than 500 points.

Today the decathlon is truly popular only in Germany. There were in 1995 approximately 1,100 U.S. athletes and 5,000 worldwide who participate in at least two decathlons per year. The Soviet Union systematically promoted the event before 1991 but the change in economic/political systems has relegated it to a "developing" world decathlon power. The United States has recently regained the world decathlon lead, mostly as a result of corporate endorsement from VISA, U.S.A. Inc., which now sponsors clinics, domestic and international decathlon competitions, and a national decathlon team.

—Frank Zarnowski

**Bibliography:** Hersh, Phil. (1992) "A Test To Withstand Pain." *Sports Illustrated* 9 (April 13): 94.

Jenner, Bruce, and Phil Finch. (1977) *Decathlon Challenge: Bruce Jenner's Story.* Englewood Cliffs, NJ: Prentice-Hall.

Kamper, Eric, and Bill Mallon. (1992) *The Golden Book of the Olympic Games.* Milan: Vallardi and Asociates.

Mallon, Bill, and Ian Buchanan. (1984) *Quest for Gold: The Encyclopedia of American Olympians.* Champaign, IL: Leisure Press.

Moore, Kenny. (1984) "He's a Perfect 10." *Sports Illustrated* 16 (18 July): 194.

Noden, Merrell. (1992) "Rise and Shine." *Sports Illustrated* 2 (14 September): 34.

———. (1992) "Talk of the Town." *Sports Illustrated* 2 (22 July): 34.

———. (1992) "Dave Is Top Dog Now," *Sports Illustrated* 3 (13 July): 30.

Rozin, Skip. (1983) *Daley Thompson: The Subject Is Winning.* London: Stanley Paul & Co.

Schenk, Christian, and Siggi Wentz. (1992) *Zehnkampf [Decathlon].* Munich: Copress Sport.

Starr, Mark. (1992) "For God and for Reebok." *Newsweek* 2 (3 August): 20.

Stengel, Richard. (1984) "Call This Briton Great." *Time* 2 (20 August): 52.

van Kuijen, Hans, ed. (1994) *Who's Who in Combined Events.* Helmond, Netherlands: van Kuijen.

Wallechinsky, David. (1984, 1988, 1992) *The Complete Book of the Olympics.* New York: Viking; Boston: Little, Brown.

Zarnowski, Frank. (1996) *Olympic Glory Denied.* Glendale, CA: Griffin Publishing.

———. (1989) *The Decathlon.* Champaign, IL: Leisure Press.

———. (1976) *The Decathlon Guide.* Emmitsburg, MD: DECA ( Decathlon Association).

———. (1975, 1976, 1978, 1980) *The Decathlon Book.* Emmitsburg, MD: DECA ( Decathlon Association).

———. (1973) *How To Organize and Run a Decathlon.* Tucson, AZ: USTFF.

Zarnowski, Frank, et al. (1980–1994) *USA Annual Decathlon/Heptathlon Handbook.* Indianapolis: USA T&F.

# Track and Field, Jumps and Throws

Various forms of competitive and achievement-oriented jumping and throwing activities are part of the overall menu of track and field events. They take place on the "field" inside or around the running track, though they have, over time, gradually assumed particular sites within the arena. The jumping events are made up of the high jump, the long jump, the triple jump (formerly called the hop, step, and jump) and the pole vault. Until relatively recently, women did not compete to any significant extent in the triple jump and pole vault. The throwing events involve the propulsion of the following implements: the shot, javelin, discus, and hammer. Women have only recently started taking part in hammer throwing competitions. Partly because athletes are restricted to limited parts of the arena, these events tend to be less popular than the more popular track events. Nevertheless, it cannot be denied that many field events can be highly spectacular—notably the pole vault and javelin.

The field events, like those which take place on the track, have a long history and have been found to exist in a variety of cultures.

## Jumps

A high jump test was the requirement of the king's warriors in Celtic Ireland about the time of Jesus Christ. Requirements of a jump to the height of the shoulder or ear are mentioned, such

*Heptathlon gold medalist Jackie Joyner-Kersee flings herself forward during the long jump during the 1992 Olympic Games.*

as 1.5 to 1.6 meters (4.9 feet to 5.3 feet). At Dessau, in Germany, 1776 through 1777, Johann Friedrich Simion introduced high jump stands with holes and pegs to support a bar, the first of its type known. There were several professional high jumpers in England and Scotland in the first half of the nineteenth century who jumped between 1.80 and 1.93 meters (5.91 to 6.33 feet) using either a crude sideways roll over the bar or a side-on scissors-style jump.

The first great amateur jumper was the Englishman Marshall Brooks, who in 1876 jumped 1.89 meters (6.20 feet). The next 25 years saw some great jumpers in Ireland and the United States, most of whom did a roll over the bar from a straight-on approach. An innovator was the American Mike Sweeney from the East Coast with his "eastern cutoff"; he jumped 1.97 meters (6.46 feet) in 1895 and 1.98 meters (6.50 feet) later as a professional. From the West Coast came George Horine with his own brand of jump, a western roll with a runup from an acute angle. He achieved 2.00 meters (6.56 feet) in 1912. Clint Larson was another exception. He jumped using a back layout and style and anticipated the modern Fosbury Flop by over 50 years. His best jump came in an exhibition of 2.07 meters (6.79 feet) in 1924.

Around 1930, a flat type of straddle jump was invented. Les Steers was one of the best exponents of this style, with 2.11 meters (6.92 feet) in 1941. The Russians invented a shoe in 1957 with a built-up sole that added leverage, but it was quickly banned because it was deemed to provide athletes with an unfair advantage over those wearing "normal" shoes. Russian, Valeriy Brumel, with a wrap-around-the-bar straddle technique, leaped 2.28 meters (7.48 feet) in 1962. Dick Fosbury and Debbie Brill of Canada revolutionized the event with their backward arch, called the Fosbury Flop and the Brill Bend. The former won the 1968 Olympic high jump. This style has seen record heights by Americans, Germans, Soviets, a Pole, Chinese, a Swede, and finally Cuban Javier Sotomayor, who has reached 2.45 meters (8.04 feet).

Women's high jumping began at Vassar College in 1895. In the early 1920s English jumpers shone. Thereafter, the record was improved by jumpers from a number of nations until Yolanda Balas of Romania made large inroads on it, improving from 1.78 to 1.91 meters (5.84 to 6.27 feet) between 1958 and 1961. Since that time Europeans have dominated the scene, and Stefka Kostadinova of Bulgaria holds the present record at 2.09 meters (6.86 feet), which was made in 1987.

Around 1791 a pole vault stand was known to exist at Schnepfenthal School in Germany. It was probably introduced by Christian Carl Andre, the gymnastic teacher, and an early recorded performance of 2.74 meters (8.99 feet) is known to have been made. It was in England, however, that the early impetus for competitive pole vaulting developed. The event was featured in the Lake District (northwest England) sports events and Robert Musgrave was credited with a vault of 3.35 meters (10.99 feet) in 1867 using a solid wooden pole. The landing area was usually on grass, although a mattress was sometimes used.

By the 1890s, sand landing pits had superseded earth in the United States. The early 1900s saw the ascendancy of U.S. vaulters, who were the first seriously to use the slightly flexible bamboo pole in about 1906. U.S. vaulters also had a hole with a backboard into which they planted their pole instead of thrusting a spiked pole to into the ground. U.S. vaulters were outstanding in these early years, as was Frenchman Fernand Gonder, who vaulted 3.74 meters (12.27 feet) in 1905. A highly talented Norwegian named Charles Hoff improved the record from 4.09 to 4.25 meters (13.42 to 13.94 feet) in 1925. By this time raised sand pits were the norm in the United States.

In the late 1930s, a Russian vaulter experimented with a flexible green bamboo pole to achieve a world-class vault. The master of the bamboo pole was Cornelius Warmerdam of the United States, who took the record from 4.54 to 4.77 meters (15.65 feet) in 1941. Raised sand and sawdust landing pits were being used at this time. Flexible Swedish steel poles were popular in the 1940s, and American Don Bragg progressed to 4.80 meters (15.75 feet) with one. However, experiments from as early as 1948 had taken place with hollow fiberglass poles, and from 1961 they ruled supreme. Landing areas became loose foam rubber from the 1950s, and a decade later, formed-foam slabs became landing areas. From a modest height of 4.83 meters (15.85 feet) with a heavy slow reactive pole, the record had shot up to 6.14 meters (20.14 feet) with longer, lighter more reactive poles. The Soviet jumper Sergey Bubka has had no equal since 1984 in this event. Pole vaulting for women was enthusiastically taken up by the Chinese in 1988 and became an international event in 1993. The world best has rapidly improved from 3.81 in 1990 to 4.28 in late 1995 by Australian Emma George.

At Dessau School, Germany, in 1776 and 1777, there was a graduated jumping ditch wider at one end than the other. In the 1790s, John Ireland, an English jumper, was credited with jumping 7.01 meters (23.00 feet); in approximately 1854, another Englishman, John Howard, claimed to have exceeded 7.30 meters (23.95 feet) and 9.01 meters (29.56 feet) with the aid of a small ramp and dumb-bells.

Jumping pits appear to have been introduced in the 1860s with broken earth into which to land. At a later date, sawdust was mixed with the sod and by 1900 sand pits were fairly common. The take-off board was originally at the pit edge to stop the earth from crumbling away. There were a number of excellent Irish jumpers in the period 1880 to 1910. Walter Newburn sprang 7.33 meters (24.05 feet) in 1898 and also had two training jumps measured at 7.82 meters (25.65 feet). Peter O'Connor was the most consistent jumper reaching 7.61 meters (24.96 feet) in 1901 with a simple knee tuck jump. The Americans came to the fore in 1900 when Meyer Prinstein, a Jew of Polish birth, achieved 7.50 meters (24.60 feet).

In the 1920s the top jumpers began to cycle their legs while jumping, a technique known as the hitch-kick, which helped them achieve a better leg shoot on landing and hence longer distances. From the 1920s, black jumpers excelled in this event, the most famous being Jesse Owens, who leaped 8.13 meters (26.67 feet) in 1935, a record that lasted 25 years. Igor Ter Ovanesyan, the Soviet jumper, was the best of the non-Americans, jumping 8.35 meters (27.39 feet) in 1967. The following year, at the Mexico City Olympics Bob Beamon of the United States achieved a phenomenal jump of 8.90 meters (29.19 feet), hailed as a jump of the twenty-first century. Two factors contributed to the distance. The altitude of 2,400 meters (7,872 feet), which offered low air resistance, and a maximum allowable following wind of 2 meters (6.5 feet) per second helped. Fellow American Carl Lewis was easily the best jumper from 1980 until the 1991 World Championships at Tokyo, when compatriot John Powell narrowly beat Lewis and claimed the world record with 8.95 meters (29.36 feet). Jumpers were helped by a hard synthetic runway that significantly aided their speed. Women have a recorded history in this event from 1895 when competitions were held at Vassar College. The English and Germans were prominent in the early 1920s, but in 1928 a Japanese woman, Kinue Hitomi, jumped the then considerable distance of 5.98 meters (19.61 feet). Fanny Blankers-Koen of the Netherlands jumped 6.25 meters (20.50 feet) in 1943, and since 1955 it has been primarily East Europeans who have held the record, with the present holder, Galina Chistyakova of Russia, at 7.52 meters (24.67 feet), made in 1988. American Jackie Joyner-Kersee twice jumped 7.49 meters (24.57 feet) in 1994.

Two records from Greek antiquity of 55 Olympic feet and 52 Delphic feet suggest a multiple jump, but it is not clear how it was performed. At the time of the first modern Olympic Games of 1896 in Athens, the triple jump was added to the program, given that it may have been an ancient Olympic event. Dreisprungen ("three jumps") took place in Bavaria from at least the fifteenth century. Triple jumping has had a long history in Scotland with mention of the event, hop, step, and jump, during the eighteenth century. Records are continuous since 1826, when Andrew Beattie jumped 12.95 meters (42.48 feet). The Scottish best improved to 14.96 meters (49.06 feet) by Tom Aitken in 1873.

The Irish were easily the best exponents of triple jumping after 1880, with Dan Shanahan reaching 15.25 meters (50.02 feet) in 1888 with two hops and a jump, Matthew Roseingrave 15.44 meters (50.64 feet), in Australia in 1895 and Dan Ahearn 15.52 meters (50.91 feet) in the United States in 1911. The Japanese became a world force in the late 1920s by way of monotonous leg-strengthening exercises. Mikio Oda won at the 1928 Amsterdam Olympics and three years later achieved a world record of 15.58 meters (51.10 feet). Chuei Nambu scored gold at the 1932 Olympics with 15.72 meters (51.56 feet) and Naoto Tajima four years later at Berlin with 16.00 meters (52.48 feet), both being world records.

Brazilian Ademar Ferreira da Silva, often referred to as a bounding rubber ball, won both the 1952 and 1956 Olympics. Jozef Schmidt of Poland was a long-legged jumper who used his great speed to win two Olympic gold medals in 1960 and 1964. In 1960 he recorded 17.03 meters (55.86 feet). The Russians brought weight training to triple jumping around 1950 and had a large number of world-class jumpers, the best of whom was Viktor Saneyev, who won three Olympic titles, 1968 through 1976, and nearly won a fourth in 1980. The year 1968 saw the use of rubberized runways, which are a boon to the triple jumper, as several world class jumpers have shattered leg bones while performing before their introduction. American Willie Banks brought charisma to the event by encouraging the crowd to clap rhythmically as he ran down the runway. It appears to have worked, as he set a world best in 1985 of 17.97 meters (58.94 feet). British star

Jonathan Edwards in 1995 leaped the longest distance ever of 18.43 meters (60.45 feet), albeit with a slight wind assistance (18.29 without being aided by wind over the permissible limit of 2.00 meters per second). Women seriously took to triple jumping in 1986, with Eastern European jumpers excelling. The long-legged Russian, Inessa Kravets, leaped 15.50 meters (50.84 feet) in 1995.

## Throws

Putting a stone of about 7.3 kilograms (16 pounds) or heavier, a shot putt, has been a sport in Europe since at least the twelfth century, especially in Scotland, Bavaria, and Switzerland. Throwing took place from behind a balk of wood. Regular competition with measured throws began in the Scottish Border Games of the 1820s. In 1827, Scotsman William Goodfellow recorded 11.43 meters (37.49 feet), and in 1842 Charles Belleny threw 12.55 meters (41.16 feet).

From 1880 to the early 1900s, the Irish were the best shot putters in the world. Their outstanding thrower was Denis Horgan, a heavily built athlete who achieved 14.88 meters (48.81 feet) in 1904. The usual practice was to throw from a 7-foot (2.13-meter) square with stopboard until 1908 when a 7-foot circle became standard. Ralph Rose of the United States was a giant of a man 1.93 meters (6 feet, 4 inches) tall and weighing 132 kilograms (291 pounds). He advanced the record to 15.54 meters (50.97 feet) in 1909. In the 1920s and 1930s, several European exponents of the event achieved records in the range 16.04 meters (52.61 feet) to 16.20 meters (53.13 feet), namely Emil Hirschfeld, Germany; Zygmunt Heljasz, Poland; and Frantisek Douda, Czechoslovakia. The 136-kilogram (300-pound) American, Jack Torrance, came along in 1934 and pushed the record up to 17.40 meters (57.07 feet).

In 1949 and 1950 the much lighter Jim Fuchs improved the record to 17.95 meters (58.88 feet) with an acute sideways lean and an explosive reaction at the front of the circle. During a European tour in 1951, Parry O'Brien was observed to start his movement across the circle from a backward position instead of the traditional sideways stance, culminating with a strong rotational drive of the arm prior to release. He was a man of exceptional dedication and determination and with the aid of his new found style, called the O'Brien

style, and regular weight training he advanced the record 16 times between 1953 and 1959 to 19.30 meters (63.30 feet). During this time, the concrete circle superseded the cinder circle.

Other Americans were taking to weight training and probably steroids, which appear to have been in circulation among the weight training fraternity from at least the early 1960s. Randy Matson, standing 2.00 meters (6 feet, 6½ inches) and with commensurate long arms, owed his success to weight training, however. As a 20-year-old in 1965, he dominated shot putting with a throw of 21.52 meters (70.59 feet) and two years later improved to 21.78 meters (71.44 feet). From 1976 the Soviets and East Germans ruled the shot circle. Aleksander Barychnikov of Russia was the first to be successful at the highest level with the rotational style of throwing reaching 22.00 meters (72.16 feet) in 1976. Udo Beyer, a large man weighing 135 kilograms (297 pounds) with a height of 1.94 meters (6 feet, 4 inches), threw a world record of 22.64 meters (74.26 feet) in 1986, and his slightly lighter East German compatriot, Ulf Timmermann, set a mark of 23.06 meters (75.64 feet) in 1988. Sometime drug offender, Randy Barnes of the United States, has the accepted world record of 23.16 meters (75.96 feet).

Women began putting the 8-pound (3.6-kilogram) shot in the United States in 1907, and in Europe a 5-kilogram (11-pound) shot was used between 1918 and 1924, after which 4 kilograms (8 pounds, 13 ounces) became the international standard. In the 1920s and 1930s, the Germans were the best, and from 1945 onward the Soviet Union has dominated the event, although East Germans and Czechs have also been prominent. The current record holder is Natalya Lisovskaya of Russia with 22.63 meters (74.25 feet) made in 1987.

The Greek poet Homer speaks of the discus being thrown by the Myceaneans at Troy, which is considered to have taken place around 1200 B.C.E. After the collapse of the Roman empire, there is no more information about discus throwing until the nineteenth century. The modern Greeks included the event in their Olympic revival games of 1859, 1870, 1875, and 1889.

The most serious revivals of the discus were the regular competitions in Gothenburg and Stockholm, commencing in the latter city in 1892 when Harald Andersson threw 26.20 meters (85.96 feet). More important was the inclusion of the discus in the first modern Olympic Games of 1896 in Athens, where Robert Garratt of the United States outthrew a local Greek. The event was peculiar to Scandinavia up until 1920, when the Americans, Germans, and Hungarians showed an interest.

The actual discus has hardly changed from 1896, when it weighed 2 kilograms (4 pounds, 6 ounces) and was made of wood with a metal rim. In the early years, the discus was thrown from a standing position from a 2.5 meter (8.2 foot) square, which by 1908 had become a circle, and all competitors either used a turn or hopped across the circle. In the United States, a 7-foot (2.1-meter) circle was used up until 1912, and a number of Americans recorded distances of between 30.00 and 40.00 meters (98.43 and 131.23 feet) between 1896 and 1906. Until 1913 the Swedes and Finns were apparently throwing with a Scandinavian 2-kilogram implement that weighed 1.97 kilograms (4 pounds, 5 ounces). Jussi Kemppainen of Finland threw 41.50 meters (136.15 feet) in 1900, but Armas Taipale (Finland) is credited with 47.85 meters (156.99 feet) in 1913 with a regular weight discus.

Improvement in throwing was slow between the years 1920 and 1941 with Americans advancing the record year by year. In 1934, Swede Harald Andersson threw 52.42 meters (171.98 feet), and the next year Willi Schroder of Germany, 53.10 meters (174.21 feet). Generally, throwers in the 1930s appreciated the fact that their discus went further if thrown into the wind. In 1948, Italian Adolfo Consolini, a highly coordinated thrower, improved the record to 55.33 meters (181.53 feet), the year he was the Olympic champion. Robert Fitch was one of the earliest throwers to use a start position with his back to the direction of throwing, and he achieved a U.S. and world record of 54.93 meters (180.22 feet) in 1946. He, like his compatriot Fortune Gordien, used a low foot placement and fast turn to advance the record to 59.28 meters (194.49 feet) in 1953.

American Al Oerter won Olympic golds at the four games between 1956 and 1968. He even returned to competition as a veteran and threw a personal best of 69.44 meters (227.82 feet) at the age of 43 in 1980. The Swedes produced a heavy-rim discus of regulation size and weight in the 1970s, which allowed more pulling power to be generated for those throwers with strong fingers.

American Jay Silvester had a different strategy. He relied heavily on weight training to provide strength and threw 70.04 meters (229.79 feet). A similar strategy has been followed by Wolfgang Schmidt of East Germany, throwing 71.16 meters (223.46 feet) in 1978, and his compatriot, Jurgen Schult, the present world-record holder, throwing 74.08 meters (243.04 feet). On Schmidt's evidence both took drugs.

Women in Europe were throwing the men's or junior men's (1.5 kilograms [3 pounds, 5 ounces]) discus in 1917 and 1921. The following year the 1-kilogram (2 pound, 3 ounce) implement came into general use. Germany and Poland had the top throwers in the 1920s and 1930s and the Soviet Union from the 1940s onward with Romania, Czech Republic, Bulgaria, and East and West Germany also having prominent throwers. The record is held by Gabriele Reinsch of East Germany at 76.80 meters (251.97 feet).

Hammer throwing was known among the Vikings 800 C.E. They threw a hammer to lay claim to land in which the best throwers claimed the largest share. A legend, referring to the eleventh century, speaks of a hammer-throwing champion in England. In the sixteenth and seventeenth centuries throwing the hammer and other similar implements was popular. Measured hammer throwing emerges as a regular sport in Scotland and Ireland from 1828. In that year, the Scotsman Adam Wilson threw 27.74 meters (91.01 feet) with a standing throw from behind a line with a wooden shafted implement 3 feet 6 inches to 4 feet (1.07 to 1.22 meters) long.

In 1878 the Amateur Athletic Club of London introduced a 7-foot throwing circle which was increased to 9 feet (2.7 meters) in 1887 probably to accommodate the turn, but it is uncertain who developed the turning technique. In Ireland, where 7- and 9-foot circles were in use, a turn appears to have been used by James Mitchell in 1886 when he threw 36.40 meters (119.42 feet). Soon after this, particularly in the United States, flexible malacca cane shafts were used to help improve distance. In 1896, John Flanagan of Ireland, but later of the United States, used two turns to achieve 44.80 meters (146.98 feet). In the same year, he was also one of the first throwers to use a double metal handle, one for each hand, and a wire instead of a wooden shaft. It was the Irish in the United States who improved the standard of throwing greatly between 1900 and 1913. John Flanagan emigrated in 1896 and achieved 56.18 meters (184.32 feet) in 1909. Matt McGrath threw 57.10 meters (187.36 feet) in 1911 and Pat Ryan 57.77 meters (189.53 feet) in 1913. These throwers were referred to as the "whales," owing to the size of their girth around their center of gravity—probably caused by their liking for beer.

In the 1920s experiments were conducted with a three-turn technique. The 1928 and 1932 Olympic winner, Pat O'Callaghan, threw 59.56 meters (195.41 feet), but it was not forwarded as a world record as Ireland was not affiliated to the International Amateur Athletic Federation (IAAF). In the mid-1930s, Sepp Christian, a German coach, devised the heel-toe turn instead of rotating on the toes, which brought four German throwers to world class. In 1938, Karl Hein threw 58.24 meters (191.08 feet), and six days later Erwin Blask took the world record to 59.00 meters (193.57 feet). In the late 1940s and early 1950s, a small tungsten-head hammer was marketed, and the record was advanced by Hungarians Imre Nemeth and Jozsef Csermak and Sverre Strandli of Norway, who threw 62.36 meters (204.59 feet) in 1953.

The following year the Soviet school of throwers emerged and with the benefit of weight training improved the record year by year. Other contributing factors were the concrete circle, which replaced cinder in 1955, providing athletes with a smoother and "quicker" surface from which to throw, and the likelihood of throwers taking steroids after 1965. Anatoliy Bondarchuk threw 75.48 meters (247.64 feet) in 1969. The four-turn throw was perfected by Aleksey Spiridonov of Russia to set a new global best of 76.66 meters (251.51 feet) in 1974. Taking steroids probably advanced the record beyond the 80 meters (262.47 feet) mark when Soviet Boris Zaychuk threw 80.14 meters (262.93 feet) in 1978 and later progressed still further to the current record of 86.74 meters (284.58 feet) by his fellow Soviet in 1986. Since the stricter clamp-down on drugs, the standard has dropped a few meters. Women's hammer throwing stems from 1988 with the countries of the old Soviet Union to the fore. Olga Kusenkova of Russia holds the world's best throw of 68.16 meters (223.62 feet) made in 1995.

Javelin throwing for distance appears to have been one of the sports described by Homer and practiced by the Myceaneans around 1200 B.C.E. The javelins thrown by the Greeks of 500 B.C.E. were thin and made of wood, with a string wound around the center of gravity. When thrown, the thrower would hold onto the end of the string. This pulling caused rotation of the javelin, giving greater stability and hence further distance. From a contemporary account, it is known that a javelin could be thrown about three-quarters of a bow-shot. This would give a distance of about 135 meters (443 feet)! The Celts in Ireland, about the time of Jesus Christ, describe a distance-throwing javelin as having a flaxen string, meaning it either had a Greek-type throwing thong or a throwing grip. Javelin throwing in warfare was comparatively common in many parts of the world through into modern times, and competitive throwing is known in Africa and South America within living memory with distances of 120 and 130 meters (394 and 427 feet) respectively having been claimed.

Modern javelin throwing was born in Scandinavia. Both the Swedes and the Finns were holding competitions from 1883. The javelin first became an international event at the unofficial 1906 Olympic Games held at Athens. The outstanding thrower in the early years was Erik Lemming of Sweden, who progressed the world best from 41.81 meters (137.17 feet) in 1897 to 62.16 meters (203.94 feet) in 1912. From thereafter until 1950, the Finns virtually dominated world javelin throwing. Jonni Myyra was their first great thrower who raised the record between 1914 and 1925 to 66.62 meters (218.57 feet) and in so doing popularized the crossover step prior to delivery.

Even more famous than Myyra was Matti Jarvinen, known as "Mr. Javelin." His career saw him advance the record to 76.47 meters (250.89 feet) between the years 1929 and 1936. When it rained arenas became flooded, and in 1938, the Finns introduced the burning off of surface water from the cinder runway by setting light to quantities of petrol. Until 1953, top-class javelins were made in Scandinavia of selected and cured wood. Aluminum and Swedish steel javelins had appeared in the late 1940s, but the revolution in aerodynamic design was pioneered by Dick Held in the United States, whose brother Bud reached 80.41 meters (263.81 feet) in 1953. His new javelin was of greater circumference and gave a 27 percent increase in surface area; he got away with it because there was no rule against it at the time (one was introduced in 1957 after his experiment). In 1957, a mediocre Spanish thrower threw over 75 meters (246 feet) with a rotational throwing technique, but the rules were quickly redrafted to stop this method before the top throwers had a chance to develop it. Speed at the moment of launching the javelin advanced the record a further 10 meters (33 feet), achieved mainly by medium height and weight throwers. The taller, heavy athlete Soviet Janis Lusis came along with his record of 91.98 meters (301.77 feet) in 1968 to set a new trend in javelin throwers.

The big strong men, of whom some probably took steroids, steadily improved the record until Uwe Hohn of East Germany threw the amazing distance of 104.80 meters (343.83 feet) in 1984, which exceeded the safe throwing area within a stadium. The IAAF took swift action in 1985 and decreed the center of gravity of the javelin be moved forward 4 centimeters (1.6 inches). This had the effect of making the javelin nose-dive earlier in its flight thus shortening the distance thrown. At the end of the first year of the new javelin being introduced the record stood at a mere 85.74 meters (281.30 feet). Steve Backley of Britain was the first to throw more than 90 meters (295 feet) with 90.98 meters (298.49 feet) in 1990. There were attempt to circumvent the rules during 1990 and 1991 by roughing the tail of the Swedish javelin and in 1992 a Hungarian javelin appeared which was covered in a thin layer of carbon fiber to cut down vibration. Both of these inventions were outlawed. The current supreme master is Jan Zelezny of Czechoslovakia. He holds the record at 95.66 meters (313.85) set in 1993. Women have a record of javelin throwing from 1912 through 1921 with the 800-gram (28.5-ounce) men's model and the regulation 600-gram (21.4-ounce) one from 1922. The Americans and Germans produced the best throwers in the 1920s and 1930s, the Soviet Union in the 1950s and 1960s and in the 1970s, particularly Ruth Fuchs of East Germany record holder first in 1972 to 1980 with 69.96 meters (229.53 feet). Countrywoman Petra Felke was the most successful in the 1980s and holds the record of 80.00 meters (262.47 feet) made in 1988.

—David Terry

**Bibliography:** Doherty, K. (1971) *Track and Field Omnibook:A Complete Guide for Coach and Athlete.* Swarthmore, PA: Tafmop Publishers.

Matthews, P. (1996) *Athletics 1995: The International Track and Field Annual.* Surbiton, UK.

Pozzoli, P. (1968) *Yearbook 1968.* Claremont, CA: Women's Track & Field World.

Quercetani, R. L. (1990) *Athletics: A History of Modern Track and Field Athletics 1860–1900 Men and Women.* Milan: Vallardi & Associati.

Zur Megede, E., and R. Hymans. (1995) *Progression of World Best Performances and Official I.A.A.F World Records.* Monaco: IAAF.

# Track and Field, Running and Hurdling

Track races tend to take center stage in the repertoire of events making up track and field competitions. In outdoor competitions these events generally range from 100 meters (109.36 yards) to 10,000 meters (6 miles, 376.11 yards). Flat races (i.e., without hurdles), which lie between these extremes, are the 200 meter (218.72 yards), 400 meter (437.44 yards), 800 meter (874.89 yards), 1,500 meter (1640.42 yards), and 5,000 meter (3 miles, 188.06 yards). Indoors, the shortest distance is usually 60 meters (65.62 yards) and the longest 3,000 meters (1 mile, 520.83 yards). Track running is usually categorized on the basis of the distance run; hence, sprints are up to 400 meters, middle distances from 800 meters to 3,000 meters, and long distances from 5,000 meters up.

Track running can be divided based on other criteria, as well, including anaerobic capacity (such as sprints) versus aerobic capacity (middle and long distances, with 800 meters balanced between the two). In addition, track races may be defined as flat or hurdle races, the latter taking place over 110 meters (120.30 yards) (100 meters for women) and 400 meters, plus the 3,000-meter (3,280.84-yard) steeplechase, which is not yet generally recognized as a women's event. The sprint and 400-meter hurdles have 10 barriers; in the steeplechase competitors have to negotiate 28 solid hurdles and 7 water jumps. Races up to 110

*Gail Devers of the United States stretches her limits during the 100-meter hurdles at the 1993 World Championships.*

meters are run along a straight track; the others are run counterclockwise around the circuit. In addition to races between individuals, track meets are usually made up of two relay (or team) races—the 4 x 100 meters and the 4 x 400 meters. These categories apply to men and women, though it is only in recent decades that women have taken part in the longer-distance track events.

The number of events the International Amateur Athletics Federation (IAAF, the international governing body) recognizes for world record purposes has diminished considerably over the last half century. The standardization and reduction in the number of race distances recognized for records is part of a gradual rationalization of track running. With a growing societal emphasis on *speed*, there has been a decline in running for distance—the furthest distance that can be run in a given time. Events such as the one-hour run are rarely run today. Apart from the 1 mile (1,609.35

meters), events measured in imperial units are no longer widely practiced.

Several forms of motivation lead athletes to participate in track. Athletes may wish to demonstrate something about themselves or to improve their personal best time. They may run against the clock to break records or significant barriers such as the 4-minute mile or the 10-second 100 meters. Racing may be motivated by the desire to beat a particular rival or win a special title or medal. Finally, and increasingly, athletes may race to make money.

## Development, Measurement, and Technology

Track racing differs from other forms of racing (for example, cross country) in that it takes place on a specially prepared circuit. The Greeks and Romans engaged in track racing. The basic unit of distance over which races were run was the *stade*, a distance of about 190 meters (210 yards) —the length of the straight sprint track. Other races were multiples of this distance, ranging from about 7 to 24 *stades*. In practice, however, the standard of measurement differed from place to place and courses, therefore, differed considerably in distance. The Greek stadium was usually a long parallelogram, the track being rectangular. Races of more than one *stade* involved athletes making a sharp turn around a socket or turning point placed on a raised spine *(spina)* along the center of the course. Associated with sprint racing was a starting gate (the *husplex)* to prevent false starts.

Other premodern track racing is associated with certain Native American nations. Although not as sophisticated as those of the Greeks, the Jicarilla, for example, had "running tracks" that were subject to modest amounts of preparation. In the Osage nation a 4-kilometer (2.5-mile) running track was constructed to keep warriors fit. A Crow running track is recorded as being 5 kilometers (3.1 miles) long and horseshoe-shaped, and a course used by the Mandan in 1892 was described as "level prairie and was cleared of every obstruction and kept in condition *for racing purposes only*" (Nabokov 1981).

Modern track running has been characterized by various applications of technology over the century and a half during which it has flourished. The first running track in England was built at Lord's Cricket Ground in London in 1837—a narrow path for two-man races, but faced with gravel and measured by surveyors. More typical, however, were races held on manicured grass surfaces. World records continued to be achieved on grass in Australia and New Zealand into the 1960s. The smooth surfaces of cricket pitches were often used for track races. In mainland Europe and North America, most running tracks were made of various combinations of cinders, clay, or shale. Certain tracks developed the reputation of being faster than others. The last Olympic Games to hold events on a cinder track was in Tokyo in 1964.

The first synthetic running track was built in the United States in 1950. Since then, such facilities have become the norm. Today, in the wealthier countries of the world, it is estimated that over 90 percent of all official track meets take place on such surfaces. It is widely regarded that synthetic tracks have contributed to the improvement of performances in all track events.

Before the invention of starting blocks, sprinters used to dig small holes in the track in order to assist them in getting a good start. The crouch start had existed in the late nineteenth century. The introduction of starting blocks was a further rationalization of the track racing environment. Invented in 1927, these were first used in Chicago in 1929. It has been estimated that starting blocks improved spring performance by 34/1000 of a second in a 100-yard (91.44-meter) race. For many years starting blocks were seen as unfair aids to the athlete—much as drug use is perceived today. Blocks were authorized by the IAAF in 1937, but their first major international presence had to wait until the 1948 Olympics in London. Starting blocks are pinned into the track and removed after the race has started. They are not used for events above 400 meters.

Track racing had been held indoors since at least 1861 when the first U.S. indoor meet was held in Cincinnati, Ohio. Gas-lit events were held in London in 1963. Today, indoor track meets are held throughout the "developed" world, a 200-meter circuit with banked curves being the norm.

Other innovations in track racing have been the refinement in timekeeping and the use of drugs. Stopwatches have given way to electronic timing, events being timed to hundredths of a second. Photo-finish electrical timekeeping has become the norm and today often determines the result and the timing of track races.

Drug use is felt to be widespread and the IAAF imposes bans on athletes having been found to have used certain "banned substances." Among the best known are anabolic steroids. The most famous drug-taker in track annals was probably Ben Johnson from Canada who, having broken the 100-meter world record in winning the Seoul Olympics with a time of 9.79 seconds, was found to have taken a banned drug. He admitted to the use of steroids, testosterone, and human growth hormone over a 10-year period. He was stripped of his medal and temporarily banned from competition. When re-admitted to the sport he was again found guilty of drug abuse. Some observers believe that the widespread use of performance-enhancing drugs is a logical extension of the achievement and record-seeking principle of modern track and field.

One technical development that has failed to be adopted in athletics is the starting gate, similar to that used in horse and dog racing. Such contraptions were experimented with in the 1930s and 1940s but, perhaps surprisingly (given the Greek antecedents alluded to above), did not find favor with athletes and their administrators.

Another innovation that could potentially improve performance is a banked track for races (especially sprints) of 200 meters or more, as found with indoor tracks. Athletes in outer lanes run more gentle curves than those on the inside, hence disadvantaging the sprinter on the inside lane. It has been shown that in a 20-second 200-meter race the runner in the inside lane suffers a penalty of 0.07 seconds. This may sound insignificant, but to a serious athlete it could mean the difference between coming first or last. Banking would reduce the disadvantage experienced by runners in the tighter inside lanes.

Among the many rules that the IAAF prescribes are the details concerning the kinds of tracks upon which major championships can be held and on which records can be set. These are quite precise. Until the 1970s many track meets were held on grass and cinder tracks, often of varying circumferences. Today's championship races must take place on a track of a particular synthetic composition that must be 400 meters in circumference. To equalize the distances athletes run, races up to 400 meters are run in lanes, and races 200 meters and 400 meters have staggered starts. In 800-meter races, the athletes usually run the first turn in lanes to avoid the congestion which might otherwise take place. Tracks for major competitions usually have eight lanes marked out.

The IAAF insists on tracks being 400 meters in circumference for the holding of championship meets and for validating record performances. This was not always the case. For example, the track at the White City Stadium, London, built for the 1908 Olympic Games, was one-third of a mile (536.45 meters); that at Stockholm (1912 Olympics) was 383 meters (418.8 yards) .

Despite these technological innovations, track athletics has not been able to fully neutralize the natural environment. Hence, 100-meter and 200-meter races accompanied by a following wind of more than 2.00 meters (2.19 yards) per second are regarded as invalid for record purposes.

Training for track racing does not necessarily take place in the same environment as racing. Sprinters may use the track relatively frequently but will also use the gymnasium and weight room to develop strength as well as speed. It is also crucial for sprinters to spend long hours finely tuning their technique, particularly that of starting, since a race of 100 meters can be won or lost at the start. Middle and long distance runners often train over varying terrain. Forests, sand dunes, and parks have formed environments for different generations of runners. Swedish trainer Gösta Holmer pioneered a form of training known as *fartlek*. This is a Swedish word meaning "speed play" in which runners change the pace at which they run as often as they feel like it. It was traditionally undertaken in the Scandinavian forests and meadows. Such training was used by the great Swedish runners of the 1940s and is today employed by athletes all over the world as part of their training regimen. This relatively unplanned approach contrasted with the "interval-running" method, often associated with the German coach, Waldemar Gerschler. This often (but not always) takes place on a track and involves running repetitions of a specific distance (for example, 200 meters, 800 meters) with a prescribed interval for "recovery." In this way an athlete might run 20 efforts of 200 meters with, perhaps, a one-minute interval between each. The great Czech runner Emil Zatopek was a well-known exponent of this approach.

## Legends and Landmarks

Track running has tended to be the most glamorous group of events in the overall track and field menu. At different periods of time, particular events and individuals have dominated the world running stage. The selection of legendary runners is largely subjective and times of performance alone are far from being the only way of comparing athletes from different decades. In the 1920s and 1930s, long-distance runners from Finland, notably Paavo Nurmi, dominated the running scene. Nurmi is regarded as having revolutionized long-distance running. He increased the amount of training beyond the conventional norm and ran with stopwatch in hand so that his pace might be regulated in the most rational way. Nurmi set 20 world records, from

2,000 meters (1 mile 427.22 yards) to 20,000 meters (12 miles 752.22 yards), but he was only one of a number of Finnish athletes who dominated global track in the 1930s. Of the 20 fastest 5,000-meter runners in the world in 1930, 12 were Finnish.

During the 1940s the Swedes dominated middle-distance running with the presence of Gunder Hägg and Arne Andersson. Hägg came close to breaking one of the legendary barriers of track athletics, the four-minute mile. Had he been exposed to more competition outside neutral Sweden in the years of World War II, he would have undoubtedly achieved it. However, it was not until 1954 that the Englishman, Roger Bannister, achieved the performance that people had dreamed of with his historic time of 3 minutes 59.4 seconds at the Oxford University running track at Iffley Road. This was arguably Bannister's major achievement for, although winning European and British Empire titles, he never achieved an Olympic victory or set any other world records. It could be argued that in the 1950s the mantle of Nurmi had been assumed by Emil Zatopek from Czechoslovakia. His severe training methods contributed to his three gold medals (5,000 meters, 10,000 meters, and marathon) at the Helsinki Olympics in 1952, a feat that remains unsurpassed. He also set 18 world records at distances from 5,000 meters to 30,000 meters (18.64 miles) .

In the 1960s the middle distances were dominated by athletes from Australia and New Zealand. Herb Elliott and Peter Snell took the 800-meter and 1,500-meter records into a new era. Elliott was coached by the enigmatic Percy Cerutty and, with a number of other Australian and New Zealand athletes, temporarily shifted the balance of distance running power to the antipodes. The other great Australian athlete of that era was Ron Clarke who, having carried the Olympic torch into the Melbourne Olympic stadium as an 18-year-old in 1956, retired from running only to return in the 1960s as a world-record holder in the 5,000 meters and 10,000 meters. The most famous of the New Zealand athletes of this period was Peter Snell, winner of two Olympic 800-meter gold medals in 1960 and 1964. In the 1980s, however, it was the British, through the exploits of Sebastian Coe, Steve Ovett, and Steve Cram, who were paramount in these events. Each

## 3 Minutes 59.4 Seconds—The 4-Minute Mile

I barely noticed the half mile, passed in 1 min. 58 sec., nor when round the next bend, Chataway went into the lead. At three-quarters of a mile the effort was still barely perceptible; the time was 3 min. 0.7 secs., and by now the crowd were roaring. Somehow I had to run that last lap in 59 seconds. Chataway led round the next bend and then I pounced past him at the beginning of the back straight, three hundred yards from the finish.

I had a moment of mixed joy and anguish, when my mind took over. It raced well ahead of my body and drew my body compellingly forward. I felt that the moment of a lifetime had come. There was no pain, only a great utility of movement and aim. The world seemed to stand still or did not exist, the only reality was the next two hundred yards of track under my feet. The tape meant finality—extinction perhaps.

My body had long since exhausted all its energy, but it went on running just the same. The physical overdraft came only from greater will power. This was the crucial moment when my legs were strong enough to carry me over the last few yards as they could never have done in previous years. With five yards to go the tape seemed almost to recede.

My effort was all over and I collapsed almost unconscious. . . . The stop-watches held the answer, the announcement came — "Result of the one mile . . . time, 3 minutes"—the rest was lost in the roar of excitement.

—Roger Bannister, *First Four Minutes*

of these athletes held the world record for the 1,500 meters, seemingly swapping it between them during the period 1979 to 1985. Coe's 800-meter record of 1 minute 41.73 seconds, set in Florence (Italy) in 1981, is (at the time of this writing) one of the longest standing world track records.

During the late 1980s and early 1990s, middle- and long-distance running has been dominated by a substantial number of African runners. The Kenyans and Ethiopians have been most prominent, but there are a growing number of world-class athletes from Morocco and Algeria. The fact that Kenya and Ethiopia have been able to produce such a long line of world-class distance runners has shattered the myth that black athletes were "natural sprinters" and could not achieve world-class performances over long distances.

Such a view reflected a simple form of racism. Although some black athletes had competed in the long distances in early Olympic Games, it was only in the 1960s that runners from Africa came to prominence. It was in the 1968 Mexico Olympics that Kenyans became synonymous with long-distance running. The greatest Kenyan runner has probably been Kipchoge Keino, but in a long line of stars it is difficult to select any single athlete who has dominated the middle and long distances the way Nurmi did. This is not surprising, given the increasingly global level of participation in track.

The United States has not produced middle- and long-distance runners of the stature of those described previously, although some observers might want to mention half-miler Malvin Whitfield, who won Olympic gold medals in both the 1948 and 1952 Olympics. On the other hand, the United States has traditionally dominated the sprint events. Jesse Owens in the 1930s and Carl Lewis in the 1980s caught the imagination of the world's media. Jesse Owens is widely regarded as the world's greatest sprinter ever. Owens is most renowned for winning gold medals for the 100 meters, 200 meters, 4 x 100 meters, and a long jump event at Olympic Games in Berlin in 1936, all with Olympic records, at a time when Adolf Hitler was preaching Aryan supremacy. Owens claims the greatest afternoon's athletic performance in athletics history. In Ann Arbor, Michigan, in May 1935, he broke the world's records for the 100 and 220 yard sprints and 220 yard hurdles (on a straight track), both of which were also recognized as world records for the slightly shorter 200 meters. He therefore broke five world running records during one afternoon—and also broke the world's long jump record at the same meet!

The Americans have never really lost their supremacy in sprinting. Carl Lewis came close to matching Owens's repertoire of skills in the more competitive years of the 1980s. Coached by Tom Tellez, Lewis won six gold medals and one silver in the Olympic Games of 1984 and 1988. In Los Angeles in 1988 he won the same events Owens had done in Berlin in 1936.

The Europeans have traditionally dominated women's sprint running, although in recent years the balance of power has shifted somewhat to the United States and Caribbean. In the postwar years, the power of the eastern Europeans was displayed in many events; in the early 1990s, the Chinese astounded the world with a number of staggering performances, including the astonishing performance of Wang Junxia, who became the first woman to break the half-hour for 10,000 meters with a time of 29 minutes 31.78 seconds. The first man to break this barrier had been Taisto Mäki of Finland in 1939. And it is difficult to ignore the phenomenal performance of the American sprinter Florence Griffith-Joyner, whose world record for the 100 meters of 10.49 must be regarded as beyond reach for many years to come. The nations and continents listed here show the global nature of track running, something not quite so evident in the jumping and throwing events.

The reasons particular countries dominate particular events are largely cultural or social. Environmental factors are not to be totally neglected, but the notion that particular ethnic groups are naturally predisposed to certain running events is today generally rejected. For example, it was once felt that the Finns were such good runners because of their access to the clear air of the coniferous forests and the continental climate of their Nordic homeland. More recently the success of Kenyan long-distance runners has been attributed to the fact that Kenyan athletes live at high altitude, hence improving their capacity to succeed at aerobic running events. Yet when neighboring high-altitude countries are compared with Kenya it is found that their per capita "production" of superior athletes is much lower than that of Kenya. Environment alone does not produce world-class runners; hard training does. (Bale and Sang, 1996)

The rate of improvement in the performance of women runners is faster than that of men. This is largely the result of the smaller numbers of women who traditionally participated in sport. Because only a small proportion of the total female population competed in track racing, there was, as a result, a small number of role models for other potential women athletes. Social conventions also traditionally inhibited women from taking part in athletics. Such conventions still apply in some parts of the world where dressing in scanty athletic clothing is considered inappropriate. The larger the number of women who compete, the greater the stimulus for better competition—and hence improved performance. That women might match men's performances was traditionally thought impossible, but the curves showing improved performances of men and women are inexorably converging.

—John Bale

**Bibliography:** Baker, William J. (1986) *Jesse Owens: An American Life.* New York: Free Press.

Bale, John, and Joe Sang. (1996) *Kenyan Running: Movement Culture, Geography and Global Change.* London: Frank Cass.

Bannister, Roger. (1955) *The First Four Minutes.* London: Putnam.

Dyer, K. F., and T. Dwyer. (1984) *Running out of Time: An Examination of the Improvements in Running Records.* Kensington: New South Wales University Press.

Eichberg, Henning. (1990) "Forward Race and the Laughter of Pygmies." In *Fin De Siècle and Its Legacies,* edited by Roy Porter and Mikluás Teich. Cambridge: Cambridge University Press, 115–131.

———. (1990) "Stronger, Funnier, Deadlier: Track and Field on the Way from the Ritual to the Record." In *Ritual and Record,* edited by John M. Carter and Arnd Krüger. Westport, CT: Greenwood Press, 123–124.

Hannus, Matti. (1990) *Flying Finns.* Helsinki: Tietosanoma.

Hoberman, John (1992) *Mortal Engines.* New York: Free Press.

Nabokov, Paul. (1981) *Indian Running.* Santa Fe, NM: Ancient City Press.

Nelson, Cordner, and Roberto Quercetani. (1985) *The Milers.* Los Altos, CA: Tafnews Press.

Prokop, Dave, ed. (1975) *The African Running Revolution.* Mountain View, CA: World Publications.

Quercetani, R. L. (1964) *A World History of Track and Field Athletics.* London: Oxford University Press.

Quercetani, Roberto L. (1990) *Athletics: A History of Modern Track and Field Athletics.* Milan: Vallardi and Associates.

Quercetani, Roberto L., and Nejet Kok. (1993) *Wizards of the Middle Distances.* Milan: Vallardi and Associates.

Wilt, Fred. (1973) *How They Train.* Los Altos, CA: Tafnews Press.

Zur Megede, E., and R. Hymans. (1995) *Progression of World Best Performances and Official IAAF World Records.* Monaco: IAAF.

# Traditional Sports, Africa

African names dot the landscape of modern sport. Senegal's Louis Phal, Nigeria's Dick Tiger, and Ghana's David Kotey head a substantial list of African boxers who have won world championships. Without Tunisian Alain Mimoun, Ethiopian Abebe Bikila, Kenyan Kipchoge Keino, and Tanzanian Filbert Bayi, recent Olympic track history would be much poorer. For several years Nigeria's Akeem Abdul Olajuwon and Sudan's Manute Bol have performed successfully (in Olajuwon's case, brilliantly) in a U.S. professional National Basketball Association that is dominated by African American athletes.

This modern prowess is built on a broad foundation of premodern, or "traditional," African experience. In the Nile River valley and on the grassy veldt of South Africa no less than in the tropical rain forests of the Congo River basin and at the edges of the massive Sahara Desert to the north, Africans played, devised local rules for various games, and competed athletically for centuries before Europeans intruded. To be sure, much traditional "sport" in Africa, as elsewhere, derived from superstitious impulses to win the favor of ancestors and the unseen deities. Like the ancient Greeks, Romans, and Britons, Africans played the fertility game. Competitive, highly ritualized games supposedly ensured productive crops and hunts as well as a fruitful marriage bed.

## Sticks and Stones

Unfortunately, little first-hand evidence survives of traditional sub-Saharan activities. Indigenous writings are virtually nonexistent; wooden artifacts have long since turned to dust; stone sculptures and monuments are few. We learn most about traditional patterns of African ludic (play) behavior from the diaries, letters, and treatises of explorers and missionaries, many of whom were unsympathetic, and from early-twentieth-century anthropologists who attempted always to fit the Africans into whatever theory of human development happened to be dominant at the time.

Egypt, however, is an exception to most generalizations about Africa, and it is certainly unique in its documentation of ancient sport. Miniature sculptures, papyrus fragments, and inscriptions and paintings on the walls of temples and tombs depict a lively sporting culture in ancient Egypt. Even pieces of equipment have survived, ranging from chariots and fish hooks to balls and board

*Various forms of wrestling were practiced all over Africa and frequently incorporated religious and social elements. This match was photographed in East Africa circa 1910.*

games. All bear witness to pharaohs and aristocrats eager to prove their superiority as huntsmen, chariot drivers, archery experts, and runners. In a pattern common to sport everywhere, these activities originated in the requirements for hunting and war. Hunters and warriors became sportsmen when the hunt ceased being a matter of mere survival and when warrior skills momentarily lost their original purpose.

For most of traditional Africa, no clear line separated hunters and warriors from the sporting impulse. Africans hunted and fought with sticks, if not spears, in hand, and in similar fashion they competed athletically. The Zulu and Mpondo of southern Africa frequently promoted stick fights within tribes and occasionally between neighboring tribes. They carried a stick in one hand (holding it in the middle) for parrying the opponent's blow, and a stick in the other hand for clouting the opponent's head. Outsiders viewing a Mpondo stick fight between two neighboring districts would find it difficult to distinguish between a deadly battle and a game. These serious stick fights were not, moreover, confined solely to sub-Saharan Africa; Egyptian sources suggest that this type of competitive activity was common in the land of the Nile as well as the Congo.

Rather than whacking each other over the head with sticks, some Africans threw sticks for distance and accuracy. Akin to the Greek javelin, this form of competition obviously originated with the spear. Among the Baganda of the present state of Uganda, the standard stick measured only about 46 centimeters (18 inches) in length. Sometimes the Baganda threw for distance, other times to hit a foe's stick. Rolling target games provided variations on the accuracy theme. In a way similar to the hoop-and-spear games enjoyed by western Native Americans, Africans everywhere rolled ball-shaped stones or roots down hills, and sometimes along level ground, while tribesmen competed with one another to hit them with spears, arrows, or stones.

Competitive stone-tossing took another form among the Kamba of Kenya and the Zulu of South Africa. They piled stones in front of several competitors and required each one to toss a stone in the air, pick up another with the same hand, and catch the airborne stone before it hit the ground. The caught stone could then be put aside and the process repeated until all the stones were tossed and caught and a winner declared. This simple game rewarded and enhanced agile hands and mental concentration.

Ball games produce similar results, but little evidence of competitive ball play can be found in traditional Africa. Among the San people of South Africa, women formed lines and excitedly passed a round object (about the size of an orange, cut from a root) back and forth, more on the order of a cooperative children's exercise than a competitive game. San men devised a competitive game using a ball made from the thickest portion of a hippopotamus's hide, the neck. They cut out a chunk and hammered into it into a round, elastic object that would bounce when thrown upon a hard surface. Then they placed a flat stone in the ground, and threw the ball hard onto the stone. When it bounced high in the sky, they pushed and shoved for an advantageous position to catch it before it hit the ground. This game is noteworthy because ball games were so rare.

Some age-old African tribes, like the Boloki of the Upper Congo River and the Bachiga of western Uganda, rowed competitively on nearby waterways; Kenya's Luo people traditionally tested their new boats by means of a race on Lake Victoria. In the mountains of East Africa, where Olympic runners have trained so effectively in recent years, the Masai of Kenya competed and excelled in the most elemental race of all, the footrace.

Another Olympic event, the high jump, seems also to have had antecedents in traditional Africa. The tall, aristocratic Watussi (Tutsi) of Rwanda and Burundi catapulted off a hardened anthill and soared at remarkable heights over a stick or rope suspended between two upright poles. More on the order of an exhibition than a contest, this achievement reportedly served as a rite of passage. Watussi male youths were regarded as men when they could clear their own height.

## Wrestling Traditions

Without doubt, wrestling was the most omnipresent of all sport in traditional Africa. Ancient Egypt again leads the way in preserving visual representations. Acrobatic gymnasts, swimmers, ball players, and stick fighters adorn the tombs along the Nile, but the dominant subject, by far, is wrestling. If one were to judge solely from the famous wall paintings in royal tombs at Beni Hasan dating from 2000 to 1500 B.C.E., one would conclude that wrestling was the national pastime in ancient Egypt. Wrestling prepared soldiers for combat and provided a ceremonial exhibition at festive events. Egyptian wrestlers evidently grappled in a no-holds-barred style, trying to trip or throw each other to the ground.

Several Egyptian etchings and paintings feature Nuba wrestlers from the Sudan (to the south) competing with Egyptians. The Nuba drew from a rich wrestling tradition. In the hilly central section of the Sudan, the larger Nuba villages held wrestling matches periodically through the harvest season from November to March. Heralds went out from a host village to its neighbors, announcing by horn and drum the forthcoming event and issuing challenges to would-be competitors. Entire villages, adorned in colorful head-dress and beads, and fortified with beer newly brewed for the occasion, descended on the central marketplace of the sponsoring village. Ceremonial dances and chants preceded the wrestling matches, which began in the early afternoon. The competitors, covered with white ashes (symbolic of sacred power), finally engaged in a catch-as-catch-can tussle, each one attempting to throw the other on his back. Victory brought a rousing cheer from village partisans, and when the matches ended shortly before nightfall, a festive party of dance, food, and strong drink followed.

In Nigeria, too, wrestling was a prominent feature of village life. With colorful rituals strikingly similar to the Nuba, the Ibo of southern Nigeria promoted wrestling contests every eighth day for three months or so during the rainy yam-growing season, then finished with a day of matches in honor of the corn deity. Ibo wrestlers were not allowed to become fatigued or angry with each other, for either condition would displease the gods and cause the crops to go bad. Good dance, drink, and physical competition supposedly made for good yams and good corn. "We think that this ceremony will help the crops to grow strong," an Ibo chieftain told an English anthropologist in 1914, "overcoming evil influences and bearing much increase" (Talbot 1967, 111).

The benefits of wrestling were by no means confined to matters of fertility. For young Ibo males, wrestling meant initiation into adulthood. Villages found the communal making of beer and food conducive to better community spirit, not to mention the cohesive effect of cheering for village representatives in the ring. Nevertheless, fertility issues were never far from the center of traditional African life. Until early in the twentieth century, most villages and small towns in southern Nigeria had elaborate shrines in honor of the local deity, who was depicted as a white life-size figure holding a sword or spear in one hand and an ax in the other. Paintings of snakes, the most ancient of fertility symbols, filled the walls and floors, and a shaman anointed a woman's womb with a feather dipped in oil. Amid all these obvious trappings of a fertility cult, two wrestlers locked their arms around each other.

The Bachama of northeast Nigeria not only embraced ceremonial wrestling, but also welcomed neighboring Jen, Bwaza, Mbula, and Bata peoples to send teams to compete with Bachama's best. Among the Bachama an imaginative myth explains the origins of wrestling. According to one version, a one-legged man came from the east leading a ram on a tether, bringing the idea of a harvest festival. He wandered from village to village, challenging all comers. He proceeded without defeat until he came to the villagers telling the yarn. One of their forefathers beat him, and from that day forward they held festivals of celebration and wrestling matches. Another version has the one-legged man losing and dying immediately, but that night his spirit appeared to the man who defeated him. The spirit denied being dead. He vowed not only to protect the village but also to return visibly to life at the next wrestling festival. Thus, for the Bachama, wrestling represented resurrection and life.

The intensity of wrestling's association with fertility cults varied from place to place in Africa, and so did wrestling styles. Unlike the intense but controlled Ibo, the Khoikhoi of southwest Africa engaged in bloody, no-holds-barred fights. Bambara wrestlers, in Mali, wore razor-sharp bracelets to intimidate and debilitate their opponents. Competitors in southeast Africa reportedly wrestled with only one arm, and from a kneeling position at that. Boys in the same region grappled from a sitting position.

Although wrestling was customarily reserved for boys and young men, women occasionally wrestled. Nuba and Ibo women did so once a year, soon after the harvest. Wrestling prowess won the females respect and attention from male youths. Anthropologists have also found evidence of young women wrestling in Senegal and Cameroon. In Benin and Gabon, girls sometimes wrestled males to whom they were betrothed. Those contests frequently turned into lightly disguised forms of sexual intimacy. When a Fon (Benin) boy defeated his fiancée, he traditionally consoled her by publicly caressing her breasts. In Gambia, the dominant female wrestler often married the male champion, thus insuring a union of the fittest genes.

## Waning and Waxing

Within the past century or so, several factors have coalesced to cause the waning of traditional African sport, especially wrestling. First, a revived, more aggressive Islam swept across Africa in the nineteenth century in opposition to the "pagan" rituals, gambling, and consumption of alcohol that usually accompanied festive sport of old. Isolated Nuba and Ethiopian scenes were the exceptions that proved the rule of scarcely any traces of wrestling traditions in north and northeast Africa, where the followers of Allah made and enforced the rules. Where Islam thrived, traditional sport declined.

British missionary schools, too, had a negative effect on native patterns of play and athletic competition. Anglican schoolmasters taught discipline and teamwork through games like soccer (association football) and cricket, two old English folk games whose codification allowed the Victorians to export them globally as carriers of Victorian values. In 1928 a Ghanaian lamented that the growth of British schools meant the dissemination of cricket and football at the expense of traditional sport. The "national character," he warned, stood "the risk of being modified, and in time altogether lost, if we give up our national games, pastimes, and customary practices" (Danquah 1928, 229).

The emergence of a capitalist mentality also worked to the detriment of native games. Particularly in the cities, new labor demands cut into old concepts of abundant free time. Wed to the seasons and time-consuming rituals, traditional sport could scarcely make the transition to urban settings. City life gauged itself according to the clock, the great symbol of modernity, and so did modern sport. Soccer, boxing, and track especially lent themselves to the urban need for orderly recreation and spectatorship.

Traditional sport is not dead, however. Albeit stripped of many of its ritualistic and mythological trappings, wrestling still thrives in Nigeria. School schedules rather than agricultural cycles now determine the time of competitive meets. A Bachama man, Julius Donald Ngbarato, won Nigeria's national wrestling championship in 1990. Ngbarato first learned his tactics in agricultural festivals along the banks of the Benue River.

Pockets of tradition remain untouched by modern ways and games. In 1962 the famous German filmmaker Leni Riefenstahl went to the remote southern valleys of the Sudan hoping to photograph the Nuba at work and play in patterns of old. A police chief on the fringe of the region informed her that she was too late. The Nuba had long since given up their traditional tribal ways, including wrestling, he insisted. Unconvinced, Riefenstahl spent two arduous days making her way into the inhospitable Nuba country. Cresting a hill late one afternoon, she looked down upon clusters of noisy village folk watching wrestlers perform their age-old rituals. To an incessant beating of drums, shrill whistles, and shouts from the spectators, the victors were carried out of the ring on the shoulders of friends. It was a ritual as old as the Nuba hills.

Traditional sport appeals to African nationalists. An old Ibo wrestler, Okonkwo, is the central character in Nigerian novelist Chinua Achebe's famous tale, *Things Fall Apart* (1959). Appearing in print just one year before Nigerian independence, *Things Fall Apart* depicts the texture of traditional life and its brutal downfall. Having beaten the previous wrestling champion, Okonkwo proudly lives off his reputation as "the greatest wrestler and warrior alive" (Achebe 1959, 122) until he lashes out at the newly arrived guardians of English law and order. The novel begins with village drums beating and flutes playing in celebration of Okonkwo's athletic prowess; it ends some 30 years later with his body hanging from a tree, a victim of modern, alien ways.

—William J. Baker

**Bibliography:** Achebe, Chinua. (1959) *Things Fall Apart.* New York: Obolensky.

Blacking, John. (1987) "Games and Sports in Pre-Colonial African Societies." In *Sport in Africa: Essays in Social History,* edited by William J. Baker and James A. Mangan. New York: Africana.

Bryant, A. T. (1949) *The Zulu People: As They Were before the White Man Came.* Pietermaritzburg, South Africa: Shuter and Shooter.

Danquah, Joseph Boayke. (1928) *Gold Coast: Akan Laws and Customs.* London: Routledge.

Decker, Wolfgang. (1992) *Sports and Games of Ancient Egypt,* trans. Allen Guttmann. New Haven, CT: Yale University Press.

Edel, May Mandelbaum. (1937) "The Bachiga of East Africa," In *Cooperation and Competition among Primitive Peoples,* edited by Margaret Mead. New York: McGraw-Hill.

Godia, George. (1989) "Sport in Kenya." In *Sport in Asia and Africa: A Comparative Handbook,* edited by Eric C. Wagner. Westport, CT: Greenwood.

Goldman, Irving. (1937) "The Bathonga of South Africa." In *Cooperation and Competition among Primitive Peoples,* edited by Margaret Mead. New York: McGraw-Hill.

Lema, Bangela. (1989) "Sport in Zaire." In *Sport in Asia and Africa,* edited by Eric C. Wagner. Westport, CT: Greenwood.

Meek, C. K. (1950) *Tribal Studies in Northern Nigeria.* New York: Humanities Press.

Paul, Sigrid. (1987) "The Wrestling Traditions and its Social Functions." In *Sport in Africa: Essays in Social History,* edited by William J. Baker and James A. Mangan. New York: Africana.

Raum, Otto F. (1953) "The Rolling Target (Hoop-and-Pole) Game in Africa: Egyptian Accession Rite or Multiple Ritual Symbolism." *African Studies* 12: 104–121, 163–180.

Riefenstahl, Leni. (1973) *The Last of the Nuba.* New York: Harper and Row.

Roscoe, John. (1966) *The Baganda: An Account of Their Native Customs and Beliefs.* New York: Barnes and Noble.

Seligman, C. G., and Brenda Z. Seligman. (1932) *Pagan Tribes of the Nilotic Sudan.* London: Routledge and Kegan Paul.

Sfeir, Leila. (1989) "Sport in Egypt: Cultural Reflection and Contradiction of a Society." In *Sport in Asia and Africa,* edited by Eric C. Wagner. Westport, CT: Greenwood.

Stevens, Jr., Phillips. (1993) "Traditional Sport in Africa: Wrestling among the Bachama of Nigeria." Paper presented at the International Conference on the Preservation and Advancement of Traditional Sport, Waseda University, Shinjoku, Japan, 11–12 March l993.

Talbot, P. Amaury. (1967) *Some Nigerian Fertility Cults.* New York: Barnes and Noble.

# Traditional Sports, Asia

The traditional Asian sports considered here comprise a diverse group. Some of the activities described are—or were—linked to local royal cults, some are explicitly connected with forms of religious worship, and some seem clearly to be linked to traditional modes of subsistence. Some seem less purely competitive than sports tend to be in a contemporary Western sense. Complicating this already complex situation is the fact that social scientists and other scholars seldom agree as to what constitutes a "traditional" phenomenon.

While bearing these problems in mind, however, it is still possible to examine a number of Asian sports that are largely regional, or even local, and that are ancient either in form or in inspiration.

## Martial Arts

Many of the Asian martial arts are discussed in considerable detail in other entries, but there are others, less well known, that should be mentioned. It seems safe to say that every region of Asia has produced some form of martial arts. Even India, which is not commonly thought to be a center for martial arts, boasts an ancient tradition of wrestling (connected to the cult of the god Hangman) and, particularly in Orissa, dance forms that are related to medieval royal and military structures. However, most Asian forms of martial arts are to be found in China, Central Asia, and Southeast Asia.

Mongol-Buh, for instance, is a Mongolian form of wrestling that attracts up to 30,000 participants at some events, in a country with barely more than two million inhabitants. Mongol-Buh resembles, to some extent, Japanese sumo, but competitors do not wrestle within a bounded ring, and the palms of the hands, unlike in sumo, may touch the ground.

Mongol-Buh, aside from its formal sporting characteristics, appeals to Mongolian patriarchal tradition, being considered one of the three "manly" sports—the other two are archery and horseback riding. The three sports are engaged in extensively by people living in the Mongolian semi-autonomous region of Inner Mongolia. Here, in July and August, the three sports are demonstrated during the course of Nadams: tribal meetings, of ancient origin, that were traditionally designed to promote negotiations over the disposition of pasture lands.

Nu-shooting, a form of archery, is popular in the southwestern provinces of China—Szechuan, Yunnan, and Kweichow. Modern competition in the sport is organized by the Chinese authorities at officially sanctioned "minority peoples" events. Both bow and arrow are wooden, and the arrowhead is bamboo: at least as currently practiced, "modernization" would violate the spirit of Nu-shooting. Skills are practiced and measured in a number of standing and kneeling positions, as well as on horseback. As with the Mongolian Nadam, skills seem likely to have been related to the needs of a nomadic and pastoral people.

Krabi-Krabong is a Thai martial art, less well known than Thai boxing, that involves the skillful wielding of swords, spears, and axes. Competitors may use a combination of weapons, and it takes much practice to master the variety of requisite techniques. Here is a "sport" which, as now presented, may more accurately be characterized as a ritual performance: a traditional music (*De-Ligua*) is played at "matches," and the action builds up to a climax according to a pre-arranged composition.

Silat, an Indonesian activity, is also highly ritualized, often being performed at explicitly religious events. Accompanied by gong music, Silat performers, either empty-handed or swinging a long ax-like weapon, dance out a choreographed sequence of movements. A related form, Penac

*A weekly fish fight held in a dilapidated tin shack on the outskirts of Bangkok. This popular Thai sport involves tiny fighting fish bred in the small ponds that dot central Thailand.*

Silat, is performed in neighboring Malaya, though performers generally use two swords and not an ax.

## Animal Sports

Animal racing—with horse, camel, buffalo, yak, and dog—is well known in Asia, particularly among the formerly nomadic inner-Asian peoples. Polo, of course, is often claimed to be Asian in origin, and forms of it are still played in Afghanistan and Northeastern Pakistan. Many traditional Central Asian animal races involve either shooting from horseback (with bow or gun) or directly competing for possession of an animal. These obviously derive from formerly subsistence-oriented activities of nomadic, pastoral peoples.

Nonracing animal sports—pitting animals against humans as in bullfighting, or one animal against another as in cockfighting, have been popular in many parts of Asia as well as in the West. Because some such activities are manifestly cruel to animals, and because most are associated with betting, animal sports receive little support from the sports authorities. Nevertheless, such pastimes continue to thrive throughout Asia.

Thailand, in particular, offers a great variety of animal sports featuring not just cocks or bulls but also crickets, beetles, and fish.

The most famous of the fish-fighting games involves the species *Betta splendens,* which, following the guppy and the goldfish, has become the world's most popular aquarium fish. The luxurious fins of the male betta, which make it attractive to aquarists, also make it provocative to other males, which constitutes the basis for the contest. Two males are placed in the same small bowl, bets are placed, and the fish rush and bite at one another until one is exhausted—or dead. The winner, usually injured during the fight, is carefully nursed back to health to fight another day, and proven champions are sold, for large sums, for breeding.

A less physical form of animal competition is the "dove-cooing contest" in which specially bred doves are judged on the quality, pitch, and duration of their calls. This sport, which has become most popular in Thailand—one fancier is said to have recently paid more than $40,000 for a prize cooer—is also popular in Malaysia, Singapore, Indonesia, India, and elsewhere. Doves were greatly prized by the Indian Mughal kings prior to the sixteenth century, and it seems that doves have long been admired, for their physical form, their calling, and their flight.

## Aerial Activities

Asia is home to a number of pastimes that might be called "aerial sports." In India, devotees of local goddesses, particularly in the south, used to engage in "hook-swinging": acts of worship that required the faithful to insert sharp hooks into their back and shoulder muscles and then swing from specially erected armatures. This, of course, can hardly be described as sport. A Korean activity is less obviously ritualistic, involving at least an element of pure recreation: during festivities celebrating the arrival of spring, women, in a standing position, compete to see how high they can swing. They manage, in some cases, to fly almost 20 meters (22 yards) off the ground.

However, of all the various Asian "aerial" activities, it is no doubt Thai kite-fighting, forms of which are also seen in Korea and China, that is the best known and most popular. The Thai form involves the use of two types of kite, one a five-pointed star, the male *chula*, the other a diamond-shaped female *pakpao*. Male kites can be as long as 2.3 meters (7½ feet) and, when aloft, require the attentions of a team of from eight to ten young boys, commanded by a captain, who sits in a sort of "fighting-chair" equipped with a pulley and levers. The male kite, which is fitted with bamboo claws and other weapons, is deliberately flown into a female kite's territory, in an attempt to capture "her." The female kite, on the other hand, is not allowed to cross into "male" territory, but, in true "double-standard" fashion, relies on smaller size and maneuverability, to flit and dodge out of range, so that the male kite eventually loses control and falls to the ground.

Though "male" and "female" kites are the most popular, not all Thai kite-flying involves a "courtship" battle. A northern Thai kite, called the *sanu*, is as tall as 1.8 meters (6 feet) and emits a singing vibration when in the air; it is judged according to both the height it attains and the quality of the melody it produces. Other Thai kites are shaped like famous figures in Thai puppetry, and are flown in events that take on the quality of scripted theater.

## Water Sports

Throughout China and Southeast Asia, boat races are popular, and have been for hundreds of years. In most cases, the boat is carved to resemble a ceremonial dragon, and the races originally formed essential parts of royal and religious rituals designed to display the naval power of kings. Today, in some regions, such races are still given religious significance, but elsewhere they are run on a purely competitive basis.

The first recorded Thai boat race took place in the seventeenth century, when King Ekatosaros decreed that every year there should be a race between the king's and the queen's royal barges. This event was, for awhile, reckoned a sort of fertility prediction, with the triumph of the queen's barge hailed as a guarantee of fertility and abundance.

In southern China, boat races are intimately connected to rituals which focus on the importance of the rains which are essential to good rice yields. Chinese "dragon-boat" races are thought to be very old, perhaps from the fifth century B.C.E. They are still popular today, primarily in southwestern parts of China.

## Outlook

Most of the sports discussed above are not highly organized, at least beyond the local level, and most are also noncommercial. Some—Nu-shooting, for instance—survive as an approved showcase activity for an ethnic minority, while others, like fish-fighting, hardly seem to be sports in any contemporary sense. Nevertheless, it should be borne in mind that takraw, for instance, while once a simple village pastime played according to many local sets of rules throughout Southeast Asia, has become a professional and internationally followed team sport. That is to say, not only are "traditional" sports interesting in their own right, they also constitute a reservoir of activities out of which the next pan-regional or even "global" pursuit may develop.

—Alan Trevithick

**See also** Animal Baiting; Buzkashi; Cockfighting; Cudgels; Kite Flying; Martial Arts; Takraw.

**Bibliography:** Japan Folklore Association. (1992) *The Energy of Asia, Reports on the Exchange of Asian Traditional Sports Demonstrations* (Japan Folklore Association cultural exchange program and conference sponsored by the Ministry of Foreign Affairs and the Japan Foundation).

Knuttgen, Howard G., Qiwei Ma, and Zhonguan Wu, eds. (1990) *Sport in China.* Champaign, IL: Human Kinetics.

Thailand Government. (1968) *Thai Games and Festivals.* Bangkok: Public Relations Department of Thailand.

Wagner, Eric A. (1989) *Sport in Asia and Africa: A Comparative Handbook.* New York: Greenwood Press.

# Traditional Sports, Europe

Traditional sports in the European context can be defined as those that had their roots in physical activities that existed before the spread of modern, internationally organized sport. A wide range of activities, only some of which still survive, were widely enjoyed in the towns and villages of Europe in the Middle Ages and the early modern period. Despite a vast amount of local variation, many of the most popular activities share broad similarities. Our knowledge of traditional games, however, is far less complete than our knowledge of modern sports. Many games were passed on through an oral tradition that declined sharply in the nineteenth century. What we do know of traditional games tends to come from visual material, such as Pieter Brueghel's paintings of children's games of the 1560s, or from literary sources, such as the inventory provided by Rabelais in 1534 in *The Life of Gargantua and His Son Pantagruel.* Charles Cotton's *The Compleat Gamester* (1674) offers the first detailed account of the varied activities that were to be found in England after the Restoration of the monarchy in 1660 and the return of the full range of traditional sports, some of which had been banned during Cromwell's Commonwealth (1649–1660). During the later seventeenth and throughout the eighteenth centuries a number of handbooks of play appeared, culminating in detailed descriptions of popular games and pastimes in Diderot's famous *Encyclopaedia* (1751–1780) and Joseph Strutt's *The Sports and Pastimes of the People of England* (1801). In addition, there were reformers like Guts Muths, whose *Games for the Young* (1796) tried to reform existing activities for new educational purposes.

As the forces of modernization broke up old communities and established a new urban industrial way of life in much of Europe, the loss of the old ways of playing was noticed by ethnographers from the later nineteenth century onward. These scholars began to record the survival of traditional games as part of a vanishing folk culture in much the same way as their colleagues collected songs and sayings. The search for "völkisch" cultural roots—a feature of the new racial nationalism of the late nineteenth and early twentieth centuries, as well as of interwar fascism—accentuated the fascination for what was seen as "gesunkenes Kulturgut" (submerged cultural tradition). Children's games survived better than many others, with the result that traditional games as a whole ran the risk of seeming puerile and trivial in comparison to the new sports that were enjoying enormous success throughout Europe after the World War I. Interest in traditional games has revived in recent years and has received official encouragement from the Council of Europe. There is an obvious danger that traditional games will lose touch with their living roots among real communities and become folkloric appendages, produced to give color to festivals that themselves are invented traditions.

Rather than attempt to trace traditional games over time or to look at them country by country, a typology based on the nature of the activity itself seems the most appropriate. But within these broad categories—"throwing," "bowling," "shooting," and so on—the range of technical and cultural variation can only be hinted at, for the attention here is directed more to what has survived than to the full range of activities that may once have existed.

## Ball Games

There is a rich variety of traditional ball games. They can either be played by hand or foot or with

*This undated miniature painting depicts an outdoor bowl game, one of the few traditional European sports that survives in some form today.*

a batting device. Traditional European team-handball games include *parkspel* on the Swedish island of Gottland, *kaatsen* in the Dutch province of Frisia, *balle pelote* in Belgium and France, *pallone elastico* in Italy, and *pelota* in Spanish Valencia or in the Basque country. Most of the ancient and violent football forms have disappeared and have been replaced by modern soccer, except for the traditional *calcio fiorentino* in Florence (Italy).

Some ball games, such as Gaelic football in Ireland, are played with both hands and feet. Gaelic football and hurling were reintroduced in the 1880s in Ireland by cultural nationalists alarmed at the spread of new British sport, and the reintroduction proved extremely successful. All kinds of batting devices are used, from racquets, as in real tennis and in France's *longue paume* game, to the sticks that are used to play *crosse*, a variant of golf played in northern France and Bel-

gium, or in the rather rough team games of shinty in Scotland and hurling in Ireland.

Other ball games make use of a tambourine (France and Italy), a forearm cover or *"bracchiale,"* as in the Italian *pallone,* or a *"chistera,"* as in the spectacular *jai alai* of the Basques.

## Bowl and Pin Games

Bowl games are played with a solid spherical object that is either rolled or thrown at a target. In pin games, targets are knocked down. Italian *bocce* and the French *jeu de boules* are now played far from their original home countries. A special case is the game of *closh*, which at the time of Erasmus (1469–1536) and Brueghel the Elder (1525–1569) was popular all over Europe. In this game a shovel-shaped bat is used to roll a heavy round bowl through an iron ring fixed in the ground. Nowadays the game is still frequently played in the Belgian and Dutch Provinces of Limburg, where it is known as *beugelen,* and in the adjacent region in Germany. Moreover, the same type of game has a variant in Portugal *(jogo do aro)* and on the Lipari Islands near Sicily *(palla-porta).* Apart from the well-known flat green bowls, which spread from England to the former British colonies, a variety of bowling games are found in Britain and in the central and southern European countries.

The modern game of ten pin bowling as played in the United States has several historical variants, some of which are highly standardized and mechanized, such as *kegeln* in Germany and bordering countries. Other pin games range from Karelian pins, in which a stick is thrown instead of a bowl, to *pendelkegeln* (Germany and Hungary), in which the bowl swung at the pins hangs on a wire.

## Throwing Games

Throwing a stick or a stone as far as possible or to hit a target is a basic human movement pattern. It appears in the modern athletic events of javelin, discus, and hammer throwing, and in shot putting. In Sweden's traditional *varpa* game the projectiles are heavy discs. Smaller discs or coins, or sometimes stones, are used in both children's and adults' throwing games. *Barra,* a particular type of javelin throwing, is practiced in northern

Spain. This iron bar weighs 3.5 kilograms (7 pounds, 11 ounces) and measures 1.5 meters (1.6 yards); it is launched after several body rotations.

Hammer throwing and tossing the caber are typical events of the well-known Scottish Highland Games. A log-throwing event virtually identical to caber-tossing is found in Portugal, where it is known as *jogo do panco,* and in Sweden, where it goes by the name of *stang-störtning.* The latter game was demonstrated at the occasion of the 1912 Olympic Games in Stockholm, together with *pärkspel, varpa,* and *glima.* Stone-putting is practiced in the traditional festivals of Swiss farmers in the Alps.

The game known as road bowls in Ireland, *klootschieten* in the Netherlands and *bosseln* or *klootschiessen* in East Frisia (Germany), is an interesting example both of the expression of regional ethnic identity and of the growing international awareness of traditional games. In 1969 these three independent groups of bowling enthusiasts joined together to form the International Bowl Playing Association.

*Toad in the hole* is the name of an English pub game, which has several continental variants such as *jeu de grenouille* in France, which in turn is called *la rana* in Spain, *jogo do sapo* in Portugal, and *pudebak* in Flanders. The toad is a thick, heavy, brass disc. The hole is enshrined within a specially made wooden box on four legs.

## Shooting Games

Shooting games have flourished in all cultures and have evolved into modern high-tech sports. Popinjay shooting, in which the target is a "jay" or set of "jays" attached to a tall mast, is depicted in many medieval and Renaissance paintings and prints and is still a very popular traditional sport in Flanders (Belgium). It was even featured in the 1900 Paris Olympic Games and the 1920 Antwerp Olympic Games.

Some present-day crossbow guilds in Flanders originated in the fourteenth and fifteenth centuries and can thus be considered as the first sports clubs in Europe. The impressive crossbow-shooting festivals of the Italian *balestrieri* (crossbow), such as are held in the magnificent city of Gubbio in the Umbrian hills and elsewhere, also have a long historical pedigree. Witnessing the pageantry of such competitions of crossbowmen

## The Play Forms of Our Forefathers and the Sport of Our Children

The Olympic Games, which stem from a modern invention, occupy the place of honor in our popular recreations. They are controlled by an official international regulation.

Although we fully approve of this, we want to point at the disdain which is shown—unjustifiedly—towards the games of strength and agility, which have contributed so much to the physical development of our forefathers and which were for them such a pleasant delight.

Here we have to safeguard a respectable tradition, as these games are deeply rooted in the inner life of our peasantry and cannot be extracted from it without grieve.

Our soccer players should not forget the game of handball or the longbow or any other games, too many to enumerate, because they all require the exercise of the eye and the hand and because they all develop dexterity, precision, nervous strengthening and body flexibility.

We call upon all our readers to inform us as completely as possible on the local forms of play and amusements which are still in use in their region, and especially those which are typical for a specific province or which are linked with the natural characteristics of the area.

We will offer a price to the fifty correspondents who will provide the best information by sending in photographic pictures and short descriptions. These results will then be published in "Ons Land" in order to contribute in this way to the revival of traditional folk games (1919, *Ons Land* 1[1]: 11).

This sad call to readers appeared in the very first issue of the first volume of the Flemish weekly *Ons Land* (Our Country) of 1919. This newspaper report illustrates the problematic relationship between traditional games and modern sport at the crucial turning point in the history of physical culture in Europe, namely the end of World War I. These traditional games were described as at risk of being ousted by the introduction of modern sports. The next issues of the magazine included six reader responses describing a number of traditional games, especially local bowl games. There was no trace, however, of the prize that was promised.

—Roland Renson

competing to win a *palio* (flag) is like stepping back into the living past.

When firearms were introduced, many archery and crossbow societies replaced their traditional weapons with culverins or carbines. These associations of riflemen, especially in Germany and Austria, but also in Denmark, are highly organized and have preserved to a notable extent their character as patriarchal men's clubs, especially in rural areas.

## Fighting Games

Wrestling is probably the oldest and the most universal traditional sport of humankind. So-called Greco-Roman wrestling, which has acquired official Olympic status, has no connection with the wrestling styles of Greek and Roman antiquity, and the type of wrestling practiced during the ancient Olympic Games has much more in common with present-day *pelivan* (Turkish wrestling) or even with modern judo.

In Europe, international competitions have already been staged, in which *glima* (game of gladness) wrestlers from Iceland were matched with adepts of the *lucha canaria* (Canary wrestling) style practiced in the Canary Islands. Moreover, an International Federation of Celtic Wrestling was founded in 1985, bringing together Icelandic *glima*, Scottish *backhold* and Breton *gouren*.

In *savate*, also called *French boxing*, both fists and feet are employed to hit the opponent; this traditional sport is structurally related to Thai kickboxing. *La canne* (stick fighting) was also once popular in France. *Jogo do pau* is a Portuguese version of stick fighting with some similarities to Japanese kendo.

Tilting, the favorite sport of the knights of medieval Europe, was officially abolished in France in 1559 when King Henry II was mortally wounded in a confrontation with his captain of the guard. However, some of its variants have survived. They include ring tilting and quintain, which can be practiced either on land or water. Ring tilting is still very popular in the Dutch Province of Zealand, quintain is practiced at the yearly festival of Foligno in Italy, and similar jousts are held on water, as in the case of the *joutes girondines* (jousts from the Gironde area) in France and the *fischerstechen* (fishermen-tilting) in Germany.

Forms of sword play have been practiced throughout Europe for centuries. Many of these sports have been highly ritualized and stylized in an endeavor to make them less lethal. Special protective gear is worn by practitioners of sports such as fencing, which has had Olympic status since the first modern Olympic Games were held in Athens in 1896. Tug of war was practiced for the last time as an Olympic event during the Antwerp Games in 1920, but it is still organized in international competition by the Tug of War International Federation (TWIF).

## Animal Games

Several animal games have gained a reputation as "blood sports" in the course of history and have been officially banned in many countries. Such cruel sports as bull-baiting and bear-baiting were popular in medieval and sixteenth- and seventeenth-century England, but these baitings, in which specially trained bulldogs were used, have not survived the so-called civilizing process. Cockfighting, however, is still very popular in the north of France. In Belgium and other countries where cockfights are illegal, these games still have their clandestine but loyal supporters. Animals are also matched in fair competitions, as in pigeon racing and dog racing. In most of these animal competitions, people train and coach the animals. In other cases, people engage in direct and hazardous confrontation with animals, as in bull-running in France and Spain, and bull-fighting in France, Portugal, and Spain. Goose-riding and other "games" in which animals such as geese, ducks, or cocks are decapitated, survive in most of the Catholic regions of Europe.

## Locomotion Games

Some traditional hill races are part of the Scottish Highland Games and the Grasmere sports festivals in the English Lake District. *Fierljeppen* (jumping for distance—with a fen-pole) has survived in the Dutch province of Frisia as a spectacular form of pole vaulting over smaller rivers. Even more spectacular, however, is the *salto del pastor* (shepherd's jump) practiced on the Canary Islands, in which a leaping pole is used to jump off cliffs and hill slopes. Among the Sami people of Norway, Sweden, and Finland, who depended almost entirely for their subsistence on their reindeer, traditional sports tend to highlight riding skills during reindeer-sledge races. The famous *Palio* of Siena, a traditional annual horse race in the very heart of the old Italian town, attracts so many visitors that it is now an internationally known tourist attraction. Traditional rowing contests (for men and women) are yearly held during the *regata storica* (ancient regatta) of Venice in Italy and during the *regatas de traineras* (whaling boats) in the bay of San Sebastian in the Spanish Basque country. In Cornwall the Falmouth Working Boat Association was formed some years ago to regulate the old style regattas for the Truro River oyster dredgers.

## Acrobatics

In all cultures, people try to keep in good physical shape by performing coded sets of physical exercises. Because of the limitations of the human neuromuscular system, which has hardly changed since the emergence of *Homo sapiens*, acrobatic performances are strikingly similar regardless of historical period or culture. The acrobatics that we see in the modern circus are, for example, very similar to those performed in the arenas of ancient Rome. Nor are the vaults and somersaults of modern gymnastics very different from the tumbling exercises described in 1599 by the Italian professional acrobat Tuccaro (1536–1604).

The *Cong-Fou* gymnastic exercises of the Chinese Taoist monks described by the French Jesuit Amiot (1779) had so much in common with the Swedish gymnastics system of Per Henrik Ling (1776–1839) that the French physician Nicolas Dally (1857) was tempted to believe that Ling had simply copied them.

Turnen, the typical German apparatus gymnastics created by Friedrich Ludwig Jahn (1778–1852), has evolved into the internationally established discipline of Olympic gymnastics. The early Turner movement nevertheless cherished so called *volkstumliche Spiele* (ethnic games) as a part of its nationalist philosophy. A striking example of traditional acrobatics are the *castells* or human pyramids formed by amateur gymnasts in Barcelona (Spain) as towering symbols of their Catalan identity.

## Conclusion

This survey of the extraordinary range of traditional sports shows the great richness of the European games heritage. *Homo Ludens* was the subject of a famous work on the play spirit in Western civilization by the great Dutch historian Johan Huizinga, who condemned the seriousness, uniformity, organization, and competitiveness of contemporary sports and civilization in comparison with a more playful and diverse world of traditional games. These have been treated as the Cinderellas of modern sport, despite the fact that most modern sports are little more than innovations based on older games. A major danger facing modern sport is that diversity will be lost as the global market and mass communications provide an ever narrower range of activities for the young. With the global village there is a risk that traditional sports will be lost forever or that they will be preserved here and there merely as examples of quaint old customs. Yet, apart from their intrinsic value, traditional sports are valuable as a kind of alternative model of sport, showing how earlier generations did things differently and providing the basis for a critique of some of the more absurd competitive excesses of modern sport.

Whereas earlier generations tended to see sport as part of a distinctive folk tradition, the recent tendency is to import sports that have deep roots in the traditions of other cultures, notably Asian. Yet judo, for all that it may be carried out under the same rules in the Netherlands as in Japan, has very different cultural associations in the two countries. Similarly, the sumo contests that from time to time are presented in Europe run the risk of appearing to be freak shows or exotic spectacles. Although it may now be possible to perform the same play "text" in any number of countries, an understanding of cultural context is far more elusive and difficult. As to the survival of existing traditional games, the enormous increase in traffic in the latter half of the twentieth century has had a strikingly destructive effect on the street as a place for play. Children, who until recently have been the most effective agency for the transmission of a living culture, increasingly live indoors, watching television and "playing" computer games, some of which bear marked similarities to older games, rolling balls and throwing objects around a screen. Pouring old wine into new bottles is always happening in cultural history, and it may be that the traditional games will live on in new forms.

—Roland Renson

See also Animal Baiting; Archery; Bowls and Bowling; Cudgels; Highland Games; Pelota; Trapball.

Bibliography: Barreau, J. J., and G. Jaoun. (1991) *Eclipses et renaissance des jeux populaires.* Rennes, France: Institut International d'Anthropologie Corporelle.

De Vroede, E., and R. Renson. (1991) *Proceedings of the Second European Seminar on Traditional Games,* Leuven 12–16 September 1990. Leuven, Belgium: Vlaamse Volkssport Centrale.

Eichberg, H. (1984) "Olympic Sport—Neocolonisation and Alternatives." *International Review for the Sociology of Sport* 19, 1: 97–106.

Endrei, W., and L. Zolnay. (1986) *Fun and Games in Old Europe,* Budapest: Corvina.

Malcolmson, R. W. (1973) *Popular Recreations in English Society, 1700–1850.* Cambridge: Cambridge University Press.

Moller, J. (1990–1991) *Gamle idraetslege i Danmark.* Vols. 1–4. Gerlev: Idraetsforsk.

Moreno, Palos C. (1992) *Juegos y deportes tradicionales en España.* Madrid: Consejo Superior de Deportes.

Renson, R., P. P. De Nayer, and M. Ostyn, eds. (1976) *The History, the Evolution and Diffusion of Sports and Games in Different Cultures, Proceedings of the Fourth International HISPA Seminar,* Leuven 1–5 April 1975. Brussels: BLOSO.

Renson, R., H. Smulders, and E. De Vroede, eds. (1978–1988) *Serie der Vlaamse Volkssport Dossiers.* Vols. 1–8. Leuven, Belgium: Vlaamse Volkssport Centrale.

Schaufelberger, W. (1972) *Der Wettkampf in der alten Eidgenossenschaft.* Vols. 1–2. Bern: Haupt.

Taylor, A. R. (1992) *The Guinness Book of Traditional Pub Games.* Enfield, UK: Guinness.

Tremaud, H. (1972) *Jeux de force et d'adresse.* Paris: Musées Nationaux.

Webster, D. (1973) *Scottish Highland Games.* Edinburgh: Reprographia Edinburgh.

# Traditional Sports, North and South America

It is a simple matter to observe that traditional sport is a ubiquitous component of cultural life across the North and South American continents. The sport of the Americas is as varied and complex as its kaleidoscope of cultures and histories. For this reason, it is not so simple to generalize with any degree of accuracy about the nature and meaning of that sport. The two continents span over 41 million square kilometers (16 million square miles), from the frozen tundra of the subarctic to the other side of the equator and the harsh chill of Tierra del Fuego; from the Bering Strait to the sunny Atlantic coast of Brazil; and from the high plateaus of the Alaskan, Rocky, and the Andean mountain ranges to the flatness of the western great basin or the marshlands of the southeast Texas coast. The vastness of the territory and the varied nature of its environment militates against generalization.

At the same time, the prehistory and written history of the so-called New World is relatively shallow in comparison to those of its Old World counterpart. Archeological science remains hard-pressed to document the presence of human life in the North and South American continents before 15,000 years ago. And it was only after European conquest just 500 years ago that the people and events of the Americas became part of a comprehensive written history. What modern science knows about life before that history is limited to what archaeologists and prehistorians can glean from unwritten records represented largely by what rocks, bones, and other material remains of lost tribes and civilizations.

The idea of traditional sport in the Americas is also complicated by the ambiguity in the term *traditional culture* as it applies to the people of North and South America. It could be argued that the only traditional cultures in the Western Hemisphere are those of Native Americans. The other, newer arrivals to the continents had their traditional cultures compromised by the realities of life in the American "melting pot." However, in fairness to the broad array of cultural styles that characterize life outside the Native American community, traditional culture and concomitantly traditional sport can be found in both Indian and non-Indian contexts in the Americas. Thus, the term traditional sport can mean both the sports of Native Americans and those folk sports brought to or developed in the New World by immigrants from the Old World and not compromised by professionalization and commercialization.

Still, any discussion about traditional sport in the Americas is restricted largely to the sport and games of Native Americans. Many of the best-known sports among non-Indian groups have relatively short histories and have evolved into what we are calling "modern" or "contemporary" sports, such as soccer (association football), basketball, football, and baseball. Many of what one might call traditional sports of American immigrant groups are more appropriately treated in the context of their countries of origin. Also, among those traditional sports that have survived relatively untainted by professionalization and commercialization many are simply variations of modern sports, such as stickball and kickball, or are relatively unknown and infrequently if ever the subject of research.

For these reasons, this entry will focus on the traditional sport of Native North and South America. This effort to generalize about and describe the multitude of such sports is tied to the following theses: that (1) there are common threads to traditional sport in the native Western Hemisphere; (2) the ball game is one of the major unifying themes in Native American history and prehistory; (3) traditional sport in Native America is part of a playful worldview that gives a particular flavor to Native American life and culture; and (4) there are many important reasons for preserving and promoting the traditional sports of the North and South American continents.

## The Literature

The literature on traditional sport in North and South America is limited at best. Until recently, American social science has devoted little attention to the general topic of sport, both modern and traditional. In the past two decades a new interest in the study of sport has emerged, and some of the new scholarship has addressed the issue of traditional or folk sport, particularly that of American Indian groups. However, as indicated earlier, not much systematic research has been done on the subject of traditional sports among non-Indian groups in the Americas.

The only treatment of Indian games and sports until recently has been for the most part that included in general ethnographic descriptions (e.g., Bureau of American Ethnology reports; see Cooper 1963a). However, because of the assump-

tion that sport was a relatively insignificant component of culture, these treatments were generally sketchy, minimal in detail, and only incidental to the broader focus of the ethnography. One exception to this tendency was the work of Stewart Culin, whose *Games of the Indians of North America* (1907) is a classic and contains detailed descriptions of many traditional sports. There were other significant contributions to the understanding of Native American traditional sport. James Mooney's lengthy article on "The Cherokee Ball Play" (1890) and Theodore Stern's monograph, *The Rubber-Ball Games of the Americas* (1949), are two examples.

In the past two decades the social sciences and the humanities in America have developed what appears to be a new interest in and a seriousness about the study of sports and games among Native Americans. This interest is reflected in the increased number of presentations, articles, and books on the subject. The latter range from the description of sport activities among particular Native American tribes (e.g., Blanchard's *Mississippi Choctaws at Play*, 1981) to the analysis of Indian sports in general (e.g., Oxendine's *American Indian Sports Heritage*, 1988). As a result of new research, American scholarship is beginning to get a clearer understanding of the scope and significance of traditional sport among the Indians of North and South America.

## Traditional Sport in Native America

The inventory of Native American traditional sports is as large and diverse as the complexity of the distribution of cultures across the two continents. In the late 1400s, North and South America were characterized by 13 distinct language families, with hundreds of languages and a comparable number of distinct cultural groups. It is assumed that each of these groups had their own forms of recreational activity and that this activity included a variety of physical skill games or sports. For that reason, it would be impossible to describe each of these here. However, there are several common themes that run through all of these activities. These themes lend themselves to the following classification: sports of physical skill, sports of mechanical skills, sports involving animals, and ball games. (Note: Anthropologists

*An early European view of a boxing match between two Hopaee Indians.*

have traditionally taken liberties with the notion of time, frequently describing past events as though they were current, a technique referred to as using the "ethnographic present" tense. I have taken that liberty here. Thus, some of the traditional sports and some of the tribal groups that are described as though they were current are no longer extant.)

## Sports of Physical Skills

It is assumed that sports of physical skills are among the oldest of human sports. These activities involve competition that stretches the limits of one's physical strength, endurance, and speed. Such activities are generally viewed as individual sports, but they do in some cases pit teams against each other. These sports include such activities as racing, swimming, wrestling, boxing, pulling, and shoving.

Foot racing is probably universal among the peoples of North and South America. The most noteworthy of these racing events are the distance events that feature endurance more than speed. Among the New World's best-known racers are the Tamahumara Indians of northern Mexico. These people have been known to run over 240 kilometers (150 miles) at a stretch and play games that involve kicking a ball or carrying a log over a course more than 120 kilometers (75 miles) in length. The Zuñi and other Pueblo Indians of the southwestern United States engage in marathon running. A form of ball racing is also common among the Pueblo peoples (Culin 1907, 666) as well as the Pima, Papago, and certain Indians of the North American Plains (e.g., Mandan). Among the Ge in South America, relay races are run in which contestants carried heavy logs said to be about one meter (three feet) in length and weigh 90 kilograms (200 pounds) (Lowie 1963a, 503). Log races are also common among the tribes of Eastern Brazil (Lowie 1963b, 392). The Tapirape have foot races in which the men of one moiety compete against those of another (Wagley and Galvao 1963, 175).

Equally common to Native America is the sport of wrestling, though it is more frequently reported among the South American than North American groups. Reagan (1932, 69–70) has described wrestling among the Navajos in which two men compete amidst great ceremony, each attempting to seize the other and throw him on his back to the ground. Similar descriptions are available for such groups among South American tribes (e.g., Ona, Bororo, Caingang, Ge, and others). Among the Yahgan and several Guiana tribes, group wrestling is common. For the Caraja, wrestling is an "indispensable part of most religious ceremonies and of all intervillage visits" (Lipkind, 1963, 191).

Competitive swimming is likewise common among Native Americans. Catlin (1841, 96) observed over 150 years ago that "the art of swimming is likewise common among Native Americans; and perhaps no people on earth have taken more pains to learn it, nor any who turn it to better account." It is said that although they were probably not the first to use the "crawl" stroke, American Indian swimmers, in particular among groups like the Mandan, have developed the technique to its full effectiveness (Oxendine 1988, 100).

Other such traditional sport activities include various forms of what is generally known as "tug-of-war," a contest in which teams pull on opposite ends of a large rope in an effort to drag the opposition across a line or through a wet, muddy, or otherwise uninviting neutral zone. Among the Ona, teams of men compete against each other in an analogous activity in which they line up in two rows and strain to shove the opposition backward in what might be called a "push-of-war" (Cooper 1963b, 122). Boxing, though not widespread, does occur among Native Americans. The Mocovi in South America, for example, engage frequently in a form of team boxing that involves fighting between teams of men and between teams of women (Metraux 1963a, 336). A similar form of pushing match using shields is popular among the Warraw (Kirchhoff 1963, 879).

Mock fights and battles are also common to Native American traditional sport. Some of these involve hurling stones, small clubs, or burning sticks. For example, among the Quimbaya of South America, a line of women face a line of men and boys, and both rows assault each other with weapons or projectiles. According to Hernandez de Alba (1963, 312), these "usually resulted in several people being wounded or even killed." Finally, Native Americans engage in a variety of competitive tests of strength involving lifting or pulling skills. One of the most interesting of these is a competition among the Cozarini of South America to demonstrate strength by pulling a heavy wooden bar through two perpendicular poles (Metraux 1963b, 357).

## Sports of Mechanical Skills

The sports of mechanical skills also involve physical skills and place a premium on hand-eye coordination. However, unlike those described above, the focus of the activities is the mastery of a piece of equipment or technique rather than some aspect of one's own body. These include competitive archery, spear-throwing, snow snake, hoop-and-pole, chunkey, and other sports that revolve around the use of a particular device. Though most focus on individual performance, some can be played as team sports.

One of the most common forms of sporting entertainment among the Indian populations of the New World is archery. The bow-and-arrow was a highly developed and widely used technology across both the North and South American continents long before European intervention. As

Oxendine (1988, 95) notes, Indian archery has taken several different forms: "traditional target shooting for accuracy, shooting at moving targets, and speed shooting." Catlin (1841, 141) observed among the Mandan a particular game of arrows in which the object was for a single archer to keep as many arrows as possible in the air at a time. Another variation of archery is that of the Goajiro of South America who competed by shooting at pieces of fruit or skin balls tossed into the air (Armstrong and Metraux 1963, 381).

One of the most popular traditional sports among the Indians of Canada and the northern United States is that of snow snake. This sport involves tossing a stick ("the snake") approximately two meters (six feet) in length across the ice. The object is to sling the stick further than the opposition. Though reserved largely for men, the sport is also played by women, but generally with smaller sticks. Although the sport is concentrated largely in northern climates and reserved for the colder months of the year, variations of snow snake are adapted to certain regions of the southwestern United States. Also, there have been reports of similar games being played by Indian groups in South America. For example, the Chaco are said to play a game in which two groups of men compete by taking turns at throwing across the ground a round piece of wood about three-quarters of one meter (30 inches) in length. The person flinging "it the farthest and the straightest obtains the prize or receives praises" (Metraux 1963a, 335–336).

Another popular traditional sport among Native Americans is the game of hoop-and-pole. The game has several variations but all involve throwing a pole, a spear, or a dart at a rolling hoop. The object is to throw the projectile in such a way that it comes to a rest close to the inert hoop; ideally underneath the hoop. Although more commonly reported in North America, the game and variations of the game appear in certain areas of the South American continent. For example, Cooper (1963a, 508) reports that a game he calls "hoop-and-pole, or more accurately hoop-and-arrow," is played by several groups "within the Guianan, Amazonian, Chacoan, and Fuegian areas." This sport involves shooting arrows at rolling fruit, hoops of solid wood or grass, or discuses of cactus.

Another version of the hoop-and-pole game is chunkey. This game is played largely by Indian groups in the southeastern United States. Similar to that of the hoop-and-pole game, the object is to toss a long stick or spear beside a rolling chunkey stone in such a way that the two come to rest at the identical spot. The Choctaws are particularly fond of this game.

## Animal Sports

When one thinks of Indians and sports involving animals, one thinks immediately of hunting and fishing. However, it is difficult to view hunting and fishing enterprises of Native Americans as sporting events; they are too closely tied to subsistence and survival. Other animals do, however, figure into the Native American repertoire of traditional sports. A few of these may pre-date European influence, but most involve the horse and thus are dated only within the past 500 years.

Horse racing and other forms of competitive horse-back riding events are popular among those groups having domesticated the horse (e.g., Navajos, Apaches, Commanches, and other Plains groups). Competitive horse racing is also reported among several South American groups including the Goajiro (Armstrong and Metraux, 1963, 381), the Mybaya, and the Mocovi (Metraux 1963a, 336).

Dog-sled racing is a popular event among Alaskans today, and some Eskimos participate, from the many regional races to the major annual event, the Iditarod. Some dog racing is reported in the modern Eskimo community (see Chance 1966, 55). However, there appears to be no mention of this sport in the early ethnographic literature, suggesting that it may be something that has developed only since European colonization of Alaska.

Dogs are the focus of at least one other sport among the Eskimos, something Oswalt (1979, 127) calls "dog baiting." A particularly temperamental or unruly member of a dog team is harnessed and held at bay by the owner. Then the dog's face is swung threateningly into the face of another harnessed dog to provoke snarling, snapping, and biting. The problem dog is thus forced to face and fight a series of his compatriots until he the owner deems he is sufficiently bloody and subdued.

Another interesting, though probably unique, sport involving animals is something that has been called the "turtle game," played by the Cashinawa of South America. This activity involves a group of men immobilizing a land turtle by binding it with cord and then attempting to repel efforts by a team of women to release the turtle (Metraux, 1963c, 679).

## The Ball Game

The ball game is the cornerstone of traditional sports among Native Americans. Widespread across both the North and South American continents, it comes in many varieties but in all cases involved the following: the competition of two teams with equal numbers of players, the movement of a ball by a team of players up and down a field, scoring points by striking or penetrating the goal of the opponent, and winning by being first to accumulate an agreed-upon total number of points.

The earliest records of the ball game come from Mesoamerica and suggest this sport may have been played by the Olmecs over 3,000 years ago. In the classic ball games of prehistoric middle America, teams representing whole communities used their hips to drive a large rubber ball up and down a well-defined ball court; thus the frequent use of the term "hip-ball game" to describe the event. The object was to strike the goal of the opponent or knock the ball through small rings that protruded out from the walls on the side boundaries of the court. Players were not allowed to touch the ball with their hands, it was a fast-moving game, and sometimes the ball play resulted in injury, even death.

Later the Mayans would play the game (*pok-ta-pok*); then the Aztecs (*tlachi*). The great ball games of the Aztecs were of economic, social, political, and religious significance. They were the setting for heavy gambling, they drew large crowds of spectators, their outcomes frequently had political consequences, and always there were elaborate ritual trappings. The ball game was important and not to be taken lightly. For example, it is reported that the emperor Axayacatl played against the lord of Xoxhimilco and laid the marketplace of Mexico against a garden belonging to this lord. He lost. The next day Mexican soldiers appeared at the palace of the fortunate winner and "while they saluted him and made him presents they threw a garland of flowers about his neck with a thong hidden in it, and so killed him" (from *Historica Chichimeca*, cited by Soustelle 1955, 160).

Archaeological evidence suggests that the Mesoamerican ball game was exported to areas far from the valley of Mexico. For example, ball courts have been found as far north as the southwestern United States, where it appears that as recently as 1500 years ago the Hohokam peoples were playing the classic ball game.

In the other direction, the game, or some variation on the game, has found its way into many areas of South America. Among the Paressi, a game is played in which a hollow rubber ball with a diameter of eight inches is propelled exclusively with the head. The object of the game is to keep the ball in the air. Points are scored when an opponent allows the ball to hit the ground (Metraux 1963b, 357). Similar games are played by the Tupari, Wayoro, and other tribes along the Guapore River (Levi-Strauss 1963, 375), the Mojo in Bolivia (Metraux 1963d, 420) and the Chane (Metraux 1963e, 482). Among the Arawak, the ball game is played by using a ball made from a rubber-like substance extracted from a gum tree. "The players had to keep it in the air without crossing a line, knocking it out of the court, or touching it with their hands and feet. Each time one of the sides failed to do this, its opponents scored a point" (Rouse 1963, 533). The Araona butt the ball with their stomachs, which they protect with bark belts (Metraux 1963d, 446).

In many ways the various types of ball games that ultimately emerge in both South and North America can be viewed as descendants of the Mesoamerican ball game. The balls are different (rubber was available prehistorically only in a limited area of the Western Hemisphere); playing fields are of different design and dimension. Equipment varies; the ball is driven by various means of kicks, butts, or sticks; and the rules are different from one setting to another. But underneath the diversity of its outward manifestations, the American ball game is in its essence still the American ball game.

The varieties of ball games played among Native Americans are many. Perhaps the most widespread of these is the game of shinny, said by Cheska (1982, 21) to be "the most universally played game on the [North American] continent." Similar to modern field hockey, shinny is played with a curved stick that is used to propel the ball. The object of the game is to drive the ball through the opponent's goal. Among many groups, shinny is played largely by women. A similar game is played in South America. The Mekranoti, for example, play a type of hockey with sticks they use to drive the game ball, usually a piece of hard fruit (Werner 1984, 142). The Chaco Indians play a similar game using a ball made of wood or plaited rope. Teams from the different bands play against each other in games that are often viewed as substitutes for open warfare (Metraux 1963a, 334).

Other ball games include double ball, football, hand-and-ball, tossed ball, and fire ball. The latter is played by members of the Iroquois tribe and involves kicking a burning ball down a field and through an opponent's goal. Among South American tribes, the Chake and several other Andean groups play a type of basketball in which the object is to pitch a small ball or round object into a basket affixed to the end of a pole (Metraux and Kirchhoff 1963, 366). The Tucuna and several other Amazonian groups in South America are said to play a type of badminton, standing in a circle, trying to keep a shuttlecock made of maize husk in the air by striking it with the palms of their hands (Nimuendaju 1963, 722). The Yahagan play a similar game using a ball of "seal gut stuffed with feathers or grass" (Cooper 1963c, 100). Among the Ge of South America, a paddle ball game is played in which participants hit a small rubber ball back-and-forth with paddles attempting to keep it from hitting the ground (Lowie 1963a, 504).

One of the most interesting American ball games is one known as the racket game, battattaway, match game, or stickball. This game, that the Choctaws refer to as *toli*, is the parent sport of lacrosse and remains popular today among several tribes in the southeastern United States. The game involves two teams who compete by moving a small ball toward the goal of the opposition by using only a racket or rackets. The team first striking or penetrating the opponent's goal a prescribed number of times wins the match. In most cases, the contests are accompanied by extensive ritual and celebratory behavior, surrounded by heavy gambling, and marked by violence and frequently bloodshed.

The racket game was played and is still played by several North American Indian groups, in addition to the Choctaw, Cherokee, Chickasaw, Creek, Catawba, and Seminole, for example. Though largely limited to the Eastern Woodlands of the United States in its distribution, stickball illustrates the major characteristics of traditional sport among the native populations of North and South America:

1. The classic versions of the racket game involved entire communities and were often major social events, times of feasting, dancing, and celebrating, as well as playing.

2. The racket game involved heavy gambling. Among the Choctaws, for example, it is said that men would actually wager their wives and children on the outcome of a match. In the large matches, the take was generally large. The distribution of these winnings had significant economic implications (Blanchard 1976).

3. There were often obvious political dimensions and significant political outcomes to stickball matches. Among the Choctaws, the word *toli* actually means "little war" and was viewed as an alternative to actual armed conflict, although in some cases the violence sparked by the *toli* contest itself led to war between the competing communities. Among the Creeks, the leadership roles and responsibilities of the different towns were often decided by the outcome of particular racket game matches (Haas 1940).

4. The game was often violent, rules were minimal, and bloodshed, both deliberate and incidental, was more the rule than the exception. There are reports of games played in the last century that had to be called off because one of the teams had been virtually decimated by injuries. Also, it was not unusual for spectators to become victims of such injuries, getting hit with an errant racket or run over by a stampeding herd of stickballers chasing an elusive ball.

5. The game was surrounded by and infused with ritual. Among the Choctaws, the formal racket games involved sorcerers, medicine people (*alickchi*), rain doctors, and drummers. Ritual surrounded the preparation of the players for the match and the game itself. The drummers added an eerie rhythm to the events of the match by their steady and constant beating. The sorcerers attempted to use their powers of malevolence to inflict harm on the players of the opposing team. The *alickchi* doctored their teams' players before the game, employing traditional methods of scratching and bloodletting to prepare them for the contest. Then during the game itself the *alickchi* used a variety of ritual techniques to increase the strength and resolve of individual team members.

6. Despite the apparent focus on the competition, winning was not the principal goal in the classic stickball match. It was as though there were an unstated assumption that ultimately fate determines the outcome of a ball game. The individual player could only do his or her best, and this became the real purpose of the game. And, unless there had been supernatural foul play, the best team won. So, discipline, quality of performance, seriousness of commitment, and those other elements that make a team the best were the goals of the individual combatants. These elements of the game were the reasons for playing. It was nice to win, but that was a matter left up to something other than the skills of any single player or team.

These characteristics of the racket game are generally shared by Native American traditional sport in general. They vary from one area to another and from one level of competition to another. But, taken all together, they illustrate very clearly the importance, seriousness, and significance of traditional sport among the native peoples of North and South America.

## Native American Traditional Sport and Worldview

The significance of traditional sport among Native Americans goes beyond the playing fields, the courts, and the tracks themselves. From the Eskimos in the Alaskan north to the Yahgan of Tierra del Fuego, sport has its roots in the very essence of Native American life, what I have referred to in another context as a "playful worldview" (Blanchard 1986). That all encompassing playfulness in Native American life sets it apart from the more serious, less playful style of industrial Europe. This contrast may lay at the heart of the clash between the native cultures of the New World and the invaders from the Old. Unfortunately, this playfulness was viewed by Europeans as an indication of indolence and sloth when in fact it was simply another way of dealing with the day-to-day realities of human life. Native American traditional sport and the seeming preoccupation of Native Americans with that sport are simply illustrations of this approach or style.

> Playful adaptation is an effective survival mechanism. Play, like work, has important functions and consequences. The critical distinction in the comparison of adaptive styles is not between work and play, but rather between levels of playfulness. More playful systems (e.g., Native America) reflect a distancing style that is indirect, flexible, curvilinear, and often circuitous. Less playful systems (e.g., Euro-American) tend to operate with a direct, inflexible, linear, and confrontational mode. Both styles ultimately lead to the achievement of adaptive goals, at least ideally, but in different ways (Blanchard 1986, 86).

Traditional sport is critical to understanding Native American life. Thus it is vital that every effort be made to salvage and preserve as many as possible of these activities as a way of preserving the distinctive quality that Native American life brings to the diversity of the human experience.

## The Current State of Traditional Sport

The preservation of traditional sport in the North and South American continents should be made a priority, both in practice and in the research and literature. Currently, traditional sport in the Americas is limited largely to rural and out-of-the-way areas and the back streets of large cities. In many cases, sports that once were an important part of community life have disappeared. Among the Mehinaku of Brazil, for example, as of the mid-1970s, the ball game of tradition was no longer being played (Gregor 1979, 20).

In some cases, there are deliberate efforts to revive these activities in some formal way. Among the Indians of the U.S. Southeast, the racket game has in the past two decades made a significant

come-back. Now, tribal groups like the Mississippi Choctaws have stickball leagues and compete on a regular basis with each other and with teams from other parts of the country. But, for the most part, there is no concerted effort to feature and preserve the traditional sports of America.

As indicated earlier, the social sciences and the humanities in the United States have taken a new interest in sports and athletics. Some of this interest has been directed to the description and analysis of traditional sport, but much remains to be done, particularly in the area of discovering and understanding those traditional sports that have survived among non-Indian minority groups in both North and South America.

Organized efforts to showcase, promote, and preserve traditional sport in the Western Hemisphere are virtually nonexistent. Some academic organizations have been founded for purposes of consolidating sport science interests. The North American Society for Sport Sociology, the Society for Sport Psychology, the North American Society for Sport History, and the Association for the Study of Play (formerly the Association for the Anthropological Study of Play) are just some of these. All of these organizations provide outlets for research and writing about traditional sport, but the latter is virtually lost in the shadows of the over-arching interest among these organizations in modern sport. Perhaps the time has come for a new organization, one bringing together persons from relevant interest groups, government personnel, representatives from selected ethnic societies, and scholars, to provide the initial impetus for preserving and promoting traditional sport in North and South America.

## Conclusion

Traditional sport is woven deeply into the fabric of folk life across the North and South American continents, both past and present. It is a statement about culture, about meaning, and about life. It assumes a special significance as an element in the intranational relations between ethnic and racial groups in the complex, pluralistic world that is the world of today's Americas. It assumes an equal significance as a part of the relationship among the nations of the Americas and with the other countries of the world. Traditional sport in North America and in South America is thus an institution that deserves greater attention than it now commands from scholars, academic organizations, special interest groups, and governments. Its promotion and preservation can play an important role in international relations and the quality of life in the twenty-first century.

—Kendall Blanchard

**See also** Mesoamerican Ball Game.

**Bibliography:** Armstrong, John M., and Alfred Metraux. (1963) "The Goajiro." *Bureau of American Ethnology Bulletin* 143, 4: 369–383.

Blanchard, Kendall. (1976) "Stickball and the American Southeast." In *Forms of Play of Native North Americans*, edited by Edward Norbeck and Claire R. Farrer. St. Paul, MN: West Publishing, 189–208.

———. (1981) *Mississippi Choctaws at Play: The Serious Side of Leisure.* Urbana: University of Illinois Press.

———. (1986) "Play as Adaptation." In *Cultural Dimensions of Play, Games, and Sport*, edited by Bernard Mergen. Champaign, IL: Human Kinetics, 79–88.

Catlin, George. (1841) *North American Indians.* Vol. I. Minneapolis: Ross and Haines.

Chance, Norman. (1966) *The Eskimo of North Alaska.* New York: Holt, Rinehart, and Winston.

Cheska, Alyce. (1982) "Ball Game Participation of North American Women." In *Her Story in Sport*, edited by Reet Howell. West Point, NY: Leisure Press.

Cooper, John M. (1963a) "Games and Gambling." *Bureau of American Ethnology Bulletin* 143, 5: 503–524.

———. (1963b) "The Ona." *Bureau of American Ethnology Bulletin* 143, 1: 107–125.

———. (1963c) "The Yahgan." *Bureau of American Ethnology Bulletin* 143, 1: 81–106.

Culin, Stewart. (1907) "Games of the North American Indians." *Annual Report of the Bureau of American Ethnology* 24. Washington, DC: Government Printing Office.

Gregor, Thomas. (1979) Mehinaku: *The Drama of Daily Life in a Brazilian Indian Village.* Chicago: University of Chicago Press.

Haas, Mary R. (1940) "Creek Intertown Relations." *American Anthropologist* 42: 479–489.

Hernandez de Alba, Gregorio. (1963) "Sub-Andean Tribes of the Cauca Valley." *Bureau of American Ethnology Bulletin* 143, 4: 297–327.

Kirchoff, Paul. (1963) "The Warraw." *Bureau of American Ethnology Bulletin* 143, 3: 869–881.

Levi-Strauss, Claude. (1963) "Tribes of the Right Bank of the Guapore River." *Bureau of American Ethnology Bulletin* 143, 3: 371–379.

Lipkind, William. (1963) "The Caraja." *Bureau of American Ethnology Bulletin* 143, 3: 179–191.

Lowie, Robert. (1963a) "The Northwestern and Central Ge." *Bureau of American Ethnology Bulletin* 143, 1: 377–417.

———. (1963b) "Eastern Brazil: An Introduction." *Bureau of American Ethnology Bulletin* 143, 1: 381–400.

Metraux, Alfred. (1963a) "Ethnography of the Chaco." *Bureau of American Ethnology Bulletin* 143, 1: 197–370.

———. (1963b) "The Paressi." *Bureau of American Ethnology Bulletin* 143, 3: 349–360.

———. (1963c) "Tribes of the Jurua-Purus Basins." *Bureau of American Ethnology Bulletin* 143, 3: 657–686

———. (1963d) "Tribes of Eastern Bolivia and the Madeira Headwaters." *Bureau of American Ethnology Bulletin* 143, 3: 381–454.

———. (1963e) "Tribes of the Eastern Slopes of the Bolivian Andes." *Bureau of American Ethnology Bulletin* 143, 3: 465–506.

Metraux, Alfred, and Paul Kirchoff. (1963) "The Northeastern Extension of Andean Culture." *Bureau of American Ethnology Bulletin* 143, 4: 349–368.

Mooney, James. (1890) "Cherokee Ball Play." *American Anthropologist* 3: 105–132.

Nimuendaju, Curt. (1963) "The Tacuna." *Bureau of American Ethnology Bulletin* 143, 3: 713–725.

Oswalt, Wendell. (1979) *Eskimos and Explorers.* Novato, CA: Chandler and Sharp.

Oxendine, Joseph B. (1988) *American Indian Sports Heritage.* Champaign, IL: Human Kinetics.

Reagan, Albert B. (1932) "Navajo Sports." *Primitive Man* 5: 68–71.

Rouse, Irving. (1963) "The Arawak." *Bureau of American Ethnology Bulletin* 143, 4: 507–546.

Soustelle, Jacques. (1955) *Daily Life of the Aztecs on the Eve of the Spanish Conquest.* Palo Alto, CA: Stanford University Press.

Stern, Theodore. (1949) *The Rubber-Ball Games of the Americas.* Seattle: University of Washington Press.

Wagley, Charles, and Eduardo Galvao. (1963) "The Tapirape." *Bureau of American Ethnology Bulletin* 143, 3: 167–178.

Werner, Dennis. (1984) *Amazon Journey: An Anthropologist's Year among Brazil's Mekranoti Indians.* New York: Simon and Schuster.

# Traditional Sports, Oceania

The term Oceania usually refers to the Pacific Basin, Micronesia, Melanesia, Polynesia, and Australia; for the purposes of this article, Indonesia is included as well.

## Australian Aboriginals

Australia is one of the oldest land masses in the world, inhabited by humans 35,000 to 40,000 years ago. The descendants of these original people, the Aborigines, numbered some 300,000 at the time of European colonization. Living in

*Balinese fighting cocks attacking in mid-air. Cock fighting is still a popular sport in many parts of Oceania; gambling is an important factor in the sport's continued appeal.*

what is generally acknowledged to be an inhospitable environment, the population was sparse, averaging only one person per 16 square kilometers (10 square miles). There are estimated to have been between 500 and 900 tribes, each one further subdivided into bands with average sizes of 20 to 25 people.

### Aboriginal Pastimes

W. E. Roth, the protector of Aborigines in Queensland, meticulously recorded the customs of the Queensland Aborigines and included thorough descriptions of their games and amusements. Since his government publication of 1897, the most extensive and authoritative analysis of the games and pastimes of the Australian Aborigines is the thesis completed by Michael Salter in 1967. Some 94 traditional aboriginal ludic

activities were identified by Salter, and of them, 11 fit Blanchard and Cheska's definition of sport. They are:

1. Tree climbing: A group game whereby competitions were held to determine the fastest to climb up and down a tree. Girls as well as boys were instructed in the physical skills necessary to perform such feats. As competitors' skills increased, the elders increased the challenge, by choosing straighter and higher trees. This activity appeared to be particularly popular among the tribes of Victoria.
2. Spear the Disc: One of the most common group games among young boys and adult males was to throw spears from a specified distance at a moving disc. Practicing a skill

obviously essential for hunting, participants scoring a bull's eye were applauded by their fellow competitors.

3. Pit Throwing: A group game particularly popular among the warlike Kalkadoons of northwestern Queensland was pit throwing. A heavy stick or bone attached to a piece of twine was thrown over an emu net into a hole dug specifically for the game. Throwers stood at a designated distance that increased in tandem with skill.

4. Returning Boomerang: Intertribal competitions in which representatives from each tribe attempted to make their boomerang complete two or three loops and land in a designated circle a few feet distant from the throwing area. The Mitakoode tribe increased the difficulty by attempting to hit a small peg placed in the ground.

5. Target and Distance Throwing: Competitions involving the throwing of sticks, boomerangs, spears, or any other object at a specific target. Trees, boughs, tree trunks, or other designated targets were used, and invariably the winner was the one who hit closest to the target. Occasionally, woomeras (a wooden rod with a hooked end designed to give additional leverage) were used to increase the distance.

6. Kangaroo Rat, or Weet Weet: In this group game, the kangaroo "rat," which was made out of a single piece of wood, was thrown so that it slid or bounced along the ground; the aim was to achieve the furthest distance and/or the greatest number of hops. Occasional references are made to umpires and awards for winners.

7. Wrestling: Wrestling exhibited many features common to modern sport: spatial boundaries often defined the competition area; precompetition preparation (and ritual) included oiling of bodies; specific rules governed the competition; winners were identified; rules of "fair" play prevailed; although contests varied by geographical location, many followed very similar rules. Though both intraband and intratribal wrestling contests apparently occurred, intertribal competitions were more prevalent.

8. Mungan-Mungan: A competitive team game between the younger boys and men played principally in what has come to be known as the Northern Territory. In the center of the designated playing areas a *wormar* (a white painted stick representing a young girl) was placed, and the object of the game was for the young boys to keep the *wormar* away from the older men. Passing and tackling were essential features of the game, which continued until one team was too exhausted to play.

9. Catchball: Catchball was the favorite and most widespread ball game and was played by both sexes. The game involved players tossing the ball back and forth while other players attempted to intercept it in the air. The playing time was determined by the physical stamina of the players. The Kalkadoons described it as "kangaroo-play," for the jumping players resembled kangaroos.

10. Football: A team game in which players varied from a few to hundreds. The most common mode of play was to kick the ball high in the air: the player tried to kick higher and farther than anyone else. The game generally ended when the players became exhausted. The ball composition varied from locale to locale and included ones made from possum's hair and kangaroo scrotums.

11. Hockey: A ball and stick game, resembling the European game of shinny, was played by both sexes and was popular among the Torres Strait Islanders and southwestern Australians. Played with a bent stick (molock with a root) and a wooden ball, there were few if any rules and usually no definite goal. The game consisted of hitting and passing, with the aim being to intercept an opponent's pass. Again, physical stamina and interest appeared to determine the length of the game.

Through "play" and "friendly contests," Aboriginal males maintained and improved their fighting prowess. Young boys imitated their elders in sham fights in which they used weapons such as toy spears, woomeras, and boomerangs. Adults participated in intertribal tournaments, called "pruns" by the Mallanpara Aborigines of Central Queensland. Although basically entertainment, such meetings followed the rules of fair play and were used to settle personal scores and tribal disagreements such as territorial disputes or theft of women. The tournaments took place in designated "battle" areas (sometimes the same area being used year after year) with the teams lining up on the opposing ends of the battlefield. Definite rules governed such "play" with, for example, spear throwing restricted to the lower legs and rest pauses being called every 10 to 15 minutes to allow players to recover and collect their weapons.

With the exception of intertribal tournaments, the rules were few, easily understood, and often temporary, and officials or referees were almost nonexistent. Victory was generally of minor significance, and winners were rarely honored, for the emphasis was maximum participation and enjoyment. Players of all skill levels were encouraged to engage in the group activities, which very rarely embraced a team concept. Competition did not dominate, and spectators were rare. Games and sports in Aboriginal culture served to solidify internal relationships and promote good will and social intercourse. Moreover, they offered a respite from work and an arena for learning cultural values.

### Effect of European Colonization

The traditional lifestyle and culture of the Aborigines was radically altered by the European settlement of Australia, and within 50 years of the arrival of the alien culture the Aboriginal population had decreased by over 80 percent. Economic, political, and educational policies were enacted to ensure that the primitive natives were "civilized." Sport was critical to this process and served as a vehicle of acculturation. Games such as cricket were effective agents of "anglicization" and inculcated European values and norms. As traditional culture was destroyed, so too were the indigenous games and sports.

The assimilation of Aborigines into European games and sports has been relatively effective and complete. In the schools and on the reserves and missions the "normal" games are now cricket, rugby, and netball. Beginning only in the mid-1980s has an appreciation of Aboriginal heritage evolved and some traditional activities revived.

National competitions restricted to Aborigines have been organized, such as the National Aboriginal Australian Rules Carnivals and interstate Aborigine Rugby League Carnivals. Occasionally, at these gatherings or other special Aborigine Sports Days, activities such as boomerang and spear throwing and fire-making contests are held for the men. Inexplicably, females are invited to compete in sack races and races whereby flour drums are balanced on their heads, which was never part of the tradition. In 1969 the Aboriginal Sports Foundation was formed, and it has received financial assistance from the federal government. The foundation is active in fostering sports competition among Aborigines but has never made any serious attempt to promote traditional sports and games.

## Melanesia

The geographical area known as Melanesia consists of a group of southeastern Pacific islands located northeast of Australia between the Equator and the Tropic of Capricorn. It extends northwest to southeast as a gigantic island crescent 5,310 kilometers (3,300 miles) long and 1,126 kilometers (700 miles) wide, and consists of coral reefs, islets, and isolated volcanic islands as well as one of the largest islands in the world—New Guinea.

### Melanesian Pastimes

Some of the earliest reports of Melanesian games come from Captain F. Barton (1880) and Reverend J. H. Holmes (1808), and Rolf Kuschel performed an exceptional case study of the games and play activities prevalent among children and adults on Beltona, an island in the British Solomon Islands, before significant contact with the outside world was made in 1938. The most comprehensive scholarly study of the Melanesians was the thesis written by Keith Lansley at the University of Alberta in 1969, and the traditional sports noted here have been gleaned from his collection of 144 activities.

1. Canoe Racing: Competitive canoe races were reported in southern New Guinea, Guadalcanal, Manus, Admiralty Island, Hall Sound, Aroma, and Gaile. The canoe was the principal means of transport in these areas, and challenge races, particularly by older children, helped to hone necessary skills.

2. Dart Throwing: A hard wooden rod with a sharp end was thrown so that it flew along the ground; the winner was the one who threw it the furthest distance. Played on a hard, flat, sandy beach, it was popular in Tanna, New Hebrides, and the Torres Strait Islands.

3. Spear Throwing: Proficiency with the spear was essential for the Melanesian male, and competitions were routinely used to develop and hone this skill. Target shooting for accuracy, distance throwing, moving targets, and challenges were the most common forms of competition. For the sport, only pointed reeds or sticks were used. Reported on Moresby Straits, Dabu, Wogeo, Kumngo, Manus, Admiralty Islands, Torres Strait Islands, Tonga, and New Hebrides.

4. Land Diving: A unique sport and a forerunner to the modern bungee jumping, land diving was reported among the natives of Maleka in the New Hebrides. A tower some 80 feet in height was constructed and the base around it cleared of debris and rocks. Vines were attached at various heights on the tower, and young men, after binding the vine around their ankles, dived head first into the prepared pit. The winner was the one diving from the highest point.

5. Racing: Ethnographers refer often to children playing and racing around, but very few, surprisingly, reported "races" of any type. In Kumngo in Central New Guinea, frequent foot races among young boys were recorded. Boys raced over different paths and the first to arrive at a designated spot was decreed the winner.

6. Foot Fighting: A rough game played by boys was found in Kumngo, Central New Guinea. The game involved ferocious kicking, with the object being to knock down all members of the opposing team.

7. Wrestling: Despite frequent citations to "rough and tumble games" by boys, organized wrestling matches are only occasionally reported. In Wogeo, New Guinea, and Manus on the Admiralty Islands, wrestling was a popular sport; however, no references are made to rules, styles, or duration of bouts.

8. Tug of War: A variety of versions of "tug of war" (pulling opposing teams) were avidly pursued by young children and men. In Tanga, the two teams stood opposing one another, joined hands and endeavored to pull the other onto the opponent's territory, while in New Hebrides a sitting version was preferred.

9. Batting the Ball: A simple ball game involving two teams was played in Central New Guinea. The ball, made of the hard fruit of the *kaui kents* tree, was thrown to the opposing team, who attempted to bat the ball back with a piece of wood. The game was played for hours with enjoyment being a significant factor.

10. Football: Various team games involving kicking the ball were played in Aoba, New Hebrides, Wogeo, New Guinea, Central New Guinea, Manus, and the Admiralty Islands. Balls ranged from native oranges, coconuts, breadfruit, or hard *konts* fruit. Few rules existed; the object was, simply, to kick the ball though a goal that was usually a couple of pieces of sticks. A highly competitive game, the team numbers varied, although they were equitable for each match.

11. Handball: A unique form of handball was recorded in New Guinea, Torres Strait Islands, Matu, Tanga, and New Hebrides. The most popular type of ball was a pig's bladder, although the fruit from the *kai* tree and balls made from pandanus and coconut palm leaves were also used. One player attempted to punch the ball for at least ten consecutive hits, while members of the opposing team tried to disrupt his juggling.

12. Shinty: A team game resembling the modern sport of field hockey was played in the Torres Strait Islands, the New Hebrides, and Fly River in New Guinea. The game involved hitting a wooden ball with a stick, often of bamboo, and was played on the beach. Few rules existed and the object appears to have been ball possession rather than scoring goals. However, the game was highly competitive and created considerable excitement.

13. Surfboard Riding: The surfboard used by Melanesians was considerably smaller than

the Polynesian version, being only 46 centimeters by 30 centimeters (18 inches by 12 inches). It could almost be called a miniature, or child's board, and was simply placed under the chest. Popular among both sexes, adults as well as children, it was reported in Northern New Guinea, the New Hebrides, Tanga, and New Ireland.

14. Cat's Cradle: This activity proliferated throughout the whole area of Melanesia. An extensive variety and quantity of string figures have been recorded.

Special mention must be made of the last two activities, which, lacking evidence of competition, do not completely satisfy the definition of sport. Surfboard riding is included here because it has generally been assumed to be an activity exclusive to Polynesians. Similarly, the making of string figures has captured the particular interest and attention of ethnographers, and more has been written about this activity than any other aspect of culture.

### Effect of European Colonization

The Europeanization of this area was specific rather than general, and links were maintained with the distant home countries rather than forged with other proximal peoples. However, in certain instances assimilation has not been complete, and the old culture has managed to survive the dominance of the new. The game of cricket on the Trobriand Islands furnishes a fascinating example. Introduced by the British missionaries with a principal aim to substitute for intertribal combats, cricket has been modified by the Trobrianders from the traditional English game, and aspects of their traditional culture have been incorporated into the game so that the sport as it is now played is distinctly "Trobriand." Full of ritual significance, the restructured game is an essential component of Trobriand culture.

### Micronesia

Derived from the Greek words *mikros* (small) and *nesos* (island), Micronesia consists of a myriad of small coral islets, reefs, and volcanic islands located in the western Pacific, north of the Equator. In size and status, Micronesia is the smallest and the least known of the Pacific island groups, which consists of the Federated States of Micronesia, the Northern Mariana Islands, and Marshall Islands. The Marianas were the first to be discovered by Europeans: in 1521 Ferdinand Magellan sailed across the Pacific in search of the Spice Islands. The first colonization of the area was by the Spanish, followed only in the past two centuries by the Germans, British, Americans, and, just before and during World War II, the Japanese. The scattered atolls extend some 2,000 miles east to west and north to south, and are populated by scattered communities.

### Micronesian Pastimes

In 1943 Herbert Krieger, curator of the United States National Museum, wrote that "games, other than those of children, were in . . . nature of athletic sports. Competitive wrestling, boxing, swimming, and diving and ball games have been recorded" (Krieger 1943, 28).

In Murdock's (1967) *Ethnographic Atlas* only a few of the various Micronesian societies were categorized as having games. The Palauans and Truckese played games of physical skill and chance. The Majuro on the Marshall Islands and Makin on the Gilbert Islands played games of physical skill only. The Ifaluk on the Central Caroline Islands engaged in games of physical skill and strategy, but none of chance. Other Micronesian societies, according to Murdock, did not have games of any type.

Embree provides an intriguing example of cultural interaction when he compares the sport of kickball in Micronesia and Thailand. On the Marshall and Gilbert Islands, the ball was made of a "stuffed cube of matting of pandanus strips" (Krieger 1943, 28), and the object of the game was to kick and keep the ball (cube) in the air as long as possible. Any number of players could be involved in the game, and the group kept time to the movements of the ball by clapping. Although Krieger states that goal lines were recognized, Embree declares that on the Marshall Islands there were no winners or losers in this game. Quite significantly, this contrasted with the very competitive sport of *sepa* or *sepak-tekraw* played in Thailand and other parts of southeast Asia. If games are a microcosm of society, then the inhabitants of the Marshall Islands lacked the competitiveness of their counterparts in Thailand.

## Polynesia

The name Polynesia comes from the Greek, and means "many islands." The sports and games of these societies are more complex, more abundant, and more competitive than in other regions.

It is impossible here to do justice to the extensive literature available on Polynesian games. The concept of competition in Polynesian sports has been substantiated in many studies, including the recent work of Gundorf Krueger, who observes:

> In the traditional culture of Hawaii the expression denoting achievement was *ho o papa*. It was bound up with a competitive philosophy that was primarily individualistic. Non-team events, combative or individual, were the predominant forms of sport. This firmly entrenched "idea of competition" is further emphasized by the Hawaiian's love of betting (Krueger 1990, 91).

The most comprehensive study of games throughout Polynesia is the master's thesis from the University of Alberta by Kevin Jones (1967). Jones collected and tabulated games and physical activities from 10 island groups within Polynesia: Hawaii, Tahiti, New Zealand, Fiji, Samoa, Niue, Rotuma, Tonga, Society, and Marquesas. He found most games to be social psychological (103), followed by political (32), economic (24), ceremonial (21), socialization (16), and family (17). Jones concluded that the "close communal and cooperative type of existence of the people, then, in which interaction between individuals and groups was a constant process, was obviously carried over into their games and physical activities" (Jones 1967, 204). Moreover, Jones's analysis of the internal characteristics revealed that the greatest number of games emphasized dexterity (78), followed by exultation (36), strategy (23), pursuit (19), enigma (15), vertigo (13), imitation (10), and chance (9). In contrast, Murdock, in the *Ethnographic Atlas* (1967), maintains that Polynesian societies had only games of physical skill, or games of physical skill and chance. Only the Hawaiians were deemed to possess games demonstrating physical skill, chance, and strategy. Jones's study reveals Murdock's analysis to be limited in scope.

## Polynesian Pastimes

Some 22 traditional Polynesian sports have been identified from Jones's work as meeting Blanchard and Cheska's definition:

1. Racing: As a competitive sport, racing was popular among the Hawaiians, Maoris, Fijians, Samoans, and Tahitians. There were even professional runners in Hawaii called *kukini* who trained assiduously and were known for their speed and endurance. While the Maoris engaged in ceremonial challenge races, the Hawaiians gambled on the outcome of the races. Prizes are frequently mentioned as being awarded to the winners, who were the fastest or who demonstrated the most stamina. Children amused themselves by imitating the activities of the adults.
2. Swimming Races: Competitive races are documented by the early ethnographers, although prizes and rules do not appear to have been prevalent.
3. Canoe races: The ready access to water made canoe racing a natural sport for the Polynesians, and the races provided opportunities for practicing skills necessary for daily survival. The Hawaiians were fond of betting on canoe races, and gambling was an integral component of this sport. The size of the canoe (single or double) and outrigger varied, and sails were sometimes placed on the canoes to increase speed. In Rotuma canoe races for women were reported.
4. Cock-Fighting: Cock-fighting was observed in Hawaii, Tahiti, Samoa, and the Society Islands. Gambling was an essential aspect of the sport, particularly in Hawaii, and people at times staked all their possessions on the outcome, although the Tahitians do not appear to have engaged in betting on these contests between birds. In Hawaii, specific training methods and fighting techniques were developed.
5. Boxing: Of all the athletic sports, boxing appears to have been a favorite among spectators and competitors alike. The sport appeared to be very "modern," with fixed rules, referees, specific arenas, and many spectators. Fights were usually terminated by knockouts, and the winner remained in

the ring to accept the next challenge. The match would continue until no one challenged; then the winner would be declared. Bare fists appear to have been the most common style, although Culin reports that the fists were wrapped in *kapa* in Hawaii. On the Society Islands, boxing was not as popular as wrestling.

6. Wrestling: The combative sport of wrestling was popular among all the Polynesians, and, like boxing, it attracted a large audience. Early explorers, ethnographers, and even missionaries were fond of this competitive sport. Particularly noteworthy in Polynesian wrestling is the wide variety of wrestling styles: upright wrestling similar to that of today; wrestling when seated; hand wrestling; standing hand wrestling; pulling hooked fingers; foot pushing; and chest pushing.

7. Fencing: Various forms of fencing, or fighting with wooden sticks, were reported among the Hawaiians, Samoans, and Maoris. Samoans also indulged in clubfights where stalks of coconut leaf were used as a substitute for clubs.

8. Tug of War: Contests of "tug of war," usually between villages and kin groups, were organized as tests of physical strength. Variations of the contest included pulling on a long rope or pole, or clasping the waist of the person in front. No rules or techniques have ever been reported, but in Hawaii prizes were awarded to the winners.

9. Ball Games: A variety of games involving a spherical object were recorded, with balls made from *kapa* being the most prevalent. Tough stalks of plantain leaves twisted closely and firmly together were also used, as were pandanus leaves stuffed with grass. The most common ball game was a kicking form where the ball was struck with the foot in an attempt to kick it beyond the goal line. In Tahiti football was played more frequently by females than males, while in Hawaii a game involving "seizing the ball" was popular.

10. Bandy: A ball and stick game similar to hockey was reported in Tahiti. The ball was made of tightly bound studs of native cloth; the hitting club was a stick 0.9 to 1.2 meters (3 to 4 feet) long. Rules and regulations were not recorded.

11. Bowling Disks (Maika): An extremely popular competitive game in Hawaii to roll spherical disks along the ground in a prescribed area. The game, which involved intense gambling, resembled modern versions of lawn bowling, where often the disks are given a bias by the thrower to round a corner. On the island of Hawaii, for example, volcanic rock was commonly shaped into disks.

12. Pitching Disks: This Polynesian version of shuffleboard was usually played by four men, two against two, with the principal object being to knock an opponent's disk off a given spot.

13. Darts: Competitive dart throwing was a popular traditional Polynesian sport that involved the total community. Despite slight variations, the Maori *teka*, the Samoan *tiak,* and the Niue *ta-tika* were similar pastimes. Basically it involved the throwing of an ordinary rod to strike and rebound along the ground the greatest distance. Specific courses are prepared, and while oftentimes open paths or village spaces are utilized, some villages constructed permanent facilities. In Tahiti it was also a common pastime for women and children.

14. Spear Throwing: On Tonga and Samoa, a distinctive variant of throwing spears, or javelins, was particularly prevalent, and involved either throwing for distance or accuracy at a specific target such as a coconut on top of a pole. Separate competitions were held for chiefs, and sometimes whole villages played against each other.

15. Tree Climbing: Numerous ethnographers note the tree climbing skills of the Polynesians, but only among the Samoans was reference made to competitions.

16. Sledding *(holua):* The Hawaiians raised this unique sport to an elaborate level of organization and status. Sledding head first down steep hillsides on special sleds at breakneck speeds, the holua was one of the most dangerous but exciting Hawaiian sports. Courses sometimes 3.2 kilometers (2

miles) long were constructed with specially layered smooth surfaces, the majority of which have been located on the Island of Hawaii. The sleds were narrow and long, 3.4 to 5.5 meters (11 to 18 feet) long, and had two long runners with upturned tips. Although staying on the sled may have been one of the primary objects, the winners were those who went the farthest. Though a competition at the *Makahiki Festival*, the sport principally engaged royalty and chiefs. However, the intense gambling associated with the competition ensured participation by all classes.

17. Surfing: Of all the sports, the most widespread and common was surf riding. Traditionally, the boards were cut with stone implements from tree trunks, with children's boards being made from breadfruit wood. The length of the boards varied, with the long ones being from 2.7 to 5.5 meters (9 to 18 feet) long; the longest ones were found only in Hawaii. Again, gambling was integral to the sport, in which the most skillful or those who first arrived on the beach were declared the winners.

18. Games: Certain activities, although they satisfy the criteria for "sports," should realistically be considered as lower level sports, or even games. They include ring-casting, checkers (konane), stone dice, find the stone, hide the stone, stone hiding, and cat's cradle.

## Traditional Sports Festivals

In this overview of traditional sports, the Makahiki Games (often compared to the ancient Greek Olympics) of the ancient Hawaiians must be recognized. This multisports festival, which lasted for four lunar months from mid-October to mid-February, was an annual event. All work ceased, and war was *kapu* (forbidden), while all Hawaiians relaxed and enjoyed sports, dancing, and feasting. Top athletes came together to compete in sports such as surfing, the *holua*, spear-throwing, wrestling, and bowling disks.

## Effect of Colonization

Among all the cultures of Oceania, the most dedicated and comprehensive attempts to preserve and maintain their traditional games and sports have been made by the Hawaiians and the New Zealand Maoris.

Sports, games, and dances are, for most Maoris, "the most real and immediate manifestation of their culture and the most tangible expression, apart from skin color, of racial identity" (Armstrong 1964, 9). Former director of physical education at the University of Otago Dr. Phillip Smithells was the first to recognize the value of Maori activities, and in 1941 he wrote a series of articles on Maori dances, hakas, and games. Some two decades later, *Maori Action Songs* (Armstrong and Ngata, 1960) and *Maori Games and Hakas: Instructions, Words and Actions* (Armstrong, 1964) were published to develop appreciation and understanding of the Maori culture among the general populace. In support of this, the Physical Education Branch of New Zealand encouraged the publication of *Games and Dances of the Maori: A Guide Book for Teachers* (Wills, 1966). As well as the action songs, poi dances and hakas, detailed descriptions of hand, knuckle, stick, and string games were included. Enhancing the adoption of the book was the inclusion of teaching techniques that were of immense value to non-Maori teachers.

The Americanization of the Sandwich or Hawaiian Islands has been complete, and it is nowhere more obvious than in Waikiki. By 1830 most of the traditional culture had disappeared, and the new American-European culture emerged. The over 100 ancient Hawaiian games and sports disappeared with the enthusiastic reception of European culture. In 1934 President Franklin D. Roosevelt became one of the first Americans to call for a revival of the traditional sports, and a once-only *Makahiki Festival* was reenacted in 1935. A more successful venture was Aloha Week. It continues today, and its most popular event is the Moloka'i-to-O'ahu canoe race. In 1977, at Waimea Falls Park, the first permanent Hawaiian games site was constructed, and the *Makahiki Festival* is now organized annually in October.

## Indonesia

Indonesia, the largest archipelago in the world, lies at the crossroads of the continents of Asia and Australia. Stretching some 6,427 kilometers

(3,977 miles) between the Indian and Pacific Oceans, there are 13,700 scattered islands, of which the largest are Sumatra, Java, Kalimantan, Borneo, and Sulawesi. Irian Jaya, which is part of the island of New Guinea, is also part of Indonesia. The Portuguese, and later the Dutch, colonized the area. Today perhaps the most fascinating aspect of Indonesia is the incredible variety of people who reside there. There are over 100 distinct ethnic groups, 300 languages, and 4 main religions: Islam, Christianity, Hinduism, and Buddhism.

The unique cultures of the Irian Jaya are now being permanently threatened by Indonesia's forced assimilation policy, transmigration, and deforestation. As part of the acculturation process the Indonesian government introduced a game from Java called "Flip the Stick," hoping through games to change the attitudes and values of the children. Although the Dani children played eagerly, the game was not adopted because of its competitive nature. Instead the children transformed it, making it noncompetitive, with no winners or losers, and emphasizing participation. Like the Trobrianders with their cricket, the Dani children resisted change, restructuring a game to suit their own needs and values.

## Indonesian Pastimes

With the thousands of islands and disparate cultural groupings, there was a rich diversity of traditional sports, although only a few traditional sports have been identified.

1. Boat racing: This was generally for men, distances were variable but not overlong, and boats from the different locales were used.
2. Bull races: Although originally from Madura, bull racing is now a popular sport in the nation's regional festival.
3. Sepak Takraw: This is an aggressive, competitive team game that appears to be a cross between volleyball and football. A hollow rattan ball is kicked, or headed, with the object being to hit the ball over the net, which is about the height of a volleyball net. A point is scored if the opponent fails to return the ball. Two or three men usually comprise a team, and at times the hits can be very acrobatic.

4. Cock-fighting: The Balinese cock-fight has maintained its popular appeal, principally because of the gambling associated with it. Villagers take great pride in their birds and have developed intense training regimes to enhance their prowess and aggressiveness. The children imitate their elders by catching crickets and organizing cricket fights.

## Conclusion

It is important to remember that the term "sport" has really quite limited application to these preindustrialized societies of Oceania. Only the Polynesians, particularly the Hawaiians, displayed complex social organizations and technologies that enabled highly organized, institutionalized competitive sports to emerge. The architectural finesse of the *holua* courses indicates the technological complexity of the society.

Competition, and the determining of winners and losers, was generally accepted in the various societies as being the essential characteristic of a sport. However, the simpler the society, the less concern with the outcome, and the more emphasis on collaborative play, turn taking, and participation. Overall, there is a certain commonality of games despite the considerable geographical separation of cultures.

—Reet Howell

**See also** Bandy; Boomerang Throwing; Boxing; Cockfighting; Darts; Hockey, Field; Shinty; Surfing; Takraw; Tug of War.

**Bibliography:** Armstrong, Alan. (1964) *Maori Games and Haka.* Wellington, NZ: A. H. and A. W. Reid.

Armstrong, Alan, and R. Ngata. (1960) *Maori Action Songs.* Wellington, NZ: A. H. and A. W. Reid.

Barton, F. R. (1908) "Children's Games in British New Guinea." *Journal of the Royal Anthropological Institute* 37: 259–279.

Basedow, H. (1925) *The Australian Aborigine.* Adelaide, Australia: F. W. Pearce and Sons.

Bevridge, P. (1883) "On the Aborigines Inhabiting the Great Lacustrine and Riverine Depression of the Lower Murray, Lower Murrumbidgee, Lower Lachlan and Lower Darling." *Journal and Proceedings of the Royal Society of New South Wales* 17: 19–74.

Birket-Smith, K. (1960) *Primitive Man and His Ways.* London: Odhams Press.

Blanchard, Kendall, and Alyce Cheska. (1985) *The Anthropology of Sport: An Introduction.* South Hadley, MA: Bergin and Garvey.

Dawson, J. (1936) *Australian Aborigines: The Language and Customs of Several Tribes of Aborigines in the Western District of Victoria.* Melbourne: G. Robertson.

Embree, J. F. (1948) "Kickball and Some Other Parallels between Siam and Micronesia." *Journal of Siam Society* 37, 1.

Firth, Raymond. (1983) "A Dart Match in Tikopia: A Study in the Sociology of Primitive Sport." In *Play, Games and Sports in Cultural Context,* edited by J. Harris and R. Park. Champaign, IL: Human Kinetics.

Geertz, C. (1972) "Deep Play: Notes on the Balinese Cockfight." In *The Interpretation of Cultures,* edited by C. Geertz. New York: Basic Books, 412–453.

Haddon, A. C. (1890) "The Ethnography of the Western Tribes of Torres Strait." *Journal of the Royal Anthropological Institute of Great Britain and Ireland* 19.

———. (1912) *Reports of the Cambridge Anthropological Expedition to the Torres Straits.* Vol. 4. Cambridge: Cambridge University Press.

Hannemann, E. F. (1959) "Games and Modes of Entertainment in the Past among the People of the Madang District." *Mankind* 5, 8: 333–345.

Harney, W. E. (1952) "Sport and Play amidst the Aborigines of the Northern Territory." *Mankind* 4, 9: 377–379

Hassell, E. (1936) "Notes on the Ethnology of the Wheelman Tribe of South-Western Australia." *Anthropos* 31: 679–711.

Holmes, J. H. (1908) "Introductory Notes on the Toys and Games of Elema, Papuan Gulf." *Journal of Royal Anthropological Institute* 37: 280–288.

Howell, Reet A., and Maxwell L. Howell. (1987) *A History of Australian Sport.* Sydney: Shakespeare Head Press.

———. (1992) *The Genesis of Sport in Queensland: From the Dreamtime to Federation.* St. Lucia: University of Queensland Press.

Howell, M. L., R. A. Howell, and K. Edwards. (1993) "Wrestling among the Australian Aborigines." Paper presented at ASSH-NASSH Joint Conference, Hawaii.

Howitt, A. W. (1904) *The Native Tribes of South-East Australia.* London: Macmillan.

Huizinga, Johan. (1950) *Homo Ludens: A Study of the Play Element in Culture.* Boston: Beacon Press.

Jones, Kevin. (1967) "Games and Physical Activities of the Ancient Polynesians and Relationships to Culture." M.A. thesis. University of Alberta, Canada.

Krieger, H. W. (1943) *Island Peoples of the Western Pacific: Micronesia and Melanesia.* Washington, DC: Smithsonian Institution.

Kruger, Gundolf. (1990) "Sport in the Context of Non-European Cultural Tradition: The Examples of Hawaii." In *Ritual and Records: Sports Records and Quantification in Pre-Modern Societies,* edited by J. M. Carter and A. Krueger. New York: Greenwood Press.

Lansley, Keith L. (1969) "The Contributions of Play Activities to the Survival of Traditional Culture in Four Melanesian Societies." M.A. thesis, University of Alberta, Canada.

McCarthy, F. D. (1958) "String Figures of Australia." *Australian Museum Magazine* 12, 8.

Mead, M. (1937) "The Samoans." In *Co-operation and Competition among Primitive Peoples,* edited by Margaret Mead. New York: McGraw-Hill.

Mitchell, D. (1967) *Ancient Sports of Hawaii.* Honolulu,HI: Bishop Museum.

Murdock, George P. (1967) *Ethnographic Atlas.* Pittsburgh: University of Pittsburgh Press.

Noble, P. D. (1979) *String Figures of Papua New Guinea.* Papua New Guinea: Institute of Papua New Guinea Studies.

Peake, L. (1990) "Retaining Cultural Games: A South East Asian Perspective." In *Sport for All: Into the 1990's,* edited by J. Standeven, K. Hardman, and D. Fisher. Champaign, IL: Human Kinetics.

Plomley, N. J. B., ed. (1966) *Friendly Mission: The Tasmanian Journals & Papers of George Augustus Robinson, 1829–34.* Kingsgrove, New South Wales: Halstead Press.

Rosenstiel, A. (1976) "The Role of Traditional Games in the Process of Socialization among the Motu of Papua New Guinea." In *The Anthropological Study of Play,* edited by D. F. Lanay and B. A. Tindall. Cornell, NY: Leisure Press.

Roth, W. E. (1897) *Ethnological Studies among the North-Western Central Queensland Aborigines.* Brisbane: Government Printing Office.

———. (1902) "Games, Sports and Amusements." *North Queensland Ethnography.* Bulletin No. 4. Brisbane: Government Printing Office.

Salter, Michael Albert. (1967) "Games and Pastimes of the Australian Aboriginal." M.A. thesis. Edmonton: University of Alberta.

Smith, W. R. (1930) *Myths and Legends of the Australian Aboriginals.* London: George G. Harrop.

Spencer, B. (1928) *Wanderings in Wild Australia.* London: Macmillan.

Sutton-Smith, Brian. (1986) "The Fate of Traditional Games in the Modern World." *Association for the Anthropological Study of Play Newsletter* 12, 2: 8–13.

Velasco, M. R. (1936) "Native Filipino Sports and Games." *Mid-Pacific Magazine* 47, 1.

Wills, D. R., ed. (1966) *Games and Dances of the Maori: A Guide Book for Teachers.* Wellington: Government Printer.

Worsnop, T. (1897) *The Prehistoric Arts, Manufactures, Works, Weapons, etc. of the Aborigines of Australia.* Adelaide: Government Printing Office.

Writer, Larry (1988). "Rurutu's Amazing Rock Litters." *Pacific Islands Monthly* (May): 24–25.

# Trampolining

For thousands of years, earthbound humans have eagerly sought new ways of escaping gravity. The sports of tumbling and acrobatics, among the oldest expressions of this yearning, were joined in the twentieth century by trampolining. To enthusiasts and serious athletes alike, trampolining offers an exhilarating form of exercise that develops

*The heights attainable on the trampoline allow maneuvers other gymnasts could not attempt. French trampolinist Lionel Pioline flies through the air in front of L'Hotel de Ville in Paris.*

balance, timing, muscular control, and coordination. These attributes also attract athletes from other sports who use trampolining as part of their conditioning programs. There are national competitions in many countries, and world trampoline championships are held every two years. In recent decades, male and female athletes from the Soviet Union and, since 1991, Russia have been the most frequent winners of world championship titles.

## Origins

The ability to jump into the air and remain airborne for as long as possible while performing maneuvers has long been a goal of acrobats, gymnasts, and tumblers. Eskimos play a game in which a group of people hold the edges of a tightly stretched walrus-skin and take turns tossing one another into the air. Elsewhere in the world, devices such as the catapult and springboard have been used by tumblers and acrobats

to attain crowd-pleasing heights. According to circus legend, it was a nineteenth-century professional tumbler named Du Trampoline who came up with the idea of adapting the safety nets used by aerialists for use as part of tumblers' routines. However apocryphal that legend (and since *trampolín* means "springboard" in Spanish, suspicion is in order) professional acrobats and tumblers used something like a trampoline for many years before the modern apparatus was invented. The American comic actor, Joe E. Brown (1892–1973), who trained on an early form of trampoline as a young man, credited the sport with allowing him to learn and perfect some of the routines he used in his performances. In 1936, an American diving and tumbling champion, George Nissen, built the prototype of the modern apparatus and the sport of trampolining, at first called "rebound tumbling," was born.

With the outbreak of World War II, the sport attracted the interest of the U.S. military, who incorporated it into the exercise program for airmen. The sport was viewed as an ideal exercise for promoting physical conditioning and mental confidence while simultaneously releasing the tensions produced by an intensive training schedule. After the war, enthusiasm for the sport spread rapidly among physical educators and gymnasts. Competitive trampolining was introduced in the United States as a special event at the 1947 Amateur Athletic Union (AAU) meet in Dallas, Texas, and was included in the Pan-American Games in 1954. Interest soon spread to Great Britain, Europe, South Africa, and Japan. The first world championships were held in Great Britain in 1964 and, beginning in 1969, have been held every two years.

## Practice

The modern trampoline consists of a resilient "bed," made of canvas, nylon, or woven webbing, attached by springs to a metal frame that suspends the bouncing surface well above the ground. The area between the bed of the trampoline and the frame is padded to prevent the athlete from landing on the springs. While there is some variation in size and shape, most full-sized trampolines measure about 3.65 meters (12 feet) by 2.45 meters (8 feet).

During training, a tumbling belt is worn around the waist and attached by ropes to overhead pulleys, enabling the trampolinist to practice somersaults and other advanced aerial routines safely. Having "spotters," people prepared to catch an out-of-control trampolinist, positioned around the trampoline is another essential to safe trampolining.

When the trampolinist lands on the bed after a bounce, the springs and elasticity of the bed absorb the impact of the body, converting the force of the impact into a recoil that propels the gymnast into the air again. Trampolinists learn to use the energy of the recoil to attain optimum heights for the performance of various routines. The heights achievable on a trampoline allow for the execution of some acrobatic maneuvers that could not even be attempted by a floor-bound gymnast. Advanced trampolinists need about 7.6 meters (25 feet) of headroom to carry out their routines.

In learning to use a trampoline, one begins by bouncing gently on the springy surface, getting a feel for the relationships among one's own weight, the force of gravity, and the resilience of the apparatus, aiming to return to the center of the bed for each landing. Because it is possible to bounce many feet into the air, it is essential to learn early how to remain in control and how to stop quickly. Stopping, which is referred to in trampolining as "killing" the bounce, is accomplished by flexing the knees on landing. This action serves to absorb the propulsive force of the recoil and keeps the trampolinist from being launched into the air again..

With experience, the trampolinist learns to perform backward and forward somersaults and twists, as well as multiples and combinations of these maneuvers. It is also possible for two, even three, people to perform on a trampoline using either alternating or simultaneous bouncing techniques. Needless to say, group trampolining demands teamwork, close coordination, and precise timing since the athletes must share the rather limited area of the trampoline bed for their take-offs and landings.

In trampoline competition, as in gymnastics, competitors are judged on their performance of compulsory and voluntary routines. In each case, a competitor performs a ten-bounce routine in which a different maneuver is completed on each of the consecutive bounces, with no extra bounces in between, and the trampolinist must land on his or her feet after the tenth maneuver of the routine. The elements of the routine are rated according to degree of difficulty and competitors gain or lose points according to their skill at performing them.

—Bonnie Dyer-Bennet

**See also** Gymnastics.

**Bibliography:** Griswold, Larry. (1966) *Trampoline Tumbling.* New York and South Brunswick, NJ: A. S. Barnes.

Hunn, David. (1979) *The Complete Book of Gymnastics.* Secaucus, NJ: Chartwell Books.

# Trap and Skeet Shooting

**See** Shooting, Clay Target

# Trapball

Trapball is one of a number of games once played widely in England, Scotland, Wales, Ireland, and France. What distinguished trapball and its variants from other batting games is that the ball was not pitched by a player. Rather, the ball was propelled into the air either by a mechanical device—the "trap"—or by some other special procedure. The ball, thus "auto-pitched," was then batted into play. Some versions of the game were scored and competitive, with team players taking turns batting and fielding. Thus, trapball and its older variants may be considered precursors to both modern cricket and baseball.

It is well documented that trapball was played in the British Isles during the fourteenth century. However, since the records in question refer to the one of the most involved mechanical versions of the game, it is probable that less sophisticated forms were played at an earlier time. Games were often associated with Christian fairs and festivals that were held around Easter, especially Shrove Tuesday, Easter Monday, and Whitsuntide. The specific origins of trapball remain unknown.

In trying to reconstruct the nature of trapball, it is well to remember with regard to medieval ball games in general that many of them were played according to highly flexible rules. It may be too much to say, as some authorities do, that British folk games were played as "savage brawls" with an "excitement akin to that aroused in battle," but trapball of whatever sort was no doubt a somewhat unregulated affair by contemporary standards. Also confounding attempts to get a clear picture of such medieval (and later) folk games is the number of regional variations.

Trapball was played by many names, some of them seen in the following list compiled by the nineteenth century English folklorist, Alice Bertha Gomme. All were ball games that were played in teams by bat or stick-wielding contestants:

| | |
|---|---|
| Bad | Bandy-cad |
| Baddin | Bandy-hoshoe |
| Bandy | Bandy-wicket |
| Bandy-ball | Bittle-battle |

*Trapball refers to any number of ball and bat games in which the ball is pitched by either mechanical devices or set on a stand. Such games can be seen as the ancestors of baseball and hockey, among other sports.*

| | |
|---|---|
| Buzz and Bandy | Kibel |
| Cat and Dog | Kirk the Gussie |
| Cat and Dog Hole | Kit-Cat |
| Catchers | Lobber |
| Cat i' the Hole | Munshets |
| Chinnup | Nur and Spel |
| Chow | Peg and Stick |
| Church and Mice | Rounders |
| Codlings | Scrush |
| Common | Shinney |
| Crab-Sowl | Sow-in-the-Kirk |
| Crooky | Stones |
| Cuck-ball | Stool-ball |
| Dab-an-Thricker | Tip-cat |
| Doddart | Trap-bat & Ball |
| Hawkey | Tribet |
| Hockey | Troap |
| Hornie Holes | Trounce Ball |
| Hummie | Trunket |
| Hurling | Waggles |
| Jowls | |

Many of these games, as the names suggest, are versions or precursors of bandy or other hockey-like games, but many others are like trap-ball in that a player must "auto-pitch" the same projectile that he then strikes.

To take an example, "tip-cat" and similarly named games, required, not a ball but, instead, a "cat"—a doubly-conical piece of wood some six inches long from tip to tip—which was lain flat on the hard ground. When struck at either end, the "cat" would spin up into the air where it could then be batted away. One can see the principle at work by rapping sharply the end of a pencil that has been lain on a hard, flat surface. After a bit of practice, the pencil will spin up into the air, but the degree of control required to produce a "battable" trajectory will quickly convince one that "tip-cat" was a game requiring considerable skill.

Another form of the game, "Knur [or nur] and Spel" is still played in the north of England, and particularly in Yorkshire. There are three versions of this game, but all are auto-pitched. In one type, the "knur," a ball only the size of a large marble, is set into a wooden and metal mechanism—the "spel." The spel, being tapped with a player's golf-like club, releases the ball. The ball, once airborne, is swatted away as far as possible, great distance being the only goal of the game.

A form of trapball imported into colonial New England was sometimes called "tribbet" and solved the "auto-pitching" problem differently. The end of a stick—or bone—was placed into a hole in the ground. A ball was then placed into the hole and the protruding end of the stick struck with the bat. This sufficed to get the ball into a hittable position.

Trapball required a "trap," a wooden device, mounted on a stand, shaped somewhat like a shoe with the "heel" portion hollowed out and a lever fixed into it on which the ball rested. One end of the lever extended out of and slightly above the "shoe" itself. When smartly struck by the bat, the level catapulted the ball—usually a hard wooden knot an inch or two in diameter—out of the trap where it could then be batted out into the field by the same player. The bat itself was often a broad and flat, almost like a racket, but it was sometimes round and only an inch and one-half in diameter.

In most forms of the game there was a batting and a fielding side. There are few indications as to team size, though six to eight on a side seems to have been general. The field was of variable dimensions and, sometimes, was marked at a given distance from the trap so that balls going outside the mark were deemed unplayable. For the most part, however, the batsman attempted to strike the ball as far as possible, while fielders attempted to catch it or, failing that, retrieve it

quickly and "bowl" it back toward the trap.

In one version an "out" occurred only if the ball struck the trap, while in another version the ball had only to come to rest within one bat's length of the trap. In most versions, apparently, if the ball were caught, the batting side "ins" were out and became fielders, but by other rules the batting side was allowed three outs before being required to relinquish its turn to the other team.

—Alan Trevithick

**See also** Bandy; Hockey, Field; Hockey, Ice; Hurling; Rounders; Shinty.

**Bibliography:** Aspin, Jehoshaphat. (1925) *A Picture of the Manners, Customs, Sports and Pastimes of the Inhabitants of England.* London: J. Harris.

Dunning, Eric, and Kenneth Sheard. (1979) *Barbarians, Gentlemen and Players.* Oxford: Martin Robinson.

Gomme, Alice Bertha. (1898) *The Traditional Games of England, Scotland, and Ireland.* London: David Nutt.

Guttmann, Allen. (1986) *Sports Spectators.* New York: Columbia University Press.

Strutt, Joseph. (1876) *The Sports and Pastimes of the People of England.* London: Chatto and Windus.

# Triathlon

The term "triathlon" describes a multisport endurance race that combines competition in three distinct disciplines. The most typical form of triathlon involves having participants swim, bike, and run (usually in that order) for specified distances. Participants win (or perform well) to the extent that they are the fastest among the competitive field to essay the entire racecourse.

The best-known triathlon is the Hawaii Ironman Triathlon (HIT). It is an ultradistance event that involves a 2.4-mile (3.9 kilometers) swim followed by 112 miles (180 kilometers) of cycling and a 26.2-mile (42 kilometers) or marathon run. As is true in the vast majority of triathlons, a participant completes the events sequentially with only brief stoppages or slowdowns (known as transitions) to change equipment and clothes.

*Developed in the California of the 1970s, the triathlon has rapidly become an institutionalized sport around the world. Here hundreds of participants jump into the Seine on the first leg of this 1989 French triathlon.*

These transitions count against the triathlete's total race time. Thus, because brief seconds or minutes can separate competitors, many triathletes train for the transitions as well as the three sports that compose the triathlon.

Most competition among triathletes occurs at shorter distances than those in ironman contests (of which the HIT is only one). Still, all triathlons are clearly endurance events taking nearly an hour to complete for the best athletes in even the shortest races. Several "levels" of distance can be specified. As the name implies, a half-ironman (or long course) triathlon usually involves a swim of about 1.2-miles (2 kilometers), a bike of 55 to 60 miles (88 to 95 kilometers), and a run of 9.3 to 13.1 miles (15 to 21 kilometers). Approximately 75 percent of triathlons in recent years have occurred at the popular international dis-

tance. These races involve 1.5-kilometer (0.93 miles) swims, 40-kilometer (24.86-mile) bike stages, and 10-kilometer (6.2-mile) run courses. A triathlon at this distance will appear in the Olympic Games scheduled for the Bimillenium in Sydney. Finally, the grossly misnamed *sprint-distance* triathlons range around 0.25 miles (400 meters) for the swim, 10 to 20 miles (15–32 kilometers) on the bike, and a 2-5-mile (3.2-kilometer) run.

The International Olympic Committee (IOC) currently has an orientation toward removing sports from the Games and only reluctantly adding new sports. Given that IOC bent, the meteoric rise of triathlon in the Olympic firmament is truly remarkable. The sport has moved from a first formal event in the mid-1970s to a full-fledged Olympic event in just over 25 years.

## Origins

The sport of triathlon emerged in California in the early 1970s (Jonas 1986; Tinley 1986). Thus, it is new enough that significant numbers of individuals acquainted with the development of triathlon since its inception can share their perceptions. This affords a unique view of the evolution of the sport precipitated through fewer reconstructive filters when compared to reports of other athletic events.

There are descriptions of the sport from triathletes in several countries (Tinley 1986; Ballesteros 1987; Lehenaff 1987). Still, although ethnographic descriptions are deemed important (Blanchard and Cheska 1985), there are few of them. There is one (somewhat dated) ethnographic description of triathlon in the United States (Hilliard 1988). It would be advantageous to have more.

Blanchard and Cheska (1985) have urged an eclectic approach at the early stages of the development of an anthropology of sport. They further suggest a cultural evolutionary model to guide the enterprise. In their work, they view sport as a cultural form that has paralleled the groups that engage in the activities. The approach is useful to an understanding of triathlon. Thus, Blanchard and Cheska (1985) offer support for a relationship between characteristics of sports and the type of culture that practices them. Their analysis does not focus on individual sports but instead on the several sports described for particular cultures.

Triathlon's recent emergence permits a tentative hypothesis that in the development of sport, ontogeny (how one sport develops) may again recapitulate phylogeny (how sports as a type of activity develops). Thus, as International Triathlon Union President Les McDonald noted, triathlon is "no longer the sport practiced by those happy-go-lucky California kids from the me-generation of the '70s and '80s." Early multisport athletes were, indeed, carefree young men who sought to combine some common elements of their lifestyle into a single race event. Those participants might be amused at the current high-tech sport that has focused on every aspect of triathlon with a single overarching concern—to increase the speed at which triathletes can complete an event. They might be agog at their sport's compiling a 134-page rulebook (Scott 1991). Clearly, for triathlon, development in sport means differentiation and complexity in much

the same way that cultural evolutionists might argue for culture.

## Practice

The work of Ingham and Loy (1993) embodies an interesting and fruitful approach to a social science attempt at understanding sport. Together they edited a volume predicated on the work of Raymond Williams that analyzes sport according to its fit to the dominant hegemony. Articles in the book examine both residual (ties to the past) and emergent (novel) aspects in various sporting subcultures with a view toward their impact on the cultural dynamic. A prime exemplar of the utility of this strategy is visible in the work of Donnelly (1993) in that volume. His chapter examines three specific sports and through them amplifies our comprehension of the dominant sports culture as well. Our understanding of triathlon may benefit from a similar analysis.

In reviewing the beginnings of triathlon (see Tinley 1986), it may seem that the sport itself emerged, in some sense, as a residual. The initial multisport event was only a small variant of a standard beach situation. One boy in the water says to another, "I'll race you to the refreshment stand." Quickly, they're off, first swimming to the shore and then running to the food vendor, perhaps eventually even racing home on their bikes. Slight formalization of that common occurrence produces an early multisport—and quintessentially amateur—event.

The dominant sport culture follows a U.S. model that supplanted a European (originally English, according to Donnelly 1993) model of the last century. The earlier culture valued sportsmanship among amateur participants (who trained and participated at their leisure). Participants often had general ability (as opposed to specific skill) and concerned themselves with "doing" more than winning. Ideally there also may have been a nostalgic hearkening to earlier times of romanticized struggle.

In contrast, the currently hegemonic U.S. model emphasizes skill, achievement (winning), and economic reward as its hallmarks. As the dominant sports culture incorporates specific athletic events, these events become increasingly commercial, bureaucratized, and professional. Training for and doing the sport and gaining sponsors become the athlete's occupation. Cognate occupations as

## Hawaii's Ironman Triathlon—Ultra Times Three

The seeds of the Hawaii Ironman Triathlon (HIT), among the most awe-inspiring sporting events in the world, were sown by early triathletes. Naval Commander John Collins had raced the earliest recorded triathlon in the Mission Bay area of San Diego around 1974. In 1977, with Navy Seal John Dunbar, he contrived to link Hawaii's most prestigious endurance events to stage a triathlon that it would take a man made of "iron" to win. The triathlon combined the difficult 2.4-mile Waikiki Rough Water Swim, the 112-mile Around-Oahu Bike Race, and the renowned Honolulu Marathon (Jonas 1986; Tinley 1986). The original 1978 HIT's twelve finishers were followed in 1979 by the first Ironwoman and 14 men, 13 of whom completed the race. Coverage by the widely read U.S. magazine, *Sports Illustrated,* fueled a tenfold participant increase in 1980.

HIT is the stuff of myth and legend. In the race's watershed year of 1982, several things happened to increase interest in the sport. Relocated to the big island of Hawaii, the year's two events inspired athletes to fantasize about the names Kona, Hawi, and the Queen K. Highway and about contesting an event that would take even the most gifted athletes eight to ten hours to complete.

Still, none of the occurrences that year shone as brilliantly as the finish to the women's contest in February. ABC television had carried the event into U.S. homes since 1980. Viewers saw women's leader Julie Moss, after a full day of racing, come within several hundred meters of the finish only to collapse from extreme glycogen depletion. Repeatedly Moss struggled on—by sheer will—until she could no longer. Finally, Kathleen McCartney passed, finishing first in front of an eerily-hushed crowd. Still, the remarkable Moss persevered, ultimately crawling the final 10 meters across the finish line into second place, history, and the hearts of those who viewed her struggle.

Moss's redoubtable courage touched deeply held values of the U.S. audience and thus caught the attention of Hollywood producers, who seized the opportunity and created a film account. Over the years literally millions have witnessed some version of that dramatic finish to the February 1982 Ironman. An Aphrodite, she beguiled those who witnessed the admixture of determination and physical depletion. Among those who watched, transfixed, was the eventual Mercury in the HIT pantheon, now Moss's husband. Mark Allen owns the course record and has won the last six times he has competed in the event.

The race has become a Mecca of triathlon, perhaps outstripping even the mystique of its counterpart in road racing, the Boston Marathon. As in the latter event, participants must qualify for the Hawaii Ironman via their performance in designated (demanding) races or by winning a slot by lottery.

—B. James Starr

spokespersons, coaches, media analysts, and clothing and equipment manufacturers or salespeople also arise.

Triathlon is moving along the path toward incorporation in the dominant sport culture. Thus, as noted above, triathlon will appear in the 2000 Olympics, only 11 years after the initial formation of an international governing body. There is a viable professional tour for both men and women competing in triathlons at various distances throughout the world. Sponsors flock to competitive triathletes and triathlons. Large corporations become title sponsors of popular triathlons or race series. Triathletes earn a living in the types of related callings noted above. There is also lower-key testimony to the intimate involvement of triathlon and commerce at Nike-town in Chicago. A major store in the chain of the international sporting goods giant, the Chicago facility closes in the evening at 8:07:45—Mark Allen's record time for the HIT.

In terms of bureaucracy, the International Triathlon Union (ITU) currently has a membership that includes nearly 120 national governing boards for triathlon, representing two million or more affiliated triathletes worldwide. National governing boards further differentiate into regional bureaucracies in some cases.

Residual components of earlier sport culture are visible in several aspects. One resistance is visible among the many triathletes who never join their national governing boards but instead pay a one-day licensing fee to participate in events sanctioned by the bureaucracy. Another residual derives from triathlon as a somewhat expensive and time-consuming pursuit. As such, it is primarily an activity of the middle class (and probably upper-middle class at that).

In addition, triathlon still has a strong commitment to its paradoxical amateurs. (These amateurs may be regarded as paradoxical due to the large investment of time, resources, and energy required to participate in their chosen sport). The national amateur age-group championships are televised each year. The sport, generalist by its very nature, is also clearly nurturant to fitness athletes such as the elderly and the physically challenged. There is often a focus in the televised HIT on a romanticized human interest side of the sport. Thus, for example, older competitors (in their seventies) have been among the featured triathletes. In 1989, the show prominently featured age-group triathlete Dick Hoyt, who completed the grueling HIT with his son Rick (who has cerebral palsy) in tow (literally on the swim). Rick rode in a specially constructed "basket" on the bike and a racing wheelchair on the run.

Without undue melodrama, there is something primal (the ultimate residual) about the sport. Here fit, healthy, and vigorous individuals striving alone yet as comrades against their personal demons, a grueling course, and even possible (although rare) death. Unsurprisingly, sublime feelings may result from such self-tests. More than just a "runner's high," the rapture that some triathletes report is probably overdetermined by both physical and psychological factors. The psychological framing includes a degree of awareness of the issues raised above. Also the framing may comprise feelings of control and of expending energy for unequivocal results based on merit (all features seen as increasingly rare nowadays).

Clearly several characteristics of triathlon are also emergent and have served to transform other sport subcultures and to become incorporated in the dominant culture. Most visible among these triathlon-based innovations are the aerobars and nondisk aerowheels that are now a common enough sight at professional bicycle races (notably time trials) and the term "cross-training." Other triathlon-based bike developments include aerodynamic drinking systems, lighter-weight materials (for bikes and their components), and new frame geometry. Advances in nutrition, clothing, and both physical and psychological features of endurance training have also diffused from triathlon to other sports. The use of heart rate monitors for training and racing provide another example of this type of technology diffusion.

In addition, there are triathlon-based novelties that are equivocal candidates for incorporation in the hegemonic sports culture. One involves the use of wetsuits in swim competitions. The emergent form of mountain bike (with the bike component off-road) or in-line skate triathlons also are of uncertain potential impact.

Despite the relative youth of this sport form, the emergence of mountain bike and ultra-endurance (e.g., double-ironman) triathlons may reflect a nostalgic search for authenticity in the sport. There is a strong belief among many triathletes that the *raison d'être* of triathlon is the intensely personal struggle to overcome the myriad sources of self-doubt. It involves dedication and fortitude that places the greatest premium on individual effort. The increasing technological orientation, bureaucratization, and commercialization of the sport detract from that focus. Interestingly, the belief also underscores the major current controversy in the sport, which concerns drafting.

Drafting occurs when one triathlete follows another too closely. The trailing athlete obtains an advantage in that the lead individual bears the brunt of the physical impact of the fluids (air/wind and water/current) around them. Although the energy savings is minimal to a trailing runner, it is highly significant on the bike (and to some extent on the swim). Drafting on the swim is usually not regarded as a problem for various reasons. During the bike phase, on the other hand, the practice has been highly regulated by the national governing boards. Thus, it is illegal to draft in most sanctioned races. Much of the effort of triathlon officials (triathlon's referees) is devoted to the prevention and elimination of bike drafting.

Currently the ITU is battling to make drafting legal, arguing primarily on the basis of commercial appeal. Most pure bike races (other than time trials) are draft-legal and commercially successful. The television presentations of the popular Tour de France include recurrent commentaries on the many tactical and strategic considerations that surround breakaways from the main peloton. Winning requires teamwork *and* individual skill. It also often involves more bike-handling skill than the draft-illegal format. A momentary lapse by one rider can cause problems for several others. This resistance to the hegemonic sport culture is currently being bitterly contested. The eventual denouement is unpredictable.

—B. James Starr

**Bibliography:** Almekinders, Louis, Sally Almekinders, and Tom Roberts. (1991) *Triathlon Training.* Winston-Salem, NC: Hunter Textbooks.

Ballesteros, Joaquin (1987) *El libro del triatlon.* Madrid: Arthax.

Blanchard, Kendall, and Alyce Cheska. (1985) *The Anthropology of Sport: An Introduction.* South Hadley, MA: Bergin & Garvey.

Cedaro, Rod, ed. (1993) *Triathlon: Achieving Your Personal Best.* New York: Facts on File.

Cook, Jeff S. (1992) *The Triathletes: A Season in the Life of Four Women in the Toughest Sport of All.* New York: St. Martin's Press.

Donnelly, Peter. (1993) "Subcultures in Sport: Resilience and Transformation." In *Sport in Social Development: Traditions, Transitions, and Transformations,* edited by Alan G. Ingham and John W. Loy. Champaign, IL: Human Kinetics.

Edwards, Sally. (1983) *Triathlon, a Triple Fitness Sport: The First Complete Guide To Challenge You to a New Total Fitness.* Chicago: Contemporary Books.

———. (1985) *The Triathlon Training and Racing Book.* Chicago: Contemporary Books.

Habernicht, Jorg. (1991) *Triathlon Sportgeschichte.* Bochum, Germany: N. Brockmeyer.

Hilliard, Dan C. (1988) "Finishers, Competitors, and Pros: A Description and Speculative Interpretation of the Triathlon Scene." *Play and Cultur,* 1: 300–313.

Horning, Dave, and Gerald Couzens. (1985) *Triathlon, Lifestyle of Fitness: Swim! Bike! Run!* New York: Pocket Books.

Ingham, Alan G., and John W. Loy, eds. (1993) *Sport in Social Development: Traditions, Transitions, and Transformations.* Champaign, IL: Human Kinetics.

Jonas, Steven. (1986) *Triathloning for Ordinary Mortals.* New York: W. W. Norton.

Lehenaff, Didier D. A. (1987) *Votre Sport le Triathlon.* Paris: Bertrand.

Plant, Mike. (1987) *Iron Will: The Heart and Soul of Triathlon's Ultimate Challenge.* Chicago: Contemporary Books.

———. (1987) *Triathlon: Going the Distance.* Chicago: Contemporary Books.

Scott, Gary P., ed. (1991) *The 1991 Triathlon Competition Guide.* Colorado Springs, CO: Triathlon Federation/USA.

Tinley, Scott, with Mike Plant. (1986) *Winning Triathlon.* Chicago: Contemporary Books.

# Trotting

**See** Horse Racing, Harness

# Truck and Tractor Pulling

The sport of truck and tractor pulling has its roots in the midwestern United States. Over a period of 40 years, it has grown into a popular motor sport as it has branched out to other regions of America. In so doing, it has cultivated a wide appeal among many diverse groups. Still, it has not abandoned its rich rural heritage, using that as a platform on which to grow. Its rural heritage has also helped it translate to other regions of the world that share a common rural culture.

## Origins

The sport can trace its roots to America's farmland, giving it a "born in America" image. Farmers had long met to test the pulling prowess of their horse teams, so it was only a matter of time before they met to do the same for their tractors.

It is even possible to pinpoint a specific geographical region out of which the sport sprang. That region is the Midwest, the country's agricultural "heartland," where no vehicle is more highly revered than the tractor. It is little wonder that it became the foundation on which a sport was built. Competitive pulling is really only an extension of what the family tractor did on the farm and what it was built to do: pull. Truck and tractor pulling, but specifically tractor pulling, is rural America's contribution to motor sports.

Those origins explain why its rural image is so persistent and why its core audience has stayed so fiercely loyal. A contest involving vehicles that many spectators grew up with can forge deep bonds and create intense loyalty. However, the sport's current array of vehicles goes far beyond tractors. There are vehicles within the sport that have no tie to the sport's rural origins and may actually be as unfamiliar to rural audiences as tractors are to urban audiences. Indeed, these vehicles have more in common with the exotic, high-performance machines one sees in drag racing, for example. As a result, pulling has reached out to motor sports arenas and spectators, showing them that pulling includes other vehicles, too.

*Truck and tractor pulling, which originated with farmers testing the strength of their tractors in the American Midwest, remains largely confined to the rural United States.*

In the process it has achieved a moderate degree of growth, cultivated a "mainstream" motor sports image, and worked at shedding its image as a "fringe" motor sport.

Still, given its rural heritage, it is not surprising that a majority of the pulling events are held at state and county fairs and that tractors are still the sport's most recognizable vehicles. Pulling has not flourished in other regions of the United States as it has in the Midwest. This may be because of cultural attitudes. At first glance, the rural South, for example, would seem to be ideal tractor pulling territory, but so far it has met with limited success. What may explain this is the South's strong stock-car racing tradition. In the South, the tractor is not the icon it is in the Midwest, and rural Southern audiences perhaps don't relate to it as intensely as rural midwesterners do. However, the South has a strong following with regard to truck pulling. In fact, trucks as pulling vehicles is the South's contribution to pulling. Thus, pulling's inroads into the South, though

scattered, are very firm, as they are in rural New England and Canada. Except for California, the western United States is largely an untapped area.

The earliest recognized motorized pulling event is reputed to have taken place in 1929; that year, events were held in both Vaughansville, Ohio, and Bowling Green, Missouri. That puts pulling among America's oldest motor sports. However, the first stirrings of organized pulling did not begin until the 1950s. As one would expect with an infant sport, it encountered growing pains, not the least of which was a hodgepodge of rules. At this stage, pulling lacked structure and was more exhibition than true competition.

## Development

In 1969 this changed. Representatives from eight Midwest pulling states met in Indianapolis to establish uniform rules and to give the activity structure. Their action turned pulling into a bona

## Yankee Ingenuity and Pulling

If there is any characteristic that is typically American, it is "Yankee ingenuity." No group of individuals is more reflective of this characteristic than American farmers, who are the most avid participants in pulling. Farmers, a self-employed lot, have always had by virtue of necessity to "do it themselves." Why should pulling be any different. The Bosse brothers, who adopted the cross-box to pulling, are only the most well-known examples. They loved to tinker and build things.

Part of this "can-do" spirit may be explained by the "homegrown" nature of the sport. Early participants were forced to do all their own "manufacturing" because what they wanted to do to their vehicles wasn't commercially available. They couldn't buy parts to "soup-up" their tractor because what they were doing to their tractors went beyond its stock nature. As a result, everything had to be homemade. And look at the Modified vehicle. Before participants invented it, that vehicle did not exist. This vehicle had to be "invented" from the ground up.

This need spawned in time a cottage industry, peopled by folks who were mechanical geniuses and had a great reservoir of Yankee ingenuity. Yet as with any skill over time, some folks became better at it than others, specialization set in, and eventually businesses were born and thrived. Some ended up building chassis, some cut tires, and others transmissions and rear ends, while still others became experts at building turbochargers, the devices that make it possible for today's Super Stock tractors to attain 1800 horsepower, compared to today's stock tractor off the assembly line that produces in the range of 125–150 horsepower.

Whereas participants in other motor sports most likely got parts "off-the-shelf," each participant in pulling was forced to be his own factory, using his lathe and other specialized equipment to custom-make parts. The Allison engine offers the best example of this phenomenon.

They stopped factory production of the Allison engine at the end of World War II, yet they play a big role today powering Modified vehicles. Some participants have gone so far as to build specialized tools just to work on these antiquated engines. That is perhaps carrying "can do" to an extreme. Still, this "do-it-yourself" attitude is a source of intense pride as participants almost get more of a thrill out of building the vehicle and the parts than what the vehicle does on the track.

As time goes on, this "do-it-yourself" trend is changing, but it is still the rule rather than the exception.

—Michael B. Camillo

fide sport and led to the formation of the National Tractor Pullers Association (NTPA), which has since grown into America's premier sanctioning body for the sport. The organization has approximately 1,500 members and sanctions more than 325 events annually.

The basic premise upon which the sport was built has never changed. It is the classic contest between an irresistible force (the pulling vehicle) and an immovable object (the sled). The goal is for the pulling vehicle to go a specified distance—most commonly 91 meters (100 yards)—while it is the sled's job to stop the vehicle. He who goes the farthest wins the contest.

There have been many changes in the sport, such as the weight classes in which the vehicles compete and new kinds of vehicles, such as pick-ups and semis. But by far the most significant changes have taken place on the side of technology, as participants climbed the horsepower ladder. In the sport's earliest years, participants competed with the same vehicle they used on the farm. The phrase "pull-on-Sunday, plow-on-Monday" with the same vehicle succinctly describes early practices. But as changes were made to the drive train and the engine, the all-purpose tractor that was used for competition one day, for farm chores the next, slipped into history. What emerged was a vehicle used strictly for pulling competition.

Another factor that changed the sport was the sled. Early on, sleds were simple, deadweight pulling platforms, loaded with concrete blocks, a tractor, or a truck. Another early type was the step-on sled. Simply stated, people were positioned along the track and stepped onto the sled as it was pulled by. What eventually took the place of these early sleds was the introduction of the mechanical weight transfer sled. The credit for this introduction goes to Billy K. Watkins (1929– ) of Illinois, who in 1970 was granted a patent for his sled. This sled is the direct ancestor of the sophisticated pulling sleds used today.

From the mid-1950s to the mid-1970s, pulling vehicles were restricted to a speed of 13 kilometers (8 miles) per hour. When this rule was abolished in 1974, the nature of the sport, with regard to both vehicle performance and fan appeal, changed dramatically. Speed entered the game and brute pulling force took a back seat.

In the beginning, organized pulling was the province of only two kinds of vehicles. One was the stock tractor, a vehicle just as it came from the factory, with no modifications to either the engine or drivetrain. Even now, there are rules that demand that pulling tractors must maintain stock sheet-metal appearance, ensuring fan identification with the vehicle. Eventually, the stock tractor went through a series of technological changes until it became today's Super Stock tractor.

The other kind of vehicle also started out as a stock tractor, but there the similarity ends. Participants took a stock tractor and replaced its engine. Examples of the engines used in this "modified" tractor came from automobiles, airplanes, even tanks. This type of vehicle is known as Modified. The Modified vehicle took another path change when two Ohio brothers, Carl Bosse (1943– ) and Paul Bosse (1945– ), adapted some engineering they saw used in other applications to the sport of pulling. What they devised was a way to hook up more than one engine and send that combined power on a single driveshaft. Their "invention" was called the crossbox and it changed the face of pulling forever.

Following the Bosse brothers, Modified competitors took stock tractors and gutted them, leaving only the frame, and then piling on engines. It led eventually to the multi-engined vehicle that is today the sport's most significant pulling vehicle from the standpoint of power.

## Outlook

Although the sport is basically a rural American phenomenon, its adoption outside America has been relatively easy, since all it takes to play is a vehicle. Early on, the United States provided the majority of pulling vehicles for those beyond its shores who were interested in the sport. Many of the vehicles that went to Europe were once owned by U.S. participants. As more and more Europeans became interested in pulling, more and more vehicles were sold overseas. That slow trickle, which began in the late 1970s, eventually built up enough vehicles that pulling was launched in Europe in 1978. As in America, the appeal of pulling in Europe is to a largely rural audience. Today, more than 10 countries in Europe participate in the sport, which is run much as it is in America. They have their own rules, though to a large extent they have used U.S. rules as their guideline. They conduct their own events and have a sanctioning body that is patterned largely after the NTPA. Their sanctioning body is the European Tractor Pulling Committee.

—Michael B. Camillo

**Bibliography:** *Puller.* (1971– ) Worthington, OH: National Tractor Pullers Association.

# Truck Racing

Truck racing includes a wide variety of motor sports in which utility and recreational vehicles compete rather than automobiles. It encompasses many types of vehicles, including pickup trucks and sport-utility vehicles.

Trucks have become widely accepted as racing vehicles since 1970. Certain types of contemporary truck racing are very similar to their automotive counterparts, or are divisions of auto-oriented racetrack sports, such as National Association of Stock Car Auto Racing (NASCAR) Super Truck racing. Other trucking sports, like Monster Trucks and truck-pulling contests, are more specifically based on the size, power, and versatility of utility vehicles.

Pickups and other utility vehicles have long been a fixture in off-road racing events, which also feature motorcycles and automobiles. Off-road racing includes rallies and other events on unpaved roads and trails or over open countryside. Many vehicles in off-road events use four-wheel drive, a mechanical system that gives a vehicle greater traction in snow, mud, sand, and other conditions by providing direct turning power from the engine to all tires, rather than just two. Four-wheel-drive vehicles are often called 4x4's.

## Origins

Contemporary truck racing has evolved from several different sources. In some ways it paral-

*A pickup competes in the Short Course Off-Road Enterprises (SCORE) World Championships, held on a short dirt-track course that duplicates the rugged terrain of longer outdoor off-road courses.*

lels the overall history of automobile racing. Off-road racing is actually the original form of automotive sport from the time before racetracks were established. Truck racing also has a distinct heritage, such as the rural tradition of using work machinery in competitive events like tractor-pulling contests.

Trucks and all-terrain vehicles were originally designed for hauling, traveling in difficult conditions, and other utilitarian purposes. They were sturdy, powerful, and versatile, but they were not usually considered suitable for general passenger transportation or recreational or competitive driving.

The first popular four-wheel-drive system was developed and marketed in the midwestern United States by blacksmiths Otto Zachow and William Besserdich after 1908. Four-wheel-drive vehicles were widely used in World Wars I and II. Among the most famous were the rugged cars known as Jeeps. After World War II, an increasing

number of people used them to explore the countryside, participate in rallies, or compete in off-road events. Pickup trucks, meanwhile, were used increasingly for general personal transportation and recreational driving. Pickups became closely associated with the rural lifestyle.

For many years, interest in these vehicles was limited to small groups of enthusiasts, and competitions were often very informal. That began to change around 1960, as light pickup trucks and other utility vehicles started to became more popular among general consumers. Manufacturers developed a wide variety of hybrids that combined characteristics of passenger cars with utility vehicles, such as the International Harvester Scout, which resembled a very large station wagon. An array of similar vehicles from Ford, General Motors, and other manufacturers were released. These new pickup trucks, vans and sport-utility vehicles placed more emphasis on comfort, handling, and speed, and some could switch from four-wheel drive to two-wheel drive for different conditions.

In the 1970s and 1980s consumer utility and recreational vehicles became major segments of the automotive market. By 1995, they were outselling conventional sedans in many regions. This prompted a parallel surge of interest in the use of these vehicles in sports. Television also made events like remote off-road races more accessible to general viewers.

## Practice

The truck-racing scene went through much flux in the 1980s and early 1990s. New sports were developed, and major racing associations added events or divisions for trucks and sport-utility vehicles. While most truck racing is focused on pickups and other small vehicles, large tractor-trailer cabs are also raced. Although not all of the new truck-racing circuits or events succeeded or survived, utility vehicles were well-established in competitive motor sports by the mid-1990s.

Pickups and other recreational and utility vehicles compete in a variety of off-road sports, from shorter timed races to longer endurance events. Among them are the Baja series of desert races, the Pikes Peak Hillclimb, and the Camel Trophy Mundo Maya '95, a grueling 20-day race through Central America.

Prominent racer and promoter Mickey Thompson (who died in 1988) developed stadium truck racing, a sport that combined off-road with closed-track racing. In 1973, Thompson formed Short Course Off-Road Enterprises (SCORE) to promote this sport, which features a short dirt-track course that duplicates the mud, hills, and other features of longer outdoor off-road courses. These dirt tracks were set up in outdoor racetracks and later in indoor stadiums. Other truck sports also take place in these venues, including truck-pulling competitions.

Trucks gained an important foothold in the world of traditional closed-track stock-car racing in 1994, NASCAR established a new Super Truck division. Super Trucks are modified pickups that adhere to rules and guidelines for engines and body construction similar to those for NASCAR stock cars. Super Truck races are much like NASCAR's Winston Cup series and other stock car events. Trucks also became more widely used

in drag-racing, and the National Hot Rod Association established a category for modified trucks used as dragsters.

More flamboyant trucking events have also gained popularity. Monster Trucking is a mix of sport and general entertainment that features powerful modified pickup trucks with gigantic tires of 66 inches or larger. They fly off ramps over old cars lined up side by side. The spectacle of the trucks crushing the cars is one of the major attractions for fans.

Monster Trucking originated in the mid-1970s when a Missouri mechanic named Bob Chandler began to modify pickup trucks by adding larger tires and special body parts from military vehicles. As the tires of his experimental trucks became ever bigger, they attracted increasing attention. In 1981, he and a friend, Jim Kramer, unofficially invented the sport of Monster Trucking by driving a modified pickup truck off a ramp to crush an abandoned car in a field. Their original Ford truck, named Bigfoot, became a popular attraction, and Monster Truck shows became a major spectator sport.

—John Townes

**Bibliography:** Geist, Bill. (1994) *Monster Trucks & Hair-in-a-Can: Who Says America Doesn't Make Anything Anymore?* New York: Putnam. Excerpted as "Really Big Trucks." *New York Times Sunday Magazine* (23 October 1994).

Stambler, Irwin. (1984) *Off Roading: Racing and Riding.* Toronto: General Publishing Co.

Voeggelin, Rick. (1995) "Pickup On This: They Race Trucks, Don't They?" *Popular Mechanics* (March).

# Tug of War

Tug of war is a contest of strength and skill that pits two teams of grunting, groaning, and grimacing competitors against each other as they pull on opposite ends of a thick rope. To the uninitiated, the spectacle seems to involve only brute strength. In actual fact there are significant elements of skill and technique and, during the event, there is a remarkable level of team cohesion as members pull together and maintain a high degree of tension on the rope. A good case can be made for tug of war demanding the most complete "total" body involvement of any athletic activity. The fingers grip around the rope, while the more powerful muscle groups of the shoulder, back, and thighs contract vigorously and violently over a period of several minutes.

Although contests like tug of war were long practiced informally in the English countryside and despite a brief Olympic career (1900–1920), the event has existed on the margins of "accepted" sport. However, in 1958 a Tug-of-War Association was formed in Great Britain; at that time, there were nearly 1,000 clubs. The record for the longest pull according to Amateur Athletic Association rules (where lying on the ground or "burying" feet are prohibited) is one of 8 minutes, 18.2 seconds, between the Royal Army Service Corps (Feltham) and the Royal Marines (Portsmouth Division) at the Royal Tournament, England, in June 1938.

## Origins

Tug of war is said to have originated in the harvest-gathering of ancient China; to have been used to train slaves to haul stones up the Sphinx; to have developed from the routines used by sailors in hoisting sails and by soldiers in hauling guns up the mountains of India's north-west frontier.

The *Dictionary of British Folk-Lore* (Gomme 1898) described the evolution of this ludic activity out of a basic catching and rhyming game. Two people, it was argued, stand facing one another and hold their linked arms in the air. They chant a series of lines during which time the rest of the play/activity group skip through. Whenever the words are ended, the arms sweep down as the two people making the "bridge" attempt to snare the person who is passing through. The person caught then places their arm around the waist of one or other of the two "bridge makers" and then the chant starts up again. The game continues until there are two teams of linked people. The climax of the activity is a competitive tugging event: "When the two parties are ranged, a tug of war takes place until one of the parties [team] breaks down or is pulled over a given mark."

According to the Rev. Dr. Gregor of Rossshire the tug of war game was orchestrated to the fol-

*Tug of war, which has been included in the modern Olympics almost from their inception, has long been a sporting activity in many cultures around the world.*

lowing rhythmic tempo where the emphasis seems more on a romantic pairing off than athletic competition.

> Apples and oranges, two for a penny,
> Come all ye good scholars, buy ever so many.
> Come choose the east, come choose the west,
> Come choose the one you like the best (Gomme 1898).

This information was complemented by a bold pencil and ink sketch showing four young ladies pulling against four others. There is no rope, but their arms are linked and intertwined and the portrait is of arched backs and a strongly contested play activity.

As early as the 1840s, tug of war appeared on the programs of various Scottish Highland

## A Sport To Speak of

Robert Palmatier and Harold Ray reveal in *Sports Talk* (1989) that tug of war contributes two sporting metaphors very much in vogue in contemporary society. The words are "anchorman" and "dig in your heels." The anchorman is the pivotal end person who gives a tug of war team its stable base. And, the digging in of one's heels is an acceptable technique used in tug of war to generate traction with the competition surface.

"Tug of war" as a symbolic figure of speech showed up in eighteen titles during one Infotrac magazine/journal search (1991–1994). For example, it appeared in *Business Week* (on Greenspan and the Federal Reserve), *Successful Farming* (the swine seedstock wars), *Family Circle* (dog problems), *Barron's* (the deutsche mark), *Facts on File* (control of the Russian newspaper *Izvestia*), *Insight* (the U.S. Congress), and *Redbook* (divorce).

Arguably, tug of war's pièce de résistance as analogous medium can be found in a full-page advertisement for American International Group, an insurance and financial services conglomerate, in a June 1995 *Economist*:

> With our financial strength, you'll be glad we're on your side. On the tough playing field of international business, you need all the leverage you can get. That's why AIG's strength and stability are so important. . . . We're ready to throw our weight behind you.

The bold, sharp and athletic color photograph shows the foremost three members of a tug of war team straining heart and muscle to bring about a shared triumph!

—Scott A. G. M. Crawford

Olympics to Olympics. In 1900, team size was six; in 1904, there were five to a team; and in 1908 teams were made up of eight athletes.

At the 1900 Paris Olympics victory went to the Sweden/Denmark combined team. Four years later at the St. Louis Olympics, when very few Europeans had either the time or money to travel to the United States, the gold medal went to the United States. Indeed, the first four teams at the St. Louis Olympics were made up by members of track and field teams or gymnastic clubs. At the 1906 Athens Olympics, Germany were the champions.

In 1908 at the London Olympics, Wallechinsky paints an picture of antagonism and accusations of chicanery. Although the Liverpool police (representing Great Britain) quickly yanked the Americans over the line, the cry went up that the British were cheats. The debate went backwards and forwards. The British policemen claimed that their heavy boots with steel cleats were standard everyday wear. The Americans saw it differently. They felt the Liverpool team was unfairly shod in "special illegal boots." The Americans were unsuccessful and British law and order prevailed with gold, silver, and bronze medals going to three teams of constabulary.

At the 1912 Stockholm Olympics, Sweden won the gold medal, and, at the 1920 Antwerp Olympics, Great Britain triumphed. Some athletes must have shown a particular talent for the event. It would be intriguing, for example, to know more about Britain's John Sewell and James Shepherd, who won silver medals in 1912 and gold medals eight years later.

> A top-class team will almost certainly comprise men with exceptionally powerful thighs and arms, great stamina and concentration, and quick reactions. When a pull is in progress, all eight men will lie back against the rope at an angle of about 35 degrees, their bodies held in a straight line from the heel of the leading foot to the top of the head (Arlott 1975).

Since 1958, there have been national outdoor championships, and European championships were inaugurated in 1965.

A 1993 publication by the British Sports Council seems to point to the event being increasingly

Games. By 1880, the Amateur Athletic Association recognized tug of war and it became (albeit more as a more sinewy sideshow than as team sport) at track and field meetings. In 1900, the event was featured at the Olympics.

David Wallechinsky has written on the brief Olympic sports history of the tug of war. The rules were simple with two teams and no weight restriction. The winning team was the one to pull the opposition six feet. The time allowed was five minutes and, in the event that no winner emerged after five minutes, victory went to the team which had pulled their opponents the farthest distance. Regulations changed from perceived as having an educational component. The sport is described as being coeducational and for all ages. Moreover, weight divisions are spelled out for youths and women, with divisions at 460 kilograms (about 1,014 pounds) and 560 kilograms (about 1,235 pounds).

In the United States, tug of war retains a niche in agricultural and county fairs, circuses, carnivals, celebrations, and picnics. It has also found a regular place in what has come to be known as corporate challenge "character building" workshops that strive to develop teamwork. Its simple organization, with group rather than individual focus, convinces many management executives that it may be a key to forging strategies for creating optimum team goals and objectives. Tug of war also continues to be a popular recreational pastime of fraternities and sororities on U.S. college campuses.

—Scott A. G. M. Crawford

**See also** War Games.

**Bibliography:** Arlott, J. A., ed. (1975) *The Oxford Companion to World Sports and Games*. London: Oxford University Press.

*Economist* (1995). AIG advertisement, 335 (24–30 June): 7920.

Gomme, G. L., ed. (1898). *A Dictionary of British Folk-Lore. Part 1: Traditional Games*. Vol. II. London: David Nutt.

Hoffman, F. W., and W. G. Bailey. (1991) *Sports and Recreations*. New York: Harrington Park Press.

John, G., and K. Campbell. (1993) *Handbook of Sports and Recreational Buildings: Outdoor Sports*. London: Sports Council.

Matthews, P., ed. (1993) *The Guinness Book of Records—1994*. New York: Facts on File.

McWhirter, N., and R. McWhirter. (1975) *Guinness Book of Records*. London: Guinness Superlatives.

Palmatier, R. A., and H. L. Ray. (1989) *Sports Talk—A Dictionary of Sports Metaphors*. Westport, CT: Greenwood Press.

Wallechinsky, D. (1991) *The Complete Book of the Olympics*. 3d ed. Boston: Little, Brown.

# Turnen

In the summer of 1811, a German teacher named Friedrich Ludwig Jahn (1778–1852) took his young pupils to the outskirts of Berlin, to a place called the Hasenheide. There he joined them in a variety of physical exercises. Along with Swedish gymnastics and English sports, these physical exercises formed the basis of modern European physical culture. Jahn proclaimed that the purpose of his "art of gymnastics" (*Turnkunst*) was to restore balance to the educational process by adding physical activity as a necessary counterweight to the excessive cerebration of nineteenth-century schools. *Turnen* was intended by him as a way for refined young men to become truly manly. These educational aims, which had already been proclaimed by the so-called Philanthropists (German educators of the late eighteenth century), were in fact secondary. Jahn's primary goals were patriotic. He envisioned *Turnen* as a way to train able-bodied defenders of the *Vaterland*. The system he referred to as "patriotic gymnastics" was an expression of political nationalism.

Jahn's immediate objective was to end the Napoleonic occupation of Germany; the anti-French element of his nationalistic program was eventually widened to include the rejection of everything non-German (which explains his choice of the invented term *Turnen* rather than the Greek term *gymnastics*). Jahn's ideas also contained racist and anti-Semitic elements. For him, the value of *Volkstum* (peoplehood) took priority over all other religious, cultural, social, and political ideals.

The *Turnbewegung* (gymnastics movement), which included elaborate celebrations of important dates in German history, had a distinctly paramilitary emphasis. Many of Jahn's disciples recalled this. "At night," observed J. J. Bornemann, "it is more difficult than it is during the day [for soldiers] to avoid dangers or defend a position." Accordingly, Jahn insisted that his followers learn to run, jump, climb, and throw in the dark as well as in broad daylight. War games were organized, with reconnaissance patrols and surprise attacks. As C. L. Dürre noted, "The idea was to orient oneself, to gain advantage, to remain alert. An excellent preparation for outpost and patrol duties as I can testify from my own experiences in the field—and at the same time a constant reminder of the great war in the service of the fatherland. . . . Attack and defense often took on a totally tactical character. Conventional plans of operation were drawn up and carried

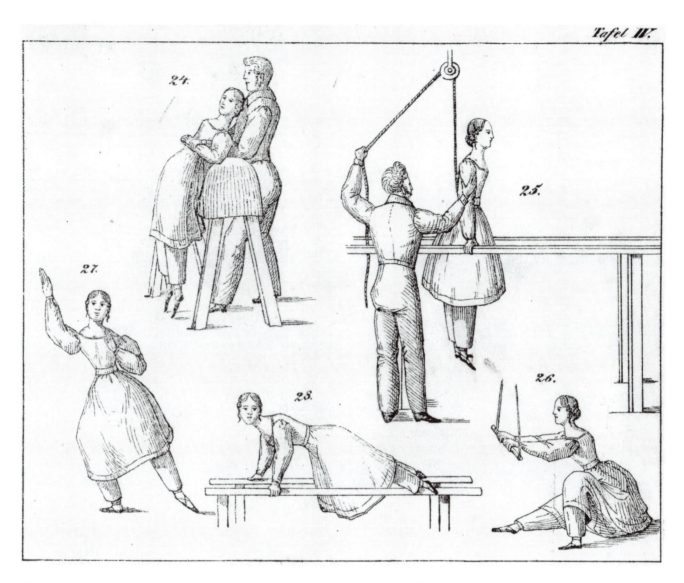

*Drawings depicting exercises from an 1835 German girls' gymnastics handbook, part of the Turnen movement founded in the early nineteenth century by Friedrich Ludwig Jahn. Jahn promoted such gymnastics as an expression of German nationalism.*

out by both sides." Jahn himself stated that his aim was to prepare young people to participate in the patriotic struggle. His colleague Friedrich Friesen also emphasized the importance of paramilitary training. It is no surprise that many *Turner* flocked to the flag when war broke out, and a number of them died in battle.

Although Jahn's ideas now seem narrowly chauvinistic, it should be recalled that nationalism in the context of French occupation had a liberal component; the war against Napoleon was, in modern terms, "a war of national liberation." Jahn's desire for the recognition of national identity was shared by the Slavs and many other subjugated peoples.

As for the gymnastic exercises themselves, it is debatable whether or not Jahn was innovative enough to be designated *Turnvater* (Father of Gymnastics). Jahn referred briefly in the introduction to his book, *Deutsche Turnkunst*, to the achievements of earlier men, including Johann Friedrich Guts Muths (1759–1839). But he failed to mention that he adopted many of the older man's exercises and modeled the grounds of the Hasenheide after those at the school in Schnepfenthal where Guts Muths taught. Indeed, a comparison of Jahn's book with Guts Muths' *Gymnastik für die Jugend* (*Gymnastics for Youth*) reveals extensive borrowing. There is no doubt that Jahn added to the range of equipment and exercises, nor is there doubt about the greater resonance of the Hasenheide compared to the school at Schnepfenthal, but the glorification of *Turnvater Jahn* as the prophet of German unity occurred only in the late nineteenth century, following the political unification of Germany in 1871.

## Jahn and His Contribution

Jahn's historical significance was and is far greater than his actual accomplishments at the Hasenheide (1811–1819). His role in the founding of patriotic student organizations and in the raising of volunteers for the war of national liberation seems less important now than his immense influence, for better or for worse, on the political and social life of nineteenth- and twentieth-century Europe. An extraordinary number of nationalities and ethnic groups, from the Low Countries to the Balkans, were inspired by Jahn and felt themselves entitled to invoke his authority.

If one wishes to do justice to a historical personality, one should begin with the contemporary assessments. Jahn was such a tempestuous and controversial person that we are fortunate to have the views of an alert, critical, and informed observer who knew him well—August Ferdinand Bernhardi, director of the Berlin school where Jahn taught. In his 1818 report, Bernhardi acknowledged that Jahn demonstrated "one-sidedness, intolerance of opposing views, vehemence, rashness," unconventionality, and the disregard of other person's feelings. "All this," he added, "is virtually of no importance compared with his devotion to the cause, his eagerness in pursuit of it, the enthusiasm he arouses, the love he feels, and the strength with which he acts upon it." Bernhardi named the idea of nationality and the appeal to history as the determining forces in Jahn's life. He emphasized Jahn's reaction to the expansion of French power under Napoleon and the consequent threat to German nationhood. He noted also Jahn's belief that Germany's political decline was directly related to the physical softness of its people. In the last analysis, Jahn was calling for physical renewal as the basis for moral renewal.

Although there are commonalities between Jahn's *Deutsches Volkstum* (German peoplehood) and Johann Gottlieb Fichte's liberal *Speeches to the German Nation*, there are important differences as well. Both men were patriots, but Fichte saw German unity as a means to a higher end; he hoped to inspire a process of universal education that would unify all humankind in a peaceful world.

In the course of time, Jahn became increasingly narrow-minded and obsessive. His speeches and writings were often full of empty pathos. They were marred by grossness, crudity, and intolerance. "It goes without saying," he wrote, "that every real man endeavors to give his children-to-be a mother from his own people. . . . Anyone who has children by a non-German wife has spurned fatherland and fatherhood."

Ironically, this fanatical patriot was distrusted, disliked, and persecuted by his own government. Once the French had indeed been driven out of Germany and Napoleon decisively defeated at the Battle of Waterloo (1815), Jahn's abrasive rhetoric was less welcome than it had been. His uncompromising approach to every question led to a number of bitter disputes over the "correct" forms of *Turnen*, most notably in the town of Breslau. The Prussian Ministry of Education decided, on June 12, 1818, to assert its authority over the Hasenheide gymnastics grounds. When Jahn defiantly announced his intention to proceed as before, he was arrested and imprisoned. *Turnen* was banned.

The ban was eventually lifted, in 1842, when King Friedrich Wilhelm IV issued a decree officially recognizing physical exercise as a necessary and indispensable part of boys' education, stipulating that *Turnen* be introduced into the curriculum. At the same time, *Turnvereine* (gymnastics clubs) became legal once again. As centers of progressive thought and action, *Turnvereine* began to spring up all over Prussia and elsewhere in Germany. In many places, these clubs took on the character of political organizations, where physical exercises were accompanied by lively discussions of political, social, intellectual, and ethical questions.

Liberal views were prevalent and members of the *Turnvereine* took prominent part in the abortive revolution of 1848. There was, however, disagreement within the ranks of the *Turner*; some asked only for a shift from absolute to constitutional monarchy while others advocated a republican form of government. Division among the *Turner* was paralleled by even wider divisions in the body politic, which resulted in the more or less complete failure of the revolution. Political repression followed.

# Development

Many gymnasts migrated to the United States during the two years of revolution and more followed when it was clear that Germany was not to have the more democratic society of which they had dreamed and for which they had fought. These immigrants established *Turnvereine* in Cincinnati, Ohio, and a number of other cities beginning in 1848. In 1851, ten of these clubs joined together to form the Socialist Gymnastic League. A special *Turn-Zeitung* (Gymnastics Newspaper) was published, with an emphasis on the discussion of American political issues. These politically active *Turner* voiced their opinions on a wide range of social questions. They were especially adamant about the evils of slavery and religious bigotry. Their attitudes were strongly expressed at the Buffalo, New York, convention of the league in 1855, where liberal-democratic views were overwhelmingly dominant. When President Abraham Lincoln called, six years later, for troops to repress the South's rebellion, the *Turner* were among the first and most enthusiastic volunteers, and they distinguished themselves on the battlefield during the Civil War.

Immediately after the war, a North American Gymnastics Association (1865) was established. One of its principal aims was the introduction of physical education into American schools. The seeds of innovative change had actually been sown years earlier when three of Jahn's disciples—Karl Beck, Karl Follen, and Franz Lieber—emigrated to the United States and began to spread the gospel of *Turnen*. In 1825, Beck was called by George Bancroft and Joseph Cogswell to teach gymnastics at the Round Hill School, which they had established in Northampton, Massachusetts. Beck also translated Jahn's *Deutsche Turnkunst* into English. Follen was employed at Round Hill School until he was appointed professor of German language and literature at Harvard. He took a broad view of his responsibilities and set up the United States' second gymnastics hall, where he gave instruction in Jahn's exercises. Lieber also worked for a time in the Boston area, where he established a swimming school.

Although the activities of Beck, Follen, and Lieber attracted wide attention, it was not until after the Civil War that German-style physical education became the norm throughout most of the United States. The North American Gymnastics Association began a physical-education training school in New York in 1866. (It was later moved to Milwaukee and then to Indianapolis.) For nearly a century, teachers trained in or committed to German gymnastics were the dominant influence on U.S. physical education.

The United States was not the only place to attract emigrants disillusioned with German politics (or pessimistic about the economic opportunities available to them in their native land). Adolf Spiess moved to Switzerland in 1833 and developed a meticulously detailed, stringently authoritarian, and widely adopted gymnastics system (which then became standard through much of Germany). Rodolfo Obermann moved from Switzerland to Italy, where a gymnastics club was organized in Turin in 1844. In the 1850s and 1860s, Carl Euler, one of Jahn's disciples, introduced *Turnen* to the Dutch and the Belgians. Others carried the standard to Russia, where clubs were established in St. Petersburg (1862) and Moscow (1889). German immigrants to Argentina founded a club in Buenos Aires in 1859 and the first Chilean *Turnverein* was established in Santiago in 1864. Brazil developed an especially active *Turner* movement.

One did not have to be a German immigrant to promote the German combination of physical education and nationalistic fervor. French pedagogues tended to scorn all things German, but, after the Prussian army defeated France in the Franco-Prussian War of 1870–1871, many Frenchmen decided that their hopes for revenge required them to imitate German physical education, which they did. Imitation was also the rule in Prague, where Jindrich Fügner and Miroslav Tyrs began the *Sokol* (Falcon) movement in Prague in 1862 as a way to preserve Czech culture *against* German influences. Elsewhere in the Austro-Hungarian Empire, suppressed nationalities organized gymnastics movements. The Slovenes opened their first club in Liubliana in 1863 and the Poles followed with a club in Lemberg in 1866. The Bulgarians opened their first club in 1879.

During the latter half of the nineteenth century, the *Turner* who had not emigrated became increasingly conservative. The Deutsche Turnerschaft (German Gymnastics Association), which they established in 1868, became a bulwark of the empire that was established in 1871. Fealty to the emperor became a central tenet of the organization. The great gymnastics festivals of the Deutsche Turnerschaft were occasions not only for massive gymnastic exhibitions but also for parades, speeches, songs, and enthusiastic declarations of patriotic loyalty. When young Germans began to discover the pleasures of modern sports like soccer, the Deutsche Turnerschaft fought tooth and nail against what it perceived to be the baleful influence of British-inspired liberal internationalism.

In response to the conservatism of the Deutsche Turnerschaft, German workers organized their own gymnastics movement. In 1893 they established the Arbeiter Turner-Bund (Workers' Gymnastics Association). There was even a gymnastics organization for German Zionists who dreamed of *Muskeljudentum* (muscular Jewishness).

By 1933, when Edmund Neuendorff became the leader of the Deutsche Turnerschaft, the organization had become so reactionary that Adolf Hitler was invited to address the great *Turnfest* (gymnastics festival) held that year in Stuttgart. Neuendorff assured Hitler that the *Turner* were marching with him, shoulder to shoulder, into a glorious future. Hitler's response was to abolish the Deutsche Turnerschaft, along with all of Germany's independent sports federations.

After the "glorious future" envisioned by Neuendorff, which featured Nazi dictatorship, World War II, and the Holocaust, the *Turnbewegung* was reconstituted, in the Federal Republic of Germany, on a democratic basis. The German Gymnastics Federation joined with the sports federations that the *Turner* had formerly opposed. Together they established the Deutscher Sportbund (German Sports Federation) on 10 December 1950. German gymnastics is no longer the dominant force in the nation's physical culture, but the Gymnastics Federation remains strong and vital.

—Horst Ueberhorst

**Bibliography:** Blecking, Diethelm, ed. *Die slawische Sokolbewegung*. Dortmund, Germany: Forschungsstelle Ostmitteleuropa, 1991.

Guttmann, Allen. *Games and Empires*. New York: Columbia University Press, 1994.

Neumann, Hannes. *Die deutsche Turnbewegung in der Revolution 1848/49 und in der amerikanischen Emigration*. Schorndorf, Germany: Karl Hofmann, 1968.

Ueberhorst, Horst. *Frisch Frei Stark und Treu*. Düsseldorf: Droste, 1973.

———. *Turner unterm Sternenbanner*. Munich: Heinz Moos, 1978.

———. *Zurück zu Jahn*. Bochum, Germany: Universitätsverlag, 1969.

# Umpires and Umpiring

What's the difference between a playground basketball game and the NBA finals? There are, of course, many differences, but one key one is the men in striped shirts, running up and down the NBA court, blowing their whistles—the referees. Whatever they are called—referee, official, umpire, linesman—they are now a key element of modern sports. In fact, the presence of umpires and the authority vested in them is one critical feature that distinguishes modern sports from traditional and informal sports and games.

Umpiring and the formal role of the independent, neutral umpire has not always been a feature of sports, although rules and some sense of authority have been a part of sporting contests for thousands of years. In the ancient Olympic Games, the event that is closest to the modern notion of sport, the judge was seen as an individual under the gods' direct control. In Imperial Rome, when the "Corpus Legis" was in effect across the empire, the "arbiter" was unknown in competitions. In sport or, more accurately, in games there was, however, a nonparticipant, a neutral figure who might be called a "master" rather than a referee or umpire. But there were no codified rules for the games to govern his decisions. In Asian societies, the situation was quite similar. In China nearly 4500 years ago, football was controlled by the emperor, while in Imperial Japan, paintings dating to the sixth century B.C.E. indicate that local contests were judged by the aristocracy, whose decisions were believed to reflect the rules established by the emperor.

The modern concept of umpiring and the modern role of the umpire emerged in Florence in the fourteenth and fifteenth centuries when Florence football spread so fast that the Senatus of Pisa issued a statement of rules and, in 1415, the Mondovi Statement was issued by the Piedmontese town of Mondov. These rules mark the start of modern umpiring because they were imposed by a neutral party, were not based on supernatural or royal authority, and required the presence of a neutral person—the umpire—whose word was expected to be accepted by all competitors.

The importance of umpiring to the evolution of sport is suggested by events in Europe in the early 1300s; Edward II of England on 13 April 1314 prohibited all ball games because of "affrays scuffled around them." Four years later, the king of France similarly prohibited the game known as soule. Thus rules, and the umpires who enforced them, brought order to sports that previously had existed only at the whim of the participants or were products of authoritarian rule.

It was not until the nineteenth century, however, that rules and umpiring became firmly established as an element of organized sport. In the eighteenth-century British colleges' "dribbling game" we get the first complete set of rules, including penalties for fouls. The first written soccer (association football) rules were codified at Cambridge in 1846. On 26 October 1863, in London's Freemason's Tavern, the Football Association was founded. Football was subsequently spread throughout the British Empire by sailors, engineers, and soldiers, as were its rules, which were followed everywhere the game was played and enforced on the field by the neutral referee.

Today, it is impossible to think of any sport without at least one on-the-field-judge. A few sports, such as Japanese sumo, have only one on-field umpire, while many others require multiple umpires, usually with one in overall command and the others providing specialized functions. In addition to on-field referees, in many competitions there are also off-field officials who rule on various matters such as drug use, meeting deadlines, using legal equipment, and wearing appropriate attire. Beyond these on- and off-field officials, there may also be official bodies that rule after the fact on matters that cannot be decided on the field. In addition, technology now influences umpiring and in some sports is beginning to replace some tasks traditionally performed by humans. For example, professional American football for a few years experimented with television replays to make decisions about on-field play, electronic timing devices are used to identify false-starts in sports such as track and swimming and to identify the winners in many sports, and the "Cyclops" electronic eye is used to detect serving faults in many major tennis tournaments. Thus, like sport in general, umpiring has become more specialized and scientific.

*Cleveland Indians' manager Al Lopez in a heated argument with umpire Bill Grieve, who had just ruled that one of two Cleveland runners who came home on a wild pitch has to go back to third. The umpire's call proved crucial; the opposing New York Yankees won the 23 June 1951 game by one run.*

# Umpires and Umpiring

The following brief survey of umpiring in a few major sports indicates the various forms umpiring now takes.

In American football a game is supervised by seven officials in the National Football League (NFL), four to seven at the college level. All officiating crews have a referee with general oversight and control of the game; the referee is assisted by umpires, linesmen, field judges, back judges, line judges, and side judges. In NFL matches they are radio connected. The referee is the sole authority for the score, and his decisions on rules and other matters pertaining to the game are final. He administers all penalties and, at the snap, is positioned behind and to the side of the offensive backfield. The umpire has jurisdiction over players' equipment and line play on both sides of the neutral zone, including noting any linemen illegally downfield. He is also responsible for the ensuring the legality of the snap, counting offensive players, and determining the legality of passes and kicks relative to the neutral zone. He is positioned 5 to 7 yards (4.5 to 6.5 meters) behind the defensive line. In addition to their primary duties, all officials have a joint responsibility for calling fouls. Each one carries a marker, which he drops when he calls a foul, and a whistle to signal that the ball is dead. At the end of the play, he reports the infraction to the referee, who enforces the prescribed penalty and uses one or more of the 47 hand signals.

In North American baseball umpires control the game. One behind home plate calls balls and strikes on the batter, determines whether a batter has been hit by a pitch or has interfered with the catcher, or vice-versa, and calls runners safe or out at home plate. He and the other three umpires, stationed near first, second, and third base, may call hit balls foul or fair; the other three call runners safe or out at the first three bases. Any umpire may call an illegal pitching motion, known as a balk. An umpire may ask for help from his fellows if he was out of position to see a play, and the first or third base umpire may be appealed to when it is a question whether a batter has taken a full swing that may account for a strike.

Basketball referees follow detailed rules based on founder James Naismith's five principles requiring a large, light ball, handled with the hands; no running with the ball; no player restricted from getting the ball when it is in play; no personal contact; and a horizontal, elevated goal. The rules are spelled out in specific detail by the governing bodies of the several branches of the sport and cover the playing court and equipment, officials, players, scoring and timing, fouls, violations, and other matters. The officials include two or three referees, two timers, and two scorekeepers.

In boxing the referee is stationed inside the ring with the boxers and regulates the bout. In some jurisdictions, the referee scores the contest along with two judges outside the ring. In most jurisdictions, however, the referee does not participate in the judging, and ringside officials score the bout. The officials award points to each boxer for each round or for punches landed, and a boxer must win a majority of scorecards to earn a decision victory.

All National Hockey League and international games and many collegiate ice hockey games are under the control of one referee, two linesmen, and various off-ice officials. Referees are responsible for calling penalties and are the final arbiters of whether a goal has been scored. Linesmen call offsides and icing infractions; they may also stop play in order to inform a referee that a team has too many players on the ice. In some U.S. college games two referees and no linesmen or two referees and one linesman are used, one of the referees being the final arbiter of disagreements.

Soccer (association football) is under control of the referee, who is assisted by two linesmen. The sole judge is the referee. He can reverse the linesmen's calls (especially an offside play). In international games (and advanced national leagues as well) there is the so-called fourth man, who sits in the stands to check the referee's actions. In Europe there are plans to link the referee, linesmen, and the fourth man with a microradio system.

Tennis requires the most officials—11 at major events. These are the chair umpire, net-cord judge, center linespersons (2), service-line persons, baseline judges (2), and sidelines persons (4). The chair umpire controls the match, keeps score, and may overrule the other officials. The 10 other officials have highly specialized functions; the net-cord, center line, and service line persons function only until a serve is in play.

Umpiring is a profession, and in all major sports umpires undergo careful training and testing, belong to professional umpiring organizations, and are paid for their services. Very few umpires are former athletes. In some sports, such as American baseball, umpiring is a full-time occupation; in other sports, such as American football, umpiring is a part-time occupation and most umpires make their living from other occupations. Once an exclusively male occupation, umpiring now includes female umpires, although their work continues to be limited mainly to sports competitions involving women athletes. There is strong resistance to women officiating at male competitions. Being a successful umpire requires a full knowledge of the rules, good eyesight, quick reflexes, the ability to make decisions, physical stamina, a steady disposition, and leadership skills. From the viewpoint of the athletes whose performance is influenced by the umpiring decisions, it is equally important that the umpire be fair. Fair does not necessarily mean that the umpire adheres rigidly to the rules, but rather that he or she is consistent from event to event and from player to player. For example, in American baseball it is well known that different umpires have different "strike zones." That is, some umpires have a "high" strike zone, others a "low" strike zone, and still others a "wide" strike zone. This means that umpires will vary in the pitches they call a strike or a ball. This variation does not bother players so long as each umpire is consistent from inning to inning and game to game. Similarly, in many major sports, umpires may be consistently inconsistent in applying certain rules from player to player. In American basketball, for example, certain star players are rarely called for certain violations such as traveling, while other players are penalized. Players accept this inconsistency on the grounds that the star players have "paid their dues."

Umpire organizations, which generally represent umpires in particular sports, are involved in recruiting, teaching, and training umpires, negotiating their salary and labor demands, and assisting in the revision of rules of play. They are also becoming involved in a new problem facing umpires in some sports—player abuse in the forms of taunting, physical threats, and physical assault, and the possibility of legal liability if an umpire's decision results in injury. In addition, the willingness of courts to become involved in decisions made by umpires or off-field officials raises questions about the "ultimate" authority of umpires.

—Marco Galdi

**See also** Law.

**Bibliography:** Brinkman, Joe, and Charlie Euchner. (1987) *The Umpire's Handbook.* New York: S. Greene.

Bunn, John William. (1967) *The Art of Officiating Sports.* 3d ed. Englewood Cliffs, NJ: Prentice-Hall.

Galdi, M., S. Gigotti, and F. Masotto (1986) *Guida al mondiale di calcio.* Rome: Lucarini Editore.

Goggioli, Girodano. (1964) *Enciclopedia dello sport.* Rome: Edizioni sportive italiene.

Guttmann, Allen (1978) *From Ritual to Record: The Nature of Modern Sports.* New York: Columbia University Press.

Heywood, William. (1969) *Palio and Ponte: An Account of the Sports of Central Italy from the Age of Dante to the XXth Century* (reprint of 1904 edition). New York: Hacker.

Holt, Richard. (1981) *Sport and Society in Modern France.* London: Macmillan.

Mackey, Helen T., and Ann M. Mackey. (1964) *Women's Team Sports Officiating.* New York: Ronald Press.

Rader, Benjamin G. (1983) *American Sports: From the Age of Folk Games to the Age of Spectators.* Englewood Cliffs, NJ: Prentice-Hall.

Thompson, William A. (1985) *Modern Sports Officiating: A Practical Guide.* 3d ed. Dubuque, IA: William C. Brown.

# Values

The value of sport and the values in sport have been the source of controversial debate at least since the time of the ancient Greeks. How can it at the same time be true that sport is both developer of moral and immoral character? Yet for every supporter, such as the French existentialist writer Albert Camus, who contended that everything he knew about ethics he had learnt from sport, there is a skeptic who, like the social historian Wray Vamplew, has asserted that the qualities instilled in sport were precisely those thought desirable in Nazi train drivers to Dachau. To unravel this apparent paradox requires the drawing of some distinctions.

In the first instance we need to be clear about the type of interest in values that differs between, say, sociologists and psychologists of sport from a philosophers' concern. Then there is the need to mark out the distinction between the ways in which a person can value sport and the value that sport has in its own right. Finally it is necessary to demarcate those values that are presupposed in the engagement in sports from those that flow as a consequence of playing them and to relate the two dimensions. The complex conceptual question "what is value?" needs to be given a preliminary airing.

While there are several competing theories that provide disparate answers to that question, an older use of the term "value" was less contested because its meaning was more restricted. The notion of value referred to the worth of something. In order for something to be of worth, it must have the capacity to confer a benefit or good to a given person or group. Conversely, something would be of no value or disvalue if it did not have the capacity to produce a benefit or good or if its effects are negative. In order to evaluate sports, however, it is necessary first to offer a description of them.

In strictly logical terms, it can be said that sports are ritually derived, rule-governed activities engaged in by humans that employ embodied capacities in the attainment of the excellent performance of codified versions of basic motor actions typically in the form of a contest. What value and disvalue they have will either be as part of this proper identification of the nature of sports or as a consequence of engagement in them.

In respect of sport, sociologists have often traced the variety of attitudes and beliefs that people have taken up in amateur and professional, elite and recreative sport and attempted to show how they differ in and between these groups with respect to, for example, age, gender, and social class. Even at this stage there are opinions and theories alike that are radically different, even incommensurable. Functionalists conceptualize "society" in organic terms. They look to cultural practices like sport as the living organs that contribute to the health of the body. In complete contrast, sociologists of sport from a Marxist position have traditionally regarded sports as potent negative ideological forces that serve to divert the working classes' attention from their parlous and exploited state. Additionally, antiracist and feminist scholars have held up sports as pernicious conservative forces that promulgate and maintain racist and sexist dispositions.

In addition to the disparate accounts from sociological perspectives, sport psychologists have attempted to ascertain the values that people purport to find in engaging in different sports in order to see where the locus of their motivations lie. Behaviorists argue that the values people develop in sport are no more than the socializing effects of the prevailing environment. Freudians may view the value of sport as practices that enable aggressive and protosexual acts motivated by life and death instincts and the pressures of society.

Whatsoever their aspirations, these social scientific inquiries, and others besides, aim to achieve the same thing: to describe as accurately as they can, the attitudes and behaviors of people in appropriate contexts. What they cannot do, and ought not aspire to do, is to settle particular questions about the goodness and badness or rightness and wrongness of the different attitudes and behaviors nor the more abstract questions about what it is for something to be right or wrong, good or bad in sports. To probe these questions is to move into the area of what value(s) is (are) itself (themselves). The branch of philosophy concerned with value is called axiology; a consideration of the nature and range of values in and of sport might therefore be called the "axiology of sport."

## Moral and Nonmoral Values; Means and Ends

When people speak of values generally, and values in sport more specifically, they commonly refer only to moral values. Yet there are a range of nonmoral values in sport, including the prudential, aesthetic, financial, and technical.

For example, prudential acts and, therefore, prudential values can easily be mistaken for moral ones. The key difference between the two is in the motivation for the act. For instance if a football player, having knocked his opponent down with a ferocious tackle, then proceeds upon completion of the play to help his adversary up in full view of the referee, it might be said that he is acting morally. However, if it then becomes clear that what he was doing was attempting to "play the referee," getting him to think well of him such that in the remainder of the game the referee would call decisions in his favor, then the act must be seen not as moral but as prudential or self regarding; as functional and therefore not moral. It is the furtherance of the player's own interests (and perhaps his team's) that has motivated his act. In other words, the act of apparent kindness to the opponent used him only as a means to the player's end.

In the case of aesthetic values, the relationship between means and ends is again important. There are a range of sports (diving, gymnastics, and trampolining to name a few) where the logical aim or end of the activity is achieved by specified means. Not just any way of traveling over the horse will do in gymnastics, and a somersault is a particular way of rotating 360 degrees according to specific aesthetic criteria. Judges look for actions that are smooth, flowing, graceful, and performed with apparent ease and economy of effort. Here, what is done is all but inseparable from the manner of doing it, whereas in most sports there is an indefinite variety of means that can achieve the ends so long as they are permitted by the rules. In order, then, to say a little more about the types of values, more needs to be said about the relationship between means and ends.

There is a famous thought experiment known as the "experience machine." A group of high-powered neuropsychologists have invented a machine wherein one may experience any and all of the experiences one desires by floating in a special vat while appropriately wired up. Periodically one may come out and change one's selections to whatever new experiences one wishes to undergo. Imagine; what would it be like to feel, as Jesse Owens did, the joy and nobility at having secured three Olympic gold medals in the hostile racist atmosphere of the Berlin stadium in the 1936 Olympics? Or what passions flowed through Nadia Comaneci having just secured the first 10 in the 1976 Olympic gymnastics final? What elation for Geoff Hurst when he scored the winning goal in overtime of the 1966 soccer World Cup as the first man ever to score three goals in the final?

What else matters to us other than how life is on the inside? In the experience machine, despite the fact that the subject has chosen the experiences, he or she is essentially passive thereafter. Yet do not human beings also desire to do certain things; to achieve the attendant satisfactions of being a successful athlete or coach, quarterback, or captain of the cricket team. The desire to be and to do such things is to be committed to various activities, roles, and relationships that define the sort of people they are. Plugging into the machine is a form of suicide since one would cease to be the person who one previously was because the strong relationship between one's experiences and one's acts no longer held. On the contrary, their status would be contingent rather than definitive. And this points up the idea that our values are emblematic of who we are; they orient us; define the parameters of what we will do and be.

By contrast, presupposed in all sporting activities, and logically prior to participation in them, is the value of personal autonomy. For the sportsmen and women who engage in these contests of skill, strength, stamina, and wit achieve, luck notwithstanding, the products of their own embodied excellences. The rules are designed to perform this function; to establish the more excellent team or performer who have or has shared the *same* test. But the rules of an activity do more than state what constitutes the sport and who has won, for they regulate conduct in the activities; they tell us about the means that may and may not be employed in order to secure victory. If boxing were merely about rendering one's opponents senseless, we might see a few more boxers bringing guns, bats, and knives into the ring with them. If the high jump were merely about jumping high, we would see people using trampolines. And yet they do not; for sport is about achieving certain ends by inefficient means. Central to the nature of sports is a gratuitous logic. In all sports, difficulties are invented just because they allow sportsmen and women to test their abilities to overcome them.

The ways of achieving victory in sports are underwritten by the most basic of moral principles and ethical virtues, such as courage, equality, fairness, freedom, honesty, and respect for all participants as persons. And there are a range of nonmoral values that are ascribed to sports, such as commitment, dedication, and discipline. The way sportsmen and women play their activities will be a function of who they are, evidenced by the manner in which they embody these ideas and dispositions. These values flow first and foremost from this relationship between the means and ends of the player, and the sports. To give a fuller account of values in sport, then, requires the recognition and understanding of the relationship between internal and external ends and the stance of the player.

## Values and Valuing; Conceptual Analysis

Many theorists in sport have posited that sports are possessed of all or some of the following values: contributive, extrinsic, inherent, instrumental, intrinsic, and relational. In attempting to clarify the terminology of value it is helpful to chart their sources.

It might be said that there are only two sources of value in sport, or anything for that matter; sports persons (subjects) and sporting practices (objects). In relation to the subject, there are two distinct types of valuing. A golfer may value her activity precisely because it represents a particular type of activity in which certain powers of concentration and complex closed skill patterns are required and where there is time to develop one's strategy without direct interference from an opponent. The source of her valuing golf is the activity itself. Her valuing of the activity is thus "intrinsic." What she values is the activity itself and nothing beyond it. Conversely, we may have another person for whom the very same game is valued because it is a way of making money, achieving social status, displaying her prowess,

and so forth. All these factors are not part of a logical description of the activity; they are contingently related to it. The nature of golf as a sport can be described without reference to them. This type of valuing is called "extrinsic"; golf is the route by which something else that is valued is secured. Confusion can be avoided if the terms "intrinsic" and "extrinsic" are used only to refer to the description of the sportsperson's stance toward sports and not the sports themselves.

There is a very close association between the nature of motivation and the nature of valuing. Many coaches lament the fact that what motivates their athletes are factors external to the activity itself. What is deeply problematic here is the contingency of the valuing and hence motivation. Stories are legion of young boys and girls of great athletic potential who have squandered their talents when the source for their motivation dried up. If what motivates the child to engage in sports is the social status, or the medals, or the glory, or the coach's praise, or simply the winning, what happens when the sport no longer achieves these ends? This is why some philosophers have been driven to the conclusion that extrinsic valuing is a weak source, since there must be something more basic beyond it. At the other end of the continuum, one can consider not the sportsperson's own dispositions, but the nature of sports themselves; whether and in what ways they are valuable.

Many, perhaps most, accounts of the value of sport may be termed "instrumental." The notion of instrumental value bears a close relation to extrinsic valuing. To say that sports are instrumentally valuable is to say they are not (or at least not necessarily) valuable in their own right, but are instrumental in achieving other things that are of value in their own right. Many academics have commented that sports, by their very nature as self-contained and scarcely related to the real world, have value only in the instrumental sense. Similarly, to say that sports are of contributive value is to say that they may contribute to the achievement of an end external to themselves. It can be seen, then, that contributory value is a form of instrumental value, but an indirect form of it.

Many different values are cited in virtue of which sports are seen as the means, as instrumentally valuable; politicians talk about the role they play in group and national identity and the recognition of rule-responsibility; physicians praise sports for their health-related value; educators praise them for their ability to achieve group solidarity; physiologists note how sports can elevate basic functions, such as lung power and cardiac output; psychologists say that sports can be a useful means for people to blow off steam in relatively harmless ways; militarists praise them for their capacity to instill loyalty and obedience to authority; religious leaders praise sports that metaphorically engender the will to fight the good fight and run the race to the finish; economists note how they can reduce lost work days; marketing moguls praise them for the success in promoting products; and so on. The sheer diversity of ends that sports can achieve is almost bewildering. One could be forgiven for thinking them to be a universal panacea.

Yet it must not be forgotten that in contrary fashion politicians also blame sport for taking up unjustifiable sums of public monies; physicians call regularly for boxing and other injurious sports to be banned; educators ask whether time ought to be spent on more intellectual pursuits; pacifists claim that sports fail in their purported cathartic task and in fact cause people to act in more aggressive and violent ways; physiologists note how endurance athletes train to levels that are harmful to their health; psychologists deplore their capacity to be destructive of self-esteem; religious leaders warn of sport's tendency to deify the body; cultural critics deride sports for the shallow narcissism they encourage. These considerations and their counter-assertions may lead us to believe that the instrumental value of sport is canceled out by the disvalue it is instrumental in bringing about.

To look only to the type of values in sport that are consequences of engagement is to ignore what is valuable in sports in and of themselves. Discussion of such value is brought together under the heading "inherent" value. The elaboration of this type of value necessitates further discussion of nature of sports themselves.

Inherent value is most easily described negatively. That is to say it is easier to say what it is not than what it is. This type of value, then, is nonderivative. Implicit in an instrumental account of the value of sports is their ability to bring about social cohesion, group identity, self-esteem, more

days at work and so on. Note the logic of this value; sports derive their value from the external ends they satisfy. It is the external ends, then, that are really valued. If this is the case it follows that if another means is more successful, effective, efficient, or simply more economic in achieving those ends, then there is every reason to engage in that activity and not sports. So if sports are found to be poor at developing self-esteem, then the psychologist may deny their value; if militarists find that brave footballers can be craven cowards in war, they cease to value them; when politicians decide that other curricular subjects are better at developing national identity, they no longer value them, and so on.

When people say they value sports for their own sake, or in their own right, they mean to say that the value is immanent in the practices themselves. These characteristics may vary from sport to sport according to their nature but some common features may be noted. Inherent in sports contests are qualities such as skillful action, powers of anticipation, tactical imagination, speed, strength, emotional intensity, and competitiveness. Each of these characteristics will take on different forms in respect of different sports. The power of anticipation in pool is vastly different from that of basketball and this will, in part, be due to the fact that one involves direct and the other indirect competition. The speed required of the rackets player will differ from that of the track sprinter and from the wide receiver in football. Each require and develop in their participants qualities in the solution of the various problems that are definitional and it is in the dialectic of this relationship that each sport displays its shape or form.

Many academics in sport have tended to move without qualification between the subject and object and therefore ignore the distinction between intrinsic and extrinsic valuing and instrumental and inherent (it should be noted that the latter are sometimes referred to as consequential and nonconsequential) value. However, a third, mediating category is conceivable. Many theorists of sport have, in making their sharp distinctions, failed to recognize the sometimes particular relationship between means and ends in sport.

In arguing that sports are often seen as means to external ends there is a failure to recognize that the relationship is not necessarily a neutral one.

There is a strong tendency to isolate a particular end and to say that sport is merely a means to achieve that end. Consider the example of pleasure. Many people value sports for the pleasure they get as a consequence of playing. It might be said that pleasure is the end to which they aim and sport is the means. Of course it might also be said that going for a walk in the country and drinking a beer might equally secure pleasure. Yet for complex activities at least, the means-end distinction interpreted thus is too crude an explanatory tool. Setting out the value of such activities in terms of means and ends often involves focusing upon certain aspects of an activity atomistically while losing the broader picture which gives them sense. Sporting activities are better conceived of as complex wholes connected in such a way that they cannot be dissected unproblematically. The satisfactions involved in activities like athletics, lacrosse, table tennis, and surfing are commonly spread over the course of a lifetime and often involve dedication, commitment, imagination, tolerance, self-sacrifice, the endurance of hardship, and so forth; they are not merely neutral routes to the securing of pleasure. When you wish to enjoy a game of baseball you do not go to play a game of tennis. This is because, again, of the differing nature of the sports (for while they are both striking games, one of them is also a fielding game and there are differences in the territories that allow an altogether different interrelationship between the contestants) and the particular motivations to play this sport rather than that. So when the track athlete runs, she runs and it will be pleasure-affording in a particular way, just as it is dissimilarly experienced by the fencer during and after a well executed parry. The pleasure derived in and through the performance is wedded uniquely to the form of action and the participant who has thus performed it. Sports under this description, both inherently and instrumentally, are valuable as instantiations of the aims of the participant who values them relationally. The relationality of this characterization is two fold; first it takes into account the sportsperson's relationship to the activity and, secondly, it takes into account the inherent and instrumental value of the activity that the athlete secures in his or her participation. Viewed in this light, sports become mixed goods; they are valuable in their own right and as particular means to potentially valuable ends.

## Values, Sports, and Society

What more can be said of values in sport other than that social scientists offer categories and descriptions of those values held by sportspersons; natural scientists offer facts of the body that can be called values but where this means no more than organic, structural, and functional benefits; and philosophers offer a conceptual framework in which all of the above accounts can be contested. In answer to this question some new, normative problems arise: "What is the relationship between values in sport and values in society?" And "which values ought to predominate in sports?" There will be no theory-neutral answer; no view from nowhere.

There can be no doubt that sports can be played, taught, coached, refereed, and administered badly or well. So, as a matter of fact, can any practice that involves contesting abilities such as education, music, art, or politics. Nothing follows necessarily from this. Much, perhaps everything, depends upon the way in which sports are enacted.

What is clear is that an exclusive concern with sport as an instrumentally valuable means to external ends constitutes a form of abuse. It is not clear how long they would survive, let alone flourish, under such alien forces. It is equally clear that, in elite sports at least, the pressure of one external end, wealth accumulation, is doing much to undermine the integrity of sports as mutual quests for excellent performances within the letter and spirit of agreed rules. Under the processes of commodification, both capitalist and communist societies, for very similar reasons, have often reduced the values of sport to one: winning. To do so is often to undermine the gratuitous logic that gives sport both its sense and its magic. Yet in contrast to this win-at-all-costs ethic, is perhaps another less pernicious logic and lobby. The noncompetitive sports movement, if not a contradiction in terms, also seeks to undermine the contesting nature of sports by exalting the process over and above the logical end. If everyone wins, no one wins, it can be said.

Sports, perhaps, are best thought to be valuable as rituals. They derive their meaning from basic actions that were once necessary for survival but are now largely obsolete under that description. We now throw, run, jump, and catch just because we can, and moreover strive do to them as excellently as they can be done. Sports are felt to be obligatory to those who come to love them; they can be played well and badly; they have consequences though they are not to be done merely for them. The value they have is perhaps best thought of as their capacity to give value to the life of people who are committed to them. To paraphrase Chesterton, "if a thing is worth doing at all, it is worth doing badly." The vast majority of sportsmen and women enjoy the value sports have and give despite their won-lost record, not because of it.

—M. J. McNamee

**Bibliography:** Coakley, J. J. (1994) *Sports in Society.* St. Louis: Mosby.

Fraleigh, W. P. (1986) *Right Actions in Sport; Ethics for Contestants.* Leeds: Human Kinetics.

Kohn, A. (1992) *No Contest: The Case against Competition.* Boston: Houghton Mifflin.

Kretchmar, R. S. (1995) *Practical Philosophy of Sport.* Champaign, IL: Human Kinetics.

Lee, M. (1993) "Why Are You Coaching Young Children?" In *Coaching Children in Sport,* edited by M. Lee. London: E & F N Spon, pp. 27–38

McNamee, M. J. (1995) "Sporting Practices, Institutions and Virtues." *Journal of Philosophy of Sport* 23: 61–83.

Midgley, M. (1974) "The Game Game." *Philosophy* 49: 231–253.

Morgan, W. P. (1993) *Leftist Theories of Sport.* Chicago: University of Illinois Press.

Pincoffs, E. L. (1986) *Quandaries and Virtues.* Lawrence: University Press of Kansas.

Sansone, D. (1988) *Greek Athletics and the Genesis of Sport.* Berkeley: University of California Press.

Seefeldt, V., and P. Vogel, eds. (1986) *The Value of Physical Activity.* Virginia: AAPHERD

Shields, D., and B. J. Bredemier. (1995) *Character Development and Physical Activity.* Champaign, IL: Human Kinetics.

Simon, R. L. (1991) *Fair Play; Sports, Values, and Society.* Boulder, CO: Westview Press.

# Vintage Auto Racing

Vintage automobile racing is a sport that combines collecting and competition. Enthusiasts restore and maintain historic old high-performance cars, and drive them in organized races. The sport emphasizes the faithful preservation of the cars' original appearance, performance characteristics, and mechanical construction.

Automobiles used in vintage racing include retired Formula One cars and other high-performance vehicles originally built for the professional racing circuits. Classic sports cars and other top-quality production street and touring vehicles are also used. The age of vintage cars ranges from extremely old automobiles to those made within the past 30 years.

It is primarily an amateur sport, with trophies awarded more often than prize money. While vintage auto races are competitive, the primary focus is on social camaraderie, the enjoyment of driving, and the opportunity to demonstrate classic vehicles in action.

## Origins

The history of vintage auto racing extends back to the early twentieth century, when new generations of cars began to replace the original pioneer vehicles. People who cherished the older cars started to collect and preserve them, and eventually formed clubs to sponsor rallies and other events. After World War II, the interest in collecting and displaying vintage cars gained new momentum, along with an overall growth of automotive racing sports.

Vintage auto racing began to evolve into a distinct sport because a growing number of collectors wanted to run their cars in actual races. Many vintage racing groups and events were subsequently organized beginning in the 1960s, and by the 1990s there were over 100 annual vintage automobile racing events in North America. The sport is also popular internationally. In 1990, the Oldtimer Grand Prix, sponsored by the Automobil Club von Deutschland at Nurburgring in Germany, attracted 100,000 spectators, who watched 600 historic cars race in 13 categories based on size, type, and age.

## Practice

Vintage auto racing has many facets. In some respects, the sport resembles other forms of automobile collecting and racing. However, vintage racing is based on specific criteria. It differs from

*Vintage auto racing is popular among those car collectors who remain faithful to the original design of cars. Racing organizations maintain close control over the types of changes that can be made in members' vehicles.*

straight collecting because the cars are actually raced, not only displayed or driven in slower, nonracing situations.

Vintage racing is also distinct from hot-rodding and other automotive sports that use modified older cars. In other sports, owners are allowed to make major changes to enhance their cars' performance, and the original vehicle might be completely transformed with a new engine and other basic alterations.

Vintage auto racers, in contrast, do not alter their cars' basic design and construction. Instead, they strive to maintain it in peak condition, exactly as it was originally built. Painting or other cosmetic restoration work duplicates the appearance of the cars when they were new. Organizations issue guidelines that restrict the kinds of changes that can be made to members' vehicles. The only deviations allowed are for specific reasons, such as the use of safer, modern tires. Original parts are encouraged in repairs. If they are no longer available, substitution parts must be very similar.

Most vintage auto racing associations are based on either geography or specific types of automobiles. The sport's overall scope is illustrated by the divisions within the Sportscar Vintage Racing Association (SVRA), a large organization in the United States that sponsors events in many categories. In SVRA, Group One includes small-bore production-based cars from 1955 through 1967, such as Alfa Romeos, Lotus Elites, and Mini-Coopers. Group 2 is for high-performance professional racing cars, such as the Formula One and the F-Libre. Group 3 includes Corvettes, Austin Healeys, Triumphs, and other production-based sports cars built from 1955 through 1962. Group 4 is comprised of classic racing cars built through 1959, including Ferraris, Elvas, and Lotuses. Group 5 includes sports racing cars built from 1960 through 1965 and FIA championship coupes built through 1972, including such specialized sports racers as the Elva MK-7, Cooper Monaco, and the Ferrari 512. Group 6 covers production sports cars and high-powered V-8's from

1963 through 1972, such as Jaguars, Cobras, and Sunbeam Tigers. Group 7 is for racing cars from 1966 through 1972, such as the Gulf Mirage and the Lola. Other rare and very old classic cars that are driven at high speeds, but not actually raced, are included in a special category.

Some organizations are more lenient in their guidelines than others. Certain clubs or events allow participants to use newly built replicas or to rebuild completely the remnants of early automobiles with parts from different cars. Other organizations are more stringent and only permit authentic old vehicles with documented histories. Safety and sportsmanship are emphasized, and drivers generally must also train and meet established standards.

Vintage racing events take many different forms. They range from local, informal gatherings to large races that attract drivers and spectators from around the world. Major vintage races are held at historic and prominent racetracks like Watkins Glen in New York, Lime Rock in Connecticut, and Sebring in Florida. They also take place at smaller tracks, or as touring races on open roads and other sites.

The races themselves are structured like their counterparts in other auto sports. The guidelines depend on the sponsor and purpose of the event. The field for some races is open to many types of cars, with eligibility based solely on times in qualifying runs. In other races, the field is strictly limited to cars of a specific type and age.

Some events loosely recapture the general spirit of older racing. Others recreate the actual routes and conditions of particular races as faithfully as possible. For example, the Mille Maglia was a historic 1,609 kilometer (1,000 mile) Italian road race that was discontinued in 1956 and has since been revived in the same location as a prominent event for vintage race cars. A separate recreation of the Mille Maglia has also been held along similar mountainous roads in California.

Vintage cars are often expensive to buy, restore, and maintain, so owners tend to be affluent or extremely dedicated. Some owners contract with professional teams to maintain the vehicles. In the 1990s a branch of the sport using retired stock cars emerged as a less expensive alternative.

—John Townes

**Bibliography:** Egan, Peter. (1993) "Vintage Racing vs. 'Real' Racing." *Road & Track Magazine* (July).

———. (1995) "The Mille Miglia and the Great Yellow Beast." *Road & Track Magazine* (November).

Lumet, Amy. (1993) "Hot Rods: How To Buy a Vintage Race Car." *Forbes Magazine*, FYI Edition (May 10).

*Vintage Motorsport Magazine.* Lakeland, FL.

Yates, Brock. (1995) "A Strange Thing Is Happening: Old Stuff Is In." *Car and Driver Magazine* (November).

# Violence

Sociologically, at least nine distinctions can be made among the forms of human violence, namely:

1. Whether the violence is actual or symbolic, that is, whether it takes the form of direct physical assault or simply involves verbal and/or nonverbal gestures of an intimidatory kind
2. Whether the violence takes a "play" or "mock" form or is "serious" or "real" in nature; this distinction might also be captured by the distinction made by P. Marsh et al. (1978) between "ritual" and "nonritual" violence, though it has to be noted that ritual and play can both have a violent content
3. Whether the violence is directed against humans, animals, or property
4. Whether or not a weapon or weapons are used
5. Where weapons are used, whether or not the assailants come directly into contact
6. Whether the violence is intentional or the accidental consequence of an action sequence that was not intentionally violent at the outset
7. Whether one is dealing with violence that is initiated without provocation or with a retaliatory response to an intentionally or unintentionally violent act
8. Whether the violence is legitimate (in accordance with a set of socially prescribed laws, rules, norms, and values) or whether it is illegitimate (involving the

contravention of laws and/or accepted social standards)

9. Whether the violence takes a "rational" (instrumental) or "affective" (emotional) form, that is, whether it is rationally chosen as a means for achieving a given goal, or engaged in as an emotionally satisfying and pleasurable "end in itself" (Elias and Dunning 1986, 224–244)

While some people subscribe to the notion that humans possess an aggressive instinct similar to the innate sexual drive (Lorenz 1963, 203–236), others argue that social relations have more to do with prompting aggressive behavior:

the potential for aggressiveness can be activated by natural and social situations of a certain kind, above all by conflict. In conscious opposition to Lorenz and others, who ascribe an aggression drive to people on the model of the sexual drive, it is not aggressiveness that triggers conflicts but conflicts that trigger aggressiveness (Elias 1988, 178).

This theory seems to hold true in the realm of sports.

## Sports-Related Violence

All sports are inherently competitive and hence conducive to aggression and violence; however, in some (such as boxing, rugby, soccer [association football], and American football) violence and intimidation in the form of a "play fight" or "mock battle" between two individuals or groups are central ingredients. Such sports involve the socially acceptable, ritualized expression of violence, but just as real battles that take place in war can involve a ritual component, so these mock battles that take place on a sports field can involve elements of, or be transformed into, non-ritual violence. This may occur when, perhaps as a result of social pressures or the financial and prestige rewards involved, people participate too seriously.

Ideally, modern sport resolves the contradiction between friendship and hostility. When people play too seriously, however, the tension level may be raised to a point where the balance between friendly and hostile rivalry is tilted in favor of the latter. In such circumstances, the rules and conventions designed to limit violence and steer it into socially acceptable channels may be suspended, and the people involved may start to fight in earnest. In soccer (association football), rugby, or American football, for example, they may play with the aim of inflicting physical damage and pain. Similarly, in boxing, where the infliction of damage and pain is a legitimate part of the contest, the contestants may continue to fight after the end of a round or even after the contest has finished. The standards governing the expression and control of violence are not the same in all societies, and in Western societies they differ between groups and sports and have not been the same in all historical periods. In fact, a "civilizing process" (Elias 1939, 1994) regarding the expression and control of violence has been central to the development of modern sports (Elias and Dunning 1986). This has principally involved a long-term shift in the balance between affective and rational violence.

In Western Europe there has been a decrease in people's desire and capacity for obtaining pleasure from attacking others. This decline in *Angriffslust* (lust for attacking) has entailed a lowering of the *Peinlichkeitsschwelle* (threshold of repugnance) regarding bloodshed and other direct manifestations of physical violence. It also entails the development of a stricter taboo on violence as part of the conscience. Guilt feelings are liable to be aroused whenever this taboo is violated. There has also been a tendency (perhaps revealed most dramatically in the abandonment of public executions) to push violence behind the scenes and to treat people who openly derive pleasure from violence as psychopaths, punishing them with stigmatization, hospitalization, and/or imprisonment. The same social process has increased the pressure on people to plan, using longer-term, more rational strategies for achieving their goals. It has also spawned an increase in socially generated competitive pressure, which encourages people to use violence in a calculated manner. This complex process can be illustrated by the development of rugby.

Rugby descended from medieval folk games in which matches were played between unrestricted numbers of people, sometimes in excess of 1,000 (Dunning and Sheard 1979, 21–62; Elias and Dunning 1986, 175–190). The boundaries of the playing

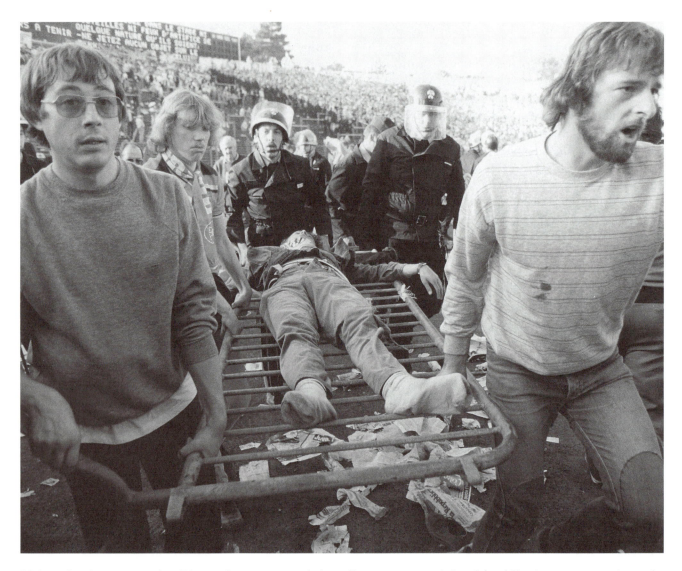

*Using a barrier as a stretcher, Liverpool supporters and riot policemen carry an injured fan following a pregame riot at the European Cup soccer final.*

area were loosely defined, and games were played over open countryside as well as through the streets of towns. The rules were oral and locally specific rather than written and instituted by a central controlling body. Despite such local variations, the folk antecedents of modern rugby shared at least one common feature: they were all play struggles involving toleration of physical violence far more severe than would be permitted or regarded as desirable by most people in today's rugby or any other comparable game.

The medieval Welsh folk game of knappan is one of those antecedents that demonstrates the levels of violence that most would find unacceptable in modern sport. According to George Owen (1603, 270–282), an early-seventeenth-century writer, the number of participants in knappan matches sometimes exceeded 2,000, and, just as in other folk games such as Cornish hurling, some participants played on horseback (Carew 1602, 73–75). The horsemen, said Owen, had "monstrouse cudgeles, of iii foote and halfe longe" and used them to beat their opponents. Others used stones. Knappan was a wild affair, which is what one would expect in a type of game characterized by: unrestricted numbers of players; loosely defined oral rules; some participants playing on horseback, others on foot; the use of sticks to hit other players as well as the ball; the players themselves controlling the matches rather than a referee; and the absence of an outside body to establish the rules and act as a court of appeal in cases of dispute.

Such games were closer to "real" fighting than modern sports. Modern sports are more abstract, more removed from serious combat (Riesman and Denney 1971, 154). The folk antecedents of modern rugby may have been "mock battles" in the sense that the lives of contending groups were not directly at risk and that the infliction of injury and death was not their central aim; nevertheless, their relatively high level of overt violence and the opportunities they afforded for inflicting pain probably constituted one of the sources of enjoyment. After all, the people of preindustrial Europe enjoyed all sorts of pastimes—cock fighting, dog fighting, bull and bear baiting, burning cats alive, prizefighting, watching public executions—which appear "uncivilized" in terms of the values that are dominant in the present-day West. Such pastimes reflected "the violent tenor of life" in Europe during the "autumn" of the Middle Ages (Huizinga 1924, 1976). These pastimes, which continued well into what historians regard as modern times, reflected the comparatively high "threshold of repugnance" that is characteristic of people in a society that stands at an earlier stage in a civilizing process.

By contrast with its folk antecedents, modern rugby, like most other present-day sports, exemplifies a game that is more civilized in at least four senses. It involves

1. Written rules that demand strict control over physical force and that prohibit it in certain forms, for example, stiff arm tackling (hitting an opponent in the throat with outstretched arm) and hacking (kicking an opponent to the ground)
2. Penalties that can be brought to bear on offenders and, as the ultimate sanction for persistent rule violation, the possibility of exclusion from the game
3. The role of referee, who, standing "outside" and "above," attempts to control the game
4. Centralized rule-making and rule-enforcing bodies (the Rugby Football Union and the International Rugby Football Board)

Two significant events occurred during the civilizing of rugby: (1) the production at Rugby School (the sport's namesake) in 1845 of the first written rules, through which an attempt was made to place restrictions on the use of hacking and other forms of physical force and to prohibit altogether the use of "navvies" (the iron tipped boots used at Rugby and other mid-nineteenth-century public schools); and (2) the formation in 1871 of the Rugby Football Union (RFU). The RFU was formed partly as a result of a public controversy over what had come to be perceived as the excessive violence and danger of the game. One of its first acts was to place, for the first time, an absolute taboo on hacking. As a result of these two pivotal occurrences, standards for controlling the game were advanced. Players were now required to exercise stricter self-control, and externally imposed sanctions encouraged their compliance with this demand (Dunning and Sheard 1979, 100–129)

Although the game was not entirely nonrational and affective in the past, the balance between rational and affective violence has changed in favor of the former. Because of the structure of modern rugby and the relatively civilized personality pattern of its players, pleasure in playing is now derived more from the expression of skill and muted forms of force than from the overt physical intimidation and infliction of pain that was characteristic of its antecedents.

Despite the fact that rugby has undergone this civilizing process, relative to most other sports it remains, along with American football and boxing, a very rough game. The limitations of the civilizing process are evident from the aggressive features that still exist in the game, such as the "ruck," which provides the opportunity for kicking and stamping on players who are lying on the ground, and the tactic of "raking" one's boot studs across their faces. The "scrum" also offers opportunities for illegitimate violence such as punching, eye gouging, and biting. Given the close packing of players during the scrum, it is difficult for the referee to control such behavior.

Rugby has probably grown more violent in recent years. It has certainly grown more competitive as is shown by the introduction at all levels of cups and leagues and by the fact that, in 1995, it became openly professional. Growing competitiveness has increased the importance of victory, which, in turn, has increased the tendency of players to play roughly (within the rules) as well as to use illegitimate violence in the pursuit of success. They do not gain pleasurable satisfaction from such violence per se but come under pressure to use it as a means of goal achievement. This form of violence is termed *instrumental violence.*

The civilizing development of rugby reflects the development of modern sports in general, particularly those that involve more or less explicit forms of combat. It is important, however, to keep in mind that the growing competitive pressure that leads to more *covert* use of rational (instrumental) violence in sport is simultaneously conducive to *overt* violence, namely that which occurs when competitors momentarily lose their self-control and strike an opponent in retaliation. The fact that the tactical use of instrumental violence often triggers such loss of self-control shows how one kind of violence can be rapidly transformed into another.

## Violence and Spectators

Violence at sports events often involves the spectators in some fashion. Players may attack spectators, spectators may commit violent acts against athletes, or spectators may fight amongst themselves. Soccer (association football) has proven to be exceptionally problematic; for example, in the 1994/95 English soccer season, Manchester United's French player, Eric Cantona, attacked a Crystal Palace fan for shouting racial slurs. And, worldwide, the sport continues to be plagued by "soccer hooliganism," which includes attacks on players, match officials, and other spectators.

A possible reason why hooliganism seems to occur more frequently in conjunction with soccer than any other sport is perhaps the fact that (when compared to rugby and American football) it has a relative lack of overt violence allowing spectators to release their aggressive feelings vicariously. However, spectator violence is a regular accompaniment of rugby in the South of France (Holt 1981, 135–136) and occurs frequently in conjunction with American football in the United States. A pattern of "celebratory rioting"—rioting when a team has won the World Series or the Super Bowl—is also well established

at major U.S. sports events, not infrequently involving the use of guns and sometimes leading to deaths (Guttmann 1978, 162–163; Murphy et al. 1990, 204–208; Williams et al. 1989, xxiii–xxiv).

The popular conception that soccer hooliganism is more frequent than spectator violence in other sports may be a function of the social composition of soccer crowds. Worldwide, the majority of soccer spectators tends to come from those lower-class segments of society in which aggressive behavior is the norm (Dunning et al. 1988, 184–216). Furthermore, in most societies, groups lower down the social scale are more likely to form intense "we group" bonds (Elias 1978, 134–148) that involve an equally intense hostility toward "outsiders." At a soccer match, of course, the outsiders are the opposing team and its supporters.

The association between hooliganism and soccer is also partly a function of the greater worldwide media exposure that the game receives. Other sports do not get as much media coverage; therefore, the violence that accompanies them is not as apparent to the general public. The media also tend to generate myth, which contributes to the public perception. For example, in the years up to the mid-1960s, the occurrence of soccer hooliganism in Central and South America, continental Europe, Scotland, Wales, and Ireland was regularly reported in the English press, together with statements to the effect that such behavior "couldn't happen in England." Spectator violence, however, had indeed been rife at English soccer matches before World War I and never died out completely (Dunning et al. 1988, 32–90). Similarly, following the 1985 Heysel tragedy, in which 39 fans died at the European Cup Final in Brussels, it came to be believed globally that soccer hooliganism was a uniquely English "disease"; yet, the worst recorded hooligan-related soccer tragedy in modern times occurred at the match between Peru and Argentina in Lima in 1964, when more than 300 people were reported to have died (Smith 1983, 181–183). Although its incidence varies between countries and within countries over time, there is not a single soccer-playing country where hooliganism has not occurred (Williams et al. 1989, 184–196). Since about 1990, soccer hooliganism has been reported more regularly in countries such as Brazil, Italy, and Portugal than in England. It would, though, be premature to conclude that soccer hooliganism in England has been cured. All that can be said with certainty is that its occurrence has been underreported and that this threat to the world's most popular team sport will not be seriously diminished anywhere until it has been tackled at its social roots.

In addition to the media, powerful groups with a commercial interest in spectator sports (e.g., sports organizations and breweries) may contribute to masking or distorting what is, in fact, a more serious incidence of sports spectator violence in North America than is generally acknowledged (Young 1991). Comparable interest groups in Europe, however, have not succeeded in similarly masking or distorting the problem of soccer hooliganism. Some critics suggest that the less centralized character of the mass media in North America may make it easier for powerful groups to mask and distort (Young 1988). It could also be the case that, because America generally is more violent than most Western European societies, sport-related violence does not stand out as clearly there as it does in less violent cultures.

In 1977, journalist Peter S. Greenberg wrote that "Fear and Loathing in the stands is certainly not a new phenomenon, but mass recreational violence has never been so rampant in the sports arenas of America" (Greenberg 1977). The judgment was backed up by U.S. sociologists Harry Edwards and Van Rackages, who wrote, also in 1977, that "sport-related violence flourishes today in crisis proportions . . . violence has indeed increased and become more malicious—particularly over the last three years" (Edwards and Rackages 1977, in Yiannakis et al. 1979, 222). During the 1980s, similarly to what happened in England regarding soccer hooliganism in the 1990s, this panic over spectator violence seems to have subsided. It is impossible to say whether the concern expressed in the United States in the 1970s was more media invention than fact. What is certain is that player and spectator violence in sport constitutes a worldwide problem and that, in its various manifestations, it represents a serious and threatening breach of the ethos of fair play.

—Eric Dunning

**See also** Rugby Union; Soccer; Spectators.

**Bibliography:** Carew, Richard. (1602) *The Survey of Cornwall.* Cited in *Barbarians, Gentlemen, and Players,* edited by Eric Dunning and Kenneth Sheard (1979). Oxford: Martin Robertson, pp. 26–28.

Coakley, Jay J. (1990) *Sport in Society: Issues and Controversies.* 4th ed. St. Louis, MO: Times Mirror/Mosby.

Dunning, Eric, Patrick Murphy, and John Williams. (1988) *The Roots of Football Hooliganism.* London: Routledge.

Dunning, Eric, and Kenneth Sheard. (1979) *Barbarians, Gentlemen and Players: A Sociological Study of the Development of Rugby Football.* Oxford: Martin Robertson.

Edwards, Harry, and Van Rackages. (1977) "The Dynamics of Violence in American Sport: Some Promising Structural and Social Considerations." *Journal of Sport and Social Issues* 7 (2): 3–31, reprinted in S*port Sociology: Contemporary Themes,* edited by Andrew Yiannakis, Thomas McIntyre, Merrill J. Melnick, and Dale P. Hart (1991). Dubuque, IA: Kendall Hunt, pp. 221–227.

Elias, Norbert. (1939) *Über den prozess der zivilisation.* 2 vols. Basle: Haus zum Falken.

———. (1988) "Violence and Civilization." In *Civil Society and the State,* edited by J. Keane. London: Verso, pp. 177–198.

———. (1994) *The Civilizing Process* (integrated edition). Oxford: Blackwell.

Elias, Norbert, and Eric Dunning. (1986) *Quest for Excitement: Sport and Leisure in the Civilizing Process.* Oxford: Blackwell.

Elias, Norbert, and John L. Scotson. (1994) *The Established and the Outsiders.* London: Sage.

Finn, Gary P. T. (1994) "Football Violence: A Societal Psychological Perspective." In *Football, Violence, and Social Identity,* edited by Richard Giulianotti et al. London: Routledge.

Giulianotti, Richard, Norman Bonney, and Mitch Hepworth. (1994) *Football, Violence, and Social Identity.* London: Routledge.

Greenberg, Peter S. (1977) "Wild in the Stands." New Times 9: 10 (November 11): 25–27, 62–64, cited in *Sport Sociology: Contemporary Themes,* edited by Andrew Yiannakis, Thomas McIntyre, Merrill J. Melnick, and Dale P. Hart (1991). Dubuque, IA: Kendall Hunt, pp. 217–221.

Guttmann, Allen. (1978) *From Ritual to Record: The Nature of Modern Sports.* New York: Columbia University Press.

Holt, R. (1981) *Sport and Society in Modern France.* London: Macmillan.

Huizinga, J. (1924; 1976) *The Waning of the Middle Ages.* London: E. Arnold.

Lorenz, Konrad. (1966) *On Aggression.* London.

Marsh, P. (1978) *Aggro: The Illusion of Violence.* London: Dent.

Marsh, P., E. Rosser, and R. Harre. (1978) *The Rules of Disorder.* London: Routledge.

Murphy, P., J. Williams, and E. Dunning. (1990) *Football on Trial.* London: Routledge.

Owen, George. (1603) *The Description of Pembrokeshire,* edited by H. Owen. Cymmrodarian Society Record Series, No. 1 (1892).

Riesman, D., and R. Denney. (1971) "Football in America: A Study in Culture Diffusion." In *The Sociology of Sport: A Selection of Readings,* edited by E. Dunning. London: Cass.

Smith, M. D. (1983) *Violence and Sport.* Toronto: Butterworths.

Williams, John, Eric Dunning, and Patrick Murphy. (1989) *Hooligans Abroad.* 2d ed. London: Routledge.

Yiannakis, Andrew, Thomas McIntyre, Merrill J. Melnick, and Dale P. Hart, eds. (1991) *Sport Sociology: Contemporary Themes.* Dubuque, IA: Kendall Hunt.

Young, K. (1988) *Sports Crowd Disorder, Mass Media, and Ideology.* Unpublished doctoral dissertation, McMaster University, Hamilton, Ontario, Canada.

———. (1991) "Sport and Collective Violence." *Exercise and Sport Sciences Reviews* 19: 539–586.

# Volkssport

Volkssport, popular sport, is neither one single sport nor a well-defined group of sports. It is as distinct in different countries as the words *volk* (Flemish, German), *narod* (Russian), *folk* (Danish), *népi* (Hungarian), and people (English) are in different languages. "Popular sport" can denote traditional, ethnic, or indigenous games as well as new games; regional sports as well as premodern folk sports; spontaneous sports of the lower classes as well as artificial folkloristic display; sport under right-wing ideologies (*völkisch*) as well as under left-wing concepts (*sport popolare*). The long history of volkssport, however, displays a comprehensive pattern that connects it with the rise and change of modern culture.

## Origins and Development

There was no volkssport before industrial modernity. In earlier times, sport denoted pastimes—hunting, falconry, and fishing—of social classes that clearly distinguished themselves from "folk," mainly the nobility and gentry. The aristocratic tournaments and the later noble exercises were exclusive, too. Meanwhile, the common people had a game culture of their own.

### Premodern Folk Games

In early modern Europe, peasants and city dwellers held their own festivities, which often centered around dances, games, and competitions of strength and agility. These games were connected with ritual festivities—often Christianized forms of pagan celebrations—like *Jul* or Christmas, erecting the May tree, Shrovetide, Midsummer dance of *Valborg* or St. John, harvest festivities, marriage, or *kermis* or wake.

Pieter Brueghel portrayed this *kermis* and other carnival activities in paintings and copperplates from the mid-sixteenth century, showing their sometimes violent, sometimes erotic, sometimes ecstatic, often grotesque and carnivalistic traits. Stand wrestling—like Breton *gouren* and Swiss *Schwingen*—was popular, with many regional variations. Races with grotesque impediments made people stumble (children's sack races are a descendant of this form). Violent ball fights through the open landscape—like Irish hurling and Breton *soule*—pitted village against village and expressed local and social identity. Mock tournaments made fun of aristocratic competitions. Aim-casting games with balls (*boule*) and plates (*palet*), sword dances and round dances, bird shooting, acrobatic shows, and animal fights were put together with theater display, music, masquerade, meals, and intoxication to form a whole festival. Bodily activities entered into "world upside down" carnivals, where the king becomes the fool and the fool becomes the king.

Early modern history is characterized by persistent attempts by the ruling classes to restrict, control, or prohibit folk-game culture. The Protestant Reformation, the Catholic Counter-Reformation, and, especially, Puritanism and Pietism, banned folk games for their pagan traits. The absolutist state reacted against elements of local autonomy expressed in festivities by trying to transform some of them into military parades, and the upper classes developed a moral critique of sexual hilarity and violent behavior.

### Modern Rise and Differentiation of Volkssport

The repression of folk games by the social elite had only limited success until the rise of industrial modernity during the nineteenth century. Gymnastics and sport were developed as more effective alternatives to folk culture than the rationalization of older folk games and were promoted by schools and the military. In the process, elements of the earlier folk culture were transformed and integrated into the new "rational"

*Thai boxing is one of the many forms of Volkssport, or "popular sport," found throughout the world.*

## Swiss Folk Wrestling as Superstition and Disorder

We have heard that the common people (*das gemeine Volk*), as peasants and farm-servants, here in Schwarzenburg for a long time have been meeting on Christmas night at the place where the religious and secular justice is administered, and hold there a wrestling match (*Schwinget*) until midnight. They challenge and try their strength against each other, and who throws the other on the ground becomes famous hereby. They also believe that who trains that night will be vigorous and healthy the coming year. They do not only put faith into this superstition, but they also, as it has often happened, damage their limbs, shed their blood, and this leads to loud crying, cursing, swearing, and other frivolous manners. Some come even from Freiburg to participate. Some have already been punished and this event has been forbidden and condemned by our decree.

—Letter of a Swiss court to the government in 1611.
(Schaufelberger 1972, vol. 1, pp. 22–23.)

body culture. This led, however, in different directions.

Certain elements of folk activity—from, for example, football (soccer), hurling, and wrestling—were transferred to new patterns of producing results and records and were thus sportified. Other elements from acrobatics and "harmless," so-called minor games were integrated into the systems of gymnastics (*volkstümliches Turnen*) and thus institutionalized for health and education. Further elements, especially from folk dance, but also from such athletic exercises as Bavarian *Fingerhakeln* and Swiss *Schwingen*, were discovered as displays of regionality and nationality or as touristic attractions and thus folklorized. Controversies about the national origin of these games and dances arose, and attempts were made to reconstruct their "authentic" forms and to keep them "pure" in the form of invented traditions. In this context, the modern concept of volkssport took form.

Under the title of volkssport a quite new framework was created for something that was valued as ancient and traditional. Certain games now became removed from their original context and specialized in clubs and associations, where they were subjected to special rules. The competitive raising of the cross or banner in Brittany, for example, became an end in itself, separate from the religious procession. The connection between game and festivity—music, dance, fool, mask, stumbling, laughter, carnivalism—disappeared and was replaced by the modern principle of discipline. Where festivity once reigned, federation, school, or museum now held sway.

The rise of volkssport also marked a new fascination with and significance of "folk" and the "popular" for modern culture, contrasting sharply the former derogatory attitudes towards *plebs* and *Pöbel* as the low and vulgar and following the new positive understanding of *Volk* by Johann Gottfried Herder (1774–1803), a literary and cultural critic who started the movement to reevaluate and reappropriate folk traditions. Volkssport broke the patterns of distinction between high and low in society—a shift related to the age of democracy, social movements, and peoples' rights, reflected in the spirit of *égalité* and *fraternité* that, for a while, characterized the French Revolution.

The reference to "folk" was, however, more than a shift of attitudes about how to approach physical culture. In social reality, volkssport could become subversive, a trend especially evident in regions of ethnic and national minorities. In Ireland in 1884, for example, the Gaelic Athletic Association first promoted hurling as a sport of liberation from the British rule and was closely connected with Republican nationalism. Beginning in the 1920s, the traditional cast and bat games *tsan, rebatta, fiolet,* and *palet* in the Valley of Aosta were organized in specialized clubs, contributing to the particular cultural identity of this Franco-Provençal province inside Italy. In Brittany a committee for *gouren* wrestling was begun in 1928, regulating classes of weight, record listing, dress, and ceremonies; like the later Federation for Breton Traditional Sport, it reflected aspirations to Breton autonomy and nationalism inside France. So, too, the Icelandic *glima* wrestling, organized since 1906 in an amateur association with regular championships, had similar significance as "national sport." And the Basque competitions of strength developed both national-folkloric and sportive traits by presenting results in lists of records and measured results.

The demarcation of class cultures in industrial society added another dimension to volkssport. In 1938, Danish Social Democratic workers' culture started *Fagenes Fest,* a festival of popular competitions such as witty races and tug-of-war between different professions. In Portugal, meanwhile, a communist-oriented practice of "popular games" still competes with a conservative tendency in the framework of *jogos tradicionais.*

The taming and standardization of folk activities by modern disciplinary sport had, thus, its limits. Volkssport has always had two faces: one disciplined, one subversive. Witness the struggle to include tug-of-war in the early modern Olympic Games; after 1920 it was excluded again because of its persistent image as nonserious folk competition. Meanwhile, however, the sportification of tug-of-war continued with the addition of championships, federations, and standardization.

## Decolonization, Festivity, and Identity

Since the 1980s, volkssport has received new attention. The first research in this field started at the Catholic University of Leuven (Belgium) in 1973 and gave rise, in 1980, to *Vlaamse Volkssport Centrale.* Supported by the Flemish Ministry of Culture, this body initiated both reconstructional studies and practical promotion of Flemish folk games. In the mid-1980s, *Idrætshistorisk Værksted* in Gerlev, sponsored by the Danish Ministry of Culture and the Danish Gymnastic and Sport Association, started to collect Danish folk games and to promote them practically and pedagogically.

A series of international festivals of volkssport made the transnational dimensions of this phenomenon visible. In 1985 the first "Eurolympics of the Small Peoples and Minorities" were hosted by Friesland in the Netherlands and included competitions in Celtic wrestling, Frisian *Streifvogelen,* and singing. In 1988, under the auspices of the Council of Europe, a seminar about traditional games was held in Vila Real (Portugal). In 1990 the first *Journée Internationale de Jeux et Sports Traditionnels* took place in Carhaix (Brittany). The festival included Breton folk games, Basque trunk hacking, Gaelic football, Icelandic *glima* and Scottish backhold wrestling, children's games, and tug-of-war. In 1992, even as it welcomed the Olympic Games, the city of Barcelona hosted a "Festival of the Particular Sports of Spain" with competitions of force, regional forms of wrestling, and Catalonian *pelota.*

---

## Raising the Cross—Laughter and Folk Riot in Brittany

Once a year in some parishes of Léon (Brittany) a *pardon,* a religious procession with heavy crosses and banners, was held.

As soon as the crosses and banners are outside the church and one has gone some steps on the way, the young people flock together around them and everybody wants to carry them. They quarrel, they pull them from each other, they even fight in the view of the Holy Sacrament which is carried in the procession. And, in order to get more freedom for their activities, the young people withdraw as far as they can from the clergy, who sometimes lose sight of them. Then they dispute, they laugh high and loud, they try the banners and crosses, they let them down and bear them in this way or let them fall, causing cries of scorn by this. The clergy are forced to leave their places in order to prevent the disorder. These are the processions of Commana and of Saint-Sauveur looking like, which one—being uninformed— would think to be popular riots (*émeutes populaires*). It is the weight of the crosses and banners which makes the glory of the carrier, letting them down in the described way. That is why the perches of the crosses and banners can never be large and heavy enough for the fancy of those who want to carry them. And one has even sometimes discovered that they put stones between the textile of the banners in order to make them heavier. . . . The respectable people (*honnêtes gens*) deplore this disorder; the political authorities have condemned and banned them. . . . But the carriers of the crosses and banners left the church in spite of the clergy's interdiction and, without doubt, by order of the elders or at least one of them, who drove them out of the church saying with loud voice, one should abandon the priests and follow the signs, with which some inhabitants had started the tour around the churchyard, while the priests, frightened by this riot, fled into the vestry.

—Report of the rector of Commana in 1777, in Fanch Peru: "Le lever de la perche en Trégor," Ar Men 6 (1986), 4.

---

The fact that the Council of Europe sponsors these types of activities and that organizations of Olympic sport try to occupy this field—as by the festival "Traditional Sports and Games of the World" in Bonn 1992—underscores the new significance of volkssport. In 1995 representatives from 24 countries set up in Copenhagen an "International Sport and Culture Association" with a plan to promote meetings of popular sport (*folkelig idræt*) and cultural festivities as a challenge to the standardization imposed by Olympic sport.

The new attraction of volkssport also illuminates a change in the relation of the Western culture to the rest of the world. During the nineteenth and twentieth centuries, sport history had consisted of the diffusion of Western sports to Africa, Asia, and Latin America and the disappearance of regional popular games and activities. This long-term colonization process has been recently counteracted by the revival—especially since the 1970s—of volkssport. The martial art *pencak silat* and the ball game *sepak takraw,* for example, found new support in Indonesia and Malaysia. Elsewhere, too, indigenous, traditional sport found new acceptance: *wushu* and *taichi* in the Chinese states and *capoeira* in Brazil, Bedouin hockey *al kora* in Libya and Algeria, drum dance *qilaatersorneq* and summer festivals *aasivik* in Greenland and the other Inuit regions. More than revival and preservation heads the agenda, however. The culture of movement in the West is increasingly marked by exercises coming from non-Western folk cultures, by *taichi, pencak silat,* Thai boxing, and *capoeira,* by *yoga* and *sufi* techniques. Even *kendo* and *sumo* have entered the Western metropoles.

The break with the long-term colonization in sports assumed dramatic forms in Eastern Europe and Middle Asia around 1989. The Soviet state had established a monopoly in standard sport as a way to achieve internal uniformity and high achievement in international competition. Folk sports among the Soviet nationalities were—with few exceptions—repressed as "nationalist," "separatist," and "religious." The resurgence of folk activities was part of the revolution that made the Soviet empire break down. The Kasakh New Year's festivity *nauryz* reappeared with its dances and games. Mongolians return—in the sign of Jingis Khan—to ancient festivities with nomad equestrianism, belt wrestling, and bow and arrow. The Tatars hold their spring time holiday *sabantuy* again, with *korash* wrestling in its center. The Baltic peoples assemble at large song festivals. And once again Inuit people from Siberia and Alaska meet in drum dance and winter festivity *kivgiq.* Thus have festivity and volkssport long marked identity and revolution.

## Inuit Festivity—Jump and Shamanism

At the end of December or the beginning of January, the Eskimo of the Chukotsky National District organize the rite known as *sayak.* The inviting family cleans their house, preparing wooden ducks and painted ceremonial paddles, blubber lamps, and a ceremonial pole in the middle of the room. The guests, all women, arrive in the twilight with reindeer meat, sugar, and other food. While the celebrant father beats the drum and sings a ritual song, they dance around the pole with free-flowing gestures and afterwards they exchange food. The next morning, the celebrant goes from house to house striking the drum and invites the women once more. This time, the dance takes on a different character, as the women stamp rhythmically; it lasts a long time and requires great physical strength and endurance. Some dancers collapse in ecstasy while the singer cries "Ogo-go-go-go-go" to "scare away" the evil spirit of death from the fallen person. In the evening there is a joint meal. The last day, young boys do the same type of dance, and in the evening girls and boys join in songs. At night, the family members paint their faces with black lines and join with the guests in meal and rituals, including a ritual healing of every member of the family, dance, and common songs. In competition everybody jumps after small paddles, which are tied high up on a thong, and tries to pull down as large a paddle as possible. Gifts are exchanged, and the evil spirits are "thrown out" with shouts and noise. Finally the shaman depicts in songs the future life of the celebrant.

During the years of Soviet power, the Eskimo economy and way of life changed with the advent of electricity, modern industrial techniques, European clothing, uniform education, and party membership. "Soviet medical institutions have driven out the shaman with his charlatan methods of 'treatment'." The victory of socialism finally brought the "breaking up and liquidation of primitive customs and beliefs" (I. K. Voblov, *Anthropological Papers of the University of Alaska* 7, 1959, pp. 71–90).

—Henning Eichberg

Because of these social dynamics, volkssport cannot be reduced to "traditional resistance" against modernity. It was itself a result of modern tendencies of sportification, pedagogization, and folklorization. However, volkssport has not only survived the Western colonization of the Third World and the modern state sport of the Soviet empire, but it has taken its actual form in revolt

## Inuit Dance—Identity and Revolution

After about 1910 the joy of *Kivgiq* dancing, and the bonding of *Kivgiq* gift giving, seemed lost to the Inupiat. We tried filling the gap with new activities, some reasonably enjoyable and some destructive. None warmed our souls in quite the same way as *Kivgiq*.—That's why I am so proud and happy to realize that *Kivgiq* is once again a strong tradition among us. I am proud to realize that during the darkest and coldest moments of winter, we again gather together by the thousands, and through traditional dance find joy and a sense of identity uniquely Inupiat. We do it without alcohol, without drugs, and with more joy.

—George Ahmaogak, mayor of North Slope Borough (Alaska), at the first visit by Siberian Inuit, 1990, in George Ahmaogak, "Remembering the Big Dances of Winter." *Uiniq* 5, 1 (May 1990): 2.)

against these tendencies. Volkssport shows premodern, modern, and transmodern traits, while contrasting with the mainstream of sport in the following respects:

The framework of volkssport is not discipline but festival.

Volkssport is connected with cultural activities of different kinds—music, joint song, dance, theater—and therefore never a "pure" discipline.

Volkssport does not aim to produce results but to foster togetherness.

Volkssport resists standardization and, instead, celebrates difference. In contrast to the display of sameness and hierarchy, it makes otherness visible.

Volkssport is linked to regional, ethnic, social, or national identities and opposes tendencies of uniformity. It opposes a "folk" view from below to colonization from above.

—Henning Eichberg

**Bibliography:** Barreau, Jean-Jacques, and Guy Jaouen, eds. (1991) *Éclipses et renaissance des jeux populaires. Des traditions aux régions dans l'Europe de demain.* Rennes: Institut International d'Anthropologie Corporelle/Institut Culturel de Bretagne.

Burke, Peter. (1978) *Popular Culture in Early Modern Europe.* London: Temple Smith.

Daudry, Pierino, ed. (1984–1993) *Lo joa' e les omo. Rivista di studi e testimonianze sui giochi, sport e cultura dei popoli.* Vols. 1–10. Châtillon/Val d'Aosta: Federaxon Esport Nohtra Tera.

Daudry, Pierino. (1990) *Jeux et jouets de la tradition valdôtaine. Giochi e giocattoli della tradizione popolare valdostana.* Aosta: Région Autonome, assessorat de l'Instruction Publique/Federaxon Esport de Nohtra Tera.

Eichberg, Henning, and Jørn Hansen, eds. (1989) *Körperkulturen und Identität.* Münster: Lit.

Elaschvili, Vassilij I. (1977) *Traditsii gruzinskoi narodnoi fizicheskoi kultury i sovremennost.* Tbilissi.

Floc'h, Marcel, and Fanch Peru. (1987) *C'hoarioù Breizh. Jeux Traditionnels de Bretagne.* Rennes: Institut Culturel de Bretagne.

Franco, Rafael Aguirre. (1978) *Juegos y deportes vascos. Enciclopedia general ilustrada del Pais Vasco, Cuerpo anexo.* 2d ed. San Sebastian: Aunamendi.

Guttmann, Allen. (1994) *Games and Empires. Modern Sports and Cultural Imperialism.* New York: Columbia University Press.

Jost, Eike, and Thomas Smidt. (1990) *Kulturelles Spiel und gespielte Kultur. Bewegungsspiel als Dramatisierung des Lebens.* Frankfurt am Main: Afra.

Mansouri, Ali Yehia. (1984) *Sport and Popular Games. Aims, Organization, Implementation.* (In Arabic.) Vol. 1. Tripoli.

Møller, Jørn. (1990–1991) *Gamle idrætslege i Danmark.* Vols. 1–4. Kastrup/Gerlev: DDSG&I/Idrætsforsk.

Redmond, Gerald. (1971) *The Caledonian Games in 19th-Century America.* Cranbury, NJ: Associated University Presses.

Renson, Roland, and Herman Smulders, eds. (1979–1986) *Serie der Vlaamse Volkssport Dossiers.* Vols. 1–7. Leuven: Katholieke Universiteit Leuven, Istitut voor Lichamelijke Opleiding/De Nederlandsche Boekandel.

Schaufelberger, Walter. (1972) *Der Wettkampf in der alten Eidgenossenschaft.* Vols. 1–2. Bern: Paul Haupt.

Stejskal, Maximilian. (1954) *Folklig idrott. En etno-sociologisk undersökning av den finlandssvenska allmogens manliga friluftslekar.* Åbo/Borgå: Svenska litteratur sällskapet i Finland.

Vroede, Erik de, and Roland Renson, eds. (1991) *Proceedings of the Second European Seminar on Traditional Games. Actes du Deuxième Séminaire Européen sur les Jeux Traditionnels.* Leuven: Vlaamse Volkssport Centrale.

# Volleyball

Volleyball, invented at the beginning of the twentieth century as a simple indoor winter game, has become an intensely competitive sport. Introduced into the Pan-American games in 1955

(Mexico City) and an Olympic event since 1964 (Tokyo), elite volleyball now involves tactics and physical skill of an advanced character. While at the recreational level volleyball maintains a universal appeal and an intuitive structure of play, at its most competitive it has increasingly emphasized specialization of players and rigorously rehearsed sequences of ball handling. Volleyball is a close cousin to basketball: both games were created in Massachusetts and both were created by men who worked for the Young Men's Christian Association (YMCA).

## Origins

William G. Morgan, who invented volleyball in 1895, was physical education director of the YMCA in the town of Holyoke, Massachusetts, and a one-time student of basketball's creator, James Naismith of Springfield, Massachusetts. Both basketball and volleyball were, in fact, invented to be pleasant and diverting indoor winter games that could augment the rather austere regimen of gymnastic exercises that comprised the greater part of late nineteenth century physical education in America. Neither man anticipated either the eventual popularity of their creations or the extraordinary competitiveness that would come to characterize top-level play.

Morgan specifically created volleyball for his clients at the YMCA. These were businessmen, for the most part, who were middle-aged, frankly stout and unathletic, and in general not up to the challenges of the somewhat more demanding basketball of the time. The original volleyball was played by two teams who pushed a slow, oversized ball back and forth over a net that was only a few inches higher than some of the players.

Because Morgan had originally used a badminton (or lawn tennis) net, he at first settled on the name "mintonette" for the new sport, but such rules as were needed were derived mainly from handball and baseball. The influence of the last is easily seen in early volleyball rules that stipulated that the game be played in nine "innings," with "three outs" allowed before a team lost the serve. In 1896, while watching a demonstration of the game, Dr. Alfred Halstead of Springfield College—a YMCA colleague of Morgan's—suggested that the name "volleyball" better suited the game's nature of pushing the ball back and forth over the net, and the new name was quickly accepted.

## Development

Volleyball, like basketball, spread very quickly and for similar reasons. Both games were simple in design, and both featured clear and intuitively appealing goals. Moreover, both games were enthusiastically promoted by the YMCA and the Young Women's Christian Association (YWCA), both of which had chapters throughout the world. Thus volleyball, like basketball, initially moved across the globe in support of a pragmatic and "muscular" Christianity. Volleyball, like its slightly older Massachusetts relative, quickly became popular throughout the world.

In the United States itself, the first national championship was played in 1922 in New York City. Twenty-three teams competed—most from no further west than Chicago—at the Brooklyn Central YMCA gymnasium. The Pittsburgh team carried away the trophy. This event was officiated by the Volleyball Rules Committee of the YMCA, as were subsequent events until 1928, when the United States Volleyball Association (USVBA) was formed.

Volleyball was introduced into Japan in 1913 by F. H. Brown, yet another YMCA organizer. Very quickly thereafter, "bareboru" became a regular feature of the Japanese sports scene and, in 1921, the Japanese Imperial Volleyball Association was developed. The YMCA was active in other parts of Asia as well, notably China, India, and the Philippines. In the Philippines, the game became very popular for awhile and volleyball was played in Manila at the so-called "Far Eastern Games" organized by the international YMCA in 1913.

During and after World War I, American soldiers played the game in Europe, not least of all because many YMCA instructors had been inducted into the Army as physical education instructors. Many YMCA and YWCA organizers stayed on after the war and the game grew in popularity through the 1920s, particularly in France where many local volleyball clubs were established. The Russians too became interested in the game, and the Soviets and their client states were to become, with Japan, major competitive players of the game.

The first international volleyball tournament

*Volleyball has developed from a purely recreational activity into a major international sport, as evidenced by this match between Cuba and the United States at the 1975 Pan American Games.*

in Europe was held in Paris in 1931. The Soviets took the first prize at that event against their most serious opponents—the Estonian team, whose country at that time had only nine years of independence left before the Soviet annexation.

By 1920, volleyball had become popular in Central and South America, particularly in Peru and Brazil. Both countries would eventually become top volleyball competitors.

Though there had been in 1936 a French attempt to establish an international volleyball organization, it was only after World War II, in 1946, that the International Volleyball Federation was formed. The federation's most active original members were France, on the one hand, and the Soviet Union, Poland, Yugoslavia, and Czechoslovakia—all communist nations—on the other. The United States showed no interest at the time in top-level volleyball, and the predominance of communist nations in top-level play insured that the game would be played in a specific and

highly politicized atmosphere for the next two decades.

For instance, during the 1949 world championships, in Prague, 11 countries competed, and the Soviets carried way both men's and women's titles. The United States did not bother to send a team at all. The Yugoslavian team did not attend either, although this had nothing to do with athletic ability or interest. Indeed, the Yugoslavians had developed considerable volleyball strength, but the Soviets wished to send them a political message via their Czechoslovakian clients. In the end, the "renegade" Yugoslavians—whose maverick leader Tito had offended socialist orthodoxy—were denied visas to travel to the championships. Sending another such message, in 1963, the Soviet bloc boycotted an international volleyball event in Albania—another "unorthodox" state. At the Albanian "championships," the only teams that played were from Albania, China, North Korea and Rumania: all socialist countries that had either broken with the Soviets ideologically or were considering doing so.

The only international volleyball played by the United States during this period was a "match" between the U.S. and Soviet embassy staffs in The Hague in 1955. According to the New York Times, the Soviets—who had proposed the friendly game—"beat the United States on the volleyball court this afternoon in an setting redolent of the spirit of coexistence, cooperation and goodwill." Perhaps the U.S. loss is unsurprising in view of the fact that the volleyball so industriously cultivated by the YMCA had been intended merely as a recreation and not as a seriously competitive game.

In 1961, the Olympic Organizing Committee voted to allow volleyball into the games. The Soviets and their clients, and the Japanese, were naturally great advocates of the change, and, at the 1964 games in Tokyo, the Japanese, Soviet, Czech and Polish teams were the main players. The Soviets edged out the Czechs for the gold medal in the men's competition, the Czech men took the silver, and the Japanese men won the bronze. However, the most exciting volleyball was undoubtedly played by the Japanese women's team. In fact, it can be fairly argued that the Japanese women's team revolutionized the game.

As one observer wrote, the Japanese played "with a ferocity and precision that have made almost a new game of a familiar playground pastime." They were never in any danger, losing only one set, during a game with the Polish team, and that only because the coach, Daimatsu Hirofumi, had taken some of his better players out of the game when he felt that the Soviet team was learning too much about the new tactics.

The Japanese women's team was formed in 1953 and sponsored by the Nichibo Spinning Mills near Osaka. Hirofumi, who worked as the company's manager in charge of office supplies procurement, drove his team very hard: practice, after work, was 6 hours a day 7 days a week, all year. The coach was known to have a hot temper, and insults and occasional kicks were part of his training formula. Though such methods were criticized by some, it has to be said that Hirofumi's 1964 team performed splendidly. One headline captures the sense of surprise that attended the Japanese victory, at least in the United States, as well as something of a lingering cold-

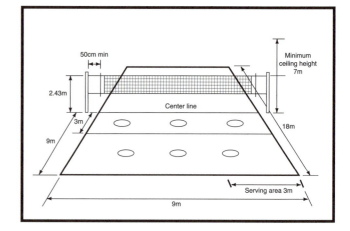

war flavor: "Celebrated Team of Office Girls Subdues Russians."

Particularly interesting to other teams was the Japanese version of the "rolling retrieve," which required that a player fall with gymnastic power and precision in order to save an incoming ball that could be up to three meters away. The player then recovered with great speed and grace to rejoin the ongoing play. Since Tokyo, volleyball has been a hard-driving "power" sport in the international arena.

At the first Olympic games to feature volleyball, the United States team came in ninth. In the 1968 Mexico City Olympics, neither the U.S. men's or women's teams made a particularly good showing—the Soviets, Japanese, Poles, and Czechs dominated—and the U.S. team did not even qualify for the Olympics again until 1984. Significantly, the first U.S. national training center for the game, near Houston, Texas, was dedicated to women's volleyball: a rare case of a sport being led, in development and top-level participation, by women. However that may be, the U.S. men's team took the gold medal at the 1984 Olympics, the women took the silver, and the United States has since been a world power in the sport.

## **Practice**

Volleyball was originally played over a net that was just 6 feet, 6 inches, but that height has been raised several times, until now the height is 7 feet, 11 and five-eighths inches for men (2.43 meters) and 7 feet, 7 and one-half inches (2.25 meters) for women. The net is 3 feet, 3 inches (1 meter) wide and is stretched across the center of a court that measures roughly 30 feet by 60 feet (9.14 meters by 18.29 meters). There is a minimum ceiling height of 23 feet (7 meters). The ball—which was first manufactured by Spaulding, the same company that first produced basketballs—is 9 to 10 ounces (250 to 280 grams) in weight and 15 to 27 inches (38 to 69 centimeters) in circumference.

Standard play is between two teams of six players—Morgan's original rules allowed for nine players. On each side of the net the teams are arrayed in two rows of three: left, center, and right forwards and left, center, and right backs. Play begins when the right back of one team serves the ball, first serve having been determined by the toss of a coin. The serve may be under- or overhanded, the player must serve within five seconds of taking a serving stance, and the served ball must not touch the net. The goal of the receiving team is to return the ball to the opposite side. They may handle the ball three times before the ball is returned and, indeed, the strategy of the game depends crucially on just such ball handling. In the basic volleying process there are a number of essential skills to be mastered.

Blocking is handled by the front line. Players in the front court area move laterally to the point where they judge the ball to be coming into their court and jump with hands outspread and arms overhead in an attempt to block the ball. Timing is obviously crucial, and many a beginner is coming back down to the gymnasium floor just as the opponents' ball moves over the net. All body contact with the net must also be avoided, which adds another level of challenge to mastering the block.

Should the block fail, or be impossible, receiving players, generally in the back court, use an underhanded stroke played close to the floor. This move is designed to "dig" the ball up into play. The move may be two handed or, in cases where quick lateral movement toward the ball is required, one handed. In either case the goal is to save the ball and to put it into play for another team member, who may choose to "set," or pass it, toward a third player. The third player, then, attempts to "spike" the ball into the opposing team's court. The set can be toward the forward ranks or toward the back, or even lateral, and much of the skill in setting consists in holding a posture that conceals the direction of the intended pass until the last possible fragment of a second.

The "spike," one of the more dramatic offensive maneuvers in volleyball, can be sent into the opposing court at speeds above 60 miles per hour (100 kilometers per hour), leaving very little reaction time for opponents. This involves a jumping attack, and an overhead smash down toward the opposite court. Rapid reaction time is essential to a good spike: should the shot be aimed down into the opponent's front court area, thus risking a successful block, or should it be fired toward back to test and hopefully defeat the "diggers"?

The serving team wins a point if the other side is unable to return the ball; if it loses, there is a "side-out" and the other team takes the serve. The players on the team that scores a side-out rotate clockwise so that each player begins the new set playing from a new position. Players must be in their appropriate positions at the moment the ball is served. After the serve, however, players may move to any position on the court and it is this feature that introduces the possibility of functional specialization into a game that was designed to be "universal" in terms of the skills required by all of its players. The post-serve movement of players is also, of course, a key matter of overall strategy in the game.

A game is won when a side has taken 15 points, so long as the other team trails by 2 points or more. Should the trailing team be within 1 point, play continues until the 2-point spread is achieved. A match consists of five games and is won with three games; three-game matches are sometimes played. Teams change sides after each game.

Beach volleyball—though played by many purely as a recreation, and by top-level players as a form of training—has developed its own competitive rules, teams, and a professional tour with corporate sponsorship. Teams may be two- or four-person and male or female. The cushioning effect of sand encourages players to attempt saving dives that would be impossible on a hard gymnasium floor, and jumping for blocks and spiking is more difficult than in standard play.

—Alan Trevithick

**Bibliography:** Baker, William J. (1982) *Sports in the Western World.* Totowa, NJ: Rowman and Littlefield.

Beal, Doug. (1985) *Spike! The Story of the Victorious U.S. Volleyball Team.* San Diego, CA: Avant Publishers.

Krout, John Allen. (1929) *Annals of American Sport.* Volume 15 of *The Pageant of America.* New Haven, CT: Yale University Press.

MacGregor, Barrie. (1977) *Volleyball.* Brighton, Sussex: EP Publishing.

Peck, Wilbur H. (1970) *Volleyball.* London: Collier Books.

Stokes, Roberta, and Mick Haley. (1984) *Volleyball Everyone.* Winston-Salem, NC: Hunter Textbooks.

Turnbull, Robert. (1964) "Celebrated Team of Office Girls Subdues Russians." *New York Times,* 24 October, 20:7.

United States Volleyball Association. (1992) *The World of Volleyball* (video). North Palm Beach, FL: The Athletic Institute.

Waggoner, Walter H. (1955) "Soviet Downs U.S. in Volleyball Match between Embassy Teams in The Hague." *New York Times,* 20 August, 3:5.

# War Games

At the nadir of Western civilization's history in a "no man's land" between the trenches that marked the killing fields of World War I, British and German soldiers emerged from their fortifications during a Christmas cease-fire to bury their dead, plant a tree, and play a game of soccer (association football). That match represented something crucial about the nature of sport. Sport and war have been inextricably linked throughout human history. War and athletic games share important historical connections.

## Origins

Many of the games that modern peoples consider sports evolved from the social practices of ancient hunting and gathering cultures, which used athletic contests as mechanisms for inculcating hunting skills, warrior training, and communal solidarity. The social organizations of sport and war share an old kinship. The aggression, competition, and teamwork that characterize primitive forms of sport also are hallmarks of primitive forms of warfare. Human cultures have invented many games simulating warfare. Recreations of war as games have athletic and nonathletic forms. From chess in Western civilization to *go* in Chinese civilization to extremely intricate computerized simulations in modern technological civilizations, nonathletic war games have evolved in diversity and complexity throughout human history. Athletic war games and sports have also developed in all human cultures. Athletic war games seek to teach physical, psychological, and social patterns, which can be applied to warfare.

## History

In hunting and gathering cultures sports such as foot races and contests of strength, which encouraged the development of the attributes necessary for warfare, represented one form of war games. Other types of war games, such as archery, spear and javelin throwing, sling-shot competitions, and other sports using war implements, familiarized people with weapons. These sports served hunting and gathering tribes as important social institutions and as a means of transmitting warrior craft from generation to generation.

As human populations began to develop agricultural civilizations (ca. 15,000–10,000 B.C.E.), their war games adapted and evolved to match newer cultural patterns of warfare. Most war games still served to create the physical and psychological stamina necessary for combat and to train people to use the increasingly sophisticated weaponry. Warrior classes in ancient Chinese, Indian, African, and Western civilizations engaged in archery; early forms of fencing; spear, javelin, and other throwing competitions; charioteering and horsemanship (excepting the American civilizations, which did not have horses). The agricultural civilizations also used war games to build the communal solidarity and to create the complex social organizations necessary for ancient warfare. These civilizations created ball games, foot and horse races, and a variety of other sports centered on the celebration of warrior prowess.

While ancient sports certainly had religious, political, and social components not immediately related to combat, most of them *were* related to war either directly or indirectly. In ancient Mesoamerica and in ancient Egypt, elaborate ball games served both as simulations of war situations and as contests to curry favor with the gods. In the Mesoamerican contests the losers, as in actual combat, sometimes faced death. Athletic champions and military conquerors were accorded similar forms of hero-worship. Indeed, the classical Greek term for an athletic contest, *agon*, also described military battles.

In Western civilization ancient Greek culture had a tremendous influence on the development of sports. The classical Greeks organized a sophisticated system of sports, which had important religious, political, and military significance. In the patriarchal cultures of ancient Greece, women were excluded from the places where men could win status, especially from sport and war. Greek athletic festivals featured games with direct military applications—chariot races, foot races, wrestling and boxing matches, duels with spears, javelin throws, and archery contests. These festivals and the Olympic Games they spawned beginning in 776 B.C.E. served as important religious ceremonies as well as celebrations of warrior prowess. The Olympics included military-related events such as foot races featuring armored runners and the violent *pankration*—a brutal fight between athletes in which almost any tactic was permitted and which sometimes led to deaths of not only the vanquished but also the victors. Olympic athletes also competed in events such as the pentathlon (a five-event contest consisting of a discus throw, a javelin throw, a standing broad jump, a foot race, and a wrestling match), which tested their warrior abilities.

The Greek athletic tradition spread throughout ancient civilization during the Hellenistic and Roman periods, and the Olympic Games continued until at least 390 C.E. Roman sports were in fact more committed to training soldiers than Greek games. Romans disliked the individualism and hero-worship that Greeks lavished on athletic champions. They preferred to run, swim, wrestle, box, race chariots, and engage in games that tested their skills with weapons and made them fit to serve in the legions rather than to concentrate on winning individual Olympic honors.

The Romans did, however, present athletic spectacles for the diversion and amusement of the citizenry and for the maintenance of public order. Romans provided "bread and circuses" in order to placate the masses. They built coliseums throughout the empire in which they staged particularly war-like contests such as chariot races, animal combats, artificial naval battles and, most popular of all the events, gladiator contests. Such brutal spectacles lasted for several centuries, although opposed by many Greek critics, some Roman intellectuals, and early Christians who were frequently martyred in the circuses. In the fifth century C.E., after the triumph of Christianity in the Roman Empire, the pagan spectacles were effectively banned. Even the Olympic Games, which the Christians associated with paganism, slowly plummeted into extinction.

Following the collapse of the Roman Empire, elite warrior classes of the medieval period—the feudal knights—engaged in games that were directly related to the dominant form of warfare— armored troops fighting on horseback. Horse racing, organized hunts, and mock combats at tournaments trained the aristocracy for battle. Just as Greek athletes had won status at the Olympics so too did European noblemen. They

*Ancient Greek athletic festivals featured games with direct military applications, including various kinds of combat. The painting on this amphora pictures contestants being monitored by an official, who holds a rod to signal fouls.*

marked their social position in the war games organized by feudal rulers. Knights competed in melees—hand-to-hand combats on foot between varying numbers of combatants. They also competed in jousts—competitions in which two mounted horsemen equipped with lances charged one another in an effort to knock their opponent from his steed. The medieval war games were shrouded in the chivalric tradition that shaped the contemporary European war culture. The medieval games were organized to reinforce chivalric notions of honor, class, and duty. Elaborate rituals were developed to connect the war games to the courtly culture of the middle ages. Knights fought for the honor of ladies or regions. No one below the rank of knight was permitted to compete. The nobility never sullied their station by competing against commoners. In spite of the fact that serious injures and deaths were not uncommon occurrences in melees and jousts, knights were obliged by chivalric conceptions of duty to participate in these sometimes fatal war games.

In early modern Europe (ca. 1400–1750) the monarchs of emerging nation-states continued to patronize war-like sports, but melees and jousts grew as obsolete as the medieval knights had when confronted by the reality of gunpowder weapons. They were replaced with more technologically up-to-date competitions such as fencing and shooting contests. In Great Britain the "manly art" of boxing was revived and organized for the first time since the collapse of the Roman Empire.

As Europeans conquered and colonized the American continents, they came into contact with indigenous Amerind peoples who also played sports related to their native styles of warfare. Various forms of ball games, wrestling, foot races, and spear-throwing and archery contests trained Native-American warriors in combat arts. North American tribes played forms of what Europeans termed "lacrosse"—an athletic ball game that served as a "little war" in which warriors demonstrated their stamina, skill, and fortitude.

Contact with Europeans often transformed or destroyed indigenous cultures and their unique sports. The ball courts of Mesoamerica declined into weed-covered fields, no longer the pitches for the life-and-death warrior games of the Aztecs and other tribes. The Spanish "civilized" native populations and banned their sports. Occasionally, Europeans appropriated native games into their own sporting cultures. The modern sport of lacrosse was developed from an ancient game by the Eastern Woodland tribes of North America. In Japan an elaborate feudal Samurai culture with sports that trained the warrior classes—similar in many respects to medieval European chivalric sports—disappeared in the nineteenth century as Japan decided to modernize and Westernize. First played by the Japanese in 1873, "modern" baseball quickly replaced "traditional" Samurai games. By the 1920s U.S. observers concluded that baseball enjoyed greater

status as the national pastime in Japan than in the United States.

The industrial revolutions and rise of nationalism, which transformed world civilizations from the late eighteenth century through the late twentieth century, altered the nature of both war and sport. The new technological patterns of warfare made combat less of a contest of physical prowess and more of a struggle of psychological stamina, social morale, and efficient machinery. Although modern armies and navies still needed physical vigor and stamina, they also began to rely more on patriotic energy, mental endurance, and teamwork. War games had always encouraged the latter as well as the former skills; however, the new modern sports (which militarists around the world insisted were essential for creating modern armed forces) stressed social and psychological recreations of warfare rather than the practice of the actual physical skills required by modern combat. If the new war games looked less like battle, they nevertheless attempted to teach modern peoples the mental and cultural skills that constituted the total warrior's craft.

The mass gymnastics movement that swept through the early-nineteenth-century German and Scandinavian states characterized one form of modern war games. Originating in the philosophical conceptions concerning Enlightenment doctrines of sound minds in sound bodies, a mass gymnastics craze in which instructors led groups through a series of exercises that were designed as athletic versions of military drills spawned the creation of *Turner* societies (as the German clubs devoted to gymnastics were called) throughout much of Germany and Scandinavia. The *Turner* movement was quickly incorporated into military drills for the new conscript armies that sought to repel Napoleon Bonaparte's (1769–1821) French legions. Nationalism and militarism ingrained mass gymnastics into German culture.

In Great Britain and its colonies the modernizing versions of traditional folk games were linked to the production of national military might. The English proclaimed that "the battle of Waterloo was won on the playing fields of Eton." Rebellious new nationalists in the United States who won their war for independence from Great Britain argued that American versions of those traditional folk sports had made a vigorous citizen army, which whipped the decadent British forces. The idea that modern Anglo-American sports manufactured military might became a powerful ideology in the industrializing world by the mid-nineteenth century. As the industrial revolution shrunk time and space and incorporated global civilizations into an interdependent economy, the new modern sports, in both their Germanic and Anglo-American variants, were introduced to the world.

Led by the United States, Great Britain, and Germany, industrialized nations adopted military athletic programs in order to modernize their armed forces. The major imperial powers of the late nineteenth and early twentieth century, including Japan, used sports to train their armies and navies. The colonial powers, including the United States, also used sports in efforts to impose Western styles of civilization on the peoples of Asia, Africa, and the Pacific.

The spread of Germanic athletics and Anglo-American sports through militarism and imperialism frequently resulted in cultural conflicts. As national militaries adopted sporting war games to prepare troops for the rigors of combat and to teach martial skills through simulated war, debates developed as to which system of athletics produced better warriors. France's defeat in the 1870–1871 Franco-Prussian War convinced many French nationalists and militarists that they would have to adopt Germanic or Anglo-American sporting practices in order to revive their nation's martial talents and restore French prestige. While various factions battled over the merits of Germanic gymnastics versus English-style physical education systems, the French public increasingly understood that some form of sporting activity would encourage *élan vital* and promote military preparedness. Although some observers, especially Anglo-American critics, sarcastically claimed the French failed to adopt any athletic style, France adapted Anglo-American games into a uniquely French sporting culture. In the 1890s France's Baron Pierre de Coubertin (1863–1937) revived the Olympic Games. Anglo-American sports provided the foundation for most of the Olympic contests. Paradoxically, Coubertin resurrected the Olympics to lessen the chance of war between nations and to build a strenuous French nationalism in case the Olympics failed to secure international peace. By

encouraging nationalism the modern Olympics have always been, at least in part, a form of war game.

During the Meiji Restoration (1868) in the midst of Japan's late-nineteenth-century race to modernize, Japanese elites borrowed Western sports in order to reorganize their educational and military systems. In particular, American baseball seized the Japanese imagination and became a symbol of the nation's modernization crusade. Inspired by American ideas that linked the skills developed by baseball to the execution of tasks required by modern warfare, Japanese leaders thought that baseball would teach the mass public the discipline, talent, and technological knowledge needed to fight modern wars.

From the mid-nineteenth century through the present, advocates of modernization in the military have promoted sport as a device for preparing nations for war. Legions of military and political officials who have encouraged industrial nations to build new modern armies and navies have also insisted that the practice of particular sports is crucial to the development of military power.

In the United States modern American football served as the war game for American martial culture. Promoted by nationalistic militarists such as Theodore Roosevelt (1858–1919), American football's ethos and structure simulated military organization. While the U.S. armed services employed a variety of sports to train warriors, football held a dominant position in American conceptions of athletic war games. The annual football match contested between the nation's two oldest military academies, the Army and the Navy, has become an important ritual in American popular culture. Indeed, analogies relating football to war have become standard in American life, and football and military languages overlap to a remarkable degree. In the Commonwealth and in former colonies of Great Britain rugby represents the same military organization and ethos exhibited in American football. In demilitarized modern Japan baseball still serves as a substitute war game.

For much of the world, militaristic ideologies find expression through soccer (association football). African, Asian, European, and Latin American nations consider the World Cup a test of national vigor and an indication of military prowess. In 1936, an Olympic match between Peru and Austria created a firestorm of South American ill will against Germany and Austria. In 1970, El Salvador and Honduras engaged in a military conflict (the "Soccer War") over a disputed World Cup qualifying match. International matches, such as the rivalry between Great Britain and Argentina following the Falklands War in 1978, have also demonstrated militaristic forms of nationalism.

In 1912 Olympic Games officials created the modern pentathlon, a war game that supposedly mimicked a soldier's duties in combat. First contested at the 1912 Olympics at Stockholm, International Olympic Committee (IOC) president Baron Pierre de Coubertin and the Swedish Olympic Committee (SOC) modeled the modern pentathlon on the ancient Greek pentathlon, which had been designed to test the skills of the athlete soldier. It combined equestrian, swimming, and running races; fencing combat; and shooting contests into an event that tested martial skills. Actually, the inclusion of sword-fighting and horsemanship in the modern pentathlon made the skills tested perhaps more appropriate to nineteenth-century cavalry officers than twentieth-century combat troops. This contest is still part of today's Olympic Games and continues to be dominated by military competitors. In the first modern Olympic pentathlon, Lieutenant George S. Patton, Jr. (1885–1945), who later became a prominent U.S. general during World War II, finished fifth. Not until 1952 at the Helsinki Olympics did a nonmilitary competitor, Sweden's Lars Hall (1927– ), capture a gold medal.

The biathlon, a combination of cross-country skiing and rifle shooting, originated during the early twentieth century in Scandinavia as a military ski patrol contest. International championships began in the 1950s, and, in 1960, the Olympic Games included the event on the winter program.

Historical connections between ideas about war and sport have shaped the athletic practices of people from the origins of human culture through the evolution of contemporary global civilizations. The presence of war games in numerous times, places, and cultures demonstrates the abiding human interest in using athletic contests to cultivate the mental, physical, and social talents necessary to engage in the deadliest of all human competitions. Both war and sport are primary expressions of human culture. They are also primary expressions that share an important historical kinship.

As the twenty-first century approaches, modern sports continue to be used throughout the world in military preparedness programs. International sporting events, particularly soccer matches and the Olympic Games, continue to create an intense nationalism that sometimes breaks out into armed conflict. The inventor of the modern Olympic Games, Baron Pierre de Coubertin, hoped that sport could be used to end war. Yet he also wanted to use sport to invigorate French nationalism. Perhaps international sport will eventually contribute to global harmony. Perhaps the effort to make sports into games for peace fails to recognize the ancient historical links between sport and war. Certainly, as long as sport continues to nurture nationalism, it will have a difficult time lessening the potential for national conflict.

—Mark Dyreson

**See also** Aggression; Biathlon; Jousting; Olympic Games, Ancient; Olympic Games, Modern; Patriotism; Pentathlon; Politics; Turnen; Violence.

**Bibliography:** Baker, William. (1982) *Sports in the Western World.* Totowa, NJ: Rowman and Littlefield.

Blanchard, Kendall. (1981) *Mississippi Choctaws at Play.* Urbana: University of Illinois Press.

Callois, Roger. (1961) *Man, Play and Games.* New York: Free Press.

Carter, John Marshall. (1988) *Sports and Pastimes of the Middle Ages.* New York: University Press of America.

Guttmann, Allen. (1978) *From Ritual to Record: The Nature of Modern Sports.* New York: Columbia University Press.

———. (1994) *Games and Empires: Modern Sports and Cultural Imperialism.* New York: Columbia University Press.

Harris, H. A. (1972) *Sport in Greece and Rome.* London: Thames and Hudson.

Hoberman, John. (1984) *Sport and Political Ideology.* Austin: University of Texas Press.

Holt, Richard. (1981) *Sport and Society in Modern France.* London: Macmillan.

———. (1989) *Sport and the British: A Modern History.* Oxford: Clarendon.

Huizinga, Johan. (1955) *Homo Ludens: A Study of the Play Element in Culture.* Boston: Beacon.

Keegan, John. (1993) *A History of Warfare.* New York: Alfred A. Knopf.

Kyle, Donald. (1987) *Athletics in Ancient Athens.* Leiden: E. J. Brill.

Lorenz, Konrad. (1966) *On Aggression.* New York: Harcourt Brace Jovanovich.

Mead, Margaret, ed. (1937) *Cooperation and Competition among Primitive Peoples*. New York: McGraw-Hill.

Mrozek, Donald. (1983) *Sport an American Mentality, 1880–1910*. Knoxville: University of Tennessee Press.

Sansone, David. (1988) *Greek Athletics and the Genesis of Sport*. Berkeley: University of California Press.

Stern, Theodore. (1949) *The Rubber Ball-Games of the Americas*. Seattle: University of Washington Press.

# Weightlifting

Competitive weightlifting today involves only two events: the snatch and the clean-and-jerk. Weightlifting can be referred to as Olympic lifting or Olympic weightlifting; it is a recognized sport in Olympic competition (men only). Olympic weightlifting is easily recognized because in both the snatch and the clean-and-jerk, the barbell is lifted to an overhead position. Weightlifting is one of two internationally recognized strength competitions; powerlifting is the other.

Weight training, which is general conditioning and development of strength, provides the physical foundation for competitive weightlifting. Weightlifting, however, goes beyond weight training. Because of the explosive nature of Olympic lifting, total body strength is required to complete the lifts effectively. Athletes must use power, strength and speed, flexibility, balance, and coordination to successfully compete the snatch and the clean-and-jerk. Proper technique provides the athlete with a competitive edge. The novice lifter should master the technique involved for both events prior to increasing the resistance on the bar.

## Origins

For centuries, man has been using weightlifting as a means of entertainment, preparation for battle, bodybuilding, and competition. The tomb of Beni Hasan revealed wall paintings showing men and women exercising with stone weights as early as 3500 C.E. Illustrations from the 2040 B.C.E. tomb records of Prince Baghti depicted movements that are strikingly similar to the one-hand snatch or swing. Ancient Greeks and Romans used different shaped and weighted stones called *halteres* for exercising. In China, weighted objects of various kinds were used for heavy exercise to prepare troops for battle.

The Greeks were the first to develop organized approaches to weight training and had weight activities that were practical and usually related to warfare. It is not surprising that they became the first bodybuilders, combining physical beauty and athletic skills. They used lifting stones, which later were replaced by a bar with a bell on each end for added resistance. (The bell clapper was removed to silence the bell, thus the term "dumbbell.") Legend has it that a Crotonan man called Milo was the first to use progressive-resistance exercise. This type of exercise is based on the idea that as the resistance increases strength increases. Milo's progressive resistance exercise consisted of daily lifting and carrying a baby calf throughout its maturation into a full-grown bull. The Romans also shared this appreciation of weight training, but with the decline and fall of the empire, the value and direction of physical exercise diminished.

During the Dark Ages, weight training became the tool of the warrior; shows of strength became popular entertainment. Large stones or trees were used in tests of strength and competition. These types of competition have remained relatively unchanged through the years in Switzerland, Spain, and Scotland as well as in the Swedish island of Gotland. History records that Richard Joy (1675 –?), the Kentish Samson, performed a harness lift of 2,254 pounds (1,025 kilograms) for King William III.

In the eighteenth century, interest in physical strength and well-being reappeared. Physical education was reintroduced to the university curriculum. The development and production of exercise apparatus along with programs using free weights and simple machines took place. Training emphasized musculature strength and endurance rather than physical development.

Professional strongmen became popular. Formalized lifts were rarely practiced as each lifter chose something that he could specialize in for entertainment purposes. Bending bars of iron, lifting every object from people to animals, and breaking chains were common fare. Felice Napoli of Italy, a circus and a fairground performer, is credited

*At the 1992 Barcelona Olympics Aleksandr Kourlovitch strains to repeat his gold medal performance of four years earlier in the over-110-kilogram class. Russians have been dominant in weightlifting since the 1960s.*

with starting the strongman boom. He influenced Professor Louis Attila, who had the foresight and vision to see weightlifting and bodybuilding as an activity in its own right. He trained many of the best-known performers of the time and crowned heads of state. He popularized the use of hollow shot leaded weights and developed the bent press or screw press. His best known students were Fredrick Muller (1867–1925), who became the great Eugene Sandow, Louis Cyr (1863–1912) known as the strongest man in the world, and Professor Edmond Desbonnet, the father of French physical culture.

Sandow became known not only for his strength but for his well-developed musculature. His emphasis on massive musculature and definition as well as strength was the initial influence leading to modern-day bodybuilding. Sandow was beaten only once by Arthur Saxon of the

Saxon Trio Strongman act who used a hollow handles weight filled with quicksilver. In this form of competition, technique had to be perfect and the weight raised absolutely level, or the quicksilver would shift making the lift almost impossible. Sandow was unsuccessful in raising the weight level. An investigation took place concerning the equipment/apparatus and a subsequent court battle ruled the contest invalid due to "trickery."

French-Canadian Louis Cyr was never beaten in any weightlifting contest. Considered to be the strongest man that ever lived, Cyr stood nearly 6 feet (1.83 meters) tall and weighed 301 pounds (136 kilograms). He made his living lifting everything from boulders to livestock. Cyr unfortunately also loved to eat and drink and as a result became grossly overweight. He died of chronic nephritis at age 49.

## Practice

Lifting as we know it today began in the mid-1800s. The development was paralleled in several countries throughout Central Europe and in the United States. Early weightlifting contests had programs consisting of "odd lifts" focusing on repetitive lifting. These included using everything from one or two finger lifts and lifting with the teeth, to the more standard snatch, press, and clean-and-jerk. One of the first attempts to have international competition took place in London in 1893. Competitors from Italy, Belgium, Britain, and Germany vied for the first "World Championship" title. The contest was decided by repetition lifting rather than aggregate totals. Lifts were judged by whether the lift was clean, or if unfair leverage or "trickery" was used.

The equipment used during the turn of the century progressed quickly. From the bar with the "dumbbells" evolved the solid globeweight introduced by Triat of France. Later, Louis Attila developed the hollow globes that could be weighted with everything from sand to quicksilver. Albert Attila, no relation to Louis, used special spiked globes weighing 220 pounds (100 kilograms) and lifted this with one hand over his head. Due to the consequences of a missed lift, this style of lifting never caught on. The French developed the first disc-loading set which was produced by M. M. Pelletier Monnier and used ideas of Professor Desbonnet. In the late 1920s Charles Rigoulot (1903–1962) used an 8-foot (2.4-meter) bar to exceed the world record for executing the clean-and-jerk; thus the advantage of a long springy bar was discovered. In 1905 the Milo Barbell Company produced the first barbell set with interchangeable plates. Rotating collars were later added.

In 1896 the first modern Olympic Games were held. Weightlifting was included but subsequently excluded in the 1900 games. Weightlifting returned to the Olympic program in St. Louis in 1904. No weightlifting was included in the 1908 (London) or 1913 (Stockholm) games. Limited U.S. participation was due to the newness of the sport and general regard that it was circus-type entertainment rather than a sport.

Father Bill Curtis, who helped to found the Amateur Athletic Union (AAU) in 1888, did much for the sport of Olympic lifting in the United States. He was one of the first to develop and use a system of weight training for overall strength and health rather than striving for higher poundage in a specific lift. W. A. Pullum, known as the "the Wizard of Weight-lifting," was the first man to concentrate on technique rather than strength. He established the first scientific weightlifters' school in 1906, and in 1912 became the first Britain to lift double his body weight. This was an unusual feat because, as a youth, he had been stricken with tuberculosis and was considered rather small. Henry Steinbon (1893–1989), a German strength expert and professional wrestler, became the chief advocate of the "quick lifts," the one-hand snatch and the clean-and-jerk. His instruction and lifting techniques were instrumental in getting the sport off the ground in the United States. Bernarr MacFadden (1868–1955), a publisher and businessman, promoted an approach of physical development through weightlifting. He promoted a regional contest with pictures in 1903 to declare "The Most Perfectly Developed Man in the World." The 1921 winner, Angelo Sicilian (1892–1972), became Charles Atlas.

The International Weightlifting Federation, formed in 1920, brought official status to the sport. Weightlifting returned to the Olympics with a new set of rules and regulations, even though a rumor suggested that it might be dropped from further games. Fourteen countries competed in Antwerp in the one-hand snatch, one-hand clean-and-jerk (opposite hand), and two-hands clean-and-jerk. From 1920 on, most of the interest would be on international lifts of the one- and two-hand snatch, one- and two-hand clean-and-jerk, and military press.

During the 1920s and 1930s lifters in the United States performed poorly compared to the international competition. They lagged far behind in technique and in program, equipment, and financial support. At the Paris 1924 contest, competitors had the choice of barbell or globe design weights and both the two-hand clean-and-press and two-hand snatch were lifts added to the competition. No U.S. weightlifters were present at either the 1924 or 1928 Olympics. The bar with the revolving sleeve was used in the 1928 Amsterdam Olympics for the first time. The press, snatch, and jerk would become the standard lifts until the press was removed in 1972.

Standardization of the lifts created a big split between Olympic weightlifting, bodybuilding, and powerlifting. The 1930s was the initiation period of bodybuilding which quickly developed in the 1940s with Mr. Universe contests. The 1946 winner of Mr. Universe was Steve Stanko, who was also the first man to total 1,000 pounds (454 kilograms) in Olympic lifts.

In 1929 the AAU assumed leadership of weightlifting and began to sanction meets. For the first time, in 1932 an AAU–sanctioned team performed at the Los Angeles Olympics. The U.S. team, coached by Bob Hoffman (1898–1985), was no match for the international lifters. However, Hoffman and the athletes at the York Barbell Club became instrumental in the Americans' rise to prominence in Olympic lifting. As developer and owner of the York Barbell Company, Hoffman coached the team for three decades, providing not only technical assistance but jobs for the lifters within his company. He is considered by many to have had the most influence on American weightlifting. From the 1930s through the 1950s lifting in the United States improved such that Americans began placing at the top of world competition.

Women entered the weightlifting scene in the 1940s, with the first recorded weightlifting meet for women held in the United States in 1947. Women have competed internationally in Olympic-style weightlifting since that time but have not yet been included in the Olympic Games. The first international competition was held in the United States with Canada, China, Great Britain, Hungary, and the United States participating. They performed to a small but enthusiastic crowd. From the start, Chinese women have consistently dominated weightlifting competition.

The development of weightlifting in the European countries was slowed as a result of World War II. In the early 1960s Eastern bloc countries considered Olympic lifting a major sport and began to dominate. This dominance has continued. During the 1970s, Vasili Alexeev (1942– ) of the Soviet Union dominated the super-heavyweight division by setting a series of world records. After a long period of controversy, the bench press was officially removed at the 1972 Olympics. Technical tricks along with poor refereeing caused a great deal of ill feelings and arguments among coaches, lifters, and officials. This left only the snatch and jerk to be performed in the Olympic set.

Olympic lifting standards have risen significantly because of the combination of increased numbers of competition opportunities, improved scientific training, and use of strength-enhancing drugs. Some countries have taken a moral and ethical stand against drug usage; they are now at a distinct disadvantage. Other countries prepared medical research to pursue new drug designs and to create methods of successfully avoiding drug detection. At the 1970 World Championships, there were massive disqualifications of athletes who used amphetamines. During the 1972 Munich Olympics, the first two positive cases of doping in weightlifting were found. In the 1976 Olympics eight disqualifications for anabolic steroid use were made. No doping was found at the 1980 Olympics in Russia when the United States boycotted, but few believe it was a clean competition. The controversy over the use of performance-enhancement drugs in lifting continues.

In a weightlifting competition today, males compete in 10 weight classes from Fly (54 kilograms [119 pounds]) to Superheavyweight (108-plus kilograms [238-plus pounds]). Women compete in 9 weight classes starting at 46 kilograms (101.5 pounds) and going up to 83-plus kilograms (183-plus pounds). Age divisions include: junior (12 through 17 years), junior (18 through 20 years), senior (21-plus), and master (35-plus). The two-hand snatch and two-hand clean-and-jerk are the only lifts included in competitive Olympic lifting.

Each lifter has three opportunities to complete a successful or legal lift for the snatch and then for the clean-and-jerk. The athlete must record one legal lift in both events to be considered in the final placing. The heaviest weight lifted for each event is used for the total of the combined lifts. The grip used for both lifts is very specific to weightlifting and is called the hook technique. This is different from a regular overhand grip in which the thumb is wrapped around the bar. The hook grip is established by first wrapping the thumb around the bar and then overlapping the thumb with the first and second finger; thus the thumb becomes a hook on the bar. Two judges and one referee indicate the success of a lift using red (no lift) and white (legal lift) lights. Red lights from two or more officials results in an unsuccessful lift attempt.

The snatch is an explosive movement when the barbell is lifted from the platform to an overhead position in one continuous motion. The intricate snatch technique makes this lift the most difficult of the two weightlifting movements. The lifter must pull the bar from the platform to chest level and then overhead with arms fully extended in one fluid motion. The body must be positioned under the bar in this movement just before the bar is extended overhead evenly. To complete this the athlete uses the squat style: The lifter is underneath the bar in a sitting position, then drives into an upright position. The split style, with one leg forward and one leg back, is not used as frequently by the lifters to get underneath the bar because it does not allow for lifting as much weight as the squat style.

The clean-and-jerk technique allows for the greatest amount of weight to be lifted. Two distinct movements are involved in this lift: the clean, which is the lifting of the weight from the platform to shoulder height, and the jerk, which is the thrusting of the weight from the chest and shoulders to an overhead position. In the clean, the weight is lifted first to waist level using the legs, hips, and back muscles. The lifter must then pull the body under the bar using a squat or a split technique. From here, the lifter stands, resting the weight on shoulders and chest. An explosive jump is used to propel the weight upward, splitting the legs to help lower the body under the bar. After the weight is overhead, the lift is completed by bringing the legs together using a series of small steps to achieve an erect stance. The lift is complete when the body becomes motionless.

Incorrect movements that are illegal and will result in disqualification of that attempt include stopping the motion of the bar after removing it from the platform (called pulling from the hang); touching the platform with any part of the body other than the feet; failure to complete extension of arms evenly and in one motion (no pause permitted); completing the lift with a press-out (bends arms while bar positioned overhead, attempts to extend arms to locked position overhead); bending and extending arms while in squat or split position (recovery); leaving the platform prior to completion of the lift; failure to wait for the referee's signal to return the bar to the platform; dropping the bar after the referee's signal; and failure to have feet and bar in line and parallel to the body at completion of the lift. Movements, specific to the snatch, which result in an unsuccessful lift attempt include pausing during the lift (motion must be continuous) and touching the head with the bar when completing the lift. Movements, specific to the clean-and-jerk, that result in disqualification of the lift include failure to place the bar on the chest prior to bringing elbows under bar; elbows or upper arms making contact with the thighs or knees; and failure to complete jerking motion in one movement.

Safety is an important factor to be considered with weightlifting. The lifter should warm up properly and be stretched before attempts are made at heavier weights. The warmup aids in prevention of injuries as well as ensuring safe lifting. When it becomes impossible to complete a lift attempt, the rules allow the athlete to drop the bar to the platform without contacting the body.

—Darlene S. Young

**See also** Bodybuilding; Powerlifting.

**Bibliography:** Fair, J. D. (1987) "Bob Hoffman, the York Barbell Company, and the Golden Age of American Weightlifting, 1945–1960." *Journal of Sport History* 14: 164–188.

Fodor, R. V. (1979) *Competitive Weightlifting.* New York: Sterling Publishing Company.

Hoffman, B. (1974) "A Century of American Weightlifting." *Strength and Health* 44, 4: 34–40, 54–55.

Kirkley, G., and J. Goodbody, eds. (1986) *The Manual of Weight-Training.* London: Stanley Paul.

Kutzer, W. F. (1979) "The History of Olympic Weightlifting in the United States." Ph.D. dissertation, Brigham Young University, Provo, Utah.

Lear, J. (1982) *The Powerlifter's Manual.* Wakefield, UK: EP Publishing.

Mentzer, M., and A. Friedberg. (1982) *Mike Mentzer's Complete Book of Weight Training.* New York: William Morrow.

Schodl, G. (1992) *The Lost Past.* Budapest, Hungary: International Weightlifting Federation.

Todd, T. (1978) *Inside Powerlifting.* Chicago: Contemporary Books.

U.S. Weightlifting Federation. (1996) *1996 Media Guide.* Colorado Springs, CO: U.S. Weightlifting Federation.

Webster, D. (1976) *The Iron Game.* Irvine, UK: John Geddes Printer.

Weiner, L. (1947) "A Preliminary Study of the History of Weightlifting in the United States of America." Master's thesis, University of Illinois, Urbana.

# Women's Sports

This article contains two entries. The first, by Gertrud Pfister, dscusses the development of women's sports in Europe; the second, by Joan Hult, concentrates on women's sports in North America. These are the regions of the world in which women's sports developed most quickly and thus influenced women's participation in sports elsewhere in the world. Women's participation in sport is also discussed throughout the encyclopedia in articles on individual sports as well as in general articles.

## Women's Sports, Europe

Body and movement culture, like gender expectations, depends on prevailing social conditions and cultural patterns. It "embodies" a society's values and norms. The many-faceted world of sports and games produces and reproduces social structures, meanings, and models of legitimacy. Gender, moreover, interacts quite independently with body and movement culture so that various combinations of gender, social class, and age decisively influence physical activities. Since most societies have been and still are dominated by men, it is hardly surprising that men have tended to take the leading role in body and movement culture. Nonetheless, women have usually been able to develop and practice their own specifically female culture alongside the men's, and there have always been some women who successfully demanded the opportunity to participate in men's sports. Questions remain, however. Have today's women, at least those in the industrialized world, really overcome the obstacles that once kept them from sports participation? Do sports now answer the social and cultural needs of girls' and women's lives?

### Preindustrial Society

The body and movement cultures of preindustrial societies are characterized by an association with religion and magic, a close relationship with economic processes and with warfare, a paucity of rules, a low level of administrative organization, and an absence of abstract records. Women participated in many if not most preindustrial physical activities, but their participation varied in accordance with the division of labor between the sexes as well as with norms, values, conceptions, and relations of power.

In ancient Greece, gymnastic exercises and sports contests evolved from the structures, values, and ideals of a bellicose aristocratic culture of aristocratic men. The men who were responsible for warfare and for the political and economic spheres were also in charge of sports. Women, whose roles were generally restricted to those of wives and mothers, were neither politically nor legally equal to men. They were prevented from exercising in public gymnasia and from witnessing—much less participating in—the Olympic Games that took place quadrennially in honor of Zeus.

At Olympia girls did run races in honor of Hera, the consort of Zeus, but this event, known as the Heraia, was a local fertility rite that lacked the prestige of the great panhellenic sports festivals. In Sparta's militaristic society, girls underwent systematic physical training designed to make them into healthy mothers of future warriors. While it is possible that some form of physical education for girls also took place outside of Sparta, gymnastics and sports contests were basically a theater for the demonstration of masculine physical prowess and beauty.

There is little evidence that Roman women participated in sports. Scattered references to foot races for girls have been found for athletic festivals in the Greek-speaking parts of the Roman Empire, and an intriguing mosaic found in a Sicilian villa seems to depict ten young aristocratic women engaged in various athletic endeavors. A very few lower-class or slave women fought as gladiators. On the whole, however, respectable Roman women seem to have avoided sports except as spectators at chariot races and gladiatorial games.

In the Middle Ages, European sports often occurred in close conjunction with religious festivals, but the regional differences and class divisions of medieval society prevented the emergence of a single, universally accepted system of

*Gold medalist Gisela Mauermayer at the 1936 Olympics. In the 1920s track and field had been the arena in which women fought for the right to compete in "male" sports.*

physical activities. Social inequalities, including those that governed gender relationships, were one consequence of a general lack of affect control, a valorization of the body as the guarantor of political and legal rights, and a general resort to physical violence as a way of settling public and private conflicts.

Despite the predominance of male power, some women achieved privileged status at court or in a nunnery. Some of these privileged women rode horseback and enjoyed the sport of falconry; some played simple ball games. Aristocratic women also played an ancillary role at the medieval tournaments that were an important aspect of the life of a medieval knight. Tournaments served not only to harden the warrior's body and prepare it for battle; they were also vivid symbolic demonstrations of social order. It was important that women be present to admire and encourage the combatants and to acknowledge men's right to rule.

In medieval towns, the most popular sports—archery, wrestling, fencing—were also related to the exigencies of warfare. That relationship meant, generally, the exclusion of women from the archery guilds that were a prominent part of urban life, but middle-class women were occasionally allowed to compete among themselves in an archery contest, especially in Flanders and in Holland. Archery matches throughout Europe were also important social events that would have been painfully incomplete had admiring female spectators been excluded.

Among the peasantry, women were so essential in the struggle for mere survival that it seemed only natural for them to share in many of the sports of their fathers, husbands, and sons. They appear in medieval art not only as dancers but also as participants in the widely popular (and wildly chaotic) game of folk football. In England, France, Germany, Switzerland, and Italy, girls and women ran races for smocks and similar prizes.

In must be admitted, however, that our picture of preindustrial body and movement culture is far from complete. If women appear far less frequently than men, one reason for their absence is that men have written the histories and interpreted the documents (which, in turn, were produced mostly by men). Scholars have only begun to write the history of women. To gather evidence of ancient and medieval women's sports, it is often necessary to glean the historical field after conventional historians have finished their harvest.

## The Eighteenth and Nineteenth Centuries

Our contemporary conceptions of sports evolved from the body and movement cultures of early modern Europe. In the late eighteenth and early nineteenth centuries, Western political, economic, and social institutions were decisively altered by new forms of technology and production, by the French Revolution and a number of similar political upheavals, and by the philosophical currents of "the Age of Reason." Work began to move from fields and households to factories and offices, changing the nature of the family, which had traditionally combined economic and domestic functions. Faith in scientific rationality, especially in the form of medicine and biology, began to replace religion as the basis of society's conception of the gender order. All these changes tended to increase rather than decrease the perceived differences between men and women. Although a few voices called for greater equality between the sexes, most Europeans believed that men and women are by nature complementary opposites. The myth of manly strength and womanly weakness was generally accepted. The doctrine of "separate spheres" sent men into the political and economic realms while women, especially those of the middle classes, were expected to devote themselves to the home and the church.

### Turnen, Gymnastics, and Sports

Modern sports are the result of the confluence of several developments in the body and movement cultures of the late eighteenth and early nineteenth centuries in Europe (and, to a lesser extent, in the United States). One such development was German gymnastics (*Turnen*), which evolved from the ideas and practices of pedagogues like Johann Christian Friedrich Guts Muths and from the political program of Friedrich Ludwig Jahn. For Jahn, *Turnen* was an expression of nationalism, a means to overcome the feudal order that had cut Germany into a patchwork of antagonistic states. His movement was also aimed at the expulsion of the French, whom Napoleon had led to a series of military victories over divided Germany.

Given his patriotic goals and emphasis on military preparedness, Jahn saw no reason to include women in his program. Besides, clambering up poles and swinging from ropes were "unseemly" activities for "the weaker sex." The exclusion of women from the ranks of the *Turnen* seemed so "self-evident" that Jahn and his followers never bothered to explain or justify it.

Like Jahn, the Swedish physical educator Per Henrik Ling (1776–1839) was influenced by GutsMuths. Ling combined the anatomical and physiological knowledge of his era with the ideas of "natural philosophy" in order to create an allegedly scientific system of simple exercises intended to promote balance, harmony, and health. The core of his system, however, included military as well as hygienic exercises. The institute that he established in Stockholm in 1813 spread his ideas throughout northern and western Europe. Although Ling envisioned his program as solely for men and boys, Swedish gymnastics eventually become the seedbed of women's physical education. In Finland, for instance, Elin Kallio (1859–1927) adapted Lingianism to the needs of girls and women. In 1896 a gymnastics federation was founded.

In France, the evolution of gymnastics took a militaristic turn under the guidance of Francisco Amoros (1770–1848), a Spanish officer who emigrated to France and established a training school at which exercises were conducted by military command. One result of his influence, which remained dominant for most of the century, was that the French, like the Germans and the Italians, associated gymnastics with bellicose nationalism. The École de Joinville (1852), where physical educators were trained, was under the army's control, and many of France's physical educators were former army officers. The predictable result of this military emphasis was the nearly total neglect of girls' and women's gymnastics in France as in every other European country.

In the course of the nineteenth century, however, there was increasing concern about the effects of industrialization and urbanization on girls' and women's health. Patriotism seemed to require that something be done. There was soon a lively debate over female physical education.

Among the first to champion physical exercise for girls was Phokion Heinrich Clias (1782–1854), a propagandist active in Switzerland, France, and England. His *Kalisthenie* (1829), from which we derive the term "calisthenics," was a landmark in the history of women's physical education. Its influence can be attributed in large part to the emphasis Clias placed on gentle exercises that enhanced female grace and beauty. German pedagogues like Johann Adolf Ludwig Werner also published books advocating gymnastics for young women. By 1850 a number of gymnastic clubs offered courses intended to make girls healthier and more attractive. It is unlikely that many girls benefited from these opportunities, and most who did came from affluent middle-class homes.

In the latter half of the nineteenth century, governments the length and breadth of Europe legislated one or another form of compulsory physical education for girls, but many of these laws remained dead letters until early in the twentieth century. It was not until late in the nineteenth century that a significant number of girls schools began to include gymnastics in their curriculum. When they did, the teachers were usually careful to limit their pupils' movements to regimented drill, which instilled obedience. To preserve "decency," German girls, for example, were not allowed to perform exercises that required them to spread their legs or to lift them above the waist.

While German girls marched and executed the standardized movements prescribed by Adolf Spiess (1810–1858) and other schoolmasters, English girls took slow walks and suffered the boredom of calisthenics. In an effort to improve the situation, the London School Board looked abroad. In 1881 Martina Bergmann (later Bergmann-Österberg; 1849–1915) was summoned from Stockholm's school of Lingian gymnastics in order to take charge of girls' physical education. It was hoped that "Swedish gymnastics" would provide inexpensive rational discipline without militaristic associations. The ideal was noncompetitive physical development without the sacrifice of femininity.

During the years when these and other gymnastic systems evolved on the continent, the British transformed their traditional physical pastimes into what we now recognize as modern sports. By the middle of the eighteenth century, there were not only written rules for horse races and for cricket matches; there were also organizations, like the Marylebone Cricket Club, that enforced the rules and standardized the contests.

By the early nineteenth century, there was also a sporting press to publicize these sports and to elevate boxers like Tom Cribb to the status of national heroes. In the course of the nineteenth century, schoolmasters at Eton, Rugby, and other public schools made a cult of cricket, crew, and football. Sports were an essential part of "muscular Christianity." They were thought to be the basis of moral manhood.

Girls and women were not entirely excluded from the nascent sports culture of the eighteenth and nineteenth centuries. Some of them participated in rural cricket matches. Aristocratic women competed in archery contests. Lower-class women in London often engaged in boxing matches, to the delight of the mostly male spectators. On the whole, however, modern sports were considered to be a masculine preserve.

## The Turn-of-the-Century Triumph of Modern Sports

Women's roles changed rapidly with the industrialization and modernization of society at the end of the nineteenth century. Feminism became a powerful force. Universities opened their doors to female students, and educated women began to enter the professions. Men discovered that more and more women were ready and willing to participate in "manly" sports. Participation was, of course, influenced by such factors as national culture and social class. In Spain, where agriculture continued to be the mainstay of the economy and where the Roman Catholic Church exercised great authority, only aristocratic or upper-middle-class women indulged in such daring pastimes as golf, tennis, and skiing. Gymnastic exercises for girls were virtually unknown and were certainly not a part of public education. In the liberal democracies of northern and western Europe, female athletes found much readier acceptance. In France, as well as in other European countries, technological improvements in the bicycle progressed to the point where large numbers of women caught "cycling fever" and a few of them actually defied convention and competed in bicycle races (which were discontinued when conservative opinion expressed outrage at such "unwomanly" forms of amusement).

There was, in fact, still widespread opposition to women's sports even in northern and western Europe. Critics relied on an arsenal of medical, moral, and aesthetic arguments. Track and field contests were condemned with special fervor because they were thought not only to encourage an unwomanly competitiveness but also to threaten a woman's health.

Despite opposition, most European countries had at least the beginnings of women's sports before the outbreak of World War I. Germany had not only women's sections of men's gymnastics clubs but also independent clubs for women and even a number of women's sports clubs. The same can be said for England and France and—to a lesser extent—for Italy. Although the economic costs of tennis, golf, and rowing tended to restrict participation in these sports to the affluent, there was also a movement for workers' sports. The German federation for workers' sports, founded in 1893, attracted a number of female members. The Czechs were also active in the field of workers' sports. In these federations, and in those of France, Belgium, and Scandinavia, female members generally had the same rights as male members, at least on paper, which was usually not the case in middle-class clubs and federations.

Track and field is an excellent place to describe more closely the barriers faced (and eventually overcome) by female athletes. In Germany, the first track and field contests for women met with strong opposition. When the Berlin sports club Comet staged a Damensportfest in 1904, the club hoped to lure a large number of sensation-hungry spectators through the turnstiles. The 400-meter (437.44-yard) race did, indeed, generate revenue and publicity, but it also raised a number of questions about the appropriateness of the race. When the race was repeated, with the added attraction of some French participants, there was less public interest than expected. The official journal of the German Track and Field Federation took the "ladies race" as an occasion to condemn women's races. The runners' style was satirized as a "duck waddle" and their efforts were written off as a misunderstanding of female emancipation. In truth, these Damensportfeste had less to do with emancipation than with voyeurism and sensationalism. Despite the failures of the first attempts to inaugurate women's track and field, interest in such events was growing.

In France as well as in Germany, athletic meets were men's affairs. Pierre de Coubertin criticized

## Women on Wheels before World War I

My friend Miss Clara Beyer and I were probably the first ladies to exhibit themselves to a scandalized public on a cycle (a three-wheeler, actually). That was in 1890. At first we had our cycles brought to the outskirts of town and rode on the deserted forest roads, the occasional passer-by hailing us with righteous indignation or with sneers and innuendo. Later we dared to ride through the town itself at dawn. Finally, one splendid afternoon, we set out bravely from the Berlin town square. Hundreds of people gathered on the instant, and a swarm of ragamuffins kept pace with us, chanting remarks of the most charming sort. In short, we ran the gauntlet which caused us to ask ourselves whether the game was worth the candle.

We were fighting a positively fanatical hatred. Pointless to compare ourselves with equestriennes: cycling remained unfeminine, though why remained unanswered. It was enough to bring us to tears. But when, once outside the town, we would speed along under the green canopy of trees, chest expanded and heart racing, we would reaffirm our eternal loyalty to cycling.

The first ladies bicycle race in September 1893 was a breakthrough. For the first time, a numerous and largely sports-minded public saw a phalanx of able female cyclists, tastefully clothed, mastering the machine. How different from seeing a lone woman cycling amidst a hooting mob! Thus the ice was broken, and now only the occasional old fogy dared describe a female bicyclist as an unfeminine creature.

And that is as it should be. Quite apart from the pleasure of the thing the rapid movement, comparable only to flying, in God s fresh air the beneficial influence of bicycling on a woman's body and spirit is utterly unmistakable.

No more missed trains, no more crowded horse-trolley, no more dearth of hackney-carriages! Free to decide to the minute when and where one wants to be! Those are the spiritual pleasures of cycling. Physically, too, we feel its benign influence. Can any migraine withstand a splendid bicycle ride? And how delectable is the modest meal in a humble country inn when we have put a goodly distance behind us!

Now, as to dress: the first thing to consign to the attic is the corset. An experienced female cyclist can only be amused by the question, "skirt or trousers?" A woman has exactly the same number of legs as a man; she uses them, especially in bicycling, in exactly the same way as a man, and should clothe them just as sensibly, giving each leg its own covering rather than placing both into one. (Has it ever occurred to anyone to put both arms into one sleeve?) The most practical garment for bicycle touring is a pair of trousers, only slightly fuller than a modern gentleman's plus-fours. Of course, one does not parade around in these upon arrival, but draws over them the skirt one has prudently brought along on the handlebars.

One piece of advice to new female disciples: in matters of cycling, seek medical advice only from a doctor who is himself a cyclist. It is quite incredible what opinions a noncycling doctor (probably a dying breed, by the way) can voice. Of course, only she whose state of health permits it should bicycle. But that is the only limitation; I admit no other.

For an older lady, the decision to clamber onto a bicycle is more difficult than for a young one. I believe that in the future, old ladies will not need to learn to ride a bicycle; they will grow old as bicycle riders. And the children who are growing up with this machine will consider it an indispensable tool, a part of their very lives.

—Condensed from Amalie Rother, *Women's Bicycling* (Munich, 1897), translated by Rodelinde Albrecht.

such meets, along with football games, as "unworthy spectacles." Despite such efforts at "guardianship" and despite the turmoil of World War I, French women staged a number of such events in the years 1914–1918. After the war, Alice Milliat (1884–1957) organized international competitions for women and an international federation to administer them. "That was a heroic time," she remembered in 1929, "when one ran 1500-meter [1,640.42-yard], 400-meter, and 300-meter [328.08-yard] races, when the same female athlete competed in six or seven events in a single day."

In England, the beginnings of women's participation in modern sports can be traced back to the women's colleges of Oxford and Cambridge, which were founded in the 1870s, and to London's polytechnical schools, where many clubs were created so that female students might do gymnastics and a variety of sports. Some of these students participated in the Jeux Olympique Féminins sponsored by Milliat, but English women were on the whole less advanced than their continental sisters.

With the increasing acceptance of women's gymnastics and sports came striking changes in dress. In the nineteenth century, as a rule, sports were done in everyday clothing, but the popularity of the bicycle forced a change in costume for safety's sake. (One solution was a long dress that could be divided and rebuttoned into a pair of makeshift trousers.) In the early decades of the twentieth century, the opposition to knee-length shorts was gradually overcome. The controversy over sports dress was not merely a debate about clothing; at issue were symbols of male power.

## Twentieth-Century Society and the Gender Order

World War I and its aftermath brought profound political, economic, and social change, including change in gender relationships. In most European nations, women moved a step forward in the direction of legal equality. Nonetheless, in countries where they achieved the right to vote and hold office, they were still regarded as "the second sex." A woman who chose to embark on a professional career suffered from discrimination; she who chose domesticity was expected to acknowledge her husband as the head of the household. Clothing reform was also less than complete. There was more freedom of movement as ankle-length dresses and tight corsets were discarded. Nudists discarded even more articles of clothing and proclaimed a new, more athletic ideal of femininity. Short hair, a tanned body, and narrow hips were thought to be fashionably "modern." The liberation of the body was purchased, however, at a cost. Women internalized aesthetic ideals, like slenderness and a youthful look, that required considerable effort. And, yet, while the "new woman" was celebrated in glamour magazines, novels, and films as an athlete, a "vamp," or a career woman, broad sections of the population clung to traditional conceptions of femininity. For women whose lives were a daily struggle for economic survival, for women who were essentially wives and mothers, the ideals propagated by the fashionable mass media were wholly unrealistic.

## Progress in Gymnastics and Women's Sports

In the postwar years, sports, which were increasingly subjected to the processes of modernization, achieved a new zenith of popularity. The globe was spanned by a network of international sports federations such as the Fédération Interna-tionale de Football Association (1904), which administered soccer (association football), and the International Amateur Athletic Federation (1912), which oversaw track and field. Despite critical opposition, sports were increasingly recognized as the religion of the twentieth century. Women were by no means immune from the fascination of sports, and large numbers of them engaged in increasingly strenuous contests.

Although few people doubted that girls and women should be physically active for the sake of their health, their participation in highly competitive sports led to fierce controversies. At their core was the debate over the compatibility of competition and motherhood. The weightiest arguments against strenuous sports came from medical experts, especially gynecologists, who inveighed against competition and against participation in "manly" sports such as soccer. (The danger was that a female might be "masculinized.") Again and again, the Cassandras of the medical profession complained about the female athlete's diminished fertility and her disinclination to bear children.

The Olympic Games were a highly visible arena for these controversies over the appropriateness and desirability of women's sports. Although Coubertin had revived the games in 1896 as a purely male enterprise and continued to oppose women's participation to the day of his death in 1937, a dozen female golfers and tennis players competed in Paris in 1900 in the Olympic Games that were held in rather confused conjunction with a world's fair. Subsequently, the number of female athletes rose slowly but continuously. Prior to World War I, women were limited to sports that the men of the International Olympic Committee deemed appropriately feminine. (Swimming and diving were introduced at Stockholm in 1912.) In the twenties, the struggle centered on track and field. While the International Amateur Athletic Federation and the International Olympic Committee wanted to keep the "core" of the games free from the contamination of female runners, jumpers, and throwers, the Fédération Sportive Féminine Internationale (FSFI), which Alice Milliat had founded in 1921, agitated for their inclusion in the Olympic Program. The FSFI held its own Jeux Olympiques in 1922 (Paris), 1926 (Göteburg), 1930 (Prague), and 1934 (London). In response to this challenge from the FSFI, the IOC reluctantly inaugurated women's track and field at the 1928 games in Amsterdam. Once the dike of discrimination was breached, no amount of argument was able to hold back the tide of women's sports at the Olympic Games. The number of sports contested by women and the number of female contestants have both grown steadily.

In Olympic sports as in others, the opportunities for women varied from country to country. In Germany, women were encouraged to participate in sports contests, including those in track and field, that had earlier been considered "unwomanly." In 1919 the German Sports Authority called upon its member clubs to create sections for female athletes. In Germany, women's soccer continued to be taboo. In France, however, where a variety of female sports federations had been founded, women not only competed in track and field, they also formed soccer teams and played in national tournaments. The rougher game of *barette*, similar to rugby, also had its French enthusiasts. In other parts of the continent, including Scandinavia, women's sports were less widely accepted. During Spain's brief republican period (1931–1939), the shackles that had inhibited the growth of women's sports were loosened, only to be tightened again when General Franco imposed a fascist dictatorship upon his people.

The national differences in opportunity can be clearly observed in the figures for between-the-wars Olympic participation. Except for the games in distant Los Angeles (1932), female athletes representing Germany constituted generally about 7 percent of their nation's Olympic team, while their Norwegian counterparts were not only far fewer in number but also much more likely to limit their participation to "feminine" sports. It was 1948 before a Norwegian woman took part in one of the track and field events while fully half of the women on Germany's 1928 team competed in them. (One of them, Lina Radke, won the first-ever 800-meter race.) It was not until after World War II that Spain sent a single female athlete to the Olympics.

Women involved in sports held differing opinions on the question of participation in the Olympic Games. With few exceptions, German sports organizations were sexually integrated., while the tendency in France and Great Britain was for women to form their own organizations.

The French, who were the dominant force in the international federation for women's sports, favored Olympic participation; the British, organized in the Women's Amateur Athletic Federation, wanted to continue the tradition of separate "Women's Olympics" (which, ironically, the French had inaugurated).

Towards the end of the 1920s, the mass media began to celebrate the achievements of female athletes. Among the early idols were the temperamental, flamboyant, unconventionally dressed French tennis player Suzanne Lenglen, the German airplane pilot Elli Beinhorn, who made headlines not only with her round-the-world flights but also by her marriage with a famed automobile racer, and Sonja Henie, the beautiful Norwegian "Ice Princess" who skated her way from the Olympic Games to a career in Hollywood. The headlines that announced Gertrude Ederle's successful swim across the English Channel were comparable to those that celebrated Charles Lindbergh's solo flight across the Atlantic.

While the achievements of female athletes continued to be met with a mix of fascination and disgust, gymnastics were gradually transformed into an almost entirely female domain. Throughout Europe, a variety of systems and schools were propagated, some emphasizing health and hygiene, some more intent on the aesthetics of human movement. Strongly criticizing modern sports and their obsession with quantified achievement, the proponents of gymnastics were concerned principally with the quality of the movement experience, the form and shape of the body, and the harmonious development of the whole person. Common also was a tendency to cultural criticism; gymnastics were affirmed as a "natural" contrast to the mad pace and artificiality of modern civilization. Although the gymnastics movement propagated a rather traditional image of womanhood, it spoke to many who believed that it offered an essentially feminine movement culture that was free from men's interference and control. For such thinkers, gymnastics meant movement without competitiveness and without role conflict.

## Women's Sports and Fascism

In the fascist ideologies espoused by the dictatorial regimes of Mussolini's Italy, Hitler's Germany,

## "The Pursuit of Beauty"

I saw an aged, aged man
    One morning near the Row,
Who sat, dejected and forlorn,
    Till it was time to go.
It made me quite depressed and bad
To see a man so wholly sad—
    I went and told him so.
I asked him why he sat and stared
    At all the passers-by,
And why on ladies young and fair
    He turned his watery eye.
He looked at me without a word,
And then—it really was absurd—
    The man began to cry.
But when his rugged sobs were stayed—
    It made my heart rejoice—
He said that of the young and fair
    He sought to make a choice.
He was an artist, it appeared—
I might have guessed it by his beard,
    Or by his gurgling voice.
His aim in life was to procure
    A model fit to paint
As "Beauty on a Pedestal,"
    Or "Figure of a Saint,"
But every woman seemed to be

As crooked as a willow tree—
    His metaphors were quaint.
"And have you not observed," he asked
    "That all the girls you meet
Have either 'Hockey elbows' or
    Ungainly 'Cycling feet'?
Their backs are bent, their faces red,
From 'Cricket stoop,' or 'Football head.' "
    He spoke to me with heat.
"But have you never found," I said,
    "Some girl without a fault?
Are all the women in the world
    Misshapen, lame or halt?"
He gazed at me with eyes aglow,
And, though the tears had ceased to flow.
    His beard was fringed with salt.

    "There was a day, I mind it well,
    A lady passed me by
In whose physique my searching glance
    no blemish could descry.
I followed her at headlong pace,
But when I saw her, face to face,
    *She had the 'Billiard eye'!"*

—From *Mr. Punch's Book of Sports*

and Franco's Spain, biological and racist ideas were revived in order to restructure the gender order and to recast masculinity and femininity as the polar opposites they were thought to be in the nineteenth century. With varying degrees of success, these regimes sought to reduce women, once again, to their wifely and maternal roles. National Socialism, that is, Nazism, in Germany exemplified the fascist approach to women's sports.

The fecund female body and the hardened male body were central to Hitler's "racial hygiene" and to his dreams of dictatorial expansionist power. In addition to health and "racial purity," Nazi physical education was intended to inculcate an ideology of racial superiority, community, military preparedness, and strong leadership. As the term "political physical education" indicates, gymnastics and sports were subordinated to politics. Physical education was a central pillar in the structure of the Nazi state. It was supposed to prepare men for their predetermined biological role as fighters and women for theirs as mothers. In Nazi discourse and in the medical lit-

erature influenced by it, discussions of women's sport centered on two questions: What enhances and what diminishes a woman's reproductive function? By providing "healthy" and "appropriate" exercises, organizations like the Bund Deutscher Mädel (Federation of German Maidens) tried to institutionalize the goals of motherhood and the health of the community. Although Nazi ideology had originally been opposed to sports competition for women, Hitler realized the propaganda advantages that were sure to accompany demonstrations of physical superiority. His regime supported female athletes in a number of ways, and the 1936 Olympic Games, which took place in Berlin, seemed to prove him right. Although the Games were staged to demonstrate—to the point of absurdity—the cult of masculinity, Germany fielded the most successful team of female athletes.

## Developments after World War II

After the devastation and deprivation of World War II, the peoples of Europe turned eagerly to sports that, even in occupied Germany, represented a more attractive world than the ubiquitous ruins of the postwar world. With the gradual return of ordinary life came a call for women to resume the domestic roles they had been forced to abandon by the exigencies of war. The 1950s were a decade that emphasized traditional ideals of home and hearth.

Simultaneous with the renewed debate about the appropriateness of women's participation in strenuous competition came the ideological struggles of the Cold War. The confrontation of communism with liberal-democratic capitalism left its mark on sports. Signs were observable everywhere in Europe, but they were especially obvious in Germany, divided down the middle by the ideological line that separated East and West. Whether they sought the role or not, the female athletes of the Federal Republic of Germany and those of the German Democratic Republic bore the banners of two embattled political-economic-cultural regimes.

## Women's Sport under Communism

The performance of the Soviet Union's female athletes at the 1952 Olympics held in Helsinki astonished the world. For nearly 40 years, athletes from the communist regimes of Eastern Europe continued to dominate the women's events at the Olympic Games (except of course, in 1984, when Romania was the only communist nation to send a team to Los Angeles). A high-water mark was reached in 1976 when the communist bloc took home from Montreal 44 of the 49 gold medals in women's events. When observers marveled at the "big red sports machine," they tended to think of the women, especially those from East Germany.

Olympic success was the result of a number of interrelated factors: the centralized search for athletic talent, which began with the systematic recruitment of children; scientific research designed to maximize performance; the concentration of economic resources on sports; the high prestige and social security granted to successful athletes; material rewards (such as trips abroad); and medical manipulation through drugs. As a result of the communist sports bureaucrats' ruthless pursuit of gold medals and world championships, women and girls were trained to the

point where, in Western eyes, they no longer seemed female. In an attempt to make their female athletes culturally acceptable, communist regimes propagated new ideals of women's roles and female physiques. "Muscular femininity" might have been their unspoken motto.

The concentration on elite athletes came at the expense of recreational sports. Facilities available to ordinary citizens were poor and teachers of physical education had far lower status than coaches of national teams. Eastern European women were triply burdened; their vocational, domestic, and political obligations left them little time or energy for sports participation. Although propagandists proclaimed the contrary, the women of the communist world were far less likely than those of the West to be involved in recreational sports.

In the West, the debate over femininity and sports was resumed. When athletes from the communist bloc introduced new acrobatic movements into women's gymnastics, many Western Europeans found the contortions ugly and unfeminine. The first reaction of the German Gymnastics Federation was to defend its ideal of femininity; since the simple, graceful, rather static movements the federation favored were unlikely to earn high scores, the federation decided in 1954 to withdraw from international competition. In time, however, the logic of modern sports forced Western women to do as the communists did or to abandon their sporting ambitions

In other sports, there were attempts to halt the trend toward "masculinization." In many European countries, women were discouraged from playing soccer. It was not until the 1970s that the Fédération Internationale de Football Association reversed itself and began to sponsor world championships for women. The International Olympic Committee (IOC) waited another 20 years before bringing women's soccer into its program. It was so difficult to disprove the myth of woman's weakness that the IOC resisted the woman's marathon race until 1984 (when Joan Benoit of the United States became the first woman to win Olympic gold for that event).

Despite the laudable effort to end sexual discrimination at the Olympic Games, the program remains unequally divided between men's and women's events. In 1988, for instance, only 26 percent of the athletes at Seoul were female; only a third of the events were for them. Even then, a woman's chances to compete in the Olympics depended on her nationality. Women were 35 percent of the British team, 18 percent of the Spanish team—and they were entirely absent from many teams representing Islamic nations; in order to win the 1,500-meter race at Barcelona in 1992, Algeria's Hassida Boulmerka had not only to outrun her rivals but also to surmount the psychological barrier of fundamentalist death threats.

## Women's Sports Today

The inequalities observable at the Olympics are paralleled by those in the lives of ordinary women interested in recreational sports. Despite the dramatic changes of recent decades, women are by no means as likely as men to be involved in sports. This is clear both from surveys and from the membership rolls of European sports federations. In England, Germany, and Norway, approximately 40 percent of adult women say that they participate in sports, but one must be attentive to the definitions employed by the researchers. In England, walking is considered a sport; in Finland, elderly berry-pickers are counted as athletes. German data are more complete and more reliable. Nearly 30 percent of all Germans are members of a sports club; 37 percent of the members are female. In Norway, girls and women are 38 percent of all club members. In Spain, however, the situation is quite different. Only 26 percent of the women claim to be athletically active (as opposed to 48 percent of the men).

To a greater degree than is the case for men, age and social class are important influences on women's sports participation. In German clubs, for instance, girls begin to cease participating in sports from their fourteenth year while boys continue to be quite active until they are at least 18. In every European nation, men and women of higher social status are more likely than the less affluent to be athletically active, but the effect of this variable is greater for women than for men. The result is that only a minuscule number of middle-aged and elderly working-class women participate in sports of any sort.

For those women who do participate, the spectrum of available options is far greater than in the past. Young women now participate in sports once thought to be exclusively male: marathon running, soccer and rugby, water polo, even boxing and weightlifting. Of course, there continues to be a gender difference in rates of participation in various sports. Men are still more likely than women to engage in sports that require aggressive body contact. Gymnastics, aerobics, and dance continue to attract far more women than men. It must also be said that the financial support for women's sports is still less than offered to men. Except in tennis and golf, opportunities for women to earn their living as openly professional athletes remain almost nonexistent. Women are radically underrepresented in sports administration at every level, from the International Olympic Committee to the local sports club. They are rarely to be found in the press box or as commentators on televised sports. There is, however, one area where women have made major gains. Although women are still a minority of the scholars engaged in the academic study of sports (about 7 percent in Germany), their voices can now be heard.

—Gertrud Pfister

**Bibliography:** Blue, Adrianne. (1987) *Grace under Pressure: The Emergence of Women in Sport.* London: Sidgwick and Jackson.

Fletcher, Sheila. (1984) *Women First: The Female Tradition in English Physical Education, 1880–1980.* Bristol, UK: Athlone Press.

Guttmann, Allen. (1991) *Women's Sports: A History.* New York: Columbia University Press.

Hargreaves, Jennifer. (1994) *Sporting Females: Critical Issues in the History and Sociology of Women's Sports.* London: Routledge.

Laget, Françoise, Serge Laget, and Jean-Paul Mazot. (1982) *Le grand livre du sport féminin.* Belville, France: F.M.T.

McCrone, Kathleen. (1988) *Playing the Game: Sport and the Physical Emancipation of English Women, 1870–1914.* Lexington: University Press of Kentucky.

Mangan, John Anthony, and Roberta J. Park, eds. (1987) *From "Fair Sex" to Feminism: Sport and the Socialization of Women in the Industrial and Post-Industrial Eras.* London: Frank Cass.

Pfister, Gertrud, and Christine Peyton, eds. (1989) *Frauensport in Europa.* Ahrensburg: Czwalina.

Pfister, Gertrud, ed. (1980) *Frau und Sport.* Frankfurt: Fischer.

# Women's Sports, North America

Great national wealth, an increasing amount of leisure time, and a tradition of highly organized amateur and professional athletics account for the obsession with sporting events in the United States. Participatory sporting and recreational activities compete for both money and time. Millions of dollars are spent watching sports; billions are spent in fitness activities and playing sport. Whereas North American sports were once an almost exclusively male domain, today girls and women are easily visible as spectators and participants at all levels of sport. This article traces the participation of females in sport from the early 1800s to the 1990s.

## 1820–1880—Agrarianism to Marketplace

The foundations of women's sport and recreation in the United States were set down in the period from the Revolutionary War to the 1820s, when the United States functioned as an agrarian society. Most men's and women's lives were interdependent and revolved around rural living and shared tasks. Typical pastimes and recreational activities for girls and women included walking, sledding, skating, equestrianism (horseback riding), swimming (more like bathing in the sea), and simple games. Outdoor sporting activities included hunting and fishing parties, fox hunting, and boating (canoeing and river boat races). For the wealthy few, there were sailing and yachting. Occasional competition could be found in horse races, foot races, spinning and corn husking contests, and similar folk games. Shuttlecock and ten-pin bowling moved toward more highly structured competition.

In the decades from 1820 to 1880, the United States transformed from an agrarian to an industrialized nation. In the process, women's lives changed significantly. Women no longer shared work with men in the same way. Consequently, for certain segments of the population—notably the middle class—the polarization of gender roles increased. The social responsibilities and behavior patterns reflected in these separate roles

form the basis for conceptions of "masculinity" and "femininity" that found powerful expression in U.S. sporting traditions.

The separation of men's and women's worlds into two separate "spheres" or cultures during the nineteenth century was reflected in a dominant pattern of men moving toward competitive sport and women toward recreation and sport for health's sake. Whereas working-class females still labored long hours, increasing leisure time allowed some women to develop club sports, engage in healthful activities, or participate in popular mass sport fads. A few bold women engaged in what were considered masculine activities. Indeed, concepts of gender appropriateness and socioeconomic status have been immensely powerful determinants in the development of women's sports in the United States and elsewhere. Which women's sports developed and which did not, as well as the type and intensity of competition, depended upon culturally ingrained traditions based on gender perceptions controlled by men. Sports were seen as a way to train young males for adulthood and enable them to develop and maintain manly characteristics of physical strength and prowess. It was also assumed that sports developed leadership qualities necessary for the marketplace. Sport for girls and women was intended to foster health, pleasant social interactions, and democratic ideals; and only incidentally character building or competition.

Exercise had been a significant aspect of pre–Civil War "health-reform" movements—several of which benefited women. Early "women's rights" advocates such as Elizabeth Cady Stanton spoke out in favor of physical education for females, and books such as Catharine Beecher's *Physiology and Calisthenics for Schools and Families* (1856) provided educators with examples of exercises to be used by girls as well as boys. Many aspects of the earlier health-reform movement were incorporated into the physical education programs that began to appear at women's colleges during the last third of the nineteenth century. As early as 1865, Vassar College opened a Department of Physical Training and secured the services of a female physician (Dr. Alida Avery) to attend to the health of the young women. Other women's colleges (for example, Goucher College) and a number of coeducational universities (including the University of Michigan) had established similar opportunities by the 1890s. From its founding in 1885, the American Association for the Advancement of Physical Education has welcomed women as active members. The association has served as the focus for advancing certain ideals and programs championed by female physical educators.

## 1880–1920—The Growth of Gender-Based and Class-Based Sport

The so-called "new woman" of the 1890s and early 1900s was characterized by an independent spirit and athletic zeal. Turning away from traditional limited domestic roles, some women began to enjoy wider professional and personal choices. Only with economic independence could patterns of social behavior change. For the first time in U.S. society, "bachelor" women, for example, could live alone in large cities, share an apartment with other women, or live at home. This freedom in lifestyle permitted the rise of the female educational establishment with its abundance of new role models and commitment to professional achievement and social goals for women. These women heralded the dawn of the feminist movement, which culminated in the passage of the Nineteenth Amendment (1920) to the United States Constitution, giving voting rights to women. As Anne O'Hagan commented in *Munsey Magazine* in 1901, "With the single exception of the improvement in the legal status of women, their entrance into the realm of sports is the most cheering thing that has happened to them in the century just past."

Political changes and economic changes were accompanied by reforms of sport attire, including "bloomers" and other trouserlike garments. Perhaps the most significant of these changes accompanied the growth of bicycling, which became ever more popular in the 1890s. Safety dictated a more "rational" form of dress, and many younger women commented on the increased sense of freedom they obtained from cycling through the countryside.

Sex-appropriate team sports were ones in which men didn't compete, such as field hockey, and ones whose rules were severely modified by

*Competitor Cassie Clark at the 1994 Olympic Festival in St. Louis. Virtually all sports—even those like weightlifting that challenge traditional notions of femininity—are now open to women.*

women for female participation, such as basketball and volleyball. Softball was tolerated because it did differ from baseball and arose from indoor baseball. Track and field, including long-distance running, was marginally acceptable in a recreational setting, but competition was discouraged.

With the invention of basketball in 1891, competitive sport became available to women. By 1892, the game was played at Smith College and had even reached California. It soon crossed class boundaries. By the 1920s, it was played as a team game both in interscholastic competition and in the developing industrial leagues. Although field hockey attracted fewer players, it spread through many women's colleges and universities after

Constance M. K. Applebee introduced the game at the Harvard Summer School of Physical Training in 1901. The United States Field Hockey Association was formed in 1922. Although the initiator of the modern Olympics, Pierre de Coubertin, steadfastly objected to women's participation in the Games, women did engage in demonstrations of tennis and golf at the 1900 Paris Games. At London in 1908, archery, figure skating, and tennis were on the program. Not until Amsterdam in 1928 (100 meters [109.36 yards]; 4 x 100 relay; high jump; discus), however, was track and field included; exaggerated reporting of the results of the 800-meter run, however, led to the elimination of that event from the women's program until Rome in 1960.

During this epoch, the socioeconomic divide widened between upper-class and working-class female athletes. Wealthy women played tennis, golf, fencing, water sports, and they participated in the winter sports of skiing, figure, and speed skating; working-class women engaged in the less feminine team sports of softball (indoor baseball) and track and field. The only truly competitive team sport other than basketball (and the mild team sport of volleyball) was field hockey, an anomaly in the history of sport for women because it was international in the scope of competition, it was vigorous, and it was played by upper-class rather than working-class women. In the late 1800s, sports like roller skating and pedestrianism enjoyed brief popularity among females. The former attracted both middle- and upper-class devotees and members of the working class, who could win cash prizes for competitions. The fleeting interest in female pedestrianism (endurance walking contests) offered some poor women substantial financial reward.

Working-class women and the daughters of recent immigrants saw sport as an arena to compete with their peers for prestige, admiration, and perhaps even money and as a psychological escape from the physical confines of their rough urban existence. The women who moved out of the gender mainstream for unique sporting experiences for money were often these women, not the elite of the society. In the twentieth century, working women might find a model for their own experiences in the industrial leagues, church-sponsored leagues, and various YWCA programs that emerged in the 1920s, 1930s, and 1940s and included basketball, track and field, softball, and bowling.

Most often women's sport was confined to private surroundings. All of the educational institution sports, however, were found in the public sector in the form of club sports. For example, ice skating and roller skating moved from private surroundings to public rinks such as New York's Central Park.

As women moved from recreational activities to sport, club facilities and competitions became necessary. The first women's club, the Ladies' Club of the Staten Island Cricket and Baseball Club, connected itself to the men's club in 1877 as an avenue to competitive tennis. Immediately accepted as a sex-appropriate sport for affluent women, tennis was taught in the colleges, and by 1900 it had appeared in public parks, playgrounds, and recreation centers throughout the country. Local and college tennis tournaments originated in 1881, and the first national tournament was organized for women in 1887. Tennis ultimately changed to a far more vigorous sport than ever imagined by the elite men who approved it for their wives and daughters. A century later, in the 1970s, women's tennis was the first women's spectator sport to break through the media and revenue barriers to find resounding public acceptance. It also became the most popular participatory sport of the 1970s.

Upper-class women participated in sex-segregated activity, but during the 1880s they also joined their husbands at country and athletic clubs and conducted local, regional, and even a few national championships through the clubs. The sports included croquet, archery, fencing, bowling, swimming, and tennis. The older, more established skating and riding clubs also gained momentum as manuals were published for both sports. Clubs were formed for the winter sports of snowshoeing, skiing, and skating. Outdoorswomen, particularly in the West, continued to enjoy fishing, hunting, hiking, riflery, camping, and mountain climbing.

## Sport Crazes and Exhibitions

When the croquet (1866) and later the archery (1870s) crazes swept the country, women donned fashionable attire to compete with and then socialize with men. Both sports had national championships for women. Croquet was so popular that candle sockets were fastened to the wickets for night play. The popularity of both sports, however, was short-lived, and more active, exciting sports like tennis gained the support of affluent women. Albeit encumbered by tight corsets, heavy petticoats, and long full skirts, women persisted in sport participation.

A large group of bold women (mostly from the laboring or immigrant class) moved outside the security of their gender roles to participate in competitive events such as horse racing, cycle races, novelty cycle/horse races, distance swimming, and riflery shooting. The most successful of these "underground" sports or perhaps more accurately "events," however, was "professional pedestrianism," the walk-run and go as-you-please races that attracted a large crowd, resulting in a large "purse." Less acceptable but nonetheless present on the fringes of sport were the "anti-feminine" exhibitions of strong women, weight lifters and body builders, wrestlers, and even a fair number of women boxers. Challenges occurred between women, and contests were conducted in many of the larger cities in the United States. Although certainly never a part of the mainstream, pugilism and wrestling were reported in the news media. The female boxers, not all beautiful and not all from the lower class, perhaps fulfilled a role similar to that of the Roller Derby women of the 1950s and 1960s.

Native American women during this era were participating in competitive sporting experiences unique to them as well as those that included mixed sports with males. Almost all the games that women played separately used modified men's rules. These games continued to be important until the tribes began to play the team sports of white women during the twentieth century. (*See* Native American Sporting Competitions.)

## Six Sports: A Snapshot

A quick glance at six major women's recreational and competitive sports in the 1880–1920 period reveals the special circumstances and development of women's sport in this era.

(1) Bicycling Mania. Two independently occurring phenomena—clothing reform and bicycling mania—interacted with and influenced each other. The happy result was that by the end of the 1890s women were able to shed the costumes of the past and feel a new independence of movement and spirit. Women were no longer strapped up like hourglasses in corsets and long skirts. The bloomer gave the average woman a sporting chance, first in cycling and then in basketball, tennis, and other sports.

The cycling rage was the most popular activity in the decades of the 1880s and 1890s for women of leisure, college women, and for professional women. The activity caused a mass exodus to the out-of-doors, not only for elite women but for any woman who could afford the price of a bicycle. The achievement of bicycle racers and the distances that some women covered (17,152 miles [28,587 kilometers] in one year) are noteworthy, but it is the freedom and the introduction to the world of sport the cycling craze gave to the average woman that are most important to sport history.

(2) Golf. From the opening tournament at Meadowbrook, Massachusetts, in 1895, golf grew in status and stature. Sportswomen loved it because it could be played during at least three seasons of the year and was thought to make women physically strong without any gender-inappropriateness. Some golf courses were built separate (just for women) but many others merely put in women's tees and men decided when women could use the course, often preventing women from playing on weekends. As the sport became more elite, colleges and high schools stopped instruction but some students formed golf clubs on their own time. The sport has stayed a sport for the "elite" even after the days of publicly built courses. The first recognized National Collegiate Championship occurred in golf in 1941—the first such action by physical educators.

(3) Swimming. Swimming is one of the oldest forms of physical activity for the female in the United States. From the Colonial period, women have been able to use the sea to their advantage and they soon organized their own bathing spots—little boxes to dress in and walk out to sea. By the early twentieth century serious swimmers were to be found in clubs such as the Women's Swimming Association in New York, home of most of the 1920s Olympians. Marathon-type swimming contests were held throughout the end of the nineteenth century. Instruction became a part of the college curriculum by the turn of the century. From the schools, the sport moved to the public arena, as more and more swimming pools

# Beginning Involvement of U.S. Women in Sport 1830–1980

| Sport | Recreation Club College (Year) | National Championship (Year) | Olympic Games (Year) | 1st National Governing Body and Present Olympic NGB (Year) |
|---|---|---|---|---|
| Archery | Pre-1830s 1870 | 1879 | 1904 1972 | National Archery Association/1879 Professional Archers Association/1961 |
| Badminton | 1879 | 1937 | | US Badminton Association/1937 American Badminton Association/1937 |
| Baseball | 1860s | | | |
| Basketball | 1892 | 1926 | 1976 | AAU/1923 USA Basketball/1974 |
| Cycling | 1878 | 1878 | 1937 | Amateur Bicycle League, America/1938 US Cycling Federation |
| Bowling | Pre-1830s | 1916 | | Womens International Bowling Association/1916 Ladies Pro Bowlers Tour Professional Women's Bowling Association/1959 US Ten Pin Bowling Federation |
| Canoe/Kayak | Pre-1830s 1910 | | 1960 | American Canoe Association/1880 US Canoe & Kayak Team |
| Crew | 1875 | 1876 | 1976 | US Olympic Women's Rowing Competition/1973 |
| Cricket | 1830s | | | |
| Croquet | 1866 | 1867 | | |
| Fencing | 1881 | 1881 | 1924 | Amateur Fencers League of America/1912 US Fencing Association |
| Field Hockey | 1897 | 1923 | 1976 | US Field Hockey Association/1922 |
| Golf | 1894 | 1895 | 1900 | Women's Professional Golf Association/1944 US Golf Association/1894 Ladies Professional Golf Association/1949 |
| Gymnastics | 1920s | 1931 | 1936 | AAU/1931 US Gymnastics Federation/1963 |
| Horseback Riding | Pre-1830s | | 1952 | US Equestrian Team/1950 American Horse Show Association/1933 |
| Ice Hockey | 1890s | | | American Girls Hockey Association/1972 |
| Ice Skating | 1850s | 1866 | | Amateur Skating Union/1921 |
| Figure Skating | | 1914 | 1924 | US Figure Skating Association/1921 |
| Speed Skating | 1930s | | 1960 | Professional Skaters Guild of America/1933 US International Speed Skating Association/1966 |
| Lacrosse | 1920s | 1933 | 1931 | US Women's La Crosse Association/1933 |
| Mountain Climbing | 1850s | | | |
| Pedestrianism | 1830s | | | |
| Racquetball | 1960s | | | American Amateur Racquetball Association |
| Roller Skating | 1880s | | | Amateur Skating Union US US Amateur Confederation of Roller Skating |
| Skiing | 1853 | | 1936 | US Ski Association National Ski Association/1904 Professional Ski Instructors of America/1961 |
| Soccer | 1890s | | 1996 | US Soccer Federation |
| Softball | 1930s | 1933 | 1996 | Amateur Softball Association/1953 International Women's Softball Association |
| Swimming & Diving | Pre-1830s | 1889 | 1920 | AAU/1914 US Swimming US Diving |
| Tennis | | 1887 | 1900 & 1920 | US Lawn Tennis Association/1889 US Professional Tennis Association/1947 American Tennis Association/1961 |
| Track & Field | 1890s | 1923 | 1928 | AAU/1923 |
| Marathon | 1950s | 1857 | 1984 | The Athletic Congress (TAC)/1974 US Track & Field Federation/1961 |
| Triathlon | 1970 | 1979 | | Triathlon Federation USA/1978 |
| Volleyball | 1897 | 1949 | 1964 | US Volleyball Association/1928 |
| Weightlifting & Body Building | 1890s | | | |
| Yachting | Pre-1830 | | 1936 | North American Yacht Racing/1897 US Yacht Racing Union/1974 |

were constructed in cities and recreational centers. The sport has remained one of the most popular in recreational and competitive modes. Using swimming skills for synchronized swimming came out of the Depression's need for new adventures in the 1933 World's Fair.

(4) Field Hockey. Field hockey and, later, lacrosse were a legacy from the women of Great Britain to the women's colleges and secondary private schools of the east, making this team sport gender acceptable. Enthusiasm for field hockey led the way to various types of international and high-level competition in the educational domain as well as the public sector, starting with a U.S. field hockey team that traveled to England in 1920.

The Field Hockey rules were brought by Constance Applebee (1873–1979), a physical educator from England who taught at Bryn Mawr College. She almost single-handedly controlled the rules during the sport's first 20 years here. After that, the United States Field Hockey Association was formed to control and promote the game and maintain the rules. As an elite sport, field hockey nonetheless provided vigorous competition, and by the end of this era field hockey players had moved into sectional national and international competition. By this time a large number of the players in these competitions were physical educators, some of whom also sponsored collegiate teams to compete against the clubs and against each other. An honorary all-American team was selected each year from 1922 forward. The varsity competition was often conducted by the very women who were anti-varsity in all other sports. It remains a favorite team sport for eastern middle-class and elite women and has moved to many sections of the country. The national tournament still occurs, with socializing the primary goal.

(5) Basketball. The real love affair in women's sport was embodied in basketball everywhere in this country, surpassing all other team sports on all levels and across all socioeconomic boundaries. In education it was the most popular sport. In popular culture, it was the favorite team sport for competition and recreational play. Basketball was the only team sport for which women completely modified men's rules to make the game more appropriate for female athletes.

Senda Berenson (1868–1954), the great leader behind the concept of the modified rules from 1892 forward and the chair of the first standard rules committee in 1899, explained that rough and vicious play seems worse in women than in men; furthermore, she believed that the game played by women's rules showed "skill, alertness, and coolness." She suggested that the selfish display of a star by dribbling and playing the entire court and rough-housing by snatching the ball could not be tolerated. Female physiological limitations were also said to demand modification of rules. By 1920 basketball was played with six players, the court divided into three equal courts with one permitted dribble, no physical contact or horizontal guarding, and no loud talking or coaching from the bench. The next 85 years were spent in discussion and debate about modifications of the basketball rules, and after each such discussion the women's rules more nearly resembled the men's. Finally in the fall of 1971, the five-player, full-court unlimited dribble won the approval of women physical educators and the Amateur Athletics Union. Throughout the next era basketball will be the major concern in relation to varsity playing and the public sector competition. Women, however, have played varsity basketball since Berkeley played Stanford in 1896. So, too, elite basketball has been played from the AAU National Championship in 1926 forward to the Olympics of the present era.

As this period ended, basketball had been completely modified, rule books published, officiating techniques developed, and from the basketball sport committee (of 1899) arose a national organization for control of all women's sport. (It later became the National Association for Girls and Women in Sport [NAGWS] and is an association within the American Alliance for Health, Physical Education Recreation and Dance [AAHPERD].) The women's pre-twentieth-century action placed much of the control of women's basketball in the educational domain until the 1970s.

(6) Bowling. Bowling, which had been played in some form much earlier, emerged as a sport for elite men and women, but as it lost favor with elite men, it also became an inappropriate sport for affluent women. It then resurfaced as an important sport for the masses by 1916, when the Women's International Bowling Congress (WIBC) was formed exclusively for women. The

WIBC was to become the largest organization for sportswomen in the world.

Bowling became the most popular sport for a majority of women by the 1930s and continued to grow until the 1970s, aided by television coverage and automatic pin setters. Surely the sport's greatest growth came after the innovation of the automatic pin setter (1950s), because it permitted daytime bowling for mothers. The sport penetrated city life. Bowling clubs rivaled the afternoon tea in some social circles, and handsome prizes were offered for play carried on in tournament style. Bowling, unlike almost any other sport, has a long and important history for the laboring, married, and professional women who played in leagues and who by the advent of World War II had become professional bowlers. Collegiate institutions have had varsity teams with as many as 500 teams (some coed and some not) sponsored by student organizations, not physical educators. Throughout the next two decades, however, women physical educators taught bowling and did sponsor telegraphic meets.

## 1920–1950—The Democratic Ideal

Post–World War I prosperity and the successful battle for women's suffrage culminating in the Nineteenth Amendment (1920) ushered in an era of economic and social optimism that shaped many areas of American life. Urbanization, greater employment for women, an increasingly mobile population with more leisure time, and relaxation of many restrictive social standards all contributed to a climate favoring greater opportunities for women in many spheres in life. Sport was one of these. The period is sometimes referred to as "the golden age of sport" because of the rapid expansion of both professional and college sport for men; growth was more limited in women's sport. During the 1920s, Helen Wills (Moody) emerged as a dominating figure in women's tennis, winning numerous U.S. Championships. In 1928, she won the British, French, and U.S. championships. Two years later, Mildred "Babe" Didrickson broke three world records in the Amateur Athletics Union (AAU) national track and field championships at the 1932 Los Angeles Olympics. Didrickson emerged victorious in the 80-meter (87.5-yard) hurdles and javelin throw.

While the Great Depression of the 1930s devastated the economy, the government (largely through the Works Project Administration [WPA]) built parks, playgrounds, and sport facilities that fostered the growth of highly competitive public leagues. Softball might well be labeled a sport of the Depression years. Although women in elite women's colleges played men's baseball in the era of the 1880s–1890s (and even a few in the 1860s), indoor baseball, which became the team sport of softball, was the truly popular sport of working-class men and all classes of women. This team sport, arising from the public rather than from the private educational domain became a part of the WPA projects in the 1930s. The federal government supported recreation programs that sponsored softball leagues. On any summer evening in Chicago, for example, you would have found thousands of women playing softball in league play, tournaments, or through the AAU competition. (The only other sport even close in numbers would have been basketball in the winter season.) The industrial leagues (in both sports) featured teams sponsored by small businesses whose company names were proudly emblazoned as advertising on the uniforms. Often, however, individuals developed their own teams. Softball from the 1930s to 1960s was a top attraction throughout the U.S. heartland, especially in Chicago. Professional baseball and softball emerged from this milieu in the 1940s and 1950s.

The decade of the 1940s further altered the sporting attitudes and behavior patterns of women, for they had experienced success as respected contributors to the nation through their work in the war plants, the armed services, and in other important positions.

## Public Domain Industrial Leagues, Olympics, and AAU

The decades from 1920 to 1950 witnessed a significant growth in recreational and competitive sport for women. Women joined company teams, industrial leagues, YWCA teams, company-sponsored basketball competition, track and field teams, bowling leagues, and summer softball leagues. Upper- and middle-class women moved in greater numbers to the recreational and competitive organizations of such diverse sports as tennis, golf, swimming, badminton, alpine skiing, skating, canoeing, and kayaking. At the grass-roots level, high schools, churches, clubs, industry, YWCA, Catholic Youth Organizations (CYO), and the Amateur Athletic Union (AAU), and National Sport Governing Bodies (NGBs) of the Olympics sponsored athletic programs, particularly in track, basketball, softball, and swimming.

Another recurring theme in the saga of women's competitive athletics in United States in this era is the struggle between leaders of the governing bodies of women's and men's athletics for control of organized amateur competition for women. The first open conflict between the men and women occurred over the U.S. women attending the first Women's Olympics (the 1922 international track and field meet in Paris). The U.S. team (made up mostly of college and private high school students) attended the event under the auspices of the AAU, with its male coaches and female chaperones. By 1923, the AAU gained jurisdiction over female athletes by having them register with AAU in order to swim or to participate in track, basketball, and gymnastics as well as other sports. This registration placed AAU in position to run local, regional, and national events for female athletes. The AAU was the single most positive force for Olympic competition for female athletes throughout the country during this era. By 1950, they offered National and local championships and had the Olympic and Pan American teams in basketball, swimming, track, and gymnastics. At the same time, the rest of the Olympic sports had their own national organizations that trained their athletes and provided the high-level competition needed for them in all the sports offered in the summer and winter Olympic Games.

By the 1920s, for the first time, female athletic heroes from the United States emerged from the Olympic Games and national championships, especially in the sports of tennis, golf, and figure skating. Americans of all social classes thrilled to their success, now heralded by national women's magazines and covered in the press and motion pictures. In addition, local heroes were found in abundance, even when national ones were limited. Media coverage even included women from track and field and other nonfeminine sporting traditions. Track and field was still considered "too masculine" for women, unless a track athlete was beautiful, in which case she became the

sweetheart of the press and magazines. Individuals like Babe Didrikson (1911–1956), for example, who was voted the finest female athlete of the first half of the twentieth century, was really not a role model or media fixture in her magnificent 1932 Olympic performance because she was not "feminine" enough and competed in "male" sports. Only after Didrikson became a professional golfer and later as the second wave of feminist values took hold was she accepted as a role model.

## Sport in the Educational Domain

In the decades between World War I and World War II, high school and college sports programs for girls and women were widely—but not exclusively—controlled by female physical educators whose aim was to foster a lifetime of participation. The primary emphasis was the health and social well-being of the participant. For the most part, intensely competitive sporting activities were shunned, for a variety of reasons. Some women physical educators argued that these activities were pursued by only a small number of very gifted women, ignoring—or giving insufficient attention to—the vast numbers of girls and women who might otherwise benefit. Other educators, echoing the assertions of physicians and others, maintained that highly competitive athletics might "masculinize" women. Some educators feared they might lose control over the programs they had developed if they emulated the entrenched male model. "A sport for every girl/Every girl in a sport"—the motto of the National Amateur Athletic Federation—exemplified such attitudes. In high schools and colleges the teachers were offering instructional programs in all the popular individual, team, and intramural sports, and they sponsored interest clubs in a variety of sports. Varsity competition flourished in rural high schools and in other pockets of the country.

Apprehensions about the male model of athletics and a desire for larger participation led high school teachers and many college leaders of physical education to endorse competitive restraints and to mandate female self-determination in athletic governance. This anticompetitive program espoused by the professional female educational establishment and other public figures had the support of such prominent leaders as Lou Henry

Hoover, wife of President Herbert Hoover. She herself was a driving force in female-focused movements with a democratic underlying purpose like the Girl Scouts of America; she also engaged in a variety of outdoor sports.

Educators characterized varsity teams as overemphasizing the "winning syndrome, corruption and commercialism rampant in men's athletics." This concept resulted in this alternative model of athletics for females, developed by women, involving play days and sports days which was a natural outgrowth of conformity and accommodation of gender roles for women.

This vision of separate competition for girls and women led to conflicts, controversy, and gender relation struggles. The women leaders viewed the AAU and varsity programs as infringements by men, However, it is imperative to note that the predominance of play days and sports days and the so-called demise of competitive athletics reported in some sport history research has been vastly exaggerated. Competitive athletics persisted throughout the period in the public domain and often in varsity sport.

Although "Every girl in a sport/A sport for every girl" remained the guiding philosophy of the National Section on Women's Athletics of the American Association for Health, Physical Education, and Recreation, not all female physical educators subscribed to it. Some states (Ohio, Kentucky, and Iowa, for example) offered local and even state girls' championships.

Girls' basketball in Iowa is perhaps the prime example of the highly competitive approach. In 1920, building upon three decades of tradition, the first state girls high school championship was held in Des Moines. The annual tournament soon became one of the major sporting events of the year. By 1985, nearly 500 Iowa schools had girls' interscholastic basketball teams. Even to watch a sport with a set of modified six-player rules, two divisions of the court, use of the limited dribble and little physical contact in guarding, townsfolk came by the thousands to watch their young athletes compete. The girls' state championship drew more crowds than the boys'. Radio broadcast (1940s) and television as early as the end of the 1950s were a part of the action.

During World War II, the necessity for physical fitness was emphasized for all citizens, and intense competition was suggested by the federal government for all high school girls, the armed forces, and the public domain. Women physical educators, therefore, helped develop federally suggested programs of fitness, and many young service women (and officers) participated themselves in such programs.

## 1950 and After—Revolution in Women's Sports

During the second half of the twentieth century, profound changes have occurred in U.S. society. Among the more significant changes have been civil rights and equal rights legislation. Major federal legislation included the 1954 Supreme Court decision requiring racial integration, the 1964 Civil Rights Act following widespread civil disturbances, the Equal Pay Acts of the 1960s, and the attempts to ratify the Equal Rights Amendment in the early 1980s. The latter stimulated an eventual array of legal successes for women's rights.

For women's sport, no federal legislation was more important than Title IX of the Education Amendments Act of 1972, which mandated parity between the genders in educational opportunities. These regulations together ushered in an age of reform and liberation—nothing short of a metamorphosis in women's lives in employment, education, and other sectors of society.

These new conceptions of equal rights and privileges for all citizens regardless of race or gender, changing cultural values regarding women, and developments fostered by the women's liberation movement, joined with the enactment of federal regulations, created a social climate conducive to the rapid rise of interest in sports of all kinds—interscholastic, intercollegiate, amateur, professional, and recreational. In the 1970s, and even more so in the 1980s, vast numbers of girls and women began to participate in sports, and, whereas formerly, dominant cultural values dictated that sports exemplifying grace and agility were most appropriate for females, sports that required strength, speed, and power now became increasingly acceptable.

### Interscholastic and Intercollegiate Athletics after 1950

During World War II, many women had gained organizational and administrative experience in the Armed Services, Red Cross, and industry. Many female physical educators counted among those who served, and a number of them increasingly recognized the need for higher standards of competition for girls and women. By the 1960s, some state high school associations had expanded opportunities for girls, and more recreational leagues and clubs opened their doors to girls (including those economically disadvantaged). By 1969, the Division for Girls and Women's Sports of the American Association for Health, Physical Education, and Recreation had begun to schedule national intercollegiate championships for college women. In 1971, the Association for Intercollegiate Athletics for Women (AIAW), which traced its organizational roots to the National Women's Basketball Committee (1989), was formed. By 1981–1982, AIAW offered national championships in 19 collegiate sports. The following year, these were jointly sponsored by AIAW and the National Collegiate Athletic Association (NCAA); and, by 1983, the AIAW had collapsed, a victim of internal disagreements and external pressures—not the least of which were fears that rapidly growing women's sports would siphon off funding that traditionally had been directed to men's intercollegiate programs.

## Title IX

In the years immediately following the passage of Title IX, considerable disagreement existed concerning the shape emerging women's programs should take. Some individuals favored emulating the model of the NCAA; others objected to recruiting, "athletic scholarships," and what they perceived as an unwholesome commercialization of school-based sports. Following the demise of the AIAW, collegiate sport for females has been governed by the regulations of the NCAA or, for smaller institutions, the National Association of Intercollegiate Athletics (NAIA). At the same time there has been a dramatic increase in the numbers of females engaged in college (and even high school) competitive programs, accompanied by a massive decline in the percentage of women who administer such programs. A sharp decline is also evident in the percentage of women who serve as the head coaches of women's sport teams.

Title IX has changed the configuration of college and university physical education and athletics. With the mergers of men's and women's physical education departments in the 1970s came the separation of athletics, intramurals, and instruction. Instructional programs were conducted with coeducational classes that favored teaching sports that were acceptable for both genders. Such sports include volleyball and softball, lifetime sports, and fitness activities. In addition, with the mergers, the women physical educators and their national organization NAGWS lost authority over rules, officiating, and governance of athletics and sports.

## Fitness and Recreation

The presence of sport in women's lives is everywhere apparent. Coincidental with the women's liberation movement, many girls and women began to adopt new lifestyles. Since the 1960s, millions of new converts have been made to such recreational, noncompetitive pursuits as aerobics, jogging, and aquacalisthenics. Backpacking, mountain climbing, bicycling, cross-country skiing, and other outdoor pursuits grew rapidly after the mid-1960s—each attracting increasing numbers of female participants.

Women have become the primary focus of the burgeoning "fitness" industry, and many women have achieved a greater sense of freedom and self-motivation as a result of their experiences in physical activity and sport. Others have become proficient at weight-lifting and other forms of physical activity that once were deemed inappropriate.

Triathlon, marathon running, distance swimming, rugby teams, soccer teams, and flag football teams now attract a sizable number of girls and women. The fast growth of these sports demonstrate that for the first time women see fitness as a personal need and sports as offering a new freedom to create personal well-being. Furthermore, women are increasingly willing and able to move into the male domain of sport without apology and with little criticism from the public. What were once "elite" sports have become less so, now offering grass-roots opportunities to a multitude of children and teenagers regardless of their economic status. Even in athletic and sport clubs where the cost is greater (figure skating, gymnastics, golf, and skiing), clubs and recreation centers attempt to provide opportunities to compete for those who could not otherwise participate.

## The Olympics

The entry of the United States into the modern Olympic Games occurred for men in 1896. Women made their first appearance almost by chance in the next two Olympic Games in golf and tennis (1900) and archery (1904). The AAU and all the national sport governing bodies were an important positive voice on behalf of female athletes for competitive athletics. As early as 1914 and 1916, the AAU maintained the records in swimming and track and by 1923 accepted women to register for other sports. In the early 1920s, basketball, track and field, and, a bit later, gymnastics, came under AAU jurisdiction. It was the beginning of the largest public programs for women in high-level competition in the country.

Women physical educators were silent regarding the gender appropriate sports in the Olympics; that is, golf, archery, swimming, gymnastics, tennis, and figure skating, but they later (1928, 1932 and 1936) protested the entry of women into the "unladylike" sport of track and male domination of competitive sport through the AAU.

In competitive athletics, this era also saw the establishment of national organizations for many sports and governance structures for the new Olympic sports as well as some intercollegiate and varsity competition. The commercialization of leisure, as evidenced by such public amusements such as dance halls, amusement parks, and variety theaters, was also well established throughout the era.

The greatest boon to Olympic sport for women was Title IX, which provided a feeder system, and the Federal Amateur Sport Act (ASA) of 1978. The act expanded the powers of the U.S. Olympic Committee to control international competition and the growth and expansion of Olympic sports in the United States. This law resulted in all sport governance groups working in harmony toward a single goal: the enactment of programs for U.S. amateur athletes at all ages and levels of abilities. The ASA made the National Sport Governing Body (NGBs) for each sport the national organization for the Olympics, Pan American Games, and World University Games,

and it ushered in an era of good feeling among the previously warring AAU and NCAA.

Women benefited from new funding for "underdeveloped sports," because all collegiate and other women's sports were classified as underdeveloped. The act is instrumental in assisting previously denied populations to achieve opportunity; women are just such a target population. With the new regulations of ASA, national festivals are sponsored each summer by the USOC. These events and tours for younger elite athletes assist young athletes as never before. Each sport (NGB) is devoting more time, energy, and money to grass-root programs as well as spending more on building a pool of young athletes. This new emphasis on grass roots has permitted team sports like soccer, handball, and volleyball to increase their numbers, not only for Olympic hopefuls but for an entire generation of young players. With increased technological assistance, equal access to training and facilities, improved financial support, increased media coverage, and increased numbers of athletes, the Olympic movement in the United States has expanded beyond all expectations.

Of the six events that comprised the 1932 women's track and field program, Mildred "Babe" Didrickson won two first-place (80-meter hurdles; javelin throw) and one second-place (high jump) medals. In London in 1948, the Netherlands' Francina "Fanny" Blankers-Koen (then 30 years old) won four of the nine women's events (100 meters, 200 meters, 80-meter hurdles, 4 x 100 meter relay). Over the years, the women's Olympic track and field program has increased markedly. At Atlanta in 1996, competitions in 271 events were scheduled. No less impressive has been the growth in the overall women's program as more and more sports have been added. During the 1960s and 1970s, swimming was dominated by Australian and U.S.—and subsequently East German—women.

## Achievements of African American Women in Athletics

During the late 1800s and early 1900s, calisthenics and sports programs developed at many historically Black colleges. Atlanta University's monthly student newspaper, *The Scroll*, announced that basketball was first introduced for women in 1899. By the 1920s and 1930s, students were engaged in track meets and basketball games with

Tuskegee Institute and other institutions. Organizations such as the Phyllis Wheatley Y.W.C.A. of Washington, D.C., promoted basketball, tennis, and other sports for local girls. In the early 1920s, Lucy Slowe challenged the assertion that tennis was "too sophisticated" for black women while capturing the national championships of the All-Black American Tennis Association.

A particularly striking success of the 1950–1990 era has been the achievements of African American women in Olympic and other high-performance sports. Indeed, there had been numerous excellent athletes in earlier decades. However, such achievements as that of Tuskegee's Alice Coachman (who won the 1948 Olympic women's high jump) and other female African American athletes rarely received the attention they merited. The remarkable performances of triple gold medalist Wilma Rudolph at Rome in 1960 did not go unnoticed, however, and she was subsequently named recipient of the Sullivan Award as the year's outstanding female athlete. At recent Olympics, Florence Griffith-Joyner and Jackie Joyner-Kersee have gained considerable media attention as well as athletic laurels.

Although they had been very successful in the 1920–1940 period at AAU National Championships in basketball and track, African American women were not found in elite sports, except tennis. During the present and past era African American women participated in all the sports of the working-class women including softball, basketball, and bowling. In addition, middle-class African Americans competed in tennis. This participation was due, in part, to the American Tennis Association (ATA), which encouraged female participation and provided the tournament outlet. Althea Gibson (1927– ) came out of the ATA, winning its National Singles Championship in 1949. She moved on to win the French Open, Wimbledon and the U.S. Open Championships, all in the 1950s. She paved the way for black men's and women's participation in previously all-white championships.

By midcentury African American athletes occupied a central position in the sport of track and field. Beginning in the 1930s black women stepped in the field abandoned by middle-class white women who deemed the sport "unfeminine." Black runners appeared on the U.S. team in the 1932 and 1936 Olympics. They won their first medals in the 1948 games.

Perhaps the greatest contribution in sport by African American athletes is their supremacy and medal counts in the Olympics of 1952–1972. Nineteen Olympians coming from Tuskegee Institute and Tennessee State won over 20 medals. Best known was Wilma Rudolph (1940–1994), whose performance in the 1960 Olympics was the first widely televised track event. With her three gold medals, she almost single-handedly rekindled U.S. interest in women doing better in the Olympic competition.

African American women competed in track and field in the Olympics from 1932 forward, but only in 1964 did they begin to compete in other sports (volleyball). Now over half of the Olympic basketball team is African American, as are most of the track athletes and a few individuals in other sports. Just a decade and a half ago only a few black basketball players were on the collegiate scene, but appearing on behalf of Delta State in the Final Four of the NCAA championships was one of them, Lucia Harris (1955– ), the first woman basketball player inducted into the men's (and now men's and women's) National Basketball Hall of Fame.

## Professional Sports

Professional sports during the period 1950–1990 reflected the exceptional gutsiness of athletes on exhibition teams; the heart and drive of those in the many team sports that failed; the love of sport reflected in participation on poorly paying teams; and the joy of spectacular commercial success and influence in the popular culture. For example, from 1936 to the 1970s, the All-American Red Heads basketball team toured the country in a manner similar to the Harlem Globetrotters. The All-American Baseball League lasted through the early years of the 1950s. A professional basketball league in the 1970s and 1980s, however, failed for lack of a large pool of talent and audience appeal. Professional bowling, golf, and tennis fared very well, with tennis becoming the most popular women's professional sport, due primarily to Billie Jean King (1944– ), who burst into national prominence at the right moment in history. In 1973, she won a great public tennis match with another professional, Bobby Riggs, in "the Battle of the Sexes," started a women's sport magazine, and almost single-handedly started the professional circuit for tennis. In the late 1990s, though, professional golf in general is growing while tennis is declining.

Other short-lived and long-lived professional teams include track and field, swimming, and, of course, the highly successful figure-skating shows. The newest professional team is a baseball team, the Silver Bullets, which competes against men's teams. The difficulty here is not having a pool of women baseball players, so softball players are attempting to turn their skills to baseball. The future looks bright, however, for basketball, for the men's National Basketball Association (NBA) has formed a women's league to begin in 1996, and the American Basketball League (ABL) will begin play in 1997. The basketball feeder system is now excellent, with collegiate basketball and Olympians and an educated audience near at hand. There are also now professional women boxers, although they are few in number and do not draw a large following. The most popular new professional sport is beach volleyball, with its double format and brief "feminine" clothing.

## Conclusion

The influx of girls and women into the sports arena is forcing changes and redefinitions of the role and function of sport in U.S. culture. These new role definitions will fuel the expansion of gender-role expectations. As the perceived female attributes of beauty and form interplay with the masculine attributes of strength and power and they merge into sporting experiences without gender, the acceptance of the female role in sport has the potential to free male and female athletes to have human experience, not sex identified or defined, leading toward a less rigidly defined sport culture.

Sport much resembles U.S. society itself in its heterogeneity and capacity for individuals to participate in diverse sports at different levels once the organized sport structure is in place. The previously divided stream of female and male athletics has become a mighty river that finally enjoys equal contributions and support from the educational domain and popular culture. Much greater media attention in the mid-1990s has sparked the imagination and awareness of girls and women to their own potential in sport. With all kinds of new sports pro-

motions and parity in athletics on the horizon, the opportunities for girls and women in the United States appear limitless.

—Joan Hult

**Bibliography:** Cahn, Susan K. (1994) *Coming on Strong: Gender and Sexuality in 20th Century Women's Sport.* New York: Free Press.

Costa, Margaret and Sharon Guthrie, eds. (1994) *Women and Sports: Interdisciplinary Perspectives.* Champaign, IL: Human Kinetics.

Cohen, Greta L., ed. (1993) *Women in Sport: Issues and Controversies.* Newbury Park, CA: Sage Publications.

Dulles, Foster Rhea. (1965) *A History of Recreation: America Learns to Play.* New York: Appleton-Century-Crofts.

Gai, Ingham Berlage. (1994) *Women in Baseball: The Forgotten History.* Westport, CT: Praeger.

Gerber, Ellen, et al. (1974) *The American Woman in Sport.* Reading, MA: Addison-Wesley.

Guttmann, Allen. (1991) *Women's Sports: A History.* New York: Columbia University Press.

Hargreaves, Jennifer. (1994) *Sporting Females: Critical Issues in the History and Sociology of Women's Sports.* New York: Routledge.

Howell, Reet, ed. (1982) *Her Story in Sport: A Historical Anthology of Women in Sports.* West Point, NY: Leisure Press.

Hult, Joan S. (1986) "The Female American Runner: A Modern Quest for Visibility." In *Female Endurance Athletes,* ed. Barbara Drinkwater. Champaign, IL: Human Kinetics.

———. (1989) "American Female Olympians as Role Models, Mentors and Leaders." In *Proceedings of the Jyvaskyla Congress on Movement and Sports in Women's Life.* Jyvaskyla, Finland: University of Jyvaskyla Press.

Hult, Joan S., and Mariana Trekell, eds. (1991) *A Century of Women's Basketball: From Frailty to Final Four.* Reston, VA: National Association for Girls and Women in Sport.

Nelson, Mariah. (1991) *Are We Winning Yet? How Women Are Changing Sports and Sports Are Changing Women.* New York: Random House.

Peiss, Kathy. (1986) *Cheap Amusements.* Philadelphia: Temple University Press.

Remley, M. L. (1990) *Women in Sport: An Annotated Bibliography and Resource Guide 1900–1990.* Boston: G. K. Hall.

Spears, Betty, and Swanson, Richard. (1988) *History of Sport and Physical Education in the United States.* Dubuque, IA: William Brown.

Struna, Nancy. (1984) "Commentary: Beyond Mapping Experience: The Need for Understanding in the History of American Sporting Women." *Journal of Sport History* 11, 1 (Spring).

Twin, Stephanie. (1979) *Out of the Bleachers.* New York: Feminist Press.

Verbrugge, Martha. (1988) *Able-Bodied Womanhood.* New York: Oxford University Press.

Vertinsky, Patricia. (1994) "Gender Relations, Women's History and Sport History: A Decade of Changing Enquiry, 1983–1993." *Journal of Sport History* 21, 1 (Spring).

———. (1990) *The Eternally Wounded Woman.* Manchester: Manchester University Press.

# Worker Sport

For millions of workers in the period between World War I and World War II, sport was an integral part of the labor movement and worker sports clubs and associations were widespread in Europe, the United States and Canada, South America, and Asia. By 1930, worker sport united well over 4 million people, making it by far the largest working-class cultural movement.

At its zenith, worker sport combined the notion of sport with socialist fellowship, solidarity, and working-class culture. The principal aims differed from country to country, yet all were agreed on the basic principles: that it would give working people the chance to take part in healthy recreation and to do so in a comradely atmosphere. Worker sport was to differ from bourgeois sport by being open to all workers, women as well as men, black as well as white. More than that, it was to provide a socialist alternative to bourgeois competitive sport, commercialism, chauvinism, and obsession with statistics and records. It was also to replace capitalist competition with socialist cooperative values and thus lay the foundation for a true working-class culture. The initial emphasis was therefore on physical activities such as gymnastics, acrobatics, tumbling, pyramid forming, mass artistic displays, hiking, cycling, and swimming.

The founders of the worker sports movement believed that sport could be revolutionary, that it was no less salient to workers than their political, trade union, and cooperative movements. While capitalism, moreover, fosters mistrust among workers of different nations, the worker sports organizations would band together internationally to create peace and international solidarity; they would turn physical culture into a new international language capable of breaking down all barriers.

It has to be remembered that worker sport was not taking place in a vacuum; it was influenced by similar forces and faced similar problems. Like other branches of the labor movement—trade unions, socialist parties, the cooperative movement, and youth organizations like the Woodcraft Folk, Young Pioneers, or Young Communist League—worker sport rose and fell almost everywhere simultaneously, reaching a peak in the 1920s and a trough in the late 1930s, fading away virtually to nothing after World War II. National peculiarities invariably added brakes and accelerators: the German and Austrian tragedies under Hitler, the relatively peaceful demise in North America, Scandinavia, and Great Britain, and the persistence of worker sport in Israel and Finland.

## Origins

Underpinning the emergence of a mass labor movement in the last quarter of the nineteenth century in North America and Western Europe was the growing predominance of regular wage-earners concentrated in large work units. By the turn of the century, the average working week in the countries of these regions was around 56 hours, compared with between 65 and 75 in the 1860s. Some of this gain was being devoted to domestic life and recreation: with more leisure and money to spend, working people could build a new family- and consumption-centered culture.

Music hall peaked after 1890, the cinema was well-established in working-class areas before 1914, and every conceivable worker institution had its own brass band. Soccer and, in America, baseball spread as participant and spectator sports, aided by the emergence of the Saturday half-holiday, which enabled athletes to circumvent the prohibitions of sabbatarian local authorities, and cheap railway excursions, which opened up new travel possibilities.

A worker sports movement began to take shape in Germany in the 1890s with the foundation of the Worker Gymnastics Association in conscious opposition to the nationalistic German Gymnastics Society (Turnen). The influence of the new association spread to North America with the migration there of entire German communities. This was followed in Germany by the Solidarity Worker Cycling Club and the Friends of Nature Rambling Association in 1895, the Worker Swimming Association in 1897, the Free Sailing Association in 1901, the Worker Track and Field Association in 1906, the Worker Chess Association in 1912 and the Free Shooting Association in 1926. Germany therefore became the hub and catalyst of the worker sports movement, with over 350,000 worker athletes in various worker clubs even before World War I.

Elsewhere, a Worker Rambling Association was set up by Austrian workers in Vienna in 1895; the same year a British Workers Cycling Club was organized around the *Clarion* newspaper. In 1898 a Socialist Wheelmen's Club came into being in the USA, and French workers started to create clubs and the umbrella Socialist Sports Athletic Federation from 1907. By 1913 there were enough members internationally for the worker sports federations of five European nations, Belgium, Britain, France, Germany, and Italy, to come together at Ghent on the initiative of the Belgian socialist Gaston Bridoux to establish the Socialist Physical Culture International.

## Development

By the time the various worker federations regrouped after World War I, two new tendencies were emerging, both of which were to cause widespread division and controversy.

The first was the growing movement away from noncompetitive recreation (physical culture) to competitive organized sport. When the Ghent International was reestablished in 1920 at Lucerne, it was renamed the International Association for Sport. The *New York Call*, the periodical of the American Socialist Party, sponsored a baseball league.

This shift towards team sports and competitions was a response to popular pressure within the working class. It may well have reflected a transfer of values from the workplace to the sphere of leisure, a reaction to the increasingly sterile nature of rationalized work. Whatever the reason, it helped to boost support for the worker sports movement.

In Germany, membership of the Worker Gymnastics and Sports Society (WGSS) in the late 1920s was 1.2 million, covering a dozen different sports, and the organization was able to open the most modern sports club in Germany, the *Bundesschule* in Leipzig (subsequently the nucleus of the German Democratic Republic's *Deutsche Hochschule für Körperkultur*). Its affiliates for cycling not only had as many as 320,000 members—the largest cycling organization in the world—but also ran a cooperative bicycle factory.

Elsewhere, the various Austrian worker sports groups combined into a single association in 1919, the Union of Worker Sport, later the Austrian Worker Sport and Cultural Association (WSCA), which grew from 100,000 to 250,000 by 1931. Its swimming affiliate gave free swimming lessons to over 10,000 working people in 1930 alone and to as many as 29,000 in 1932. The Czechoslovak Worker Gymnastics Association put on sports festivals in Prague in which some 35,000 took part and 100,000 attended. In Britain, the British Workers Sports Federation showed a steady growth after its formation in 1923, and the Clarion Cycling Club set up the National Workers Sports Association (NWSA) in 1930, the same year as the Workers Wimbledon Tennis Championships were held. As evidence of its commitment to organized sport, the NWSA entered a team, the London Labor Football Club, in a London soccer league. In 1934, the NWSA played host to worker athletes from Austria, Belgium, Czechoslovakia, Palestine, and Switzerland at its Dorchester Sports Festival; in turn, British workers went abroad to worker festivals. Even in relatively small countries like Denmark, Finland, Norway, and Switzerland, membership figures were impressive: 20,000, 41,000, 65,000, and 27,000, respectively, by 1930.

The second postwar tendency was the mounting division between social democrats or socialists, on the one hand, and communists, on the other, over leadership and aims of the worker sports movement. A number of worker sports organizations broke away from the Lucerne Sports International (LSI), a branch of the Bureau of the Socialist International, after the formation of the International Association of Red Sports and Gymnastics Associations, better known as Red Sport International (RSI), in Moscow in 1921 as a branch of the Communist International or Comintern.

Relations between the two worker sports internationals were hostile right from the start, the RSI accusing its "reformist" rival of diverting workers from the class struggle through its policy of political neutrality in sport. True, the socialists were not trying to make the sports movement into an active revolutionary force; instead, it was to be a strong, independent movement within capitalist society that would be ready, after the revolution, to implement a fully developed system of physical culture. The RSI, on the other hand, wished to build a sports international that would be a political vehicle of the class struggle; it did not want merely to produce a better sports system for workers in a capitalist world. The LSI countered that the RSI only aspired to undermine it and take it over, so it banned all RSI members from its activities and all contacts with the Soviet Union (indeed, the British Labour Home Secretary J. R. Clynes refused entry visas to Soviet soccer players in 1930).

The two internationals therefore developed separately and, as with the parent political movements, spent too much time and energy fighting each other rather than the common enemy. By the time they eventually came together, in 1936, it was too late to save the worker sports movement from fascist repression (the German WGSS had been one of the first targets for the Nazis in 1933, the Austrian WSCA was suppressed a year later, and the Czechoslovak association two years after that).

## The Worker Olympics

While the worker sports movement did not take issue with much of the Coubertin idealism concerning the modern Olympic Games, it did oppose the Games themselves and counterposed them with its own Olympiads on the following grounds.

First the bourgeois Olympics encouraged competition along national lines, whereas the worker Olympics stressed internationalism, worker solidarity, and peace. While the International Olympic Committee (IOC) barred German and Austrian athletes from the 1920 and 1924 Games, for example, the 1925 Worker Olympics were held in Germany under the slogan "No More War."

Second, while the Olympics restricted entry on the grounds of sporting ability, the worker games invited all, putting the emphasis on mass participation, and extended the events to include poetry and song, plays, artistic displays, political lectures, and pageantry.

Third, the IOC Games were criticized for being confined chiefly to the sons of the rich and privileged (through the amateur code and the domination of national Olympic committees by the upper classes). Baron de Coubertin himself had always opposed women's participation and readily accepted the cultural superiority of whites

over blacks. The longest-serving IOC presidents, Baillet-Latour and Avery Brundage, both collaborated with the Nazi regime and were unabashedly anti-Semitic. By contrast, the Worker Olympics were explicitly against all chauvinism, racism, sexism, and social exclusivity; they were truly amateur, organized for the edification and enjoyment of working women and men, and illustrated the fundamental unity of all working people irrespective of color, creed, sex, or national origin.

Finally, the labor movement did not believe that the Olympic spirit of true amateurism and international understanding could be attained in a movement dominated by an aristocratic-bourgeois leadership. It was therefore determined to retain its cultural and political integrity within the worker's own Olympic movement.

### Prague, 1921

The first of such international Olympic festivals was hosted by the Czechoslovak Worker Gymnastics Association in Prague, 26–29 June 1921, and advertised as the first unofficial Worker Olympics. It attracted worker athletes from 13 countries: Austria, Belgium, Britain, Bulgaria, Czechoslovakia, Finland, France, Germany, Poland, Switzerland, the USA, USSR, and Yugoslavia. In addition to sport, the Olympics featured mass artistic displays, choral recitals, political plays and pageants, and culminated in the singing of revolutionary songs.

### Frankfurt, 1925

The first official Worker Olympics were arranged by the 1.3 million strong Lucerne Sport International in Germany, seven years after the end of World War I. They were billed by the organizers as a festival of peace. As a British representative put it, if wars are won on the playing fields of Eton, peace can be won on the democratic sports fields of the Workers International Olympiads.

The Winter Games, held in Schreiberhau (now Riesengebirge), attracted contestants from 12 countries, while the summer Frankfurt Games had representatives from 19 countries and over 150,000 spectators. Both winter and summer events included traditional competitive sports like skiing, skating, track and field, gymnastics, and wrestling, although the organizers stated their intention of avoiding the quest for records and idolization of individual "stars." All the same, they did not discount top performances and the world record for the women's 100-meter (109.36-yard) relay was broken. But the accent was on mass participation and socialist fellowship. For example, every athlete took part in the opening and closing artistic display, and the atmosphere was festive and unashamedly political. The opening ceremonies and victory rituals dispensed with national flags and anthems, featuring instead red flags and revolutionary hymns like the "Internationale." The centerpiece of the festival was an artistic display, accompanied by mass choirs and featuring the multiperson pyramids and tableaux symbolizing working-class solidarity and power in the class struggle. It culminated in the dramatic presentation, "Struggle for the World" (*Kampf um die Erde*), using mass speaking and acting choruses that portrayed sport as a source of strength for the creation of a new world.

Despite the success of the Frankfurt Games, they were marred by continuing rivalry between socialists and communists, and were confined to LSI affiliates, excluding all worker associations belonging to the communist RSI as well as socialist groups and athletes who had had contacts with RSI members (including those who had been to the Soviet Union or played host to Soviet sport groups). Beside Soviet athletes, they therefore excluded as many as 250,000 Germans and 100,000 Czechoslovaks, some of whom staged counterdemonstrations during the Frankfurt Games.

### Moscow, 1928

As a counter to both the socialist games of Frankfurt and the "bourgeois" Olympics of Amsterdam in 1928, the communist sports movement put on the First Workers Spartakiad in Moscow. It was launched on 12 August 1928 by a parade of 30,000 banner- and torch-carrying women and men marching in colorful formation through Moscow's Red Square to Dinamo Stadium (the largest Soviet stadium at the time). Despite the boycott by both socialist and bourgeois sport groups, some 600 worker athletes from 14 countries (15 percent of the total entry of 4,000) were said to have taken part. The foreign athletes came from Algeria, Argentina, Austria, Britain (26 participants), Czechoslovakia, Estonia, Finland, France (32 participants), Germany, Latvia, Norway, Sweden, Switzerland, and Uruguay.

The comprehensive sports program of 21 sports (the bourgeois Olympics of 1926 comprised only 17) covered track and field, gymnastics, swimming, diving, rowing, wrestling, boxing, weightlifting, fencing, cycling, soccer, basketball, and shooting. Although standards were not as high as those at the Amsterdam Olympics, Soviet sources claim that in virtually all events the Spartakiad winners surpassed the records set at the Frankfurt Workers Olympics. But the emphasis was not wholly on sport; the festival included a variety of pageants and displays, carnivals, mass games, motorcycle and automobile rallies, and demonstrations of folk games, folk music, and dancing. In addition, there were poetry readings and mock battles between the "workers of the world" and the "world bourgeoisie" (in which everyone participated, there being no passive spectators for this "sports theater" finale).

The winter counterpart to the Spartakiad took place in late 1928 in Moscow with 636 participants in skiing, speed skating (women and men), biathlon, and a special skiing contest for postal workers, rural dwellers, and border guards.

### Vienna, 1931

Although the social democrats had held a worker sport festival at Nuremberg in 1928 (with limited success), their next venture was to represent the zenith of the worker sport movement. The LSI, as sponsor, now had over 2 million members, including 350,000 women (over a sixth of the total) and arranged a festival in winter at Mürzzuschalg and in summer at Vienna that far outdid in spectators, participants, and pageantry the 1932 "bourgeois" Olympics at Lake Placid and Los Angeles.

As the invitation of the Austrian hosts to the Vienna Games announced in German, French, Czech, and Esperanto, the program was to include a children's sport festival, a meeting of the Red Falcon (*Sokol*) youth group, 220 events in all sport disciplines, Olympic championships, national championships, friendly matches, city games, a combination run and swim through Vienna, artistic displays, dramatic performances, fireworks, a festive parade, and mass exercises.

Some 80,000 worker athletes from 23 countries came to "Red Vienna," and on the opening day as many as a quarter of a million spectators watched 100,000 men and women parade through the

## Vienna Olympics, 1931

# TO WORKER ATHLETES OF THE WORLD!

## COME TO THE WORKER OLYMPICS IN RED VIENNA!

Children's sport festival.
Meeting of the Red Sokol youth group.
220 events in all sports disciplines.
Olympic championships.
National competitions.
Friendly matches. City Games.
Combination run and swim through Vienna.
Artistic displays. Dramatic performances.
Fireworks. A festive parade. Mass exercises.

streets to the new stadium constructed by the Viennese socialist government. As many as 65,000 later watched the soccer finals and 12,000 the cycling finals. This time the sports program and ceremony were more in line with the "bourgeois" Olympics. An Olympic flame was borne into the stadium (carried from Mount Olympus); each delegation marched into the stadium as a separate nation (though under a red flag); and the sports program roughly paralleled that of the "bourgeois" Olympics—though open to all, irrespective of ability, thereby demonstrating sport for all.

By design the Vienna Olympiad coincided with the opening of the Fourth Congress of the Socialist International and was pointedly noted that, whereas the political International assembled no more than a few hundred delegates, the sports International brought together the masses themselves. Indeed, there was no other element of the labor movement in which popular participation was more manifest: congresses might pass resolutions about proletarian solidarity and revolutionary energy, but worker sport provided practical application of those ideas.

### Barcelona (1936) and Antwerp (1937)

Alarmed at the popularity and growing strength of the worker sports movement, bourgeois governments stepped up their repressive actions. When communist workers tried to organize a Sec-

ond Spartakiad in Berlin in 1932, they first ran into visa problems (all Soviet and some other athletes were refused visas to enter Germany) and then, when several hundred worker athletes had managed to reach Berlin, the Games were banned.

Under attack from fascism, the socialists and communists at last came together in a popular front and jointly organized a third Worker Olympics, scheduled for Barcelona in Republican Spain from 19 to 26 July 1936. They were to be in opposition to the "Nazi Olympics" held in Berlin a week later. The Catalonia Committee for Worker Sport received promises of attendance from over 1,000 French worker athletes (the socialist government of Leon Blum gave equal funds to Barcelona and Berlin teams), as well as 150 from Switzerland, 100 from the Soviet Union, 60 from Belgium, 12 from the United States, 6 from Canada, and more from other countries. The Spanish Olympic Committee declared that it would boycott Berlin and take part in Barcelona.

But the third Worker Olympics never took place. On the morning of the scheduled opening ceremony, the Spanish fascists staged their military putsch. Some worker athletes remained in Spain to fight in the International Brigade during the Spanish Civil War, and many who returned home (like the Canadians, who included the national high jump champion Eva Dawes) were banned from sport by their national federations—while those athletes who had given the Nazi salute to Hitler in the Berlin Olympic opening ceremony returned as national heroes.

After the abortive Barcelona Games, the communist and socialist coalition rescheduled the third Worker Olympics for Antwerp in 1937. While the Antwerp Games were not as large as those at Vienna or as the intended Barcelona Games would have been, they did present an imposing display of worker solidarity. Despite the barriers put in their way by increasingly hostile and fascist regimes, special trains carried an estimated 27,000 worker athletes from 17 countries (including the Soviet Union) to Antwerp—an astonishing achievement in Europe in 1937. Some 50,000 people filled the stadium on the final day, and the traditional pageant through the city attracted over 200,000. Following this success, a fourth Worker Olympics was planned for Helsinki in 1943, but war brought down the curtain on the period of worker Olympic festivals.

## The Post–World War II Era

The worker sports movement survived World War II bowed but undefeated; the radically changed circumstance of the postwar world inevitably brought a transformation of the movement. Basically, the new role was one of selective cooperation and amalgamation with the national sports federations and clubs, by contrast with the prewar separate development. The new situation was brought about by a number of factors. In the first place, the Soviet Union had broken its isolation: it emerged from World War II a victor, its military and political power having penetrated into Central and Eastern Europe. In the conditions of international friction, or Cold War, that ensued, with two rival blocs facing each other in a divided Europe, sport became a relatively harmless arena for international competition, for "defeating" one's ideological opponent. Within the Soviet Union, domestic sport was now thought powerful enough to take on the world, and victories over bourgeois countries (especially the United States) would demonstrate the vitality of the Soviet system and Soviet-style communism. That the political aim eventually failed should not obscure the success of the sporting venture.

Second, with the process of decolonialization and mounting democratization of both the Olympic movement and bourgeois sport generally, with fewer sports and clubs being confined to middle- and upper-class white males, the belief grew that international sport, particularly the Olympic Games, could be opened up to working people, women, and ethnic groups; further, it might be used for peace, democracy, and the isolation of racist systems like South African apartheid.

Third, largely as a result of the above, the emphasis within worker sport switched to campaigning inside "bourgeois" organizations for funds, playgrounds, open spaces, and facilities for working people, and for women's sport, against commercialism and chauvinism. In France, for example, the aim was no longer for the Fédération du Sport et Symnique Travailliste (GFSGT) to replace bourgeois sport, but to take part in building a national sports system based on the needs of all.

All the same, a separate worker sports movement did manage to survive. Immediately after the war, the socialists in Western Europe set up the International Worker Sports Committee (IWSC) in London in 1946. Despite a peak of 2.2 million members in 14 countries in the late 1940s, however, the IWSC never attained the importance that the prewar movement had had, partly because individual member associations were weak, with the exception of those in Finland, France, and Austria. The most influential worker sports organization today is that in Israel: Hapoel (The Worker) is Israel's largest and strongest sports organization; it is the only instance (outside remaining communist states) where a worker sports organization controls its country's sport.

The worker sports movement needed to expand if it was to fulfill its cultural and political mission. But the needs of growth presented complex problems. Organized sport, like the working class itself, is a product of modern industrial society, and in a bourgeois world a large proportion of working men and women are steeped in and subscribe to society's dominant values.

Nonetheless, the worker sports movement did try to provide an alternative experience based on workers' own culture and inspired by visions of a new socialist culture. To this end it organized the best sporting program it could, regardless of the level, whether a Sunday bike ride or a Worker Olympic festival, founded on genuinely socialist values. Its story is as much a part of the history of sport and of the labor movement as is Coubertin's Olympics or trade unionism.

—James Riordan

**Bibliography:** Gruneau, Richard. (1983) *Class, Sports and Social Development.* Amherst: University of Massachusetts Press.

Hoberman, John. (1984) *Sport and Political Ideology.* London: Routledge and Kegan Paul.

Holt, Richard. (1981) *Sport and Society in Modern France.* London: Macmillan.

———. (1990) *Sport and the Working Class in Modern Britain.* Manchester: Manchester University Press.

Jones, Stephen. (1988) *Sport, Politics, and the Working Class: Organised Labour and Sport in Inter-War Britain.* Manchester: Manchester University Press.

Kidd, Bruce. (1995) "Worker Sport in the New World. The Canadian Story." In *The Story of Worker Sport,* edited by Arnd Krüger and James Riordan. Champaign, IL: Human Kinetics.

Kolasky, John. (1979) *The Shattered Illusion.* Toronto: Peter Martin.

Krüger, Arnd, and James Riordan, eds. (1996) *The Story of Worker Sport.* Champaign, IL: Human Kinetics.

———. (1985) *Der Internationale Arbeitersport.* Cologne: Pahl-Rugenstein.

Kruger, Arnd. (1985) "The Rise and Fall of the International Worker Sports Movement." In *Proceedings of the 11th HISPA Congress.* Glasgow: Jordanhill College Press.

Moustard, René. (1983) *Le Sport Populaire.* Paris: Le sport en plein air.

Murray, William. (1987) "The French Workers' Sports Movement." *International Journal of the History of Sport* 4.

Naison, Mark. (1979) "Lefties and Righties: The Communist Party and Sports during the Great Depression." *Radical America* 13, 4.

Riess, Steven. (1982) "Working-Class Sports in America, 1882–1920." Paper delivered to the American Historical Association, San Francisco (12 August).

Riordan, James. (1977) *Sport in Soviet Society.* Cambridge: Cambridge University Press.

———. (1984) "The Workers' Olympics." In *Five Ring Circus: Money, Power and Politics at the Olympic Games,* edited by Alan Tomlinson and Gary Whannel. London: Pluto Press.

———. (1991) *Sport, Politics and Communism.* Manchester: Manchester University Press.

Simri, Uriel. (1995) "Hapoel—The World's Only Ruling Worker Sports Organisation (Israel)." In *The Story of Worker Sport,* edited by Arnd Kruger and James Riordan. Champaign, IL: Human Kinetics.

Teichler, H. J., and G. Hauk, eds. (1987) *Illustrierte Geschichte des Arbeitersports.* Berlin: Verlag Karl Hofmann.

Ueberhorst, Horst. (1973) *Frisch, Frei, Stark und Treu. Die Arbeitresportbewegung in Deutschland, 1893–1933.* Dusseldorf: Droste Verlag.

Wheeler, Robert. (1978) "Organised Sport and Organised Labour: The Worker Sports Movement." *Journal of Contemporary History* 13.

# Wrestling, Freestyle

In freestyle wrestling, competitors may take a wide variety of holds on both the upper body and legs, but in contrast to the many forms of belt wrestling, the rules of freestyle do not allow competitors to grasp the opponent's clothing to secure a hold. A freestyle wrestler can win the bout either by pinning the opponent or by scoring points for successful tactics. The modern sport, which is practiced in the Olympic Games, the World Games, and National Collegiate Athletic Association (NCAA) and Amateur Athletic Union (AAU) competitions, represents a tradition thousands of years old and manifested worldwide. Its tactics, heroes, and lore have had remarkable impact on literature, art, and history.

## Origins

The origin of wrestling cannot be isolated in space or time: the many manifestations of the sport are spread so widely that the only meaningful inquiry about its origins will seek them in the nature of humankind or, quite plausibly, in the ethology of animal behavior. Ethologists find nonlethal combat among a number of animal species; its apparent purposes range from play to the establishment of hierarchy. Wrestling is virtually unique among combat sports in allowing the opportunity for full physical confrontation with limited possibility of serious injury, and its relative safety as an outlet for aggression and test of physical superiority may best explain its origin and its wide and enduring popularity.

Depictions of wrestling appear as early as 3000 B.C.E. in the ancient Near East, offering a rich source of evidence for the early history of the sport. Virtually all the tactics seen in modern freestyle wrestling, including the most sophisticated throws, can be found among the 406 wrestling pairs depicted on the walls of the Middle Kingdom tombs at Beni Hasan in the Nile valley, and both sculpture and literature from Mesopotamia show that the sport was popular there in antiquity. References to wrestling festivals are frequent in epics and hymns of ancient and medieval India, and in a story remarkably akin to the Greek legend of the female warrior and athlete Atalanta, Marco Polo tells of a Tartar princess who challenged her hapless suitors to a wrestling contest. Wrestling was part of the Olympics of ancient Greece since the eighteenth Olympiad in 704 B.C.E. Hundreds of vases, sculptures, and coins depict wrestling, and the sport finds frequent mention in Greek literature. The Greeks appear to have been the first to structure their competitions as a formal elimination tournament; while wrestling bouts were common in other ancient societies at religious or royal occasions, the Greeks were keenly interested in the emergence of a single winner from a group of competitors and structured the encounters accordingly. It is worth noting that the earliest surviving work in Western literature, the *Epic of Gilgamesh,* describes wrestling, as does the earliest surviving work of Greek literature, Homer's *Iliad.*

A number of types of freestyle wrestling seen today appear to be the direct descendants of ancient forms. The Nuba of the lower Sudan have held wrestling festivals for centuries, if not millennia, and there appears to be remarkable continuity between the costumes of the Nubian wrestlers seen in Egyptian sculpture and the gourd-strung skirts that the Nuba wrestlers still wear. A highly popular folk wrestling of India performed on the mud surface of the *akhara* also continues an ancient tradition. Freestyle wrestling has been popular in the British Isles for many centuries, and the Lancashire style in particular has had a profound influence on modern wrestling. In this tradition, often called "catch as catch can," contestants begin standing and continue the contest on the ground if neither contestant scores a fall from standing. A Scottish variant of the Lancashire style begins with the contestants standing chest to chest, grasping one another with arms locked around the body, and the contest continues on the ground if a fall does not follow. In the Irish collar-and-elbow style, wrestlers begin the bout by grasping the collar with one hand and the elbow with the other; if neither man achieves a fall from this position, open wrestling continues, both standing and on the ground, until a fall is scored. Irish immigrants brought this style to the United States, where its tactics were widely adopted. Because of the heavy Irish settlement in northwest Vermont, the collar-and-elbow style became the predominant tactic of the region, and the success of Vermont's George William Flagg, who became the wrestling champion of the Army of the Potomac, further popularized the Irish style.

## Development

It is perhaps due to the popularity and relatively high status of professional Greco-Roman wrestling in nineteenth century Europe and its frequent international meets that the emergence of amateur competition, particularly in freestyle wrestling, was slow in Europe. The Olympics of 1896 featured only one bout, a heavyweight Greco-Roman contest, and freestyle did not appear until the St. Louis Olympics of 1904, where there was competition in seven weight categories. Since 1921, the Fédération Internationale des Luttes Amateurs (FILA), with headquarters in Lausanne, Switzerland, has set the rules, scoring, and procedures that govern wrestling competition at the World Games and the Olympics,

*In this Greek bronze statue of the Hellenistic era, the standing wrestler uses his opponent's arm to force him to the ground while preventing him from escaping by stepping over one of his legs and pressing his head down.*

and these were adopted by the Amateur Athletic Union (AAU) in the United States for its freestyle competitions.

Freestyle wrestling spread rapidly in the United States after the Civil War, and by the 1880s its tournaments drew hundreds of participants. Urbanization, increased industrialization, and the disappearance of the frontier formed the context in which this highly individual combat sport—along with boxing—found new and heightened popularity. A professional circuit, by no means corrupted into the staged theatrics of its later years, emerged in this era, as did amateur organizations: about the time of the first New York Athletic Club tournament in 1878, professional championship bouts offered purses of up to $1,000. 1900 saw the first intercollegiate wrestling match, held between Yale University

## Wrestling Theory and Practice
### Akhara

What is an *akhara*? It is a place of recreation for youth. It is a shrine of strength where earth is turned into gold. It is a sign of masculinity and the assembly hall of invigorated youth. Strength is measured against strength and moves and counter moves are born and develop. . . . An *akhara* is where one prays and where offerings are given and distributed. Its earth is saluted and taken up to anoint one's shoulders and head. And then one wrestles and the sound of slapping thighs and pounding chests fills the air. Grunts and groans of exertion echo ominously. One trounces and in turn is trounced. Exercise is done. Laziness and procrastination are drowned in sweat.

—Ratan Patodi, *The Art of Indian Wrestling*
(translated by Joseph S. Alter)

and the University of Pennsylvania. Professional wrestlers formed the National Wrestling Alliance in 1904, and in 1911, for the famous rematch of George Hackenschmidt and Frank Gotch, the gate was $87,000. With the first Eastern Intercollegiate Wrestling Association tournament in 1905 a rapidly expanding roster of tournaments for college and secondary school wrestlers began; management of the Eastern Association remarkably remained under student leadership for over 30 years. In 1927, R. G. Clapp of the University of Nebraska formulated rules for intercollegiate wrestling and in the following year, the first NCAA wrestling tournament took place; its rules, which were quickly adopted by the Eastern Association, diverged from the international style of FILA and AAU competition.

Time limits for bouts and a system for determining a victor when neither wrestler has gained a fall are developments of the twentieth century. Nineteenth-century championship bouts, especially in Greco-Roman wrestling, could last for many hours, which spectators found tedious. Although the AAU rules then in use called for the referee to determine the victor if no fall had occurred after fifteen minutes of wrestling, at early Eastern Intercollegiate Wrestling Association Tournaments, bouts continued until a fall was scored, even if that meant half an hour or more of wrestling. By 1911, rudimentary guidelines for

determining victory by the referee's decision in intercollegiate matches emerged, also keeping those bouts to a maximum of fifteen minutes. This time length has decreased steadily over the century; in 1996, FILA bouts consist of two periods of three minutes each with a sixty-second rest period between the periods, and intercollegiate bouts consist of one three-minute period, followed by two periods of two minutes each. Intercollegiate rules, unlike FILA rules, do not allow a rest period.

## Practice

Under modern international rules, a wrestler scores a fall on his opponent and immediately wins the bout by holding his shoulders motionless on the mat long enough to allow the referee to ascertain the total control needed for a fall. U.S. intercollegiate rules specify that the shoulders must be *pinned:* motionless for one full second for college competition and two seconds for secondary school contests. Under earlier FILA rules, rolling an opponent across his shoulders counted for a fall; under current rules, this tactic counts for two points. Both the international and intercollegiate practices mark a departure from ancient Greek usages in which touching the back to the ground or stretching an opponent prone constituted a fall; the Greeks also required three falls to determine the winner. In both antiquity and modern times, disputes over whether or not a fall occurred have not been uncommon.

Scoring systems, weight categories, and definition of permissible tactics have varied widely over time and place in the history of wrestling. Under current FILA rules, if neither wrestler scores a fall, victory is determined by the number of points scored for successful tactics. These include taking the opponent to the mat or exposing his shoulders to the mat. Up to five points are awarded for "grand technique," in which one wrestler lifts his opponent in an arc of great amplitude or height and returns him to the mat with his shoulders exposed in danger of a fall. NCAA rules allow up to three points for a "nearfall" but do not award extra points for "grand technique." In both FILA and NCAA rules, when one wrestler scores fifteen points more than his opponent, the judges will stop the bout and declare him the winner by technical superiority. Intercollegiate wrestling since 1915 has recorded the time each contestant has had his opponent under his control on the mat, and for some time in the early years of wrestling, this was the major criterion for determining a victor in the absence of a fall; its significance for scoring has steadily declined to the present, when "time advantage" counts for one point at most.

Reflecting contemporary values of sporting ethics and recreational hygiene, FILA and intercollegiate rules from their earliest years stressed the safety of the competitors. Holds and tactics that jeopardized life or limb or whose object was punishment of the opponent, rather than leverage, have been consistently illegal. These include the full nelson, strangleholds, twisting hammerlocks, the flying mare with the opponent's arm locked, and slamming the opponent to the mat. Modern rules have gone farther in banning virtually any hold that pressures a joint in a direction contrary to its normal movement. These refinements stand in stark contrast to the roughness of ancient Greek wrestling, which allowed strangleholds and granted Olympic titles in 456 and 452 B.C.E. to a wrestler named Leontiskos, whose principal tactic was breaking his opponent's fingers. The Greeks viewed their combat sports as both training and surrogates for the heroism of warfare; not surprisingly their notions of fair play differed from those of the twentieth century, when combat took on a different character. While contemporary FILA and intercollegiate rules forbid rough tactics, they also rigorously penalize wrestlers for attempting to stall, insisting that both athletes try to stay near the center of the mat and wrestle aggressively. Whereas ancient Greek wrestling had no weight categories, nor do many of the popular forms of wrestling today worldwide, modern FILA and intercollegiate rules divide contestants into ten different weight categories.

The significance of winning the bout differs widely from culture to culture. Whereas the ancient Greek poet Pindar twice spoke of the disgrace that accompanied the defeated wrestler, anthropologists report that despite the importance of wrestling to the Nuba of present-day Sudan, defeat is borne gracefully. Among the nomadic Mongolians, the wrestler who lost in the festivals had to give his clothing to his opponent and hold a banquet for him and all his kin; in con-

## Observations on Wrestling

### Abe Lincoln Wrestles

"He was at least two inches taller than I was," said Mr. Lincoln, "and somewhat heavier, but I reckoned that I was the most wiry, and soon after I had tackled him, I gave him a hug, lifted him off the ground, and threw him flat on his back. That settles his hash."

—Benjamin Perley Poore, in *Reminiscences of Abraham Lincoln*.

### Plato on Wrestling

The tactics of upright wrestling, a disentangling of necks, hands and sides, practiced with love of victory and with decorous disposition for the sake of strength and health, are completely worthwhile and not to be overlooked.

—Plato, *Laws* 796a

### Jacob and the Man

Jacob was left alone. And a man wrestled with him until the break of dawn. When he saw that he had not prevailed against him, he wrenched Jacob's hip at its socket, so that the socket of his hip was strained as he wrestled with him. Then he said, "Let me go, for dawn is breaking." But he answered, "I will not let you go, unless you bless me." Said the other, "What is your name?" He replied, "Jacob." Said he, "Your name shall no longer be called Jacob, but Israel, for you have striven with God and man and have prevailed."

—Genesis 32:25–29 (translated by the Jewish Publication Society)

trast, a Muslim chant sung at Turkish popular tournaments reminded victors and defeated that on the last day, all stood equal in the Prophet's band. The intensely individualistic nature of the sport makes it an excellent touchstone for a society's posture towards the polarities of competition and cooperation.

The great and famous of both history and myth have often appeared as wrestlers; such stories surface in widely diverse contexts, and even when apocryphal serve as evidence of the popularity and status of the sport. Wrestling was regularly a rite of passage for gods, heroes, and kings. Perhaps the best-known wrestler in Western civilization is the biblical Jacob from the book of Genesis, who can become the patriarch Israel only after wrestling all night with a mysterious being identified in the biblical text merely as "a man" ('iysh). The Sumerian hero Gilgamesh, whose epic antedates Genesis, only emerges as a serious and determined leader after wrestling the formidable Enkidu. Arabic literature depicts Muhammad as a mighty wrestler, who bests a skeptic in wrestling. Greek mythology sets the control of the universe as the prize of the wrestling between Zeus and his father Kronos, and the exploits of both Herakles and Theseus frequently include wrestling contests against man and beast. Numerous kings, at least in legend, have been wrestlers: Shulgi of Sumer may be the first king on record to boast of his wrestling prowess, and Ptolemy II and III of Egypt (third century B.C.E.) appear in artwork as victorious wrestlers. The eighth century C.E. Byzantine king Basil I, according to court historians, defeated a boastful Bulgarian wrestler, and at the Field of the Cloth of Gold pageant in 1520, Francis I of France threw Henry VIII of England in a wrestling bout. A late Greek tradition tells that the philosopher Plato wrestled in the Isthmian games, a major athletic festival. Modern democratic societies also desire such signs of fitness to lead. Although the stories of George Washington as a wrestler are of dubious provenance, contemporary sources tell of Abraham Lincoln's wrestling prowess.

Major figures emerged in Europe and the United States in the late nineteenth century as opportunities for honor and large cash rewards increased. The European Greco-Roman champion George Hackenschmidt won a series of widely watched freestyle bouts in England against the Turkish champion Muhammed Madrali. Hackenschmidt was a sufficient sensation to be recorded in early films, some of which are still extant. In 1905 he toured the United States, defeating Tom Jenkins for the world freestyle championship. The United States, meanwhile, was producing a number of professional strongmen: Martin "Farmer" Burns, "Strangler" Lewis, and Frank Gotch, who handed Hackenschmidt the only two defeats of his career of over 2,000 matches, the first arguably by using foul tactics.

In modern international wrestling, wrestlers from the former Soviet Union have had remarkable success, with strong showings also from Japan, Turkey, Iran, Sweden, Finland, and the United States. The Russian Alexandr Medved won three Olympic gold medals between 1964 and 1972, plus ten world championships. Outstanding U.S. gold medalists include Doug Blubaugh, Ben Peterson, John Peterson, Dan Gable, and John Smith, who was first in the 1988 Olympics in addition to winning six world championships between 1987 and 1992. Oklahoma State University, the University of Oklahoma, Iowa State University, and the University of Iowa have secured the greatest share of team NCAA championships; in recent years a substantial number of intercollegiate champions have moved on to Olympic contests with great success.

—Michael B. Poliakoff

See also Arm Wrestling; Sumo; Traditional Sports, Africa; Traditional Sports, North and South America; Traditional Sports, Oceania; Wrestling, Greco-Roman.

**Bibliography:** Alter, Joseph S. (1992) *The Wrestler's Body.* Berkeley: University of California Press.

Armstrong, Walter. (1893) *Wrestling.* London: Longmans, Green.

Caroll, Scott T. (1988) "Wrestling in Ancient Nubia." *The Journal of Sport History* 15, 2: 121–137.

Hackenschmidt, George. (1909) *The Complete Science of Wrestling.* London: Athletic Publications.

Keen, Clifford, Charles Speidel, and Raymond Swartz. (1964) *Championship Wrestling*, 4th ed. New York: Arco Publishing.

Morton, Gerald W. (1985) *Wrestling to Rasslin: Ancient Sport to American Spectacle.* Bowling Green, OH: Bowling Green State University Press.

Niebel, Benjamin W., and Douglas A. Niebel. (1982) *Modern Wrestling. A Primer for Wrestlers, Parents, and Fans.* University Park: Pennsylvania State University Press.

Poliakoff, Michael B. (1987) *Combat Sports in the Ancient World: Competition, Violence, and Culture.* New Haven, CT: Yale University Press.

Sayenga, Donald, and Philip Badger. (1975) *The Easterns. 70 Years of Wrestling.*

Wilsdorf, Helmut. (1939) *Ringkampf im alten Agypten.* Wuerzburg: Konrad Triltsch Verlag.

Wilson, Charles Morrow. (1959) *The Magnificent Scufflers: Revealing the Great Days When America Wrestled the World.* Brattleboro, VT: Stephen Greene Press.

# Wrestling, Greco-Roman

The modern sport of Greco-Roman wrestling is governed by all the rules and procedures of international freestyle wrestling, with the added restriction that no holds below the waist are allowed. Despite its name, Greco-Roman is not an ancient form of wrestling but is principally a development of nineteenth-century Europe, where it achieved high popularity as both an amateur and professional sport and appeared in the first modern Olympics. It has maintained its popularity into present times, especially among wrestlers in Europe and the Far East.

## Origins

The formalization of the elements of Greco-Roman wrestling into the sport known today is a recent phenomenon. Sixteenth-century drawings of wrestling ascribed to Albrecht Dürer and Fabian von Auerswald's "Wrestler's Art" depicts leg holds inadmissible in Greco-Roman wrestling, suggesting that freestyle, rather than Greco-Roman, was that era's mainstream form of wrestling. A number of indigenous forms of wrestling in Europe that restrict holds to the upper body may have contributed to the development of the Greco-Roman style. The British style of Cumberland and Westmoreland wrestling, for example, allows a variety of trips that are not permitted in Greco-Roman, but its restriction of arm holds to the upper torso is quite similar; so also in Devon and Cornwall, the wrestlers take their holds above the waist.

Although British authors often referred to the style as French wrestling or old Norman, the continental name, Greco-Roman, reflected the classicizing tendency of European athletic movements of the eighteenth and nineteenth centuries that desired the support of ancient models for their contemporary practices. It was widely, though mistakenly, believed that the Greeks had a separate wrestling competition called upright wrestling in which only upper body holds were permitted. Johann Friedrich Guts Muths' eigh-

teenth-century *Gymnastics for Youth,* for example, moves from a description of "orthopale" (a term Plato uses for the standing part of wrestling) to a description of schoolboy wrestling in which no mention is made of any holds on the legs. By the late nineteenth century, Greco-Roman wrestling enjoyed great prestige and popularity in continental Europe.

## Development

Despite the similarities of Greco-Roman to several regional British forms of wrestling and its brilliant promotion by William Muldoon in the United States after the Civil War, the sport never achieved lasting popularity in the English-speaking world, yielding place to the more natural and unstructured freestyle forms. The 1911 *Encyclopedia of Sports and Games* dismissed it as "[a] system, dignified by the high sounding Greco-Roman title (though it bears but the faintest resemblance to the wrestling of either the ancient Greeks or Romans) . . . foisted upon the British public in 1870." Its popularity in Europe, on the other hand, was such that virtually all nineteenth-century capital cities hosted international tournaments, often with enormous prizes for the victors. At the czar's tournament, competitors received 500 francs per month merely to train and compete; up to 5,000 francs in prize money awaited the victor.

A number of nineteenth-century Greco-Roman strongmen, remarkable both as athletes and as public figures, appeared in the later half of the nineteenth century. Notable among them were Paul Pons of France, Kara Ahmed of Turkey, and Stanislaus Zbyszko of Poland, who received a law degree from the University of Vienna before devoting himself exclusively to first Greco-Roman, and later freestyle wrestling, on the professional circuit. Like his contemporary George Hackenschmidt, he was the favorite and familiar of aristocrats and royalty. William Muldoon, who had been a successful barroom freestyle wrestler in post–Civil War New York, traveled from the United States to France to fight in the Franco-Prussian War and there learned the Greco-Roman style. His Greco-Roman championship bouts in the United States were remarkable in their ability to draw substantial crowds, but subsequent U.S. wrestling celebrities in the United States were almost exclusively freestyle wrestlers.

*Yuri Melnichenko of Kazakhstan emerged victorious from this match with the United States' Dennis Hall to win a gold medal in Greco-Roman wrestling at the 1996 Olympics in Atlanta.*

The greatest Greco-Roman wrestler of the nineteenth century was indisputably George Hackenschmidt, an athlete of prodigious strength born in Estonia, who later gained the ring name the Russian Lion. Trained in civil engineering and the author of several books on physical culture, his combined Greco-Roman and freestyle career included more than 2,000 victories. In 1898, at the age of 21 with some 15 months of wrestling training, he defeated the experienced Paul Pons in a match in St. Petersburg. In 1900, as a professional, he won the St. Petersburg and the Moscow tournaments and a series of international tournaments thereafter. In England he defeated the American Tom Jenkins in alternate Greco-Roman and freestyle bouts and shortly after this 1904 bout turned exclusively to freestyle to compete more effectively in England, Australia, and the United States. After retiring from the ring, he became the physical education adviser to the British House of Lords.

Greco-Roman wrestling appeared at the first modern Olympics in 1896 in Athens, where three contestants competed in the heavyweight class, with Karl Schuhman of Germany taking the first place over Georgios Tsitas of Greece. Freestyle, by comparison, did not appear in the Olympics until the 1904 games in St. Louis. During this century, the former Soviet Union, Bulgaria, Romania, Japan, Sweden, and Finland have shown remarkable success in Olympic competition. Carl Westergren of Sweden is the only Greco-Roman wrestler to win three gold medals (1920, 1924, and 1932); Ivar Johansson, also of Sweden, took gold medals in Greco-Roman competition in 1932 and 1936 and a freestyle gold medal in 1932. The United States, whose national wrestling is exclusively freestyle, entered its first Greco-Roman team in 1952 and has succeeded in winning only two gold medals, when Steve Fraser and Jeffrey Blatnick won in the 1984 Los Angeles Olympics.

## Practice

In the Greco-Roman style, wrestlers may not take holds below the waist or even use their legs actively in holds; thus the leg takedowns and trips fundamental to freestyle wrestling are barred. The arm drags, bear hugs, and headlocks of freestyle wrestling, on the other hand, are a central part of the Greco-Roman wrestler's repertoire and are carefully refined. Far from creating a dull contest, the restriction of holds to the upper body has encouraged the use of a spectacular series of throws called souples, in which the offensive wrestler lifts his opponent in a high arch while falling backward to a bridge on his own neck and bringing his opponent's shoulders into contact with the mat. Even in wrestling on the mat (*par terre*), the Greco-Roman wrestler must seek ambitious body-lock and gut-wrench holds to attempt to turn his opponent for a fall. The ability to arch backward from a standing position onto one's own neck confidently and safely while lifting and turning the opponent to the mat is crucial for success. The rules of the International Amateur Wrestling Federation (Fédération Internationale des Luttes Amateurs) strictly prohibit stalling, and after 15 seconds of inconclusive action on the ground, the bout must resume with both wrestlers in a neutral standing position and working toward a throw.

Until the formalization of the federation's rules in 1921, Greco-Roman bouts were notorious for their length. On the professional circuit, bouts of two or three hours were not uncommon, and although Hackenschmidt sometimes scored falls in a matter of seconds, his bouts regularly lasted between 20 and 40 minutes. William Muldoon's epic bout with Clarence Whistler at New York's Terrace Garden Theater in 1881 lasted some eight hours before ending in a draw; his match with William Miller at Gilmore's Garden lasted 9 hours and 35 minutes. Even the early Olympic bouts were prolonged: in 1912, Anders Ahlgren of Sweden and Ivar Boehling of Finland battled for nine hours in the finals before the officials declared the match a draw and awarded both men a silver medal.

Under modern rules, a bout consists of two periods of three minutes each, and a point system identical to that of international freestyle determines the victor in the absence of a fall. As in freestyle, a fall is scored when one wrestler holds his opponent's shoulders motionless on the mat long enough for the referee to ascertain total control. The age categories, weight classes, and dress follow the same rules as freestyle.

The Greco-Roman bouts of the professional circuit were characterized by a high level of brutality: body slams, choke-holds, head-butting, and even the introduction of caustic substances to weaken an opponent were known. At the end of the nineteenth century, the rules were quite simple: gouging with the nails, punching with the fist, and violently slamming one's arms together around the opponent's stomach were the few tactics explicitly forbidden. Today, all tactics that jeopardize the life or limb of an opponent are strictly forbidden, and notwithstanding spectacular back arches, bridges, and throws, Greco-Roman matches proceed with a very high level of safety.

—Michael B. Poliakoff

**See also** Wrestling, Freestyle.

**Bibliography:** Fleischer, Nat. (1936) *From Milo to Londos, The Story of Wrestling through the Ages.* The Ring Athletic Library 13. New York: C. J. O'Brien.

Jaenecke, C. (1899) *Der Griechisch-Roemische Ringkampf in seiner heutigen Gestaltung.* Hamburg, Germany: J. F. Richter.

Martell, William A. (1973) *Greco-Roman Wrestling.* Champaign, IL: Human Kinetics.

Morton, Gerald W., and George M. O'Brien. (1985) *Wrestling to Rasslin: Ancient Sport to American Spectacle.* Bowling Green, OH: Bowling Green University Popular Press.

Petrov, Rajko. (1986) *Freestyle and Greco-Roman Wrestling.* Lausanne, Switzerland: Fédération Internationale des Luttes Amateurs.

Wilson, Charles Morrow. (1959) *The Magnificent Scufflers. Revealing the Great Days When America Wrestled the World.* Brattleboro, VT: Stephen Greene Press.

# Wushu

Composed of two characters, wushu is the Chinese term usually translated as "martial arts." "Wu" is associated with military and warfare; "shu" with the skill, way, or methods of doing an activity. As a classifying term, wushu covers the Chinese martial traditions from their origins in early stone-age cultures to a wide variety of martially inspired practices seen today. (The term

*Chinese soldiers practice martial arts using leather belts.*

*gongfu,* or *kung-fu,* often used in the West to refer to Chinese martial arts, is actually composed of two Chinese characters referring to the time and effort required to accomplish a task. The term can be applied to any human activity and is applied to martial arts only because of the time and effort required to become skilled in these arts.)

## Origins and Development

Chinese martial traditions have evolved along with the technological and social changes that have occurred during China's long history. Fighting arts required a variety of defensive and offensive specializations, from basic hand-to-hand combat to complex techniques of large-scale warfare. Although primarily composed of fighting arts, wushu has long been associated with physical conditioning, dance, drama, meditative exercise, and competitive exhibition. Wushu developed as a vital aspect of China's culture and

came to influence the martial traditions of neighboring countries and eventually the rest of the world.

The Chinese martial arts grew out of the need for protection against other people and dangerous animals. As Chinese society grew more complex, so did its martial systems. The first fighting methods utilized the body parts most appropriate for the task: hands, feet, elbows, knees, and head. Rudimentary skills were developed and supplemented by the use of hunting and farming tools made of wood and stone, including the club, spear, and knife. As the basic technology developed and metals came into use, a spectrum of weaponry became available. Chinese society came to place more and more emphasis on warfare, and the martial arts became a specialized profession for many. However, with the advent of modern firearms in China, traditional martial arts were more commonly practiced as forms of exercise and sport.

Martial arts enjoy a growing popularity throughout the world today. Although they can be found in all cultures, martial arts of Asian origin are the better known because of their sophisticated repertoire of techniques coupled with philosophies of self-cultivation. The histories of the most popular Asian martial art styles indicate a profound Chinese influence. For example, Okinawan karate derived from China's Fujian province and the founder of Korean Tae Kwon Do studied wushu while serving in the military in Manchuria. For this reason, an overview of the development of Chinese wushu helps clarify the significance of today's martial arts.

Rudimentary forms of Chinese martial arts took root in the early Neolithic times as products of a survival instinct. These basic fighting methods served to protect individuals, families, and clans. They also provided entertainment, as in games of "head butting" in which contestants donned animal horns. By the Zhou Dynasty (1122?–256 B.C.E.), wushu had already reached a highly advanced level. Excavations of the period have uncovered an array of arms and armor, including spears, halberds, chariots, bows, arrows, helmets, swords, and knives. Other artifacts depict not only sophisticated military organization, but a culture in which martial arts were greatly valued for their eminent role in securing or maintaining political stability. In the fifth century B.C.E., the crossbow and iron weapons came into use, ushering in new modes of fighting arts. Military treatises, such as Sun Tsu's *The Art of War*, detailed military tactics and maneuvers that are still studied today for their insights and practicality.

In the following centuries, China remained the exemplar of refined culture, and all surrounding countries looked to her for knowledge and inspiration. But with China's cultural greatness came threats of foreign invasion by those seeking her riches. Internal conflicts likewise erupted due to inevitable social inequities that developed among economic groups. Chinese history flows through dynastic cycles in which imperial armies were almost always fighting with invading barbarians and/or native rebel groups. Long years of turmoil have taught the Chinese to rely on martial arts as a security measure. Those who possessed the most advanced systems felt that they had an advantage in protecting their empire, clan, or family. Therefore, the fighting systems that

## Martial Arts and the American Imagination

The significant place the martial arts have found in the American imagination is a product of the ease with which the characteristics of these arts and their practitioners have been merged with mythic patterns concerning warriors in American culture. The martial arts have such a resonance in the popular imagination due to the fact that their outward appearance is so different, but their symbolic structure is flexible enough to be melded into a new, syncretic cultural entity.

The American fascination with the martial arts is equally a product of the split between what we wish we were and what we are. Our affinity for these arts is the complex result of individual needs and cultural conditioning. Despite our convictions that we are engaging in something very new, we are in reality recreating and perpetuating a mythic pattern that has great resonance within us.

In seeking skill, we deal with lack of control.
In the celebration of the individual, we find social definition.
In an activity of iconoclasts, we find boundary and structure.
In the new and strange, we unconsciously recreate an old and familiar mythic pattern.

—John Donohue, "Wave People: The Martial Arts and the American Imagination." *Journal of Asian Martial Arts* 3, 1 (1994): 22.

evolved were highly secretive and taught only to selected individuals or groups.

The fighting systems that developed reflect the concerns and social positions of their creators. For example, the imperial army developed arts geared for large-scale military engagements. They often focused on long-range weapons, such as the crossbow and archery. Their maneuvers usually required a fast cavalry to carry out their objectives. But all too often the imperial political-military structure crumbled, leaving the commoners to fend for themselves. Other groups developed their own highly effective fighting systems. These groups often organized themselves around a common social bond, be it linguistic, social, or philosophic.

Because specially gifted individuals are credited with the creation of specific martial systems, their own families often retained hold of the tradition by passing on their knowledge from generation to generation. Their concerns were primarily for the security of family and clan. Their limited resources kept their focus on developing skills an individual fighter could employ, including weapons such as sword, spear, or knife. The conflicts they encountered were often with individuals or with small groups, so open-hand boxing skills were also of great importance.

Martial art styles were usually named for the people, places, or philosophic ideas associated with them. There are a few hundred known Chinese styles, but many more styles and substyles remain to be categorized. For simplicity, martial art styles are sometimes placed into general categories, such as Northern/Southern, Internal/External, or Daoist/Buddhist, and sometimes they are categorized according to their place of origin.

Of special importance in the evolution of some Chinese martial arts is their association with temples. During times of turmoil, temples were often places of refuge. They attracted a variety of people from all segments of Chinese society, including martial experts who came from near and far to live together, often discussing and comparing their knowledge. Some temples, such as the Shaolin, became "universities" where leading experts contributed to the preservation and evolution of the martial arts.

Some martial traditions have become extinct due to the rise of modern weaponry. Nonetheless, in China many martial arts remain intact. The continued popularity of these arts is due, in part, to their pervasive presence in Chinese culture. Their historical importance, already noted in preceding paragraphs, has been the subject of many literary endeavors, including a separate "martial arts" genre. As moving art forms, the martial arts are valued living expressions of their developers' creativity and genius. Martial art forms are also cherished for their therapeutic benefits, and in China the majority of people practicing a martial art do so primarily for this reason. However, the martial arts can be found in theatrical productions, self-defense classes, military training programs, entertainment industries, meditative practices, and sporting events.

## Outlook

In China today, modern forms of entertainment are limited. Televisions, computers, and electronic games, for example, are luxuries few can afford. Modern health care is also limited due to high costs. Therefore, wushu, as a form of exercise and sport, offers an attractive alternative. Martial art exhibitions have a long-standing tradition in China. Competitions were held regularly in provinces, and now competitions are featured at the national level as well. During the present decade, international teams have been formed. Coaching of routines standardized by government regulations are taught in specialized martial art schools and in colleges having departments dedicated to wushu.

Competitive martial art exhibitions have transformed traditional solo routines by incorporating gymnastic elements for greater visual effects. Matches between individuals, usually judged on a point system, place limitations on the type of techniques used. Overall, martial sports have selectively adapted elements from traditional systems, thus presenting only one aspect of what the field of martial arts entails. Political and financial concerns play an increasing role in the sport as world participation in Asian martial arts increases.

China was the exemplar of refined culture to surrounding Asian countries for many centuries. This holds true for Chinese martial traditions as well. The martial arts in Japan, Korea, and Indonesia, for example, were influenced by encounters with Chinese people, such as those occurring during trade, immigration, or war. Knowledge of Asian martial arts likewise spread to the rest of the world, the movie industry being the most significant popularizer.

The martial arts are practiced for a variety of reasons in all parts of the world today. Some see wushu as a violent activity and are either attracted to it or seek to suppress its practice for this reason. Martial sports are popular with those who enjoy competitions. Such sporting events range from full-contact bouts with no rules, to no-contact tournaments with rules to prevent injures and ensure fairness in judging. However, major problems continue to plague martial sports since there is no one internationally recognized system for teaching, ranking, or judging. Still others desire to learn martial arts for the many potential physical and psychological benefits offered. More than ever, individuals are attracted to the study of wushu not simply as a physical activity, but as a way of self-discovery. Therefore, despite its organizational disarray as a sport, wushu will certainly increase in popularity.

—Michael A. DeMarco

**See also** Martial Arts.

**Bibliography:** Boudreau, Francoise, Ralph Folman, and Burt Konzak. (1995) "Psychological and Physical Changes in School-Age Karate Participants: Parental Observations." *Journal of Asian Martial Arts* 4, 4: 50–69.

Dreager, Donn, and Robert Smith. (1969) *Comprehensive Asian Martial Arts.* Tokyo: Kodansha International.

Donohue, John. (1991) *The Forge of the Spirit: Structure, Motion, and Meaning in the Japanese Martial Tradition.* New York: Garland Publishing.

Donohue, John. (1992). "Dancing in the Danger Zone: The Martial Arts in America." *Journal of Asian Martial Arts* 1, 1: 86–99.

Donohue, John. (1994). *Warrior Dreams: The Martial Arts and the American Imagination.* Westport, CT: Bergin and Garvey.

Haines, Bruce. (1995) *Karate's History and Traditions.* Rev. ed. Tokyo: Charles E. Tuttle.

Harrison-Pepper, Sally. "The Martial Arts: Rites of Passage, Dramas of Persuasion." *Journal of Asian Martial Arts* 2, 2: 90–103.

Holcombe, Charles. (1992) "Theater of Combat: A Critical Look at the Chinese Martial Arts." *Journal of Asian Martial Arts* 1: 4, 64–79.

Kauz, Herman. (1992) *A Path to Liberation: A Spiritual and Philosophical Approach to the Martial Arts.* New York: Overlook Press.

Pieter, Willy. (1994) "Research in Martial Sports: A Review." *Journal of Asian Martial Arts* 3, 2: 10–47.

Reid, Howard, and Michael Croucher. (1983) *The Way of the Warrior: The Paradox of the Martial Arts.* Woodstock, NY: Overlook Press.

Rosenberg, Daniel. (1995) "Paradox and Dilemma: The Martial Arts and American Violence." *Journal of Asian Martial Arts* 4, 2: 10–33.

Sutton, Nigel. (1993). "Gongfu, Guoshu and Wushu: State Appropriation of the Martial Arts in Modern China." *Journal of Asian Martial Arts* 2, 3: 102–114.

# Yachting

Yachting has been an Olympic sport since 1900. Although the term "yachting" tends to be more often applied to larger boats, and the term "sailing" to smaller boats, the International Olympic Committee continues to use the word yachting, even though all eight current Olympic classes are day boats (they do not have overnight accommodations) ranging in length from 11 to 27 feet (3.3 to 8.1 meters). All Olympic races are held by class in which competitors race each other in identical boats in a fleet race. Generally, the smaller and simpler boats are the least expensive, and so have the larger world following, leading to larger Olympic fleets. Sailboard fleets have had over 50 countries competing. The types of classes used in Olympic racing are regularly reviewed and changed, and some separate classes for women began in 1988.

## Origins

Sailing figured in several of the pre-1896 Olympic Games revivals. This is not surprising because the people who organized sports then were usually wealthy, and sailing was an early sport to be organized by the upper classes. The first modern Olympic Games, in Athens in 1896, were scheduled to include yachting races, but they were canceled due to rough seas, although the swimming—also held on the open sea—went ahead.

The first Olympic yachting races held were in 1900, in France, at Meulan and Le Havre, when seven classes (1/2, 1/2–1, 1–2, 2–3, 3–10, 10–20 tons, and open) were raced. Only six nations (France, Germany, Great Britain, Netherlands, Switzerland, and the United States) competed, perhaps because the events had been announced only four months before the games. No yachting events were held at the 1904 St. Louis Games, but the sport was back on the program in 1908 and has remained an Olympic sport ever since.

## Development

In 1908, most Olympic events were held in London, but sailing venues were Ryde, on the Isle of Wight, for most classes, and on the Clyde in Scotland, for the 12 meter event. Five classes were used (6, 7, 8, 12, and 15 meters) and five nations took part. There were no entries for the 15 meter class; only one 7 meter entry, which had among the crew Frances Rivett-Carnac, who thus became the first Olympic yachtswoman; and both 12 meters had British crews. In 1912, races were held for 6-, 8-, 10-, and 12 meter boats, with a total of 21 boats from five nations. No games were held in 1916 because of World War I.

In 1920, Olympic yachting began to have small boat (dinghy) racing, which has continued in some form ever since. An astonishing 14 classes raced (12-foot dinghy and 18-foot dinghy; two versions of the 6, 8, 10, and 12 meters; 6.5 and 7 meters; and 30 and 40 square meter classes. Seven classes had only one entrant, and this created a major move toward the use of one-design classes (where all boats in the fleet are of the same type and exactly alike) from 1924 on. In 1924, a 12-foot Voetsjol class became the first Olympic single-hander, and 6 and 8 meter boats were also raced. Each country was allowed only one entrant per class, and the 12-foot dinghy had 17 competitors. The same three classes were used in 1928, when Crown Prince Olaf of Norway (1903–1991) won the 6 meter, thus keeping alive the aristocratic links of the sport. A Frenchwoman, Virginie Heriot, was a member of the gold medal–winning crew in the 8 meter race, the first time a woman had won a contested medal.

In 1932, in Los Angeles, the Star class was raced for the first time. It remains an Olympic class to this day. Other classes were the Snowbird (a single hander, each of which was provided by the organizing committee, and exchanged after each race among the 11 competitors), and the 6 and 8 meter. In 1936, in Kiel, the Olympia-Jolle replaced the Snowbird as the single hander. A total of 26 nations raced 59 boats.

Following the canceled Olympics of 1940 and 1944, the 1948 games began to look more like modern racing. First, the classes were Firefly, Dragon, Star, Swallow, and 6 meter. Second, the winner in the Firefly class was Paul Elvstrom (1928– ), who continued to compete in the Olympic Games until 1988. Third, the courses were, for the first time, started into the wind. Seventy-five boats competed.

In 1952, the Finn made its first appearance as the single-hander, replacing the Firefly. Finns

*France's* Ville de Paris *(right) forces New Zealand's* Challenge *(left) to go wide around the mark during the Louis Vuitton Cup race in 1992.*

remain an Olympic class to this day. The 5.5 meter replaced the Swallow, and there were 93 boats from 19 nations. In 1956, the 12 square meter Sharpie class replaced the 6 meter and the number of nations competing rose to 28, although the number of boats dropped to 71, doubtless because of the event's location in Australia. In 1960, the Flying Dutchman class made its debut, replacing the Sharpie. The Dragon class was won by Prince Constantin of Greece (1940– ), who was thrown into the water—in traditional style—following his victory. The entries numbered more than 100 boats for the first time—128 boats from 46 nations. The same classes (Finn, Flying Dutchman, Star, Dragon, and 5.5 meter) were used in 1960, 1964, and 1968, but entries were down in 1964 to 40 nations and 109 boats because the location was in Japan.

In 1964, for the first time, communication with onshore coaches (whether by shouting or over radio) was banned, and semiprofessional sailors—people who made their living as sail makers—began to dominate events. In 1972, the Soling and Tempest joined the competition classes, and the 5.5 meter was dropped. All buoy roundings were photographed in an attempt to have evidence for protests, if necessary. The six classes at these games consisted of four keelboats and two centerboarders; this did not reflect contemporary yacht racing which was, and is, mostly held in centerboard dinghies.

The lack of correlation between Olympic classes and classes most popular with the general public showed some correction in 1976 when the classes raced at Kingston on Lake Ontario, Canada, were Finn, Flying Dutchman, 470, Soling, Tempest, and Tornado (the first catamaran raced in the Olympics). The Star came back in 1980 to replace the Tempest, but yachting was more seriously affected than most sports in the

## Paul Elvstrom—Four Gold Medals in a Row

Yachting champion Paul Elvstrom was born on February 25, 1928, in Hellerup, Denmark, and began racing at the age of 10. At 20, he entered an Olympic Games yachting event for the first time. He competed in the Firefly class, a 12-foot centerboard dinghy with two sails, usually crewed by two people but chosen for these games as the single-handed dinghy. He had never seen a Firefly prior to the games, and he retired from the first race, incorrectly thinking he had broken a rule. In the remaining races, he never finished lower than twelfth place in a fleet of 21, and he won the gold medal for Denmark.

In 1952, he was back on the Danish team, this time in the Finn class, the new single-hander. Because of the relatively large sail area, the Finn class needs great strength and endurance to sail well. Elvstrom was one of the first in yachting to realize that strength training would be beneficial. He had built a training bench to practice hiking out over the side (leaning out to keep the boat more upright and prevent capsizing). As a result, he was so much better than his 27 opponents that after six races his lead was so great, he did not even need to start the seventh. He did start, and he won, and a second gold medal was his.

In 1956, Elvstrom won his third gold medal, again in the Finn class, in very windy conditions. After this win, he went on to win world championships outside the Olympics in three different classes: 5-0-5, Finn, and Snipe. But Elvstrom suffered from excruciatingly painful headaches and was sometimes so nervous before a race that he passed out. Owing to these problems, Elvstrom had to be persuaded to participate in the 1960 games. No one had ever won four consecutive gold medals in any sport in the Olympics, and trying to become the first to do

so put fantastic pressure on this man. Elvstrom collapsed before the sixth race but went on to win it and clinch the gold medal. He was physically unable to take part in the seventh race, but it did not matter.

Elvstrom really did retire after that, but as an observer at the 1964 games, he once again realized the fun to be had in yachting competition. In 1968, he was back at the games, this time in the Star class, where he happily finished fourth. In 1972, he again did not win a medal, coming thirteenth in the Soling class. He began to concentrate on writing about sailing and on running his sailboat equipment business. He became perhaps best known to sailors by his quadrennially published books, explaining new yachting rules. These books are always accompanied by a set of small plastic boats, used to illustrate many a protester's case in protest meetings the world over.

In 1982, having won a further five world championships (in 5.5 meter, Star, Soling, 1/2 ton and Flying Dutchman classes) Elvstrom received the Bronze Olympic Order for his extraordinary efforts in yachting. Two years later, at the age of 56, he entered the Olympic yachting again, with his youngest daughter, Trine, crewing for him in the Tornado catamaran class. They narrowly missed the bronze medal and had so much fun they entered the 1988 games, Elvstrom's eighth Olympics. Although they did not win a medal, Elvstrom had completed a 40-year span of Olympic competition at the age of 60. In 1990, he was awarded the Beppe Croce Trophy of the International Yacht Racing Union for lifetime dedication to the sport of yachting.

—Shirley H. M. Reekie

---

boycott of that year because the events were held at Tallinn, in Estonia, which several countries refused to recognize as being part of the Soviet Union. The number of boats, 53, was the lowest since 1956.

In Los Angeles in 1984, an entirely new type of sailing was added: sailboarding. Other classes remained the same. Despite the boycott at these games, 174 boats from 62 nations took part. In 1988, a new type of event was added: one for women only in the 470 class. This idea was extended to a women-only class of sailboarders in 1992 and a women's single-hander, the Europe, was added to the men's Finn. For 1996, the classes are Europe (women), Finn (men), Laser, 470 (men), 470 (women), sailboard (men), sailboard (women), Soling (men and women), Star

(men and women), and Tornado (men and women). Of the eight different classes, two are keelboats, one is a catamaran, one is a sailboard, and four are centerboard dinghies, which closely approximates to world popularity of the various types of racing boats.

—Shirley H. M. Reekie

**See also** Sailing.

**Bibliography:** Johnson, Peter. (1989) *The Sail Magazine Book of Sailing.* New York: Knopf.

Knox-Johnston, Robin. (1990) *History of Yachting.* Oxford, UK: Phaidon.

Richey, Michael W., ed. (1980) *The Sailing Encyclopedia.* New York: Lippincott & Crowell.

Aberdare, The Rt. Hon. Lord. (1980) *The Willis Faber Book of Tennis & Rackets.* London: Stanley Paul.

*Aboyne Highland Games: Results of Principal Competitions 1867–1927.* (1928) Aberdeen, UK: Aberdeen Press and Journal.

Abrahams, R. L. A. (1995) "Golf." In *The Theater of Sport,* edited by K. B. Kaitz. Baltimore, MD: Johns Hopkins University Press.

Abt, S. (1989) *In High Gear.* Mill Valley, CA: Bicycle Books.

———. (1991) *Tour de France: Three Weeks to Glory.* New York: Bicycle Books.

Abt, Vicki, James F. Smith, and Eugene Martin Christiansen. (1985) *The Business of Risk.* Lawrence: University Press of Kansas.

Achebe, Chinua. (1959) *Things Fall Apart.* New York: Obolensky.

Acker, William R. B. (1965) *Japanese Archery.* Rutland, VT: Tuttle.

Adams, Bernard. (1980) *The Badminton Story.* London: British Broadcasting Publications.

Adams, F. (1844) *The Seven Books of Paulus Aegineta.* London: Sydenham Society.

Adams, L., and E. Goldbloom. (1991) *Racquetball Today.* St. Paul, MN: West Publishing.

Adams, R. C., and J. A. McCubbine. (1991) *Games, Sports, and Exercises for the Physically Disabled.* 4th ed. Philadelphia: Lea and Febiger.

Adams, Richard E. W. (1977) *Prehistoric Mesoamerica.* Boston: Little, Brown.

Adelman, Melvin L. (1986) *A Sporting Time: New York City and the Rise of Modern Athletics, 1820–1870.* Urbana: University of Illinois Press.

Aepli, Beat. (1988) *Bumerang.* Zell, Switzerland: ZKM.

Agbogun, Jacob B. (1970) "A History of the British Commonwealth Games." M.A. thesis, University of Alberta, Canada.

Ainslie, Tom. (1970) *Complete Guide to Harness Racing.* New York: Trident Press.

Aitkin, Brian W. W. (1989) "The Emergence of Born-Again Sport." *Studies in Religion* 18 (Autumn/Fall): 391–405.

Alderson, Frederick. (1972) *Bicycling: A History.* Newton Abbott, UK: David and Charles.

Alger, S. L. (1992) "Sports without Limits: Barcelona '92." *Sports 'N Spokes* 18, 4: 12–33.

Allanson-Winn, R. G., and C. E. Walker. (1903) *English Cane, Staff and Single Stick.*

Allen, A. (1981) *Sports for the Handicapped.* New York: Walker and Company.

Allen, E. John B. (1993) *From Skisport to Skiing: One Hundred Years of an American Sport, 1840–1940.* Amherst: University of Massachusetts Press.

Allen, G. H. (1905) *Land's End to John O'Groats.* London: Fowler.

Allen, R. C. Stafford. (1962) *Theory of Flight for Glider Pilots.* New York: Barnes & Noble.

Allison, Lincoln. (1993) *The Changing Politics of Sport.* Manchester, UK: Manchester University Press.

Allison, Lincoln, ed. (1986) *The Politics of Sport.* Manchester, UK: Manchester University Press.

Allison, Maria T. (1980) "Competition and Cooperation: A Sociocultural Perspective." *International Review of Sport Sociology* 15: 93–104.

Almekinders, Louis, Sally Almekinders, and Tom Roberts. (1991) *Triathlon Training.* Winston-Salem, NC: Hunter Textbooks.

Alter, Joseph S. (1992) *The Wrestler's Body: Identity and Ideology in North India.* Berkeley: University of California Press.

Altham, H. S., and E. W. Swanton. (1962) *A History of Cricket.* 2 vols. 5th ed. London: Allen & Unwin.

Altherr, Thomas L. (1978) "The American Hunter-Naturalist and the Development of the Code of Sportsmanship." *Journal of Sport History* 5: 7–22.

Amateur Trapshooting Association. (1995) *1996 Official Trapshooting Rules.* Vandalia, OH: American Trapshooting Association.

American College of Sports Medicine. (1992) *ACSM Fitness Book.* Champaign, IL: Leisure Press.

American Drug Free Powerlifting Association. (1994) *Lifter's Rulebook.* Mountaintop, PA: American Drug Free Powerlifting Association.

An Old Wykehamist (J. A. Fort). (1907) *Winchester Fives.* Winchester, UK: P. & G. Wells.

Anderson, Bob, ed. (1975) *Sportsource.* Mountain View, CA: World Publications.

Anderson, Dan. (1982) *American Freestyle Karate: A Guide to Sparring.* Hollywood, CA: Unique Publications.

Anderson, Earl R. (1980) "Footnotes More Pedestrian Than Sublime: A Historical Background for the Foot-Races in

Evelina and Humphry Clinker." *Eighteenth Century Studies* 14, 1: 56–68.

Anderson, Gary L. (1972) *Marksmanship.* New York: Simon and Schuster.

———. (1995) "Olympics 1996, Where Shooting Will Be Seen Differently." In *Gun Digest 1996,* edited by Ken Warner. Northbrook, IL: DBI Books.

Anderson, J. K. (1985) *Hunting in the Ancient World.* Berkeley: University of California Press.

Andre, J., and D. N. James. (1991) *Rethinking College Athletics.* Philadelphia: Temple University Press.

Andresen, Jack. (1974) "Skate Sailing." In *Sailing on Ice.* New York: A. S. Barnes.

Andry, N. (1741) *L'orthopedie, ou l'art de prevenir et corriger dans les deformites de corps.* Paris: Dupont.

Anglo, Sydney. (1961) "Archives of the English Tournament: Score Cheques and Lists." *Journal of the Society of Archivists* 2, 4: 153–162.

———. (1968) *The Great Tournament Roll of Westminster.* Oxford: Clarendon.

Anshel, M. (1990) *Sport Psychology: From Theory to Practice.* Scottsdale, AZ: Gorsuch Scarisbrick.

Antal, Laslo. (1983) *Competitive Pistol Shooting.* East Ardsley, Wakefield, UK: EP Publishing.

Antal, Laslo, and Ragnar Skanaker. (1985) *Pistol Shooting.* Liverpool, UK: Laslo Antal & Ragnar Skanaker.

Apollodorus. (1975) *The Library of Greek Mythology.* Translated by Keith Aldrich. Lawrence, KS: Coronado Press.

Appenzeller, Herbert. (1975) *Athletics and the Law.* Charlottesville, VA: Michie.

———. (1993) *Managing Sports and Risk Management Strategies.* Durham, NC: Carolina Academic Press.

Applin, Albert G. (1982) "From Muscular Christianity to the Marketplace: The History of Men's and Boys' Basketball in the United States, 1891–1957." Ph.D. dissertation, University of Massachusetts.

Araúz de Robles, Santiago. (1974) *Sociología del toreo.* Madrid: Prensa Española.

Arbena, Joseph L., ed. (1988) *Sport and Society in Latin America: Diffusion, Dependency, and Mass Culture.* Westport, CT: Greenwood Press.

Arévalo, José Carlos, and José Antonio del Moral. (1985) *Nacido para morir.* Madrid: Espasa-Calpe.

Arlott, John A., ed. (1975) *The Oxford Companion to World Sports and Games.* London: Oxford University Press.

Arms, Robert L., Gordon W. Russell, and Mark L. Sandilands. (1979) "Effects on the Hostility of Spectators of Viewing Aggressive Sports." *Social Psychology Quarterly* 42: 275–279.

Armstead, Lloyd D. (1990) *Whitewater Rafting in Western North America.* Chester, CT: Globe Pequot Press.

Armstrong, Alan. (1964) *Maori Games and Haka.* Wellington, NZ: A. H. and A. W. Reid.

Armstrong, Alan, and R. Ngata. (1960) *Maori Action Songs.* Wellington, NZ: A. H. and A. W. Reid.

Armstrong, John M., and Alfred Metraux. (1963) "The Goajiro." *Bureau of American Ethnology Bulletin* 143, 4: 369–383.

Armstrong, Walter. (1893) *Wrestling.* London: Longmans, Green.

Arnaud, Pierre, and Thierry Terret. (1993) *Le reve blanc, olympisme et sport d'hiver en France: Chamonix 1924 Grenoble 1968.* Bordeaux: Presses Universitaires de Bordeaux.

Arnheim, Daniel D. (1989) *Modern Principles of Athletic Training.* St. Louis, MO: Times Mirror/Mosby College Publishing.

Arnold, P. J. (1991) "The Preeminence of Skill as an Educational Value in the Movement Curriculum." *Quest* 43 (April): 66–67.

———. (1994) "Sport and Moral Education." *Journal of Moral Education* 23, 1: 75–89.

Arthur, Harold. (1898) "Tilting in Tudor Times." *Archaeological Journal* 55: 296–320.

Ashe, Arthur R. Jr. (1988) *A Hard Road to Glory: A History of the African-American Athlete.* 3 vols. New York: Warner Books.

Aspin, Jehoshaphat. (1925) *A Picture of the Manners, Customs, Sports and Pastimes of the Inhabitants of England.* London: J. Harris.

Atkinson, Graeme. (1982) *Everything You Ever Wanted To Know about Australian Rules Football But Couldn't Be Bothered Asking.* Melbourne, Australia: Five Mile Press.

Auguet, Roland. (1972) *Cruelty and Civilization: The Roman Games.* London: Allen & Unwin.

Aurelianus, Caelius. (1547) In *Medici antiqui omnes.* Venice: Aldus.

Axton, W. F., and Wendy Lee Martin. (1993) *Field Hockey.* Indianapolis, IN: Masters.

Aylward, J. D. (1956) *The English Master at Arms.* Notes and Queries no. 198. London: Routledge and Kegan Paul.

Azoy, G. Whitney. (1982) *Buzkashi: Game and Power in Afghanistan.* Philadelphia: University of Pennsylvania Press.

Baade, Robert. (1995) "Stadiums, Professional Sports and City Economies: An Analysis of the United States Experience." In *The Stadium and the City,* edited by John Bale and Olof Moen. Keele, UK: Keele University Press, 277–294.

Bailey, W. S., and T. D. Littleton. (1991) *Athletics and Academe.* New York: Macmillan.

Bainbridge, F. A. (1931) *The Physiology of Muscular Exercise,* 3d ed. Rewritten by A. V. Bock and D. B. Dill. New York: Longmans, Green.

Baker, L. H. (1945) *Football: Facts and Figures.* New York: Farrar & Rinehart.

Baker, William J. (1982) *Sports in the Western World.* Totowa, NJ: Rowman & Littlefield.

———. (1986) *Jesse Owens: An American Life.* New York: Free Press.

———. (1988) *Sports in the Western World.* Revised edition. Urbana: University of Illinois Press.

———. (1994) "To Pray or To Play? The YMCA Question in the United Kingdom and the United States, 1850–1900." *International Journal of the History of Sport* 11 (April): 42–62.

Baker, William J., and James A. Mangan, eds. (1987) *Sport in Africa: Essays in Social History.* New York: Africana Publishing.

Balakrishnan, P. (1995) *Kalarippayattu: The Ancient Martial Art of Kerala.* Trivandrum: Shri C.V. Govindankutty Nair Gurukkal, C.V.N. Kalari, Fort.

Bale, John. (1982) *Sport and Place.* London: Hurst.

———. (1989) *Sports Geography.* New York: Spon.

———. (1991) *The Brawn Drain: Foreign Student-Athletes in American Universities.* Urbana: University of Illinois Press.

———. (1993) *Sport, Space and the City.* New York: Routledge.

———. (1994) *Landscapes of Modern Sport.* Leicester, UK: Leicester University Press.

Bale, John, and Joe Sang. (1996) *Kenyan Running: Movement Culture, Geography and Global Change.* London: Frank Cass.

Bale, John, and Joseph Maguire, eds. (1993) *The Global Sports Arena.* London: Frank Cass.

Balikci, Asen. (1978) "Buzkashi." *Natural History* 87, 2: 54–63.

———. (1978) "Village Buzkashi." *Afghanistan Journal* 5, 1: 11–21.

Ballesteros, Joaquin. (1987) *El libro del triatlon.* Madrid: Arthax.

Ballou, Ralph B., Jr. (1988) "Grasslands: America's Aintree." Paper presented at the annual meeting of the North American Society for Sport History, Tempe, AZ, May 20–23.

Baltzell, E. Digby. (1995) *Sporting Gentlemen: Men's Tennis from the Age of Honor to the Cult of the Superstar.* New York: Free Press.

Bancroft, J. (1925) *The Respiratory Function of the Blood.* Part I. London: Cambridge University Press.

Bandura, Albert (1973) *Aggression: A Social Learning Analysis.* Englewood Cliffs, NJ: Prentice-Hall.

Bandy, Susan J., ed. (1988) *Coroebus Triumphs: The Alliance of Sport and the Arts.* San Diego, CA: San Diego State University Press.

Bane, Michael. (1996) *Over the Edge: An Odyssey of Extreme Sports.* New York: Macmillan.

Banner, Lois. (1983) *American Beauty.* Chicago, IL: University of Chicago Press.

Bannister, Roger. (1955) *The First Four Minutes.* London: Putnam.

Barber, G., ed. (1984) *Olympic Gold 84.* Kensington, New South Wales: Bay Books.

Barber, Richard. (1974) *The Knight and Chivalry.* Ipswich, UK: Boydell Press.

Barker, Juliet R. V. (1986) *The Tournament in England, 1100–1400.* Woodbridge, UK: Boydell Press.

Barna, Victor. (1962) *Table Tennis Today.* London: Arthur Barker.

Barnes, H. (1988) "Lacrosse, the Creator's Game." In *Persons, Minds and Bodies: A Transcultural Dialogue amongst Physical Education, Philosophy and the Social Sciences,* edited by S. Ross and L. Charette. North York, Ontario: University Press of Canada, 153–160.

Barnes, John. (1988) *Sports and the Law in Canada.* Markham, Ontario: Butterworths.

Barnett, S. (1990) *Games and Sets: The Changing Face of Sport on Television.* London: British Film Institute.

Baron, L., M. A. Straus, and D. Jaffee. (1988) "Legitimate Violence, Violent Attitudes, and Rape: A Test of the Cultural Spillover Theory." In *Human Sexual Aggression: Current Perspectives,* edited by R. A. Prentsky and V. L. Quinsey. New York: New York Academy of Sciences, 79–110.

Barreau, J. J., and G. Jaoun. (1991) *Eclipses et renaissance des jeux populaires.* Rennes, France: Institut International d'Anthropologie Corporelle.

Barrett, J. Lee. (1986) *Speed Boat Kings.* Ann Arbor: Historical Society of Michigan.

Barton, F. R. (1980) "Children's Games in British New Guinea." *Journal of the Royal Anthropological Institute* 37: 259–279.

Basedow, H. (1925) *The Australian Aborigine.* Adelaide, Australia: F. W. Pearce and Sons.

Bass, Howard. (1958) *The Skating Age.*

———. (1968) *Winter Sports.* South Brunswick, N.J.: A. S. Barnes.

Bateman, Derek, and Derek Douglas. (1986) *Unfriendly Games: Boycotted and Broke, The Inside Story of the 1986 Commonwealth Games.* Glasgow, UK: Mainstream Publishing Projects and Glasgow Herald.

Bauer, Erwin A. (1975) *Cross-Country Skiing and Snowshoeing.* New York: Winchester Press.

Beach, Bell. (1912) *Riding and Driving for Women.* New York: Charles Scribner's Sons.

Beal, Becky. (1995) "Disqualifying the Official: An Exploration of Social Resistance through the Subculture of Skateboarding." *Sociology of Sport Journal* 12: 252–267.

Beal, Doug. (1985) *Spike! The Story of the Victorious U.S. Volleyball Team.* San Diego, CA: Avant Publishers.

Bealle, Morris A. (1957) *The Softball Story.* Washington, DC: Columbia Publishing.

———. (1962) *The New 1962 Compact Edition of the Softball History.* Washington, DC: Columbia Publishing.

Bean, Dawn, ed. (1963–1978) *Synchro-Info.* Santa Ana, CA.

———. (1979–1992) *Synchro.* Santa Ana, CA.

# Bibliography

Bean, George E. (1956) "Victory in the Pentathlon." *American Journal of Archaeology* 60: 361–368.

Beaufort, Duke of. (1890) *The Badminton Library of Sports and Pastimes.* London: Longmans, Green.

Beddoes, Richard, Stan Fischler, and Ira Getler. (1974) *Hockey: The Story of the World's Fastest Sport.* New York: Macmillan.

Bedford, Julian. (1989) *The World Atlas of Horse Racing.* London: Hamlyn.

Bellak, Laszlo. (1990) *Table Tennis: How a New Sport Was Born.* (Self-published.)

Benedict, Jeffrey, Todd Crosset, and Mark A. McDonald. (1994) "Student-Athletes Reported for Sexual Assault: A Survey of Campus Police Departments and Judicial Affairs." Paper presented at the conference of the North American Society for the Sociology of Sport, Savannah, GA.

Bennett, Bruce L. (1985). "This Is Our Heritage: 1960–1985," *Research Quarterly for Exercise and Sport.* Centennial Issue (April): 102–120.

Bennett, Tiny. (1970) *The Art of Angling.* Ontario, Canada: Prentice-Hall.

Bent, Newell. (1929) *American Polo.* New York: Macmillan.

Berg, Karin. (1993) *Ski i Norge.* Olso, Norway: Aventura.

Bergamín, José. (1981) *La música callada del toreo.* Madrid: Turner.

Bergan, Ronald. (1982) *Sports in the Movies.* London and New York: Proteus Publishing.

Bergmann, Richard. (1950) *Twenty-One Up.* London: Sporting Handbooks.

Berkowitz, Leonard. (1969) *Roots of Aggression.* New York: Atherton Press.

Berlioux, Monique. (1983) *1896–1984: L'Olympisme par L'Affiche; Olympism through Posters.* Lausanne, Switzerland: International Olympic Committee.

Berman, Neil David. (1981) *Playful Fictions and Fictional Players: Game Sport, and Survival in Contemporary American Fiction.* Port Washington, NY: Kennikat.

Bernard, C. (1927) *An Introduction to the Study of Experimental Medicine.* Translated by H. M. Green. New York: Macmillan.

Berry, Herbert. (1991) *The Noble Science: A Study and Transcription of Sloane MS. 2530, Papers of the Masters of Defence of London, Temp. Henry VIII to 1590.* Cranbury, NJ: University of Delaware Press.

Berry, Robert C., and Wong, Glenn M. (1986) *Law and Business of the Sports Industries.* Boston, MA: Auburn House.

Berryman, Jack W. (1995). *Out of Many, One: A History of the American College of Sports Medicine.* Champaign, IL: Human Kinetics.

Besford, Pat (1971) *Encyclopedia of Swimming.* New York: St. Martin's Press.

Besford, Pat, ed. (1971) *Encyclopedia of Swimming.* New York: St Martin's Press.

Best, D. (1974) *Expression in Movement and the Arts: A Philosophical Enquiry.* London: Lepus.

Best, G. (1971) *Mid-Victorian Britain: 1851–1875.* London: Weidenfeld and Nicolson.

Betts, John R. (1974) *America's Sporting Heritage: 1850–1950.* Reading, MA: Addison-Wesley.

Bevridge, P. (1883) "On the Aborigines Inhabiting the Great Lacustrine and Riverine Depression of the Lower Murray, Lower Murrumbidgee, Lower Lachlan and Lower Darling." *Journal and Proceedings of the Royal Society of New South Wales* 17: 19–74.

Bilik, S. E. (1956) *The Trainers Bible.* New York: TJ Reed and Co. (originally published in 1917).

Billiard Congress of America. (1995) *Billiards: The Official Rules & Records Book.* Iowa City, IA: Billiard Congress of America.

Birley, Derek. (1979) *The Willow Wand: Some Cricket Myths Explored.* London: Queen Anne Press.

Birrell, Susan J. (1978) "Sporting Encounters: An Examination of the Work of Erving Goffman and Its Application to Sport." Ph.D. dissertation, University of Massachusetts, Amherst.

Bishop, J. G. (1992) *Fitness through Aerobic Dance.* Scottsdale, AZ: Gorsuch Scarisbrick Publishing.

Bissinger, H. G. (1990) *Friday Night Lights: A Town, a Team, a Dream.* Reading, MA: Addison-Wesley.

Bjarkman, Peter C. (1994) *Baseball with a Latin Beat: A History of the Latin American Game.* Jefferson, NC: McFarland.

Blacking, John. (1987) "Games and Sports in Pre-Colonial African Societies." In *Sport in Africa: Essays in Social History,* edited by William J. Baker and James A. Mangan. New York: Africana.

Blackwood, Caroline. (1987) *In the Pink.* London: Bloomsbury

Blaikie, David. (1984) *Boston: The Canadian Story.* Ottawa: Seneca House Books.

Blair, Wesley. (1984) *The Complete Book of Target Shooting.* Harrisburg, PA: Stackpole Books.

Blanchard, Kendall. (1976) "Stickball and the American Southeast." In *Forms of Play of Native North Americans,* edited by Edward Norbeck and Claire R. Farrer. St. Paul, MN: West Publishing, 189–208.

———. (1981) *The Mississippi Choctaws at Play: The Serious Side of Leisure.* Urbana: University of Illinois Press.

———. (1986) "Play as Adaptation." In *Cultural Dimensions of Play, Games, and Sport,* edited by Bernard Mergen. Champaign, IL: Human Kinetics, 79–88.

———. (1995) *The Anthropology of Sport: An Introduction.* 2d ed. Westport, CT: Greenwood Press.

Blanchard, Kendall, and Alyce Cheska. (1985) *The Anthropology of Sport: An Introduction.* South Hadley, MA: Bergin & Garvey.

Blannin, A. (1877) *Hasty Notes of a Flying Trip with the Victorian Rifle Team to England and America in 1877.* Melbourne, Australia: Privately printed.

Blasco Ibáñez, Vicente. (1911) *The Blood of the Arena.* Chicago: McClurg.

Blazic, Branko, and Zorko Soric. (1975) *Team Handball.* Winnipeg, Canada: Winnipeg Free Press.

Blecking, Diethelm, ed. (1991) *Die slawische Sokolbewegung.* Dortmund, Germany: Forschungsstelle Ostmitteleuropa.

Blondin, A. (1977) *Sur le Tour de France.* Paris: Mazarine.

Bloodgood, Lida L. Fleitmann. (1953) *Hoofs in the Distance.* New York: D. Van Nostrand.

Bloom, M. (1977) *Cross Country Running.* Mountain View, CA: World Publications.

Bloss, Margaret Varner, and R. Stanton Hales. (1994) *Badminton.* Dubuque, IA: Brown & Benchmark.

Blue, Adrianne. (1987) *Grace under Pressure: The Emergence of Women in Sport.* London: Sidgwick and Jackson.

Bø, Olav. (1993) *Skiing throughout History.* Oslo, Norway: Det Norske Samlaget.

Boeheim, Wendelin. (1890) *Handbuch der Waffenkunde.* Graz: Akad. Druck und Verlagsanstalt.

Boggan, Tim. (1976) *Winning Table Tennis.* Chicago, IL: Henry Regnery.

Bolin, Anne. (1992) "Vandalized Vanity: Feminine Physiques Betrayed and Portrayed." In *Tatoo, Torture, Adornment and Disfigurement: The Denaturalization of the Body in Culture and Text,* edited by F. Mascia-Lees. Albany: State University of New York Press, 79–90.

———. (1992) "Flex Appeal, Food and Fat: Competitive Bodybuilding, Gender and Diet." *Play and Culture* 5, 4: 378–400. Reprinted in *Building Bodies* (1996), edited by P. Moore. New Brunswick, NJ: Rutgers University Press.

———. (Forthcoming) "Beauty or the Beast: The Subversive Soma." In *Athletic Intruders: Women, Culture and Sport,* edited by A. Bolin and J. Granskog. Albany: State University of New York Press.

Bomann-Larsen, Tor. (1993) *Den evige sne: en skihistorie om Norge.* Oslo, Norway: Cappelens.

Bombin-Fernandez, Luis, and Rudolfo Bozas-Urrutia. (1976) *El gran libro de la pelota.* 2 vols. Madrid: Tipografia Artictica.

Bond, Bob. (1980) *The Handbook of Sailing.* New York: Knopf.

Bonhomme, Guy. (1991) *De la paume au tennis.* Paris: Gallimard.

Bonington, C. (1976) *Everest the Hard Way.* London: Hodder.

Booth, Douglas. (1991) "War off Water: The Surf Life Saving Association and the Beach," *Sporting Traditions: Journal of the Australian Society for Sports History* 7, 2: 135–162.

———. (1994) "Surfing '60s: A Case Study in the History of Pleasure and Discipline," *Australian Historical Studies* 26: 262–279.

———. (1995) "Ambiguities in Pleasure and Discipline: The Development of Competitive Surfing," *Journal of Sport History* 22, 3: 189–206.

Borassatti, Giustiniano. (1753) *Il ginnasta in pratica, ed in teorica.* Venice, Italy: Gio Battista Rossi.

Borelli, G. A. (1710) *De motu animalium.* Batavia, The Netherlands: Lugduni.

Borhegyi, Stephan F. de. (1960) "America's Ballgame." *Natural History* 69: 48–59.

Bose, Mihir. (1990) *A History of Indian Cricket.* London: Deutsch.

Bottenburg, Maarten van. (1992) "The Differential Popularization of Sports in Continental Europe." *Netherlands Journal of Social Science* 28, 1 (April): 3–30.

———. *Verborgen Competitie.* (1994) Amsterdam, The Netherlands: Bert Bakker.

Boudreau, Francoise, Ralph Folman, and Burt Konzak. (1995) "Psychological and Physical Changes in School-Age Karate Participants: Parental Observations." *Journal of Asian Martial Arts* 4, 4: 50–69.

Bouissac, Paul. (1973) *La mesure des gestes.* The Hague: Mouton.

Bourdieu, P. (1988) "Program for a Sociology of Sport." *Sociology of Sport Journal* 5: 153–161.

Boutros, Labib. (1981) *Phoenician Sport. Its Influence on the Origin of the Olympic Games.* Amsterdam, The Netherlands: J. C. Gieben.

Bowen, Rowland. (1970) *Cricket: A History of Its Growth and Development throughout the World.* London: Eyre and Spottiswoode.

Bowers, Carolyn O., Jacquelyn K. Fie, and Andrea B. Schmid. (1981) *Judging and Coaching Women's Gymnastics.* 2d ed. Palo Alto, CA: Mayfield.

Boydston, Jeanne. (1990) *Home and Work: Housework, Wages, and the Ideology of Labor in the Early Republic.* New York: Oxford University Press.

Brabazon of Tara, Lord. (1966) "Tobogganing." *Winter Sports.* London: Lonsdale Library.

Brailsford, Dennis. (1991) *Sport, Time, and Society: The British at Play.* London: Routledge.

Brasch, Rudolph. (1970) *How Did Sports Begin? A Look at the Origins of Man at Play.* New York: David McKay.

Braunwart, Bob, and Bob Carroll. (1981) *The Alphabet Wars: The Birth of Professional Football, 1890–1892.* Canton, OH: Professional Football Researchers Association.

Bredemeier, Brenda Jo, and David L. Shields. (1994) *Character Development and Physical Activity.* Champaign, IL: Human Kinetics.

Bredemeier, Brenda Jo, David L. Shields, and Michael D. Smith. (1986) "Athletic Aggression: An Issue of Contextual Morality." *Sociology of Sport Journal* 3, 1: 15–28.

Brenner, Reuven, and Gabrielle A. Brenner. (1990) *Gambling and Speculation: A Theory, a History, and a Future of Some Human Decisions.* New York: Cambridge University Press.

Bridges, E. Lucas. (1948) *Uttermost Part of the Earth.* London: Hodder and Stoughton.

Brinkman, Joe, and Charlie Euchner. (1987) *The Umpire's Handbook.* Lexington, MA: S. Greene.

Brock, A. J. (1939) *Greek Medicine.* London: J. M. Dent.

Brohm, Jean-Marie. (1978) *Sport: A Prison of Measured Time.* Translated by Ian Fraser. London: Ink Links.

Brokaw, I. (1925) *The Art of Skating.* New York: American Sports Publishing.

Brookes, Christopher. (1978) *English Cricket: The Game and Its Players through the Ages.* London: Weidenfeld and Nicolson.

Brooks, Christine. (1994) *Sports Marketing: Competitive Business Strategies for Sports.* Englewood Cliffs, NJ: Prentice-Hall.

Brown, G., ed. (1979) *New York Times Encyclopedia of Sports: Volume 12.* Danbury, CT: Grolier.

———. (1979) *New York Times Encyclopedia of Sports—Winter Sports.* Danbury, CT: Grolier.

———. (1979) *New York Times Encyclopedia of Water Sports.* Danbury, CT: Arno Press.

Brown, Les (1971) *Television: The Business behind the Box.* New York: Harcourt Brace Jovanovich.

Brown, Nigel. (1959) *Ice Skating: A History.* New York: A. S. Barnes.

Brown, Paul. (1930) *Aintree: Grand Nationals Past and Present.* New York: Derrydale Press.

———. (1931) *Spills and Thrills.* New York: Charles Scribner's Sons.

———. (1935) *Hits and Misses.* New York: Derrydale Press.

———. (1936) *Ups and Downs.* New York: Charles Scribner's Sons.

———. (1949) *Polo.* New York: Scribners.

Brown, Richard D. (1976) *Modernization.* New York: Hill & Wang.

Brownfoot, J. N. (1992) "Emancipation Exercise and Imperialism: Girls and Games Ethnic in Colonial Malaya." In *The Cultural Bond—Sport, Empire, Society,* edited by J. A. Mangan. London: Frank Cass.

Bryant, A. T. (1949) *The Zulu People: As They Were before the White Man Came.* Pietermaritzburg, South Africa: Shuter and Shooter.

Bryson, Lois. (1987) "Sport and the Maintenance of Masculine Hegemony." *Women's Studies International Forum* 10: 349–360.

Buckley, W. E., et al. (1988) "Estimated Prevalence of Anabolic Steroid Use among Male High School Seniors." *Journal of the American Medical Association* 260, 23: 3441–3445.

Budden, Paul. (1992) *Looking at a Far Mountain: A Study of Kendo Kata.* London: Ward Lock.

Bunn, John William. (1967) *The Art of Officiating Sports.* 3d ed. Englewood Cliffs, NJ: Prentice-Hall.

Bura, Fabian. (1960) *Die Olympischen Spiele auf den Briefmarken der Welt.* Cologne, Germany: N. J. Hoffmann Verlag.

Burette, J. (1748) *Dissertazione del Disco.* Venice: Aldus.

Burgess, Hovey. (1976) *Circus Techniques: Juggling, Equilibristics.* New York: Drama Book Specialists.

Burke, Edmund Holley. (1957) *The History of Archery.* New York: William Morrow.

Burke, Peter. (1978) *Popular Culture in Early Modern Europe.* New York: Harper & Row.

Burkert, Walter. (1979) *Structure and History in Greek Mythology and Ritual.* Berkeley and Los Angeles: University of California Press.

Burns, Grant. (1987) *The Sports Pages: A Critical Bibliography of Twentieth-Century American Novels and Stories Featuring Baseball, Basketball, Football, and Other Athletic Pursuits.* Metuchen, NJ: Scarecrow Press.

Buss, A. H. (1961) *The Psychology of Aggression.* New York: Wiley.

Butler, L. St.J., and P. J. Wordie, eds. (1989) *The Royal Game.* Fordhead, Kippen, Stirling, UK: Falkland Palace Real Tennis Club.

Buxton, Meriel. (1987) *Ladies of the Chase.* London: Sportsman's Press.

Byles, J. B., and S. Osborn. (1898) "First Aid." In *The Encyclopedia of Sport,* edited by The Earl of Suffolk and Berkshire, H. Peck, and F. E. Aflalo. New York: G. P. Putnam's Sons.

Byrom, Glen, ed. (1980) *Rhodesian Sports Profiles, 1907–1979.* Bulawayo: Books of Zimbabwe.

Cagnatus, M. (1602) *De sanitate tuenda.* Padua.

Cahn, Susan K. (1994) *Coming on Strong: Gender and Sexuality in Twentieth Century Women's Sport.* New York: Free Press.

Caillois, Roger (1961) *Man, Play, and Games.* New York: Free Press of Glencoe.

Cambria, Rosario. (1974) *Los toros: Tema polémico en el ensayo español del siglo XX.* Madrid: Gredos.

Cameron, Alan. (1973) *Porphyrius the Charioteer.* Oxford: Clarendon Press.

———. (1976) *Circus Factions: Blues and Greens at Rome and Byzantium.* Oxford: Clarendon Press.

Camogie Association of Ireland. (1990) *Playing Rules and Constitution.* Dublin, Ireland: Camogie Association.

Campbell, J. F. (1892) *Popular Tales of the West Highlands.* Vol. 3. Paisley, UK: Alexander Gardner.

Campbell, Robert. (1967) *Skeet Shooting with D. Lee Braun.* New York: Rutledge Books.

———. (1969) *Trapshooting with D. Lee Braun and the Remington Pros.* New York: Rutledge Books.

Canape, J. (1541) *L'anatomie du movement des muscles.* Paris: Gallen.

Cañete, C., and D. Cañete. (1976) *Arnis (Eskrima): Philippine Stickfighting Art.* Cebu City, Philippines: Doce Pares Publications.

Cardano, G. (1551) *De subtilitate et de rerum varietate.* Libri XXI. Paris: Gallen.

Carey, James, ed. (1988) *Media, Myths, and Narratives: Television and the Press.* Newbury Park, CA: Sage Publications.

# Bibliography

Carhart, Arthur Hawthorne. (1949) *Fresh Water Fishing.* New York: A. S. Barnes.

Carlile, Forbes. (1963) *Forbes Carlile on Swimming.* London: Pelham.

Carlson, L. H., and J. J. Fogarty. (1987) *Tales of Gold: An Oral History of the Summer Olympic Games.* New York: Contemporary Books.

Caroll, Scott T. (1988) "Wrestling in Ancient Nubia." *Journal of Sport History* 15, 2: 121–137.

Carpenter, Linda Jean. (1995) *Legal Concepts in Sport: A Primer.* Reston, VA: AAHPERD.

Carr, Raymond. (1976) *English Foxhunting: A History.* London: Weidenfeld and Nicholson.

Carroll, Nick, ed. (1991) *The Next Wave: A Survey of World Surfing.* Sydney, Australia: Angus and Robertson.

Carroll, Noel. (1979) *Sport in Ireland.* Dublin, Ireland: Department of Foreign Affairs.

Carter, John Marshall. (1988) *Sports and Pastimes of the Middle Ages.* New York: University Press of America.

Carter, John Marshall, and Arnd Krüger, eds. (1990) *Ritual and Record.* Westport, CT: Greenwood Press.

Cashman, Richard, and Michael McKernan, eds. (1981) *Sport: Money, Morality and the Media.* Sydney, Australia: University of New South Wales Press.

Cashman, Richard, et al., eds. (1996) *The Oxford Companion to Australian Cricket.* Melbourne, Australia: Oxford University Press.

Caskey, George B., and David G. Wright. (1966) "Coasting and Tobogganing Facilities: A Manual and Survey on Construction and Operations." *Management Aids* 62. Wheeling, WV: National Recreation and Park Association.

Castañer, Sonia. (1979) *Historia de los juegos deportivos panamericanos.* Havana, Cuba: Dirección Nacional de Propaganda.

Casten, C., and P. Jordan. (1990) *Aerobics Today.* St. Paul, MN: West Publishing.

Castle, Egerton. (1897) *Bibliotheca Artis Dimicatroi.* London.

———. (1969) *Schools and Masters of Fence: From the Middle Ages to the Eighteenth Century.* London: Arms and Armour Press and York, PA: George Shumway.

Catlin, George. (1841) *North American Indians.* Vol. 1. Minneapolis, MN: Ross and Haines.

Catton, Bruce. (1972) *Waiting for the Morning Train: An American Boyhood.* Garden City, NY: Doubleday.

Cavallo, Dominick. (1981) *Muscles and Morals: Organized Playgrounds and Urban Reform, 1880–1920.* Philadelphia: University of Pennsylvania Press.

Cayleff, S. E. (1995) *Babe, The Life and Legend of Babe Didrikson Zaharias.* Urbana: University of Illinois Press.

Ceballos, Francisco. (1969) *El polo en la Argentina.* Buenos Aires, Argentina: Remonta.

Cedaro, Rod, ed. (1993) *Triathlon: Achieving Your Personal Best.* New York: Facts On File.

Champion, Walter T. (1990) *Fundamentals of Sports Law.* Rochester, NY: Clark, Boardman and Callahan.

———. (1993) *Sports Law in a Nutshell.* St. Paul, MN: West Publishing.

Chance, Norman. (1966) *The Eskimo of North Alaska.* New York: Holt, Rinehart, and Winston.

Chandler, Joan. (1988) *Television and National Sport: The United States and Britain.* Urbana: University of Illinois Press.

Chany, Pierre. (1985) *La fabuleuse histoire du Tour de France.* Paris: O.D.I.L.

Chapel, C. E. (1949) *Field, Skeet and Trapshooting.* New York: Coward-McCann.

Chapman, David L. (1994) *Sandow the Magnificent: Eugene Sandow and the Beginnings of Bodybuilding.* Urbana: University of Illinois Press.

Chaves Nogales, Manuel. (1937) *Juan Belmonte, Killer of Bulls.* New York: Doubleday.

Chelladurai, P. (1984) "Discrepancy between Preferences and Perceptions of Leadership Behavior and Satisfaction of Athletes in Varying Sports." *Journal of Sport Psychology* 6: 27–41.

———. (1993) "Leadership." In *Handbook of Research in Sport Psychology,* edited by R. N. Singer, M. Murphey, and L. K. Tennant. New York: Macmillan, 647–771.

Cheng, Man-ching. (1956) *Tai Chi Chuan: A Simplified Method of Calisthenics for Health and Self Defence.* Taipei: Shih Chung Tai-chi Chuan Center.

Cheska, Alyce. (1982) "Ball Game Participation of North American Women." In *Her Story in Sport,* edited by Reet Howell. West Point, NY: Leisure Press.

Chick, Garry, John W. Loy, and Andrew W. Miracle. (1995) "Sport, War and Rape." Paper presented at the annual meeting of the American Anthropological Association, Washington, DC.

Chiefari, Janet, and Nancy Wightman. (1981) *Better Synchronized Swimming for Girls.* New York: Dodd, Mead.

Chimits, Xavier, and François Granet. (1994) *The Williams Renault Formula 1 Motor Racing Book.* New York: Dorling Kindersley.

Choi, Hong Hi. (1993) *Taekwon-do: The Korean Art of Self-Defence.* 3d ed. 15 vols. Mississauga, Ontario: International Taekwon-Do Federation.

Christophersen, Pedro F. (1948) *Teoría y práctica del juego de polo.* Buenos Aires, Argentina: Asociatión Argentina de Polo.

Christout, Marie-Francoise. (1965) *Le merveilleux et le theatre du silence en France à partir du XVIIe siècle.* The Hague: Mouton.

Christy, Eva. (1907) *Modern Side Saddle Riding.* 3d ed. London: Vinton & Co.

———. (1932) *Cross-Saddle and Side-Saddle.* Philadelphia: J. B. Lippincott.

Chu, Donald. (1989) *The Character of American Higher Education and Intercollegiate Sport.* Albany: State University of New York Press.

Churbuck, D. C. (1988) *The Book of Rowing.* Woodstock, NY: Overlook Press.

Claflin, Edward. (1978) *The Irresistible American Softball Book.* New York: Dolphin Books.

Clancy, Foghorn. (1952) *My Fifty Years in Rodeo.* San Antonio, TX: Naylor.

Claramunt, Fernando (1989). *Historia ilustrada de la tauromaquia.* Madrid: Espasa-Calpe.

Clark, Coleman. (1933) *Modern Ping-Pong.* New York: John Day.

Clark, R. W. (1977) *Men, Myths and Mountains.* London: Weidenfeld & Nicolson.

Clark, R. W., and E. C. Pyatt. (1957) *Mountaineering in Britain: A History from the Earliest Times to the Present Day.* London: Phoenix House.

Clarke, John, and Chas Critcher. (1985) *The Devil Makes Work: Leisure in Capitalist Britain.* Urbana: University of Illinois Press.

Clarke, Mrs. J. Stirling. (1857) *The Habit and the Horse.* London: Smith, Elder & Co.

Claudy, C. H. (1910) "Skate-Sailing for Life." *St. Nicholas* 37 (February): 298.

Claussen, Wally van B. (1926) *Practical Suggestions for Making and Using Skate Sails.* Distributed by the Skate-Sailing Association of America.

Clement, Annie. (1986) *Legal Responsibility in Aquatics.* Aurora, OH: Sport and Law Press.

———. (1988) *Law in Sport and Physical Activity.* Dubuque, IA: Brown/Benchmark.

Clephan, R. Coltman. (1918) *The Tournament. Its Periods and Phases.* London: Methuen.

Clerici, Gianni. (1974) *The Ultimate Tennis Book.* Chicago, IL: Follett.

Clias, P. H. (1825) *An Elementary Course of Gymnastic Exercises.* London: Sherwood Gilbert and Piper.

Coakley, Jay J. (1990) *Sport in Society.* St. Louis: Missouri Times Mirror.

———. (1994) *Sport in Society: Issues and Controversies.* St. Louis, MO: Mosby-Year Book.

Coates, Austin. (1983) *China Races.* Hong Kong: Oxford University Press.

*Codex Mendoza.* (1938) London: Waterlow and Sons.

Coffey, John. (1987) *Canterbury XIII.* Canterbury, New Zealand: Coffey.

Cohen, Greta L., ed. (1993) *Women in Sport: Issues and Controversies.* Newbury Park, CA: Sage Publications.

Cohen, Stanley. (1977) *The Game They Played.* New York: Farrar, Straus & Giroux.

Cohn, Nik. (1981) *Women of Iron.* Wideview Books.

Coleman, Charles L. *The Trail of the Stanley Cup.* Vol. 1, 1893–1926 (1966). Vol. 2, 1927–1946 (1969). Vol. 3, 1947–1967 (1976). Montreal and Sherbrooke: National Hockey League.

Coleman, Jim. (1987) *Hockey Is Our Game: Canada in the World of International Hockey.* Toronto, Canada: Key Porter Books.

Coles, Robert. (1975) "Football as a Surrogate Religion." In *A Sociological Yearbook of Religion,* no. 3, edited by Michael Hill.

Collins, Bud, and Zander Hollander, eds. (1994) *Bud Collins' Modern Encyclopedia of Tennis.* Detroit, MI: Visible Ink Press.

Collins, M. F., and C. S. Logue. (1976) *Indoor Bowls.* London: Sports Council.

Collins, Tony. (1995) "The Origins of Payment for Play in Rugby Football." *International Journal of the History of Sport* 12, 1 (April): 33–50.

Collins, Valeria. (1993) *Recreation and the Law.* New York: E. & F. N. Spon.

Colquhoun, I., and H. Machell. (1927) *Highland Gatherings.* London: Heath Cranton.

Colwin, Cecil. (1992) *Swimming into the Twenty-first Century.* West Point, NY: Leisure Press.

*Compendium of the Results of the Pan American Games from Buenos Aires 1951 to Indianapolis 1987.* (1989) 4th ed. Mexico City: Pan American Sports Organization.

Connell, R. W. (1987) *Gender and Power: Society, the Person and Sexual Politics.* Stanford, CA: Stanford University Press.

———. (1995) *Masculinities.* Berkeley: University of California Press.

Conover, Garrett, and Alexandra Conover. (1995) *A Snow Walker's Companion: Winter Skills from the Far North.* Camden, ME: Ragged Mountain Press.

Conrad, Jack Randolph. (1957) *The Horn and the Sword: The History of the Bull as a Symbol of Power and Fertility.* New York: E. P. Dutton.

Cook, Jeff S. (1992) *The Triathletes: A Season in the Life of Four Women in the Toughest Sport of All.* New York: St. Martin's Press.

Cook, T. A. (1894) *Notes on Tobogganing at St. Moritz.* New York: Scribner.

Coolidge, W. A. B. (1908) *The Alps in Nature and History.* London: Methuen.

Cooper, John M. (1963) "Games and Gambling." *Bureau of American Ethnology Bulletin* 143, 5: 503–524.

——— (1963) "The Ona." *Bureau of American Ethnology Bulletin* 143, 1: 107–125.

———. (1963) "The Yahgan." *Bureau of American Ethnology Bulletin* 143, 1: 81–106.

Cooper, Kenneth. (1968) *Aerobics.* New York: M. Evans.

———. (1970) *The New Aerobics.* New York: M. Evans.

———. (1972) *Aerobics for Women.* New York: M. Evans.

———. (1977) *The Aerobics Way.* New York: M. Evans.

Cooper, Pamela. (1995) "26.2 Miles in America: The History of the Marathon Footrace in the United States." Ph.D. dissertation, University of Maine.

Cooper, Phyllis. (1980) *Feminine Gymnastics.* 3d ed. Minneapolis: Burgess.

Cope, Myron. (1974) *The Game That Was.* New York: Thomas Y. Crowell.

Copley-Graves, Lynn. (1992) *Figure Skating History: The Evolution of Dance on Ice.* Columbus, OH: Platoro Press.

Corcoran, John, and Emil Farkas. (1983) *Martial Arts: Traditions, History, People.* New York: Gallery Books.

Cosell, Howard, with Peter Bonventre. (1985) *I Never Played the Game.* New York: William Morrow.

Cosentino, Frank. (1969) *Canadian Football: The Grey Cup Years.* Toronto, Canada: Musson.

———. (1995) *The Passing Game: A History of the CFL.* Winnipeg: Bain & Cox.

Cossío, José María de. (1961) *Los toros. Tratado técnico e histórico.* 4 vols. Madrid: Espasa-Calpe.

Costa, Margaret, and Sharon R. Guthrie, eds. (1994) *Women and Sport: An Interdisciplinary Perspective.* Champaign, IL: Human Kinetics.

Cote, J., J. H. Salmela, and S. Russell. (1995) "The Knowledge of High-Performance Gymnastic Coaches: Methodological Framework." *Sport Psychologist* 9: 67–75.

Coulton, Jill. (1981) *Sport Acrobatics.* New York: Sterling.

Counsilman, James, and Brian Counsilman. (1994) *The New Science of Swimming.* Englewood Cliffs, NJ: Prentice-Hall.

Cousins, G. (1975) *Golf in Britain.* London: Routledge and Kegan Paul.

Cox, Richard H. (1994) *Sport Psychology: Concepts and Applications.* 3d ed. Madison, WI: Brown & Benchmark.

———. (1995) *The Internet as a Resource for the Sports Historian.* Frodsham: Sports History Publishing.

Cox, Richard William. (1991) *Sport in Britain: A Bibliography of Historical Publications, 1800–1988.* Manchester, UK, and New York: Manchester University Press.

Craig, Darrell. (1988) *Iai: The Art of Drawing the Sword.* Tokyo: Charles E. Tuttle.

Craven, John, ed. (1969) *Football the Australian Way.* Melbourne, Australia: Lansdowne Press.

Crawford, S. A. G. M. (1975) "Joe Scott: Otago World Champion Pedestrian." *New Zealand Journal of Health, Physical Education, and Recreation* 83 (November).

———. (1990) "Film as Art, Artifice and Illusion." *Aethlon: Journal of Sport Literature* 7, 2 (Spring): 47–55.

———. (1991) "Sports Heroes in the Film Medium— *Chariots of Fire* to *Hoosiers*." *Journal of Physical Education and Sport Science* 3, 1 (January): 45–54.

———. (1991) "An Analysis of Athletic Themes in British Literature and Cinema." *Journal of Physical Education and Sport Science* 3, 11 (July): 62–69.

———. (1991) "An Examination of Post World War II Boxing Movies." *Illinois Journal* 29 (Spring): 6–8.

———. (1991) "Contemporary Canadian Sport Films." *Journal of International Council for Health, Physical Education and Recreation* 27, 1 (Fall): 29–31.

———. (1991) "The Black Actor as Athlete and Mover: An Historical Analysis of Stereotypes, Distortions and Bravura Performances in American Action Films." *Canadian Journal of History of Sport* 22, 2 (December): 23–33.

———. (1992) "The Bad Coach in Contemporary Sporting Films: An Analysis of Caricature, Character, and Stereotype." *Applied Research in Coaching and Athletics,* 46–61.

Craydon, Ron. (1995) *The Story of Table Tennis—The First 100 Years.* Hastings, UK: English TTA.

Creelman, William A. (1950) *Curling Past and Present: Including an Analysis of the Art of Curling by H. E. Wyman.* Toronto, Canada: McClelland and Stewart.

Cripps, Cecil. (1990) *Racing the Wind!* Melbourne, Australia: Vetsport Promotions.

Cripps-Day, Francis H. (1919) *The History of the Tournament in England and in France.* London: Bernard Quaritch.

Croft, Peter. (1990) *Clayshooting.* London: Ward Lock.

Cromartie, Warren. (1991) *Slugging It Out in Japan: An American Major Leaguer in the Tokyo Outfield.* New York: Kodansha International.

Cross, Gary. (1990) *A Social History of Leisure since 1600.* State College, PA: Venture.

Crosset, T. W. (1995) *Outsiders in the Clubhouse—The World of Women's Professional Golf.* Albany: State University of New York Press.

Crossman, Jim. (1978) *Olympic Shooting.* Washington, DC: National Rifle Association of America.

Crouch, Tom. (1983) *The Eagle Aloft.* Washington, DC: Smithsonian Institution Press.

Crowther, Nigel B. (1985) "Studies in Greek Athletics, Parts I and II," special issues of *Classical World* 78, 5 (May–June): 497–558 and 79, 2 (November–December): 73–135.

Cruise, David, and Alison Griffiths. (1991) *Net Worth: Exploding the Myths of Pro Hockey.* Toronto, Canada: Penguin Books Canada.

Cuddon, John Anthony. (1979) *International Dictionary of Sports and Games.* New York: Schocken Books.

Culin, Stewart. (1907) *Games of the North American Indians.* Twenty-fourth Annual Report of the Bureau of American Ethnology. Washington, DC: Government Printing Office.

Cullum, Grove. (1934) *Selection and Training of the Polo Pony.* New York: Scribners.

Cumming, John. (1981) *Runners and Walkers: A Nineteenth Century Sports Chronicle.* Chicago, IL: Regnery Gateway.

Cummings, Parke, ed. (1949) *The Dictionary of Sports.* New York: A. S. Barnes.

Cunningham, C. D., and W. W. Abney. (1887) *The Pioneers of the Alps.* London: Sampson, Low, Marston, Searle, and Rivington.

Cunningham, Hugh. (1980) *Leisure in the Industrial Revolution c.1780–c.1880.* New York: St. Martin's Press.

Curl, James Stephen. (1980) *A Celebration of Death: An*

*Introduction to Some of the Buildings, Monuments, and Settings of Funerary Architecture in the Western European Tradition.* New York: Charles Scribner's.

Curtis, Sam, Earl Perry, and Norman Strung. (1976) *Whitewater!* London and New York: Collier Macmillan.

Cutright, Paul Russell. (1985) *Theodore Roosevelt: The Making of a Conservationist.* Urbana: University of Illinois Press.

Cuyler, P. L. (1979) *Sumo: From Rite to Sport.* New York: Weatherhill.

Dale, T. F. (1915) *Polo at Home and Abroad.* London: London and Counties.

Daly, J. A. (1988) "A New Britannia in the Antipodes: Sport, Class and Community in South Australia." In *Pleasure, Profit, Proselytism: British Culture and Sport at Home and Abroad,* edited by J. A. Mangan. London: Frank Cass.

D'Amoric, Georges. (1898) *French Cane Fighting.* London: n.p.

Danaher, Mary A. (1978) *The Commemorative Coinage of Modern Sports.* Cranbury, NJ: A. S. Barnes.

Daniels, J. L. (1981) "World of Work in Disability Conditions." In *Rehabilitation Counseling,* edited by R. M. Parker and C. E. Hansen. Boston: Allyn and Bacon, 169–199.

Dank, Milton. (1977) *The Glider Gang.* Philadelphia: J. B. Lippincott.

Danquah, Joseph Boayke. (1928) *Gold Coast: Akan Laws and Customs.* London: Routledge.

Darden, Ellington. (1982) *The Nautilus Bodybuilding Book.* Chicago, IL: Contemporary Books.

Darnell, Eric, and Benjamin Ruhe. (1985*) Boomerang: How To Throw, Catch, and Make It.* New York: Workman Press.

Davidson, Judith A. (1985) "Sport and Modern Technology: The Rise of Skateboarding, 1963–1978." *Journal of Popular Culture* 18, 4: 145–157.

Davidson, J. A., and D. Alder. (1993) *Sport on Film and Video.* Metuchen, NJ: Scarecrow Press.

Davies, Richard O. (1994) *America's Obsession: Sports and Society since 1945.* Fort Worth, TX: Harcourt Brace.

Davis, Charlotte, and Dawn Bean. (1988) *Three Month Curriculum for Synchronized Swimming.* Indianapolis, IN: U.S. Synchronized Swimming.

Davis, Parke H. (1911) *Football, the American Intercollegiate Game.* New York: Scribner's Sons.

Davis, Pat. (1983) *Guinness Book of Badminton.* London: Guinness Superlatives Ltd.

Dawney, Hugh. (1984) *Polo Vision.* London: J. A. Allen.

Dawson, J. (1936) *Australian Aborigines: The Language and Customs of Several Tribes of Aborigines in the Western District of Victoria.* Melbourne, Australia: G. Robertson.

De Beaumont, Charles L. (1970) *Fencing: Ancient Art and Modern Sport.* South Brunswick, NJ: A. S. Barnes.

de Bondt, Cees. (1993) *"Heeft yeman lust met bal, of met reket te spelen . . .?" Tennis in Nederland 1500–1800.* Hilversum, The Netherlands: Uitgeverij Verloren.

De Capriles, Jose R., ed. (1965) *AFLA Rulebook.* Worcester, MA: Heffernan Press.

De Lorme, T. L., and A. L. Watkins. (1951) *Progressive Resistance Exercise.* New York: Appleton Century Crofts.

De Marco, Michael A. (1992) "The Origin and Evolution of Taijiquan." *Journal of Asian Martial Arts* 1, 1: 8–25.

De Vroede, E., and R. Renson. (1991) *Proceedings of the Second European Seminar on Traditional Games,* Leuven 12–16 September 1990. Leuven, Belgium: Vlaamse Volkssport Centrale.

Decarpentry, Albert Eugene Edouard. (1987) *Academic Equitation.* London: J. A. Allen.

Decker, Kate Delano-Condax. (1995) *Riding: A Guide for New Riders.* New York: Lyons & Burford.

Decker, Wolfgang. (1990) "The Record of the Ritual: the Athletic Records of Ancient Egypt." In *Ritual and Record,* edited by John Marshall Carter and Arnd Krüger. New York: Greenwood Press, 21–30.

———. (1992) *Sports and Games of Ancient Egypt,* translated by Allen Guttmann. New Haven, CT: Yale University Press.

———. (1995) *Sport in der Griechischen Autike.* Munich, Germany: C. H. Beck.

DeGlopper, Donald R. (1974) *City on the Sands: Social Structure in a Nineteenth-Century Chinese City.* Ann Arbor, MI: University Microfilms.

Del Rey, Pat. (1977) "Apologetics and Androgyny: The Past and the Future." *Frontiers* 3: 8–10.

———. (1978) "The Apologetic and Women in Sport." In *Women and Sport: From Myth to Reality,* edited by C. A. Oglesby. Philadelphia: Lea and Febiger, 107–11.

Delahaye, M. (1986) *La Boxe-Française.* Paris: Editions Française Reder.

———. (1986) *Savate, Chaussoun, et Boxe-Française.* Paris: Editions Française Reder.

Delaney, Trevor. (1984) *The Roots of Rugby League.* Keighley, UK: Delaney.

———. (1993) *Rugby Disunion.* Keighley, UK: Delaney.

Delgado Ruiz, Manuel. (1986) *De la muerte de un dios: La fiesta de los toros en el universo simbólico de la cultura popular.* Barcelona: Nexos.

Dencher, Stepehen. (1988) *Sporting Art in Eighteenth Century England.* New Haven, CT: Yale University Press.

DeNeui, D. L., and D. Sachau. (1996) "Spectator Enjoyment of Aggression in Intercollegiate Hockey Games." *Journal of Sport & Social Issues* 20: 69–77.

Denholm-Young, Noel. (1948) "The Tournament in the 13th Century." In *Studies in Medieval History,* edited by Richard Hunt. Oxford: Clarendon, 240–268.

Denlinger, K., and L. Shapiro. (1975) *Athletes for Sale.* New York: Thomas Y. Crowell.

Dent, C. T. (1876) "Two Attempts on the Aiguille du Dru." *Alpine Journal* 7: 65–79.

———. (1892) *Mountaineering.* London: Longman.

Deonna, W. (1953) *Le symbolisme de l'acrobatie antique*. Brussels, Belgium: Berchem.

DePauw, K. P. (1984) "Commitment and Challenges: Sports Opportunities for Athletes with Disabilities." *Journal of Physical Education, Recreation and Dance* (February): 34–35.

———. (1990) "PE and Sports for Disabled Individuals in the United States." *Journal of Physical Education, Recreation and Dance* (February): 53–57.

Derderian, Tom. (1994) *Boston Marathon: The History of the World's Premier Running Event*. Champaign, IL: Human Kinetics.

Derwald, Richard, and Kathy Derwald. (1990) "The Night Women's Bodybuilding Died." *Natural Physique* 4, 3: 44–45, 95.

Dheensaw, Cleve. (1994) *The Commonwealth Games*. Victoria, British Columbia: Orca Book Publishers.

Di Donna Prencipe, Carmen, ed. (1986) *"Letteratura e sport": Acts of the Convegno di Foggia 22–23 maggio 1986*. Bologna: Nuova Universale Cappelli.

Diagram Group. (1982) *Sports Comparisons*. New York: St. Martin's Press.

Diamond, Dan, and Joseph Romain. (1988) *Hockey Hall of Fame: The Official History of the Game and Its Greatest Stars*. Toronto, Canada: Doubleday Canada.

Diamond, Dan, ed. (1992) *The Official National Hockey League Stanley Cup Centennial Book*. Toronto, Canada: McClelland & Stewart.

Dickerson, G. (1991) *The Cinema of Baseball: Images of America, 1929–1989*. Westport, CT: Meckler.

Dickson, Paul. (1994) *The Worth Book of Softball*. New York: Facts On File.

Diem, Carl. (1941) *Asiatische Reiterspiele*. Berlin: Deutscher Archiv-Verlag.

———. (1967) *Weltgeschichte des Sports*. 2 vols. Stuttgart: Cotta Verlag.

———. (1971) *Weltgeschichte des Sports*. 3d ed., 2 vols. Frankfurt: Cotta.

Digel, H. (1992) "Sports in a Risk Society." *International Review for the Sociology of Sport* 26, 2: 257–273.

Dingman, Richard A. (1984) *Patterns*. Cambridge, MA: Mind-Dog Books.

———. (1994) *The Little Book of Juggling*. Philadelphia: Running Press Publishers.

———. (1996) *The Ultimate Juggling Book*. Philadelphia: Running Press Publishers.

Disston, H. (1961) *Know about Horses—A Ready Reference Guide to Horses, Horse People, and Horse Sports*. New York: Bromhall House.

Dixon, Peter. (1970) *Soaring*. New York: Ballantine Books.

Dizard, Jan. (1994) *Going Wild: Hunting, Animal Rights, and the Contested Meaning of Nature*. Amherst: University of Massachusetts Press.

Dizikes, John. (1981) *Sportsmen and Gamesmen*. Boston: Houghton Mifflin.

Dizionario del calcio. (1990) *La Gazzetta dello Sport (Dictionary of Association Football)*. Milan, Italy.

Dobereiner, P. (1973) *The Glorious World of Golf*. London: Hamlyn.

Dodds, E. King. (1909) *Canadian Turf Recollections and Other Sketches*. Toronto, Canada: Self-published.

Dodge, Tom, ed. (1980) *A Literature of Sports*. Lexington, MA: D. C. Heath.

Doherty, K. (1971) *Track and Field Omnibook: A Complete Guide for Coach and Athlete*. Swarthmore, PA: Tafmop Publishers.

Doherty, W. J. (1931) *In the Days of the Giants*. London: Harrap.

Doniger O'Flaherty, Wendy. (1981) *The Rig Veda. An Anthology*. New York and London: Penguin Books.

Donlon, J. G. (1990) "Fighting Cocks, Feathered Warriors, and Little Heroes." *Play & Culture* 3, 4: 273–285.

———. (1990) "Gamecock Imagery in Contemporary Discourse." *Aethlon: The Journal of Sports Literature* 8, 1: 157–162.

———. (1992) "Fightin' Cocks in Words and Pictures: Some Notes on Roosters and Symbolic Representation." *Centaur: The Journal of Human/Animal Interface* 1: 55–63.

———. (1993) "Cajun Cockpits." *Journal of Material Culture* 2: 25–36.

Donnelly, Peter. (1993) "Subcultures in Sport: Resilience and Transformation." In *Sport in Social Development: Traditions, Transitions, and Transformations*, edited by Alan G. Ingham and John W. Loy. Champaign, IL: Human Kinetics Publishers, 119–145.

Donohue, John. (1991) *The Forge of the Spirit: Structure, Motion, and Meaning in the Japanese Martial Tradition*. New York: Garland.

———. (1992) "Dancing in the Danger Zone: The Martial Arts in America." *Journal of Asian Martial Arts* 1, 1: 86–99.

———. (1994) *Warrior Dreams: The Martial Arts and the American Imagination*. Westport, CT: Bergin & Garvey.

Donohue, John, and Kimberley Taylor. (1994) "The Classification of the Fighting Arts." *Journal of Asian Martial Arts* 3: 10–37.

Doughty, Robin W. (1975) *Feather Fashions and Bird Preservation: A Study in Nature Protection*. Los Angeles: University of California Press.

Douglass, William, ed. (1978) "The St. Louis Fronton Revisited." *Basque Studies Newsletter* 19, 2 (November).

Drackett, Phil. (1987) *Flashing Blades: The Story of British Ice Hockey*. Ramsbury, UK: Crowood Press.

Draeger, Donn F (1973) *Classical Bujutsu: The Martial Arts and Ways of Japan*. Vol. I. New York and Tokyo: Weatherhill.

———. (1973) *Classical Budo: The Martial Arts and Ways of Japan*. Vol. II. New York: Weatherhill.

———. (1974) *The Martial Arts and Ways of Japan*. Vols. 1–3. New York: Weatherhill

Draeger, Donn F., and Robert W. Smith. (1969) *Asian Fighting Arts*. Tokyo: Kodansha.

———. (1969, 1980) *Comprehensive Asian Martial Arts*. Tokyo: Kodansha.

Drowatzky, John N. (1984) *Legal Issues in Sport and Physical Education Management*. Champaign, IL: Stipes.

Dryden, Ken. (1983) *The Game: A Thoughtful and Provocative Look at a Life in Hockey*. Toronto, Canada: Macmillan of Canada.

Dryden, Ken, and Roy MacGregor. (1989) *Home Game: Hockey and Life in Canada*. Toronto, Canada: McClelland and Stewart.

Dubay, Pierre. (1978) *Arc et Arbalète*. Paris: Albin Michel.

Duchartre, Pierre-Louis. (1929) *The Italian Comedy*. Translated by R. T. Weaver. London: Harrap.

Duchesne, G. (1855) *De l'electrisation localisée*. Paris: Balliere.

Duchesne, J. (1648) *Ars medica dogmatica hermetica*. Frankfurt, Germany: n.p.

Duckworth, W. L. N. (1962) *Galen on Anatomical Procedures, Books X–XV*. Cambridge: Cambridge University Press.

Dudycha, Douglas, et al. (1983) *The Canadian Atlas of Recreation and Exercise*. Waterloo, IA: University of Waterloo, Department of Geography.

Duff, Robert W., and Lawrence K. Hong. (1984) "Self Images of Women Bodybuilders." *Sociology of Sport Journal* 1: 374–380.

Dulles, Foster Rhea. (1965) *A History of Recreation: America Learns To Play*. New York: Appleton-Century-Crofts.

Dundes, Alan. (1994) *The Cockfight: A Casebook*. Madison: University of Wisconsin Press.

Dunning, Eric. (1986) "Sport as a Male Preserve: Notes on the Social Sources of Masculine Identity and Its Transformations." *Theory, Culture & Society* 3, 1: 79–90.

Dunning, Eric, and K. Sheard. (1979) *Barbarians, Gentlemen and Players: A Sociological Study of the Development of Rugby Football*. Oxford: Martin Robertson.

Dunning, Eric, ed. (1971) *The Sociology of Sport: A Selection of Readings*. London: Cass.

Dunning, Eric, and Christopher Rojek, eds. (1992) *Sport and Leisure in the Civilizing Process: Critique and Counter-Critique*. London: Macmillan.

Dunphy, Don. (1988) *Don Dunphy at Ringside*. New York: Henry Holt.

Dunsmore, Susi. (1983) *"Sepak Raga" (Takraw): The Southeast Asian Ball Game*. Occasional Paper No. 4. Sarawak: Sarawak Museum.

Dupree, Louis. (1970) "Sports and Games in Afghanistan." *American Universities Field Staff Reports*. South Asia Series XIV (1).

Duquin, Mary E. (1982) "The Importance of Sport in Building Women's Potential." *Journal of Physical Education, Recreation, and Dance* 53: 18–20, 36.

Durán, Fray Diego. (1971) *Book of the Gods and Rites of the Ancient Calendar*. Translated by Fernando Horcasitas and Doris Heyden. Norman: University of Oklahoma Press.

Durant, Will. (1939) *The Life of Greece*. New York: Simon and Schuster.

Durkheim, Emile. (1961 [1912]) *The Elementary Forms of the Religious Life*. New York: Collier.

Dyer, Jack, and Brian Hansen. (1968) *The Wild Men of Football*. Melbourne, Australia: Southdown Press.

Dyer, K. F. (1982) *Catching Up the Men: The Social Biology of Female Sporting Achievement*. St. Lucia: University of Queensland Press.

Dyer, K. F., and T. Dwyer. (1984) *Running out of Time: An Examination of the Improvements in Running Records*. Kensington, Australia: New South Wales University Press.

Eaton, D. H. (1920) *Trapshooting: The Patriotic Sport*. Cincinnati, OH: Sportsmen's Review Publishing.

Eaves, G. (1969) *Diving: The Mechanics of Springboard and Firmboard Techniques*. New York: A. S. Baines and Company.

Ebert, Joachim. (1963) *Zum Pentathlon der Antike*. Berlin: Akademie Verlag.

Ebert, R. (1991) *Movie Home Companion*. Kansas City, MO: Andrews and McMeel.

Edel, May Mandelbaum. (1937) "The Bachiga of East Africa," In *Cooperation and Competition among Primitive Peoples*, edited by Margaret Mead. New York: McGraw-Hill.

Edelman, Robert. (1993) *Serious Fun: A History of Spectator Sports in the U.S.S.R.* New York: Oxford University Press.

Edinburgh, Duke of. (1982) *Competition Carriage Horse Driving*. Macclesfield, UK: Horse Drawn Carriages Limited.

Edginton, Christopher R., D. Jordan, D. DeGraaf, and S. Edginton. (1995) *Leisure and Life Satisfaction: Foundational Perspectives*. Dubuque, IA: Brown & Benchmark.

Edwards, E. H., ed. (1977) *Encyclopedia of the Horse*. New York: Crescent Books.

Edwards, Harry. (1973) *The Sociology of Sport*. Homewood, IL: Dorsey Press.

———. (1986) "The Collegiate Athletic Arms Race: Origins and Implications of the 'Rule 48' Controversy." In *Fractured Focus*, edited by R. E. Lapchick. Lexington, KY: Lexington Books.

Edwards, R. Wayne. (1984) "Team Handball: A Familiar Name but a Different Game." *Journal of Physical Education, Recreation, and Dance* 55, 2: 27–28.

Edwards, Sally. (1983) *Triathlon, a Triple Fitness Sport: The First Complete Guide To Challenge You to a New Total Fitness*. Chicago, IL: Contemporary Books.

———. (1985) *The Triathlon Training and Racing Book*. Chicago, IL: Contemporary Books.

Egerton, David. (1933) "Eton Fives." In *Rackets, Squash Rackets, Tennis, Fives and Badminton*, edited by Lord Aberdare. London: Seeley Service & Co.

# Bibliography

Eichberg, Henning. (1973) *Der Weg des Sports in die Industrielle Zivilisation.* Baden-Baden: Nomos Verlagsgesellschaft.

———. (1978) *Leistung, Spannung, Geschwindigkeit.* Stuttgart: Klett-Cotta.

———. (1984) "Olympic Sport—Neocolonization and Alternatives." *International Review of Sport Sociology* 19, 1: 97–105.

———. (1988) *Leistungsraume.* Munster, Germany: Lit Forlag.

———. (1990) "Forward Race and the Laughter of Pygmies." In *Fin De Siècle and Its Legacies,* edited by Roy Porter and Mikluás Teich. Cambridge: Cambridge University Press, 115–131.

———. (1990) "Stronger, Funnier, Deadlier: Track and Field on the Way from the Ritual to the Record." In *Ritual and Record,* edited by John M. Carter and Arnd Krüger. Westport, CT: Greenwood Press, 123–124.

Eichel, Wolfgang. (1953) "Die Entwicklung der Körperübungen in der Urgemeinschaft." *Theorie und Praxis der Körperkultur* 2: 14–33.

Eifermann, Rivka R. (1973) "Rules in Games." In *Artificial and Human Thinking,* edited by Alice Elithorn and David Jones. San Francisco: Jossey-Bass, 147–161.

Einthoven, W. (1903) "The Galvanometric Registration of the Human Electrocardiogram." *Arch. Ges. Physiol.* 99: 472–480.

Eisen, George, and Wiggins, David K., eds. (1994) *Ethnicity and Sport in North American History and Culture.* Westport, CT: Greenwood Press.

Eitzen, D. S. (1993) *Sport in Contemporary Society.* New York: St. Martin's Press.

Eitzen, D. S., and G. Sage. (1993) *Sociology of North American Sport.* 5th ed. Dubuque, IA: Wm. Brown.

Elder, Donald. (1956) *Ring Lardner: A Biography.* New York: Doubleday.

Elias, Norbert. (1939) *Über den prozess der zivilisation.* Volume 1 of 2 vols. Basle: Haus zum Falken.

———. (1986) "An Essay on Sport and Violence." In *Sport and Leisure in the Civilizing Process,* edited by Norbert Elias and Eric Dunning. Oxford: Basil Blackwell, 150–174.

———. (1991) *The Symbol Theory.* London: Sage.

———. (1994) *The Civilizing Process.* Oxford: Blackwell.

Elias, Norbert, and Eric Dunning. (1986) *Quest for Excitement: Sport and Leisure in the Civilizing Process.* Oxford: Blackwell.

Embree, J. F. (1948) "Kickball and Some Other Parallels between Siam and Micronesia." *Journal of Siam Society* 37, 1.

Emery, C. R. (1972) *The Story of the Pan American Games.* Kansas City, MO: Ray-Gay.

Emery, D., and S. Greenberg. (1986) *The World Sports Record Atlas.* New York: Facts On File.

Endrei, W., and L. Zolnay. (1986) *Fun and Games in Old Europe.* Budapest: Corvina.

Engel, C. E. (1950) *A History of Mountaineering in the Alps.* London: Allen & Unwin.

English Bowling Association and British Crown Green Association. (1992) *Know the Game: Bowls.* London: A. and C. Black.

Esmas, Marjorie R. (1984) "Tourism as Ethnic Preservation: The Cajuns of Louisiana." *Annals of Tourism Research* 11.

Espy, Richard. (1979) *The Politics of the Olympic Games.* Berkeley: University of California Press.

Evans, Jeremy. (1983) *Complete Guide to Windsurfing.* London: Bell & Hyman.

Everton, Clive. (1979) *The Story of Billiards and Snooker.* London: Cassell.

Fabian, L., and J. Hiser. (1986) *Racquetball: Strategies for Winning.* Dubuque, IA: Eddie B.

Fagen, Robert M. (1981) *Animal Play Behavior.* New York: Oxford University Press.

Fahlberg, L., and L. Fahlberg. (1994) "A Human Science for the Study of Movement: An Integration of Multiple Ways of Knowing." *Research Quarterly for Exercise and Sport* 65, 2: 100–103.

Fair, J. D. (1987) "Bob Hoffman, the York Barbell Company, and the Golden Age of American Weightlifting, 1945–1960." *Journal of Sport History* 14: 164–188.

Falla, Jack. (1981) *NCAA: The Voice of College Sports.* Mission, KS: National Collegiate Athletic Association.

Fanck, Arnold, and Hannes Schneider. (1925) *Wunder des Schneeschuhs.* Hamburg, Germany: Enoch.

Faris, Nabih Amin, and R. P. Elmer. (1945) *Arab Archery.* Princeton, NJ: Princeton University Press.

Farkas, Emil, and John Corcoran. (1985) *The Overlook Martial Arts Dictionary.* Woodstock, NY: Overlook Press.

Farmer, Charles J. (1977) *The Digest Book of Canoes, Kayaks and Rafts.* Northfield, IL: DBI Books.

Farrington, S. Kip, Jr. (1972) *Skates, Sticks and Men: The Story of Amateur Hockey in the United States.* New York: David McKay.

Federal Aviation Agency. (1985) *Commercial Glider Pilot Practical Test Standards.* Washington, DC: Office of Flight Operations.

———. (1987) *Flight Instructor Practical Test Standards for Gliders.* Washington, DC: Office of Flight Standards.

———. (1987) *Private Glider Pilot Practical Test Standards.* Washington, DC: Office of Flight Standards.

Fédération Equestre Internationale. *Rules for Dressage Events of the Fédération Equestre Internationale.* Lausanne, Switzerland: Fédération Equestre Internationale.

Fédération Internationale d'Inter-crosse. (1991) *Dobry en Polska.* Unpublished proceedings of conference in Legnica, Poland.

Fédération Internationale de l'Automobile (FIA). (1995) *1996 Formula One Technical Regulations.* Paris: FIA

———. (1995) *1996 Formula One World Championship Sporting Regulations.* Paris: FIA.

Fédération Internationale de Luge. (1992) *International Luge Racing Regulations.* English version provided by the U.S. Luge Association, Lake Placid, NY.

Fédération Internationale de Natation Amateur. (1946– ) *FINA Handbook.* Lausanne, Switzerland: Fédération Internationale de Natation Amateur.

———. (1995) *Synchronized Swimming Judges' Training Manual.* Lausanne, Switzerland: Fédération Internationale de Natation Amateur.

Fernández Suárez, Alvaro. (1961) *España, arbol vivo.* Madrid: Aguilar.

Ferreiro Toledano, Abraham. (1986) *Centroamérica y el Caribe a través de sus juegos.* Mexico City: Artes Gráficas Rivera.

———. (1992) *Historia de los once juegos deportivos panamericanos, 1951–1991.* Mexico City: Pro Excelencia del Deporte.

Ferrill, Arthur. (1985) *The Origins of War: From the Stone Age to Alexander the Great.* London: Thames and Hudson.

Ffoulkes, Charles. (1912) "Jousting Cheques of the 16th Century." *Archaeologia* 58: 31–50.

Fiddian, Marc. (1977) *The Pioneers.* Melbourne, Australia: Victorian Football Association.

Figone, Albert J. (1989) "Gambling and College Basketball: The Scandal of 1951." *Journal of Sport History* 16, 1: 44–61.

Fine, G. A. (1987) *With the Boys.* Chicago: University of Chicago Press.

Finley, Moses I., and Henri W. Pleket. (1976) *The Olympic Games: The First Thousand Years.* London: Chatto & Windus.

Finn, Michael. (1982) *Iaido: The Way of the Sword.* London: Paul H. Compton.

———. (1984) *Jodo: The Way of the Stick.* Boulder, CO: Paladin Press.

———. (1985) *Kendo No Kata: Forms of Japanese Kendo* Boulder, CO: Paladin Press.

———. (1987) *Kendo: The Way and Sport of the Sword.* London: Elite International Publications.

———. (1988) *Martial Arts: A Complete Illustrated History.* Woodstock, NY: Overlook Press.

Finney, Ben, and John Houston. (1966) *Surfing: The Sport of Hawaiian Kings.* Johannesburg, South Africa: Hugh Keartland Publishers.

Firth, Raymond. (1983) "A Dart Match in Tikopia: A Study in the Sociology of Primitive Sport." In *Play, Games and Sports in Cultural Context,* edited by J. Harris and R. Park. Champaign, IL: Human Kinetics.

Fischer, Leo H. (1940) *How To Play Winning Softball.* New York: Prentice-Hall

Fischler, Stan, and Shirley Fischler. (1979) *Fischler's Ice Hockey Encyclopedia.* Rev. ed. New York: Thomas Y. Crowell.

———. (1983) *Everybody's Hockey Book.* New York: Charles Scribner's Sons.

Fiske, John. (1991) "Bodies of Knowledge: Panopticism and Spectatorship." Unpublished keynote address at the annual meetings of the North American Society for the Sociology of Sport, Milwaukee, WI.

Fitsell, J. W. (1987) *Hockey's Captains, Colonels and Kings.* Erin, Ontario: Boston Mills Press.

Fittis, R. S. (1891) *Sports and Pastimes of Scotland.* Paisley, UK: Alexander Gardner.

Fitz-Barnard, L. (1983) *Fighting Sports.* Surrey, UK: Saiga Publications.

Fleckenstein, Josef, ed. (1985) *Das ritterliche Turnier im Mittelalter.* Göttingen, Germany: Vandenhoeck and Ruprecht.

Fleischer, Nat. (1929) *Jack Dempsey: The Idol of Fistiana.* New York: Ring Athletic Library.

———. (1936) *From Milo to Londos: The Story of Wrestling through the Ages.* The Ring Athletic Library 13. New York: C. J. O'Brien.

———. (1960) *50 Years at Ringside.* London: Corgi.

Fleischer, Nat, and Sam Andre. (1980) *A Pictorial History of Boxing.* London: Hamlyn.

Fletcher, Sheila. (1984) *Women First: The Female Tradition in English Physical Education, 1880–1980.* Bristol, UK: Athlone Press.

Flint, Rachel Heyhoe, and Netta Rheinberg. (1976) *Fair Play: The Story of Women's Cricket.* London: Angus and Robertson.

———. (1978) *Field Hockey.* Woodbury, NY: Barron's.

*Flos duellatorum in armis, sine armis, equester, pedester; il fior di battaglia di maestro Fiore dei Liberi da Premariacco. Testo inedito del MCCCX publicato ed illustrato a cura di Francesco Novati.* (1902) Bergamo: Istituto Italiano d'Arti Grafiche (original 1410).

Floyd, P., et al. *Wellness: A Lifetime Commitment.* Winston-Salem, NC: Hunter Textbooks.

Fodor, R. V. (1979) *Competitive Weightlifting.* New York: Sterling.

Forbes, Susan L., and Lori A. Livingston. (1994) "From Frances Dove to Rosabelle Sinclair and Beyond: The Introduction of Women's Field Lacrosse to North America." In *Proceedings of the 10th Commonwealth & International Scientific Congress,* edited by F. I. Bell and G. H. Van Gyn. Victoria, Canada: University of Victoria, 83–86.

Forbes, W. Cameron. (1911) *As to Polo.* Boston: Privately printed.

Ford, Emma. (1992, 1995) *Falconry: Art and Practice.* London: Cassell.

Forget, J. P. (1995) *The Complete Guide to Western Horsemanship.* New York: Howell Book House.

Fostle, D. W. (1988) *Speedboat.* Mystic, CT: Mystic Seaport Museum Stores.

Foucault, Michel. (1979 [1977]) *Discipline and Punish.* Harmondsworth: Penguin.

Fox, J. C. (1967) *The Indianapolis 500.* New York: World.

Fox, John W. (1991) "The Lords of Light Versus the Lords of

# Bibliography

Dark: The Postclassic Highland Maya Ballgame." In *The Mesoamerican Ballgame*, edited by Vernon L. Scarborough and David R. Wilcox. Tucson: University of Arizona Press.

Fox, Stephen. (1994) *Big Leagues: Professional Baseball, Football, and Basketball in National Memory*. New York: Morrow.

Fraleigh, W. (1984) *Right Actions in Sport: Ethics for Contestants*. Champaign, IL: Human Kinetics.

France, Ministre de l'Education Nationale. (1989) *L'Education physique et sportive à l'école:Les sports de combat les jeux d'opposition à l'école elementaire*. Paris: Ministre de l'Education Nationale.

Francis, Lorna. (1993) *Aerobic Dance for Health and Fitness*. Madison, WI: Brown and Benchmark.

Frankenberg, R. (1990) *Village on the Border*. Prospect Heights, IL: Waveland Press.

Fraser, I. (1968) *The Annals of Thames Hare and Hounds*. London: Thames & Hudson.

Frazer, James George. (1890) *The Golden Bough: A Study of Magic and Religion*. London: Macmillan.

Frederic, Louis. (1991) *A Dictionary of the Martial Arts*. Translated and edited by Paul Crompton. Rutland, VT, and Tokyo: Charles Tuttle.

Fredriksson, Kristine. (1985) *American Rodeo*. College Station, TX: Texas A&M University Press.

Freedman, Harold, and Lemon, Andrew. (1990) *The History of Australian Thoroughbred Racing*. Melbourne, Australia: Southbank Communications.

Freeman, Garth. (1987) *Petanque: The French Game of Bowls*. Leatherhead, UK: Carreau Press.

Freeman, J. Richardson. (1991) "Purity and Violence: Sacred Power in the Teyyam Worship of Malabar." Ph.D. dissertation, University of Pennsylvania.

Freidel, David, Linda Schele, and Joy Parker. (1993) *Maya Cosmos: Three Thousand Years on the Shaman's Path*. New York: William Morrow.

French, Richard. (1975) *Antivivisection and Medical Science in Victorian England*. Princeton, NJ: Princeton University Press.

Frey, James H., ed. (1987) "Gambling on Sports." *Arena Review* 11, 1: 8–14.

Friary, Richard. (1990) "Lying on the Wind: Ice Skate Sailing." *Speedskating Times* Part 1, 1, 5 (April): 6; Part 2, 1, 6 (May): 6.

———. (1996) *Skate Sailing*. Indianapolis: Masters Press.

Friddle, Martha C., and Linda A. Bowlby. (1994) *The Sidesaddle Legacy*. Bucyrus, OH: World Sidesaddle Federation.

Frith, David. (1987) *Pageant of Cricket*. Melbourne, Australia: Macmillan.

Froboess, F. (1956) *Fell's Official Guide to Diving*. New York: Frederick Fell.

Fujii, Okimitsu. (1987) *ZNKR Seitei Iai*. London: Kenseikai Publications.

Fukushima, Sho. (1980) *Men's Gymnastics*. London and Boston: Faber & Faber.

Funken, Liliane, and Fred Funken. (1979) *Rüstungen und Kriegsgerät im Mittelalter. 8.–15. Jahrhundert.* München: Mosaik Verlag.

Gabriel, Richard A. (1990) *The Culture of War: Invention and Early Development*. New York: Greenwood Press.

Gaelic Athletic Association. (1991) *Rules*. Dublin: GAA.

Gai, Ingham Berlage. (1994) *Women in Baseball: The Forgotten History*. Westport, CT: Praeger.

Gaines, Charles, and George Butler. (1974) *Pumping Iron*. New York: Simon and Schuster.

———. (1983) "Iron Sisters." *Psychology Today* 17: 65–69.

Galdi, M., S. Gigotti, and F. Masotto. (1986) *Guida al mondiale di calcio*.

Galen. *On the Natural Faculties*. (1916) Translated by A. J. Brock. Loeb Classical Library. London: W. Heinemann.

———. *De sanitate tuenda*. (1951) Translated by R. M. Green. Springfield, IL: Charles C. Thomas.

Galenson, David W. (1993) "The Impact of Economic and Technological Change on the Careers of American Men Tennis Players, 1960–1991." *Journal of Sport History* 20, 2 (Summer): 127–150.

———. (1995) "Does Youth Rule? Trends in the Ages of American Women Tennis Players, 1960–1992." *Journal of Sport History* 22, 1 (Spring): 46–59.

Gallop, Rodney. (1970) *A Book of the Basques*. Reno: University of Nevada Press

Gallup, Elizabeth M. (1995) *Law and the Team Physician*. Champaign, IL: Human Kinetics.

Galtung, Johan. (1984) "Sport and International Understanding: Sport as a Carrier of Deep Culture and Structure." In *Sport and International Understanding*, edited by M. Illmarinen. Berlin, Germany: Springer-Verlag, 12–19.

Gangadharan, N., trans. (1985) *Agni Purana*. Delhi, India: Motilal Banarsidass.

Gantz, Jeffrey. (1981) *Early Irish Myths and Sagas*. New York: Dorsett Press.

Gantz, Timothy. (1993) *Early Greek Myth. A Guide to the Literary and Artistic Sources*. Baltimore and London: Johns Hopkins University Press.

Gardiner, E. Norman. (1978) *Athletics of the Ancient World*. Chicago, IL: Ares Publishers (originally 1930).

Garnett, Michael. (1983) *A History of Royal Tennis in Australia*. Mt. Waverley, Victoria: Historical Publications.

———. (1991) *Royal Tennis for the Record*. Romsey, Victoria: Historical Publications.

Gate, Robert. (1984) *Gone North*. Ripponden, UK: Gate.

———. (1989) *Rugby League, An Illustrated History*. London: Arthur Barker.

Gavin, James. (1992) *The Exercise Habit*. Champaign, IL: Leisure Press.

Geertz, Clifford. (1972) "Deep Play: Notes on the Balinese

Cockfight." In *The Interpretation of Cultures,* edited by Clifford Geertz. New York: Basic Books, 412–453.

Georgano, G. N., ed. (1971) *The Encyclopedia of Motor Sport.* New York: Viking Press.

George, J. J. (1995) "The Fad of North American Women's Endurance Swimming during the Post–World War I Era." *Canadian Journal of History of Sport* 26, 1 (May): 52–72.

George, Nelson. (1992) *Elevating the Game: Black Men and Basketball.* New York: HarperCollins.

Gerber, Ellen W. (1971). *Innovators and Institutions in Physical Education.* Philadelphia: Lea & Febiger.

Gerber, Ellen, et al. (1974) *The American Woman in Sport.* Reading, MA: Addison-Wesley.

German National Equestrian Federation. (l985) *The Principles of Riding: The Official Instruction Handbook of the German National Equestrian Federation.* London: Threshold Books.

———. (l986) *The Advanced Techniques of Riding: The Official Instruction Handbook of the German National Equestrian Federation.* London: Threshold Books.

Gibson, J. H. (1993) *Performance versus Results.* Albany: State University of New York Press.

Giddens, Robert. (1950) *Ice Hockey: The International Game.* London: W. & G. Foyle.

Giel, Debra. (1988) "Freestyle Skiing: From 'Hotdogging' to Olympic Demonstration Event." *Physician and Sportsmedicine* 16, 2 (February): 189–190, 195–196.

Gillman, P., ed. (1993) *Everest.* Boston: Little, Brown.

Gillmeister, Heiner. (1990) *Kulturgeschichte des Tennis.* Munich, Germany: Wilhelm Fink Verlag.

Gillmore, Russell S. (1974) "Crack Shots and Patriots: The National Rifle Association and America's Military Sporting Tradition, 1871–1929." Ph.D. dissertation, University of Wisconsin, Madison.

Glanville, Brian. (1980) *The History of the World Cup.* London: Faber and Faber.

Gleason, G. R. (1967) *Judo for the West.* South Brunswick, NJ: A. S. Barnes.

Godia, George. (1989) "Sport in Kenya." In *Sport in Asia and Africa: A Comparative Handbook,* edited by Eric C. Wagner. Westport, CT: Greenwood.

Godwin, T., and C. Rhys. (1981) *The Guinness Book of Rugby Facts and Feats.* Enfield, UK: Guinness Superlatives.

Goldberger, Alan L. (1984) *Sports Officiating, A Legal Guide.* Champaign, IL: Human Kinetics.

Goldman, B., P. Bush, and R. Klatz. (1984) *Death in the Locker* Room. South Bend, IN: Icarus Press.

Goldman, Irving. (1937) "The Bathonga of South Africa." In *Cooperation and Competition among Primitive Peoples,* edited by Margaret Mead. New York: McGraw-Hill.

Goldman, R., with P. Bush and R. Klatz. (1984) *Death in the Locker Room: Steroids, and Sports.* South Bend, IL: Icarus Books.

Goldman, R., and R. Klatz. (1992) *Death in the Locker Room.* Chicago, IL: Elite Sports Medicine.

Goldstein, Warren. (1989) *Playing for Keeps: A History of Early Baseball.* Ithaca, NY: Cornell University Press.

Golesworthy, Maurice. (1957) *The Encyclopaedia of Association Football.* London: Robert Hale.

Gomme, Alice Bertha. (1898) *The Traditional Games of England, Scotland, and Ireland.* London: David Nutt.

Gomme, Alice Betha, ed. (1964) *The Traditional Games of England, Scotland, and Ireland.* Vol. 2. New York: Dover.

Gomme, G. L., ed. (1898) *A Dictionary of British Folk-Lore. Part 1: Traditional Games.* Vol. 2. London: David Nutt.

Goodbody, John. (1983) *The Illustrated History of Gymnastics.* New York: Beaufort.

Goodger, B. C., and J. M. Goodger. (1977) "Judo in the Light of Theory and Sociological Research." *International Review of Sport Sociology* 12, 1: 5–34.

Goodman, Susan F., and Ian McGregor. (1994) *Legal Liability and Risk Management.* North York, Ontario: Risk Management Associates.

Gordon, B. (1935) "Grecian Athletic Training in the Third Century (AD)." *Annals of Medical History* 7 (November): 513–518.

Gordon, Barclay F. (1983) *Olympic Architecture: Building for the Summer Games.* New York: John Wiley & Sons.

Gordon, Neil F., and Larry W. Gibbons. (1990) *The Cooper Clinic Cardiac Rehabilitation Program.* New York: Simon and Schuster.

Gordon-Watson, M. (1987) *The Handbook of Riding.* New York: Alfred A. Knopf.

Gorman, J., K. Calhoun, and S. Rozin. (1994) *The Name of the Game: The Business of Sport.* New York: John Wiley and Sons.

Gorn, Elliott J. (1985) "'Gouge and Bite, Pull Hair and Scratch': The Social Significance of Fighting in the Southern Backcountry." *American Historical Review* 90 (February): 18–43.

———. (1986) *The Manly Art: Bare-Knuckle Prize Fighting in America.* Ithaca, NY: Cornell University Press.

Gorn, E. J., and W. Goldstein. (1993) *A Brief History of American Sports.* New York: Hill and Wang.

Gourlay, John. (1931) *The Grasslands International Steeplechase, 1930.* Gallatin, TN: Grasslands Downs.

Grace, Peter. (1991) *Polo.* New York: Howell.

Graham, Cooper C. (1986) *Leni Riefenstahl and Olympia.* Metuchen, NJ, and London: Scarecrow Press.

Graham, Stedman, Joe Goldblatt, and Lisa Delpy. (1995) *The Ultimate Guide to Sport Event Management and Marketing.* Burr Ridge, IL: Irwin Professional Publishing.

Gray, Jennifer. (1993) *Coaching Synchronized Swimming Figure Transitions.* Maidenhead, Berkshire, UK: Standard Studio Publishers.

Grayson, Edward. (1994) *Sport and the Law.* 2d ed. London: Butterworths.

# Bibliography

Great Britain, War Office. (1886) *Manual of Instruction for Single Stick Drill*. London: Harrison and Sons.

Green, Harvey. (1986) *Fit for America: Health, Fitness, Sport and American Society*. New York: Pantheon.

Greenberg, Martin J. (1989) *Sports Biz—An Irreverent Look at Big Business in Pro Sports*. Champaign, IL: Leisure Press.

———. (1993) *Sport Law Practice*. Charlottesville, VA: Michie.

Gregor, Thomas. (1979) *Mehinaku: The Drama of Daily Life in a Brazilian Indian Village*. Chicago: University of Chicago Press.

Grey, D. (1970) *Rope Boy*. London: Victor Gollancz.

Grice, Tony. (1994) *Badminton for the College Student*. Boston: American Press.

Griffith, C. R. (1926) *Psychology of Coaching*. New York: Scribners.

———. (1928) *Psychology and Athletics*. New York: Scribners.

Griffiths, Trevor R. (1993) *Grand Prix*. London: Bloomsburg Publishing.

Grimsley, W., ed. (1971) *A Century of Sports*. New York: Associated Press.

———. (1971) *Great Moments in Sport*. New York: Plimpton Press.

Grinnell, George Bird. (1913) *Hunting at High Altitude*. New York: Harpers & Brothers.

Griswold, Larry. (1966) *Trampoline Tumbling*. New York and South Brunswick, NJ: A. S. Barnes.

Grombach, John V. (1956) *Olympic Cavalcade*. New York: Ballantine Books.

Grosse, Susan J., and Donna Thompson, eds. (1993) *Leisure Opportunities for Individuals with Disabilities: Legal Issues*. Reston, VA: AAHPERD.

Gruneau, Richard. (1983) *Class, Sports and Social Development*. Amherst: University of Massachusetts Press.

Gruneau, Richard, and David Whitson. (1993) *Hockey Night in Canada: Sport, Identities, and Cultural Politics*. Toronto, Canada: Garamond Press.

Grusky, O. (1963) "The Effects of Formal Structure on Managerial Recruitment: A Study of Baseball Organization" *Sociometry* 26: 345–353.

Guiney, David, and Patrick Puirseal. (1965) *The Guinness Book of Hurling Records*. Dublin: Macmillan.

Gundling, Beulah, and Jill White. (1988) *Creative Synchronized Swimming*. Champaign, IL: Leisure Press.

Gunter, Charles R. (1978) "Cockfighting in East Tennessee and Western North Carolina." *Tennessee Folklore Bulletin* 44 (December): 160–169.

Gurney, Gerald N. (n.d.) *Table Tennis: The Early Years*. St. Leonards-on-Sea, East Sussex, UK: International Table Tennis Federation.

Guthrie, C. (1940) *A History of Medicine*. London: Nelson.

Guts Muths, J. Chr. (1793) *Gymnastik für jugend*. (1804) 2d ed. Schnepfenthal.

Guttmann, Allen. (1978) *From Ritual to Record: The Nature of Modern Sports*. New York: Columbia University Press.

———. (1986) *Sport Spectators*. New York: Columbia University Press.

———. (1988) *A Whole New Ball Game*. Chapel Hill: University of North Carolina Press.

———. (1991) *Women's Sports: A History*. New York: Columbia University Press.

———. (1992) *The Olympics: A History of the Modern Games*. Urbana: University of Illinois Press.

———. (1994) *Games and Empires: Modern Sports and Cultural Imperialism*. New York: Columbia University Press

Gyarfas, Tamas, ed. (1977– ) *International Swimming and Water Polo*. Belgrade, Yugoslavia.

Haarstad, Kjell. (1993) *Skisportens oppkomst i Norge*. Trondheim, Norway: Tapir Forlag.

Haas, Mary R. (1940) "Creek Intertown Relations." *American Anthropologist* 42: 479–489.

Habashi, Zaki. (1976) "King Tutankhamun, Sportsman in Antiquity." In *The History, the Evolution and Diffusion of Sports and Games in Different Cultures*, edited by Roland Renson, Pierre Paul De Nayer, and Michael Ostyn. Brussels: BLOSO, 71–83.

Habernicht, Jorg. (1991) *Triathlon Sportgeschichte*. Bochum, Germany: N. Brockmeyer.

Hackenschmidt, George. (1909) *The Complete Science of Wrestling*. London: Athletic Publications.

Hackensmith, C. W. (1966) *History of Physical Education*. New York: Harper & Row.

Haddon, A. C. (1890) "The Ethnography of the Western Tribes of Torres Strait." *Journal of the Royal Anthropological Institute of Great Britain and Ireland* 19.

———. (1912) *Reports of the Cambridge Anthropological Expedition to the Torres Straits*. Vol. 4. Cambridge: Cambridge University Press.

Haigh, Gideon. (1993) *The Cricket War: The Inside Story of Kerry Packer's World Series Cricket*. Melbourne, Australia: Text Publishing.

Haines, Bruce. (1995) *Karate's History and Traditions*. Rev. ed. Tokyo: Charles E. Tuttle

Haining, Peter. (1976) *The Compleat Birdman*. New York: St. Martin's Press.

Halberstam, David. (1985) *The Amateurs*. New York: Penguin Books.

Hales, Diane. (1979) *A History of Badminton in the United States from 1878–1939*. Pomona: California State Polytechnic University.

Haley, N. (1970) *How To Teach Group Riding*. New York: A. S. Barnes.

Hänel, Erich. (1910) *Der Sächsischen Kurfürsten Turnierbücher*. Frankfurt: Keller.

Hanesworth, Robert D. (1967) *Daddy of 'Em All: The Story of Cheyenne Frontier Days*. Cheyenne, WY: Flintlock.

Hankinson, A. (1977) *The Mountain Men: An Early History of Rock Climbing in North Wales*. London: Heinemann Educational.

———. (1988) *A Century on the Crags: The Story of Rock Climbing in the Lake District*. London: J. M. Dent.

Hanna, Glenda. (1991) *Outdoors Pursuits Programming—Legal Liability and Risk Management*. Edmonton: University of Alberta Press.

Hannemann, E. F. (1959) "Games and Modes of Entertainment in the Past among the People of the Madang District." *Mankind* 5, 8: 333–345.

Hannus, Matti. (1990) *Flying Finns*. Helsinki: Tietosanoma.

Haralambos, K. M. (1990) *The Byerley Turk*. London: Threshold.

Harbour, Dave. (1979) "Trophy Bass: The Challenge and the Prize." In *L. Underwood's Bass Almanac*, edited by L. Underwood. Garden City, NY: Doubleday, 200–212.

Harding, W. (1975) *Downward Bound: A Mad Guide to Rock Climbing*. Englewood Cliffs, NJ: Prentice-Hall.

Hardy, Stephen. (1982) *How Boston Played: Sport, Recreation and Community, 1865–1915*. Boston: Northeastern University Press.

Hare, C. E. (1939, 1949) *The Language of Field Sport*. London: Country Life Ltd.; New York: Charles Scribner's Sons.

Hargreaves, J. (1986) *Sport, Power and Culture: A Social and Historical Analysis of Popular Sports in Britain*. New York: St. Martin's Press.

———. (1993) "The Victorian Cult of the Family and the Early Years of Female Sport." In *The Sport Process*, edited by E. G. Dunning, J. A. Maguire, and R. E. Pearton. Champaign, IL: Human Kinetics.

———. (1994) *Sporting Females: Critical Issues in the History and Sociology of Women's Sports*. London: Routledge.

Harney, W. E. (1952) "Sport and Play amidst the Aborigines of the Northern Territory." *Mankind* 4, 9: 377–379.

Harper, W. (1972) "Giving and Taking." Paper presented at the February meeting of the Philosophic Society for the Study of Sport, Brockport, NY.

———. (1973–1976) *The Play Factory Advocate*, vols. 1–4. Emporia, KS: William A. Harper.

———. (1985) "The Philosopher in Us." In *Sport Inside Out: Readings in Literature and Philosophy*, edited by D. Vanderwerken and S. Wertz. Fort Worth, TX: Texas Christian University Press, 449–545.

Harris, D. V., and B. L. Harris. (1984) *The Athlete's Guide to Sports Psychology: Mental Skills for Physical People*. New York: Leisure Press.

Harris, Harold A. (1964) *Greek Athletes and Athletics*. London: Hutchinson.

———. (1972) *Sport in Greece and Rome*. London: Thames and Hudson.

———. (1972) "The Method of Deciding Victory in the Pentathlon." *Greece and Rome* 19: 60–64.

———. (1975) *Sport in Britain*. London: Hutchinson.

Harris, Janet C., and Roberta J. Park, eds. (1983) *Play, Games and Sports in Cultural Contexts*. Champaign, IL: Human Kinetics.

Harris, Marvin. (1979) *Good To Eat: Riddles of Food and Culture*. New York: Simon and Schuster.

Harris, Peter B. (1975) *The Commonwealth*. London: Longman.

Harrison, David. (1993) *Sea Kayaking Basics*. New York: Hearst Marine Books.

Harrison, E. J. (1955) *The Fighting Spirit of Japan*. London: W. Foulsham.

Harrison, Henry. (1988) *Play the Game: Ten Pin Bowling*. London: Ward Lock.

Harrison, James C. (1968) *Care and Training of the Trotter and Pacer*. Columbus, OH: U.S. Trotting Association.

Harrison-Pepper, Sally. "The Martial Arts: Rites of Passage, Dramas of Persuasion." *Journal of Asian Martial Arts* 2, 2: 90–103.

Harste, Ann K. (1990) "Soccer on Ice." *The Physician and Sports Medicine* 18 (November): 32.

Hart, James E., and Robert J. Ritson. (1993) *Liability and Safety in Physical Education and Sport: A Practitioner's Guide to the Legal Aspects of Teaching and Coaching in Elementary and Secondary Schools*. Reston, VA: AAHPERD.

Hart, M. (1972) *Sport in the Socio-Cultural Process*. Dubuque, IA: Wm. C. Brown.

Hart, Stan (1985) *Once a Champion: Legendary Tennis Stars Revisited*. New York: Dodd, Mead.

Harte, Chris. (1993) *A History of Australian Cricket*. London: Deutsch.

Hartley, R. A. (1988) *History & Bibliography of Boxing Books*. Alton, Hampshire, UK: Nimrod Press.

Harvey, Jean, and Francois Houle. (1994) "Sport, World Economy, Global Culture, and New Social Movements." *Sociology of Sport Journal* 11: 337–355.

Hashman, Judy Devlin. (1984) *Winning Badminton*. London: Ward Lock.

Hassell, E. (1936) "Notes on the Ethnology of the Wheelman Tribe of South-Western Australia." *Anthropos* 31: 679–711.

Haw, Sarah. (1993) *The New Book of the Horse*. New York: Howell Book House.

Hawes, Lorin L. (1975) *All About Boomerangs*. Sydney, Australia: Hamlyn Group.

Hawley, F. Frederick. (1987) "Cockfighting in the Piney Woods: Gameness in the New South." *Sport Place* (Fall).

———. (1989) "Cockfight in the Cotton: A Moral Crusade in Microcosm." *Contemporary Crises*.

Hay, Douglas. (1975) "Poaching and the Game Laws on Crannock Chase." In *Albion's Fatal Tree: Crime and Society in Eighteenth-Century England*, edited by Douglas Hay et al. New York: Pantheon Books.

Hayes, Alice M. (1910) *The Horsewoman: A Practical Guide to Side-saddle Riding and Hunting*. London: Hurst and Blackett.

# Bibliography

Haynes, Bailey C. (1989) *Bill Pickett, Bulldogger: The Biography of a Black Cowboy.* Norman and London: University of Oklahoma Press.

Heads, Ian. (1992) *True Blue.* Sydney, Australia: Ironbark.

Heald, C. B. (1931) *Injuries and Sport.* London: Oxford University Press.

Healey, Deborah. (1989) *Sport and the Law.* Kensington, Australia: New South Wales University Press.

Heath, Ernest Gerald. (1973) *A History of Target Archery.* Newton Abbot, UK: David & Charles.

Heath, Fran. (1989) *Synchronized Swimming Routine Choreography.* Edmonton: Synchro Swim Alberta.

Heathcote, J. M., et al. (1890; rpt. 1903) *Tennis. Lawn Tennis. Rackets. Fives.* London: Longmans, Green.

Heine, Michael. (1995) *Gwich'in Tsii'in: A History of Gwich'in Athapaskan Games.* Ph.D. dissertation, University of Alberta.

Heinrich, Fritz. (1978) "Wer hat das Trickskifahren erfunden?" *Leibesübungen-Leibeserziehung* 32, 1: 6–8.

Heller, Peter. (1974) *"In This Corner!": Forty World Champions Tell Their Stories.* New York: Dell.

Hellison, D. (1973) *Humanistic Physical Education.* Englewood Cliffs, NJ: Prentice-Hall.

Helly, Louis. (1966) *Cent ans de ski français.* Grenoble, France: Cahiers de l'Alpe.

Hemingway, Ernest. (1932) *Death in the Afternoon.* New York: Charles Scribner's Sons.

Henderson, Joe. (1988) *Total Fitness: Training for Life.* Dubuque, IA: W. C. Brown.

Henderson, Noel. (1989) *European Cycling: The 20 Classic Races.* Brattleboro, VT: Vitesse Press.

Henderson, Robert W. (1947) *Bat, Ball, and Bishop: The Origin of Ball Games.* New York: Rockport.

———. (1948) *The King's Book of Sports in England and America.* New York: New York Public Library.

Hendricks, William. (1974) *William Hendricks' History of Billiards.* Roxana, IL: William Hendricks.

Hennessy, John. (1983) *Torvill & Dean.* New York: St. Martin's Press.

Henning, H. N. (1983) *International Swimming and Water Polo.* Budapest, Hungary. Part 1, 2–7; Part 2, 2–7, 49–51, 57–59, 65–67.

Henshaw, Richard. (1979) *The Encyclopaedia of World Soccer.* New York: New Republic Books.

Hernandez de Alba, Gregorio. (1963) "Sub-Andean Tribes of the Cauca Valley." *Bureau of American Ethnology Bulletin* 143, 4: 297–327.

Herrigel, Eugen. (1948) *Zen in der Kunst des Bogenschiessens.* Konstanz: Weller. (English translation by R. F. C. Hull [1953]. *Zen in the Art of Archery.* New York: Pantheon.)

Hervey, John. (1947) *The American Trotter.* New York: Coward-McCann.

Hervey, John, et al. (1931) *Racing at Home and Abroad.* London: London & Counties Press.

Herxheimer, H. (1932) *Grundriss der Sportmedizin fÿr Arzte und Studierende.* Leipzig, Germany: Georg Thieme.

Herzog, H. (1985) "Cockfighting in Southern Appalachia." *Appalachian Journal* 12: 114–148.

———. (1988) "Cockfighting and Violence in the South. In *The Encyclopedia of Southern Culture,* edited by W. Ferris. Chapel Hill: University of North Carolina Press.

———. (1993) "'The Movement Is My Life': The Psychology of Animal Rights Activism." *Journal of Social Issues* 49: 103–119.

Hess, Felix. (1968) "The Aerodynamics of Boomerangs." *Scientific American* (November): 124–136.

———. (1975) *Boomerangs: Aerodynamics and Motion.* Groningen, Netherlands: Privately printed.

Hewitt, Foster. (1961) *Hockey Night in Canada: The Maple Leafs' Story.* 2d ed. Toronto, Canada: Ryerson Press.

Heywood, William. (1969) *Palio and Ponte: An Account of the Sports of Central Italy from the Age of Dante to the Twentieth Century* (reprint of 1904 edition). London: Methuen.

Hick, Daniel, ed. (1992) *L'Empire du sport.* Aix-en-Provence, France: Centre des Archives d'Outre Mer.

Hickie, T. V. (1993) *They Ran with the Ball: How Rugby Football Began in Australia.* Melbourne, Australia: Longman Cheshire.

Hickok, Ralph. (1971) *Who Was Who in American Sports.* New York: Hawthorn Books.

———. (1992) *The Encyclopedia of North American Sports History.* New York: Facts On File.

———. (1995) *A Who's Who of Sports Champions: Their Stories and Records.* Boston and New York: Houghton Mifflin.

Higgs, R. J. (1981) *Laurel and Thorn: The Athlete in American Literature.* Lexington: University Press of Kentucky.

———. (1982) *Sports.* Westport, CT: Greenwood Press.

———.(1995) *God in the Stadium: Sport and Religion in America.* Lexington: University Press of Kentucky.

Higgs, Robert J., and Neil D. Isaacs. (1977) *The Sporting Spirit: Athletes in Literature and Life.* New York: Harcourt, Brace.

Hill, A. V. (1927) *Living Machinery.* New York: Harcourt, Brace.

———. (1927) *Muscular Movement in Man: The Factors Governing Speed and Recovery from Fatigue.* New York: McGraw-Hill .

Hilliard, Dan C. (1988) "Finishers, Competitors, and Pros: A Description and Speculative Interpretation of the Triathlon Scene." *Play and Culture,* 1: 300–313.

Hinman, Bob. (1971) *The Golden Age of Shotgunning.* New York: Winchester Press.

Hirst-Fisher, Robin. (1990) *Intermediate Riding Skills.* New York: Howell Book House.

Hitchcock, F. C. (1962) *Saddle Up.* London: Stanley Paul.

Hoberman, John M. (1984) *Sport and Political Ideology.* Austin: University of Texas Press.

———. (1992) *Mortal Engines.* New York: Free Press and Toronto: Maxwell Macmillan Canada.

Hobsbawm, E. J. (1990) *Nations and Nationalism since 1780: Programme, Myth and Reality.* Cambridge: Cambridge University Press.

Hobsbawm, E. J., and T. Ranger, eds. (1983) *The Invention of Tradition.* Cambridge: Cambridge University Press.

Hobson, Richard. (1993) *Riding—The Game of Polo.* London: J. A. Allen.

Hobusch, Erich. (1980) *Fair Game: A History of Hunting, Shooting, and Animal Conservation.* New York: Arco Publishing.

Hodges, David, Doug Nye, and Nigel Roebuck. (1981) *Grand Prix.* New York: St. Martin's Press.

Hoeger, W., and S. Hoeger. (1992) *Lifetime Physical Fitness and Wellness.* Englewood, CO: Morton Publishing.

Hoff, Feliks F. (1983) *Iai-Do: Blitzschnell die Waffe Ziehen und Treffen.* Berlin: Verlag Weinmann.

Hoffman, B. (1974) "A Century of American Weightlifting." *Strength and Health* 44, 4: 34–40, 54–55.

Hoffman, F. (1708) *Dissertationes physico-medicae.* The Hague: Van der Kloot.

Hoffman, F. W., and W. G. Bailey. (1991) *Sports and Recreations.* New York: Harrington Park Press.

Hoffman, Shirl J., ed. (1992) *Sport and Religion.* Champaign, IL: Human Kinetics.

Hogan, M., and E. Turner. (1988) *Skills and Strategies for Winning Racquetball.* Champaign, IL: Leisure Press.

Holcombe, Charles. (1992) "Theater of Combat: A Critical Look at the Chinese Martial Arts." *Journal of Asian Martial Arts* 1: 4, 64–79.

———. (1993) "The Daoist Origins of the Chinese Martial Arts." *Journal of Asian Martial Arts* 2, 1: 10–25.

Holland, Anne. (1991) *Classic Horse Races.* London: MacDonald.

Hollander, Zander, ed. (1979) *The Modern Encyclopedia of Basketball.* Garden City, NY: Dolphin Books.

———. (1993) *The Complete Encyclopedia of Hockey.* 4th ed. Detroit, MI: Visible Ink Press.

Hollander, Zander, and David Schulz. (1978) *The Jai Alai Handbook.* Los Angeles, CA: Pinnacle Books.

Holliman, Jennie. (1975 [1931]) *American Sports (1785–1835).* Philadelphia: Porcupine Press.

Holloway, Jean Barrett, et al. (1994) "Strength Training for Female Athletes: A Position Paper: Part I." *National Strength and Conditioning Association Journal* 11, 4: 43–55.

Hollum, Diane. (1984) "Equipment." In *The Complete Book of Speed Skating.* Hillside, NJ: Enslow Publishers.

Holmes, J. H. (1908) "Introductory Notes on the Toys and Games of Elema, Papuan Gulf." *Journal of Royal Anthropological Institute* 37: 280–288.

Holt, Richard. (1981) *Sport and Society in Modern France.* London: Macmillan, and Hamden, CT: Anchor.

———. (1989) *Sport and the British: A Modern History.*

Oxford: Clarendon and New York: Oxford University Press.

———. (1990) *Sport and the Working Class in Modern Britain.* Manchester, UK: Manchester University Press.

Holt, R., P. Lanfranchi, and J. A. Mangan, eds. (1996) *European Heroes: Myth, Identity, Sport.* London: Frank Cass.

Holum, D. (1984) *The Complete Handbook of Speed Skating.* Hillside, NJ: Enslow Publishing.

Hopkins, C. Howard. (1951) *History of the Y.M.C.A. in North America.* New York: Association Press.

Hopper, C. A. (1984) "Socialization of Wheelchair Athletes." In *Sports and Disabled Athletes,* edited by C. Sherrill. Champaign, IL: Human Kinetics, 197–202.

Horn, T. S., ed. (1992) *Advances in Sport Psychology.* Champaign, IL: Human Kinetics.

Horneber, Ralf. (1993) *Olympic Target Rifle Shooting.* Translated by Bill Murray. Munich, Germany: F. C. Meyer Verlag.

Horning, Dave, and Gerald Couzens. (1985) *Triathlon, Lifestyle of Fitness: Swim! Bike! Run!* New York: Pocket Books.

Horse Capture, George. (1989) *Powwow.* Cody, WY: Buffalo Bill Historical Center.

Husing, Ted. (1935) *Ten Years before the Mike.* New York: Farrar and Rinehart.

Houblon, Doreen Archer. (1938) *Side-Saddle.* London: Country Life.

Howat, Gerald. (1980) *Village Cricket.* London: David and Charles.

Howell, M. L., R. A. Howell, and K. Edwards. (1993) "Wrestling among the Australian Aborigines." Paper presented at ASSH-NASSH Joint Conference, Hawaii.

Howell, Max, and Reet Howell (1988) *The Greatest Game under the Sun.* Brisbane, Australia: Queensland Rugby Football League.

Howell, N., and Max L. Howell. (1969) *Sport and Games in Canadian Life: 1700 to Present.* Toronto, Canada: Macmillan.

Howell, Reet, ed. (1982) *Her Story in Sport: A Historical Anthology of Women in Sports.* West Point, NY: Leisure Press.

Howell, Reet A., and Maxwell L. Howell. (1987) *A History of Australian Sport.* Sydney, Australia: Shakespeare Head Press.

———. (1992) *The Genesis of Sport in Queensland: From the Dreamtime to Federation.* St. Lucia: University of Queensland Press.

Howitt, A. W. (1904) *The Native Tribes of South-East Australia.* London: Macmillan.

Hughes, Robert, and Jay J. Coakley. (1991) "Positive Deviance among Athletes: The Implications of Overconformity to the Sport Ethic." *Sociology of Sport Journal* 8: 307–325.

Huizinga, Johan. (1950, 1955) *Homo Ludens: A Study of the*

*Play Element in Culture.* Boston: Beacon Press and London: Roy Publishers.

———. (1971) "The Play Element in Contemporary Sport." In *The Sociology of Sport: A Selection of Readings,* edited by Eric Dunning. London: Cass.

Hult, Joan S. (1986) "The Female American Runner: A Modern Quest for Visibility." In *Female Endurance Athletes,* edited by Barbara Drinkwater. Champaign, IL: Human Kinetics.

———. (1989) "American Female Olympians as Role Models, Mentors and Leaders." In *Proceedings of the Jyvaskyla Congress on Movement and Sports in Women's Life.* Jyvaskyla, Finland: University of Jyvaskyla Press.

Hult, Joan S., and Mariana Trekell, eds. (1991) *A Century of Women's Basketball: From Frailty to Final Four.* Reston, VA: National Association for Girls and Women in Sport.

Humber, William. (1983) *Cheering for the Home Team: The Story of Baseball in Canada.* Toronto, Canada: Oxford University Press.

Humphrey, John H. (1986) *Roman Circuses: Arenas for Chariot Racing.* London: B. T. Batsford.

Humphreys, Duncan. (1996) "Snowboarders: Bodies Out of Control and in Conflict." *Sporting Traditions,* forthcoming.

Hunn, David. (1979) *The Complete Book of Gymnastics.* Secaucus, NJ: Chartwell Books.

Hunt, J. (1953) *The Ascent of Everest.* London: Hodder.

Hyland, Anne. (1990) *Equus: The Horse in the Roman World.* New Haven, CT: Yale University Press.

Hyland, Drew. (1990) *Philosophy of Sport.* New York: Paragon House.

*IAAF* [International Amateur Athletic Federation] *Bulletin* (1973–1986) In French and English.

Imus, Brenda. (1992) *From the Ground Up: Horsemanship for the Adult Rider.* New York: Howell Book House.

Ingham, Alan G., and John W. Loy, eds. (1993) *Sport in Social Development: Traditions, Transitions, and Trans-formations.* Champaign, IL: Human Kinetics Publishers.

Ingleton, Geoffrey Chapman, ed. (1952) *True Patriots All or News from Early Australia as in a Collection of Broadsides.* Sydney, Australia: Angus and Robertson.

Innes, Steven, ed. (1988) *Work and Labor in Early America.* Chapel Hill: University of North Carolina Press.

Inokuma, Isao, and Sato Nobuyuki. (1986) *Best Judo.* New York: Kodansha International.

Inosanto, Dan. (1980) *The Filipino Martial Arts.* Hollywood, CA: Know How Publications.

International Badminton Federation. (1994) *IBF Statute Book.* Cheltenham, UK: International Badminton Federation.

International Conference Proceedings. (1989) *The Olympic Movement and the Mass Media: Past, Present and Future Issues.* Calgary, Alberta: Hurford Enterprises.

International Gymnastics Federation. (1993) *Code of Points for Artistic Gymnastics for Men.* Switzerland: FIG.

International Gymnastics Federation, Women's Technical Committee. (1993) *Code of Points for Artistic Gymnastics for Women.* Switzerland: FIG.

International Shooting Union. (1995) *General Technical Rules and Special Technical Rules.* Munich, Germany: International Shooting Union.

International Skiing Federation. (1992) *FIS Freestyle. General Rules and Regulations. Rules for Specific Competitions.* Berne, Switzerland: International Skiing Federation.

———. (1993) *FIS Freestyle. General Rules for Scoring. Judging Manual.* Berne, Switzerland: International Skiing Federation.

Irwin, John. (1973) "The Natural History of an Urban Scene," *Urban Life and Culture* 2, 2: 131–160.

Isaacs, Neil D. (1975) *All the Moves: A History of College Basketball.* Philadelphia: Lippincott.

———. (1977) *Checking Back: A History of the National Hockey League.* New York: W. W. Norton.

Italia, Bob. (1991) *In-line Skating.* Minneapolis, MN: Rockbottom.

Itzkowitz, David C. (1977) *Peculiar Privilege: A Social History of English Foxhunting.* Hassocks, UK: Harvester.

Ivry, Benjamin. (1988) *Regatta: A Celebration of Oarsmanship.* New York: Simon and Schuster.

Izenberg, Jerry. (1972) *How Many Miles to Camelot? The All-American Sports Myth.* New York: Holt, Rinehart and Winston.

Jable, J. Thomas. (1978) "The Birth of Professional Football: Pittsburgh Athletic Clubs Ring in Professionals in 1892," *Western Pennsylvania Historical Magazine* 62 (April): 131–147.

Jackson, Alastair. (1989) *The Great Hunts: Foxhunting Centres of the World.* Newton Abbot, UK: David and Charles.

Jackson, Donald F. (1991) "Philostratos and the Pentathlon." *Journal of Hellenic Studies* 111: 178–81.

Jaenecke, C. (1899) *Der Griechisch-Roemische Ringkampf in seiner heutigen Gestaltung.* Hamburg, Germany: J. F. Richter.

James, Bill. (1988) *The Bill James Historical Baseball Abstract.* New York: Villard Books.

James, C. L. R. (1963) *Beyond the Boundary.* London: Hutchinson.

Jamieson, D. A. (1943) *Powderhall and Pedestrianism.* Edinburgh, Scotland: W. and A. K. Johnstone.

Jamison, Wesley, and William Lunch. (1992) "Rights of Animals, Perceptions of Science, and Political Activism: Profile of American Animal Rights Activists." *Science, Technology & Human Values* 17, 4: 438–458.

Japan Folklore Association. (1992) *The Energy of Asia, Reports on the Exchange of Asian Traditional Sports Demonstrations* (Japan Folklore Association cultural exchange program and conference sponsored by the Ministry of Foreign Affairs and the Japan Foundation).

Jarvie, G. (1986) "Highland Gatherings, Sport and Social Class." *Sociology of Sport* 3: 344–355.

# Bibliography

———. (1991) *Highland Games: The Making of the Myth.* Edinburgh, UK: Edinburgh University Press.

———. (1992) "Highland Gatherings, Balmorality and the Glamour of Backwardness." *Sociology of Sport* 2: 167–178.

Jasper, James, and Dorothy Nelkin. (1992) *The Animal Rights Crusade: The Growth of a Moral Protest.* New York: Free Press.

Jayasankaran, J. (1995) "Offside: Red Faces Follow Match Fixing Revelations." *Far Eastern Economic Review* 158, 2: 20.

Jefferson, Rufus C. (1957) *Skate Sailing.* North Minneapolis, MN: Harrison & Smith.

Jenner, Bruce, and Phil Finch. (1977) *Decathlon Challenge: Bruce Jenner's Story.* Englewood Cliffs, NJ: Prentice-Hall.

Jeziorski, R. J. (1994) *The Importance of School Sports in American Education and Socialization.* New York: University Press of America.

John, G., and K. Campbell. (1993) *Handbook of Sports and Recreational Buildings: Outdoor Sports.* London: Sports Council.

Johnson, Cecil. (1994) *Guts: Legendary Black Rodeo Cowboy Bill Pickett.* Fort Worth, TX: Summit Group.

Johnson, Don, ed. (1991) *Hummers, Knucklers, and Slow Curves: Contemporary Baseball Poems.* Urbana: University of Illinois Press.

Johnson, Jack. (1977) *Jack Johnson: In the Ring and Out.* London: Proteus.

Johnson, Peter. (1989) *The Sail Magazine Book of Sailing.* New York: Knopf.

Jonas, Steven. (1986) *Triathloning for Ordinary Mortals.* New York: W. W. Norton.

Jones, C. (1976) *Climbing in North America.* Berkeley: University of California Press.

Jones, Donald G. (1992) *Sports Ethics in America; A Bibliography, 1970–1990.* New York: Greenwood Press.

Jones, J. R. (1960) *Encyclopaedia of Rugby Football.* London: Sportsmans Book Club.

Jones, Kevin. (1967) "Games and Physical Activities of the Ancient Polynesians and Relationships to Culture." M.A. thesis, University of Alberta, Canada.

Jones, S. G. (1988) *Sport, Politics and the Working Class— Organised Labour and Sport in Inter-War Britain.* Manchester, UK: Manchester University Press.

Joseph, L. H. (1949) *Gymnastics from the Middle Ages to the Eighteenth Century.* Ciba Symposia 10, 5. Summit, NJ: Ciba Pharmaceutical Products.

Josselyn, John. (1883) "An Account of Two Voyages to New-England" (1675). *Massachusetts Historical Society Collections*, 3d series, 349.

Jou, Tsung Hwa. (1983) *The Tao of Tai-Chi Chuan: Way to Rejuvenation.* Edited by Shoshana Shapiro. Warwick: Tai-Chi Foundation.

Joyner, Stephen. (1993) *Complete Guide and Resource to In-line Skating.* Cincinnati, OH: Betterway.

Judd, Dennis, and Peter Slinn. (1982) *The Evolution of the Modern Commonwealth 1902–1980.* London: Macmillan Press.

Juergens, George. (1966) *Joseph Pulitzer and the "New World World."* Princeton, NJ: Princeton University Press.

Jung, Emil Bernard. (1980) *Combined Driving.* New York: Publisher.

Kailasapathy, K. (1968) *Tamil Heroic Poetry.* Oxford: Clarendon Press.

Kaiser, Ronald A. (1986) *Liability and Law in Recreation, Parks and Sports.* Englewood Cliffs, NJ: Prentice-Hall.

Kamper, Erich, and Bill Mallon. (1992) *The Golden Book of the Olympic Games.* Milan, Italy: Vallardi and Associates.

Kano, Jigoro. (1932) "The Contribution of Judo to Education." *Journal of Health and Physical Education* (November).

———. (1937) *Judo (Jujutsu).* Tokyo: Board of Tourist Industry, Japanese Government Railways.

———. (1986) *Kodokan Judo.* Tokyo and New York: Kodansha.

Kaplan, H. Roy (1986) "Sports, Gambling, and Television: The Emerging Alliance." In *Fractured Focus: Sport as a Reflection of Society*, edited by Richard E. Lapchick. Lexington, MA: D. C. Heath.

Karkkainen, P. (1992) "Pesäpallo—Finnish Baseball: History and Presentation of the National Game." Presented at the first International Society of History in Sports and Physical Education seminar, "Sport and Cultural Minorities," 8–13 June, Turku, Finland.

Karl, Dennis. (1990) *Glorious Defiance.* New York: Paragon Books.

Karr, Elizabeth Platt. (1884) *The American Horsewoman.* Boston and New York: Houghton Mifflin.

Katz, Donald. (1994) *Just Do It: The Nike Spirit in the Corporate World.* New York: Random House.

Katz, E. (1979) *The International Film Encyclopedia.* London: Macmillan.

Kauz, Herman. (1992) *A Path to Liberation: A Spiritual and Philosophical Approach to the Martial Arts.* New York: Overlook Press.

Keegan, John. (1993) *A History of Warfare.* New York: Alfred A. Knopf.

Keen, Clifford, Charles Speidel, and Raymond Swartz. (1964) *Championship Wrestling,* 4th ed. New York: Arco Publishing.

Keen, Maurice. (1984) *Chivalry.* New Haven, CT, and London: Yale University Press.

Kellerman, Annette. (1918) *How To Swim.* London: William Heinemann.

Kelly, J. F. (1961) *Dealing with Horses.* New York: Arco Publishing.

Kelly, J. R., and G. Godbey. (1992) *The Sociology of Leisure.* State College, PA: Venture.

Kelver, Gerald O. (1975) *100 Years of Shooters and Gunmakers of Single Shot Rifles.* Brighton, CO: Gerald Kelver.

# Bibliography

Kendall, Paul G. (1933) *Polo Ponies.* New York: Derrydale Press.

Kennedy, Fred. (1952) *The Calgary Stampede Story.* Calgary, Canada: T. Edwards Thonger.

Kenney, Karen. (1982) "The Realm of Sports and the Athletic Woman, 1850–1900." In *Her Story in Sport: A Historical Anthology of Women in Sports,* edited by Reet Howell. West Point, NY: Leisure Press, 107–140.

Kerr, John. (1890) *History of Curling, Scotland's Ain' Game and Fifty Years of the Royal Caledonian Curling Club.* Edinburgh, UK: David Douglas.

———. (1904) *Curling in Canada and the United States, a Record of the Tour of the Scottish Team, 1902–1903, and the Game in the Dominion and the Republic.* Edinburgh, UK: George A. Morton.

Khalsa, Nanak Dev Singh. (1991) *Gatka: As Taught by Nanak Dev Singh Khalsa.*

Kidd, Bruce. (1995) "Toronto's Sky Dome: The World's Greatest Entertainment Centre." In *The Stadium and the City,* edited by John Bale and Olof Moen. Keele, UK: Keele University Press, 175–196.

———. (1995) "Worker Sport in the New World. The Canadian Story." In *The Story of Worker Sport,* edited by Arnd Krüger and James Riordan. Champaign, IL: Human Kinetics.

Killip, S., and R. Stennett. (1990) *Use of Performance Enhancing Substances by London Secondary School Students, Report 90-03.* London and Ontario, Canada: Board of Education for the City of London.

Kimberley, Earl of. (1936) *Polo.* Philadelphia: Lippincott.

King, Bill. (1982) *Rodeo Trails.* Laramie, WY: Jelm Mountain Press.

Kinsella, W. P. (1982) *Shoeless Joe.* New York: Ballantine Books.

Kirchoff, Paul. (1963) "The Warraw." *Bureau of American Ethnology Bulletin* 143, 3: 869–881.

Kirk, Geoffrey S. (1970) *Myth, Its Meaning and Function in Ancient and Other Cultures.* Berkeley and Los Angeles: University of California Press.

Kirkley, G., and J. Goodbody, eds. (1986) *The Manual of Weight-Training.* London: Stanley Paul.

Kirksmith, Tommie. (1991) *Ride Western Style: A Guide for Young Riders.* New York: Howell Book House.

Kirsch, George. (1989) *The Creation of American Team Sports: Baseball and Cricket, 1838–1872.* Urbana: University of Illinois Press.

Kiyota, Minoru, and Kinoshita Hideaki. (1990) *Japanese Martial Arts and American Sports: Cross-Cultural Perspectives on Means to Personal Growth.* Tokyo: Bunsei Press.

Klein, Alan. (1986) "Pumping Irony: Crisis and Contradiction in Bodybuilding." *Sociology of Sport Journal* 3, 2: 112–133.

———. (1991) *Sugarball: The American Game, The Dominican Dream.* New Haven, CT: Yale University Press.

———. (1993) *Little Big Men: Gender Construction and Bodybuilding Subculture.* Albany: State University of New York Press.

Klein, Jeff Z., and Karl-Eric Reif. (1987) *The Klein and Reif Hockey Compendium.* Rev. ed. Toronto, Canada: McClelland and Stewart.

Kleinman, S., ed. (1986) *Mind and Body: East Meets West.* Champaign, IL: Human Kinetics.

Klemola, H. (1963) *Tahkon latu. Lauri Pihkala eilen ja tänään* [Tahko's trail: Lauri Pihkala in the past and present]. 75-vuotispäivän juhlakirja. Helsinki, Finland: Otava.

Klimke, Reiner. *Basic Training of the Young Horse.* (1985) London: J. A. Allen.

Klopsteg, Paul E. (1934) *Turkish Archery and the Composite Bow.* Evanston, IL: Author (second edition in 1947).

Knauff, Thomas L. (1990) *Transition to Gliders.* Iceland: Prentsmidja Arna Valdemarssonar hf.

———. (1994) *Glider Basics from First Flight to Solo.* Iceland: Prentsmidja Arna Valdemarssonar hf.

Knox-Johnston, Robin. (1990) *History of Yachting.* Oxford, UK: Phaidon.

Knuttgen, Howard G., Qiwei Ma, and Zhonguan Wu, eds. (1990) *Sport in China.* Champaign, IL: Human Kinetics.

Koeberle, Brian E. (1990) *Legal Aspects of Personal Fitness Training.* Canton, OH: Professional Reports.

Koehler, Robert W. (1987) *Law, Sport Activity and Risk Management.* Champaign, IL: Stipes Publishing.

Kohlberg, L. (1981) *The Philosophy of Cognitive Moral Development.* New York: Harper & Row.

Kohn, A. (1986) *No Contest: The Case against Competition.* Boston: Houghton Mifflin.

Kolasky, John. (1979) *The Shattered Illusion.* Toronto, Canada: Peter Martin.

Koppett, Leonard. (1968) *24 Seconds To Shoot: An Informal History of the National Basketball Association.* New York: Macmillan.

———. (1981) *Sports Illusion, Sports Reality: A Reporter's View of Sports, Journalism and Society.* Boston: Houghton Mifflin.

———. (1994) *Sports Illusion, Sports Reality.* Urbana: University of Illinois Press.

Kotter, K. (1984) "Le bobsleigh et la federation internationale de bobsleigh et de tobogganing." *Message-Olympique* (June): 59–66.

Kovaks, Maureen Gallery, trans. (1989) *The Epic of Gilgamesh.* Stanford, CA: Stanford University Press.

Kozar, Andrew J. (1992) *The Sport Sculpture of R. Tait McKenzie.* Champaign, IL: Human Kinetics.

Krause, Richard. (1994) *Leisure in a Changing America: Multicultural Perspectives.* New York: Macmillan.

Kretchmar, S. (1975) "From Test to Contest: An Analysis of Two Kinds of Counterpoint in Sport." *Journal of the Philosophy of Sport* 2: 23–30.

———. (1985) "'Distancing': An Essay on Abstract

Thinking in Sport Performances." In *Sport Inside Out: Readings in Literature and Philosophy,* edited by D. Vanderwerken and S. Wertz. Fort Worth: Texas Christian University Press, 87–102.

———. (1994) *Practical Philosophy of Sport.* Champaign, IL: Human Kinetics.

Krieger, H. W. (1943) *Island Peoples of the Western Pacific: Micronesia and Melanesia.* Washington, DC: Smithsonian Institution.

Krieger, Pascal. (1989) *Jodo: The Way of the Stick.* Gland, Switzerland: Sopha Diffusion.

Kroll, Walter P. (1982) *Graduate Study and Research in Physical Education.* Champaign, IL: Human Kinetics.

Kronfeld, Robert. (n.d.) *Kronfeld on Gliding and Soaring.* London: John Hamilton.

Krout, John Allen. (1929) *Annals of American Sport.* Volume 15 of *The Pageant of America.* New Haven, CT: Yale University Press.

Krüger, Arnd. (1975) *Sport und Politik.* Hannover, Germany: Fackelträger Verlag.

———. (1985) "The Rise and Fall of the International Worker Sports Movement." In *Proceedings of the 11th HISPA Congress.* Glasgow, UK: Jordanhill College Press.

Krüger, Arnd, and James Riordan, eds. (1985) *Der Internationale Arbeitersport.* Cologne, Germany: Pahl-Rugenstein.

———. (1996) *The Story of Worker Sport.* Champaign, IL: Human Kinetics.

Krüger, Arnd, and John McClelland, eds. (1984) *Die Anfänge des Modernen Sports in der Renaissance.* London: Arena Publishers.

Kruger, Gundolf. (1990) "Sport in the Context of Non-European Cultural Tradition: The Examples of Hawaii." In *Ritual and Records: Sports Records and Quantification in Pre-Modern Societies,* edited by J. M. Carter and A. Krueger. New York: Greenwood Press.

Kruger, N. C. (1962) *Avicenna's Poem on Medicine.* Springfield, IL: Charles C. Thomas.

Kuhaulua, Jesse. (1973) *Takamiyama.* Tokyo: Kodansha International.

Kurup, K. K. N. (1973) *The Cult of Teyyam and Hero Worship in Kerala.* Indian Folklore Series No. 21. Calcutta, India: Indian Publications.

Kutzer, W. F. (1979) "The History of Olympic Weightlifting in the United States." Ph.D. dissertation, Brigham Young University, Provo, Utah.

Kydd, Rachael. (1979) *Long Distance Riding Explained.* New York: Arco.

Kyle, Donald. (1987) *Athletics in Ancient Athens.* Leiden, The Netherlands: E. J. Brill.

———. (1990) "Winning and Watching the Greek Pentathlon." *Journal of Sport History* 17: 291–305.

———. (1993) *Athletics in Ancient Athens.* Revised edition. Leiden, The Netherlands: E. J. Brill.

Kyle, Donald G., and Gary D. Starks, eds. (1990) *Essays on Sport History and Sport Mythology.* College Station: Texas A & M Press.

La Curne de Sainte Palaye, Jean B. (1759–1781) *Mémoires sur l'ancienne chevalerie.* Paris: Duchesne.

Labanowich, S. (1987) "The Physically Disabled in Sports." *Sports 'N Spokes* 12, 6: 33–42.

Laffaye, Horacio Alberto. (1989) *El polo internacional argentino.* Buenos Aires, Argentina: Privately printed.

———. (1995) *Diccionario de Polo.* Weston: Polo Research.

LaFrance, David G. (1995) "Labor, the State, and Professional Baseball in Mexico in the 1980s." *Journal of Sport History* 22, 2: 111–134.

Laget, Françoise, Serge Laget, and Jean-Paul Mazot. (1982) *Le grand livre du sport féminin.* Belville, France: F.M.T.

Laget, S. (1990) *La saga du Tour de France.* Paris: Gallimard.

Laitinen, E. (1983) *Pesäpallo: Kansallispeli 60 vuotta* [Pesäpallo: a national game in 60 years]. Saarijärvi, Saarijärven: Offset Ky.

Lake, Fred, and Hal Wright. (1974) *A Bibliography of Archery.* Manchester, UK: Manchester Museum.

LaMarca, Laura, ed. (1993– ) *Synchro USA.* Indianapolis, IN: United States Synchronized Swimming.

Lambranzi, Gregorio. (1716) *Neue und curieuse theatralische Tanz-schule.* Nuremberg, Germany: Wolrab English translation by D. de Moroda. Brooklyn, NY: Dance Horizons, 1966.

Lanfranchi, Pierre, ed. (1992) *Il calcio e il suo pubblico.* Naples, Italy: Edizioni Scientifiche Italiane.

Lansley, Keith L. (1969) "The Contributions of Play Activities to the Survival of Traditional Culture in Four Melanesian Societies." M.A. thesis, University of Alberta, Canada.

Lapchick, Richard E. (1975) *The Politics of Race and International Sport, The Case of South Africa.* Westport, CT: Greenwood Press.

———. (1986) *Fractured Focus: Sport as a Reflection of Society.* Lexington, MA: D. C. Heath.

Lapchick, Richard E., and J. B. Slaughter. (1989) *The Rules of the Game: Ethics in College Sports.* New York: Macmillan.

Laptad, Richard E. (1972) *A History of the Development of the United States Gymnastics Federation.* U.S. Gymnastics Federation.

Lardner, Ring. (1916) *You Know Me Al.* New York: George Doran.

Larner, G. E. (1910) *Larner's Text Book on Walking for Pleasure, Exercise, Sport.* London: Health and Strength.

Larson, James F., and Heung-Soo Park. (1993) *Global Television and the Seoul Olympics.* Boulder, CO: Westview Press.

Latham, J. D., and W. F. Paterson. (1970) *Saracen Archery.* London: Holland Press.

Lawrence, Elizabeth Atwood. (1982) *American Rodeo: An Anthropologist Looks at the Wild and the Tame.* Knoxville: University of Tennessee Press.

# Bibliography

Lear, J. (1982) *The Powerlifter's Manual.* Wakefield, UK: EP Publishing.

Lebroucher, H. (1910) *Manuel de la Boxe Française.* Paris: Libraire de Jules Tanull.

LeClerc, D. (1729) *Histoire de le medicine.* Amsterdam, The Netherlands: Van der Kloot.

LeCompte, Mary Lou. (1982) "The First American Rodeo Never Happened." *Journal of Sport History* 9 (Summer): 89–96 .

———. (1985) "Wild West Frontier Days, Roundups and Stampedes: Rodeo before There Was Rodeo." *Canadian Journal of History of Sport* 12 (December): 54–67.

———. (1993) *Cowgirls of the Rodeo: Pioneer Professional Athletes.* Urbana: University of Illinois Press.

———. (1994) "Hispanic Roots of American Rodeo." *Studies in Latin American Popular Culture* 13 (Spring): 1–19.

Lee, Hugh M. (1988) In *The Archaeology of the Olympics. The Olympics and Other Festivals in Antiquity,* edited by Wendy J. Raschke. Madison: University of Wisconsin Press, 110–118.

Lee, Mabel. (1983) *A History of Physical Education and Sports in the U.S.A.* New York: John Wiley and Sons.

Lee, Mabel, and Bennett, Bruce L. (1960) "This Is Our Heritage: 75 Years of the American Association for Health, Physical Education and Recreation." *Journal of Health, Physical Education and Recreation* 34 (4): 25–85.

Leech, Arthur B. (1875) *Irish Riflemen in America.* London: Edward Stanford.

Lefebvre, L. M., and M. W. Passer. (1974) "The Effects of Game Location and Importance of Aggression in Team Sport." *International Journal of Sport Psychology* 5: 102–110.

Lehenaff, Didier D. A. (1987) *Votre Sport le Triathlon.* Paris: Bertrand.

Lema, Bangela. (1989) "Sport in Zaire." In *Sport in Asia and Africa,* edited by Eric C. Wagner. Westport, CT: Greenwood.

Lenk, H. (1979) *Social Philosophy of Athletics.* Champaign, IL: Stipes.

Leonard, W. M. (1993) *A Sociological Perspective of Sport.* New York: Macmillan.

Lesser, Alexander. (1933) *The Pawnee Ghost Dance Hand Game: A Study of Cultural Change.* Columbia University Contributions to Anthropology 16. New York: Columbia University Press.

Lester, Gary. (1988) *The Story of Australian Rugby League.* Sydney, Australia: Lester Townsend.

LeUnes, A. D., and J. R. Nation. (1989) *Sport Psychology: An Introduction.* Chicago, IL: Nelson-Hall.

Levers de Miranda, Angel. (1962) *Ritos y juegos del toro.* Madrid: Taurus.

Levine, Peter. (1985) *A. G. Spalding and the Rise of Baseball: The Promise of American Sport.* New York: Oxford University Press.

———. (1992) *Ellis Island to Ebbets Field: Sport and the American Jewish Experience.* New York: Oxford University Press.

Levi-Strauss, Claude. (1963) "Tribes of the Right Bank of the Guapore River." *Bureau of American Ethnology Bulletin* 143, 3: 371–379.

Lewis, J. Lowell. (1992) *Ring of Liberation: A Deceptive Discourse in Brazilian Capoeria.* Chicago: University of Chicago Press.

Lewis, R. M. (1991) "American Croquet in the 1860s: Playing the Game and Winning." *Journal of Sport History* 18, 3 (Winter): 365–386.

Leyenaar, Ted J. (1978) *Ulama: The Perpetuation in Mexico of the Pre-Spanish Ball Game Ullamaliztli.* Translated  by Inez Seeger. Leiden, The Netherlands: Brill.

Leyenaar, Ted J., and Lee A. Parsons. (1988) *Ulama: The Ballgame of the Mayas and Aztecs.* Leiden, The Netherlands: Spruyt, Van Mantgem & De Does.

Liang, T. T. (1977) *T'ai Chi Ch'uan for Health and Self Defense: Philosophy and Practice.* New York: Vintage Books.

Ligget, P. (1988) *The Tour de France.* London: Harrap.

———. (1992) *The Complete Book of Performance Cycling.* London: Collins Willow.

Lipkind, William. (1963) "The Caraja." *Bureau of American Ethnology Bulletin* 143, 3: 179–191.

Lipski, S., and G. McBoyle (1991) "The Impact of Global Warming on Downhill Skiing in Michigan." *East Lakes Geographer* 26: 37–51.

Littauer, M. A., and J. H. Crouwel. (1979) *Wheeled Vehicles and Ridden Animals in the Ancient Near East.* Leiden, The Netherlands: E. J. Brill.

———. (1985) *Chariots and Related Equipment of the Tomb of Tut'ankhamun.* Oxford: Griffith Institute.

Little, K. M. (1956) *Polo in New Zealand.* Wellington, New Zealand: Whitcomb and Tombs.

Littre, M. P. E. (1819–1861) *Oeuvres completes d'Hippocrate.* Paris: Bailliere.

Lloyd, Janis M. (1986) *Skiing into History 1924-1984.* Toorak, Australia: Ski Club of Victoria.

Logan, G. A., and Wallis, E. L. (1960) "Recent Findings in Learning and Performance." Paper presented at the southern section meeting, California Association for Health, Physical Education and Recreation, Pasadena.

Loken, Newton C., and Robert J. Willoughby. (1977) *Complete Book of Gymnastics.* 3d ed. Englewood Cliffs, NJ: Prentice-Hall.

Longrigg, Roger. (1972) *The History of Horse Racing.* New York: Stein and Day.

———. (1975) *The Turf: Three Centuries of Horse Racing.* London: Eyre Methuen.

———. (1977) *The English Squire and His Sport.* New York: St. Martin's Press.

Lorenz, Konrad. (1966) *On Aggression.* New York: Harcourt Brace Jovanovich.

Lovesey, Peter, and Tom McNab. (1969) *The Guide to British*

*Track and Field Literature 1275–1968.* London: Athletics Arena.

Lowden, John. (1992) *Silent Wings at War.* Washington, DC: Smithsonian Institution Press.

Lowerson, John. (1993) *Sport and the English Middle Classes, 1870–1914.* Manchester, UK: Manchester University Press.

Lowie, Robert. (1963) "The Northwestern and Central Ge." *Bureau of American Ethnology Bulletin* 143, 1: 477–417.

———. (1963) "Eastern Brazil: An Introduction." *Bureau of American Ethnology Bulletin* 143, 1: 381–400.

Lowry, Dave. (1986) *Bokken: Art of the Japanese Sword.* Burbank, CA: Ohara Publications.

Loy, John W. (1968) "The Nature of Sport: A Definitional Effort." *Quest* 10: 1–15.

———. (1969) "Game Forms, Social Structure, and Anomie." In *New Perspectives of Man in Action*, edited by R. C. Brown and B. J. Cratty. Englewood Cliffs, NJ: Prentice-Hall, 181–199.

———. (1992) "The Dark Side of Agon: Men in Tribal Groups and the Phenomenon of Gang Rape." Presidential address, annual meeting of the North American Society for the Sociology of Sport, Toledo, OH, November.

Loy, John W., and Garry Chick. (1993) "A Cross-Cultural Test of the Cultural Spillover Theory of Rape." Paper presented at the annual meeting of the Society for Cross-Cultural Research, Washington, DC.

Loy, John W., Barry D. McPherson, and Gerald Kenyon. (1978) *Sport and Social Systems.* Reading, MA: Addison-Wesley.

Lucas, John A. (1968) "Pedestrianism and the Struggle for the Sir John Astley Belt, 1878–1879." *Research Quarterly* 39, 3 (October): 588.

———. (1980) *The Modern Olympic Games.* New York: A. S. Barnes.

———. (1992) *Future of the Olympic Games.* Champaign, IL: Human Kinetics.

Lucas, John A., and R. A. Smith. (1978) *Saga of American Sport.* Philadelphia: Lea and Febiger.

Ludwig, Ruth. (1995) *Balloon Digest.* Indianola, IA: Balloon Federation of America

Lueras, Leonard. (1984) *Surfing, the Ultimate Pleasure.* New York: Workman Publishing.

Lugs, Jaroslav. (1968) *A History of Shooting.* Middlesex, UK: Spring Books.

Lukowich, Ed, Eigil Ramsfjell, and Bud Sumerville. (1990) *The Joy of Curling: A Celebration.* Toronto, Canada: McGraw-Hill Ryerson.

Lumpkin, A., S. Stoll, and J. Beller. (1995) *Sport Ethics: Applications for Fair Play.* St. Louis, MO: Mosby.

Lund, Thomas A. (1980) *American Wildlife Law.* Berkeley: University of California Press.

Lundholm, Jean K., and Mary Jo Ruggieri. (1976) *Introduction to Synchronized Swimming.* Minneapolis, MN: Burgess Publishing.

Lunn, Arnold. (1927) *A History of Skiing.* London: Oxford University Press.

Luther, Carl J. (1926) "Geschichte des Schnee- und Eissports." In *Geschichte des Sports aller Volker und Zeiten*, edited by G. A. E. Bogeng. Leipzig, Germany: Seeman, 2: 497–557.

MacAloon, John J. (1981) *This Great Symbol: Pierre de Coubertin and the Origins of the Modern Olympic Games.* Chicago: University of Chicago Press.

*The Maccabi: A Photographic History. On the Occasion of the 13th Maccabiah — A Photographic Exhibition of the 12 Maccabiot 1932–1985.* (n.d.) Ramat Gan, Israel: Pierre Gildesgame Maccabi Sports Museum.

Macdonald, Janet. (1993) *Teaching Side-saddle.* London: J. A. Allen.

Macdonald, Janet, and Valerie Francis. (1979) *Riding Side-saddle.* London: Pelham Books.

MacGregor, Barrie. (1977) *Volleyball.* Brighton, Sussex: EP Publishing.

McGregor, Ian, and Joseph MacDonald. (1990) *Risk Management Manual for Sport and Recreational Organizations.* Corvallis, OR: NIRSA.

Mackey, Cleo. (1979) *The Cowboy and Rodeo Evolution.* Dallas, TX: Cleo Mackey Publishing.

Mackey, Helen T., and Ann M. Mackey. (1964) *Women's Team Sports Officiating.* New York: Ronald Press.

Maclean, J. C., and P. Chelladurai. (1994) "Dimensions of Coaching Performance: Development of a Scale." *Journal of Sport Management* 9, 2 (May): 194–207.

Maclennan, H. D. (1993) *Shinty: 100 Years of the Camanachd Association.* Nairn, UK: Balnain Books.

Magriel, Paul, ed. (1951) *Memoirs of the Life of Daniel Mendoza.* London: Batsford.

Maguire, Joseph. (1992) "Towards a Sociological Theory of Sport and the Emotions." In *Sport and Leisure in the Civilizing Process*, edited by E. Dunning and C. Rojek. Toronto, Canada: University of Toronto Press.

Main, Jim. (1974) *Australian Rules Football.* Melbourne, Australia: Lansdowne Press.

Malcolmson, Robert W. (1973) *Popular Recreations in English Society 1700–1850.* Cambridge: Cambridge University Press.

Maliszewski, Michael. (1996) *Spiritual Dimensions of the Martial Arts.* Tokyo: Charles E. Tuttle.

Mallon, Bill. (1988) *The Olympic Record Book.* New York: Garland Publishing Company.

Mallon, Bill, and Ian Buchanan. (1984) *Quest for Gold: The Encyclopedia of American Olympians.* Champaign, IL: Leisure Press.

Mallwitz, Alfred. (1988) In *The Archaeology of the Olympics. The Olympics and Other Festivals in Antiquity*, edited by

Wendy J. Raschke. Madison: University of Wisconsin Press, 79–109.

Maloy, Bernard P. (1988) *Law in Sport—Liability Cases in Management and Administration*. Dubuque, IA: Brown/Benchmark.

Mandel, F. (1925) *Chirurgie der Sportunfalle*. Berlin, Germany: Urban and Schwarzenberg.

Mandell, Richard D. (1971) *The Nazi Olympics*. New York: Macmillan.

———. (1976) *The First Modern Olympics*. Berkeley: University of California Press.

———. (1976) "The Invention of the Sports Record." *Stadion* 2, 2: 250–264.

———. (1984) *Sport, A Cultural History*. New York: Columbia University Press.

———. (1988) *Sport*. New York: Columbia University Press.

Mandle, W. F. (1977) "The IRB and the Beginnings of the Gaelic Athletic Association." *Irish Historical Studies* 20 (September): 418–438.

———. (1987) *The Gaelic Athletic Association and Irish Nationalist Politics 1884–1924*. London: Croom Helm.

Mangan, J. A. (1981) *Athleticism in the Victorian and Edwardian Public School*. Cambridge: Cambridge University Press.

———. (1986) *The Games Ethic and Imperialism*. New York: Viking.

Mangan, J. A., ed. (1992) *The Cultural Bond: Sport, Empire and Society*. London: Frank Cass.

———. (1995) *Tribal Identities: Nationalism, Europe, Sport*. London: Frank Cass.

Mangan, J. A., and James Walvin, eds. (1987) *Manliness and Morality: Middle-Class Masculinity in Britain and America, 1800–1940*. Manchester, UK: Manchester University Press.

Mangan, John Anthony, and Roberta J. Park, eds. (1987) *From "Fair Sex" to Feminism: Sport and the Socialization of Women in the Industrial and Post-Industrial Eras*. London: Frank Cass.

Manley, Michael A. (1988) *History of West Indian Cricket*. London: Deutsch.

March, Harry A. (1934) *Pro Football: Its "Ups" and "Downs."* Albany, NY: J. B. Lyon.

Marchaj, C. A. (1988) "Land and Hard-water Sailing Craft." In *Aero-Hydrodynamics of Sailing*. Camden, ME: International Marine Publishing.

Marchiano, Armando. (1983) *Bocce, che passione!* Padua, Italy: Casa Editrice MEB.

Marples, M. (1954) *A History of Football*. London: Secker and Warburg.

Marsh, Peter. (1982) "Social Order on the British Soccer Terraces." *International Social Science Journal* 34: 247–256.

Marshall, Julian. (1878) *Annals of Tennis*. London: "The Field Office"; reprint. Baltimore, MD: Racquet Sports Information & Service, 1973.

Martell, William A. (1973) *Greco-Roman Wrestling*. Champaign, IL: Human Kinetics.

Martens, R. (1987) *Coaches Guide to Sport Psychology*. Champaign, IL: Human Kinetics.

———. (1991) *Successful Coaching*. Champaign, IL: Leisure Press.

Martens, R., R. S. Vealey, and D. Burton. (1990) *Competitive Anxiety in Sport*. Champaign, IL: Human Kinetics.

Martin, Arthur E. (1990) *Life in the Slow Lane*. Portsmouth, NH: Peter E. Randall.

Martin, David E., and Roger W. H. Gynn. (1979) *The Marathon Footrace: Performers and Performances*. Springfield, IL: Charles C. Thomas.

Martin, Joan L., Ruth E. Tandy, and Charlene Agne-Traub. (1994) *Bowling*. Madison, WI: William C. Brown and Benchmark.

Martin, Lawrence. (1990) *The Red Machine: The Soviet Quest To Dominate Canada's Game*. Toronto: Doubleday Canada.

Martins, Ernst. (1989) *80 Years of I.I.H.F./I.E.H.V.* Munich: International Ice Hockey Federation.

Masayoshi, Shigeru Nakajima. (1983) *Bugei Ju-Happan: The Spirit Of Samurai*. Tokyo: G.O. Ltd.

Mason, Bernard. (1974) *Boomerangs: How To Make and Throw Them*. New York: Dover.

Mason, Tony. (1980) *Association Football and English Society, 1863–1915*. Brighton, UK: Harvester.

———. (1995) *Passion of the People: Football in South America*. London: Verso.

Mason, Tony, ed. (1989) *Sport in Britain: A Social History*. Cambridge: Cambridge University Press.

Massengale, John D., and Swanson, Richard A. eds. (In press). *History of Exercise Science and Sport*. Champaign, IL: Human Kinetics.

Mastro, J. (1985) "Psychological Characteristics of Elite Male Visually Impaired and Sighted Athletes." Ph.D. dissertation, Texas Woman's University.

Mathews, Peter, ed. (1986) *The Official Commonwealth Games Book*. Preston, UK: Opax Publishing and the Commonwealth Games Consortium.

Mathisen, James. (1990) "Reviving 'Muscular Christianity': Gil Dodds and the Institutionalization of Sport Evangelism." *Sociological Focus* 23 (August): 233–329.

Matthews, P. (1982) *The Guinness Book of Athletics—Facts and Feats*. Fakenham, UK: Fakenham Press.

———. (1996) *Athletics 1995: The International Track and Field Annual*. Surbiton, UK: n.p.

Matthews, P., ed. (1993) *The Guinness Book of Records—1994*. New York: Facts On File.

Matthiessen, Peter. (1950) *Wildlife in America*. New York: Viking.

Matz, David. (1991) *Greek and Roman Sport. A Dictionary of Athletes and Events from the Eighth Century B.C. to the Third Century A.D.* Jefferson, NC: McFarland.

# Bibliography

Maximilian I. (1875) *The Triumph of the Emperor Maximilian I.* Edited by Alfred Aspland. London: Holbein Society.

Maxwell, Doug, et al. (1980) *The First Fifty. A Nostalgic Look at the Brier.* Toronto, Canada: Maxcurl Publications.

Mayhew, Bob, and John Birdsall. (1990) *The Art of Western Riding.* New York: Howell Book House.

Maynard, David N. (1994) "The Divergent Evolution of Competitive Cycling in the United States and Europe." In *The Masks of Play,* edited by Brian Sutton-Smith and Diana Kelly-Byrne. New York: Leisure Press, 78–87.

Maynard, Russell. (1986) *Tanto: Japanese Knives and Knife Fighting.* Burbank, CA: Unique Publications.

Mazzeo, K. S., and L. M. Mangili. (1993) *Fitness through Aerobics and Step Training.* Englewood, CO: Morton Publishing.

McCagy, Charles, and Arthur Neal. (1974) "The Fraternity of Cockfighters: Ethical Embellishments of an Illegal Sport." *Journal of Popular Culture* 8: 557–569.

McCarthy, F. D. (1958) "String Figures of Australia." *Australian Museum Magazine* 12, 8.

McConnell, C. D. (1996) "Sport Management and Change." Master of Business Studies thesis, Massey University, Albany Campus, Auckland, NZ.

McConnell, Harold. (1984) "Recruiting Patterns of Midwestern Major College Football." *Geographical Perspectives* 53: 27–43.

McConnell, R. C. (1995) *Sport Leadership—More Than Sport Management.* Albany, Auckland, NZ: Massey University.

———. (1996) "Sport Team Leadership." Ph.D. dissertation, Massey University, Albany, Auckland, NZ.

McCormack, G. (1991) "The Price of Affluence: The Political Economy of Japanese Leisure." *New Left Review* 188: 121–134.

McCormick, P. J. (1943, 1944) "Two Medieval Catholic Educators." *Catholic University Bulletin* 12, 13.

McCrone, Kathleen. (1988) *Playing the Game: Sport and the Physical Emancipation of English Women, 1870–1914.* Lexington: University Press of Kentucky and London: Routledge.

McDonald, John. (1993) *The First 100: A Century of Swimming in Victoria.* Melbourne: Swimming Victoria.

McElligott, Tom J. (1984) *The Story of Handball: The Game, the Players, the History.* Dublin, Ireland: Wolfhound Press.

McFarlane, Brian. (1994) *Proud Past: Bright Future: One Hundred Years of Canadian Women's Hockey.* Toronto, Canada: Stoddart Publishing.

McGehee, R. V. (1994) "Los Juegos de las Américas: Four Inter-American Multisport Competitions." In *Sport in the Global Village,* edited by Ralph C. Wilcox. Morgantown, WV: Fitness Information Technology.

McGinnis, Vera. (1974) *Rodeo Road: My Life as a Pioneer Cowgirl.* New York: Hastings House.

McGregor, Craig. (1968) *Profile of Australia.* Chicago, IL: Henry Regnery.

McGurn, James. (1987) *On Your Bicycle.* London: John Murray.

McIntosh, Peter C. (1952, 1979) *Physical Education in England since 1800.* London: Bell & Hyman.

———. (1963) *Sport in Society.* London: C. A. Watts.

———. (1979) *Fair Play: Ethics in Sport and Education.* London: Heinemann.

McIntyre, W. David. (1977) *The Commonwealth of Nations: Origins and Impact, 1869–1971.* Minneapolis: University of Minnesota Press.

McKee, S. (1994) *Coach.* Mechanicsburg, PA: Stackpole Books.

McKendrick, Neil, John Brewer, and J. H. Plumb. (1982) *The Birth of a Consumer Society: The Commercialization of Eighteenth-Century England.* Bloomington: Indiana University Press.

McKenzie, R. T. (1909) *Exercise in Education and Medicine.* Philadelphia: W. B. Saunders.

McLish, Rachel. (1984) *Flex Appeal.* New York: Warner Books.

McNally, Tom. (1993) *The Complete Book of Fly Fishing.* 2d ed. Camden, ME: Ragged Mountain Press.

McNamee, Graham, with Robert G. Anderson. (1926) *You're On the Air.* New York: Harper and Brothers.

McPhee, Hilary, and Brian Stoddart. (1995) *Liberation Cricket: West Indies Cricket Culture.* Manchester, UK: Manchester University Press.

McPherson, Barry D., James E. Curtis, and John W. Loy. (1989) *The Social Significance of Sport: An Introduction to the Sociology of Sport.* Champaign, IL: Human Kinetics.

McQuillen, John A., Jr. (1975) "American Military Gliders in World War II in Europe." Ph.D. dissertation, St. Louis University.

McWhirter, N. (1979) *Guinness Book of Women's Records.* New York: Sterling Press.

McWhirter, N., and R. McWhirter. (1975) *Guinness Book of Records.* London: Guinness Superlatives.

———. (1995) *Guinness Book of Records.* Enfield, Middlesex: Guinness Superlatives.

Mead, Margaret, ed. (1937) *Cooperation and Competition among Primitive Peoples.* New York: McGraw-Hill.

Meanwell, W. E., and K. K. Rockne. (1931) *Training, Conditioning and the Care of Athletes.* Madison, WI: W. E. Meanwell.

Meek, C. K. (1950) *Tribal Studies in Northern Nigeria.* New York: Humanities Press.

Mehl, Erwin. (1964) *Grundriss der Weltgeschichte des Schifahrens.* Stuttgart, Germany: Hoffmann.

Meier, K. (1975) "Cartesian and Phenomenological Anthropology: The Radial Shift and Its Meaning for Sport." *Journal of the Philosophy of Sport* 2: 51–73.

———. (1980) "An Affair of Flutes: An Appreciation of Play." *Journal of the Philosophy of Sport* 7: 24–45.

———. (1988) "Embodiment, Sport, and Meaning." In

*Philosophic Inquiry in Sport*, edited by W. Morgan and K. Meier. Champaign, IL: Human Kinetics, 93–101.

Meisel, Willy. (1956) *Soccer Revolution*. London: Phoenix.

Meisels, Penina. (1992) *Polo*. San Francisco, CA: Collins.

Mendenhall, Thomas C. (1980) *Highlights from 150 Years of American Rowing*. Indianapolis, IN: U.S. Rowing.

———. (1981) *A Short History of American Rowing*. Cambridge, MA: Charles River Press.

Mendez, C. *The Book of Bodily Exercise*. (1660 [1553]) Translated by F. Guerra. (1960) New Haven, CT: Elizabeth Licht.

Menestrier, Claude François. (1669) *Traité des tournois, joustes, carrousels et autres spectacles publiques*. Lyon: Muguet.

———. (1683) *De la chevalerie ancienne et moderne*. Paris: R. J. B. de la Caille.

Menke, F. G. (1950) *The All Sports Record Book*. New York: A. S. Barnes.

———. (1960) *The Encyclopedia of Sports*. 2d rev. ed. New York: A. S. Barnes.

———. (1975) *The Encyclopedia of Sport*. 5th ed. South Brunswick, NJ, and New York: A. S. Barnes.

Mentzer, M., and A. Friedberg. (1982) *Mike Mentzer's Complete Book of Weight Training*. New York: William Morrow.

Merchant, Larry. (1973) *The National Football League Lottery*. New York: Holt, Rinehart, and Winston.

Mercuriale, G. *De arte gymnastica libri sex*. (1672 [1569]) Edited by Andrea Frisii. Amsterdam, The Netherlands: Juntarum.

Mercurialis, Hieronymus. (1569) *Artis gymnasticae libri sex*. Venice, Italy: Giunti.

Messenger, Christian. (1981) *Sport and the Spirit of Play in American Fiction: Hawthorne to Faulkner*. New York: Columbia University Press.

———. (1990) *Sport and the Spirit of Play in Contemporary American Fiction*. New York: Columbia University Press.

Messner, M. A. (1992) *Power at Play: Sports and the Problem of Masculinity*. Boston: Beacon Press.

———. (1993) "Theorizing Gendered Bodies: Beyond the Subject/Object Dichotomy." In *Exercising Power: The Making and Remaking of the Body*, edited by Cheryl Cole, John Loy, and Michael Messner. Albany: State University of New York Press.

Messner, M. A., and D. F. Sabo. (1994) *Sex, Violence and Power in Sports: Rethinking Masculinity*. Freedom, CA: Crossing Press.

Messner, M. A., and D. F. Sabo, eds. (1990) *Sport, Men, and the Gender Order: Critical Feminist Perspectives*. Champaign, IL: Human Kinetics.

Metcalfe, Alan. (1987) *Canada Learns To Play: The Emergence of Organized Sport, 1807–1914*. Toronto, Canada: McClelland and Stewart.

Metheny, Eleanor. (1965) *Connotations of Movement in Sport and Dance*. Dubuque, IA: Brown.

———. (1968) *Movement and Meaning*. New York: McGraw-Hill.

———. (1972) "The Symbolic Power of Sport." In *Sport and the Body: A Philosophical Symposium*, edited by E. Gerber. Philadelphia: Lea and Febiger, 221–226.

Metraux, Alfred. (1963) "Ethnography of the Chaco." *Bureau of American Ethnology Bulletin* 143, 1: 197–370.

———. (1963) "The Paressi." *Bureau of American Ethnology Bulletin* 143, 3: 349–360.

———. (1963) "Tribes of Eastern Bolivia and the Madeira Headwaters." *Bureau of American Ethnology Bulletin* 143, 3: 381–454.

———. (1963) "Tribes of the Eastern Slopes of the Bolivian Andes." *Bureau of American Ethnology Bulletin* 143, 3: 465–506.

———. (1963) "Tribes of the Jurua-Purus Basins." *Bureau of American Ethnology Bulletin* 143, 3: 657–686.

Metraux, Alfred, and Paul Kirchoff. (1963) "The Northeastern Extension of Andean Culture." *Bureau of American Ethnology Bulletin* 143, 4: 349–368.

Mewshaw, Michael. (1993) *Ladies of the Court: Grace and Disgrace on the Women's Tennis Tour*. New York: Crown Publishers.

Meyer, Robert G. (1984) *The Complete Book of Softball: The Loonies Guide to Playing and Enjoying the Game*. New York: Leisure Press.

Meyrick, Samuel Rush. (1824) *A Critical Inquiry into Antient Armour*. London: R. Jennings.

Mezo, Ferenc. (1956) *The Modern Olympic Games*. Budapest, Hungary: Pannonia Press.

Michaelis, Hans-Thorald. (1985) *Schützengilden*. Munich: Keyser.

Michaud, Roland, and Sabrina Michaud. (1988) *Horsemen of Afghanistan*. London: Thames and Hudson.

Michener, James A. (1976) *Sport in America*. New York: Random House.

Middlehurst, Tony. (1990 [1977]) *The Iron Redskin*. n.p.: Sparkford, Foulies.

Mifune, Kyuzo (1961) *Canon of Judo: Principle and Technique*. Tokyo: Seibundo-Shinkosha.

Miles, Eustace. (1901) *The Game of Squash*. New York: E. P. Dutton.

Miles, Henry Downes. (1906) *Pugilistica*. 3 vols. Edinburgh, UK: John Grant.

Miles, Richard. (1968) *The Game of Table Tennis*. Philadelphia: J. B. Lippincott.

Miller, David LeRoy. (1970) *Gods and Games: Toward a Theology of Play*. New York: World.

Miller, E. D. (1928) *Modern Polo*. London: Hurst and Blackett.

Miller, James Edward. (1990) *The Baseball Business: Pennants and Profits in Baltimore*. Chapel Hill: University of North Carolina Press.

Miller, Richard. (1967) *Without Visible Means of Support*. Los Angeles: Parker.

# Bibliography

Miller, Stephen G. (1991) *Arete, Ancient Writers, Papyri and Inscriptions on the History and Ideals of Greek Athletics and Games.* 2d, expanded edition. Los Angeles: University of California Press.

Milner, Mordaunt. (1990) *The Godolphin Arabian.* London: J. A. Allen.

Miracle, Andrew W., and C. Roger Rees. (1994) *Lessons of the Locker Room: The Myth of School Sports.* Amherst, NY: Prometheus Books.

Miroy, Neville. (1986) *The History of Hockey.* Laleham on Thames, UK: Lifeline.

Mishkind, Marc E., et al. (1987) "The Embodiment of Masculinity: Cultural, Psychological and Behavioral Dimensions." In *Changing Men: New Directions in Research on Men and Masculinity,* edited by Michael S. Kimmel. Newbury Park, CA: Sage Publications, 37–52.

Mitani, Y. (1986) *Muso Jikiden Eishin Ryu.* Tokyo: Kendo Nihon.

Mitchell, D. (1967) *Ancient Sports of Hawaii.* Honolulu, HI: Bishop Museum.

Mitchell, Timothy. (1991) *Blood Sport. A Social History of Spanish Bullfighting.* Philadelphia and London: University of Pennsylvania Press.

Mitchell, W. O. (1993) *The Black Bonspiel of Willie MacCrimmon.* Toronto, Canada: McClelland and Stewart.

Mizerak, Steve, with Michael E. Panozzo. (1990) *Steve Mizerak's Complete Book of Pool.* Chicago: Contemporary Books.

Moller, J. (1990–1991) *Gamle idraetslege i Danmark.* Vols. 1–4. Gerlev, Denmark: Idraetsforsk.

Moncreiffe, I. (1954) *The Scottish Annual and Book of the Braemar Gathering.* Arbroath, UK: Herald Press.

Money, Keith, and Curry, John. (1978) *John Curry.* New York: Alfred A. Knopf.

Monnazzi, G. (1982) "Paraplegics and Sports: A Psychological Survey." *International Journal of Sports Psychology* 13: 85–95.

Monsaas, Judith A. (1985) "Learning To Be a World-Class Tennis Player." In *Developing Talent in Young People,* edited by Benjamin S. Bloom. New York: Ballantine Books.

Montagu, Ivor. (1936) *Table Tennis.* London: Sir Isaac Pitman and Sons.

Montesinos, Enrique, and Sigfredo Barros. (1984) *Centroamericanos y del Caribe: Los más antiguos juegos deportivos regionales del mundo.* Havana, Cuba: Editorial Científico-Técnica.

Moon, Y., and D. Shin. (1990) "Health Risks to Golfers from Pesticide Use on Golf Courses in Korea." In *Science and Golf,* edited by A. Cochran. London: Spon, 358–363.

Mooney, James. (1890) "Cherokee Ball Play." *American Anthropologist* 3: 105–132.

Moore, Katharine Elizabeth. (1986) "The Concept of British Empire Games: An Analysis of Its Origin and Evolution from 1891 to 1930." Ph.D. dissertation, University of Queensland, Australia.

———. (1989) " 'The Warmth of Comradeship': The First British Empire Games and Imperial Solidarity," *International Journal of the History of Sport* 6, 2 (September): 242–251.

Moorhouse, Geoffrey. (1983) *Lord's.* London: Hodder and Stoughton.

———. (1989) *At the George.* London: Hodder.

Moorhouse, H. B. (1987) "Scotland against England: Football and Popular Culture." *International Journal of the History of Sport* (4 September).

Moreno, Palos C. (1992) *Juegos y deportes tradicionales en España.* Madrid: Consejo Superior de Deportes.

Morgan, Paul, and Helene Morgan. (1992) *The Ultimate Kite Book.* New York and London: Simon and Schuster and Dorling Kindersley.

Morgan, W. (1982) "Play, Utopia, and Dystopia: Prologue to a Ludic Theory of the State." *Journal of the Philosophy of Sport* 9: 30–42.

Morgan, William J. and Klaus V. Meier, eds. (1988) *Philosophic Inquiry in Sport.* Champaign, IL: Human Kinetics.

———. (1995) *Philosophic Inquiry in Sport.* 2d ed. Champaign, IL: Human Kinetics.

Moriarty, Dick, Mary Moriarty, Marge Holman, and Ray Brown. (1994) *Canadian/American Sports, Fitness and the Law.* Toronto, Ontario: Canadian Scholars' Press.

Moriarty, P., with C. Sparks. (1959) *Springboard Diving.* New York: Ronald Press.

Morris, George. (1990) *Hunter Seat Equitation.* New York: Doubleday.

Morrison, A. (1995) *The Impossible Art of Golf: An Anthology of Golf Writing.* New York: Oxford University Press.

Morrow, Don. (1989) "Lacrosse as the National Game." In *A Concise History of Sport in Canada,* edited by D. Morrow et al. Toronto, Canada: Oxford University Press, 45–68.

———. (1992) "The Institutionalization of Sport: A Case Study of Canadian Lacrosse, 1844–1914." *International Journal of the History of Sport* 9, 2: 236–251.

Mortimer, Roger. (1971) *The Encyclopaedia of Flat Racing.* London: Richard Hall.

Morton, Gerald W., and George M. O'Brien. (1985) *Wrestling to Rasslin: Ancient Sport to American Spectacle.* Bowling Green, KY: Bowling Green University Popular Press.

Mosher, M. (1979) "The Team Captain." *Volleyball Technical Journal* 4, 3: 7–8.

Mosher, S. D. (1991) "Fielding Our Dreams: Rounding Third in Dyersville." *Sociology of Sport Journal* 8, 3 (September): 272–280.

Mossiman, T. (1985) "Geo-Ecological Impacts of Ski-Piste Construction in the Swiss Alps." *Applied Geography* 5: 29–38.

Motolin'a (Fray Toribio de Benavente). (1970) *Memoriales e historia de los Indios de la Nueva Espa–a: Estudio preliminar por Fidel de Lejarza.* Madrid, Spain: Ediciones Atlas.

Mott, Frank Luther. (1962) *American Journalism: A History 1690–1960.* 3d ed. New York: Macmillan.

Mott, Morris, and John Allardyce. (1989) *Curling Capital: Winnipeg and the Roarin' Game, 1876 to 1988.* Winnipeg, Canada: University of Manitoba Press.

Moustard, René. (1983) *Le Sport Populaire.* Paris: Le sport en plein air.

Mrozek, Donald. (1983) *Sport and American Mentality, 1880–1910.* Knoxville: University of Tennessee Press.

Mujumdar, D. C. (1950) *Encyclopedia of Indian Physical Culture.* Baroda, India: Good Companions.

Mullan, Michael. (1995) "Opposition, Social Closure and Sport: The Gaelic Athletic Association in the 19th Century." *Sociology of Sport Journal* 12: 268–289.

Muller, E. A., and W. Rohmert. (1963) *Die Geschwindigkeit der Muskelkraft Zunahme bei Isometrischen Training.*

Mullin, Bernard, Steve Hardy, and William Sutton. (1993) *Sport Marketing.* Champaign, IL: Human Kinetics .

Mummery, A. F. (1895) *My Climbs in the Alps and Caucasus.* London: Fisher Unwin.

Munson-Williams-Proctor Institute. (1980) *The Olympics in Art: An Exhibition of Works of Art Related to Olympic Sports.* Utica, NY: Munson-Williams-Proctor Institute.

Murdock, George P. (1967) *Ethnographic Atlas.* Pittsburgh, PA: University of Pittsburgh Press.

Murphy, S. M. (1995) *Sport Psychology Interventions.* Champaign, IL: Human Kinetics.

Murray, Bill. (1994) *Football: A History of the World Game.* London: Scolar Press.

Murray, Mimi. (1979) *Women's Gymnastics: Coach, Participant, Spectator.* Boston: Allyn and Bacon.

Murray, W. H. (1981) *The Curling Companion.* Glasgow: Richard Drew Publishing.

Murray, William. (1987) "The French Workers' Sports Movement." *International Journal of the History of Sport* 4.

Museler, Wilhelm. *Riding Logic.* (1937) London: Methuen.

Myzk, William. (1987) *The History and Origins of the Virginia Gold Cup.* The Plains, VA: Piedmont Press.

Nabokov, Paul. (1981) *Indian Running.* Santa Fe, NM: Ancient City Press.

Naismith, James. (1941) *Basketball: Its Origin and Development.* New York: Association Press.

Naison, Mark. (1979) "Lefties and Righties: The Communist Party and Sports during the Great Depression." *Radical America* 13, 4.

Nafziger, James A. R. (1988) *International Sports Law.* Irvington, NY: Transnational Publishers.

Nalda, Jose Santos. (1986) *Iaido—Todas Las Bases y Los Katas Exigidos Para Cinto Negro.* Barcelona: Editorial APas.

Nansen, Fridtjof. (1890) *Paa Ski over Gronland; en Skildring af den Norske Gronlands-Ekspedition 1888–1889.* Oslo, Norway: Aschehoug.

Narayan, R. K. (1972) *The Ramayana.* Harmondsworth, UK, and New York: Penguin Books.

Nasaw, David. (1985) *Children of the City: At Work and at Play.* Garden City, NY: Doubleday.

Nash, J., ed. (1931) *Interpretations of Physical Education: Mind-Body Relationships.* New York: Barnes.

Nash, Roderick. (1989) *The Rights of Nature: A History of Environmental Ethics.* Madison: University of Wisconsin Press.

National Aeronautic Association. (1995) *World and United States Aviation and Space Records.* Arlington, VA: National Aeronautic Association.

National Museum of Roller Skating. (1983) *First Fifty Years: American Roller Skates 1860–1910.* Lincoln, NE: National Museum of Roller Skating.

National Rifle Association Staff. (1978) "Silhouette Shooting Comes of Age." *American Rifleman* (May): 35–40.

National Sporting Clays Association. (1965) *Sporting Clays.* Houston, TX: NSSA / NSCA.

Nattrass, Susan M. (1974) "The Development of International Clay Pigeon Shooting." M.A. thesis, University of Alberta, Edmonton.

Nauright, J., and T. J. Chandler, eds. (1996) *Making Men: Rugby and Masculine Identity.* London: Frank Cass.

Neale, Denis. (1970) *Table Tennis: The Way to the Top.* London: Arthur Barker.

Neft, David S., and Richard M. Cohen. (1991) *The Sports Encyclopedia: Pro Basketball.* New York: Grosset & Dunlap.

Neft, David S., Richard M. Cohen, and Rick Korch. (1992) *The Sports Encyclopedia: Pro Football.* New York: St. Martin's Press.

Neft, David S., Roland T. Johnson, and Richard M. Cohen. (1974) *The Sports Encyclopedia: Pro Football.* New York: Grosset & Dunlap.

Neil, C. L. (1903) *Walking.* London: Pearson.

Neil, Graham I. (1976) *Modern Team Handball.* Montreal, Canada: McGill University Press.

Nelson, Cordner, and Roberto Quercetani. (1985) *The Milers.* Los Altos, CA: Tafnews Press.

Nelson, Mariah. (1991) *Are We Winning Yet? How Women Are Changing Sports and Sports Are Changing Women.* New York: Random House.

Nelson, Randy F., ed. (1989) *Martial Arts Reader: Classic Writings on Philosophy and Technique.* Woodstock, NY: Overlook Press.

Nesbitt, Lloyd. (1993) "The In-line Skating Experience." *Physician and Sportsmedicine* 21 (August): 81–82.

Netherby, Steve. (1974) *The Experts' Book of Fresh Water Fishing.* New York: Simon and Schuster.

Neumann, Hannes. (1968) *Die deutsche Turnbewegung in der Revolution 1848/49 und in der amerikanischen Emigration.* Schorndorf, Germany: Karl Hofmann.

Newcomb, Horace, ed. (1994) *Television: The Critical View.* 5th ed. New York: Oxford University Press.

Newell, Gordon. (1987) *Ready All! George Yeoman Pocock and Crew Racing.* Seattle: University of Washington Press.

Nicholson, G. (1977) *The Great Bike Race.* London: Methuen.

Nickerson, Elinor. (1982) *Racquet Sports, An Illustrated Guide.* Jefferson, NC: McFarland.

Nideffer, R. M. (1985) *Athlete's Guide to Mental Training.* Champaign, IL: Human Kinetics.

Niebel, Benjamin W., and Douglas A. Niebel. (1982) *Modern Wrestling. A Primer for Wrestlers, Parents, and Fans.* University Park: Pennsylvania State University Press.

Niedner, Felix. (1881) *Das deutsche Turnier im 12. und 15. Jahrhundert.* Berlin: Weidmann.

Nimuendaju, Curt. (1963) "The Tacuna." *Bureau of American Ethnology Bulletin* 143, 3: 713–725.

Noble, P. D. (1979) *String Figures of Papua New Guinea.* Papua New Guinea: Institute of Papua New Guinea Studies.

Noel, Eugenio. (1914) *Escritos antitaurinos.* Madrid: Taurus.

Noll, Greg, and Andrea Gabbard. (1989) *Da Bull: Life over the Edge.* South Laguna, CA: Bangtail Press.

Noren, Arthur T. (1940) *Softball.* New York: A. S. Barnes.

Novak, Michael. (1976) *The Joy of Sports: End Zones, Bases, Baskets, Balls, and the Consecration of the American Spirit.* New York: Basic Books.

Noverr, D. A., and L. E. Ziewacz, eds. (1987) *Sport History.* New York: Markus Wiener.

Nye, Doug. (1992) *The Autocourse History of the Grand Prix Car 1966–1991.* Richmond, UK: Hazleton Publishing.

Nye, Peter. (1988) *Hearts of Lions: The History of American Bicycle Racing.* New York: W. W. Norton.

Nygren, Helge, Antero Raevuori, and Tarmo Maki-Kuuti. (1983) *Pitka latu: vuosisata suomalaista hiihtourheilua.* Porvoo: Soderstrom.

Maolfabhail, Art. (1975) *Camán: Two Thousand years of Hurling in Ireland.* Dundalk: Croom Helm.

Obata, Toshishiro. (1986) *Naked Blade: A Manual of Samurai Swordsmanship.* Westlake Village, CA: Dragon Enterprises.

———. (1987) *Crimson Steel: The Sword Technique of the Samurai.* Westlake Village, CA: Dragon Enterprises.

O'Brien, A., and M. O'Bryan. (1976) *Bobsled and Luge.* Canada: Colban.

Ogilvie, Robert S. (1985) *Competitive Figure Skating: A Parent's Guide.* New York: Harper & Row.

Oh, Sadaharu. (1984) *Sadaharu Oh: A Zen Way of Baseball.* New York: Times Books.

O'Hanlon, Timothy. (1982) "School Sports as Social Training: The Case of Athletics and the Crisis of World War I." *Journal of Sport History* 9 (Spring): 1–24.

O'Hara, John. (1994) "Horse-Racing and Trotting." In *Sport in Australia: A Social History,* edited by Wray Vamplew and Brian Stoddart. Melbourne, Australia: Cambridge University Press.

Oleksak, Michael M. (1991) *Beisbol: Latin Americans and the Grand Old Game.* Grand Rapids, MI: Masters Press.

Oliveira, Nuno. (1983) *Classical Principles of the Art of Training Horses.* Australia: Howley and Russell.

Oliver, Guy. (1992) *The Guinness Record of World Soccer: The History of the Game in over 150 Countries.* London: Guinness Publishing.

Olivera, Eduardo A. (1932) *Origenes de los deportes britanicos en el Rio de la Plata.* Buenos Aires, Argentina: L. J. Rosso.

Olivova, Vera. (1984) *Sports and Games in the Ancient World.* New York: St. Martin's Press.

*Olympic Gold 84.* (1994) Kensington, New South Wales: Bay Books.

*Olympic Sports: A Handbook of Recognized Olympic Sports.* (n.d.) New York: U.S. Olympic Committee.

*One Hundred Years of Golf.* (1971) Dunedin: Otago Golf Club.

Oppenheim, Francois. (1970) *The History of Swimming.* North Hollywood, CA: Swimming World.

Oriard, Michael. (1982) *Dreaming of Heroes: American Sports Fiction 1868–1980.* Chicago: Nelson-Hall.

———. (1993) *Reading Football: How the Popular Press Created an American Spectacle.* Chapel Hill: University of North Carolina Press.

———. (1993) *Sporting with the Gods: The Rhetoric of Play and Game in American Culture.* New York: Cambridge University Press.

Orlick, T. (1986) *Psyching for Sport: Mental Training for Athletes.* Champaign, IL: Human Kinetics.

———. (1990) *In Pursuit of Excellence.* Champaign, IL: Human Kinetics.

Orlick, T., and J. Partington. (1988) "Mental Links to Excellence." *Sport Psychologist* 2: 105–130.

Orme, Nicholas. (1983) *Early British Swimming, 55 BC–AD 1719, with the First Swimming Treatise in English, 1595.* Exeter: University of Exeter.

Osgood, William, and Leslie Hurley. (1975) *The Snowshoe Book.* 2d ed. Brattleboro, VT: Stephan Greene Press.

Osterhoudt, Robert G. (1991) *The Philosophy of Sport: An Overview.* Champaign, IL: Stipes Publishing.

Oswalt, Wendell. (1979) *Eskimos and Explorers.* Novato, CA: Chandler and Sharp.

Otake, Ritsuke. (1978) *The Deity And The Sword* Vols. 1, 2, and 3. Trans. Donn F. Dreager, Terue Shinozuka, and Kyoichiro Nunokawa. Tokyo: Minato Research and Publishing Co.

Ours, Robert. (1984) *College Football Almanac.* New York: Harper & Row.

Owen, George. (1603) *The Description of Pembrokeshire.* Edited by H. Owen. Cymmrodarian Society Record Series 1 (1892).

Owen, Rosamund. (1984) *The Art of Side-Saddle Riding.* London: Trematon Press.

Ownby, Ted. (1990) *Subduing Satan: Religion, Recreation, and Manhood in the Rural South, l865–1920.* Chapel Hill: University of North Carolina Press.

Oxendine, Joseph B. (1988) *American Indian Sports Heritage.* Champaign, IL: Human Kinetics.

Padura, Leonardo. (1989) *Estrellas del béisbol.* Havana: Editora Abril.

Page, Harry S. (1929) *Between the Flags.* New York: Derrydale Press.

Pagen, Dennis. (1989) *Hang Gliding Flying Skills.* Mingoville, PA: Sport Aviation Publications.

———. (1993) *Performance Flying.* Mingoville, PA: Sport Aviation Publications.

———. (1995) *Hang Gliding Training Manual.* Mingoville, PA: Sport Aviation Publications.

Palmatier, R. A., and H. L. Ray. (1989) *Sports Talk — A Dictionary of Sports Metaphors.* Westport, CT: Greenwood Press.

Palmedo, Roland, ed. (1937) *Skiing: The International Sport.* New York: Derrydale.

Palmer, A. J. (1977) *The International Shooting Union, Official History 1907–1977.* Wiesbaden, Germany: International Shooting Union.

Palmer, W. J. (1987) *The Films of the Seventies: A Social History.* Metuchen, NJ: Scarecrow Press.

Panofsky, Erwin. (n.d.) *Tomb Sculpture: Four Lectures on Its Changing Aspects from Ancient Egypt to Bernini.* New York: Harry Abrams.

Pape, Max. (1982) *The Art of Driving.* New York: J. A. Allen.

Paraschak, Victoria. (1983) "Discrepancies between Government Programs and Community Practices: The Case of Recreation in the Northwest Territories." Ph.D dissertation, University of Alberta.

———. (1990) "Organized Sport for Native Females on the Six Nations Reserve, Ontario from 1968 to 1980: A Comparison of Dominant and Emergent Sport Systems." *Canadian Journal of History of Sport* 21, 2: 70–80.

———. (1991) "Sport Festivals and Race Relations in the Northwest Territories of Canada." In *Sport, Racism and Ethnicity,* edited by Grant Jarvie, 74–93. London: Falmer Press.

———. (1995) "The Native Sport and Recreation Program, 1972–1981: Patterns of Resistance, Patterns of Reproduction." *Canadian Journal of History of Sport* 26, 2: 1–18.

Pare, A. (1582) *Opera ambrosii parei regis primarii et parisiensis chirurgi.* Paris: Jacques de Puys.

Parish, David, and John Anthony. (1981) *Target Rifle Shooting.* East Ardsley, Wakefield, UK: EP Publishing.

Park, Roberta J., and Helen M. Eckert, eds. (1991). *New Possibilities, New Paradigms?* Academy Papers No. 24. Champaign, IL: Human Kinetics Books.

Park, Yeon Hee, and Jeff Liebowitz. (1993) *Fighting Back: Taekwondo for Women.* East Meadow, NY: Y. H. Park.

———. (1993) *Taekwondo for Children: The Ultimate Reference Guide for Children Interested in the World's Most Popular Martial Art.* East Meadow, NY: Y. H. Park.

Park, Yeon Hee, Yeon Hwan Park, and Jon Gerrard. (1989) *Tae Kwon Do: The Ultimate Reference Guide to the World's Most Popular Martial Art.* New York: Facts On File.

Parkhouse, Bonny. (1991) *The Management of Sport.* St. Louis, MO: Mosby Year Book.

Parks, Janet, and Beverly Zanger, eds. (1990) *Sport and Fitness Management.* Champaign, IL: Human Kinetics.

Parr, Andrew. (1991) *Sandyachting — A History of the Sport and Its Development in Britain.* Pembrokeshire, UK: Gomer Press.

Parrish Art Museum. (1968) *A Salute to the Olympics — Sports in Art.* Southampton, NY: Parrish Art Museum.

Parry, J. (1988) "Physical Education, Justification, and the National Curriculum." *Physical Education Review* 11: 106–118.

Paterson, W. F. (1984) *Encyclopaedia of Archery.* New York: St. Martin's Press.

Paul, Sigrid. (1987) "The Wrestling Traditions and its Social Functions." In *Sport in Africa: Essays in Social History,* edited by William J. Baker and James A. Mangan. New York: Africana.

Paul, William Wayne. (1974) "The Social Significance of the Asian Martial Arts." M.A. thesis, San Francisco State University.

Paulo, Karen. (1990) *America's Long Distance Challenge.* North Pomfret, VT: Trafalgar Square.

Payne-Gallwey, Ralph. (1903) *The Cross-bow.* London: Longman.

Peak, Robert. (1984) *Golden Moments: A Collection of United States 1984 Commemorative Olympic Issues.* Washington, DC: United States Postal Service.

Peake, L. (1990) "Retaining Cultural Games: A South East Asian Perspective." In *Sport for All: Into the 1990's,* edited by J. Standeven, K. Hardman, and D. Fisher. Champaign, IL: Human Kinetics.

Pearson, Kent. (1979) *Surfing Subcultures of Australia and New Zealand.* St. Lucia, Australia: University of Queensland Press.

Pearton, Robert. (1986) "Violence in Sport and the Special Case of Soccer Hooliganism in the United Kingdom." In *Sport and Social Theory,* edited by C. Roger Rees and Andrew W. Miracle. Champaign, IL: Human Kinetics, 67–83.

Peck, Wilbur H. (1970) *Volleyball.* London: Collier Books.

Peiss, Kathy. (1986) *Cheap Amusements.* Philadelphia: Temple University Press.

Pérez Medina, Ramón G. (1992) *Historia del baseball panameño.* Panamá: Dutigrafía.

Pérez, Louis A., Jr. (1994) "Between Baseball and Bullfighting: The Quest for Nationality in Cuba, 1868–1898." *Journal of American History* 81, 2: 493–517.

Perkin, Harold. (1989) "Teaching the Nations How To Play: Sport and Society in the British Empire and Commonwealth." *International Journal of the History of Sport* 6, 2: 145–155.

Perrin, J. (1985) *Menlove: The Life of John Menlove Edwards.* London: Victor Gollancz.

———. (1986) *On and Off the Rocks.* London: Victor Gollancz.

Peterson, Harold L. (1962) *Treasury of the Gun.* New York: Golden Press.

Peterson, Robert W. (1990) *Cages to Jump Shots: Pro Basketball's Early Years.* New York: Oxford University Press.

Petrov, Rajko. (1986) *Freestyle and Greco-Roman Wrestling.* Lausanne, Switzerland: Fédération Internationale des Luttes Amateurs.

Pettavino, Paula J., and Geralyn Pye. (1994) *Sport in Cuba: The Diamond in the Rough.* Pittsburgh: University of Pittsburgh Press.

Pfister, Gertrud, ed. (1980) *Frau und Sport.* Frankfurt, Germany: Fischer.

Pfister, Gertrud, and Christine Peyton, eds. (1989) *Frauensport in Europa.* Ahrensburg, Germany: Czwalina.

Phillips, Ann-Victoria (1979) *The Complete Book of Roller Skating.* New York: Womman.

Phillips, Dennis J. (1989) *Teaching, Coaching, and Learning Tennis: An Annotated Bibliography.* Metuchen, NJ: Scarecrow Press.

Phillips, Keith, ed. (1990) *The New BBC of Bowls.* London: BBC.

Phillips, Mark. (1993) *Horse and Hound Book of Eventing.* New York: Howell Book House.

Pieter, Willy. (1994) "Research in Martial Sports: A Review." *Journal of Asian Martial Arts* 3, 2: 10–47.

Pigafetta, Antonio. (1969) *Magellan's Voyage, A Narrative Account of the First Circumnavigation.* New Haven, CT: Yale University Press.

Piggott, Derek. (1977) *Understanding Gliding.* New York: Barnes & Noble.

Pihkala, L. (1932) *Peäpallo itsekurin ja päällikkmielen kouluna* [Pesäpallo as a school self-discipline and commander-spirit]. Pesäpalloilijan vuosikirja.

Pilley, D. (1989) *Climbing Days.* London: Hogarth Press.

Pines, Philip A. (1980) *The Complete Book of Harness Racing.* New York: Arco Publishing.

Pirazzini, Ezio. (1971) *Storia dei motomondiali. I giorni del coraggio.* Bologna, Italy: Edizioni Calderini.

———. (1977) *Addio campione. I cavalieri dell'impossibile.* Bologna, Italy: Edizioni Calderini.

Pistilli, Alberto. (1991) *Storia del motociclismo mondiale dalle origini ad oggi. Fuori strada.* Milan, Italy: Vallardi Associati.

Plant, Mike. (1987) *Iron Will: The Heart and Soul of Triathlon's Ultimate Challenge.* Chicago, IL: Contemporary Books.

———. (1987) *Triathlon: Going the Distance.* Chicago, IL: Contemporary Books.

Plomley, N. J. B., ed. (1966) *Friendly Mission: The Tasmanian Journals & Papers of George Augustus Robinson, 1829–1834.* Kingsgrove, New South Wales, Australia: Halstead Press.

Plotnicki, Ben A., and Andrew J. Kozar. (1970) *Handball.* Dubuque, IA: Kendall/Hunt.

Podhajsky, Alois. (1973) *The Complete Training of Horse and Rider.* London: Wilshire.

Pointer, Larry. (1985) *Rodeo Champions: Eight Memorable Moments of Riding, Wrestling, and Roping.* Albuquerque: University of New Mexico Press.

Polednik, Heinz. (1969) *Weltwunder Skisport.* Wels, Germany: Welsermuhl.

Poliakoff, Michael B. (1987) *Combat Sports in the Ancient World: Competition, Violence and Culture.* New Haven, CT: Yale University Press.

Pollard, Jack. (1988) *Australian Horse Racing.* Sydney, Australia: Angus & Robertson.

Pope, Steven. (1995) "An Army of Athletes: Playing Fields, Battlefields, and the American Military Sporting Experience, 1890–1920." *Journal of Military History* 59 (July): 435–456.

Porquet, Jean-Luc, and Dominique Pouillet. (1987) *Le boomerang: Son histoire, sa fabrication, ses techniques.* Bourges, France: Editions Hoebecke.

Porter, David L., ed. (1987) *The Biographical Dictionary of American Sports: Baseball.* New York: Greenwoood.

———. (1987) *Biographical Dictionary of American Sports: Football.* Westport, CT: Greenwood Press.

———. (1988) *Biographical Dictionary of American Sports.* Westport, CT: Greenwood Press.

———. (1992 and 1995) *Biographical Dictionary of American Sports.* Westport, CT: Greenwood Press.

———. (1995) *African-American Sports Greats—A Biographical Dictionary.* Westport, CT: Greenwood Press.

Porter, Willard. (1982) *Who's Who in Rodeo.* Oklahoma City, OK: Powder River.

Poynter, Dan. (1992) *Parachuting: The Skydiver's Handbook.* Santa Barbara, CA: Para Publishing.

Pozzoli, P. (1968) *Yearbook 1968.* Claremont, CA: Women's Track & Field World.

Pranin, Stanley. (1991) *The Aiki News Encyclopedia of Aikido.* Tokyo: Aiki News.

———. (1992) *Takeda Sokaku and Daito-ryu Aiki Jujutsu.* Tokyo: Aiki News.

———. (1993) *Aikido Masters: Prewar Students of Morihei Ueshiba.* Tokyo: Aiki News.

Prebish, Charles S. (1993) *Religion and Sport: The Meeting of Sacred and Profane.* Westport, CT: Greenwood.

Presas, Remy A. (1993 [1974]) *Modern Arnis: Philippine Martial Art.* Manila, Philippines: Modern Arnis.

Price, S. D. (1974) *Get a Horse! Basics of Back-Yard Horsekeeping.* New York: Viking Press.

Pridgen, T. (1938) *Courage: The Story of Modern Cockfighting.* Boston: Little, Brown.

*A Profile of Water Skiing in the United States.* (1994) Winter Haven, FL: American Water Ski Association.

Prokop, Dave, ed. (1975) *The African Running Revolution.* Mountain View, CA: World Publications.

Pronger, B. (1990) *The Arena of Masculinity: Sports,*

*Homosexuality and the Meaning of Sex.* London: Gay Men's Press.

Pryce, Robert. (1989) *Scotland's Golf Courses.* Aberdeen, UK: Aberdeen University Press.

Puirseal, Padraig. (1983) *The G.A.A. in Its Time.* Dublin, Ireland: Puirseal.

Pullum, Bill, and Frank T. Hanenkrat. (1973) *Position Rifle Shooting.* New York: Winchester Press.

———. (1995) *The New Position Rifle Shooting.* Peachtree City, GA: Target Sports Education Center.

Pyatt, E. (1980) *The Guinness Book of Mountains and Mountaineering Facts and Feats.* London: Guinness Superlatives.

Pye, J. K. (1971) *A Grand National Commentary.* London: J. D. Allen.

Pyke, F. S. (1991) *Better Coaching.* Canberra: Australian Coaching Council.

Quercetani, Roberto L. (1964) *A World History of Track and Field Athletics.* London: Oxford University Press.

———. (1990) *Athletics: A History of Modern Track and Field Athletics 1860–1900, Men and Women.* Milan, Italy: Vallardi & Associati.

Quercetani, Roberto L., and Nejet Kok. (1993) *Wizards of the Middle Distances.* Milan, Italy: Vallardi & Associati.

Race Walking Association. (1962) *The Sport of Race Walking.* Ruislip, UK: Race Walking Association.

Rackham, George. (1968) *Synchronized Swimming.* London: Faber & Faber.

Rader, Benjamin G. (1983) *American Sports: From the Age of Folk Games to the Age of Spectators.* Englewood Cliffs, NJ: Prentice-Hall.

———. (1984) *In Its Own Image: How Television Has Transformed Sports.* New York: Free Press.

———. (1990) *American Sports: From the Age of Folk Games to the Age of Televised Sports.* 2d ed. Englewood Cliffs, NJ: Prentice-Hall.

———. (1992) *Baseball: A History of America's Game.* Urbana: University of Illinois Press.

Radnige, Keir. (1994) *Ultimate Encyclopaedia of Soccer.* London: Hodder and Stoughton.

Raitz, Karl B., ed. (1995) *The Theater of Sports.* Baltimore, MD: Johns Hopkins University Press.

Raj, J. David Manuel. (1971) *Silambam Technique and Evaluation.* Karaikudi.

———. (1975) *Silambam Fencing from India.* Karaikudi.

———. (1977) "The Origin and Historical Development of Silambam Fencing: Ancient Self-Defense Sport of India." Ph.D. dissertation, University of Oregon.

Ramazzini, B. (1940 [1713]) *De Morbis Artificiorum.* Translated by W. C. Wright. Chicago, IL: University of Chicago Press.

Ramsey, F., T. Paul, and F. Murray. (1982) *Fundamentals: Concepts in Exercise and Fitness.* Dubuque, IA: Kendall/Hunt.

Rappelfeld, Joel. (1992) *The Complete Blader.* New York: St. Martin's.

Raschke, Wendy J., ed. (1988) *The Archaeology of the Olympics. The Olympics and Other Festivals in Antiquity.* Madison: University of Wisconsin Press.

Raum, Otto F. (1953) "The Rolling Target (Hoop-and-Pole) Game in Africa: Egyptian Accession Rite or Multiple Ritual Symbolism." *African Studies* 12: 104–121, 163–180.

Ray, Slim. (1992) *The Canoe Handbook.* Harrisburg, PA: Stackpole Books.

Read, Charles. (1929) *Squash Rackets.* London: Heinemann.

Reagan, Albert B. (1932) "Navajo Sports." *Primitive Man* 5: 68–71.

Redmond, G. (1971) *The Caledonian Games in Nineteenth Century America.* Cranbury, NJ: Fairleigh Dickinson University Press.

———. (1982) *The Sporting Scots of Nineteenth Century Canada.* East Brunswick, NJ: Fairleigh Dickinson University Press.

Redmond, Gerald, ed. (1978) *Edmonton '78: The Official Pictorial Record of the XI Commonwealth Games.* Edmonton, Alberta, Canada: Executive Sport Publications.

———. (1986) *Sport and Politics.* Champaign, IL: Human Kinetics Publishers.

Reed, P., and R. Muggerridge. (1984) *Savate, the Martial Art of France.* Phoenix, AZ: Paladin Press.

Reekie, Shirley H. M. (1986) *Sailing Made Simple.* Champaign, IL: Leisure Press.

Rees, C. Roger, and Andrew W. Miracle. (1984) "Conflict Resolution in Games and Sports." *International Review of Sport Sociology* 19: 145–156.

Rees, C. Roger, Frank M. Howell, and Andrew W. Miracle. (1990) "Do High School Sports Build Character? A Quasi-Experiment on a National Sample." *Social Science Journal* 27: 303–315.

Regan, Tom. (1985) *The Case for Animal Rights.* Berkeley: University of California Press.

Reichler, Joseph, ed. (1992) *The Complete and Official Record of Major League Baseball.* New York: Macmillan.

Reid, Howard, and Michael Croucher. (1983) *The Fighting Arts: Great Masters of the Martial Arts.* New York: Simon and Schuster.

———. (1983) *The Way of the Warrior: The Paradox of the Martial Arts.* Woodstock, NY: Overlook Press.

Reid, J. C. (1971) *Bucks and Bruisers: Pierce Egan and Regency England.* London: Routledge.

Reid, Philip. (1974) *Victor Barna.* Lavenham, Suffolk, UK: Eastland.

Reilly, Robin L. *Japan's Complete Fighting System—Shin Kage Ryu.* Tokyo: Charles E. Tuttle.

Reisman, Marty. (1974) *The Money Player.* New York: William Morrow.

Remley, M. L. (1990) *Women in Sport: An Annotated Bibliography and Resource Guide 1900–1990.* Boston: G. K. Hall.

René d'Anjou. (1827) *Les tournois du roi René*. Edited by Jean Jacques Champollion-Figeac et al. Paris: C. Motte.

Renson, Roland. (1976) "The Flemish Archery Gilds: From Defense Mechanisms to Sports Institutions." In *The History, the Evolution and Diffusion of Sports and Games in Different Cultures*, edited by P. P. De Nayer, M. Ostyn, and R. Renson. Brussels: BLOSO, 135–159.

———. (1977) "Play in Exile: The Continental Pastimes of King Charles II (1630–1685)." In *HISPA VIth International Congress*. Dartford, UK: Dartford College of Education, 508–522.

Renson, Roland, H. Smulders, and E. De Vroede, eds. (1978–1988) *Serie der Vlaamse Volkssport Dossiers*. Vols. 1–8. Leuven, Belgium: Vlaamse Volkssport Centrale.

Renson, Roland, P. P. De Nayer, and M. Ostyn, eds. (1976) *The History, the Evolution and Diffusion of Sports and Games in Different Cultures, Proceedings of the Fourth International HISPA Seminar,* Leuven 1–5 April 1975. Brussels: BLOSO.

Rhodes, Reilly, ed. (1990) *Sport in Art from American Museums*. New York: Universe Publishing.

Riboni, Guiseppe. (1862) *Broadsword and Quarter-Staff without a Master*. Chicago, IL: E. B. Myers.

Rice, Grantland. (1954) *The Tumult and the Shouting: My Life in Sport*. New York: A. S. Barnes.

Richardson, Ernie, Joyce McKee, and Doug Maxwell. (1962) *Curling, An Authoritative Handbook of the Techniques and Strategy of the Ancient Game of Curling*. Toronto, Canada: Thomas Allen.

Richardson, L. N. (1953) *Jubilee History of the International Cross-country Union 1903–1953*. Ambergate, UK: ICCU.

———. (1965) *International Cross Country Union 1903–1953*. Ambergate, UK: ICCU.

Richey, Michael W., ed. (1980) *The Sailing Encyclopedia*. New York: Lippincott & Crowell.

Rieder, Ulrike. (1993) *Correct Vaulting* (U.S. ed.). Bainbridge Island, WA: American Vaulting Association.

Riefenstahl, Leni. (1973) *The Last of the Nuba*. New York: Harper & Row.

Riess, Steven A. (1980) *Touching Base: Professional Baseball and American Culture in the Progressive Era*. Westport, CT: Greenwood.

———. (1982) "Working-Class Sports in America, 1882–1920." Paper delivered to the American Historical Association, San Francisco, CA (12 August).

———. (1989) *City Games: The Evolution of American Urban Society and the Rise of Sports*. Urbana and Chicago: University of Illinois Press.

Riffer, Jeffrey K. (1985) *Sports and Recreational Injuries*. Colorado Springs, CO: Shepard's/McGraw-Hill.

Rigauer, B. (1981) *Sport and Work*. New York: Columbia University Press.

Riger, Robert. (1967) *Man in Sport: An International Exhibition of Photography*. Baltimore, MD: Baltimore Museum of Art.

Riordan, James. (1977) *Sport in Soviet Society*. Cambridge: Cambridge University Press.

———. (1984) "The Workers' Olympics." In *Five Ring Circus: Money, Power and Politics at the Olympic Games,* edited by Alan Tomlinson and Gary Whannel. London: Pluto Press.

———. (1991) *Sport, Politics and Communism*. Manchester, UK: Manchester University Press.

Riske, Milt. (1984) *Cheyenne Frontier Days*. Cheyenne, WY: Frontier Printing.

Ritchie, Andrew. (1975) *King of the Road: An Illustrated History of Cycling*. London: Wildwood Press.

Riviere, Bill. (1985) *The Open Canoe*. Boston and Toronto: Little, Brown.

Rivola, Luigi, and Gianna Rivola. (1991) *Storia del motociclismo mondiale dalle origini ad oggi. (Su strada)*. Milan, Italy: Vallardi Associati.

Roberts, Chris. (1992) *Powwow Country*. Helena, MT: American and World Geographic Publishing.

Roberts, John M., and Brian Sutton-Smith. (1962) "Child Training and Game Involvement." *Ethnology* 1, 2: 166–185.

Roberts, John. M., and Garry E. Chick. (1979) "Butler County Eight Ball: A Behavioral Space Analysis." In *Sports, Games, and Play: Social and Psychological Viewpoints*, edited by J. H. Goldstein. Hillsdale, NJ: Erlbaum, 65–99.

Roberts, John M., and Herbert Barry III. (1976) "Inculcated Traits and Game-Type Combinations: A Cross-Cultural View." In *The Humanistic and Mental Health Aspects of Sport, Exercise, and Recreation*, edited by Timothy T. Craig. Chicago: American Medical Association, 5–11.

Roberts, John M., Malcolm J. Arth, and Robert R. Bush. (1959) "Games in Culture." *American Anthropologist* 59: 497–504.

Roberts, Kenneth G., and Philip Shackelton. (1983) *The Canoe: A History of the Craft from Panama to the Arctic*. Toronto, Canada: Macmillan of Canada and Camden, ME: International Marine.

Roberts, Ned H., and Kenneth L. Waters. (1967) *The Breech-Loading Single-Shot Match Rifle*. New York: D. Van Nostrand.

Roberts, Randy. (1979) *Jack Dempsey: The Manassa Mauler*. Baton Rouge: Louisiana State University Press.

———. (1983) *Papa Jack: Jack Johnson and the Era of White Hopes*. New York: Free Press.

Roberts, Randy, and James Olson. (1989) *Winning Is the Only Thing: Sports in America since 1945*. Baltimore, MD: Johns Hopkins University Press.

Robinson, Rachel Sargent. (1979 [1955]) *Sources for the History of Greek Athletics*. Chicago: Ares Publishers.

Roden, Donald. (1980) "Baseball and the Quest for National Dignity in Meiji Japan." *American Historical Review* 85, 3: 511–534.

Rodenas, Paula. (1991) *Random House Book of Horses and Horsemanship*. New York: Random House.

Rogers, Fairman. (1900) *Manual of Coaching.* Philadelphia: J. B. Lippincott.

Roller, Lynn E. (1981) "Funeral Games for Historical Persons." *Stadion* 7: 1–17.

———. (1981) "Funeral Games in Greek Art." *American Journal of Archeology* 85: 107–119.

Ronberg, Gary. (1974) *The Hockey Encyclopedia.* New York: Macmillan.

Rooney, John. (1972) *A Geography of American Sport: From Cabin Creek to Anaheim.* Reading, MA: Addison-Wesley.

———. (1978) *The Recruiting Game: Toward a New System of Intercollegiate Sport,* 2d ed. Lincoln: University of Nebraska Press.

Rooney, John F., Jr., and Richard Pillsbury. (1992) *Atlas of American Sport.* New York: Macmillan.

*Roots of the Greyhound* (1990). Abilene, KS: Greyhound Hall of Fame.

Roper, S. (1994) *Camp 4: Recollections of a Yosemite Rock Climber.* Seattle, WA: The Mountaineers.

Roscoe, John. (1966) *The Baganda: An Account of Their Native Customs and Beliefs.* New York: Barnes & Noble.

Rose, Laura, ed. (1995) "Major Steeplechase Exhibit in Works at National Museum of Racing." *National Sporting Library Newsletter* 43: 3.

Rose, Stuart. (1931) *The Maryland Hunt Cup.* New York: Huntington Press.

Rosen, Charles. (1978) *The Scandals of '51: How Gamblers Almost Killed College Basketball.* New York: Holt, Rinehart, and Winston.

Rosenberg, Daniel. (1995) "Paradox and Dilemma: The Martial Arts and American Violence." *Journal of Asian Martial Arts* 4, 2: 10–33.

Rosenstiel, A. (1976) "The Role of Traditional Games in the Process of Socialization among the Motu of Papua New Guinea." In *The Anthropological Study of Play,* edited by D. F. Lanay and B. A. Tindall. Cornell, NY: Leisure Press.

Rosenzweig, Roy. (1983) *Eight Hours for What We Will: Workers and Leisure in an Industrial City, 1870–1920.* Cambridge: Cambridge University Press.

Rosiniski, José. (1974) *Formula 1 Racing: The Modern Era.* New York: Madison Square Press.

Rossell, John E., Jr. (1954) *The Maryland Hunt Cup: 1894–1954.* Baltimore, MD: Sporting Press.

———. (1974) *The Maryland Hunt Cup, Past and Present.* Baltimore, MD: Sporting Press.

Rost, J. C. (1991) *Leadership for the Twenty-First Century.* New York: Praeger.

Roth, Bernhard A. (1977) *The Complete Beginner's Guide to Canoeing.* Garden City, NY: Doubleday.

Roth, W. E. (1897) *Ethnological Studies among the North-Western Central Queensland Aborigines.* Brisbane, Australia: Government Printing Office.

———. (1902) "Games, Sports and Amusements." *North Queensland Ethnography.* Bulletin No. 4. Brisbane, Australia: Government Printing Office.

Rotundo, E. A. (1993) *American Manhood: Transformations in Masculinity from the Revolution to the Modern Era.* New York: Basic Books.

Rouse, Irving. (1963) "The Arawak." *Bureau of American Ethnology Bulletin* 143, 4: 507–546.

Rouse, Paul. (1993) "The Politics and Culture of Sport in Ireland: A History of the GAA Ban on Foreign Games 1884–1971, Part 1 1884–1921." *International Journal of the History of Sport* 10, 3 (December): 333–366.

Rowe, Peter. (1988) *American Football: The Records.* Enfield, UK: Guinness.

Rowland, B. J. (1970) *Handball: A Complete Guide.* London: Faber and Faber.

Royster, Charles. (1979) *A Revolutionary People at War: The Continental Army and American Character, 1775–1783.* New York: W. W. Norton.

Rozin, Skip. (1983) *Daley Thompson: The Subject Is Winning.* London: Stanley Paul.

Ruck, Rob. (1987) *Sandlot Seasons: Sport in Black Pittsburgh.* Urbana and Chicago: University of Illinois Press.

———. (1990) *The Tropic of Baseball: Baseball in the Dominican Republic.* New York: Carroll & Graf.

———. (1993) "Baseball in the Caribbean." In *Total Baseball,* 3d ed., edited by John Thorn and Pete Palmer. New York: HarperCollins.

Rugby Fives Association. (n.d.) *Fives: An Introduction to the Game of Rugby Fives.* Sutton Valence, UK: Rugby Fives Association.

———. (1994) *Fives: Courts, Fixtures and Players.* Sutton Valence, UK: Rugby Fives Association.

Ruhe, Benjamin. (1977) *Many Happy Returns.* New York: Viking Press.

Rühl, Joachim K. (1985) "Das Turnier als friedfertiger Krieg." In *Sport im Spannungsfeld von Krieg und Frieden,* edited by Hartmut Becker. Clausthal-Zellerfeld, Germany: DVS, 31–53.

———. (1986) "Wesen und Bedeutung von Kampfansagen und Trefferzählskizzen für die Geschichte des spätmittelalterlichen Turniers," in *Sport zwischen Eigenständigkeit und Fremdbestimmung,* edited by Giselher Spitzer and Dieter Schmidt. Bonn: Peter Wegener, 86–112.

———. (1988) "Zur Leistungsquantifizierung im spätmittelalterlichen Turnier." *Brennpunkte der Sportwissenschaft* 2 , 1: 97–111.

———. (1989) "Behind the Scenes of Popular Spectacle and Courtly Tradition: The Ascertainment of the Best Jouster." In *Proceedings of the XIIth HISPA Congress,* edited by Roland Renson et al. St. Augustin, Germany: Academia, 39–48l

———. (1989) "Preliminaries to German Tournament Regulations of the 15th Century." *British Society of Sports History Bulletin* 9: 90–101.

———. (1990) "German Tournament Regulations of the 15th Century." *Journal of Sport History. Special Issue: German Sport History* 17, 2: 163–182.

———. (1990) "Sports Quantification in Tudor and Elizabethan Times." In *Ritual and Record. Sports Records and Quantification in Pre-Modern Societies*, edited by Marshall Carter and Arnd Krüger. New York: Greenwood, 65–86.

———. (1993) "Measurement of Individual Sport-Performance in Jousting Combats." In *Proceedings of the 1991 International ISHPES Congress*, edited by Roland Renson. Madrid: INEF Madrid, 226–238.

Rummelt, Peter. (1986) *Sport im Kolonialismus, Kolonialismus im Sport*. Cologne, Germany: Pahl-Rugenstein.

Rundell, Michael. (1985) *The Dictionary of Cricket*. London: Allen & Unwin.

Rupp, Virgil. (1987) *Let 'Er Buck*. Pendleton, OR: Pendleton Roundup Committee.

Russell, G. W. (1993) *The Social Psychology of Sport*. New York: Springer-Verlag.

Rutherford, J. (1983) *Indianapolis Year Book*. Indianapolis, IN: Carl Hungess Publishing.

Ruxin, Robert H. (1983) *An Athlete's Guide to Agents*. Bloomington: Indiana University Press.

Ryan, A. J. (1968) "Medical History of the Olympic Games." *Journal of the American Medical Association* 205, 11 (September): 715–720.

Ryan, B. S. (1994) "Re-defining Amateurism in English Rugby Union." M.S. thesis, University of Leicester, UK.

Ryan, Joan. (1995) *Little Girls in Pretty Boxes: The Making and Breaking of Elite Gymnasts and Figure Skaters*. New York: Doubleday.

Ryckman, R. M., et al. (1985) "Physical Self-Efficacy and Actualization." *Journal of Research in Personality* 19: 288–298.

Ryser, Otto, and James Brown. (1990) *A Manual for Tumbling and Apparatus Stunts*. 8th ed. Dubuque, IA: Wm. C. Brown.

Saar, G. Van. (1914) *Die Sportverletzungen*. Stuttgart, Germany: F. Enke.

Sabo, Don. (1985) "Sport, Patriarchy, and Male Identity: New Questions about Men and Sport." *Arena Review* 9, 2: 1–30.

Sabo, D., and R. Runfola, eds. (1980) *Jock: Sports and Male Identity*. Englewood Cliffs, NJ: Prentice-Hall.

Safrit, Margaret J., and Eckert, Helen M. eds. (1987). *The Cutting Edge in Physical Education and Exercise Science Research*. Academy Papers No. 20. Champaign, IL: Human Kinetics Publishers.

Sagar, Ann. (1993) *Vaulting: Develop Your Riding & Gymnastic Skills*. London: B. T. Batsford.

Sage, G. H. (1990) *Power and Ideology in American Sport: A Critical Perspective*. Champaign, IL: Human Kinetics.

Sahlin, Alexander. (1989) *Skridskosegling: Teknik och Prylar*, 2d ed. Distributed by the Skate-Sailing Section of the Swedish Ice Sailing Association. English version, *Skate Sailing: Techniques and Equipment*, distributed by the Skate-Sailing Association of America.

Salmela, J. H. (1992) *The World Sport Psychology Source Book*. 2d ed. Champaign, IL: Human Kinetics.

Salter, Michael A. (1967) "Games and Pastimes of the Australian Aboriginal." M.A. thesis. Edmonton, Alberta, Canada: University of Alberta.

———. (1980) "Play in Ritual: An Ethnohistorical Overview of Native North America." In *Play and Culture*, edited by Helen B. Schwartzman. West Point, NY: Leisure Press, 70–82.

———. (1994) "Iroquoian Snow-Snake: A Structural-Functional Analysis." Paper presented at the 2d International Sport History and Physical Education Studies Seminar, Lillehammer, Norway.

Sammons, Jeffrey T. (1988) *Beyond the Ring: The Role of Boxing in American Society*. Urbana and Chicago: University of Illinois Press.

Sandercock, Leonie, and Ian Turner. (1982) *Up Where, Cazaly?* Sydney, Australia: Grenada.

Sandiford, K. (1994) *Cricket in the Victorian Age*. Aldershot, UK: Scolar Press.

Sansone, David. (1988) *Greek Athletics and the Genesis of Sport*. Berkeley: University of California Press.

Santorio, S. (1614) *De medicina statio aphorismi*. Venice, Italy.

Saotome, Mitsugi. (1993) *Aikido and the Harmony of Nature*. Boston and London: Shambhala.

Sasamori, J., and G. Warner. (1964) *This Is Kendo*. Tokyo: Charles E. Tuttle.

Sassoon, Siegfried. (1928) *Memoirs of a Foxhunting Man*. London: Faber.

Sasuly, Richard. (1982) *Bookies and Bettors: Two Hundred Years of Gambling*. New York: Holt, Rinehart, and Winston.

Sautter, Erwin A. (1993) *Curling—Vademecum*. Zumikon, Switzerland: Erwin A. Sautter-Hewitt.

Sayenga, Donald, and Philip Badger. (1975) *The Easterns. 70 Years of Wrestling*.

Scanlon, Thomas F. (1984) *Greek and Roman Athletics: A Bibliography*. Chicago: Ares Publishers.

Scarborough, Vernon L., and David R. Wilcox, eds. (1991) *The Mesoamerican Ballgame*. Tucson: University of Arizona Press.

Schaad, Cornelius G. (1930) *Ping-Pong: The Game [and] Its Tactics and Laws*. Boston: Houghton Mifflin.

Schaer, Alfred. (1901) *Die Altdeutschen Fechter und Spielleute*. Strassburg, Germany: K. J. Trubner.

Schaufelberger, W. (1972) *Der Wettkampf in der alten Eidgenossenschaft*. Vols. 1–2. Bern: Haupt.

Schenk, Christian, and Siggi Wentz. (1992) *Zehnkampf [Decathlon]*. Munich, Germany: Copress Sport.

Schiff, Sol. (1939) *Table Tennis Comes of Age*. New York: Henry Holt.

Schmid, Andrea Bodo. (1976) *Modern Rhythmic Gymnastics*. Palo Alto, CA: Mayfield.

Schmid, Andrea Bodo, and Drury, Blanche J. (1977) *Gymnastics for Women*. 4th ed. Palo Alto, CA: Mayfield.

Schneider, E. C. (1939) *Physiology of Muscular Activity.* Philadelphia: W. B. Saunders.

Schobel, H. (1966) *The Ancient Olympic Games.* London: Studio Vista.

Schodl, G. (1992) *The Lost Past.* Budapest, Hungary: International Weightlifting Federation.

Schröter, Harald. (1983) *Roger Ascham, Toxophilus: The Schole of Shootinge. London 1545.* St. Augustin: Richarz.

Schubert, George W., Rodney K. Smith, and Jesse C. Trentadue. (1986) *Sports Law.* St. Paul, MN: West Publishing.

Schuetz, Richard J., Jr. (1976) "Sports, Technology, and Gambling." In *Gambling and Society: Interdisciplinary Studies on the Subject of Gambling*, edited by William R. Eadington. Springfield, IL: Charles C. Thomas.

Schullery, Paul. (1988) *The Bear Hunters Century: Profiles from the Golden Age of Bear Hunting.* Harrisburg, PA: Stackpole Books.

Schwarzenegger, Arnold. (1985) *Encyclopedia of Modern Bodybuilding.* New York: Simon and Schuster.

Scott, Bob. (1976) *Lacrosse: Technique and Tradition.* Baltimore, MD: Johns Hopkins University Press.

Scott, D. (1974) *Big Wall Climbing: Development, Techniques and Aids.* New York: Oxford University Press.

Scott, Gary P., ed. (1991) *The 1991 Triathlon Competition Guide.* Colorado Springs, CO: Triathlon Federation/USA.

Segal, Erich. (1984) "'To Win or Die': A Taxonomy of Sporting Attitudes," *Journal of Sport History* 11: 25–31.

Segar, William. (1602) *Honour, Military and Ciuill.* London: Barker.

Seligman, C. G., and Brenda Z. Seligman. (1932) *Pagan Tribes of the Nilotic Sudan.* London: Routledge and Kegan Paul.

Serjeant, Richard, and Alex Watson, eds. (1965) *The Gliding Book.* London: Nicholas Kaye.

Seunig, Waldemar. *The Essence of Horsemanship.* (1983) UK: J. A. Allen.

Seymour, Harold. (1960–1990) *Baseball.* 3 vols. New York: Oxford University Press.

———. (1990) *Baseball: The People's Game.* New York: Oxford University Press.

Sfeir, Leila. (989) "Sport in Egypt: Cultural Reflection and Contradiction of a Society." In *Sport in Asia and Africa,* edited by Eric C. Wagner. Westport, CT: Greenwood.

Shamos, Mike. (1995) "A Brief History of the Noble Game of Billiards." In *Billiards: The Official Rules & Records Book.* Iowa City, IA: Billiard Congress of America, 1–5.

Shapiro, James E. (1980) *Ultramarathon.* New York: Bantam Books.

Sharkey, B. J. (1984) *Physiology of Fitness.* Champaign, IL: Human Kinetics.

———. (1990) *Physiology of Fitness.* 3d ed. Champaign, IL: Human Kinetics.

Shecter, Leonard. (1969) *The Jocks.* Indianapolis: Bobbs-Merrill.

———. (1970) *The Jocks.* 2d ed. New York: Bobbs-Merrill.

Sheffield, R., and R. Woodward. (1980) *The Ice Skating Book.* New York: Universe Books.

Sherer, Karl Adolph. (1978) *70 Years of L.I.H.G./I.I.H.F.: The Seventy-Year History of the International Ice Hockey Federation.* Munich, Germany: International Ice Hockey Federation.

———. (1983) *75 Years of I.I.H.F./I.E.H.V.* Munich, Germany: International Ice Hockey Federation.

Shermer, Michael. (1993) *Race Across America: The Agonies and Glories of the World's Longest and Cruelest Bicycle Race.* Waco, TX: WRS Publishing.

Sherrill, C. (1984) "Social and Psychological Dimensions of Sports for Disabled Athletes." In *Sports and Disabled Athletes,* edited by C. Sherrill. Champaign, IL: Human Kinetics, 21–33.

———. (1986) *Adapted Physical Educational and Recreation.* 3d ed. Dubuque, IA: William C. Brown.

Sherrill, C., et al. (1988) "Use of the Personal Orientation Inventory with Disabled Athletes." *Perceptual and Motor Skill* 67: 262–266.

———. (1990) "Self-Actualization of Elite Blind Athletes: An Exploratory Study." *Journal of Visual Impairment and Blindness* (February): 55–60.

Shields, D. L., and B. J. Bredemeier. (1995) *Character Development in Physical Activity.* Champaign, IL: Human Kinetics.

Shindachi, T. (1892) "'Ju-jitsu,' The Ancient Art of Self-Defence by Sleight of Body." *Transactions and Proceedings of the Japan Society (of London)* 1: 4–21.

Shioda, Gozo. (1985) *Aikido Jinsei* [My Aikido Life]. Tokyo: Takeuchi-shoten-shinsha.

Shipley, Stan. (1993) *Bombardier Billy Wells: The Life and Times of a Boxing Hero.* Tyne and Wear, UK: Bewick.

Shishida, Fumiaki. (1992) "Martial Arts Diary by Admiral Isamu Takeshita and Morihei Ueshiba in about 1926" (in Japanese with English abstract). *Research Journal of Budo* 25, 2: 1–12.

Shishida, Fumiaki, and Tetsuro Nariyama. (1985) *Aikido Kyoshitsu* [Aikido Class]. Tokyo: Taishukan.

Shropshire, Kenneth L. (1990) *Agents of Opportunity: Sports Agents and Corruption in Collegiate Sports.* Philadelphia: University of Pennsylvania Press.

———. (1990) *Careers in Sports Law.* Chicago: American Bar Association.

Sillitoe, A. (1968) *The Loneliness of the Long Distance Runner.* New York: Knopf.

Silver, George. (1972) "Paradoxes of Defense and Brief Instructions." In *Three Elizabethan Fencing Manuals, Scholars Facsimilars and Reprints*, edited by J. L. Jackson. New York: Delmar, 489–634.

Simon, R. (1991) *Fair Play: Sports, Values, and Society.* Boulder, CO: Westview Press.

Simri, Uriel. (1995) "Hapoel—The World's Only Ruling Worker Sports Organisation (Israel)." In *The Story of Worker Sport,* edited by Arnd Krüger and James Riordan. Champaign, IL: Human Kinetics.

Singapore Amateur Sepak Takraw Association. (1978) *Status Report on Sepak Takraw in Singapore.*

Singer, C. (1956) *Galen on Anatomical Procedures, Books I–VIII and five chapters of Book IX.* London: Oxford University Press.

Singer, Peter. (1975) *Animal Liberation: A New Ethics for Our Treatment of Animals.* New York: Avon Books.

Sipes, Richard G. (1973) "War, Sports and Aggression: An Empirical Test of Two Rival Theories." *American Anthropologist* 75: 64–86.

SIRC (1993) *Sport Leadership: Leadership Dans Sport.* Gloucester, Ontario, Canada: Sport Information Centre.

Sisson, Mark. (1989) *Training and Racing Biathlons.* Los Angeles, CA: Primal Urge Press.

Sissons, Ric. (1988) *The Players: A Social History of the Professional Cricketer.* Sydney, Australia: Pluto Press.

*Skating* (Colorado Springs, CO).

Skeeter, Brent. (1988) "The Climatically Optimal Major League Baseball Season in North America." *Geographical Bulletin* 30, 2: 97–102.

Skelton, Betty. (1988) *Side Saddle Riding: Notes for Teachers and Pupils.* London: Sportsman Press.

Slatta, Richard W. (1990) *Cowboys of the Americas.* New Haven, CT, and London: Yale University Press.

Slusher, Howard. (1967) *Man, Sport and Existence: A Critical Analysis.* Philadelphia: Lea & Febiger.

Smith, A. Ledyard. (1961) "Types of Ball Courts in the Highlands of Guatemala." In *Essays in Precolumbian Art and Archaeology,* edited by Samuel K. Lothrop et al. Cambridge, MA: Harvard University Press, 100–125.

Smith, Beverly. (1994) *Figure Skating: A Celebration.* Toronto, Canada: McClelland & Stewart.

Smith, Charles F. (1932) *Games and Games Leadership.* New York: Dodd, Mead.

Smith, D., with J. H. Bender. (1973) *Inside Diving.* Chicago: Henry Regnery.

Smith, David B. (1981) *Curling: An Illustrated History.* Edinburgh, UK: John Donald.

Smith, Herb A. (1975) *Boomerangs: Making and Throwing Them.* Littlehampton, UK: Gemstar.

Smith, Lawrence B. (1931) *Better Trapshooting.* New York: E. P. Dutton.

Smith, Leroi ("Tex"). (1982) *Karting.* New York: Arco Publishing.

Smith, Myron J., comp. (1986) *Baseball: A Comprehensive Bibliography.* Jefferson, NC: McFarland.

———. (1994) *The College Football Bibliography.* Westport, CT.: Greenwood.

Smith, N. L. (1979) *Almanac of Sports and Games.* New York: Facts On File.

Smith, Page, and Charles Daniel. (1975) *The Chicken Book.* Boston: Little, Brown.

Smith, Peter K. (1982) "Does Play Matter? Functional and Evolutionary Aspects of Animal and Human Play." *Behavioral and Brain Sciences* 5: 139–184.

Smith, Raymond. (1969) *The Hurling Immortals.* Dublin, Ireland: Spicer.

Smith, Robert. (1972) *Illustrated History of Pro Football.* New York: Grosset & Dunlap.

Smith, Robert A. (1972) *A Social History of the Bicycle.* New York: American Heritage Press.

Smith, Robert W. (1966) *A Complete Guide to Judo: Its History and Practice.* Rutland, VT: Charles E. Tuttle.

———. (1995) "Cheng Manqing and Taijiquan: A Clarification of Role." *Journal of Asian Martial Arts* 4, 2: 50–65.

Smith, Ronald A. (1988) *Sports and Freedom: The Rise of Big-Time College Athletics.* New York: Oxford University Press.

———. (1994) *Big-Time Football at Harvard, 1905: The Diary of Coach Bill Reid.* Urbana: University of Illinois Press.

Smith, W. R. (1930) *Myths and Legends of the Australian Aboriginals.* London: George G. Harrop.

Smoll, F. L., and R. E. Smith. (1989) "Leadership Behaviors in Sport : A Theoretical Model and Research Paradigm." *Journal of Applied Social Psychology* 19: 1522–1551.

———. (1996) *Children and Youth in Sport: A Biopsychosocial Perspective.* Madison, WI: Brown & Benchmark.

Smout, T. C. (1986) *A Century of the Scottish People, 1830–1950.* New Haven, CT: Yale University Press.

Snook, G. A. (1984) "The History of Sportsmedicine, Part 1." *American Journal of Sports Medicine* 12, 252 (July/August).

Snouffer, Chet. (1994) *The Leading Edge.* Newsletter of the Free Throwers Boomerang Society, 1980–1994. Delaware, OH: Leading Edge Boomerangs.

Snyder, E., and E. Spreitzer. (1976) "Correlates of Sport Participation among Adolescent Girls." *Research Quarterly* 47: 804–809.

———. (1978) *Social Aspects of Sport.* Englewood Cliffs, NJ: Prentice-Hall.

Snyder, E., and S. Kivlin. (1975) "Women Athletes and Aspects of Psychological Well-Being and Body Imagery." *Research Quarterly* 46: 191–199.

Soar, P., ed. (1984) *The Hamlyn World Encyclopaedia of Football.* London: Hamlyn.

Soaring Society of America. (1991) *SSA Membership Handbook.* Hobbs, NM: Soaring Society of America.

Sobel, Lionel. (1977) *Professional Sports and the Law.* New York: Law-Arts Publishers (1981 supplement).

Sollier, A., and Zsolt Gyobiro. (1969) *Japanese Archery: Zen Is Action.* New York: Walker/Weatherhill.

Solomon, M. (1983) "Vainless Quest: Myth, Metaphor and Dream in *Chariots of Fire.*" *Communication Quarterly* 31, 4 (Fall): 274–280.

Soucie, D. (1994) "Effective Managerial Leadership in Sport Organizations." *Journal of Sport Management* 8: 1–13.

*A Sound Mind in a Sound Body—A History of Maccabi.* Ramat Gan, Israel: Pierre Gildesgame Maccabi Sports Museum.

Soustelle, Jacques. (1955) *Daily Life of the Aztecs on the Eve of the Spanish Conquest.* Palo Alto, CA: Stanford University Press.

Souza, Ken, with Bob Babbitt. (1989) *Biathlon: Training and Racing Techniques.* Chicago: Contemporary Books.

Spalding, Albert G. (1911; reprint, 1992) *America's National Game.* New York: American; Lincoln: University of Nebraska Press.

Sparshott, Francis. (1988) *Off the Ground. First Steps to a Philosophical Consideration of the Dance.* Princeton, NJ: Princeton University Press.

Speak, M. A. (1998) "Social Stratification and Participation in Sport in Mid-Victorian England with Particular Reference to Lancaster, 1840–1870." In *Pleasure, Profit, Proselytism: British Culture and Sport at Home and Abroad,* edited by J. A. Mangan. London: Frank Cass.

Spears, B. (1981) "Tryhosa, Melpomene, and Nadia: The IOC and Women's Sport." In *Olympism,* edited by J. Segrave and D. Chu. Champaign, IL: Human Kinetics, 81–88.

Spears, Betty. (1976) "Women in the Olympic Games: An Unresolved Problem." In *The Modern Olympics,* edited by P. J. Graham and H. Ueberhorst. New York: Leisure Press.

Spears, Betty, and Swanson, Richard A. (1995). *History of Sport and Physical Activity in the United States.* 4th ed. Madison, WI: Brown & Benchmark.

———. (1988) *History of Sport and Physical Education in the United States.* Dubuque, IA: William Brown.

Spencer, B. (1928) *Wanderings in Wild Australia.* London: Macmillan.

Sperber, Murray. (1991) *College Sports, Inc.: The Athletic Department vs. the University.* New York: Henry Holt.

———. (1993) *Shake Down the Thunder: The Creation of Notre Dame Football.* New York: Henry Holt.

Sperling, Susan. (1988) *Animal Liberators: Research and Morality.* Berkeley: University of California Press.

*Sport and the Law* (supplement to the official proceedings of the International Athletic Foundation Symposium on Sport and Law, Monte Carlo [1991]). (1995) Monaco.

Springwood, Charles. (1996) *Cooperstown to Dyersville: A Geography of Baseball Nostalgia.* Boulder, CO: Westview.

Squires, Richard C. (1969) *How To Play Platform Tennis.* New York: Devin-Adair.

———. (1978) *The OTHER Racquet Sports.* New York: McGraw-Hill.

St. John, Bob. (1977) *On Down the Road: The World of the Rodeo Cowboy.* Englewood Cliffs, NJ: Prentice-Hall.

Staal, Frits. (1993) "Indian Bodies." In *Self as Body in Asian Theory and Practice,* edited by Thomas P. Kasulis et al. Albany: State University of New York Press, 59–102.

Stafford, R. (1990) *Racquetball: The Sport for Everyone.* 3d ed. Memphis, TN: Stafford.

Stahl, E. E. (1733) *De motu corpori humani.* Erfurt, Germany: Moeller.

Stambler, Irwin. (1984) *Off Roading: Racing and Riding.* Toronto, Canada: General Publishing.

Stamp, Don. (1971) *The Challenge of Archery.* London: Adam & Charles Black.

Standl, Hans. (1976) *Pistol Shooting as a Sport.* Translated by Anita Pennington. New York: Crown Publishers.

Stark, P. (1987) "Barrel Jumping." *Outside* (January): 55.

Steadward, R., and C. Walsh. (1984) "Training and Fitness Programs for Disabled Athletes: Past, Present, and Future." In *Sports and Disabled Athletes,* edited by C. Sherrill. Champaign, IL: Human Kinetics, 3–17.

Steele, M. (1985) "What We Know When We Know a Game." In *Sport Inside Out: Readings in Literature and Philosophy,* edited by D. Vanderwerken and S. Wertz. Fort Worth, TX: Texas Christian University Press, 78–86.

Steere, Michael (1985) *Scott Hamilton: A Behind-the-Scenes Look at the Life and Competitive Times of America's Favorite Figure Skater.* New York: St. Martin's Press.

Stein, Henri. (1925) *Archers d'autrefois; archers d'aujourd'hui.* Paris: Longuet.

Stein, J. U. (1982) "New Vistas in Competitive Sports for Athletes with Handicapping Conditions." *Exceptional Educational Quarterly* (May): 28–34.

Steinkraus, W., ed. (1976) *The U. S. Equestrian Team Book of Riding.* New York: Simon and Schuster.

Stern, Theodore. (1949) *The Rubber Ball-Games of the Americas.* Monographs of the American Ethnological Society, no. 17. Seattle: University of Washington Press.

Sternberg, Dick. (1982) *The Art of Fresh Water Fishing.* Minnetonka, MN: Cy DeCosse.

Stevens, John. (1995) *The Secrets of Aikido.* Boston, and London: Shambhala.

Stevens, Phillips, Jr. (1993) "Traditional Sport in Africa: Wrestling among the Bachama of Nigeria." Paper presented at the International Conference on the Preservation and Advancement of Traditional Sport, Waseda University, Shinjoku, Japan, 11–12 March 1993.

Stewart, Bob. (1983) *The Australian Football Business.* Kenthurst, Australia: Kangaroo Press.

Stewart, G. T. (1983) "Whymper of the Matterhorn: A Victorian Tragedy." *History Today* 33: 5–13.

Stewart, Ken. (1994) *The Glider Pilot's Manual.* UK: Airlife Publishing.

Stoddart, B. (1994) "Golf International: Considerations of Sport in the Global Marketplace." In *Sport in the Global Village,* edited by R. C. Wilcox. Morgantown, WV: Fitness Information Technology.

Stokes, Roberta, and Mick Haley. (1984) *Volleyball Everyone.* Winston-Salem, NC: Hunter Textbooks.

Stokvis, Ruud. (1989) "De Populariteit van Sporten." *Amsterdams Sociologisch Tijdschrift* 15, 4 (March): 673–696.

Stoll, S. K. (1993) *Who Says It's Cheating?* Dubuque, IA: Kendall Hunt.

Stone, William J. (1987) *Adult Fitness Programs: Planning, Designing, Managing, and Improving Fitness Programs.* Glenview, IL: Scott, Foresman.

Strauss, R. (1987) *Drugs and Performance in Sports.* Philadelphia: W. B. Saunders.

Strehly, Georges. (1892) *L'acrobatie et les acrobates, texte et dessins.* Paris: Delagrave.

Stremski, Richard. (1986) *Kill for Collingwood.* Sydney, Australia: Allen & Unwin.

Strickland, Charles. (1995) *Western Riding.* Pownal, VT: Storey Communications.

Strong, Roy C. (1958) "Elizabethan Jousting Cheques in the Possession of the College of Arms I, II." *The Coat of Arms* 5, 34: 4–8; 5, 35: 63–68.

Struna, Nancy. (1984) "Commentary: Beyond Mapping Experience: The Need for Understanding in the History of American Sporting Women." *Journal of Sport History* 11, 1 (Spring).

———. (1996) *People of Prowess: Sport, Leisure, and Labor in Early Anglo-America.* Urbana: University of Illinois Press.

Strutt, Joseph. (1969) *The Sports and Passtimes of the People of England.* First published in 1801. 1903 edition reissued with a preface by N. and R. McWhirter. London.

Subramanian, N. (1966) *Sangam Polity.* Bombay, India: Asian Publishing House.

Sucher, Harry V. (1990) *Harley Davidson.* London: Bison Books.

Sugden, John, and Alan Bairner. (1993) "National Identity, Community Relations and the Sporting Life in Northern Ireland." In *The Changing Politics of Sport,* edited by Lincoln Allison. Manchester, UK: Manchester University Press.

———. (1993) *Sport, Sectarianism and Society in a Divided Ireland.* Leicester, UK: Leicester University Press.

Suino, Nicholas. (1994) *Eishin-Ryu Iaido: Manual of Traditional, Japanese Swordsmanship.* New York: Weatherhill.

———. (1995) *Practice Drills for Japanese Swordsmanship.* New York: Weatherhill.

Suits, B. (1972) "What Is a Game?" In *Sport and the Body: A Philosophical Symposium,* edited by E. Gerber. Philadelphia: Lea and Febiger, 16–22.

———. (1978) *The Grasshopper: Games, Life and Utopia.* Toronto, Canada: University of Toronto Press.

Sullivan, Dean A., comp. and ed. (1995) *Early Innings: A Documentary History of Baseball, 1825–1908.* Lincoln: University of Nebraska Press.

Sullivan, George. (1965) *The Compete Guide to Softball.* New York: Fleet Publishing.

———. (1975) *Paddle. The Beginner's Guide to Platform Tennis.* New York: Coward, McCann & Geoghegan.

Summerfield, K., and A. White. (1989) "Korfball: A Model of Egalitarianism." *Sociology of Sport Journal* 6, 2 (June): 144–151.

Sunadomari, Kanemoto. (1969) *Aikido Kaiso Ueshiba Morihei* [A Biography of Morihei Ueshiba: The Founder of Aikido]. Tokyo: Kodansha.

Surtees, Robert Smith. (1901 [1838]) *Jorrocks Jaunts and Jollities.* London: Downey.

Sutton, Nigel. (1991) *Applied Tai Chi Chuan.* London: A. & C. Black.

———. (1993) "Gongfu, Guoshu and Wushu: State Appropriation of the Martial Arts in Modern China." *Journal of Asian Martial Arts* 2, 3: 102–114.

Sutton-Smith, Brian. (1986) "The Fate of Traditional Games in the Modern World." *Association for the Anthropological Study of Play Newsletter* 12, 2: 8–13.

Sutton-Smith, Brian, and John M. Roberts. (1980) "Play, Games, and Sports." In *Handbook of Cross-Cultural Psychology, Volume 4: Developmental Psychology,* edited by Harry C. Triandis and Alastair Heron. Boston: Allyn and Bacon, 425–471.

Swaddling, Judith. (1984) *The Ancient Olympic Games.* Austin: University of Texas Press.

Swan, Margaret, Donald Kane, and Dawn Bean. (1984, 1989) *Coaching Synchronized Swimming Effectively.* Champaign, IL: Human Kinetics.

Sweet, Waldo E. (1987) *Sport and Recreation in Ancient Greece: A Sourcebook with Translations.* Oxford: Oxford University Press.

Swift, Sally. (1985) *Centered Riding.* New York: St. Martin's Press/Marek.

Talbot, P. Amaury. (1967) *Some Nigerian Fertility Cults.* New York: Barnes & Noble.

Talhoffer, Hans. (1887) *Fechtbuch aus dem Jahre 1467. Gerichtliche und andere.*

Tamasu, Hikosuke. (1993) *Songs of International Friendship.* Tokyo: Kimihiko Tamasu.

Taylor, A. R. (1992) *The Guinness Book of Traditional Pub Games.* Enfield, UK: Guinness.

Taylor, G. (1860) *The Swedish Movement Cure.* New York: Macmillan.

Taylor, J., ed. (1932) *Selected Writings of John Hughlings Jackson.* London: Hodder and Stoughton.

Taylor, Kim. (1992, 1994) *Kim's Big Book of Iaido.* Vols. 1–5 Guelph: Sei Do Kai.

Taylor, Nick. (1987) *Bass Wars: A Story of Fishing Fame and Fortune.* New York: McGraw-Hill.

Tegner, Bruce. (1967) *The Complete Book of Judo.* New York: Bantam Books.

Teichler, H. J., and G. Hauk, eds. (1987) *Illustrierte Geschichte des Arbeitersports.* Berlin, Germany: Verlag Karl Hofmann.

Tejada-Flores, L. (1967) "Games Climbers Play." *Ascent* 1: 23–25.

Tek, Peter Lim Tian. (1995) "Principles and Practices in Taijiquan." *Journal of Asian Martial Arts* 4, 1: 65–72.

Telander, R. (1989) *The Hundred Yard Lie: The Corruption of College Football and What We Can Do To Stop It.* New York: Simon and Schuster.

Tellington, W., and L. Tellington-Jones. (1979) *Endurance and Competitive Trail Riding.* Garden City, NY: Doubleday.

Terret, Thierry. (1995) "Professional Swimming in England before the rise of Amateurism, 1837–75." *International Journal of the History of Sport* 12, 1 (April): 18–32.

Thailand, Government of. (1968) *Thai Games and Festivals.* Bangkok: Public Relations Department of Thailand.

Theberge, N. (1988) "Making a Career in a Man's World: The Experiences and Orientations of Women in Coaching." *Arena Review* 12 (2): 116–127.

Thelin, John R. (1994) *Games Colleges Play: Scandal and Reform in Intercollegiate Athletics.* Baltimore, MD: Johns Hopkins University Press.

Thimm, Captain Carl A. (1896) *Complete Bibliography of Fencing and Duelling as Practiced by All European Nations from the Middle Ages to the Present Day.* London: John Lane; reprint 1992, London: James Cummins.

Thom, W. (1813) *Pedestrianism.* Aberdeen, UK: D. Chalmers.

Thomas, C. (1983) *Sport in a Philosophic Context.* Philadelphia: Lea and Febiger.

Thomas, D. Q., and N. E. Rippe. (1992) *Is Your Aerobics Class Killing You?* Chicago: Chicago Review Press.

Thomas, Jacques. (1985) *Magie du boomerang.* Lyon, France: L'imprimerie des Beaux-Arts.

———. (1991) *The Boomerangs of a Pharaoh.* Lyon, France: Jacques Thomas.

Thomas, L. (1969) *Book of the High Mountains.* New York: Simon & Schuster.

Thomas, Lowell, and Ted Shane. (1940) *Softball: So What?* New York: Frederick A. Stokes.

Thomas, Mary L. (1993) *Fair Lady Aside.* Rev. ed. Bucyrus, OH: World Sidesaddle Federation.

Thomas, Sir William Beach. (1936) *Hunting England.* London: Batsford.

Thompson, Brett, ed. (1980) *Olympiad: A Graphic Celebration.* San Diego, CA: A. S. Barnes.

Thompson, E. P. (1967) "Time, Work-Discipline, and Industrial Capitalism." *Past and Present* 38: 56–97.

Thompson, Lee. "The Modernization of Sumo as a Sport." Ph.D. dissertation, Osaka University, 1989.

Thompson, William A. (1985) *Modern Sports Officiating : A Practical Guide.* 3d ed. Dubuque, IA: William C. Brown.

Thompson, S., and J. Finnigan. (1990). "Egalitarianism in Korfball Is a Myth." *New Zealand Journal of Health Physical Education and Recreation* 23, 4: 7–11.

Thorn, John, and Peter Plamer, eds. (1993) *Total Baseball.* New York: Outlet Books.

Thornes, John. (1977) "The Effect of Weather on Sport." *Weather* 32: 258– 269.

Thorpe, Jim, in collaboration with Thomas Collison. (1932) *Jim Thorpe's History of the Olympics.* Los Angeles, CA: Wetzel.

Tijerino, Edgard. (1989) *Doble play.* Managua, Nicaragua: Editorial Vanguardia.

Timmons, Grady. (1989) *Waikiki Beachboy.* Honolulu, HI: Editions Limited.

Tinley, Scott, with Mike Plant. (1986) *Winning Triathlon.* Chicago: Contemporary Books.

Tissot, C. J. (1781) *Gymnastique medicinale et chirurgicale.* Paris: Dupont.

Todd, Jan. (1991) "Bernarr MacFadden: Reformer of Feminine Form." *Iron Game History* 1, 4/5: 3–8.

Todd, Terry. (1978) *Inside Powerlifting.* Chicago, IL: Contemporary Books.

———. (1987) "Anabolic Steroids: The Gremlins of Sport." *Journal of Sport History* 14.

———. (1995) "Mac and Jan." *Iron Game History* 3, 6: 17–19.

Tomiki, Kenji. (1991) *Budo-ron* [Budo Theory]. Tokyo: Taishukan.

Toole-Scott, R. (1960) *Circus and Allied Arts, a World Bibliography.* Vol. 2. Derby, UK: Harpur and Sons, 19–24.

Torres, Angel. (1976) *La historia del béisbol cubano, 1878–1976.* Los Angeles: Torres.

*Tout sur le saut de barils.* (1980) Courtesy of Gilles Leclerc, Association Canadienne de Saut de Barils, St. Bruno, Canada.

Trefethen, James B. (1967) *Americans and Their Guns.* Harrisburg, PA: Stackpole.

Tremaud, H. (1972) *Jeux de force et d'adresse.* Paris: Musées Nationaux.

Trench, Charles C. (1972) *A History of Marksmanship.* Chicago: Follett.

———. (1974) *A History of Angling.* Chicago: Follett.

———. (1980) *A History of Marksmanship.* New York: Exeter Books.

Trollope, Anthony. (1952 [1865]) *Hunting Sketches.* London: Benn.

Trubiano, Ernie. (1982) *The Carolina Cup, 50 Years of Steeplechasing and Socializing.* Columbia, SC: R. L. Bryan.

Trulson, Michael E. (1986) "Martial Arts Training: A Novel 'Cure' for Juvenile Delinquency." *Human Relations* 39: 1131–1140.

Tryckare, Tre, Ewart Cagner, and Bernt Dybern. (1976) *The Lore of Sportfishing.* New York: Crown.

Tuer, David F., and Howard F. Hunt. (1986) *Encyclopedic Dictionary of Sports Medicine.* New York and London: Chapman and Hall.

Turner, C., and T. Soper. (1990) *Methods and Practice of Elizabethan Swordplay.* Carbondale: Southern Illinois University Press.

Turner, Michael, and Gerry Cranham. (1992) *Great Jockeys of the Flat.* Middlesex, UK: Guiness.

Turner, Stephen. (1986) *Windsurfing*. New York: Gallery.

Turoff, Fred. (1991) *Artistic Gymnastics: A Comprehensive Guide to Performing and Teaching Skills for Beginners and Advanced Beginners*. Dubuque, IA: Wm. C. Brown.

Tutko, T. A., and J. W. Richards. (1971) *Psychology of Coaching*. Ottawa: Coaching Association of Canada.

Twin, Stephanie. (1979) *Out of the Bleachers*. New York: Feminist Press.

Tygiel, Jules. (1983) *Baseball's Great Experiment: Jackie Robinson and His Legacy*. New York and Oxford: Oxford University Press.

Tylor, Edward B. (1879) "The History of Games." *Fortnightly Review, London*, 25, n.s. (1 January –1 June): 735–747. Also in *The Study of Games*, edited by Elliot Avedon and Brian Sutton-Smith. (1971) New York: John Wiley.

Tynan, Kenneth. (1955) *Bull Fever*. New York: Harper & Bros.

Tzachou-Alexandri, Olga, ed. (1989) *Mind and Body, Athletic Contests in Ancient Greece*. Athens: Greek Ministry of Culture.

Uberstine, Gary A. (1988) *Law of Professional and Amateur Sports*. New York: Clark Boardman.

Ueberhorst, Horst. (1969) *Zurück zu Jahn*. Bochum, Germany: Universitätsverlag.

———. (1973) *Frisch, Frei, Stark und Treu. Die Arbeitresportbewegung in Deutschland, 1893–1933*. Dusseldorf, Germany: Droste Verlag.

———. (1978) *Turner unterm Sternenbanner*. Munich, Germany: Heinz Moos.

Ueshiba, Kisshomaru. (1977) *Aikido Kaiso Ueshiba Morihei Den* [A Biography of Morihei Ueshiba: The Founder of Aikido]. Tokyo: Kodansha.

———. (1981) *Aikido no Kokoro* [The Spirit of Aikido]. Tokyo: Kodansha.

Ukah, Matthias O. (1990) "Socio-cultural Forces in Growth of All African Games." *Journal of the International Council for Health, Physical Education and Recreation* 26, 2: 16–20.

Ulmann, Jacques. (1965) *De la gymnastique aux sports modernes*. Paris: Presses Universitaires de France. (1977) 3d ed. Paris: Vrin.

———. (1971) *De la gymnastique aux sports modernes*. 2d ed. Paris: Vrin.

Ulmrich, Ekkehart, ed. (1992) *100 Jahre Skitechnik—40 Jahre Interski-Kongresse*. Planegg, Germany: Deutscher Skiverband.

Umphlett, W. Lee, ed. (1975) *The Sporting Myth and the American Experience: Studies in Contemporary Fiction*. Lewisburg, PA: Bucknell University Press.

———. (1983) *American Sport Culture: The Humanistic Dimensions*. Lewisburg, PA: Bucknell University Press.

———. (1991) *The Achievement of American Sport Literature: A Critical Appraisal*. Rutherford, NJ: Fairleigh Dickinson University Press.

Underdown, David. (1985) *Revel, Riot and Rebellion: Popular Politics and Culture in England 1603–1660*. Oxford: Oxford University Press.

Union Internationale de Tir. (1993) *Special Technical Rules for Clay Target Shooting*. Munich, Germany: UIT.

United States Badminton Association. (1995) *Badminton '95* (USBA Official Media Guide). Colorado Springs, CO: United States Badminton Association.

———. (1996) *60 Years: 1936–1996, 60th Jubilee Fact Book*. Colorado Springs, CO: United States Badminton Association.

U.S. Fish and Wildlife Service. (1993) *1991 National Survey of Fishing, Hunting, and Wildlife Associated Recreation*. Washington, DC: Government Printing Office.

United States Olympic Committee. (1988) *Seoul-Calgary 1988*. Sandy, UT: Commemorative Publications.

U.S. Synchronized Swimming. (1944– ) *Official Synchronized Swimming Handbook*. Indianapolis, IN: U.S. Synchronized Swimming.

U.S. Weightlifting Federation. (1996) *1996 Media Guide*. Colorado Springs, CO: U.S. Weightlifting Federation.

Unsworth, W. (1982) *Everest*. Harmondsworth, UK: Penguin.

———. (1992) *Encyclopaedia of Mountaineering*. London: Hodder & Stoughton.

———. (1994) *Hold the Heights: The Foundations of Mountaineering*. Seattle, Washington: The Mountaineers.

Urick, Dave. (1988) *Lacrosse: Fundamentals for Winning*. New York: Sports Illustrated Winner's Circle Books.

Uzorinac, Zdenko. (1981) *From Sarajevo to Novi Sad*. Zagreb: Graficki zavod Hrvatske.

Vaage, Jakob. (1952) *Norske ski erobrer verden*. Oslo, Norway: Gyldendal Norsk Forlag.

———. (1979) *Skienes Verden*. Oslo, Norway: Hjemmenes.

Vale, Juliet. (1982) *Edward III and Chivalry. Chivalric Society and Its Context. 1270–1350*. Woodbridge, UK: Boydell Press.

Vale, Malcolm G. A. (1981) *War and Chivalry*. London: Gerald Duckworth.

Vamplew, Wray. (1976) *The Turf: A Social and Economic History of Horse Racing*. London: Allen Lane.

———. (1988) *Pay Up and Play the Game: Professional Sport in Britain 1875–1914*. Cambridge: Cambridge University Press.

———. (1989) "Horse Racing." In *Sport in Britain: A Social History*, edited by Tony Mason. Cambridge: Cambridge University Press.

Vamplew, Wray, and Brian Stoddart, eds. (1994) *Sport in Australia: A Social History*. Cambridge: Cambridge University Press.

Vamplew, Wray, Katherine Moore, John O'Hara, Richard Cashman, and Ian F. Jobling, eds. (1992) *The Oxford Companion to Australian Sport*. Melbourne, Australia: Oxford University Press.

van Buitenen, J. A. B. (1973–1978) *The Mahabharata*, vols. 1–3. Chicago and London: University of Chicago Press.

Van Buskirk, Kim, ed. (1987) *Coaching Intermediate Synchronized Swimming Effectively.* Champaign, IL: Human Kinetics.

Van Dalen, Deobold B., and Bennett, Bruce L. (1971). *A World History of Physical Education.* 2d ed. Englewood Cliffs, NJ: Prentice-Hall.

Van der Smissen, Betty. (1990) *Legal Liability and Risk Management for Public and Private Entitites—Sports and Physical Education, Leisure Services, Recreation and Parks, Camping and Adventure Activities.* Cincinnati, OH: Anderson Publishing.

Van Hyning, Thomas E. (1995) *Puerto Rico's Winter League: A History of Major League Baseball's Launching Pad.* Jefferson, NC: McFarland.

van Kuijen, Hans, ed. (1994) *Who's Who in Combined Events.* Helmond, Netherlands: van Kuijen.

Van Mele, Veerle, and Roland Renson. (1992) *Traditional Games in South America.* Schorndorf: Hofmann.

Van Steenwyk, E. (1980) *Quarter Horse Winner.* Chicago: Albert Whitman.

Vanderwerken, David, and Spencer K. Wertz, eds. (1985) *Sport Inside Out: Readings in Literature and Philosophy.* Fort Worth: Texas Christian University Press.

Vanhouse, Norman. (1986) *BSA Competition History.* n.p.: Sparkford Foulis Haynes Publishing.

Vealey, R. S. (1994) "Current Status and Prominent Issues in Sport Psychology Intervention." *Medicine and Science in Sport and Exercise* 26: 495–502.

Velasco, M. R. (1936) "Native Filipino Sports and Games." *Mid-Pacific Magazine* 47, 1.

Vennum, Thomas, Jr. (1994) *American Indian Lacrosse: Little Brother of War.* Washington, DC: Smithsonian Institution.

Verbrugge, Martha. (1988) *Able-Bodied Womanhood.* New York: Oxford University Press.

Vernam, Glenn R. (1994) *Man on Horseback.* New York: Harper & Row.

Verrini, Michele, and Enzo Lucchi, eds. (1974) *Il libro del motocross.* Verona, Italy: Mondadori.

Versi, A. (1986) *Football in Africa.* London: Collins.

Vertinsky, Patricia. (1990) *The Eternally Wounded Woman: Women, Doctors and Exercise in the Late Nineteenth Century.* Manchester, UK: Manchester University Press.

———. (1994) "Gender Relations, Women's History and Sport History: A Decade of Changing Enquiry, 1983–1993." *Journal of Sport History* 21, 1 (Spring).

Veysey, Lawrence. (1965) *The Emergence of the American University.* Chicago: University of Chicago Press.

Victoria Commonwealth Games Society. (1994) *Let the Spirit Live On: XV Commonwealth Games.* Victoria, British Columbia: Victoria Commonwealth Games Society.

Vida, F. (1976) *Storia dello Sci Italia, 1896–1975.* Milan, Italy: Milano Sole.

Vincent, Ted. (1981) *Mudville's Revenge: The Rise and Fall of American Sport.* New York: Seaview Press.

Viney, Nigel, and Neil Grant. (1978) *An Illustrated History of Ball Games.* London: Heinemann.

Voigt, David Quentin. (1983) *American Baseball,* 3 vols. University Park: Pennsylvania State University Press.

Vokey, John R., and Gordon W. Russell. (1992) "On Penalties in Sport as Measures of Aggression." *Social Behavior and Personality* 20: 219–225.

Volti, Rudi. (1992) *Society & Social Change.* New York: St. Martin's Press.

Von Achenbach, Benno. (n.d.) *Anspannen und Fahren.* Germany.

Voy, R. (1991) *Drugs, Sport, and Politics.* Champaign, IL: Leisure Press.

Wadler, G. I., and B. Hainline. (1989) *Drugs and the Athlete.* Philadelphia: F. A. Davis.

Wagenvoord, James. (1968) *Flying Kites in Fun, Art and War.* New York: Macmillan.

Wagg, Stephen, ed. (1995) *Giving the Game Away: Football, Politics, and Culture on Five Continents.* London: Leicester University Press.

Wagley, Charles, and Eduardo Galvao. (1963) "The Tapirape." *Bureau of American Ethnology Bulletin* 143, 3: 167–178.

Wagner, Eric A., ed. (1989) *Sport in Asia and Africa: A Comparative Handbook.* Westport, CT: Greenwood Press.

Wagner, Peter. (1976) "Puritan Attitudes towards Physical Education in l7th Century New England." *Journal of Sport History* 3 (Summer): 139–151.

Wagner, Philip. (1983) "Sport: Geography and Culture." In *Time and Space in Geography,* edited by Allen Pred. Lund, Sweden: Gleerup, 85–108.

Waicukauski, Ronald J., ed. (1982) *The Law and Amateur Sport.* Bloomington: Indiana University Press.

Walker, Stella A. (1972) *Sporting Art; England 1700–1900.* London: Studio Vista.

Wallechinsky, David. (1984) *The Complete Book of the Olympics.* New York: Viking Press.

———. (1988) *The Complete Book of the Olympics.* Revised ed. New York: Viking.

———. (1991) *The Complete Book of the Olympics.* 3d ed. Boston: Little, Brown.

Wallechinsky, David, Irving Wallace, and Amy Wallace. (1977) *The Book of Lists.* New York: William Morrow.

Walton, G. M. (1992) *Beyond Winning: The Timeless Wisdom of Great Philosopher Coaches.* Champaign, IL: Leisure Press.

Walvin, James. (1978) *Leisure and Society, 1830–1950.* London: Longman.

Wann, Daniel L. (1993) "Aggression among Highly Identified Spectators as a Function of Their Need To Maintain Positive Social Identity." *Journal of Sport and Social Issues* 17: 134–143.

Ward, Carl. (1994) *Hockey.* London: Blandford.

Warehime, R. G., D. K. Routh, and M. L. Foulds. (1974) "Knowledge about Self-Actualization and the Presentation of Self as Self-Actualized." *Journal of Personality and Social Psychology* 30, 1: 155–162.

Warner, Gordon, and Donn F. Draeger. (1982) *Japanese Swordsmanship: Technique and Practice.* New York and Tokyo: Weatherhill.

Watanabe, Tadashige. (1993) *Shinkage-ryu Sword Techniques, Traditional Japanese Martial Arts.* Vols. 1 and 2. Trans. by Ronald Balsom. Tokyo: Sugawara Martial Arts Institute

*Water Skier.* (1989) AWSA 50th Anniversary Edition. Winter Haven, FL: American Water Ski Association.

Waterman, Charles F. (1981) *A History of Angling.* Tulsa, OK: Winchester Press.

Watjen, Richard. (1958) *Dressage Riding.* UK: J. A. Allen.

Watman, M. (1968) *History of British Athletics.* London: Robert Hale.

Watney, Mrs. B. M. I. (1981) *The British Driving Society Book of Driving.* London: British Driving Society.

Watson, G. (1990) *The Tour de France and Its Heroes.* London: Stanley Paul.

Watson, J. N. P. (1977) *The Book of Foxhunting.* London: Batsford.

———. (1986) *The World of Polo.* Topsfield, MA: Salem House.

Watson, Ken (1950) *Ken Watson on Curling.* Toronto, Canada: Copp Clark Publishing.

Watson, R. P. (1899) *Memoirs of Robert Patrick Watson: A Journalist's Experience of Mixed Society.* London: Smith, Ainslie.

Watson, Roderick, and Martin Gray. (1978) *The Penguin Book of the Bicycle.* Harmondsworth, UK: Penguin Books.

Webb, Ida. (1976) "Women's Hockey in England." In *The History, the Evolution and Diffusion of Sports and Games in Different Cultures,* edited by R. Benson, P. P. de Mayer, and M. Ostyn. Brussels, Belgium: n.p.

Weber, E. (1971) "Gymnastics and Sports in Fin de Siecle France: Opium of the Classes." *American Historical Review* 76 (February).

Webster, D. (1959) *Scottish Highland Games.* Glasgow, UK: Collins (1973, Edinburgh, UK: Reprographia Edinburgh).

———. (1976) *The Iron Game.* Irvine, UK: John Geddes Printer.

Webster, F. A. M. (1929) *Athletics of Today.* London: Frederick Warne.

Weeks, Bob. (1995) *The Brier: The History of Canada's Most Celebrated Curling Championship.* Toronto, Canada: Macmillan Canada.

Weider, Betty, and Joe Weider. (1981) *The Weider Book of Bodybuilding for Women.* Chicago, IL: Contemporary Books.

Weiler, Ingomar. (1974) *Der Agon im Mythos: Zur Einstellung der Griechen zum Wettkampf.* Darmstadt, Germany: Wissenschaftliche Buchgesellschaft.

———. (1981) *Der Sport bei den Völkern der alten Welt.* Darmstadt: Wissenschaftliche Buchgesellschaft.

Weiler, Paul C., and Gary Roberts. (1993) *Sports and the Law: Cases, Materials, and Problems.* St. Paul, MN: West Publishing.

Wein, Chaim. (n.d.) *The Maccabiah Games in Eretz Israel.* Israel: Maccabi World Union and the Wingate Institute for Physical Education and Sport.

Weinberg, R. S., and D. Gould. (1995) *Foundations of Sport and Exercise Psychology.* Champaign, IL: Human Kinetics.

Weiner, L. (1947) "A Preliminary Study of the History of Weightlifting in the United States of America." Master's thesis, University of Illinois, Urbana.

Weiss, J. Bernard. (n.d.) *Gliding and Soaring Flight.* London: Sampson Low, Marston.

Weiss, M. R., and B. J. L. Bredemeier. (1986) "Moral Development." In *Physical Activity and Well Being,* edited by V. Seefeldt. Reston, VA: American Alliance for Health, Physical Education, Recreation, and Dance, 373–390.

———. (1990) "Moral Development in Sport." *Exercise and Sport Sciences Review* 18: 331–378.

Weiss, Paul. (1969) *Sport: A Philosophic Inquiry.* Carbondale: Southern Illinois University Press.

Weissbein, S. (1910) *Hygiene des Sport.* Leipzig, Germany: Greuthlein.

Weistart, John C., and Cym H. Lowell. (1979) *The Law of Sports.* Indianapolis: Bobbs-Merrill.

Welch, Ann, and Lorne Welch. (1965) *The Story of Gliding.* London: John Murray.

Welsh, Peter C. (1967) *Track and Road: The American Trotting Horse.* Washington, DC: Smithsonian Institution Press.

Welsh, Robin. (1969) *A Beginner's Guide to Curling.* London: Pelham Books.

———. (1985) *International Guide to Curling.* London: Pelham Books.

Wenz, Betty, ed. (1980) *Sports Medicine Meets Synchronized Swimming.* Reston, VA: American Alliance for Health, Physical Education, Recreation and Dance.

Werner, Dennis. (1984) *Amazon Journey: An Anthropologist's Year among Brazil's Mekranoti Indians.* New York: Simon and Schuster.

Werner, Doug. (1993) *Snowboarder's Start-Up.* Ventura, CA: Pathfinder.

Werner, Steve, and the editors of *Plane & Pilot* Magazine. (1995) *The Plane & Pilot International Aircraft Directory.* Tabb Books.

Wertz, S. (1991) *Talking a Good Game: Inquiries into the Principles of Sport.* Dallas, TX: Southern Methodist University Press.

West, Trevor. (1991) *The Bold Collegians.* Dublin, Ireland: Lilliput.

Westbrook, Adele, and Oscar Ratti. (1974) *Secrets of the Samurai.* Rutland, VT: Charles E. Tuttle.

———. (1979) *Aikido and the Dynamic Sphere.* Rutland, VT, and Tokyo: Charles E. Tuttle.

# Bibliography

Westerblad, C. A. (1909) *Ling, the Founder of Swedish Gymnastics*. London: J. M. Dent.

Westover, Craig, and Tamara Westover. (1979) "Cabogganing." *Canoe* 7, 1: 60–61.

Weyand, A. M. (1926) *Football, Its History and Development*. New York: D. Appleton.

Whannel, Garry. (1992) *Fields in Vision: Television Sport and Cultural Transformation*. London: Routledge.

Whedon, Julia. (1988) *The Fine Art of Ice Skating*. New York: Harry N. Abrams.

Wheeler, Robert. (1978) "Organised Sport and Organised Labour: The Worker Sports Movement." *Journal of Contemporary History* 13.

White, Andy. (1994) "The Professionalization of Rugby Union Football in England: Crossing the Rubicon?" M.S. thesis, University of Leicester, UK.

White, Francis. (1635) *A Treatise of the Sabbath-Day*. London: n.p.

Whiting, Robert. (1989) *You Gotta Have Wa*. New York: Macmillan.

Whitlock, H. H. (1957) *Race Walking*. London: Amateur Athletic Association.

Whittingham, Richard. (1984) *What a Game They Played*. New York: Harper & Row.

Whymper, E. (1871) *Scrambles amongst the Alps in the Years 1860–1869*. London: Murray.

Wickelgren, Ingrid. (1994) "In-line Injuries Soar." *Current Science* 80 (23 September): 8–9.

Widmeyer, W. Neil, and Jack S. Birch. (1984) "Aggression in Professional Ice Hockey: A Strategy for Success or a Reaction to Failure?" *Journal of Psychology* 117: 77–84.

Wiemers, Jutta. (1994) *Equestrian Vaulting*. London: J. A. Allen & Co.

Wiley, Carol, ed. (1992) *Women in the Martial Arts*. Berkeley, CA: North Atlantic Books.

Wiley, Mark V. (in press) *Martial Culture of the Philippines*. Tokyo: Charles E. Tuttle.

Williams, J. M., ed. (1993) *Applied Sport Psychology: Personal Growth to Peak Performance*. 2d ed. Mountain View, CA: Mayfield.

Willis, W. H. (1941) "Athletic Contests in the Epic," *Transactions and Proceedings of the American Philological Association* 72: 392–317.

Willoughby, D. P. (1970) *The Super Athletes*. New York: A. S. Barnes.

Wills, D. R., ed. (1966) *Games and Dances of the Maori: A Guide Book for Teachers*. Wellington, New Zealand: Government Printer.

Wills, Maralys. (1992) *Higher Than Eagles*. Marietta, GA: Longstreet Press.

Wills, Philip. (1974) *Free as a Bird*. New York: Barnes & Noble.

Wilsdorf, Helmut. (1939) *Ringkampf im alten Ägypten*. Wuerzburg, Germany: Konrad Triltsch Verlag.

Wilson, Charles Morrow. (1959) *The Magnificent Scufflers: Revealing the Great Days When America Wrestled the World*. Brattleboro, VT: Stephen Greene Press.

Wilson, K. (1981) *Hard Rock*. 2d ed. London: Granada Publishing.

Wilson, Lillie. (1991) "At the Senior Olympics." *American Demographics* (May).

Wilt, Fred. (1973) *How They Train*. Los Altos, CA: Tafnews Press.

Wind, H. W. (1975) *The Story of American Golf*. New York: Alfred A. Knopf.

Winner, Ken, and Roger Jones. (1980) *Windsurfing with Ken Winner*. San Francisco, CA: Harper & Row.

Wirth, Dick. (1982) *Ballooning, the Complete Guide to Riding the Winds*. New York: Random House.

*Wisden Cricket Almanac* (annual from 1864).

Wittenberg, Jeffrey D. (1987) *Product Liability: Recreation and Sports Equipment*. New York: Law Journal Seminars-Press.

Wofford, James C. (1995) *Training the Three-Day Event Horse and Rider*. New York: Howell Book House.

Wong, Glenn M. (1994) *Essentials of Amateur Sports Law*. Westport, CT: Praeger.

Wood, Clement, and Gloria Goddard. (1940) *The Complete Book of Games*. Garden City, NY: Garden City Publishing.

Wood, T., and R. Cassidy. (1927) *The New Physical Education: A Program of Naturalized Activities for Education toward Citizenship*. New York: Macmillan.

Woodford, M. H. (1960, 1972) *A Manual of Falconry*. London: Adam & Charles Black.

Woodruff, Hiram. (1847) *The Trotting Horse of America*. Philadelphia: John C. Winston.

Woolfe, Raymond G., Jr. (1983) *Steeplechasing*. New York: Viking.

Woolum, J. (1992) *Outstanding Women Athletes*. Phoenix, AZ: Oryx Press.

Worsnop, T. (1897) *The Prehistoric Arts, Manufactures, Works, Weapons, etc. of the Aborigines of Australia*. Adelaide, Australia: Government Printing Office.

Wulff, Lee. (1982) "Fly Fishing: An Angler's Perspective." In *Water Swift and Smal*, edited by G. LaFontaine and D. Seybold. Tulsa, OK: Winchester Press, 121–137.

Wythe, Major G., Captain Joseph Mills Hanson, and Captain C. V. Burger, eds. (1919) *The Inter-Allied Games of 1919*. New York: Games Committee.

Yalouris, Nicholas, ed. (1979) *The Eternal Olympics: The Art and History of Sport*. New Rochelle, NY: Caratzas Brothers.

Yambao, Placido. (1957) *Mga Karunungan sa Larong Arnis* [Knowledge in the Art of Arnis]. Manila: University of the Philippines.

Yasser, Raymond L. (1985) *Torts and Sports: Legal Liability in Professional and Amateur Athletics*. Westport, CT: Quorum Books.

# Bibliography

Yasser, Raymond, James R. McCurdy, and C. Peter Goplerud. (1994) *Sport Law, Cases and Materials.* Cincinnati, OH: Anderson Publishing.

Yeo, Stephen, and Eileen Yeo, eds. (1981) *Popular Culture and Class Conflict 1590–1914. Explorations in the History of Labour and Leisure.* Atlantic Highlands, NJ: Humanities Press.

Yokohama, S. Sugahara. (1964) *Olympic Games Stamps.* Tokyo: Chuokoron Jigyo Shuppan.

Young, David C. (1984) *The Olympic Myth of Greek Amateur Athletics.* Chicago: Ares Publishers.

Young, M. (1992 and 1994) *The Guinness Book of Sports Records.* New York: Facts On File.

Young, Nat. (1983) *The History of Surfing.* Sydney, Australia: Palm Beach Press.

Young, Scott. (1990) *The Boys of Saturday Night: Inside Hockey Night in Canada.* Toronto, Canada: McClelland and Stewart.

Young, T. R. (1986) "The Sociology of Sport: Structural Marxist and Cultural Marxist Approaches." *Sociological Perspectives:* 3–28.

Yukawa, Yoshi. (1990) *Japanska Svard.* Stockholm: Berghs.

Yukl, G. A. (1981) *Leadership in Organizations.* Englewood Cliffs, NJ: Prentice-Hall.

Yur'yev, A. A. (1985) *Competitive Shooting.* Translated by Gary L. Anderson. Washington, DC: National Rifle Association of America.

Zander, G. (1879) *L'etablissement de gymnastique medicale mechanique.* Paris: Bailliere.

Zapata Cabañas, Gabriel. (1990) *Yucatán en torneos nacionales e internacionales de béisbol amateur.* Mérida, Yucatán, México: Maldonaldo.

Zarnowski, Frank. (1973) *How To Organize and Run a Decathlon.* Tucson, AZ: USTFF.

———. (1975, 1976, 1978, 1980) *The Decathlon Book.* Emmitsburg, MD: DECA ( Decathlon Association).

———. (1976) *The Decathlon Guide.* Emmitsburg, MD: DECA ( Decathlon Association).

———. (1989) *The Decathlon.* Champaign, IL: Leisure Press.

———. (1996) *Olympic Glory Denied.* Glendale, CA: Griffin Publishing.

Zarnowski, Frank, et al. (1980–1994) *USA Annual Decathlon/Heptathlon Handbook.* Indianapolis, IN: USA T&F.

Zarrilli, Phillip B. (1986) "From Martial Art to Performance: *Kalarippayattu* and Performance in Kerala." *Sangeet Natak* 81–82, 5–41; 83, 14–45.

———. (1989) "Three Bodies of Practice in a Traditional South Indian Martial Art. *Social Science and Medicine* 28, 12: 1289–1309.

———. (1992) "To Heal and/or To Harm: The Vital Spots in Two South Indian Martial Arts, Part I and Part II." *Journal of Asian Martial Arts* 1, 1: 36–67; 1:2, 1–15.

———. (1994) "Actualizing Power(s) and Crafting a Self in *Kalarippayattu,* a South Indian Martial Art and the Yoga and Ayurvedic Paradigms," *Journal of Asian Martial Arts* 3, 3: 10–51.

———. (1995) "The Kalarippayattu Martial Master as Healer: Traditional Kerala Massage Therapies." *Journal of Asian Martial Arts* 4, 1: 66–83.

———. (in press) *"When the Body Becomes All Eyes": Paradigms and Discourses of Practice and Power in Kalarippayattu, a South Indian Martial Art.* New Delhi, India: Oxford University Press.

Zeigler, E. F. (1977) *Physical Education and Sport Philosophy.* Englewood Cliffs, NJ: Prentice-Hall.

———. (1984) *Ethics and Morality in Sport and Physical Education: An Experiential Approach.* Champaign, IL: Stipes.

Zeigler, Earl. (1987) "Sport Management: Past, Present, Future." *Journal of Sport Management* 1, 1: 4–24.

Zeman, Brenda. (1988) *To Run with Longboat: Twelve Stories of Indian Athletes in Canada.* Edmonton: GMS Ventures, Inc.

Zen Nippon Kendo Renmei. (1990) *Zen Nippon Kendo Renmei Iai.* Tokyo: Kendo Nihon.

Ziegler, Earle, ed. (1973) *A History of Sport and PE to 1900.* Champaign, IL: Stipes.

Ziethen, Karl-Heinz. (1981) *4,000 Years of Juggling.* Sainte-Genevieve, France: Michel Poignant P. L.V.

Ziethen, Karl-Heinz, and Andrew Allen. (1985) *Juggling: The Art and Its Artists.* Berlin, Germany: Werner Rausch & Werner Luft.

Zolna, Ed, and Mike Conklin. (1981) *Mastering Softball.* Chicago, IL: Contemporary Books.

Zuccoli, Carlo. (1992) *The Fields of Triumph: Guide to the World of Racing.* Milan, Italy: Monographic.

Zucker, H. M., and L. J. Babich. (1987) *Sports Film: A Complete Reference.* Jefferson, NC: McFarland.

Zur Megede, E., and R. Hymans. (1995) *Progression of World Best Performances and Official I.A.A.F World Records.* Monaco: IAAF.

*Zweikampfe darstellend.* Edited by Gustav Hergsell and J. G. Calve. Prague, Poland: Gustav Hergsell and J. G. Calve.

# Illustration Credits

455 Wendy Gavin Gregg, Millwood, Virginia.
459 American Horse Shows Association, New York.
461 Photo by Sandy Clements, United States Pony Clubs, Lexington, Kentucky.
464 Tish Quirk, Carlsbad, California.
468 The World Sidesaddle Federation, Bucyrus, Ohio.
472 Nelson and Owen Photography, San Jose, California.
475 American Horse Shows Association, New York.
478 Al Bello/Allsport.
483 Corbis Bettmann.
490 Archive Photos.
497 Kim Taylor, Guelph, Ontario, Canada.
500 UPI/Bettmann.
504 Corel Corporation.
508 UPI/Corbis-Bettmann.
520 UPI/Corbis-Bettmann.
522 The Bettmann Archive.
525 The Bodleian Library, Oxford (top).
525 The Herald's College, London (bottom).
527 Reuters/Corbis-Bettmann.
532 Corbis-Bettmann.
536 Markus Boesch/Allsport.
542 Vandystadt/Allsport.
546 UPI/Bettmann.
548 Yasuhiro Sakaue, Fukushimashi, Japan.
552 Reuters/Corbis-Bettmann.
554 Korfalverbond, The Netherlands.
560 Corbis-Bettmann.
566 A. R. Parr.
577 Corbis-Bettmann.
583 Photofest.
587 United States Luge Association, Lake Placid, New York.
594 Karen Christensen/David Levinson, Great Barrington, Massachusetts.
600 UPI/Corbis-Bettmann.
606 AP/Wide World Photos.
611 Markus Boesch/Allsport.
614 Phillip B. Zarrilli, Los Angeles, California.
622 Royal Photo Company Collection, Photographic Archives, University of Louisville, Kentucky.
637 Photo by Stuart Weiner, courtesy of the Bowers Museum of Cultural Art, Santa Ana, California.
645 Corbis-Bettmann.
648 Corel Corporation.
654 UPI/Corbis-Bettmann.
658 Allsport.
664 Culver Pictures, Inc.
680 Peter Arnold, Inc.

684 Allsport.
690 The Metropolitan Museum of Art.
699 Archive Photos.
707 Nathan Bilow/Allsport.
713 National Paddleball Association, Flint, Michigan.
716 UPI/Corbis-Bettmann.
724 Richard Holt, Overijssel, Belgium.
733 Archive Photos.
736 British Museum.
738 U.S. Modern Pentathlon Association, San Antonio, Texas.
744 Corbis-Bettmann.
751 Reuters/Corbis-Bettmann.
754 UPI/Corbis-Bettmann.
759 Reuters/Jonathon Bainbridge/Archive Photos.
765 The Greenwood Press, San Francisco, California.
767 Reuters/Corbis-Bettmann.
772 Lorraine Connor, Allsport.
776 Reuters/Corbis-Bettmann.
786 Archive Photos.
788 Allsport.
791 Corel Corporation.
800 Allen Guttmann, Amherst, Massachusetts.
804 Vandystadt/Allsport.
810 The Bettmann Archive.
819 Wellesley College Archives.
829 Allsport.
833 Reuters/Corbis-Bettmann.
848 Corel Corporation.
851 Corel Corporation.
857 Corbis-Bettmann.
862 Sport Sail, Inc., Boulder, Colorado.
864 George Therihult, New London, New Hampshire.
869 Al Bello/Allsport.
872 The Master and Fellows of University College, Oxford.
875 Bob Krist/Corbis.
880 Pascal Rondeau/Allsport.
884 Tim Defrisco/Allsport.
887 Glenn Matheson, San Antonio, Texas.
891 Corbis-Bettmann.
893 Reuters/Corbis-Bettmann.
895 Corel Corporation.
902 Reuters/Corbis-Bettmann.
905 U.S. Amateur Confederation of Roller Skating, Lincoln, Nebraska.
908 U.S. Amateur Confederation of Roller Skating, Lincoln, Nebraska.
915 Corel Corporation.
919 Chris Cole/Allsport.
923 USDA Forest Service/Corbis.

# Illustration Credits

928    Corel Corporation.
931    Rod Kieft/Nature's Bounty.
934    Anton Want/Allsport.
937    UPI/Corbis-Bettmann.
939    R. E. Barber, Denver, Colorado.
945    Reuters/Corbis-Bettmann.
960    Jamie Squire/Allsport.
966    UPI/Corbis-Bettmann.
971    From *Old-Fashioned Sports Illustrations* (Mineola, New York: Dover Publications, Inc., 1988)
973    Mike Cooper/Allsport.
976    UPI/Corbis-Bettmann.
978    Corel Corporation.
982    Reuters/Bettmann.
985    Corel Corporation.
991    UPI/Bettmann.
994    Reuters/Corbis-Bettmann.
999    Ken Levine/Allsport.
1006    Jae Kyn Lee, Brookfield, Wisconsin.
1009    Courtesy of the *Journal of Asian Martial Arts* and Via Media Publishing.
1011    Eric Bartholomay/Allsport.
1015    UPI/Corbis-Bettmann.
1018    Reuters/Corbis-Bettmann.
1028    American Platform Tennis Association, Inc., Upper Montclair, New Jersey.
1029    American Platform Tennis Association, Inc., Upper Montclair, New Jersey.
1031    Heiner Gillmeister, Bruehl, Germany.
1034    Tim Boggan, Merrick, New York.
1040    From *Winter Sports in Switzerland* by E. F. Benson, illustrated by C. Fleming Williams (London: G. Allen & Co., 1913)

1046    Richard Martin/Allsport.
1050    Reuters/Gary Hershorn/Archive Photos.
1057    Gail Devers/Allsport.
1063    Frobenius-Institute, Frankfurt on the Main, Germany.
1068    UPI/Corbis-Bettmann.
1071    Corbis-Bettmann.
1077    Corbis-Bettmann.
1084    Corbis-Bettmann.
1094    Gerard Planchenault/Allsport.
1098    Reuters/Bettmann.
1103    Kevin Levine/Allsport.
1106    Mike Powell/Allsport.
1108    Corbis-Bettmann.
1111    Tafel IV in *Kleines Handbuch der Gymnastik für Mädchen,* by K. L. Heldermann, Leipzig, 1835.
1118    UPI/Bettmann.
1129    Stephen Dunn/Allsport.
1132    Reuters/Nick Didlick/Archive Photos.
1137    Archive Photos.
1143    UPI/Corbis-Bettmann.
1150    British Museum.
1155    Simm Bruty/Allsport.
1160    Gertrud Pfister, Berlin, Germany.
1171    Tony Duffy/Allsport.
1190    The Walters Art Gallery, Baltimore, Maryland.
1195    Allsport.
1197    Reuters/Corbis-Bettmann.
1204    Corel Corporation.

**Andrea Abbas**
*Keele University, Keele, UK*
*Masculinity*

**Harvey Abrams**
*State College, Pennsylvania*
*Art*
*Literature*

**E. John B. Allen**
*Plymouth State College, Plymouth,*
*New Hampshire*
*Skiing, Alpine*
*Skiing, Nordic*

**Gary Anderson**
*International Shooting Union*
*Shooting, Pistol*
*Shooting, Rifle*

**G. Whitney Azoy**
*Lawrenceville School, Lawrenceville,*
*New Jersey*
*Buzkashi*

**William J. Baker**
*University of Maine, Orono, Maine*
*Basketball*
*Traditional Sports, Africa*
*Religion*

**John Bale**
*Keele University, Keele, UK*
*Environment*
*Geography*
*Track and Field, Running and Hurdling*

**Ralph B. Ballou, Jr.**
*Middle Tennessee State University,*
*Murfreesboro, Tennessee*
*Horse Racing, Steeplechase*

**Robert Knight Barney**
*Centre for Olympic Studies, University of*
*Western Ontario, Canada*
*Olympic Games, Modern*

**Dawn Bean**
*United States Synchronized Swimming*
*Swimming, Synchronized*

**A. Gilbert Belles**
*Western Illinois University,*
*Macomb, Illinois*
*Handball, Court*
*Handball, Team*

**Kendall Blanchard**
*University of Tennessee,*
*Martin, Tennessee*
*Anthropology*
*Traditional Sports, North and South*
*America*

**Tim Boggan**
*USA Table Tennis*
*Tennis, Table*

**Anne Bolin**
*Elon College, Elon, North Carolina*
*Bodybuilding*

**Gherardo Bonini**
*European Community Historical Archives,*
*Florence, Italy*
*Motocross*
*Motorcycle Racing*

**Douglas Booth**
*University of Otago,*
*Dunedin, New Zealand*
*Surfing*

**Linda A. Bowlby**
*World Sidesaddle Federation*
*Horseback Riding, Sidesaddle*

**Maynard Brichford**
*University Archives, Urbana, Illinois*
*African Games*
*Politics*

**Anthony Bush**
*Waltham Cross, UK*
*Polo, Bicycle*

**Michael B. Camillo**
*World Pulling International,*
*Worthington, Ohio*
*Truck and Tractor Pulling*

**Kevin Carr**
*Amherst College,*
*Amherst, Massachusetts*
*Judo*
*Jujutsu*

**Richard Cashman**
*University of New South Wales,*
*Kensington, Australia*
*Cricket*

**Joan M. Chandler**
*University of Texas, Dallas*
*Media*

**Timothy J. L. Chandler**
*Kent State University, Kent, Ohio*
*Camogie*
*Hurling*
*Rugby Fives*

**Jeffery A. Charlston**
*George Washington University,*
*Washington, D.C.*
*Skating, In-Line*

**Karen Christensen**
*Great Barrington, Massachusetts*
*Cricket sidebar*

**Garry Chick**
*University of Illinois,*
*Urbana-Champaign, Illinois*
*Aggression*
*Billiards*
*Definitions*
*Formula 1 Auto Racing*
*Mesoamerican Ballgame*

**Annie Clement**
*Cleveland State University,*
*Cleveland, Ohio*
*Law*

**Tony Collins**
*Sheffield Hallam University,*
*Sheffield, UK*
*Rugby League*

# The Contributors

**Mary Conti**
*American Horse Shows Association*
  *Horseback Riding, Eventing*
  *Horseback Riding, Hunters and Jumpers*
  *Horseback Riding, Vaulting*
  *Horseback Riding, Western*

**Pamela Cooper**
*Allentown, Pennsylvania*
  *Marathon and Distance Running*

**Frank Cosentino**
*York University, Toronto, Canada*
  *Football, Canadian*

**Sally Crawford**
*National Louis University/*
*Full Circle Fitness*
  *Aerobics*
  *Conditioning*
  *Exercise*

**Scott A. G. M. Crawford**
*Eastern Illinois University,*
*Charleston, Illinois*
  *Associations*
  *Barrel Jumping*
  *Coursing*
  *Croquet*
  *Darts*
  *Diving*
  *Golf*
  *Highland Games*
  *Horseback Riding, Gymkhana*
  *Indy Auto Racing*
  *Korfball*
  *Movies*
  *Netball*
  *Pedestrianism*
  *Polo, Water*
  *Race Walking*
  *Shinty*
  *Skating, Ice Speed*
  *Sled Dog Racing*
  *Swimming, Distance*
  *Tug of War*

**Simon J. Crawford**
*Illinois Wesleyan University*
  *Parachuting*

**Michael Cronin**
*Sheffield Hallam University,*
*Sheffield, UK*
  *Bobsledding*

**Lewis C. Cuyler**
*Berkshire Sculling Association,*
*Pittsfield, Massachusetts*
  *Rowing*

**Michael G. Davis**
*Truman State University,*
*Kirksville, Missouri*
  *Tai Chi*

**Wolfgang Decker**
*Deutsche Sporthochschule Köln,*
*Cologne, Germany*
  *Chariot Racing*

**Lisa Delpy**
*George Washington University,*
*Washington, D.C.*
  *Management and Marketing*

**Michael A. DeMarco**
*Journal of Asian Martial Arts*
  *Wushu*

**Richard Dingman**
*International Jugglers Association*
  *Juggling*

**Jon Griffin Donlon**
*Baton Rouge, Louisiana*
  *Cockfighting*
  *Hunting*

**Peter Donnelly**
*McMaster University,*
*Hamilton, Ontario, Canada*
  *Mountain Climbing*
  *Rock Climbing*

**Andrew Doyle**
*Auburn University, Montgomery,*
*Auburn, Alabama*
  *Intercollegiate Athletics*

**Margaret Carlisle Duncan**
*University of Wisconsin,*
*Milwaukee, Wisconsin*
  *Tae Kwon Do*

**Eric Dunning**
*Centre for Research into Sport and*
*Society, University of Leicester, UK*
  *Spectators*
  *Violence*

**Tom Dunning**
*University of Tasmania, Launceston,*
*Tasmania, Australia*
  *Animal Baiting*

**Brooke Dyer-Bennet**
*Monterey, Massachusetts*
  *Drag Racing*

**Bonnie Dyer-Bennet**
*Berkshire Reference Works (staff)*
  *Biathlon*
  *Trampolining*

**Mark Dyreson**
*Weber State University, Ogden, Utah*
  *Armed Forces Games*
  *Technology*
  *War Games*

**Henning Eichberg**
*Gerlev Idrætschøjskole,*
*Slagelse, Denmark*
  *Volkssport*

**Raymond Farrell**
*British Association for Sport & Law,*
*Manchester Metropolitan University, UK*
  *Law*

**Albert J. Figone**
*Humboldt State University,*
*Humboldt, California*
  *Gambling*

**Dennis J. Foster**
*Masters of Foxhounds Association*
*of America*
  *Foxhunting sidebar*

**Joel S. Franks**
*San Jose State University,*
*San Jose, California*
  *Ethnicity*

**Richard Friary**
*Skate Sailing Association*
  *Sailing, Ice Skate*
  *Sailing, Icewing and Roller Skate*

**Marco Galdi**
*ANSA News Agency, Rome, Italy*
  *Umpires and Umpiring*

# The Contributors

**David W. Galenson**
*University of Chicago, Chicago, Illinois*
*Tennis*

**Heiner Gillmeister**
*University of Bonn, Bonn, Germany*
*Tennis, Real*

**Matti Goksøyr**
*Norges Idrettshøgskole, Oslo, Norway*
*Ski Jumping*

**Allen Guttmann**
*Amherst College, Amherst, Massachusetts*
*Diffusion*
*Modernization*
*Ritual*
*Sumo*

**Astrid Hagenguth**
*New York, New York*
*Skating, Figure*

**Steve Hick**
*Falls Church, Virginia*
*Cudgeling*

**Hajime Hirai**
*Shiga University, Shiga, Japan*
*Baseball, Japanese*

**Richard Holt**
*De Montfort University, UK, and*
*Katholieke Universiteit, Leuven, Belgium*
*Patriotism*
*Cycling sidebar*

**Ronald L. Holt**
*Weber State University, Ogden, Utah*
*Martial Arts*

**Peter A. Horton**
*School of Physical Education, Singapore*
*Geography sidebar*

**Maxwell Howell**
*University of Queensland,*
*Indooroopilly, Australia*
*Football, Australian*

**Reet Howell** (deceased)
*Queensland University of Technology,*
*Australia*
*Traditional Sports, Oceania*

**Joan Hult**
*University of Maryland,*
*College Park, Maryland*
*Speedball*
*Women's Sports, North America*

**Duncan Humphreys**
*University of Otago,*
*Dunedin, New Zealand*
*Skateboarding*
*Snowboarding*

**Steven J. Jackson**
*University of Otago,*
*Dunedin, New Zealand*
*Lacrosse*

**Wesley V. Jamison**
*University of Arkansas,*
*Fayetteville, Arkansas*
*Animal Rights*

**Ian F. Jobling**
*University of Queensland,*
*Brisbane, Australia*
*Swimming, Speed*

**Don Johnson**
*East Tennessee State University,*
*Johnson City, Tennessee*
*Literature*

**Gary Kemp**
*University of Waikato,*
*Hamilton, New Zealand*
*Olympic Games, Modern, sidebar*

**Jane Kidd**
*British Equestrian Centre,*
*Kenilworth, Warwickshire, UK*
*Horseback Riding, Dressage*

**Donald G. Kyle**
*University of Texas, Arlington*
*Olympic Games, Ancient*
*Pentathlon, Ancient*

**Horacio A. Laffaye**
*Yale University School of Medicine,*
*New Haven, Connecticut*
*Polo*

**Mary Lou LeCompte**
*University of Texas, Austin, Texas*
*Rodeo*

**Michael Letters**
*University of Queensland,*
*Brisbane, Australia*
*Football, Gaelic*

**David Levinson**
*Human Relations Area Files,*
*New Haven, Connecticut*
*Extreme Sports*
*Stickball*

**Katherine Lincoln**
*Bernardsville, New Jersey*
*Carriage Driving*

**Sigmund Loland**
*Norges Idrettshøgskole, Oslo, Norway*
*Skiing, Freestyle*

**John Lowerson**
*University of Sussex,*
*Brighton, Sussex, UK*
*Bowls and Bowling*
*Foxhunting*
*Hockey, Field*

**John W. Loy**
*University of Otago,*
*Dunedin, New Zealand*
*Aggression*
*Definitions*
*Sociology*

**Stu Luce**
*National Air Racing Group*
*Air Racing*

**Ruth P. Ludwig**
*Balloon Federation of America*
*Ballooning*

**John McClelland**
*University of Toronto, Ontario, Canada*
*Acrobatics*

**C. D. (Kit) McConnell**
*Auckland, New Zealand*
*Leadership*

**R. C. McConnell**
*Massey University (Albany),*
*Auckland, New Zealand*
*Coaches and Coaching*
*Leadership*

# The Contributors

**Richard V. McGehee**
*Southeastern Louisiana University,
Hammond, Louisiana*
   *Baseball, Latin American
   Gymnastics
   Pan American Games*

**Heather McMorrow**
*United States Luge Association*
   *Luge*

**Michael McNamee**
*Cheltenham and Gloucester College of
Higher Education, UK*
   *Values*

**Teresa Baksh McNeil**
*Cuyamaca College, El Cajon, California*
   *Jai Alai
   Pelota*

**Anita H. Magafas**
*Western Illinois University,
Macomb, Illinois*
   *Horseback Riding, Endurance*

**Maurice Mars**
*University of Natal Medical School,
Kwa Zulu Natal, South Africa*
   *Drugs and Drug Testing*

**Tony Mason**
*University of Warwick, Coventry, UK*
   *Soccer*

**Walter Miller**
*Monument, Colorado*
   *Soaring*

**Andrew W. Miracle**
*Texas Christian University,
Fort Worth, Texas*
   *Aggression*

**Timothy Mitchell**
*Texas A & M University,
College Station, Texas*
   *Bullfighting*

**Linda Mojer**
*American Amateur Racquetball Association*
   *Racquetball*

**William J. Morgan**
*University of Tennessee,
Knoxville, Tennessee*
   *Philosophy*

**Morris Mott**
*Brandon University,
Manitoba, Canada*
   *Curling
   Hockey, Ice*

**Susan Nattrass**
*Bedford, Nova Scotia, Canada*
   *Shooting, Clay Target*

**John Nauright**
*University of Queensland,
Brisbane, Australia*
   *Football, Gaelic*

**Dennis Pagen**
*United States Hang Gliding Association*
   *Hang Gliding*

**Victoria Paraschak**
*University of Windsor, Ontario, Canada*
   *Native American Sporting Competitions*

**Roberta J. Park**
*University of California, Berkeley*
   *Physical Education*

**A. R. Parr**
*Broad Haven, Pembrokeshire, Wales*
   *Sand Yachting*

**Katharine A. Pawelko**
*Western Illinois University,
Liverpool, UK*
   *Tobogganing*

**Benny Josef Peiser**
*Liverpool John Moores University,
Liverpool, UK*
   *Karate*

**Gertrud Pfister**
*Institut für Sportwissenschaft,
Berlin, Germany*
   *Women's Sports, Europe*

**Richard Pillsbury**
*Georgia State University,
Atlanta, Georgia*
   *Stock Car Racing*

**Philip A. Pines**
*Trotting Horse Museum,
Goshen, New York*
   *Horse Racing, Harness (Trotting)*

**Bill Plummer**
*American Softball Association*
   *Softball*

**Michael Poliakoff**
*Pennsylvania Department of Education,
Harrisburg, Pennsylvania*
   *Wrestling, Freestyle
   Wrestling, Greco-Roman*

**S. W. Pope**
*Journal of Sport History*
   *Basketball*

**Rudi Prusok**
*American Single Shot Rifle Association*
   *Shooting, Single-Shot*

**Rivka Rabinowitz**
*Pierre Gildesgame Maccabi Sports
Museum, Ramat Gan, Israel*
   *Maccabiah Games*

**Benjamin G. Rader**
*University of Nebraska, Lincoln, Nebraska*
   *Baseball, North American*

**Gerald Redmond**
*University of Alberta, Edmonton, Canada*
   *Commonwealth Games*

**Shirley H. M. Reekie**
*San Jose State University,
San Jose, California*
   *Sailboarding
   Sailing
   Yachting*

**Roland Renson**
*Katholieke Universiteit, Leuven, Belgium*
   *Archery
   Traditional Sports, Europe*

**Mary E. Ridgway**
*University of Texas, Arlington, Texas*
   *Disabled Sports*

**James Riordan**
*University of Surrey,
Guildford, Surrey, UK*
   *Worker Sport*

# The Contributors

**Joachim K. Rühl**
*Deutsche Sporthochschule Köln,*
*Cologne, Germany*
> *Jousting*

**Allan J. Ryan**
*American College of Sports Medicine*
> *Medicine*

**Yasuhiro Sakaue**
*Fukushima University,*
*Fukushimashi, Japan*
> *Kendo*

**Thomas F. Scanlon**
*University of California,*
*Riverside, California*
> *Mythology*

**Andy Seeley**
*US Amateur Confederation*
*of Roller Skating*
> *Skating, Roller*

**Roland Seiler**
*Sport Science Institute,*
*Magglingen, Switzerland*
> *Orienteering*

**K. G. Sheard**
*Centre for Research into Sport and*
*Society, University of Leicester, UK*
> *Rugby Union*

**Ron Shepherd**
*East Melbourne, Victoria, Australia*
> *Cycling*

**Stan Shipley**
*University of London, UK*
> *Boxing*

**Fumiaki Shishida**
*Waseda University,*
*Tokorozawa, Japan*
> *Aikido*

**Martti Silvennoinen**
*University of Jyväskylä, Jyväskylä, Finland*
> *Baseball, Finish*

**Ronald A. Smith**
*Pennsylvania State University,*
*University Park, Pennsylvania*
> *Football, American*

**Chet Snouffer**
*U.S. Boomerang Association*
> *Boomerang Throwing*

**Kathleen M. Spence**
*U.S. Badminton Association*
> *Badminton*

**B. James Starr**
*Howard University, Washington, D.C.*
> *Duathlon*
> *Triathlon*

**Sharon Kay Stoll**
*University of Idaho, Moscow, Idaho*
> *Ethics*

**Nancy L. Struna**
*University of Maryland,*
*College Park, Maryland*
> *Leisure*

**Kim Taylor**
*University of Guelph, Ontario, Canada*
> *Iaido*

**David Terry**
*Ruislip, Middlesex, UK*
> *Cross-Country Running*
> *Track and Field, Jumps and Throws*

**George Theriault**
*New London, New Hampshire*
> *Sailing, Parawing*

**Jeffrey R. Tishman**
*Associated Press Archives*
> *Fencing*
> *Pentathlon, Modern*

**John Townes**
*Berkshire Reference Works (staff)*
> *Arm Wrestling*
> *Canoeing and Kayaking*
> *Falconry*
> *Flying Disc*
> *Footbag*
> *Gay Games*
> *Ice Boating*
> *Karting*
> *Kite Flying*
> *Motor Boating*
> *Rafting*
> *Senior Games*
> *Shuffleboard*
> *Skiing, Water*

> *Tennis, Paddle*
> *Tennis, Platform*
> *Truck Racing*
> *Vintage Auto Racing*

**Alan Trevithick**
*Berkshire Reference Works (staff)*
> *Asian Games*
> *Bandy*
> *Horseshoes*
> *Paddleball*
> *Pigeon Racing*
> *Snowshoe Racing*
> *Takraw*
> *Traditional Sports, Asia*
> *Trapball*
> *Volleyball*

**Horst Ueberhorst**
*Wachtberg-Niederbachern, Germany*
> *Turnen*

**Wray Vamplew**
*De Montfort International Centre for*
*Sports History and Culture, Leicester, UK*
> *History*
> *Horse Racing, Thoroughbred*

**Robin S. Vealey**
*Miami University, Oxford, Ohio*
> *Psychology*

**Mark V. Wiley**
*Charles E. Tuttle Publishing Company,*
*Tokyo, Japan*
> *Martial Arts, Philippines*

**Ian D. W. Wright**
*Squash Rackets Association, UK*
> *Squash Rackets*

**Daniel G. Yoder**
*Western Illinois University,*
*Macomb, Illinois*
> *Commercialization*
> *Fishing, Freshwater*
> *Fishing, Saltwater*

**Darlene Young**
*Western Illinois University,*
*Macomb, Illinois*
> *Powerlifting*
> *Weightlifting*

# The Contributors

**Philip B. Zarilli**
*University of Wisconsin,*
*Madison, Wisconsin*
   *Martial Arts, South Asia*

**Frank Zarnowski**
*Mount St. Mary's College,*
*Emmitsburg, Maryland*
   *Track and Field, Decathlon*

**Dean A. Zoerink**
*Western Illinois University,*
*Macomb, Illinois*
   *Rounders*

# Index

# Index

Boston Braves, 98
Boston Bruins, 427, 429
Boston Celtics, 104
Boston Conference in the Interest of Physical Training, 744
Boston Garden Rodeo, 811
*Boston Gazette,* 621
Boston Marathon, 600, 602, 603, 605, 1100
*Boston Medical and Surgical Journal,* 745, 749
Boston Normal School of Gymnastics, 745
Boston Red Sox, 97
Boswell, Henry, 896
*Bota luzea,* 733
Botafogo soccer club (Brazil), 950
*Bote luzea,* 1032
Botham, Ian, 785, 873
Bouin, Jean, 220
Boule, 1136. *See also* Pétanque
Boulmerka, Hassiba, 10, 1169
Boulogne, Joseph, 316
Bourdieu, P., 619
Bournemouth Rowing Club, 767–768
Boutros, Labib, 671
Bowden, Norris, 899
Bowditch, Henry Pickering, 745
Bowerman, Bill, 604–605
Bowlby, Linda A., 470
Bowls/bowling, **139–147**, 1071
    British tradition, 141–144
    Latin/European tradition, 139–141
    origins, 139, 141–142, 144
    ten-pin, 144–146
    traditional Oceanic, 1090
    women, 143, 146, 1172, 1175–1176, 1181
Box lacrosse, 562
Boxe française, 223, 225
Boxing, **147–153**
    Africa, 151, 1062
    Cuba, 86
    and cudgeling, 225
    and Filipino martial arts, 612
    and gambling, 369, 370–371
    movies, 55, 663, 665–666
    and politics, 755
    and race/ethnicity, 149, 294, 296, 298, 299, 621
    and religion, 797
    traditional Oceanic, 1089–1090
    umpiring, 1117
    and violence, 147, 570–571, 1131
    women, 152, 1173, 1182
Boy Scouts, 224, 894
Boyle, R., 328
*The Boy's Own Book,* 816
Brabazon of Tara, Lord, 1044
Brabec, Eric, 175
Bradman, Sir Douglas, 212
Braemar Royal Highland Society, 411
Bragg, Arthur, 716
Bragg, Don, 1051
Branham, John F., 439
Brant, Peter, 763
Brasch, R., 39, 204, 383, 767
Brayton, Scott, 503
Brazil

aerobics, 6
capoeira, 1140
field hockey, 421
gymnastics, 1113
ice hockey, 430
kendo, 550
polo, 760
rodeo, 815
soccer, 253, 726, 755, 949, 950, 952, 954, 1134
tennis, 1020
traditional sports, 1077
volleyball, 1143
Breal, Michel, 599
Bredemeier, Brenda Jo L., 13, 14, 288
Breeding, 446, 448, 751
Breen, Ellen, 919
Breen, George, 993
Brehon Laws (Ireland), 490
Brennand, Bill, 25
Brenner, Gabrielle A., 369, 370
Brenner, Reuven, 369, 370
Brezek, John, 49
Brichford, Maynard, 11
Bridges, E. Lucas, 618
Brier, 230
Brill, Debbie, 1051
Brisick, Jamie, 989
Bristow, Lily, 662
Britain. *See* Great Britain
British American Football League, 252
British Association for Sport and Law, 568
British Athletics Federation (BAF), 569, 570
British Balloon and Airship Club (BBAC), 72
British Boy Scouts, 224
British Columbia Lions, 349
British Commonwealth Games, 196
British Crown Green Amateur Association, 143
British Darts Organization (BDO), 246
British Driving Society, 174
British Empire and Commonwealth Games, 196
British Empire Games, 196
British Equestrian Federation (BEF), 463–464
British Field Sports Society, 361–362
British Horse Society (BHS), 457, 464
British Ice Hockey Federation, 427
British Isles Bowls Council, 143
*British Journal of Sports History,* 415
British Kandahar Ski Club, 916
British Open Championships (squash rackets), 974
British Pétanque Association, 141
British Physical Training and Recreation Act, 755
British public schools
    and Australian football, 343–344
    and cricket, 210
    and cross-country running, 219
    and cudgeling, 223
    and field hockey, 419, 420
    and mountain climbing, 659

and patriotism, 724
and rugby, 334, 346, 832, 833–834, 838, 842, 1133
and rugby fives, 825, 826, 827
and soccer, 250, 945, 946
and spectators, 968–969
and squash rackets, 972
and tennis, 1018
and women's sports, 1162
British Rowing Association, 380
British Show Jumping Association (BSJA), 464
British Society for Sports History (BSSH), 415
British Sports Council, 1109–1110
British Ten-Pin Bowling Association, 145
British Thai Boxing and Kickboxing Federation, 571
British Workers Cycling Club, 1184
British Workers Sports Federation, 1184
Brittany, 1136, 1138, 1139
Broadwick, "Tiny," 720
Brock, A. J., 628
Brody, Tal, 594
Broeukheuysen, Nico, 554
Brohm, J., 618
Bronowski, Jacob, 161
Bronson, Charles, 962
Bronzed Aussies, 988
Brooke, Robert, 463
Brooklyn Dodgers, 88, 89, 96–97
Brooklyn Excelsiors, 92
Brooks, Marshall, 1050
Broomhall, Jayne, 686
Broughton, Jack, 147
Broun, Heywood, 623
Brown, Christy, 258
Brown, Doris, 221
Brown, Elwood S., 52, 251–252
Brown, F. H., 1142
Brown, G., 264
Brown, Jim, 962
Brown, Joe, 805, 807
Brown, Joe E., 1094
Brown, Joyce, 185
Brown, Tim, 898
Browne, Terrence, 74, 76
Brownfield, Kim, 258
Brownfoot, Janice, 684
Browning, Kurt, 899
Browning, Todd, 258
Brownlow, Charles, 345
Brownlow Medal, 345
Brueghel, Pieter, 43, 895, 1070, 1071, 1136
Brumel, Valeriy, 1051
Brundage, Avery, 11, 403, 700, 701–702, 716, 718, 1185
Brunet, Andrée, 899
Brunet, Pierre, 899
Bryson, Lois, 15
Bu, 82
Bubka, Sergey, 1051
Buckingham, Second Duke of, 359
Buckley, W. E., 271
Budd, Arthur, 828
Buddhism, 41, 301, 606, 608
    and aikido, 21

# Index

# Index

# Index

# Index

# Index

# Index

# Index

# Index

# Index

# Index

# Index

# Index

# Index

# Index

# Index

# Index

Walker, Weldy, 93
Walking, 785–786
Wallace, Bill, 543
Wallace, John H., 275
Wallach, Eli, 962
Wallaroo Football Club (Jau), 837
Wallechinsky, David, 264, 785, 1109
Waller, Fred, 927
Waller, Ken, 129
Wallis, E. L., 201
Walton, G., 574
Walton, Izaak, 319
Walton, Philip, 384
Wang Junxia, 1061
Wang Tao, 1039
Wann, Daniel L., 15
War games, **1149–1154**. *See also* Military influences
Warbrick, Doug, 988
Warby, Kenneth Peter, 649
Ward, I., 412–413
Waring, Thomas, 44
Warmerdam, Cornelius, 1051
Warner, Charles Dudley, 485
Warne-Smith, Ivor, 345
Warrnambool-Melbourne cycle race, 235
Waseda College, 81
Washington, Booker T., 745
Washington, George, 362
Washington, Kenny, 340
Washington Huskies, 511
Watanabe, Akira, 645
Watanabe, Emi, 897
Water polo, **766–770**
Water skiing, 307, **927–930**
Waterloo Cup (coursing), 204
Waterman, Charles F., 319, 320, 321, 325, 326, 328, 329
Watkins, A. L., 631
Watkins, Billy K., 1104
Watson, Big Bill, 1048
Watson, John, 762
Watson, Ken, 230
Watson, Robert Patrick, 991
Watson, Tom, 386–387
Wayman, Tommy, 763
Wayoro people, 1080
Weah, George, 954
*Web and the Rock*, 584
Webb, Matthew, 990–991, 993
Weber, Franz, 918
Weber, Max, 640, 752
Webster, D., 409, 410, 412
Wedell, James, 23
Weet weet, 1085
Weider, Ben, 128
Weider, Joe, 128, 129, 133
Weight management, 303
Weightlifting, 576–577, **1154–1158**
people with disabilities, 258
powerlifting, 130, 770–774, 1157
women, 130, 771, 1157, 1171, 1173
*See also* Bodybuilding
Weiler, Ingemar, 669, 670, 671, 672, 673
Weiss, M. R., 288
Weiss, Paul, 248, 740
Weissbein, Siegfried, 631

*Der Weisse Rausch*, 915
Weissflog, Jens, 913–914
Weissmuller, Johnny, 990, 995, 996
Weistart, John, 565
Weizmann, Chaim, 593
Wellesley College, 745
Wellness revolution, 303
Wembley Stadium, 60
Werner, Dennis, 1080
Werner, Johann Adolf Ludwig, 1162
Wertz, S., 286
West, Benjamin, 896
West Indies, 213–214, 294, 683, 684
cricket, 211, 212, 213–214, 725
West Side Tennis Club (United States), 1023
Westchester Cup, 758, 760–761
Westchester Hare and Hounds (United States), 220
Westerblad, C. A., 630
Westergren, Carl, 1195
Western Canada Hockey League, 426–427
Western Canada Rugby Football Union, 348, 349
Western Harness Racing Association (United States), 435
Western horseback riding, **474–477**
Western States Trail Ride. *See* Tevis Cup
Westernization. *See* Diffusion
Weston, Edward Payson, 600
Weymann, Charles, 23
Wham-O, 329–330, 332
Wheelchair sports, 46, 254–255, 257, 258–259
Wheelchair Sports, USA, 255
Whillans, Don, 805, 807
The Whip (Great Britain), 174
Whistler, Clarence, 1196
Whitbread Round the World Race, 854
White, Andrew D., 335
White, Andy, 837, 838, 839
White, Anita, 554
White, Byron "Whizzer," 339
White, Cheryl, 447
White, Francis, 578
*White Fang*, 931–932
White House Conference on Aging, 871
*White Men Can't Jump*, 106
Whitehead, James, 585
White-water rafting. *See* Rafting
White-water sports, 172
Whitfield, Fred, 813
Whitfield, Malvin, 1061
Whiting, Robert, 81
Whitmore, James, 214
Whitten, Ted, 345
Whitworth, Kathy, 385
Whymper, Edward, 659, 660
Wickham, Alick, 996
*Wide World of Sports*, 264–265, 624
Widmark, Richard, 75–76
Widmeyer, W. Neil, 14
Wiener Eislauf Verein (Austria), 897
Wigger, Deena, 884
Wightman, Hazel, 68
Wilber, Doreen, 46
Wilbye, Harald, 707

Wilcox, David R., 636
*The Wild One*, 655
Wild-water canoe racing, 173
Wiley, Mark, 610, 612
Wilhelm, Friedrich, IV (Kaiser of Germany), 1112
Wilhelmina (Queen of Netherlands), 554
Willard, George "Jess," 68
Willard, Nancy, 585
William (Crown Prince of Prussia), 120, 122
William IV (King of England), 380
*William Hendricks' History of Billiards*, 110
William the Conqueror (King of England), 42, 311, 463
Williams, David, 345
Williams, Doug, 61
Williams, Esther, 990, 995, 999
Williams, John, 46, 1134
Williams, Percy, 197
Willingdon, Lord, 197
Willis, W. H., 672
Willoughby, D. P., 991
Wills, D. R., 1091
Wills, Helen, 1176
Wills, Sir Alfred, 657, 658, 659
Wills, Thomas Kentworth, 343, 345
Wilson, Adam, 1054
Wilson, August, 585
Wilson, Horace, 251
Wilson, Rufus Rockwell, 402
Wimbledon, 1017, 1018, 1019–1020, 1021, 1022
Winchester College. *See* British public schools
Winchester Fives, 825, 826
Windsurfing. *See* Sailboarding
Winged Wheelers, 348
Wingert, Will, 333
Wingfield, Walter, 1019
Winmau World Masters, 246
Winner, Ken, 849
Winnipeg Blue Bombers, 349
Winnipeg Football Club, 348
Winston Cup, 977, 978, 979, 980
Winter Olympics. *See* Olympic Games
Wirkola, Bjorn, 912
*Wisden*, 210
Wisden, John, 210
Wise, Bernard, 220
Wise, John, 720
*The Witchery of Archery*, 45
Wittgenstein, 740
Wittman, Steve, 25
Witzig, John, 987
Wodehouse, P. G., 387
Wolde, Mamo, 10, 600, 604, 700
Wolfe, Thomas, 584
Wolsey, Thomas, 795
*Women and Sport: Interdisciplinary Perspectives*, 289
*Women of Trachis*, 671
Women's Amateur Athletic Federation, 1166
Women's Fast Pitch National Championship (Native American), 682